Shakespeare's
Stanley Epitaphs
in
Tong Shropshire

Ask who lies here, but do not weep;
He is not dead, he doth but sleep.
This stony register is for his bones;
His fame is more perpetual than these stones.
And his own goodness, with himself being gone,
Shall live when earthly monument is none.

Not Monumental Stone preserves our fame,
Nor sky-aspiring pyramids our name.
The memory of him for whom this stands
Shall outlive marble and defacers' hands.
When all to time's consumption shall be given,
Standley, for whom this stands, shall stand in Heaven.

Shakespeare's
Stanley Epitaphs
in
Tong Shropshire

**on the tomb of Sir Thomas & Sir Edward Stanley
in St Bartholomew's Church Tong
with their first ever biographies**

Helen Moorwood

Visits to St Bartholomew's Church, Tong can be arranged by contact with the Tong Parochial Church Council, Tong Vicarage, Tong, Shifnal, Shropshire TF11 8PW. Extensive information on the church and relevant publications is available on appropriate websites. The guidebook *St Bartholomew's Church Tong Shropshire* (Published by RJL Smith & Associates) is available from the church.

© Helen Moorwood 2013

Published 2013
by RJL Smith & Associates, Much Wenlock, Shropshire

ISBN 978-0-9573492-2-3

Cover design by Eberhard Strabel, Sauerlach, near Munich, Bavaria
Tong Castle c.1731 (adaptation from *Bucks's Views*, 1760)
Stanley tomb, sketch by Francis Sandford, 1664 © College of Arms, Dugdale's Diary, C35, p. 41
Shakespeare 'Old Player' portrait © Ian Wilson
Sir Edward Stanley's effigy © RJL Smith

In Memoriam

To my dear husband
Alan Moorwood
†2011
who had to put up with
Shakespeare & Sir Edward Stanley
as 'rivals' for attention
for so many years

To everyone at
Gawthorpe Hall

Helen Moorwood
helen@moorwood.de
www.moorwood.de

All profits from the sale of this book will be donated
to the Restoration Fund of St Bartholomew's Church, Tong.

Contents

Illustrations

Illustrations

Preface

This book plays the role of 'prequel' to a re-investigation of the 'Lancastrian Shakespeare' theory, which claims that young William Shakespeare spent some time in Lancashire with the Catholic Hoghtons (of Hoghton Tower and Lea, where he was a servant, 'William Shakeshafte', associated with 'instruments of music' and 'play-clothes') and the Catholic Heskeths (of Rufford Old Hall). These two 400-year-old family traditions were researched and presented for the first time by a scholar in 1985 (E. A. J. Honigmann, *Shakespeare: the 'lost years'*). The family that has now emerged as crucial in explaining Shakespeare's ancestry and early biography is the Stanley family, Earls of Derby, 'Kings of Lancashire' and Lords of Man. It has long been known that Ferdinando, Lord Strange, 5th Earl of Derby, was Shakespeare's patron in Strange's Players during his successes in London in the early 1590s. It was known and recorded by several near-contemporaries that William Shakespeare had written two Verse Epitaphs for Ferdinando's cousin Sir Edward Stanley's family tomb in Tong, Shropshire, although the authorship subsequently came to be doubted – erroneously. These two stories have now come together with many more Stanley details to shed light on several Shakespeare mysteries. In this book the full story of Sir Edward Stanley and the Shakespeare Epitaphs is investigated.

My husband Alan's main (slightly amused) complaint whenever I ventured to talk to him about my 'Shakespeare research' was: 'The answer to all your questions is – the Earl of Derby'. The 'hero' of this book was not the Earl of Derby, but he was pretty close to several of them. Sir Edward Stanley was the grandson of the 3rd, the nephew of the 4th and the first cousin of the 5th and 6th Earls of Derby. He also happened to be rather closely related to all the main Earl Alternative Authorship Candidates: William Stanley, 6th Earl of Derby, of course, whose father-in-law was Edward de Vere, 17th Earl of Oxford ('hero' of the 2011 film *Anonymous*); and Roger Manners, 5th Earl of Rutland (the Russian candidate). Sir Edward was also related through his mother Lady Margaret née Vernon and his wife Lady Lucy née Percy to several characters in Shakespeare's Lancastrian History Plays; and candidates for the 'Dark Lady' of the Sonnets (Mary née Fitton, Elizabeth née Vernon, Penelope Rich née Devereux). He can thus be seen as a pivotal figure in the Shakespeare-Stanley constellation. The Tong Epitaphs alone prove that Shakespeare was Shakespeare, and he could have met all the aristocratic candidates via the Stanleys, not least via Sir Edward.

The final chapter of this book presents the first-ever biographies of father Sir Thomas Stanley (c.1534-1576) and son Sir Edward Stanley (1562-1632), on whose tomb in St Bartholomew's, Tong, Shropshire appear two Verse Epitaphs attributed by several in the 17th century to Shakespeare. This is now certain beyond all reasonable doubt, and the only sensible explanation is that Shakespeare and Stanley had known each other since their youth together in Lancashire. Dashing off a couple of epitaphs for his family tomb in c.1603, when they were both at James's coronation, was merely a logical outcome of their long friendship.

Sir Thomas's and Sir Edward's identities and biographies have been successfully separated from those of several other contemporary namesakes, who have rather muddled the situation until now. Sir Thomas was the 2x-great-grandson of the victor at Bosworth, Baron Thomas Stanley, 1st Earl of Derby (3rd creation), of Lancashire, who appears in Shakespeare's *Richard III*. It seemed ironically appropriate that I was proofreading this book at the same time as this king's skeleton was unearthed from under a car park in Leicester. Henry VII's victory at Bosworth (thanks to the Stanley armies from Lancashire and Cheshire) turned out to provide a crucial event for the ancestries of Sir Edward Stanley and William Shakespeare. On the battlefield Henry promised to reward all who had fought for him that day – and he did. Lord Thomas Stanley (whose second wife was Lady Margaret Beaufort, mother of Henry VII) was created 1st Earl of Derby and awarded vast lands; soldier Shakeshafte was awarded an estate in Warwickshire (John Shakespeare more or less told us this when he applied for the impalement of his wife's Cheshire Arderne arms in 1599); Thomas Arderne of (Alvanley and) Harden (Tameside, near Stockport, just over the River Tame from Lancashire) was awarded an estate in Leicestershire. Their descendants never forgot their origins, and William Shakespeare incorporated many of their ancestors in his Lancastrian 'king plays'.

Preparing this book has been a historical detective story in itself. Sorting out previous muddles concerning the Tong Epitaphs was one major step towards establishing many other Shakespeare-Stanley links, which form an integral part of what has become known as the 'Lancastrian Shakespeare' theory. Concomitant to this is the 'Catholic Shakespeare' theory. At the end of some day in the not too distant future, William Shakespeare's ancestry and biography during his 'lost years' will need to be rewritten. But first, the focus in this book is on presenting all relevant documentation that proves beyond all reasonable doubt that Shakespeare wrote the Verse Epitaphs in Tong in c.1603 for his friend Sir Edward Stanley.

My entry point to this historical detective story was Alexander Standish of Duxbury (1567-1622), a contemporary of Sir Edward Stanley and William Shakespeare. He can be seen on the Family Tree in Appendix 12b, appearing there because in his widowerhood he had a liaison with twice-widowed Countess Alice Stanley née Spencer. Her first husband had been Ferdinando Stanley, Lord Strange, 5th Earl of Derby until his death by poisoning in 1594. Their eldest daughter Anne had inherited her right of succession to the Tudor throne from her father Ferdinando, and was indeed confirmed as heiress presumptive to Queen Elizabeth in 1596. Alice's second husband, from 1600 until his death in 1617, was Sir Thomas Egerton (from Cheshire), Elizabeth's Master of the Rolls, later her and James's Lord Chancellor, 1st Viscount Brackley, Lord Ellesmere. Alexander Standish's mother was Margaret Hoghton, a half-sister of Alexander Hoghton who wrote his will in 1581 naming a servant William Shakeshafte (young William Shakespeare, according to 'Lancastrian Shakespeare') three times in connection with musical instruments and play-clothes. It was easy to imagine that Alexander and William might well have met at Hoghton Tower when Alexander was visiting his uncle Alexander Hoghton and William Shakeshafte was perhaps playing a musical instrument and dressing in play-clothes. More details about Alexander appear in Chapter I. Introduction.

Alexander was also the closest relative in Duxbury of Pilgrim Father Captain Myles Standish when he sailed on The Mayflower in 1620 – but that is another long story, which will be covered elsewhere. The only relevant part of Myles's story for this book is that it involved all the same local families as those involved in 'Lancastrian Shakespeare', with Standishes, Hoghtons and Heskeths, along with the Stanleys, appearing on both sides of the religious divide during Elizabeth's and James's reigns.

I had known all my life about the tradition at Hoghton Tower that 'young Shakespeare spent a couple of years' there – I grew up in Darwen, just round the corner of Darwen moors, along the River Darwen. It never occurred to me until relatively recently that I would be the one to find confirmation of this beyond all reasonable doubt. Nor did it ever occur to me until relatively recently that I would find myself convinced of the 'Catholic Shakespeare' theory, particularly having grown up in the Congregationalist Church and been told as a child that I shouldn't play with Catholic children! But so it came about. Research into my Grandma Duxbury's family led back to the Duxburys of Duxbury and the Standishes of Duxbury, who had taken over from them as Lords of the Manor. The Standishes of Duxbury revealed Alexander's Hoghton mother and his fascinating liaison with Countess Alice Stanley. References and a visit to her tomb in Harefield led me to the Stanley tomb in Tong. And so this book was born.

Details of all mentioned above will be given in sequels to this book (some on my website), but here, as stated above, we will concentrate on the story behind the Shakespeare Verse Epitaphs on the Stanley tomb in St Bartholomew's Church, Tong, Shropshire.

Helen Moorwood
Sauerlach near Munich, Bavaria, March, 2013

Acknowledgements

My deep thanks and acknowledgements go to the following for all their help and support in my various pursuits over the past dozen years and more, and/or permission to quote freely from their writings:

Lancashire, Duxbury to Shakespeare: Ray Aspden (Duxbury family history); the Revd John Cree (organizer of the Myles Standish Festival at St Laurence's, Chorley in 2005); Alan Duxbury (Duxbury family history); Margaret Flannery (for equipping me with local large-scale maps); G. A. (Tony) Foster (Vice-President, Lancashire Family History & Heraldry Society): Jim Heyes (former Research Librarian at Chorley Library; author of *A History of Chorley*); Phil Hudson (Editor of *Lancashire History Quarterly*); W. J. (Bill) Taylor (Vice-President of the Lancashire Family History & Heraldry Society); W. (Bill) Walker (my guide round Duxbury; author of *Duxbury in Decline* and *St George's, Chorley*).

Stanley epitaphs and tombs: David Dixon (holder of the keys to St Bartholomew's Parish Church, Tong); the Venerable, the Very Revd Dr Robert (Bob) Jeffery (for a wonderful set of articles pertaining to the Tong epitaphs, assembled for his book *Discovering Tong: Its History, Myths and Curiosities*); Joyce Frost (for painstakingly transcribing and publishing the Revd J. E. Auden's notes in *Auden's History of Tong*); Lilian Wright (for her invaluable articles on the Stanleys at Eynsham and Sir Edward's burial and plaque in St Leonard's Parish Church, Eynsham); Simon Watney (Church art historian, for his enlightening articles on Shakespearean epitaphs on the Stanley and other tombs); Sylvia Ladymann (guide to Countess Alice Stanley's tomb in Harefield Church, Middlesex); David Baker (historian at St Mary's Church, Walthamstow, Essex, home of Lady Lucy's tomb).

Shakespeare's Lancashire Links via Stanleys: Professor Barry Coward (author of *The Stanleys: Lords Stanley and Earls of Derby, 1385-1672*); Professor Leo Daugherty (author of the first-ever biography in 2004 of William Stanley, 6th Earl of Derby for the *ODNB*, and subsequent books on the Stanleys and Shakespeare, who told me on one occasion that we were the only two people interested in William Stanley); Carol Curt Enos (indefatigable researcher and author on 'Lancastrian Shakespeare' and 'Catholic Shakespeare'; compiler of the *Shakespeare Encyclopedia*, extracts in Appendix 7; has provided constant support); Professor E. A. J. Honigmann (sadly deceased in 2011; without his scholarly spadework, this book would never have been written; he also kindly sent me a copy of his book on *John Weever*, another important Lancashire link); Sir Bernard de Hoghton (owner of Hoghton Tower, who inherited the family tradition that 'Shakespeare was here for a couple of years'); John Idris Jones (for his articles on the Salusburys and *The Phoenix and the Turtle*); Mary S. Lovell (author of *Bess of Hardwick, First Lady of Chatsworth*, which revealed the full story of Sir Thomas's plan to rescue Mary, Queen of Scots from Chatsworth); Professor Peter Milward SJ (indefatigable supporter of 'Lancastrian Shakespeare' and prolific author on 'Catholic Shakespeare', who valuably provided me with much support and many of his publications); Sylvia Morris (Shakespeare blogger; former Head of Shakespeare Centre Library and Archive at Shakespeare Birthplace Trust, who belatedly 'discovered' the Tong epitaphs); Lyn Williams (an invaluable contact at The New Globe, whose enthusiasm led to her participation in the course on 'Shakespeare's Lancashire Links' at Alston Hall); Dr Ian Wilson (proposer of one 'Dark Lady'; for permission to use his Shakespeare 'Old Player' portrait); Professor Richard Wilson (enthusiastic supporter of 'Lancastrian Shakespeare' and 'Shakespeare North').

Libraries & Halls: thanks to the staff at the Lancashire Record Office, Preston (renamed Lancashire Archives); Chetham's Library, Manchester (Dr Michael Powell); John Rylands University Library, Manchester; Alston Hall near Preston (Lancashire Adult Learning; for organizing the three-day residential course 'Shakespeare's Lancashire Links' in 2004); Stonyhurst College (for guided tours); Rufford Old Hall (courtesy of the National Trust); and successive former librarians at Knowsley Hall Amanda Askari and Emma Tate (for support and guided tours, before both retired because of motherhood) and Dr Brendan Cole.

Webmasters: for their enthusiasm and highly relevant contributions: Tony Christopher (another guide around Duxbury, founder of the website mylesstandish.info); Frances Coakley (Manx Notebook); Peter Duxbury (founder of A Duxbury Family Website; sadly deceased in 2005; the website taken over by Ronald D[uxbury] Taylor); Stephen Pearson (Shakespeare Family Genealogy); Brian S[tanley] Roberts (Stanley Family Genealogy).

Finally, my heartfelt acknowledgement of the patience, support and expertise of John Smith of RJL Smith & Associates, who first took the photographs of the Stanley tomb in Tong Church (some of them 'impossible') and then painstakingly saw this book through to publication.

Chapter I
Introduction

St Bartholomew's Church, Tong, Shropshire has the distinction of containing more (authenticated) epitaphs written by Shakespeare for inclusion on a tomb or gravestone than any other church in England. This record is not too difficult to ascertain or beat because at Tong there are two Verse Epitaphs and the only other epitaph in stone is Shakespeare's own for himself on his gravestone in Stratford Parish Church. Several other tombs provide relevant contemporary details, but the most important epitaphs under discussion in this book are those in Tong on the magnificent tomb with marble effigies of **Sir Thomas Stanley** (died 1576) and his widow Lady Margaret (died 1596); and the alabaster effigy on the lower tier of their son **Sir Edward Stanley Jr** (died 1632), who commissioned the tomb and received the epitaphs from Shakespeare c.1601–03.

Because of the different materials used it is likely that the marble effigies were commissioned and completed first and the lower effigy later, yet all well within the lifetime of **Sir Edward Jr**. Other pieces of visible and documented evidence that **Sir Edward Jr** commissioned his own effigy in Tong are that:

1. He is depicted as c. forty years old, which he was in 1601–03.
2. He sold Tong Castle and moved away permanently to Eynsham in Oxfordshire in 1603.
3. John Weever reported in c.1626 that 'Sir Edward...yet living... hath already made his owne monument...'. His effigy must have been placed in storage somewhere, with instructions.
4. Daughter Petronella presumably fulfilled her father's wishes when he died in 1632 at Eynsham.

The names of the three chief Stanley protagonists in this book are always given in **bold**, to make sure we know who we are reading about. This saves always having to repeat 'of Tong' or other places where they lived at various times, and serves to distinguish them from other contemporary (Sir) Thomas and (Sir) Edward Stanleys who enter the story. Those consistently in bold are **Sir Edward Sr** (d. 1604), younger brother of **Sir Thomas**, therefore uncle of **Sir Edward Jr**. This was also useful for myself as a reminder when writing this book. If one or other of these names did not appear in bold on any single page, I had obviously strayed too far away from their lives.

The wives of **Sir Thomas** (Margaret Vernon) and **Sir Edward Jr** (Lucy Percy) are not in bold. This is solely for the reason that their identities have never been doubted, their deaths and burials are well authenticated and they have never been confused with others of the same name. Reasons for other occasional uses of bold are given before the relevant section.

To pre-empt the main conclusions at the end of this book, it is highly likely that (Sir) **Edward Stanley Jr** (born 1562, knighted 1603) met William Shakespeare (born 1564) when they were both rather young (when Shakespeare was working in Lancashire for the upper gentry families of Hoghton and Hesketh and later almost certainly involved in Derby's Players, later Strange's Players in the 1580s), and continued to meet on many occasions. On one occasion around 1601–03, most likely at the latest in 1603 at James I's coronation or in 1604 in the procession, delayed until the following year because of an outbreak of plague, Shakespeare dashed off a

Ia. Stanley coat of arms
Argent. On a bend azure three stags' heads cabossed or
(Victoria County History, Vol.6)

couple of epitaphs for **Sir Edward Jr** for inclusion on his tomb, at that time presumably in the making. **Sir Edward Jr** had many close relatives who were writing poetry and plays in the 1580s to early 1600s, who admired many of the works produced, earlier or later, by Shakespeare, Spenser, Jonson, etc., some of whom received dedications from these and others. They all enter this story in one way or another.

The main mystery [for me] was why the history of the Tong Shakespeare epitaphs had not been explained satisfactorily before. One main answer lay in historical events, when so many Stanley records and monuments were destroyed. Records disappeared because of neglect or fire; monuments were desecrated during the Civil War. The Victorian era and vogue of restoration changed the position of many tombs in many churches, unfortunately without leaving adequate documentation, etc. and so forth. But enough documentary details have survived to provide a fairly authentic history of the tomb at Tong and biographies of the main protagonists.

Hunting around in archives and libraries [and tombs in churches] for a decade or so, preceded by a lifetime of reading and being inspired by Shakespeare, etc. brought me into contact with others interested in similar matters. I believe that we MIGHT in the future come a little closer to understanding Shakespeare's contacts and through them also come a little closer to some of the inspirations that he turned into dramatic miracles, which so many of us have enjoyed on the page and stage ever since. I am ready, as a former Girl Guide, to Be Prepared to stick my neck out, with the full expectation that it might be chopped off—metaphorically— by Stratford. Several characters who appear in this book literally had their heads chopped off in Tudor and Stuart times.

The main surprise for me, and I can only assume for any potential reader, is that this tomb and the Shakespeare epitaphs in Tong have been generally ignored by so many in the twenty-first century who are otherwise interested in all or most Shakespearean matters. For example, I have just been through the indexes, yet again, of major post-2000 biographies or books re-examining certain aspects of Shakespeare's life on my shelves, one of which accompanied a successful TV series, one has been a best seller, or at least has been prominent in airport bookshops. Another won a prize and two explore his Catholicism or other contemporary influences. None of them contained a single mention of Tong or the tomb of **Sir Thomas** and **Sir Edward Stanley Jr**, which are the central focuses of this book.

In chronological order of publication these were: Michael Wood, *In Search of Shakespeare* (2003) – accompanying the BBC TV series with the same title; Richard Wilson, *Secret Shakespeare: Studies in theatre, religion and resistance* (2004) – influences on Shakespeare; Stephen Greenblatt, *Will in the World* (2005) – the best seller; James Shapiro, *1599: A Year in the Life of William Shakespeare* (2005) – the prize winner; Clare Asquith, *Shadowplay: The Hidden Beliefs and Coded Politics of William Shakespeare* (2005) – Shakespeare's Catholicism. This is not to say that they are not worth reading – of course they all are – but there will be no quotes from any of these about the Shakespeare epitaphs in Tong. The same applies to more recent books and the latest updates of various major Shakespeare websites. The year 2007 produced several more books on Shakespeare's biography: at least by Bill Bryson, *Shakespeare: the world as a stage*, very entertaining, but again no mention of the epitaphs at Tong; Germaine Greer on Mrs Shakespeare, *Shakespeare's Wife*; Charles Nicholl, *The Lodger: Shakespeare on Silver Street*. Even more recently has come James Shapiro's latest offering, *Contested Will: Who Wrote Shakespeare?* (Faber, 2010).

This book aims to fill this black hole in recent 'full' Shakespeare biographies inasmuch as it presents many details that have not so far been put together about those whose effigies are on the Stanley tomb in Tong. It also explores various possible occasions for an encounter between **Sir Edward Stanley Jr** and Shakespeare when the former might have requested epitaphs from the latter; also with **Sir Edward Stanley Sr**, brother of **Sir Thomas**, who for several, sometimes long periods, deputised in Lancashire for his elder brother Henry, 4th Earl of Derby.

I take this opportunity to give my opinion on the recent controversy on Shakespeare's religious beliefs. We have his friend and rival Ben Jonson's line that he was 'for any religion, as being well versed in both'. ('Both', in this context, meant Protestant and Catholic.) I see no reason to disbelieve this. Whatever Shakespeare's hidden beliefs, his dramatic, poetic and diplomatic talents ensured that he, unlike many of his contemporaries in the theatre world (e.g. Ben Jonson), never spent time in gaol (as far as we know). However, as will emerge in this book, he was certainly surrounded by Catholic families. Among these were many of the Stanleys who appear in the following pages.

I repeat that this book should never have needed to be written, because all the major facts about all the main participants were recorded or written at the time (sixteenth and seventeenth centuries), and all published at the latest by the early twentieth century. One constant question on my part was why I should be the first person to write the first reasonably full biographies of **Sir Thomas** and **Sir Edwards Sr** and **Jr**. The main answer I came up with can be summarised in one word: Lancashire. This was the home of their immediate male forebears back to the fourteenth century and several of mine back to even earlier. The main question from any reader might be 'Why should she have bothered?' and the main answer to this is that I happen to have enjoyed learning about **Sir Thomas**'s and **Sir Edward Sr** and **Jr**'s biographies. I felt all the time that I was in the middle of a detective story. Uncovering the story of **Sir Edward Sr** presented the greatest adventure, especially when separating him from other Sir Edwards who had their own adventures, sometimes rather spectacular.

During the genealogical journey through and among my humble families in Lancashire, I had hit on a few Early Modern prominents (none of them claimed as my ancestors). Mixed among these were William Shakespeare (with his father's ancestors in Preston and his step-mother Mary Arderne's ancestors in North Cheshire) and Pilgrim Father Captain Myles Standish (from Duxbury near Chorley, regarded by many US citizens as one of the founders of the US), all of which ultimately led to this book. The only common ancestry I might claim with one of these was Myles Standish, although we need to go back to a Duxbury-Standish marriage in c.1350–54. Maybe a little bit of one of my fingernails contains the same DNA as Myles Standish and his descendants?

Someone famous —I am afraid I forget who — said that 'biographies are novels with an index'. This was true and cruel at the same time. Anyone setting out on writing a biography does their best; they might be right in some places and wrong in others. This book is certainly not an attempt at a novel, but it does have an index. It also rewrites a little bit of history. I confess I was inspired to a certain extent by Josephine Tey, *A Daughter of Time* (1951), which was a novel (without an index) which presented a strong case for a certain rehabilitation of Richard III from the image of him — hunch-backed and evil — presented in standard history, not least by Shakespeare in *Richard III*. The Battle of Bosworth turned out to be extremely important in the ancestry of the Stanley Earls of Derby and the Shakespeares. Shakespeare was himself a 'son of time', writing during the Tudor and Stuart period when everyone had to bear in mind the punishment of stepping over a certain boundary that conflicted with the interests of the government. To a certain extent, then, I am at the same time pro and contra the image presented by previous Shakespeare biographers about Shakespeare himself. We all agree that he was a dramatic and verbal genius, but he must have been rather devious, just to survive. I believe that his association with various Stanleys, who were constantly walking a similarly dangerous line, may have contributed to the obfuscation of Shakespeare's own position.

It is too early to attempt to write full biographies of these three Stanleys. All that can be done for the moment is begin to put together a jigsaw puzzle of various pieces of their lives that are on record, in documents and references located so far. Alas, the characters and personal feelings of these two knights will probably always remain a mystery, as they left behind no personal letters to or from them and no diaries or even account books. They did appear at least with their names, however, in several documents and reports in various places; and it is these details that are presented in this book.

It should not be surprising that many of these reports come from Lancashire, because that is where **Sir Thomas** (c.1535–76) started life, as the second son of Edward, 3rd Earl of Derby, 'King of Lancashire' and Lord of Man. N.B. **Sir Thomas**'s year of birth is unknown and c.1534 is calculated from the known birth of his elder brother Henry, Lord Strange, in c. September 1531, followed by two daughters. **Sir Thomas**'s birth might, of course, have been a year earlier or a few years later. He spent most of his young adulthood in Lancashire and the Isle of Man, with a two (+?, perhaps three or four) year spell in the Tower of London from November 1570, until he moved to Tong, Shropshire in c.1574–75, where he died and was buried not too long afterwards (1576).

Ib. Armorial bearings of Stanley, Earl of Derby

Argent, on a bend azure three stags'/bucks' heads cabossed or. Plus a griffin and a stag attired (with antlers) rampant at either side, an earl's coronet, an eagle and child as the crest and the motto *sans changer*.

His only surviving son and heir **Sir Edward Jr** (1562–1632) kept up his links with Lancashire from his main residence at Tong, but seems to have spent most of his last years at Eynsham in Oxfordshire from 1603 (when he sold Tong Castle) until 1632, when he died and was buried there by his only unmarried daughter. **Sir Thomas** and **Sir Edward Jr** therefore spent less than thirty years altogether at Tong Castle, during the nearly hundred years from **Sir Thomas**'s birth (c.1534) to **Sir Edward**'s death (1632), so it is hardly surprising that the largest mark they left in Tong, still there four centuries later, was not a series of family papers or local reports by others, but the most solid monument possible: a magnificent tomb. **Sir Edward Jr**, in particular, also left behind many mysteries.

The research on the tomb in Tong arose directly from research on 'Shakespeare's Lancashire Links', the provisional title of a forthcoming book by the current author (which will act as a kind of sequel). This book on the Tong epitaphs extracts relevant sections from 'Shakespeare's Lancashire Links' (suitably adapted to the current context) and pursues biographical details of **Sir Thomas** and **Sir Edward Jr** — and some of their close relatives — in more detail.

Notes for biographies of two of the people mentioned in the text have been, since early 2004, on the website [www.the-bard.info], courtesy of the Duxbury website [www.duxburymk.net], whose founder and webmaster, Peter Duxbury (a sixth cousin of mine, we worked out), sadly died in September 2005, and to whom I here pay tribute for his unstinting support. This website has meanwhile been taken over by a 'cousin', Ronald Duxbury Taylor, in Hong Kong. The two highly relevant people are Alexander Standish of Duxbury, Esquire (1570–1622), a close relative of many in the 'Shakespeare in Lancashire' story; and Countess Alice of Derby née Spencer (c.1560–1637), wife/widow of Ferdinando Stanley (1558/9–1594), Lord Strange, later 5th Earl of Derby, patron of Shakespeare in Strange's Players. Alice and Ferdinando moved constantly in Shakespeare circles and Ferdinando was a first cousin of **Sir Edward Jr** (their fathers were brothers). It was the close relationship between widower Alexander Standish Esquire and widow Countess Alice (documented in Alexander's *Inquisition post mortem* in 1623) that was my 'smoking gun' several years ago to 'Shakespeare's Lancashire Links'. I quote (extract from the website):

1623: inquisition post mortem
Lancashire Inquisitions,
Lancashire and Cheshire Record Society, vol. xxiv, No. 56, pp. 397–400.

Alexander Standish, of Duxbury, Esquire
Inquisition taken at Chorley, 11 Sept. 21 James (1623) before *Edward Rigby*, Esq., Escheator, after the death of *Alexander Standish*, of Duxbury, Esq., by the oath of *Thomas Worthington*, of Worthington Esq., etc. etc.... who say that Alexander Standish long before his death was seised in

his demesne as of fee of the manor of Duxbury; and of 13 messuages, 13 gardens, 1 water-mill, 200 acres of land, 50 acres of meadow, 150 acres of pasture, 12 acres of wood, 20 acres of moor, and 12s. free rent in Duxbury, etc. etc.... The said *Alexander Standish* was also seised as of fee of the reversion of the manor of Anlezargh, and of the reversion of 12 messuages, 12 gardens, 1 water-mill, 240 acres of land, 30 acres of meadow, 130 acres of pasture, 8 acres of wood, 500 acres of furze and heath, 200 acres of moor, 100 acres of marsh, and **3s. free rent in Anlezargh, after the death of *Alice* Countess of *Derby*, who holds the said manor and other the premises in Anlezargh for life; the said Countess is yet living at Anlezargh.** . . etc. etc.

When I first read this, many moons ago while investigating the Duxburys and Standishes of Duxbury, my main question was, 'Who exactly was Countess Alice?' And how did she fit into the picture of Alexander's life? I now know exactly who Countess Alice was and how she fitted into Alexander's story. Some day, whenever time permits, I will write full biographies of Alexander and Alice, including more details discovered in the meantime. Meanwhile many notes for these biographies are on the Duxbury website and also on the website [mylesstandish.info].

Via various routes (geographical and through documents), all this led to a visit to Tong in the summer of 2004, where David Dixon gave a much valued personal tour of the church and immediately afterwards attended my course on 'Shakespeare's Lancashire Links' at Alston Hall near Preston, a residential College of Higher Education run by Lancashire County Council. Several years later came the completion of this book. As soon as possible I intend to publish a monograph on another person who enters the story: *The Travels of Sir William Stanley, 6th Earl of Derby*, first cousin of **Sir Edward Stanley Jr**, and, incidentally, an Alternative Authorship Candidate for some of Shakespeare's Works. He certainly didn't write them as they were performed, but it has become increasingly obvious that they must have known each other and that William Stanley's travels and writings were probably well known to Shakespeare. The latter might even have 'borrowed' some of the former's travel reminiscences, particularly when writing *Love's Labour's Lost*. It has also become increasingly accepted that the most likely wedding celebration for which *A Midsummer Night's Dream* was written and performed in the presence of Queen Elizabeth was the marriage on 26 January 1595 between William Stanley, 6th Earl of Derby, and Elizabeth de Vere, daughter of Edward, 17th Earl of Oxford (another Alternative Authorship Candidate).

The most essential background reading to 'Lancastrian Shakespeare' still remains today the book by E.A.J. Honigmann, *Shakespeare: the 'lost years'* (Manchester University Press, 1985; 2nd edition, with a new preface, 1998). Chapter VII is devoted to the seven surviving Shakespeare epitaphs, including those in Tong Church. The other chapters tackle different aspects of what has become known as 'Shakespeare in Lancashire' or the 'Lancastrian Shakespeare theory'. In brief, this builds on the provably old and persistent traditions passed down in two Lancashire gentry families, the de Hoghtons of Hoghton Tower and the Heskeths of Rufford, both not far from Preston, that Shakespeare had spent some time with their families in his youth. In the case of the de Hoghton tradition this was 'a couple of years' and with the Heskeths 'a short time'. The main point of controversy is whether or not the 'William Shakeshafte' mentioned in Alexander Hoghton's will in 1581, in conjunction with 'playclothes' and 'instruments of musics', was actually young William Shakespeare. I believe that he was, and will present all the newly discovered evidence in *Shakespeare's*

Ic. Shakespeare after Droeshout
Droeshout produced his drawing for the *First Folio*, 1623. It is accepted as one of only two indisputably genuine portraits of Shakespeare, the other being the 'Chandos Portrait' in the National Gallery, London.

Lancashire Links. This is not, however, essential to pursuing **Sir Thomas** and **Sir Edward Sr** and **Jr**; Honigmann's book was, and still is.

The publication of Professor Honigmann's book in 1985 created something of a furore in Shakespeare academic circles, but most of the ideas proposed have since been accepted by an ever growing number of academics, particularly those allied to the cause of 'Catholic Shakespeare', which has produced a number of scholarly books in recent years. The briefest possible summary of Honigmann's book, which sparked off a revival of research in this area, is his Contents list:

> I. Introduction; II. Hoghton of Hoghton Tower; III. Sir Thomas Hesketh of Rufford; IV. John Cottom of Tarnacre; V. John Weever and the Hoghtons; VI. Shakespeare and Lord Strange's Men; VII. The Shakespeare epitaphs and the Stanleys; VIII. Thomas Savage of Rufford; IX. The Phoenix and the Turtle; X. Shakespeare's religion; X. Conclusion.

> Appendix A: Extracts from wills: 1. Alexander Hoghton (1581); 2. Sir Thomas Hesketh (1588); 3. Thomas Savage (1611); 4. John Cottom (1616); 5. John Weever (1632).
> Appendix B: Genealogical tables: 1. Hoghton of Hoghton Tower; 2. Butler of Middle Rawcliffe; 3. Cottam (Cottom) of Tarnacre; 4. Salusbury of Lleweni and Rug.
> Appendix C: *A Midsummer Night's Dream*, *Henry VI* Parts 2 and 3, and the Stanley family.

It will be noted that the wills reproduced by Honigmann were all written during the lifetime of **Sir Edward Jr**, and that the Stanley family plays rather a large role in Honigmann's book.

One oddity about the tomb in Tong Church is that only **Sir Thomas** and his wife Margaret née Vernon were buried there, also possibly their first son Henry, who 'died an infant', although it is possible that he was buried in Lancashire, where **Sir Thomas** was living before he moved to Tong in c.1574–5 after his release from the Tower. This oddity became apparent when the Stanley vault was opened in 1891. The coffins assumed to be those of **Sir Thomas** and Lady Margaret were found cut open and their bodies no longer there. Yet another oddity is why **Sir Edward Jr**'s effigy appears below those of his parents, but no effigy of his wife. One explanation for no wife here is that his wife and four of their seven daughters were buried and commemorated on a tomb at Walthamstow in Essex in 1601, the most likely date for **Sir Edward Jr**'s commissioning of his own tomb. He then died and was buried, however, at Eynsham in Oxfordshire in 1632 (with a memorial inscription on a tablet, but no effigy). Their first and only son Thomas, who 'died in infancie', had been buried at Winwick in Lancashire. None of their three surviving daughters was buried at Tong or Eynsham. Finding explanations for all these anomalies provided a detective story on its own, quite apart from the Shakespeare epitaphs.

The composition of the text for the inscription on the tomb can be dated with certain accuracy to post-1600 (because of the inclusion of daughter Venetia, who was born in December of that year). One can also probably date **Sir Edward**'s commissioning of some part of the tomb at Tong to 1603 at the latest, when he sold Tong Castle and other estates in the Midlands and left for another of his estates in Oxfordshire. The main mystery is thus why his effigy is in Tong Parish Church, when **Sir Edward** was not buried there, and why and when his parents' bodies disappeared from the vault. Where did they disappear to?

A note about names and titles.

Sir Thomas Stanley is always referred to as this, because he was already knighted in 1553 by Queen Mary before he turned twenty; his younger brother **Sir Edward Sr** is always referred to as this, because he was also knighted fairly young, in 1560 in Ireland. It is necessary to distinguish him from his nephew **Edward Jr**, who was referred to variously by contemporaries as '**Edward Stanley, Esq.**', '**Edward Stanley son of Sir Thomas** deceased', '**Master Edward Stanley**', '**Edward Stanley of Winwick**' and '**Edward Stanley of Tong**'. These were before his knighthood in 1603, after which he was fairly consistently referred to as '**Sir Edward Stanley**' of Eynsham.

Confusions in some previous accounts of the Earls of Derby have arisen because of a multitude of (Sir) Edward Stanleys, with at least three during the period 1603-1609 and numerous earlier ones. The uncle of **Sir Edward Stanley Jr** of Eynsham was **Sir Edward Sr**, who died in 1604 and was buried at Ormskirk. His death has been widely reported as in 1609, but the meticulous research of Brian S. Roberts leaves no doubt that the only believable date was 1604, in the Parish Register of Ormskirk. This is given on the Stanley Family Genealogy website. This is not to mention another contemporary (Sir?) Edward Stanley of Hooton, who fought for the Spanish during the Dutch War of Independence at the end of the sixteenth century and subsequently became a Jesuit priest (if these two were indeed one and the same). Another Edward Stanley stormed the walls at the Siege of Zutphen in 1586 and was knighted. Either he or yet another Sir Edward Stanley died in combat in Ireland in 1597. And there seems to have been yet another Edward Stanley, who died in Portugal in 1590, his origin not yet identified (but presumably another Catholic Stanley in exile). This is apart from several more contemporary Edward Stanleys (not knights), predominantly in Lancashire and Staffordshire. Details of some of these are given in Chapter XXII. Other (Sir) Edward Stanleys.

If this book achieves nothing else, it will serve to have (hopefully) sorted out not only 'our' two **Sir Edwards** from all their namesakes, but also to have distinguished between three contemporary Sir Thomas Stanleys: 'our' **Sir Thomas Stanley** of Winwick and Tong, Thomas Stanley who was Bishop of Man and Rector of Winwick (in his case 'Sir' was an honorary title awarded to bishops) and Sir Thomas Stanley who was 2nd Lord Monteagle, son of the Stanley victor at Flodden in 1513. And several of these — or their close relatives — have been connected with Shakespeare circles in one way or another.

A note on sources.
These were initially all books, mainly those that provided transcriptions or authoritative references to contemporary documents from authoritative sources. Only during later revision did I venture into a few massive sessions of googling. There is an enormous amount online on many characters mentioned in the following pages, but very little on **Sir Thomas** and **Sir Edward**, and as often as not it was a misidentification. There were, however, a few gems here and there, which it would have taken months of researching in libraries to find, and these are quoted, with the source fully acknowledged.

A note about references to 'the author'.
I fully realise it is normal practice in academic circles to refer to oneself as this, but it proved hopeless in many cases. So many authors are referred to that it would often have been more confusing than helpful to the 'general reader'. Apologies, therefore, for the intrusion of my name or initials HM when making comments on other authors' work. This leads directly to the next note.

A note on footnotes and end notes.
I fully recognise their usefulness on occasion, but in general I hate the things. I therefore made every effort to include all relevant details within the text, as long as they did not interrupt the flow and lead to too many words in brackets. Where footnotes are used, they are immediately below the relevant text.

One final note on the order of chapters, with each one more or less standing on its own.
When I first embarked on writing this book it seemed sensible to present the material under these headings, even though they by no means follow the chronology of **Sir Thomas** and **Sir Edward**'s lives. Only when we reach the time-line at the end of the book can we put all the details together chronologically. Before then, the reader is invited to join in solving the jigsaw puzzle or detective story. For convenience to the reader conclusions are given at the end of several chapters, based on the 'new' details presented up to that point. The impatient reader could therefore skip through the book, just reading the chapter conclusions, the time-line and the biographies of the two knights on the tomb

at the very end, which present as much as can be written with a high degree of certainty at the moment. If some of the details and conclusions presented on the way provide repetitions in several chapters, please accept my apologies; and yet no apologies are really due, because they had to be presented. When one arrives at similar conclusions from different directions, the main conclusion is that the 'real' historical story is lurking somewhere at the centre.

Id. Effigy of Sir Edward Stanley in St Bartholomew's Church, Tong
© RJL Smith

Chapter II
The Stanley tomb in Tong today, *Guidebook* in hand:
St Bartholomew's Church, Tong, Shropshire

II–1. Introduction

I visited St Bartholomew's, Tong and scrutinised the Stanley tomb in August 2004 by appointment. This visit ultimately resulted in this book. I predict that this book MIGHT result in many visits to the church by others. If this were to be the case, it would be advisable, before any visit, to consult the local authorities who actually have the key to the church, which is not always automatically open, for obvious reasons. Today (in 2012) permission for the opening of the church can be obtained most easily via email from the various authorities given on their website.

The visitor to the Collegiate and Parish Church of St Bartholomew's, Tong, Shropshire, is confronted with a multitude of tombs, memorials and other features. With some justification it has been called 'The Westminster Abbey of the Midlands', although to be fair one should also include several other Midlands churches and cathedrals under this nomenclature. One thing that makes St Bartholomew's rather special is that it contains a Stanley monumental tomb on which there are two verse epitaphs claimed by several in the seventeenth century (in still existing MSS) to have been written by William Shakespeare. We might remember that Shakespeare died in 1616, but the memory of his poetic and dramatic works lived on throughout the seventeenth century, suppressed throughout the Civil Wars but revived after the Restoration. Those who reported on the Shakespeare authorship of these two verse epitaphs were therefore either contemporaries of William Shakespeare himself, or of his children and grandchildren, some of whom survived into the Restoration period.

Anyone who has followed Shakespearean research over the past few years will know that it has been widely (although by no means universally) accepted that young William spent a period in his youth in Lancashire, under the patronage of the Hoghton and Hesketh families, before moving to the patronage of the Stanley family of Lancashire, Earls of Derby. If this was indeed historically true, then the verse epitaphs in Tong can be regarded as a natural result of this patronage. The Stanleys of Tong were from Lancashire.

There are only seven surviving epitaphs in existence that have been attributed to William Shakespeare's authorship. (All attributions are fairly reliable, although all, of course, have been disputed). Amongst these seven, the only three actually visible today in stone are the one he wrote for himself (in the Parish Church in Stratford, where he was buried, on a stone set in the floor, replaced when it 'wore out') and the two in Tong on the Stanley tomb. These two are the originals from c.1603 and are still eminently visible. The other four have survived only in documentary details. Reams have been written about all of these, with most details devoted to Shakespeare himself, of course, and whether or not he could possibly have written such a doggerel verse for himself and similar doggerel verses in praise of others. I know of no better summary of these than the one by E. A. J. Honigmann,

Shakespeare, the 'lost years', Chapter VII, 'The Shakespeare Epitaphs and the Stanleys', pp. 77-83.

A revisit to the Stanley tomb in Tong seems to be appropriate, with an examination of what can actually be seen today, and what others have written about this over the centuries.

~~~~~~~~~~~~

II–2. Current Guides to St Bartholomew's Church, the Stanley tomb & the history of Tong

There is no better initial guide around all these monuments and features in the church than the guidebook: *St Bartholomew's Church Tong Shropshire*, 2002, 22 pp. The text was researched and compiled by the Very Reverend Dr Robert Jeffery, Vicar of Tong 1978–87, subsequently Dean of Worcester and Sub-Dean of Christ Church, Oxford. The excellent photographs were taken by R.J.L. Smith of Much Wenlock, who also edited and published the guidebook and this book in your hands. Much of the text was based on the historical notes of a previous Vicar of Tong, the Revd John Ernest Auden (who happens to have been the uncle of poet W. H. Auden). Since writing the guidebook, Dr Jeffery has written *Discovering Tong*: *Its History, Myths and Curiosities*, published for the Tong Parochial Church Council, 2007. Between these two publications the Notes of the Revd Auden were transcribed, edited and published by Mrs Joyce Frost, wife of the Revd George Frost, another former Vicar of Tong. The relevant sections from the Revd Auden's 'Notes' appear in Chapter IV. The Revd J.E. Auden's *History of Tong* re the Stanley Tomb. R.J.L. Smith has taken additional photographs for the book now in the reader's hand, most specifically all details of the Stanley tomb. Excellent as these books are, they are all, by definition, histories of the whole parish, including many other details on the history of the church itself. In this book in general and this chapter in particular, we concentrate on the Stanley tomb and the people in effigy thereon, plus others actually named in the Monumental Inscription (MI) on the tomb.

There is little remaining doubt that:

a) the tomb was commissioned in 1601–02 by **Sir Edward Stanley Jr**, probably shortly after he had commissioned the Stanley tomb in Walthamstow, Essex, during his bereavement, having just lost his wife and four young daughters in mid-1601;

b) the text of the MI was almost certainly written by **Sir Edward Stanley Jr** himself, including what he considered the most important details about his immediate family;

c) he had known William Shakespeare for many years and followed his adolescent and early adult career from Lancashire to London, including his great successes on the stage and in various publications;

d) when they met again (almost certainly in London) during or shortly after the construction of the tomb, William Shakespeare wrote the two verse epitaphs for inclusion in suitable available spaces.

Several mysteries still remain, of course, which will be explored in future chapters.

~~~~~~~~~~~~

II–3. The architectural features of the tomb today

For the moment let us concentrate on the tomb as it appears today and be absolutely certain who is depicted by the effigies.

The tomb is constructed from marble and alabaster and a mixture of other stones, in two tiers. The bottom tier contains the life-size effigy of **Sir Edward** (1562–1632) and the top one the life-size effigies of his parents **Sir Thomas** (c.1534–76) and Lady Margaret Stanley née Vernon (c.1535–96). This **Sir Edward** is called **Jr** whenever it is necessary to distinguish him from his uncle

IIa. The Stanley tomb today
© RJL Smith.

IIb. Before the 1892 retoration
On the top of this very elaborate tomb (left) are the effigies of Sir Thomas Stanley and his wife Margaret Vernon. Underneath is the effigy of their son Sir Edward Stanley, who commissioned the tomb. As originally designed, the four pillars had golden balls on the top and carved figures at each corner. Some of these figures survive elsewhere in the church.

(Jeffery, Discovering Tong, p. 90).

Sir Edward Sr (c.1535–40 to 1604). The latter only marginally enters the story of the tomb itself, and no other Sir Thomas Stanley and Sir Edward Stanley enters the story of this tomb at all. Indeed, one of the main aims of this book was to identify as definitely as possible details for the biographies of **Sir Thomas** and **Sir Edward** on the tomb, distinguishing them from all the other contemporary Sir Thomas and Sir Edward Stanleys with whom they have frequently been muddled.

We will meet some other contemporary Sir Edward Stanleys in more detail later in this book (Chapter XXII. Other (Sir) Edward Stanleys). The reason for there being so many contemporary (Sir) Edward Stanleys was partly because of Edward Stanley, 3rd Earl of Derby (1508–72). He named his third (surviving) son after himself — this was **Sir Edward Sr**. However, there had also been other previous Sir Edward Stanleys from side branches, who predictably produced sons and grandsons with the same name. And so in every generation throughout the whole Tudor period there were two, three or more (Sir) Edward Stanleys. Sir Thomases were almost as numerous, descended from Thomas, 1st Baron Stanley and his son and heir Thomas 2nd Baron Stanley, 1st Earl of Derby (3rd creation), the one who appears in Shakespeare's *Richard III*.

The top tier is supported on four round columns on each side, with additional support coming from interior trusses on eight ornamental square columns. On the top four corners are obelisks. We will read later that there were originally other decorative features, which have since disappeared or been moved for a variety of reasons.

One description of the Stanley tomb by an expert on church monuments is as follows:

> [The tomb] consists of two excellent recumbent white marble effigies of **Sir Thomas** and Lady Stanley on top of a broad black and grey convex-sided sarcophagus with elegant white clasps, supported by eight marble Tuscan columns with four cross-arches. These are decorated with beautifully carved miniature emblems suspended by lively ribbonwork on their pilasters and spandrels. Housed under the cross-arches is a narrow, convex-sided, black and white sarcophagus resting on lions' feet and carrying the alabaster effigy of their son, lying on a traditional folded rush mat. His head rests on a pillow and his right hand on his chest, in contrast to the effigies of his parents whose hands are joined in prayer, signifying that the monument was

IId. Sir Edward Stanley Jr (lower tier)
[see also colour section] © RJL Smith

made in **Sir Edward**'s lifetime. The four black obelisks now on the top corners originally stood at floor level. Their places were formerly occupied by the four vandalised allegorical figures now placed high up on the adjacent screen to the Vernon chapel on the south side of the tomb.
(Simon Watney, 'Sky aspiring pyramids', *Church Monuments*, vol. XX, 2005, pp.103–4.)

IIc. Lady Margaret and Sir Thomas Stanley (upper tier)
[see also colour section] © RJL Smith

This does not solve any mysteries still remaining, but gives us a few new words from architectural jargon when describing tombs, e.g. pilasters and spandrels. It also provides a rap on the knuckles to anyone who has ever looked at a tomb and confused marble with alabaster: **Sir Thomas** and his wife are in marble; **Sir Edward** is in alabaster. Watney has also identified the columns as Tuscan rather than Dugdale's 'Corinthian' (see Chapter V. Two early recordings).

Both knights are wearing Elizabethan armour, which already poses a slight problem. There is no (surviving documentary) record (discovered so far) of either ever having fought in a war or military or naval campaign, unlike several of their close relatives and friends, who certainly did. Regular tournaments were held at Court, which required armour. Whether or not **Sir Thomas** or **Sir Edward** participated in any of these tournaments remains unknown, although there is no doubt that both were at court when they were knighted by the monarch (**Sir Thomas** in 1553 by Queen Mary and **Sir Edward** in 1603 by King James). The armour might thus be merely conventional as the suitable attire for a knight in effigy on an Elizabethan/Jacobean tomb.

We should perhaps remember that **Sir Thomas** and particularly his son **Sir Edward** lived during the time of Sir Francis Drake, Sir Walter Raleigh & Co. The latter have gone down in popular history as heroes, and we all remember them not least from the history we learnt at school. None of us learnt at school about any Stanley knights, least of all these two on the tomb in Tong. Yet **Sir Thomas** and **Sir Edward** have one distinction that places them apart from all other Elizabethan (and Marian and Jacobean) knights, which makes them unique — their tomb is the only one in the whole country that displays two verse epitaphs attributed to Shakespeare.

One large clue about the date of the tomb comes from the portrayal of **Sir Edward** as a man of around forty, with a full head of hair, and certainly not that of a sixty-nine-year-old, his age at death. This on its own suggests that he commissioned his effigy, and maybe the whole tomb, around 1601 or soon afterwards. His effigy could have been carved from life, his father's from a sketch from memory or maybe a portrait (he died in 1576), and his mother's perhaps also from a portrait (she died in 1596). No portraits of any of them have survived, so their effigies are the sole pictorial record.

~~~~~~~~~~~~~~~~~

II–4. The Monumental Inscription

According to the guidebook the inscription on the side of the tomb reads:

> Thomas Stanley, second son of Edward Earl of Derbie, Lord Stanley and Strange Descended from the Familie of the Stanleys Married Margaret Vernon one of the daughters and cohairs of Sir George Vernon of Nether Haddon in the Countie of Derbie Knight. By whom he had Issue Two Sons Henry and Edw: Henry died an infant and E survived to whom Thos Lordships Descended and Married the La Lucie Percie second daughter to Thomas Earl of Northumberland by her had issue 7 daughters and one soone Shee and her 4 daughters 18 Arabella 16 Marie 15 Alice and 13 Priscilla are interred under a monument in ye Churche of Waltham in ye countie of Essex. Thomas his soone died in infancie and is Buried in Ye parishe Church of Winckle in Ye Countie of Lanca: Ye other Three Petronella Francis and Venesie are living.
>
> (*Guidebook*, pp. 12–13.)

As can be seen from photographs, the MI is on three panels along the bottom of the top tier. The text immediately above, as given in the guidebook, is indeed a (fairly) faithful transcription, but in modernized spelling, all running on and with a few discrepancies. Anyone actually peering at the tomb (or the photos in this book) will immediately notice that the original text is all in capital letters. It seems useful, therefore, to give an accurate rendition of the text as it actually appears on the tomb. This is always referred to in this book as the MI, to distinguish it from the two verse epitaphs at the head and foot.

THOMAS STANDLEY KNIGHT SECOND SOONE OF ED'
EARLE OF DERBIE LO: STANLEY AND STRANGE
DESCENDED FROM Yᴱ FAMILIE OF Yᴱ STANLEYS MARIED
MARGARET VERNON ONE OF Yᴱ DAVGHTERES AND
COHAIRS OF Sᴿ GEORGE VERNON OF NETHER HADDON
IN THE COVNTIE OF DARBIE KNIGHT

BY WHOM HE HAD ISSVE · 2 · SOONS HENRI AND
EDW: HENRIE DIED AN INFANT · E · SVRVIVED TO WHOM
THOS LORDSHIPES DESENDED & MARIED Yᴱ LA: LVCIE PERCIE
SECOND DAVGHTEᴿ TO THO. EARLE OF NORTHVMBELAND
BY HIR HE HAD ISSVE · 7 · DAVGHTERS & ONE SOONE. SHEE
AND HIR · 4 · DAVGTER. ¹⁸ ARBELLA. ¹⁶ MARIE. ¹⁵ ALIS. & ¹³ PRISCILLA.

ARE INTERRED VNDER A MONNIMENT IN Yᴱ CHVRCHE
OF WALTHAM, IN Yᴱ COVNTIE OF ESSEX . THOˢ HIS SOON
DIED IN HIS INFANCIE A IS BVRIED IN Yᴱ PARISHE CHVRCHE
OF WINWICKE IN Yᴱ COVNTIE OF LANCA: Yᴱ OTHER THREE .
PETRONELLA, FRANCIS, AND VENESIE ARE YET LIVINGE .
[All superscripts in the MI actually appear immediately above the relevant letter/word.]

With so much detail given about the family, this MI was obviously composed by someone with intimate knowledge of all concerned, and there is no reason to suppose that the original text was by anyone other than **Sir Edward Jr** himself. He obviously thought at the time that he had given all necessary details for 'eternity'. At what point the various abbreviations and idiosyncrasies of spelling and punctuation in later versions crept in will never be known, but one might assume that the person inscribing these words into the spaces available was responsible for several slight anomalies. He was just doing his job as an artisan, not necessarily as a highly literate transcriber.

~~~~~~~~~~~~~~~~~

II–5. The two verse epitaphs at the head and foot (by Shakespeare?)

The guidebook tells us (p.13): 'The words at each end of the monument are reputed to have been written for it by William Shakespeare. This claim has been well authenticated: successive Earls of Derby patronised Shakespeare and his players. The verses read:

Ask who lyes heare but do not weep He is not dead he doth but sleep This stoney register is for his bones His fame is more perpetual than these stones And his own goodness with himself being gone Shall lyve when earthlie monument is none

Not monumental stone preserves our Fame Nor sky aspyring pyramids our name The memory of Him for whom this stands Shall outlive marble and defacers Hands When all to tyme's consumption shall be geaven Standley for whom this stands shall stand in Heaven.'

This is true, but the verses do actually appear in verse form on the tomb. My conclusion, having examined at least a dozen later printed renditions of the verse epitaphs on the tomb, is that very few people reporting about the Tong epitaphs actually visited St Bartholomew's to view the tomb and see the epitaphs for themselves. All was based on hearsay and (sometimes) inadequate reports or copies of transcriptions. Given that these verses have been quoted many times, with a whole variety of deviant spellings and punctuation, it seems to be in order to provide an accurate version of how they actually appear in gilt lettering on the tomb.

(At the foot):
ASK WHO LYES HEARE, BVT DO NOT WEEP,
HE IS NOT DEAD, HE DOOTH BVT SLEEP
THIS STONY REGISTER, IS FOR HIS BONES
HIS FAME IS MORE PERPETVALL THÊ THEISE STONES
AND HIS OWNE GOODNES W^T HIM SELF BEING GON
SHALL LYVE WHEN EARTHLIE MONAMENT IS NONE

(At the head):
NOT MONVENTALL STONE PRESERVES OVR FAME
NOR SKY ASPYRING PIRAMIDS OVR NAME,
THE MEMORY OF HIM FOR WHOM THIS STANDS
SHALL OVTLYVE MARBL, AND DEFACERS HANDS
WHEN ALL TO TYMES CONSVMPTION SHALL BE GEAVEN
STANDLY FOR WHOM THIS STANDS SHALL STAND IN HEAVEN

II-6. More details from the guidebook

So much, then, can be deduced from just looking at the tomb today. The guidebook also gives the following paragraph (p.12), a masterpiece of succinctness, with some preliminary elaborations on details in notes:

The monument was originally beside the high altar, beneath which the Stanleys are buried in lead coffins.[i] **Sir Thomas Stanley** was the Governor of the Isle of Man.[ii] **Sir Edward Stanley**, their son, was married to Lady Lucy Percy whose father was executed by Elizabeth I in 1572 for plotting against her. Her grandfather had been executed by Henry VIII.[iii] **Sir Edward Stanley**, who was regarded by the Puritans as a dangerous papist,[iv] died in 1632 having sold Tong Castle to Sir Thomas Harries in 1613.[v]

Notes by HM:

[i] The original and the present position of the tomb can be seen on the plan of the church in the guidebook. **Sir Thomas** and Lady Margaret were indeed buried in the Stanley vault beneath the altar (in 1576 and 1596 respectively), but when this was opened in 1891, their bodies were not there, their

coffins having been cut open. There were also remains in lime in a small coffin of what was presumed might have contained the body of their infant son Henry. A full report of the opening of the vault appears in Chapter IV. The Revd J.E. Auden's *History of Tong* re the Stanley tomb.

[ii] Sir Thomas Stanley held the position of Governor of the Isle of Man in 1562–66. It had been a hereditary post within the family since his ancestor Sir John Stanley had been awarded the title of Lord of Man in 1405. The Governor from then on was always appointed by the Stanleys.

[iii] The story of the Percys, Earls of Northumberland, has been researched and told many times (all Earls in the *Old* and *New/Oxford DNB*, for starters, and recently on a multitude of genealogical websites), but bears retelling here briefly from the perspective of Lucy and her husband. Lucy's grandfather was Sir Thomas Percy, who was executed at Tyburn in 1537 for his role in the Pilgrimage of Grace in 1536. His older brother Henry Algernon Percy, 6th Earl (betrothed for a while to Anne Boleyn and therefore long in disfavour with Henry VIII), fearing the effect on the fortunes of the family, voluntarily surrendered his estates to the crown and on his death, childless, on 29 June 1537, the title fell into abeyance. Sir Thomas's widow married Sir Richard Holland of Denton near Manchester, Lancashire, which already gives a Lancashire connection in Stanley territory for Lucy in her step-grandfather. Her grandmother died in 1567 when Lucy was only about four or five, but presumably the Percy family retained memories and perhaps some contact with their Lancashire in-laws.

When the title was restored by Catholic Queen Mary, along with the estates, it passed to 6th Earl Henry's nephew Thomas, eldest son of Henry's younger brother Sir Thomas. This Thomas, now 7th Earl of Northumberland, was Lucy's father, married since 1558 to Anne Somerset, daughter of Henry Somerset, 2nd Earl of Worcester.

Those immediate relatives actually known by Lucy (c.1562–1601), second daughter of Thomas the 7th Earl and wife of **(Sir) Edward Jr**, were the following [one might presume that their stories were known rather well to her husband]:

a) Her father Thomas Percy, 7th Earl of Northumberland (1528–72) was beheaded in 1572 in York for his involvement in the Northern Rebellion of 1569, which was largely between those with Protestant (supporting Elizabeth) and Catholic (supporting Mary, Queen of Scots) allegiances, although of course more complicated. For his participation in supporting Mary, Queen of Scots and his ensuing 'martyrdom' he was later beatified by the Catholic Church. He died without leaving a male heir when Lucy was under ten, but her mother lived until 1596. She, however, as a staunch Catholic, had been one of the main instigators of and participants in the Northern Rebellion and after the suppression of this she was forced into exile in Flanders, where she died at Namur. Three of her daughters (including Lucy) were left behind in England and raised by their paternal uncle Henry Percy, 8th Earl of Northumberland at Petworth, Sussex. Lucy's marriage to **Edward Stanley** in c.1581 was therefore presumably arranged by her uncle Henry.

b) Henry Percy (1532–85), Lucy's uncle, was later incarcerated in the Tower of London, where he was found shot in his cell in 1585. The official verdict was suicide, but at the time and ever since there have inevitably been suspicions as to whether it was suicide or murder.

c) Henry, 9th Earl (1564–1632), son and heir of Henry, 8th Earl, was Lucy's first cousin, with whom she grew up. He was an exact contemporary of Lucy, her husband **(Sir) Edward Jr** and Shakespeare. He has gone down in popular history as 'The Wizard Earl' because of his interest in alchemy, science and astronomy, amongst many other areas, including patronage of the arts. In 1594 he married Dorothy Devereux (c.1564–1619), sister of Robert Devereux, 2nd Earl of Essex. His other sister was Penelope Devereux (1563–1607), who is generally accepted as the inspiration for Stella in Sir Philip Sidney's *Astrophel and Stella*. (Penelope appears in 'Appendix 3. Shakespeare's Dark Lady of the Sonnets — Sir Edward's cousin-in-law Penelope Rich?'.) Henry, 'The Wizard Earl', was involved in politics and Catholic plots inasmuch as he sent a relative Sir Thomas Percy to James VI's court in Scotland, promising support for his succession to Elizabeth's throne if he would be tolerant to Catholics. This backfired in the Gunpowder Plot, when another Thomas Percy was one of the main conspirators and one of those shot during his attempt to escape through the Midlands. Because of this association, Henry 'The Wizard Earl' was sent to the Tower of London, where he spent 17 years. Lucy had died in the meantime, but her husband lived until 1632 throughout all these events.

[iv] Sir Thomas was undoubtedly a papist (see the oft-given 1575 quote referring to his meeting 'papists gentilmen' in Tong, mentioned in several later chapters, including Chapter XXVIII. Timeline). His younger brother **Sir Edward Stanley Sr** might have been described as an 'arch-papist' on occasion and Richard Topcliffe, Elizabeth's chief persecutor of Catholics, growled on one occasion that 'all Stanleys are traitors'. I fear that in this case, however, any reference to a Sir Edward Stanley being an 'arch-papist' might have referred to one of the several other contemporary Sir Edward Stanleys. I have encountered no references to son **Sir Edward Jr** being actively papist, although he was certainly surrounded by many who were, including several involved in the Gunpowder Plot in 1605, who were executed. These included a Percy (mentioned above) and Sir Everard Digby, a childhood friend of the Stanleys and father of Sir Kenelm Digby, the future husband of **Sir Edward Jr**'s daughter Venetia. Also the 4th Lord Monteagle who 'betrayed' the Gunpowder Plot to the government authorities was a 'cousin' of some degree to **Sir Edward Stanley Sr** and **Jr**. Although himself a Parker, he was the inheritor through marriage of the Stanley title of Lord Monteagle of Hornby Castle near Lancaster, which had been bestowed on Sir Edward Stanley, brother of the 1st Earl of Derby, by Henry VIII after his instrumental role in the victory over the Scots at Flodden in 1513. This lay in the meantime nearly a century in the past, but there is more than adequate evidence that the Stanleys, Lords Monteagle, and the Stanleys, Earls of Derby had stayed in constant contact and very much remembered their joint roots in Lathom, Lancashire. The very fact that **Sir Edward Stanley Jr** lived on to a natural death in 1632 in Eysnham, Oxon, aged almost seventy, and that his uncle **Sir Edward Sr** lived on to a natural death in 1604, aged well into his sixties, buried at Ormskirk, implies in itself that they were never actively involved in any 'papist conspiracies' in the 1580s, 1590s or early 1600s.

[v] Under other circumstances the precise date of the sale of Tong Castle would probably be semi-irrelevant, but it seems to be rather relevant in this book, considering that we are on a detective hunt which concerns Shakespeare (who retired from the London theatre at the latest by 1613 and died in 1616). **Sir Edward Jr** did indeed sell Tong Castle to Sir Thomas Harries. The almost certain date is 1603, but various details in the aftermath of this sale concerning the Manor of Tong dragged on for a few more years, including the dates 1613 and 1623. This perhaps explains why at least three different dates for the sale have been reported in previous accounts. The Revd Dr Jeffery agrees (personal communication), and some day we might together produce all the relevant documents from archives, to the boredom of most readers, but with the satisfaction that we have produced an explanation of previous errors.

~~~~~~~~~~~~~~~~

II–7. A few more questions, whilst still looking at the tomb

Even without knowledge of the Stanley bodies in the vault (or not there), just looking at the tomb today might raise a few more questions for the inquisitive visitor.

Question One.
Why is only the effigy of Sir Edward Jr, and not his wife Lucy, on the lower tier of the tomb?
This question has indeed been asked by at least one long-time resident of Tong. Any explanation for this must be based on the following facts:

a) His wife Lucy had died in early-mid 1601 at Walthamstow, Essex, along with four of their daughters. He had buried them there with a monumental tomb and effigies of them all. He had also written a MI for this tomb, recording the family history.
b) He very obviously commissioned the tomb in Tong, or at least his own effigy for this, after he had buried his wife and four daughters.
c) He still had three surviving daughters, and in 1601–03 might well have expected that they and he himself might live on for many more years — which they did.
d) He sold Tong Castle in 1603 and moved to Eynsham Abbey in Oxfordshire, where he died in 1632.
e) His later son-in-law Sir Kenelm Digby wrote in his memoirs that his father-in-law had rather withdrawn from public life after the death of his wife Lucy.
f) He was buried at Eynsham in 1632 by his unmarried daughter Petronella.

In the middle of all these facts various possible explanations emerge, among which are the following tentative suggestions.
a) It might well have been the case that he and his wife were already separated for a while. They certainly were by her death.
b) When he commissioned the tombs for his wife at Walthamstow and his parents at Tong, he still had no idea what he might do with the rest of his remaining life.
c) When he commissioned his own effigy in c.1602, he had still not decided what the final form of the tomb at Tong should be.
d) The next thirty years were so turbulent that he perhaps never came to a decision about the best solution.
e) When Petronella buried him, she decided to place her father's effigy in Tong (according to his last wishes?), united in death with her mother, Lucy, at least by two almost identical MIs.

Questions Two and Three.
Why were there two verse epitaphs and not just one? And were they really by Shakespeare?
These can be tentatively answered now, before they are pursued in more detail. The fact that there are two epitaphs and two male effigies led to the early general assumption that there was one each for **Sir Thomas** and **Sir Edward**. However, with **Sir Thomas**'s death in 1576, when William Shakespeare was only twelve, it is highly unlikely that he ever met him, and certainly not at an age when Shakespeare was writing poems or epitaphs. If both were written for **Sir Edward Jr**, then one must wonder why there were two. Were they offered as alternatives, but he included them both? We will never know, but the last line in the second epitaph leaves no doubt that this one was written for a Stanley:

'Standly for whom this stands, shall stand in heaven'.

This includes a pun on the name. It is not just since the advent of slipping keys on a typewriter and modern careless spelling and typos that Stanley often comes out as Standl(e)y. It occurs as this several times in contemporary MSS, allowing puns on anything including 'stand', e.g. 'stand fast', 'of high standing', etc. The name actually came from Stoneleigh in Staffordshire (meaning the 'stoney meadow', from Anglo-Saxon), the original home before one Stanley moved to Cheshire, with a later branch founded in Lancashire at the time of John of Gaunt (who appears as 'time-honoured Lancaster' in *Richard II*). This Lancashire branch subsequently became the Earls of Derby, when 2nd Baron Thomas Stanley was created 1st Earl of Derby (third creation, and a title available rather conveniently, because the main family seat was at Lathom in the hundred of West Derby) by his step-son Henry VII after his victory over Richard III at Bosworth Field in 1485. He appears in *Richard III* as 'Lord Stanley, called also Earl of Derby' and **Sir Edward Jr**'s gt-gt grandfather George, Lord Strange, also receives an off-stage role as a hostage during the battle. Shakespeare gives a dramatic but rather dubious historical account of the battle and the events leading up to it. For a more reliable historical account of the Stanley participation, one needs to consult historians on the Lancashire Earls of Derby.

As to whether the epitaphs really were by Shakespeare, the *Guidebook* (p.13) tells us:

> The words at each end of the monument are reputed to have been written for it by William Shakespeare. This claim has been well authenticated; successive Earls of Derby patronised Shakespeare and his players.

[Details of this authentication and the relevant Earls of Derby will be pursued in later chapters.]

The perspicacious observer of the tomb will note that the second epitaph, whoever wrote it, had actually seen the tomb, or at least knew of its planned features. This hint is 'sky-rising pyramids', mirroring the pyramids/obelisks on the top four corners. The inclusion of 'marble' is probably insignificant, because virtually all tombs as elaborate as this were made at least partly of marble. If the epitaphs were by Shakespeare, this would in itself push the date of the commissioning and the potential completion of the tomb, and the composition of the epitaphs back to well before 1616, the year of Shakespeare's death. Further confirmation of early rather than later completion comes from **Sir Edward**'s face, which, as noted above, is certainly not that of a sixty-nine-year-old (his age at death), but more like a forty-year-old, his age in 1602. A near contemporary example of another tomb depicting a relative as a thirty-year-old, although nearer eighty when she died, is that of Countess Alice née Spencer in Harefield Church, Middlesex. She was the widow of **Sir Edward**'s first cousin Ferdinando, 5th Earl of Derby.

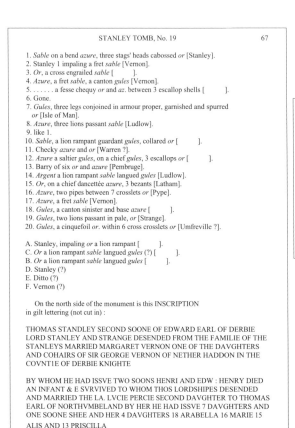

STANLEY TOMB, No. 19   67

1. *Sable* on a bend *azure*, three stags' heads cabossed *or* [Stanley].
2. Stanley 1 impaling a fret *sable* [Vernon].
3. *Or*, a cross engrailed *sable* [   ].
4. *Azure*, a fret *sable*, a canton *gules* [Vernon].
5. . . . . . . a fesse chequy *or* and *az.* between 3 escallop shells [   ].
6. Gone.
7. *Gules*, three legs conjoined in armour proper, garnished and spurred *or* [Isle of Man].
8. *Azure*, three lions passant *sable* [Ludlow].
9. like 1.
10. *Sable*, a lion rampant guardant *gules*, collared *or* [   ].
11. Checky *azure* and *or* [Warren ?].
12. *Azure* a saltier *gules*, on a chief *gules*, 3 escallops *or* [   ].
13. Barry of six *or* and *azure* [Pembruge].
14. *Argent* a lion rampant *sable* langued *gules* [Ludlow].
15. *Or*, on a chief dancettée *azure*, 3 bezants [Latham].
16. *Azure*, two pipes between 7 crosslets *or* [Pype].
17. *Azure*, a fret *sable* [Vernon].
18. *Gules*, a canton sinister and base *azure* [   ].
19. *Gules*, two lions passant in pale, *or* [Strange].
20. *Gules*, a cinquefoil *or.* within 6 cross crosslets *or* [Umfreville ?].

A. Stanley, impaling *or* a lion rampant [   ].
C. *Or* a lion rampant *sable* langued *gules* (?) [   ].
B. *Or* a lion rampant *sable* langued *gules* [   ].
D. Stanley (?)
E. Ditto (?)
F. Vernon (?)

On the north side of the monument is this INSCRIPTION in gilt lettering (not cut in) :

THOMAS STANDLEY SECOND SOONE OF EDWARD EARL OF DERBIE LORD STANLEY AND STRANGE DESENDED FROM THE FAMILIE OF THE STANLEYS MARRIED MARGARET VERNON ONE OF THE DAVGHTERS AND COHAIRS OF SIR GEORGE VERNON OF NETHER HADDON IN THE COVNT1E OF DERBIE KNIGHTE

BY WHOM HE HAD ISSVE TWO SOONS HENRI AND EDW : HENRY DIED AN INFANT & E SVRVIVED TO WHOM THOS LORDSHIPES DESENDED AND MARRIED THE LA. LVCIE PERCIE SECOND DAVGHTER TO THOMAS EARL OF NORTHVMBELAND BY HER HE HAD ISSVE 7 DAVGHTERS AND ONE SOONE SHEE AND HER 4 DAVGHTERS 18 ARABELLA 16 MARIE 15 ALIS AND 13 PRISCILLA

IIe. Shields on the tomb
Showing previous marriage alliances
(Griffiths, *History of Tong*, 1885, p.67)

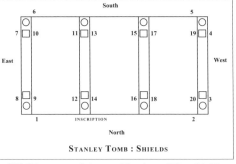

STANLEY TOMB : SHIELDS

IIf. Diagram of the positioning of the shields
(Griffiths, *History of Tong*, 1885)

Chapter III
The Revd Dr Robert Jeffery on
'The Shakespeare Connection' with Tong

III–1. Introduction

We met the Very Reverend Dr Robert Jeffery in the last chapter as the author of the text for the *Guidebook* of 2002. His book *Discovering Tong: Its History, Myths and Curiosities* (2007) covers the history of the village and parish as well as the church, with just four pages on the Stanley tomb in 'Part 4. Literary Tong, Chapter 12, The Shakespeare Connection.' Most notable is that he includes the attribution of the authorship of the epitaphs to Shakespeare rather more forcefully than the Revd J.E. Auden, who used the word 'allegedly'. Auden's comment was at a time (c.1900) when there was great scepticism. The magisterial Sir Sidney Lee had published his biography of Shakespeare in 1898, which did not even mention the Tong epitaphs. During the whole of the nineteenth century there had been resistance to accepting the idea that Shakespeare had consorted in any intimate way with Catholics, whereas **Sir Thomas Stanley** and some of his relatives were certainly rather ardent Catholics.

In my opinion Dr Jeffery in 2007 gave the best and most thoroughly researched outline to date of the various attributions of the Tong epitaphs to Shakespeare, and the even larger number of doubts. He also admirably pointed out many of the muddles that had been introduced and perpetuated over the last couple of centuries. Most of his Chapter 12 is therefore reproduced here.

IIIa. Engraving of Tong Castle, c.1731
Samuel and Nathaniel Buck,*Views of Ruins of Castles & Abbeys in the Midlands 1726-1739* (pub. 1760), usually known as *Buck's Views*. This was still largely the Tudor version before later restoration and thus contained many elements that would have been familiar to Sir Thomas and Sir Edward Stanley.

I hope this does not detract from sales of his book. It should be noted that his Chapter 12 has eight pages, out of a total of 210. The other 202 pages are equally packed with interesting history and excellent illustrations.

His eight pages here are accompanied by a series of notes by myself. My notes are in no way a criticism of Dr Jeffery's work, but aim to highlight various muddled points which, it is hoped, are now solved in later chapters of this book in the reader's hand, devoted totally to the Tong epitaphs. They also aim to add, as appropriate, some details from Lancashire unknown to Dr Jeffery. His notes appear in round brackets; my own notes are in bold with Roman numerals in square brackets. His Notes for this Chapter all appear on page 154, the eighth page of his chapter. It seemed sensible here to include his Notes immediately under each section.

~~~~~~~~~~~~

III–2. *Discovering Tong*: 'The Shakespeare Connection' — Part One

At the beginning of Jeffery's Chapter 12 appear the verse epitaphs, as given in Chapter II. The Stanley tomb in Tong today, followed by:

> In Chapter 7, we noted how this Tomb has been moved and the connections between the Vernon and Stanley families' history was outlined. But what is the origin of the Shakespearian attribution and can it be justified? The attribution is early. There is a document of 1620 which copies out these words, stating that they are by Shakespeare.**(1) [i]** Sir William Dugdale, in his survey of Tong in 1663, acknowledged the Shakespearian origin.**(2) [ii]** The Revd R. W. Eyton and Archdeacon Cranage, following him, both have real doubts. Eyton writes about the first verse:
>
> *'This was probably an early effort by the poet of genius for Sir Thomas Stanley died in December 1576 when Shakespeare was not yet 13 years old.'*
> On the second verse he writes:
> *'The opposite end of the tomb there exist six lines which I cannot but help thinking to have been an imitation of the former and by an inferior poet. Possibly they are in praise of Sir Edward Stanley (son of Sir Thomas) to whose memory the monument is in part devoted for they speak of who lies beneath. Now Sir Thomas Stanley is said to have been buried not at Tong but at Walthamstow.'* (Eyton)
>
> This reveals vast confusions. Eyton may not have known that the tomb had been moved. We know that the inscription on Sir Thomas' coffin, which was found in the Sanctuary, confirms that he was buried at Tong. Secondly, the Thomas referred to on the side of the tomb is the son of Edward. Moreover, the inscription on the tomb states that this Thomas died in infancy and is not buried at Walthamstow, but *'in ye parish of Winwick in ye countie of Lancs'*.**[iii]**
>
> In 1929, a Mrs Esdaile wrote a pamphlet entitled ***Shakespeare's verses in Tong Church***. She asserted the authenticity of Shakespeare's verses. She pointed out that doggerel rhymes, like those on Shakespeare's own memorial in Stratford-on-Avon Church, were written because they were easy for the stone carvers. She mentioned the Shakespeare connections with the Stanleys. *A Midsummer Night's Dream* was written for the wedding of Fernando (*sic*, Ferdinando) (Fourth [*sic*, Fifth] Earl of Derby) in 1588. Fernando had taken over the patronage of Shakespeare's company of players in that year.**(3) [iv]**
>
> **(1)** This is a transcription of the words on the tomb and has a note in a later hand at the top stating 'Inscriptions transcribed in the 1620s' but the provenance is not at all clear.**[i]**
> **(2)** See the footnotes on the epitaph in ***Complete Sonnets and Poems*** ed. by Colin Burrow pp. 723–724.**[ii]**
> **(3)** Mrs Esdaile ***Shakespeare's Verses in Tong Church*** (*The Times*, 1929).**[iv]**
>
> (Jeffery, *Discovering Tong*, pp.147–148; notes for this chapter on p.154.)

Notes by HM:

[i] **'There is a document of 1620 which copies out these words, stating that they are by Shakespeare'.** I confess that this was one of my first encounters with huge muddles. Dr Jeffery points out that the provenance is not clear. Unfortunately, he does not say where he found it. I strongly suspect that this transcription was rather later than 1620, a copy of a copy, with the original transcription 'known' from other sources to have been 'transcribed in the 1620s'. The first known transcription discovered so far was by poet and antiquarian John Weever, which is covered in full in the following Chapters IV, V and VII, all relating to John Weever. The dates of c.1626 and 1630 have been attributed by others to Weever's transcription of the verse epitaphs, so a couple of decades later the attribution to the writer 'in a later hand' might have just taken a pot-shot at a transcription 'in the 1620s'. In any case this was before the death of **Sir Edward** in 1632 (and obviously before the death of Weever, who died in the same year). Weever's transcription did not, however, include any reference to Shakespeare.

[ii] Colin Burrow produced this edition for Oxford in 2002. Since then Oxford has produced *The Complete Works* (2005), eds. Wells and Taylor, including a section on the Sonnets and Poems. I have yet to read a commentary by any Shakespeare scholar that demonstrates knowledge of the biographies of **Sir Thomas** and **Sir Edward Jr** beyond what is on the MI on the tomb; nor any comment revealing more than a perfunctory knowledge of Sir William Dugdale. However, someone in the (mid?) seventeenth century thought they knew that someone had transcribed the verses in c.1620 and also knew that they were by Shakespeare. This must have preceded Sir William Dugdale's 1663 MS, which was the first to produce a partial transcription of the MI **plus** a transcription of the verse epitaphs, with a very definite attribution of authorship to Shakespeare, included in his diary of notes for his *Visitation of Shropshire* in 1663. See Chapter V. Two early recordings of the inscription and epitaphs; Chapter VI. Seven seventeenth-century recordings; Chapter VII. How reliable was Sir William Dugdale?

[iii] The Revd R.W. Eyton wrote this in his monumental *Antiquities of Shropshire* (1841). As Dr Jeffery writes, he perpetrated so many errors and anomalies about the tomb and the inscriptions that it can be dismissed as contributing nothing relevant to the debate on authenticity of Shakespeare authorship. This quote does, however, reveal that the transcription 'in 1620' was perhaps a copy of Weever's transcription. In this Eyton also falsely gave the place of **Sir Thomas**'s burial as Walthamstow.

[iv] I have been an admirer of Mrs Esdaile's contribution since Dr Jeffery sent it to me. I consider it so valuable in the whole Shakespeare/Stanley debate that it is reproduced in full in Chapter IX. Katherine Esdaile's contribution. However, one must remember that she wrote it in 1929, a date well before a flood of publications on Shakespeare and Stanleys appeared during the rest of the century. In fact there are several errors in one of her sentences: '*A Midsummer Night's Dream* was written for the wedding of Fernando (*sic*, Ferdinando) (Fourth [*sic*, Fifth] Earl of Derby) in 1588'.

'Fernando' was almost always called Ferdinando, and he was the Fifth, not 'Fourth' Earl of Derby. One correction was by Jeffery, one by myself. Also, her unequivocal statement that *Dream* was written for this wedding is by no means the accepted story. In fact, there has been much debate for the last several decades about which wedding it was written for and first performed at, with no one supporting Ferdinando's in 1588. The two main current contenders are:

a) The wedding of William Stanley, 6th Earl of Derby and Elizabeth de Vere, daughter of Edward de Vere, 17th Earl of Oxford (both of these Earls are Alternative Shakespeare Authorship candidates!!) at Greenwich on 26 January 1595.

b) The wedding of Thomas Berkeley and Elizabeth Carey at Blackfriars on 19 February 1596.

William Stanley was the brother of Ferdinando, and took over the Earldom when his brother died in 1594, by suspected poisoning. The arguments for a premiere at the Stanley wedding (cogent for all who believe in 'Shakespeare in Lancashire') appear in E. A. J. Honigmann, *Shakespeare: the 'lost years'*, Appendix C. This is of potential relevance, of course, to the Stanley Tong Epitaphs, because **Sir Thomas of Winwick and Tong** was the uncle of Ferdinando and William, the latter being therefore a first cousin of **Sir Edward Jr**, with whom he always stayed in contact.

III–3. *Discovering Tong*: 'The Shakespeare Connection'— Part Two

The Revd Dr Jeffery continues:

> Recent research takes us further. In 1985 Prof. E. Honigmann published a book entitled *'Shakespeare: The Lost Years'*(4) It contains a whole chapter on the Stanley Tomb.[v] He begins by quoting E. K. Chambers, who dismisses the Shakespearean authorship:

> 'It is clear that one set of verses cannot be Shakespearean if it relates to Sir Edward Stanley who owned Tong (he died in 1632) and on internal evidence there is no temptation to accept either of them as his.' **(5)**

> Chambers is following the errors of Eyton and Cranage. Honigmann is clear that Shakespeare belonged to a Roman Catholic family. When he was 15, his father was made bankrupt. William had to leave school. His schoolmaster put him in touch with his brother, John Cottam, a Jesuit priest, who was working secretly with Catholic families in Lancashire. He was based at Hoghton Hall.[vi] Part of this theory relies on the assumption that the reference of a legacy to a servant called Shakeshaft, which appears in Alexander Hoghton's will, refers to William Shakespeare.**(6)** But there were large numbers of people called Shakeshaft in the Preston area at that time. Ackroyd, in his recent biography of Shakespeare, comments:

> *'It seems more than a coincidence. What would be more natural than that Cottam should recommend his most brilliant pupil, also a Catholic to be schoolmaster to the Hoghton children.'* **(7)** [vii]

> **(4)** Honigmann, *Shakespeare: The Lost Years* (1985)
> **(5)** E. K. Chambers, *William Shakespeare - A study of the Facts and Problems* (1930)
> **(6)** See also R. Wilson, *Secret Shakespeare* (2003) and S. Greenblatt *Will in the World* (2004). Too much can be made of the Roman Catholic connection. At this period many people observed religious practices that were most convenient to them. Ben Jonson, who was a Catholic for many years and ended up as an Anglican, said he was 'for any religion as being versed in both'. Shakespeare was godfather to one of his children and probably held similar views.
> **(7)** See Ackroyd, *Shakespeare: the Biography* (2005) especially Chapters 7 and 15.
> (Jeffery, Discovering Tong, p. 149; notes p.154.)

Notes by HM:
I am afraid that even more confusions are revealed here, particularly when seen from the Lancashire end of the story:

[v] *Shakespeare: the 'lost years'* by E. A. J. Honigmann does indeed include a whole chapter on the Shakespeare epitaphs, but on all seven of them, not just the two at Tong, and he has very little to say about the tomb itself. There are therefore four valuable pages there, but only four. These are quoted from in later chapters of this book. There was a second edition in 1998, with a valuable New Preface. He suspected, as indeed happened, that many suggestions in the first edition of his book would be greeted with scepticism and suspicion. Only by the second edition in 1998 had some of the theories presented gained ground. These were debated at length in a conference on 'Lancastrian Shakespeare' at Lancaster University and Hoghton Tower in August 1999, the papers from which were duly published in *Theatre and Religion: Lancastrian Shakespeare*, Richard Dutton, Alison Findlay and Richard Wilson (Eds), 2 Vols, Manchester University Press, 2003. Unfortunately there was nothing

here on the Tong epitaphs.

[vi] 'His schoolmaster put him in touch with his brother, John Cottam, a Jesuit priest, who was working secretly with Catholic families in Lancashire. He was based at Hoghton Hall.' A few muddles here, I am afraid, in which brothers John (schoolmaster) and Thomas (priest) Cottam have been confused. Thomas Cottam (priest) seems also to have been confused with other Catholic/Jesuit priests, some of whom, but by no means all, worked 'secretly with Catholic families in Lancashire'. Exactly who was based at 'Hoghton Hall' and which Hoghtons were mainly concerned presents another muddle:

a) The schoolmaster at Stratford Grammar School was John Cottam. He returned to Lancashire in early 1581 and appears in the list of 30 servants of Alexander Hoghton in his will of 1581, another one being William Shakeshafte.

b) Thomas Cottam the priest was John Cottam's brother. Thomas went into exile, returned on a mission, was arrested soon after landing in 1580 and executed in 1582. There is therefore no way that he could have been 'working secretly with Catholic families in Lancashire' at the time under consideration. Honigmann devotes a whole chapter to this family in Chapter IV. John Cottom of Tarnacre. Cottam and Cottom were, of course, interchangeable spellings of their name, along with several other renderings.

c) Alexander Hoghton mentioned above, who wrote the crucial will in 1581, was called 'of Lea', and he did indeed own the manor and the hall of Lea (near Preston), but the new Hoghton family residence was Hoghton Tower (never called 'Hoghton Hall'), built by his elder brother Thomas Hoghton 'The Exile' before fleeing into exile in 1569.

d) Richard Hoghton of Park Hall, Charnock (near Preston) was another (half-)brother. It was he who was suspected of harbouring Catholic priests, including Jesuit Edmund Campion along with his papers, and it was he who visited his (half-)brother Thomas Hoghton 'The Exile' in the Spanish Netherlands in the late 1570s. Incidentally, one of their sisters, Margaret Hoghton, married Thomas Standish of Duxbury, whose son Alexander Standish of Duxbury was my 'entry-ticket' to the Hoghtons. All the Hoghtons mentioned above were his uncles. (Materials for his biography have been on the Duxbury Family Website since 2004.)

e) Edmund Campion SJ was the most famous Jesuit to reach Lancashire in the Mission to England in 1580 led by himself and Robert Persons SJ. He was in the Preston area from Easter to Whitsuntide 1581, moving about secretly of necessity, but the name associated most frequently with him was indeed Hoghton. All Hoghtons denied this (of course) and no proof was ever found.

Biographies of all Catholics/Jesuits mentioned above are in the *Catholic Encyclopedia*. Consideration of the roles of the Cottams, Edmund Campion and the Hoghtons is given in Appendix 5. 'Shakespeare in Lancashire' by Peter Milward SJ.

Having sorted out these muddles, we can turn to another problem. If young Shakespeare/Shakeshafte did spend the traditional 'couple of years' with the

IIIb. View of Tong Castle
Viewed from Ruckley in the west of Tong Parish, after restoration in the 18th century. It survived until the 20th century but, in a dilapidated state, was blown up in 1954. The M54 now runs through the site. The full story plus more illustrations in Jeffery, *Discovering Tong,* 2007.

Hoghtons (until the Hoghton will in August 1581), it is difficult to fit all these dates together. If the Hoghton family tradition is based on the truth, then young Shakespeare must already have been with them since 1579. Thomas Cottam did not arrive back in England until 1580 and John Cottam did not return to Lancashire until January 1581. With the best will in the world it is difficult to believe that six months or one year would remain in family memory as 'a couple of years'. It seems that we should seek another route by which young William Shakeshafte/Shakespeare reached the Hoghtons.

[vii] *'to be schoolmaster to the Hoghton children'* in the quote from Ackroyd. We have another problem here, because Alexander Hoghton, who wrote the 'famous' will in 1581, never had any children from either of his two marriages. He even dictated in his will, shortly before he died, 'my wife and children, if it shall please almighty God to bless me with any'. He did, however, have a large household — 30 'servants' are named in his will. (Honigmann, *'lost years'*, pp. 135–142.) These are all given here, with the (sur)names in *italics* of Lancashire families who play a significant role in the 'Catholic Shakespeare in Lancashire' story. Maybe one or more of these might provide a clue to the other route by which young William reached the Hoghtons. Additions in brackets and italics are mine:

> [...] the longest liver of these my servants, that is to wit, Thomas Barton, William Rigby, Roger Livesey, John *Hoghton*, Henry Bounde, William Clough, Thomas Coston, John Kitchen, James Pemberton, Robert Tomlinson, Richard Fishwick, John *Cotham [presumed to be the Stratford schoolmaster, with brother Thomas, a priest–HM]*, Thomas Barker, Henry Browne, Miles Turner, Richard Snape, James Greaves, Thomas Sharp, George Bannister, John *Beseley [two Besely sons were Jesuit priests–HM]*, Thomas Ward, Robert Bolton, John Snape, Roger Dickinson, *Fulk Gillom, [turned up later at Rufford Old Hall with the Heskeths–HM] William Shakeshafte [assumed to be one and the same as William Shakespeare, who moved from the Hoghtons to the Heskeths–HM]*, Thomas *Gyllom*, William Ascroft, Roger *Dugdale [assumed to be a relative, however distant, of Sir William Dugdale's father from Great Mitton, 8 miles from Hoghton Tower–HM]* & Margery *Gerrard [presumably/perhaps from the family very closely associated with **Sir Thomas Stanley** and **Sir Edward Stanley Sr** and **Jr**–HM]*.
>
> [...] my trusty and loving friends John *Talbot* of Salebury *[local tradition associates this family with the Talbots, Earls of Shrewsbury–HM]*, Edward Standish of Standish, Esquire *[a staunch Catholic, friend of the Earls of Derby and kinsman of the Alexander Standish of Duxbury mentioned above–HM]*, Thomas Fleetwood son & heir apparent of the said John Fleetwood & my brother-in-law *Bartholomew Hesketh [brother of Richard Hesketh, who carried the letter in 1593 from Catholic exiles to Ferdinando, 5th Earl of Derby, Shakespeare's patron in Derby's Players–HM]* to be supervisors of this my last will & testament.

III–4. *Discovering Tong*: 'The Shakespeare Connection'— Part Three

The Revd Dr Jeffery continues:

> Hoghton also employed 'players'. There is in existence a copy of Hall's Chronicles, which belonged to Hoghton. It is heavily annotated by a hand which some suspect to be that of William Shakespeare.**[i]** At this time the Lancashire recusants were being persecuted, this may have led Shakespeare to return to Stratford.
>
> The long connections with the Stanley family make the commission of the epitaph on the tomb more likely, but the dating has confused people. The discovery that the tomb was not erected until 1602 makes the Shakespeare authorship more probable.**(8)** We should note that there are several other epitaphs by Shakespeare, including his own, with the rhyme of 'bones' and 'stones'. Recently Simon Watney has discovered the tomb of Sir William Gostwick at St Laurence Church, Willington, Bedfordshire. This tomb has the identical first verse as the Tong inscription. This leads him to question the Shakespearian authorship.**(9) [ii]** At the same time there is evidence that the Gostwicks and the Stanleys knew each other, and both had recusant

connections.**(10)** Gostwick may have borrowed the verse from Stanley, or the author may have sold it to both of them. Gostwick died in 1615.

We know that Shakespeare composed at least six other epitaphs, as well as his own. However, the Shakespearean connection with the tomb is not just on the Stanley side: there is also a Vernon connection. The accounts of the Earl of Rutland, for 31st March 1613, records payments to Shakespeare and the actor Richard Burbage for an '*Impressa*' made for the Earl. Burbage was a painter; an Impressa was a symbolic design for a shield.**[iii]** We know that the Earl of Rutland was a friend of the Earl of Southampton, who was a patron of Shakespeare. In the early 1590s Southampton and Rutland were known to '*pass the time in London merely going to plays every day*'. This was Robert [*sic*, Roger] Manners 5th Earl of Rutland who died in 1612. The Impressa was made for his brother, the 6th Earl. Dorothy Vernon was the wife of their great uncle and the sister of Thomas Stanley's wife. Moreover, the Earl of Southampton's wife was a Vernon.**(11) [iv]**

The Stanley tomb has also attracted the attention of those who wish to undermine Shakespeare as the author of the plays. One theory ascribes them to William, Earl of Derby, arguing that he wrote the words on this tomb in 1632. The evidence above undermines this and other theories.**(12) [v]**

In passing we may note two other Shakespeare connections. Both the father of Richard Vernon and the father of Anne Talbot (wife of Henry Vernon) appear in *Henry VI Part I* in passages relating to the Percy rebellion and the battle of Shrewsbury.

(8) See Chapter 7 and Introductory essay to the verse by Stanley Wells in **The Complete Oxford Shakespeare** pp. 81–82.

(9) S. Watney **Sky Aspiring Pyramids**.**[ii]**

(10) I am grateful to Mrs Christine Buckley for pointing this out.

(11) See (7) above p. 469.

(12) One persistent American enquirer wanted the tomb 'opened' on the assumption that **Edward Stanley** was Shakespeare, not knowing he is buried at Eynsham or that the tomb had been moved.

(Jeffery, Discovering Tong, pp. 149–150; notes p.154.)

Notes by HM:

[i] This suggestion appears in Ackroyd, *Shakespeare: the Biography* (2005), p.76.

[ii]This article appears in *Church Monuments* by Simon Watney, see Chapter II. The tomb today.

[iii] The Shakespeare in these Rutland accounts was only named as 'Mr Shakespeare'. Burbage was a painter, which makes it logical for him to have been involved in making an Impres(s)a. As far as we know, William Shakespeare was not a painter. There was, however a John Shakespeare, who was a 'bit-maker' at the court in London, a job which involved making exactly such things as Impresas. Strong evidence has also emerged in recent years that John Shakespeare of Stratford married several years before normally assumed, and also almost certainly produced at least two extra brothers for William in addition to those who appear in Stratford Parish Registers, which do not start until 1558. Much of this research has been by Stephen Pearson, a genealogist specialising in Shakespeares in the Midlands, webmaster and author of many contributions on The Shakespeare Family History Website. His article 'Wherefore Art Thou, Grandfather?' is particularly recommended. The 'Grandfather' in this case refers to a hunt for William Shakespeare's grandfather, who, Pearson proves, cannot possibly have been farmer Richard Shakespeare of Snitterfield, the one in the conventional story.

[iv] These family connections are explored in several later chapters in this book. Chapter XXVI. The Earls of Rutland, Sir Thomas & Sir Edward and Shakespeare, is devoted entirely to these connections.

[v] The current leading proponent of William Stanley, 6th Earl of Derby, as Shakespeare is John Raithel, webmaster of The URL of Derby. The author of the first ever scholarly biography of William Stanley was Professor Leo Daugherty, for the *New/Oxford Dictionary of National Biography* (2004). He may be regarded as the current leading expert on William Stanley. Of course he dismisses the idea completely that William Stanley was William Shakespeare, but in his latest book on William Stanley he presents many recently discovered close connections, not least via the poet Richard Barnfield: *Shakespeare, Richard Barnfield and the Sixth Earl of Derby*, Cambria, 2010. His introduction is on a web page devoted to this publication.

~~~~~~~~~~~~

III–5. *Discovering Tong*: John Milton, Shakespeare and the Stanleys

At this point (p.150) Jeffery leaves the Stanley tomb in Tong and explores a few other Shakespeare/Stanley connections:

> In 1630 John Milton published a poem in Shakespeare's second folio.[i] It has echoes of the verses on the Stanley Tomb. The poem is entitled: *An Epitaph on the Admirable Dramatick Poet. W Shakespeare.*
>
> What needs my Shakespeare, for his Honour'd bones,
> The labour of an age in piled Stones?
> Or that his hallow'd reliques should be hid
> Under a star-ypointing pyramid?
> Dear son of memory, great heir of fame,
> What need'st though such weak witnes of thy name?
> Thou, in our wonder and astonishment
> Hast built thyself a live long monument.
> For whilst to the shame of slow endeavouring art,
> Thy easy numbers flow; and that each heart
> Hath, from the leaves of thy unvalued book,
> Those delphick lines with deep impression took;
> Then thou, our fancy of itself bereaving,
> Dost make us marble with too much conceiving;
> And, so sepulcher'd in such pomp dost lie,
> That Kings, for such a Tomb, would wish to die. **(13) [ii]**
>
> Did Milton know about Shakespeare's verse at Tong, or is this simply the sort of architectural/cultural language current at the time? There were connections. One link was Shropshire. Milton's father's landlord was the Earl of Bridgewater of Ludlow Castle, where *Comus* was performed in 1634.[iii] John Milton's father must have known Shakespeare because he became a trustee of the Blackfriar's Theatre in 1608 at the time that Shakespeare's 'King's Men' were performing there. Milton also knew Alice Spencer, wife of Ferdinand, Earl of Derby.[iii] Professor Campbell in an essay on the young Milton also reports on the Stanley Epitaph.**(14) [iv]** At the same time, a recent biographer of Milton refers to 'The Pseudo-Shakespearean verses' at Tong. We shall never know the truth of this matter.**(15)**
>
> **(13)** Ed. C.C. Clarke *Milton's Poetical Works*
> **(14)** G. Campbell *Shakespeare and the Youth of Milton* in the Milton Quarterly Vol 33 no 4. **[iv]**
> **(15)** G. J. Schiffhorst *John Milton*

(Jeffery, *Discovering Tong*, pp.150–1; notes p.154.)

Notes by HM:

[i] This is a mere quibble: he wrote it in 1630 and it was published in 1632 in the Second Folio. Several websites give many details of this Sonnet.

[ii] There are as many variations in spelling and punctuation in versions of this Sonnet as there are of the verse epitaphs in Tong. The main difference is that this Sonnet only appeared in print and was not written on a tomb.

[iii] These two facts are linked. The Earl of Bridgewater was the son-in-law of Countess Alice Stanley née Spencer. Frances Stanley (b.1583), the second daughter of Ferdinando, 5th Earl of Derby and Alice, married in 1602 John Egerton, 2nd Viscount Brackley, 1st Earl of Bridgewater. He was the son

of Thomas Egerton (from Cheshire), 1ˢᵗ Viscount Brackley, Lord Chancellor Ellesmere, who in 1600 had married widowed Alice, a second marriage for her and third for him. When married to Ferdinando (who died in 1594) Alice was **Sir Edward Jr**'s cousin-in-law and they often met when back in Lancashire (*Derby Household Books*). At this time Alice was still battling away in court against her brother-in-law William Stanley, 6ᵗʰ Earl, over who should receive the Derby family properties. This was finally solved in 1609, with about half going to each. **Sir Edward Jr** must have been involved in this because he was in possession of extensive Derby properties, which, if he produced no male heir, would revert to the Earldom.

[iv] Campbell, *Milton Quarterly* 33.4 (1999) pp. 95–105. This article is meanwhile online. It is quoted from several times in Chapter VI. Seven seventeenth-century recordings.

III–6. Lady Venetia Digby, John Aubrey & Ben Jonson

The last sentence in the inscription on the side of the tomb, referring to **Sir Edward**'s three surviving daughters, reads:

> Petronella, Francis and Venesie are yet living.
> [...] successive Earls of Derby patronised Shakespeare and Venetia, who was born in 1600 at Tong Castle, is the most famous. Lady Venetia Digby, as she became, was a great beauty and was the subject of a long poem *Eupheme* by Ben Jonson. Van Dyck painted her portrait. She died in 1633. The words at each end of the monument are reputed to have been written for it by William Shakespeare and his players.
>
> (*Guidebook*, p.13)

Dr Jeffery adds more in *Discovering Tong*. Venetia can have had nothing (as a beauty) to do with Shakespeare writing the Epitaphs, if he did indeed write them about the time of the presumed commissioning and construction of the tomb (1601–03). She was born in December 1600. However, it is worth considering Venetia in the context of the Epitaphs as to whether her future life sheds any light on her father's previous life. One thing is certain: **Sir Edward Stanley Jr** was close friends with the Digbys.

> This last, Venetia, was born at Tong in 1600 and after her mother's death was sent, with her sister Frances, to live at Gayhurst, where her neighbours were the Digby family. As a child, she played with Kenelm Digby. His father was one of the members of the Gunpowder Plot and executed in 1606. When Edward Stanley inherited Eynsham Abbey, he moved there with his daughters and Kenelm went abroad. So the Digby connection was severed. She was one of the great beauties of her age, and became the subject of scurrilous comments by the diarist John Aubrey. He says that she stayed at '*Enstone near Oxford*' (he must have meant Eynsham) but '*as private as that place was, it seems her beautie could not lye hid*'. According to Aubrey, all the eligible young men were after her. When she stayed in London, over the door of her lodgings were written the words: '*Pray do not come neer, for dame Venetia Stanley Lodgeth Here*'. Aubrey continued:
> '*...She had a most lovely and sweet turne'd face, delicate darke-brown haire. She had a perfect helthy constitution; strong; good skin; well proportioned; much inkling to a Bona Roba (near altogether) her face, a short ovail, darke – browni-brown about which much sweetness, as also in the opening of her eie-lids. The colour of her cheeks was just that of the damask rose, which is neither too hott nor too pale. She was a just stature, not very tall.*' **(16)**
> This leads Aubrey's biographer to comment:
> '*One would have said that Aubrey was himself in love with Venetia Stanley did one not know that he was only seven at the time of her death in 1633.*' **(17)**
> Venetia became a well-known courtesan, and was for a time the mistress of both the Earl of Dorset and Sir Edmund Wilde of Droitwich. In 1624, she secretly married her childhood friend Sir Kenelm Digby, who she thought had died in a battle at Angers in 1620. Digby was handsome but a very eccentric figure. He wrote cookery books, invented strange medicines, fought battles,

and was the model for Ben Jonson's **The Alchemist**. This marriage led Eyton to comment that had Sir Edward retained Tong, Kenelm and Venetia might have inherited.... **(18)**

After their marriage, she seems to have been a devoted wife, a caring mother, and a supporter of good causes, especially helping poor Catholic families. She died quite young, in 1633, of a cerebral haemorrhage. Aubrey described the event:

'*Sir Kenelm had severall Pictures of her by Vandyke etc. He had her hands cast in playster, and her feet and face. See Ben Jonson's 2nd volume, where he hath made her live in poetry, in his drawing of her both Body and mind Sitting, and ready to be drawn*

> *What makes these Tiffany, silkes and lawne,*
> *Embroideries, feathers, fringes, lace.*
> *When ever limbe take like face etc.*

She dyed in her bed suddenly. Some suspected that she was poisoned. When her head was opened there was found to be little braine, which her husband imputed to her drinking viper-wine; but spiteful women would say 'twas a viper husband who was jealous of her that she woud steale a limpe'.**(19)**

The poem referred to is 'Eupheme the Picture of her Mind'. Aubrey gives us the following epitaph to Sir Kenelm, written by a Mr Ferrar:

> *Under this stone the matchless Digby lies*
> *Digby the great, the valiant, and wise;*
> *This Age's Wonder, for his Noble Parts;*
> *Skill'd in six Tongues and learned in all the Arts*
> *Born on the day he died th'eleventh of June*
> *On which he bravely fought at Scandaroon*
> *Tis rare that one and self-same day should be*
> *His day of birth, of death, of Victory.*

Digby also wrote his own account of his romance with Venetia in a document entitled 'The Courtship of Theogenes and Stelliana'.

(16) Ed. O. Lawson [*sic*, Oliver Lawson Dick,] **Aubrey's Brief Lives** [Secker and Warburg, 1949.]
(17) D. Tylden-Wright **John Aubrey: a life** [Harper Collins, 1991.]
(18) R. W. Eyton **Antiquities of Shropshire** [7 vols, London 1854-60.]
(19) For the Van Dyke paintings see A. Sumner '**Venetia Digby on her Deathbed**' [Chapter from Catalogue accompanying an Exhibition at Dulwich Picture Gallery, London, 1995–96; *History Today*, October 1995.]

(Jeffery, Discovering Tong, pp. 151-3; notes p. 154.)

~~~~~~~~~~~~~~~~~~~~~~~~~~

III–7. Venetia's sisters, mother, aunt and a few in-laws

To add to Jeffery's information, the other two surviving sisters are also worth mentioning early in this book, although not as much information has survived about them as their rather famous sister Venetia. Something of the family of their grandmother Margaret Vernon also seems to be in order. Daughter Petronella never married. One presumes she stayed at Eynsham to look after her father. She certainly buried him there, and commissioned a memorial for him. (Later in this book we will visit Eynsham, to bury **Sir Edward Jr** again.) One wonders why she did not arrange for him to be buried in the Stanley vault in Tong under his effigy and with his parents, in the ready-made tomb; or why not with his dear wife at Walthamstow? We will presumably never know.

We do, however, know a little about the third sister, Frances, who married Sir John Fortescue of Salden, Buckinghamshire. We also know a lot about the Percy family, **Sir Edward Jr**'s in-laws, Earls of Northumberland; also about the Vernon family of Haddon Hall, one of whose members, Margaret, of course, married **Sir Thomas Stanley**, with her effigy on the tomb in Tong; also about the Manners family of Belvoir, Earls of Rutland, one of whose members married Margaret's sister Dorothy. Dorothy was the younger heiress by several years. Her marriage provided something of a scandal when she eloped with John Manners, second son of the 1st Earl of Rutland of Belvoir Castle.

When I wrote to Professor Peter Milward SJ in Tokyo with an earlier copy of the summary of the brief biographies of **Sir Thomas** and **Sir Edward Jr**, I received in his answer:

> Now I feel a special interest in the wives of the two Stanleys father and son. You merely mention the wife of Sir Edward as Margaret Vernon, whose sister Dorothy inherited Haddon Hall and married John Manners, second son to the first Earl of Rutland. This brief mention calls to my mind a drama I once watched in my boyhood about the romantic elopement of John and Dorothy with the setting at Haddon Hall[...].What is more, the family of Vernon has deep recusant connections and reverberations. As for Rutland, it was the fifth Earl, Roger Manners, who was not only a royal ward like Shakespeare's Southampton and as such subjected to indoctrination by Sir William Cecil, Master of the Wards, but also one of the candidates for the authorship of Shakespeare's comedies. Then, as for the younger Stanley, his wife was Lucy Percy, whom you mentioned as "from a family distinguished by numerous Catholic Northern rebellions", and implicitly dramatized by Shakespeare in his two Parts of *Henry IV* (as interestingly explored by Lily Campbell in her book on *Shakespeare's Histories*, 1947). I would like to know more about her. Incidentally, it was largely thanks to their recusant wives that the old families of England, whose husbands were under stronger pressure to conform, succeeded in remaining true to the "old faith" at least till the eighteenth century, when so many fell by the wayside.
>
> It is of further interest for me to see how the younger Sir Edward surrounded himself with recusants and even with "Gunpowder Plotters". You mention the plotter Thomas Percy, his associate Sir Everard Digby, as well as his son Sir Kenelm, and Sir John Fortescue, from whose nephew another John Shakespeare acquired the London Gatehouse replete with Catholic associations (as discussed by Ian Wilson in *Shakespeare, The Evidence* (1993)). Really, you have hit on a real gold mine for further Shakeapearian studies!
>
> (Peter Milward, SJ, Personal letter, June 25, 2010)

Whether I have hit on a 'gold mine' or not remains to be seen, but his comments were encouraging. It does seem to have affected Father Peter that someone investigating this recusant background, herself with a solid Non-conformist background, might be more believable for the Shakespeare academic community than a Jesuit. Time might tell. Perhaps it should be added that Father Peter (as we agreed I should call him) can absolutely justifiably be regarded as the reviver of the 'Catholic Shakespeare' theory, with his book *Shakespeare's Religious Background* in 1973, followed by dozens of monographs on the subject, most, although not all, published by the Renaissance Institute, Sophia University, Tokyo, which he founded.

My acknowledgement of the enormous help given to me by the Very Revd Dr Jeffery during the preparation of his book in 2007 was given earlier in this book, and I hope that this chapter has confirmed my appreciation. I just needed to put all together with my own research on the relevant Stanleys in Lancashire and Cheshire archives and on some of the other people involved at various stages in the relevant Stanleys' lives.

Inevitably, all these characters will return again and again when covering the story from different angles. By the end of this book, we will have amassed enough material to be able to write the very first and fairly full biographies of **Sir Thomas**, his son **Sir Edward Jr** and his brother **Sir Edward Sr**, who does not appear on the tomb, nor received an epitaph from Shakespeare, but certainly played an important role in the lives of his brother and nephew.

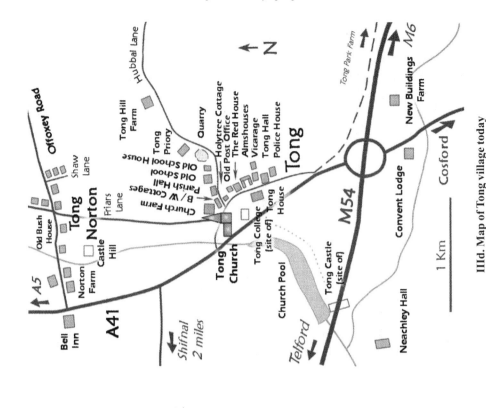

IIId. Map of Tong village today
© Robert Stallard (Jeffery, *Discovering Tong*, p. 122)

IIIc. Map of Tong, 1739
Although this was at the time of the Duke of Kingston, a later owner, the fields would have been little different from during the Stanley ownership. © Robert Stallard (Jeffery, *Discovering Tong*, p. 34)

Chapter IV
The Revd J.E. Auden's *History of Tong* — the Stanley tomb

IV-1. A brief history of the Revd J.E. Auden's research and publication(s)
IV-2. Auden's assessment of the authenticity of Shakespeare authorship of the
     verse epitaphs vs the assessment of others in the nineteenth and twentieth centuries
IV-3. Relevant extracts re the Stanleys on the tomb
IV-4. Later records by Auden of some relevance to the Stanleys
IV-5. The restoration of Tong church in 1887 to 1892
IV-6. Sir William Dugdale and heraldry in St Bartholomew's
IV-7. Postscript – the Vernons and a few suspect dates

IV–1. A brief history of the Revd J.E. Auden's research and publication(s)

The Revd John Ernest Auden (1860–1946) was the Vicar of Tong from 1896 until 1913 and must rank as the most important historian until this time of the parish of Tong, St Bartholomew's Church and the families associated with the church and the village over the centuries. He was appointed Vicar of Tong shortly after the restoration of the church and the opening of the Stanley vault in 1891–92, and acquired full written reports of this. His account is thus reproduced in full.

Auden published historical tracts on many subjects in various historical journals, but, for whatever reason, never published his main findings about the people with effigies on the Stanley tomb. He left behind a large quantity of handwritten Notes, deposited by his daughter in 'what was then the Shropshire Local History library, now part of Shropshire Archives' (*Auden's History*, Vol. 1, p. 3). Perhaps most surprising is that Auden's notes on Tong were not published until 2003–2005. They had been photocopied by Jeffery, but still awaited a wider audience. The daunting project of transcribing, typing, editing and publishing Auden's Notes was undertaken admirably by Joyce Frost, wife of the Vicar of Tong at this time, the Revd George Frost, since retired. These were taken through to publication by David Dixon, Church Warden, via Arima Publishing, with all proceeds dedicated to the St Bartholomew's Restoration Fund. Let us be pleased that this initiative was undertaken and that these are now readily available. The latest editions can be purchased from the church:

> *Auden's History of Tong, Volumes 1* and *2: Notes on the Parish of Tong collected by J. E. Auden, Vicar of Tong, 1896-1913*, edited by Joyce Frost. *Vol. 1* first appeared in 2003; 2nd edition, subtitle *Notes on the History of Tong from the Parish Books,* with index, 2005; *Vol. 2*, subtitle *The Third Note Book of John Ernest Auden*, 2005 (Arima Publishing).

All page numbers below are given from the 2005 edition(s). These stand as a worthy memorial to the Revd J.E. Auden and his successors in Tong, particularly those named above. I seem to be one of the few people who has actually read every word of these 2003–05 publications, and checked some of the details against other historical documentary sources. Happily, the judgment is that most of Auden's basic conclusions were fundamentally sound about the Stanleys of Tong, but that unfortunately he got a few dates wrong — and he also got a few Sir Edward Stanleys muddled up — very understandably.

Please let me hastily add that this is no criticism of his prodigious work. This was mainly based in Shropshire. And yet **Sir Thomas Stanley** and his brothers Henry, 4th Earl of Derby and **Sir Edward Sr** came from Lancashire, to which county one needed to make a few forays to research the Stanleys. And Lady Margaret née Vernon, the wife of **Sir Thomas** and mother of **Sir Edward Jr**, was from Derbyshire. The latter's wife Lucy née Percy and four of their daughters died in Essex in early-mid 1601, after which **Sir Edward Jr** ended up moving around the homes of himself and various relatives in Buckinghamshire, Lancashire, London and his own estate in Eynsham, Oxfordshire, where he died in 1632. Auden was hardly in a position to explore all the archives in Record Offices of these counties at the turn of the nineteenth to twentieth centuries, quite simply because these Record Offices had not yet been created.

Perhaps another significant detail is that Auden appears not to have actually read the last will and testament of Lady Margaret and her only surviving son **Sir Edward Stanley Jr**. Copies of these, now stored in the collections of the Prerogative Court of Canterbury at the National Archives in Kew, proved to be rather revealing. Two later chapters in this book are devoted to these: Chapter XVIII. Sir Thomas's (1576) and Lady Margaret's (1596) last wills and testaments and Chapter XXVII. Sir Edward Stanley's last will and testament, 1632.

Meanwhile, let us examine the Revd J.E. Auden's findings and judgments.

IV–2. Auden's assessment of the authenticity of Shakespeare authorship of the verse epitaphs vs the assessment of others in the nineteenth and twentieth centuries

The Revd J.E. Auden was cautious in his judgment of the authenticity of Shakespeare authorship, steering a middle course between total acceptance and/or total rejection. One must remember that he was writing in Victorian times, within a century after other researchers had made many startling discoveries about John and William Shakespeare's biographies. When the claim by Sir William Dugdale came to light in the eighteenth century of his assertion that the Epitaphs on the Stanley tomb were by Shakespeare, this was followed up by nineteenth-century historians attempting to establish the documented 'facts' about Shakespeare's life. Most were queried (and often rejected), with many dismissed as 'mere' tradition, hearsay, folklore, imaginative inventions in retrospect, etc.. The Shakespeare Verse Epitaphs for the Stanleys in Tong were usually dismissed under one of these categories — take your pick. This also applied throughout most of the twentieth century, when the Shakespeare epitaphs were dismissed by several eminent Shakespeare scholars as unauthentic or at best possible, but highly dubious.

One needs only to refer to Sir Sidney Lee (English), the magisterial biographer of Shakespeare in 1898, *A Life of William Shakespeare* (now available free online as an eBook from Project Gutenberg), and Professor Sidney Schoenbaum (American), another magisterial biographer of Shakespeare in the late twentieth century, with his almost 'final word' in *William Shakespeare: A Compact Documentary Life, Revised Edition with a New Postscript*, New York, Oxford U.P., 1987. Neither placed any value on the claim of Shakespeare's authorship of the verse epitaphs in Tong; indeed, they never even mentioned them in their final tomes.

IVa. View of Tong Church
(old engraving)
(Jeffery, *Discovering Tong*, p.17)

It was therefore interesting to read the judgment of the *éminence grise* of Stratford,

Professor Dr Stanley Wells, in his writings in the *Oxford Shakespeare* during the late 1990s and early Noughties: the Shakespeare biographies by Lee and Schoenbaum (mentioned above) are still the only ones recommended by him. To do Wells justice, however, he does nod in the direction of the Stanley verse epitaphs in Tong in *The Complete Works* (2005), apparently influenced at least in part by all the research of the last two decades into 'Lancastrian Shakespeare'.

Back to the Revd J.E. Auden. Like so many other vicars in possession of parish registers before they were finally made public, he was also a historian. He was, of course, Anglican. It is interesting to note that his nephew, poet W. H. Auden, was of an Anglo-Catholic family.

In her introductions to the two volumes Mrs Frost makes the following pertinent remarks:

> Anyone writing about Tong today values and trusts Auden. As the list of his publications at the end of the biography given here shows, he was too much of a historian to have called these Notes a full-blown 'History of Tong', but they tell us so much about Tong and are so interesting that it seems well worthwhile to make them available for all. When Auden died he left his Notes to his daughter, and she gave them to what was then the Shropshire Local History Library, now part of Shropshire Archives, who store and protect them appropriately. I gratefully acknowledge their permission to reprint them in this way. (*Auden's History*, Vol. 1, p. 3.)
>
> In copying these notes I have kept to the quite remarkable assortment of spellings in the original documents, although this gave the computer considerable hiccups. Headings and dates have been highlighted for clarity. Apart from a very few footnotes of my own in square brackets [like this], the footnotes are all those of John Auden himself. (*Auden's History*, Vol. 2, p. 4.)

I fully sympathise with Mrs Frost's comments on spellings, footnotes and hiccups for the computer, which were multiplied by often complicated formatting to include my own footnotes, attempting to distinguish them from Auden's and Mrs Frost's.

~~~~~~~~~~~~~~~

IV–3. Relevant extracts re the Stanleys on the tomb

The only Stanleys referred to by Auden are those whose effigies appear on the tomb. The Vernons, ancestors of Lady Margaret, receive rather more attention because so many of them lived and are commemorated in Tong. Details of her father George Vernon's ancestry are given, including thumbnail sketches of Sir Richard Vernon of Tong and Haddon (1390/1–1451/2), whose tomb is in the church, Sir William Vernon of Tong and Haddon (d.1467), Sir Henry Vernon of Tong and Haddon (d.1515), rebuilder of Tong Castle, whose tomb is in the church, and Richard Vernon of Tong and Haddon, who died in 1517 leaving a son George, not yet three years old. Their biographical details are not repeated here. We start with George, whose elder daughter Margaret married **Sir Thomas Stanley**. [All names in **bold** in the following quotes are from Mrs Frost transcribing Auden.]

> **GEORGE VERNON, KNIGHT**, of Tong and Haddon, "the king of the Peak", born 1514, married
> **(1)** Margaret, daughter and heiress of Gilbert Talboys, knight, and by her had Margaret, born 1540, and Dorothy, born 1545.
> **(1)** [Daughter] Margaret inherited Tong, and married in 1558, Thomas Stanley, Knight, second son of Edward, Earl of Derby.
> **(2)** Dorothy inherited Haddon, and married, circa 1568, John Manners, second son of the Earl of Rutland. Her eldest child George was born in 1569 and she died 24 June 1584. John Manners died 4 June 1611.
> George Vernon married (2ndly) Matilda daughter of Ralph Longford, knight, but by her had no issue. He died in 1565 and was buried at Bakewell.
>
> **THOMAS STANLEY, KNIGHT**, of Tong, *jure uxoris*, [by right of his wife] MARGARET VERNON.

Apparently he did not take up his residence at Tong for about 9 years after he inherited the property in 1565. For in the Taylor mss. in the Shrewsbury School Library, (also quoted in Owen and Blakeway's *History of Shrewsbury* (p. 365), is the following note:

'AD 1575 Now latlie by credible report Sir Thomas Stanley is cum to dwell in this cuntrie, and many papists gentilmen resorte unto hym.'[See HM Note [i] below.]

His son and heir Edward Stanley was born in 1562, and on his birth Thomas' father, the Earl of Derby, made a deed of settlement granting to Sir Thomas for life all his manors and lands in the counties of Chester, Warwick, Oxford and Devon with remainder to his wife Margaret for life, with remainder to their son Edward for life.

Sir Thomas Stanley died 21 December 1576, being succeeded by his only son, Edward, then aged 14. Of the vast possessions of Sir Edward Stanley, Erdeswick writing circa 1596, speaks of him as 'now Lord of Harlaston', and says of Cubleston 'Edward Stanley is now owner thereof,' and of West Bromwich, 'now one of the Stanleys hath the seat of his house there.' But in 1603 he sold Harlaston to Sir Edward Brabazon, and about the same time, the manor of West Bromwich to his cousin Sir Richard Sheldon, and Tong to **Sir Thomas Harris**. (See HM Note [ii] below.)

Sir Edward Stanley married Lucy, 2nd daughter of Thomas, Earl of Northumberland, by whom he had one son and seven daughters, of whom only 3 daughters grew up:

(? was the son buried in the vault with his grandfather?)

Venetia, born 1600, married Sir Kenelm Digby, died 1633.

Frances, married Sir John Fortescue.

Petronella, died unmarried.

Sir Edward Stanley died in 1632, at Eynsham, co. Oxford, aged 70, leaving his property to his daughter Petronella. **[iii]**

(*Auden's History*, Vol. 1, pp. 15-17)

[i] Auden includes other comments on Margaret and Dorothy Vernon and 'Catholic Sir Thomas Stanley' in his criticism of all the mistakes made in two previous Guides of Tong:

Criticism of Two Guides of Tong
1. By T. P. Marshall. Reviewed by J. E. Auden.
2. *History of Tong Church etc*. by G. H. Boden, Verger. Reviewed by J.H. Clarke.
This book is simply and solely a mass of extracts taken from writings of others without the slightest acknowledgement or allusion to those authors.

[*Auden's History*, Vol. 1, pp. 57–64.)

[ii] Auden also provides details of the alienation of the manor of Tong in 1607 after **Sir Edward** had sold Tong Castle in 1603. This date has often been confused with the sale of the castle.

The king gave licence to Sir Edward Stanley to alienate the manor of Tong to Thomas Harries, Sergeant-at-Law, afterwards knight and baronet, which Harris had one son and three daughters. The son died in his youth. (*Originalia*, 6 & 7 Jas. I, 1st 9 1607-9).

(*Auden's History*, Vol. 1, p. 18.)

[iii] This age of Sir Edward at his death is now queried. We will read later, in the inscription on **Sir Edward Stanley Jr**'s memorial at Eynsham, placed there by his daughter Petronella, that he was actually aged 69, in his 70th year. This allows a more accurate birth date in mid- to late-1562: after 18 June [his own death] and before December [aged 14 at his father's death in December 1576]. From now on his birth is therefore given as mid-late 1562. Auden was not aware that Eynsham was one Stanley property entailed by fail-male to revert to the Earldom of Derby, should **Sir Edward** die without a male heir.

~~~~~~~~~~~~~~~

IV-4. Later records by Auden of some relevance to the Stanleys

No Parish Registers have survived for the period when **Sir Thomas** and **Sir Edward** were living at

Tong Castle; therefore there is no record of the burial of **Sir Thomas**, his wife Lady Margaret (who may or may not have died in Tong) and infant son Henry, nor the baptisms of **Sir Edward** and Lucy's children. However, a record has survived from 1630 (still within the lifetime of **Sir Edward Jr**) of the history of the registers and other books and religious objects owned by the church. Presumably **Sir Edward** knew some of these earlier objects well, even if not those purchased in 1630, when he was living at Eynsham, Oxon.

[...] The Churchwardens in 1630 were Roger Austen of Ruckley Grange and Thomas Halfpenny. They seem to have found the parish ill provided with books or a place to keep them in[1], and the former at once set about getting what was necessary; the Churchwardens' book begins thus:

'This booke was bestowed by Roger Austen of Ruckley Grandge, one of the Churchewardens for the Towne and P'she of Tonge in Com. Salop, for the use of the Churchwardens for the keepinge of theire Accompts of the Churche hereafter. In the Syxte yeare of the Raigne of our Sovraigne Lorde Charles now kynge of England. Anno Dm. 1630.'

And in his accounts for 1630 are the following entries:

Paid for a chest lidde	xx d.
Given to the Joyner for plaining it	vi d.
For three lockes three hinges with nayles and setting on for a coffer	v s.
Paid for a register booke of parchment, being twelve skins made into sixe and thirtie leaves	vii s.
For two Journeys to Bridgenorth for a regester booke in kausing it to be made and fechinge it spent	xii d

Into this chest were put all the goods belonging then to the Church, for Mr Austen writes:
Memorandum: that these thinges hereafter nominated are left in a chest newlye repaired by Roger Austen one of the Churchwardens of the P'ishe of Tonge 1630.
Imp: one Bible, one Comunion booke, two bookes of homilies, one booke of Canons, a booke called a defence of the Apologie of the Church of England, The Paraphrase of Erasmus,[2] a regester booke.
Item: one Comunion Cuppe with a cover,[3] a cloth of silke and one of diaper for the Comunion table.
Item: fower towels.
Item: a pulpett cloth of blacke, and a cloth of blacke to cover the Bere at anye Buriall.
Item: a surplus.

This chest, with its three locks to prevent Vicar or Churchwardens opening it unless all three were present and agreed, is still in the vestry, and the Register purchased by Roger Austen is the earliest extant. For, though William Mytton (died 3 Sept. 1746) quotes in his M.S. extracts from the Shropshire Registers 'a Roll beginning in 1588 imperfect,' which he found at Tong, it has now disappeared, and the first existing register is headed: "The regester for the p'ish of Tong beginninge the 19th. May ano. Domin. 1629." The vicar of Tong at the time was the Revd George Meeson described in an Elizabethan clergy list of 1602 as "no preacher, no degree." (i.e. held no degree and was not licensed by his Bishop to preach.) However he wrote a good clear hand as may be seen from his signature.

(*Auden's History*, vol. 2, pp. 12-15.)

Footnotes by the Revd J.E. Auden:
[1] Thomas Cromwell's injunction came into operation Sept. 29, 1538. On Sept. 5, having recently been appointed Vicar General, issued a series of injunctions, including this one:
*That you and every parson, vicare of curate shall for every churche kepe **one booke or registere** wherein ye shall write the day and yere of every weddyng, christenying and burying made within your parishe for your tyme, and so for every man suceedyng you likewise. And shall insert every persons name that shall be so weddid, christened or buried. (State Papers).*

Then followed directions for the provision by the parish of 'one sure coffer with two locks and keys,' in which to keep the book. Entries were to be made every Sunday, in the presence of at least one warden, of all the weddings, etc., made the whole week before.

The 70th Canon of 1603 enjoined that the Registers be kept in a '**sure coffer with three locks and keys**'.

[2] By a proclamation of **1541 every parish was ordered to 'buy and provide Bibles** of the largest and greatest volume, and cause the same to be set and fixed in the Parish Church.' The price of the Bible unbound was settled at 10s. –'i.e. about £6. 10s. 0d. of our money' [*as Auden writes in c. 1900*] or 12s. 'Well and sufficiently bound, trimmed and clasped.' This was the Great Bible.

The 'English Order of Communion' appeared in 1548. It was not a full Communion Office, but an English form for the people, grafted on to the Latin Office for the Mass.

The First Book of Homilies was printed in 1547, and is ascribed to Cranmer, Ridley, Latimer, Bonner and the latter's chaplain. The Second Book was published in 1563 and was mainly the work of Jewel.

The Constitutions and Canons Ecclesiastical were published in 1604, and 'the Book of the said Canons was ordered to be provided at the charge of the Parish'.

The Paraphrase of Erasmus was in 1547 ordered to be placed beside the Gospels in some convenient place in every church that the parishioners might read it.

Bishop Jewel's 'Defence of the Apologie of the Churche of Englande, conteininge an Answeare to a certain Booke lately set forth by Mr. Hardinge', was also ordered to be kept in churches.

[3] On June 2, 1553 Tong possessed a **chalice of copper** partially gilt, all that was left by the King's Commissioners of the goods which no doubt had once belonged to the church, the gifts of pious benefactors.

Fulke Eyton e.g. by his will dated 1454 bequeathed to the Warden and Priests of the College of Tong his '**best Basin and Eure of Silver**', and '**to the Chapell of our Lady of Tong his Chalice and his blew vestiment of damaske of his armes.**' William Fitzherbert in 1451 bequeathed 'a gown for making vestments'. Before 1855 there were at Tong Castle 'two mediaeval thuribles which were said to have been formerly used in Tong church' and bought at the sale of the Duke of Kingston's property in 1764. (H.F.J. Vaughan in S.A.S.T. vol. 2, (1879).)

IV–5. The restoration of Tong church in 1887 to 1892

Auden provides details of the restoration of the church and inspection of the Stanley tomb in 1887–92.

1887. The Revd G. C. Rivett-Carnac began the restoration of the church and effected a great many improvements under the guidance of Mr. Street as architect. The following is from a letter of William Dalrymple Maclagan, the late Archbishop of York (1891-1909), then Bishop of Lichfield (1878-1890).

'Sept. 17, 1887. I am glad to hear of the good progress you are making in the restoration of your very fine church, and I sincerely trust that there will be no difficulty in raising a sufficient fund for so good a purpose. The church is well worthy of all the care that can be bestowed on it, and I am thankful to know that you are dealing with the matter wisely and not attempting too much.'

The Restoration Committee, however, found that the undertaking was beyond their resources, and so the work was not finished till the late Earl of Bradford took the matter in hand.

The following are the notes left by the Revd J. H. Courtney Clarke in his Church Register.

1891

June 8   Chancel closed for restoration

June 19   Workmen opened the Durant Vault in the Chancel and Stanley Vault in the sacrarium. The former contained 10 coffins, viz. 1 to 3, illegible:

4) Geo. Durant, B. 1776, D. 1844.

5) Rose Durant, B. 1776, D. 1844.

6) Maria Durant. B. Nov. 22, 1800, died April 15, 1833.

7) Cecil son of George Durant died March 24, 1832 aged 6 months.

8) Belle B. Sept. 25, 1807, died Sept. 6, 1835.

9) Mark Hanbury Durant, son of Geo. and Marianne Durant B. Nov. 5, 1808, died Aug. 22, 1815.

10) Benjamin Charnock Payne died 14 May, 1793 age 38.

[Some of the details above, and extra details below, although irrelevant to the Stanleys, are reproduced here mainly to demonstrate the meticulousness of the Revd Courtney Clarke's notes].

The Stanley vault contained:

1) a complete coffin of 'The Right Hon. Gervas Lord Pierrepoint died May 22, 1715'.

2) the lead coffin cut open of **Sir Thomas Stanley** with the inscription on a lead plate 'Hic jacet **Thomas Stanley, Miles**, filius secundus Edwardi comitis Darbi, maritus Margarite filie et une heredum Georgii Vernon militis, qui obiit vicessimo primo die decembris anno regni reginae Elizabeth – decimo nono; anno Domini milesimo quingentessimo septuagessimo sexto.[i]' Anima misereatur Deus. Amen Per me Johannem in Lathomum.[ii].

3) A lead coffin cut open with no name on it.[iii].

4) A square box containing remains in lime. This box might have contained the bones of the little son of **Sir Thomas**.

Notes by HM:

[i] Mrs Joyce Frost quotes from Auden:

Here lies Sir Thomas Stanley, Knight, second son of Edward, Earl of Derby, husband of Margaret, daughter and co-heir of George Vernon, Knight, who died on the 21st December in the 19th year of the reign of Queen Elizabeth AD 1576. God have mercy on his soul. Amen. By me, John Lathom. (Translation from Griffiths, p. 65)

[ii] Lathom is the modern spelling, although it regularly appeared as Latham in contemporary MSS.

In the reign of Henry the 4th Sir John Stanley (who died 1414), married Isabel the daughter and heire of Sir Thomas Latham, who for her dowrie amongst many other lands, brought the sumptuose seate called Latham House, whichever since hath been the seate of the Stanleys.

(Gough's *Middle*, p.23).

[iii] From surrounding evidence, this was most likely the coffin of **Sir Thomas**'s wife, Margaret Vernon, who, although married a second time, requested in her will to be buried next to her first husband. The big surprise was that neither of the Stanley bodies was there.

June 20   The old floor was found 9 in. under present floor in the chancel, and below the arch of the Durant Vault.

June 29   Mr. Ewan Christian visited the church and decided to raise the chancel floor over the vaults and not to fill them up. The Willoughby slab to be removed from the centre of the chancel between the vestry and south door to the floor east of stalls on north side. The screen and stalls to be raised and moved east to clear pillars. The lead coffin on north side of Stanley vault supposed to be Sir T. Stanley, but much broken, is in the shape of stone coffins, and Mr. Christian considers it much older than the other lead coffins.

June 30   In excavating the chancel floor 2 skulls, arms and thighs were found, one beneath the other at the east end of the north stalls, they both lay with head to south and feet to north and were in position as originally laid. The lower one was not disturbed, the upper one was placed in the Stanley Vault behind the oldest coffin.

	The original floor 9 in. below the floor just removed, shewed the tiles laid according to the correct pattern at the back of the stalls.
July 3	Closed Stanley Vault. Opened Willoughby Vault situated in centre of chancel between south and vestry doors.

[Further entries for July 7 and 8 are not included here, as irrelevant for the Stanleys.]

1892

Feb. 15	Nave of the church closed for restoration.

[Entries for Feb. 20, 22, Mar. 8, 22, April 7, irrelevant for the Stanleys].

April 26	It was settled to raise and repair bookcase in vestry and make a new cupboard for surplices underneath. To floor vestry with oak blocks on concrete. To increase weight of Great Bell from 2 tons 1 cwt. 1 qr. present weight to 50 cwt. To turn Stanley Tomb east and west, and to repair it and other tombs. To remove organ westward to within 2 feet of north screen. To make the floor in the stall of the Vernon chantry of oak blocks.
April 26	Figures removed from top of pillars on Stanley Tomb because they did not belong there. Mr. Bridgman of Lichfield had seen similar figures on a tomb at Long Melford, Suffolk, which he thinks were designed by the same man.

(Auden's History, vol. 2, pp. 178-182.)

The Great Bell subsequently arrived and was put in place, with Reopening Services on 23 June. The early history of the Great Bell, with a date of 1518 on it — and therefore in place and tolling during the time of **Sir Thomas** and **Sir Edward** in Tong — told in *Auden's History*, Vol.1, pp.180-82.

IV–6. Sir William Dugdale and heraldry in St Bartholomew's

Sir William Dugdale, Norroy King of Arms, was at Tong Church in September 1663, when making his Heraldic Visitation of Shropshire. He records that in the south window of the chancel were (1) the arms of Pembruge impaling Lingen, (2) of Pembruge, (3) Lingen, (4) Fitzalan, (5) Vernon, (6) Vernon, (7) Pype, and (8) De la Bere. And in the north window was (1) Trussel impaling Ludlow, (2) Ludlow impaling Lingen, Vernon impaling a blank, (8) De la Bere impaling Fizalan. These have all entirely disappeared. Dugdale also describes the monuments, saying of the Stanley tomb that the inscription on it was written by Shakespeare — (Harleian M.S. 5816 foll. quoted in Eyton ii pp 250.

(Auden's History, Vol. 2, pp. 57-58.)

Auden was mistaken in quoting the Harleian MS as Dugdale's MS notes. Dugdale's Notes were then, as now, at the College of Arms. The one in the Harleian MS was one of those attributed to Sir Francis Fane, which appears in Chapter VI. Seven seventeenth-century recordings, four attributed to Shakespeare. He was aware of the Dugdale MSS, but never succeeded in distinguishing adequately between this transcription and the one quoted by Eyton:

> In a volume of still unpublished M.S. by Sir Wm. Dugdale is a passage dealing with the Stanley monument. After quoting the prose epitaph in full Dugdale continues. "Shakespeare [in the margin], These following verses were made by William Shakespeare, the late famous tragedian". Dugdale's text is followed by a series of drawings of Shropshire antiquities made by Francis Sandford, and in Sandford's sketch of the Stanley monument at Tong we see the pyramids with their finial balls and spikes in their original position; the allegorical figures, now sadly defaced and banished to the niches on the arch dividing the Vernon Chapel from the south aisle, standing on the canopy; and the whole composition from the side a view which, wedged as the tomb now is between the earlier Vernon monument, it is today impossible to photograph.

(Auden's History, Vol. 2, p. 59.)

All praise to Mr R.J.L. Smith, who miraculously succeeded in the 'impossible' for this book! Albeit with twenty-first-century technology.

IV–7. Postcript — the Vernons and a few suspect dates

The Revd J.E. Auden stuck to the facts he had discovered about the relevant Stanleys and Vernons. In the case of the Vernons, it seems that he was not very interested in a local legend, part of the folklore surrounding the Vernons of Haddon Hall, concerning a romantic elopement. As with much folklore, the story probably contains grains of truth, but has been embellished in the retelling. One recent account is on Tudorplace. This website also provides a rather detailed biography of Sir George and the various posts he held — also various 'legends' surrounding him. For this, one can only express thanks at making them so accessible. If this 'legend' of the elopement were to be true, then we have another detail to add to the biography of **Sir Thomas**: the story of a celebration of the betrothal of **Sir Thomas** and Margaret Vernon, with the (eminently logical) extrapolation that they married near Haddon Hall not too long afterwards. If one puts a few dates together, however, one runs into a few problems.

Putting these problems on one side for the moment, we can enjoy the legendary story, which starts with a 'wicked father' (perhaps not so wicked but distinctly obstreperous), a damsel in distress restricted to her fireside (hints of Cinderella?), romantic incidents in a forest with a young man dressed as a forester (hints of Robin Hood?), the hero and heroine escaping, and all living happily ever after. Let us remember that this took place not too far away from the site of many Robin Hood legends and that the elaborations on the basic story must have been related during the seventeenth to nineteenth centuries. The late eighteenth and early nineteenth centuries saw the development of the Romantic movement and also the concomitant enormous popularity of Grimm's fairy tales, first published in 1812 in German, with numerous editions during the following years and translations into English in print ever since. Maybe these inspired a 'Prince Charming' and hiding in the woods?

> **Dorothy Vernon** was the daughter of **Sir George Vernon**, known as "King of the Peak," because of his immense wealth. His eldest [*sic*, elder] dau., Margaret, was betrothed to **Lord Stanley**'s youngest [*sic*, second] son. The Stanleys owned much land in Lancashire and should the two families unite their wealth would have been considerable. **Dorothy** was five years younger than her sister; she was supposed to be the "*most beautiful of all beautiful women*". **John Manners** had been trying to gain **Dorothy**'s hand, but her father refused his suit, calling John "*that nobody, the second son of a mushroom earl*". **Sir George** thought that the **Earl of Rutland**, who had recently been raised to the peerage, was an upstart who had married money in the form of the De Roos heiress. Furthermore, the Manners were Protestants, whereas the Vernons were Catholics. Dorothy had no wish to be sacrificed to her father's ambitions; she wanted **John Manners** and must have pleaded often with her father, but **Sir George** had her put under close surveillance and she was refused any communication with the world outside the Hall. However, legend tells us that John Manners dressed up as a forester and hunted the woods around Haddon. **Dorothy** must have eluded her guardians on occasions, to meet him and plan their future development. One night at Haddon Hall, a festive evening was held in honour of **Margaret**'s forthcoming marriage. There was music, dancing and singing, plenty of food and wine. Some time during the general confusion and merrymaking **Dorothy** was able to slip away, unobserved, to the side of the ballroom, going out of a small door, ever afterwards known as 'Dorothy's Door', outside and down the balustraded steps, along the Lower Garden to the little bridge over the River Wye, where **John Manners** was waiting with swift horses to take them to Aylestone, in Leicestershire, where they could be married. That is the story legend gives us and often legend is so different from the truth, but in this case the facts seem just as romantic. **Dorothy**, it seems, after much pleading, weeping and argument, was able to wear down her

father's resistance to the Manners family and **John** in particular. **Sir George** told her she could marry **John** but only on condition she went as far away from Haddon as possible, he would not allow her to disgrace the name of the Hall; she could go to Aylestone, a small Manor owned by the Vernons, here no one would know her. He told her he would not attend the wedding neither would he have anything to do with the pair of them. So **John** and **Dorothy** went to Aylestone where they were married by the priest, **William Heathcott**, without ceremony or any big reception, but it seems these things were unimportant, for **Dorothy** and her husband lived very happily together.

There is a Dorothy Vernon's pew in Aylestone Church, which probably means that they lived at Aylestone for a time. Dorothy's father must have relented for she inherited most of the Vernon lands and they went to live at Haddon Hall, the tenants now calling Sir John "King of the Peak". The ancient castellated mansion of Haddon Hall, exhibits the architecture of various periods, having been built at several times by the families of Vernon and Manners.

(Tudorplace, website)

Now for the problems with dates. Let us remind ourselves of the Vernon dates given by Auden (above). Those now queried are in ***bold italics***.

GEORGE VERNON, KNIGHT, of Tong and Haddon, 'the king of the Peak', ***born 1514***, married: 1) Margaret, daughter and heiress of Gilbert Talboys, knight, and by her had two daughters: Margaret, born 1540, and Dorothy, ***born 1545***.
Margaret inherited Tong, and married in 1558, Thomas Stanley, Knight, second son of Edward, Earl of Derby.
Dorothy inherited Haddon, and ***married, circa 1568***, John Manners, second son of the Earl of Rutland. Her eldest child George was born in 1569 and she died 24 June 1584.
John Manners died 4 June 1611.

Birth date of Sir George Vernon. Auden gives 1514 and Tudorplace gives c.1503. This need not trouble us too much, although it would be good to know the sources for this discrepancy. However, it gives us his age at the date of birth of his elder daughter Margaret Vernon as 26 or 37. (1540, in exactly or about this year, is the date given by both and otherwise generally accepted, although I have yet to discover the original source). In turn, his age at the birth of his second daughter Dorothy, if in 1545, would have been 31 or 42. Whichever of Sir George's dates of birth is correct, the long gaps could easily be accounted for by several hypothetical miscarriages (although no children dying young are reported).

Marriage of Sir Thomas and Margaret. If Auden is correct, they married in 1558, which would provide the date of the celebration of their forthcoming betrothal, and hence the story of the elopement as earlier in this year, or not too long before. How old were they both in this year? We know that the date of birth of their son Edward was 1562, because of the settlement in 1562/3 by Edward, 3rd Earl of Derby of lands on his second son Sir Thomas for his son Edward (full details in Chapter IX. Main Derby historians: Seacome). We know that the year of birth of Sir Thomas's elder brother Henry, Lord Strange was 1531, which makes a date of birth of (Sir) Thomas in c.1534 a rather reasonable supposition. We know that Sir Thomas was knighted in 1553. This gives their ages at marriage in 1558 as Sir Thomas aged 24, already a knight for 4/5 years, and Margaret aged 18. These ages seem rather reasonable for customs and conventions of the time, but certain inevitable questions arise: What was Sir Thomas doing between being knighted aged c.19 in London and marrying aged 24 in Derbyshire? Where did he meet her? Or was this an arranged marriage? If the latter, who met whom to arrange this? In any case, what did he do before he settled down to marriage and a life in the 1560s of fulfilling family duties, personal duties to his wife and family, and public duties as the second son of the Earl of Derby? Alas, we will probably never know, and 1553-8 will remain as 'lost years' in his life.

Date of birth of (Sir) John Manners, the aspiring husband of young Dorothy. All accounts of the Manners family, Earls of Rutland (detected and examined so far) give his year of birth as c.1534,

IVb. View of Tong Castle and Church, 1823
by E. Reynolds (Jeffery, *Discovering Tong*, p. 18)

which would make him aged 23/24 in 1557/8, the year of the elopement. As he had apparently fallen in love with her at least a year or so before, this would also seem a reasonable age to fall in love with a young woman who was supposed to be the '*most beautiful of all beautiful women*'. The main problem with dates comes with the age of Dorothy during the whole of this period.

Date of birth of Dorothy. Auden and Tudorplace give this as 1545, five years after the birth of her elder sister Margaret. In itself, this seems a reasonable assumption, but if the celebration of the betrothal of **Sir Thomas** and Margaret at Haddon Hall, and thus the scenario for Dorothy's eloping, was in 1557/8, she would have been aged 12/13. If the last event really was in 1557/8 and Dorothy really was born in 1545, then (Sir) John must have fallen desperately in love with her when she was aged around 10/11, she would have been escaping to a secret rendezvous in the forest aged around 11/12 and eloped aged around 12/13. These ages seem rather unlikely.

Dates of Dorothy's marriage and birth of her children. Auden gives the date of marriage as 1568 and the birth of first son George Manners as 1569. Yet Sir George Vernon wrote his will in 1565 and died on 31 August 1565 (Tudorplace gives these details). If there is any truth in the elopement story, it must have happened before this, at the latest in 1564. If the elopement was during a celebration of the betrothal of **Sir Thomas** and Margaret, this pushes it back to 1561 because they were definitely married by this year before they had their first son Edward in mid-late 1562. However, Dorothy and John's first child George was not born until 1569. Daughter Grace was then born, with a third child John born in 1576.

An interim conclusion is that there may well be some truth behind the elopement story, but that some of the dates assumed so far must be wrong. This is echoed in the account of the story by a historian of Derbyshire, who provides dates somewhat different from above, e.g. Sir George Vernon's death in 1567, not 1565. He also awards Sir George vast lands (thirty manors), divided between his two daughters, details of some of which have not yet surfaced in the story of lands owned by **Sir Edward Jr**, inherited from his mother.

> Sir George Vernon had time on his side. Succeeding to the Haddon estates in 1517, the eighth year of Henry VIII's reign, he died in the ninth year of Elizabeth I, having served four sovereigns. The last of the Haddon Vernons, he seems almost to have set out to stamp his

personality indelibly on the place, earning himself the half-admiring, half-fearful epithet of 'King of the Peak' for his lavish life-style and autocratic bearing. Of many stories — some possibly apocryphal — told of him, the most typical is of his having his men hang a murderer caught in the act without bothering with the formalities of a trial.

When Sir George died in 1567 he owned thirty manors, and in the absence of a son they were divided between his two daughters, Dorothy, wife of Sir John Manners, and Margaret, married to Thomas Stanley, the Earl of Derby's second son. Dorothy inherited Haddon, from which she had allegedly eloped.

The elopement story is well known, though the details vary. But the basic scenario has Dorothy slipping away from her sister's wedding reception, down the steps from the ballroom — now known as 'Dorothy Vernon's steps' and on to a bridge across the Wye, where her lover John Manners was waiting to carry her away to Aylestone in Leicestershire, where they were married immediately. That Sir George was bent on forcing Dorothy into a loveless marriage with another man is the usual explanation for the need for an elopement, but a more plausible theory stresses a religious conflict between the families, the Vernons being Protestant and the Manners Roman Catholics.

The story does not seem to have appeared in print before 1822, and then as the plot of a romantic novel,[i] which has led many people to the conclusion that the authoress invented the whole story, supporting that by rightly pointing out that neither the bridge nor the steps existed in Dorothy's times. Against this scepticism is a body of opinion holding the view that the novelist got hold of an authentic local tradition and worked it into her story, adding the steps and the bridge as acceptable literary licence.

The story is good enough to be true, whether it is or not. Readers may believe it if they wish; after all this time, there seems little chance of the truth ever being established. All we know for certain is that Sir John Manners married Dorothy Vernon at Aylestone in Leicestershire; that Dorothy died in 1584, twenty-seven years before her husband, and that they are reunited in effigy on a splendid tomb chest in Bakewell Church.

(Roy Christian, *Notable Derbyshire Families*.
Pub. The Derbyshire Heritage Series, 1987, pp.14-16.)

[i] One can browse to one's heart's content via Google about this and several subsequent novels during the following century, an opera by Arthur Sullivan, a black and white silent movie, and sundry other fictitious versions of the 'Dorothy's elopement' story. David Trutt, *Haddon Hall's Dorothy Vernon: the story of the legend*, 2006, an eBook online tells the story of the development of the legend and is particularly recommended.

In any case, Dorothy definitely inherited Haddon Hall on her father's death and she and her husband John Manners kept the male line going. Their grandson John inherited the title of 8th Earl of Rutland in 1641 when his three Manners cousins at Belvoir Castle had all died *osp*. This story is covered in detail in Chapter XXVI. The Earls of Rutland, Sir Thomas & Sir Edward and Shakespeare.

The most important figure for **Sir Edward Jr**'s later story was his cousin Grace Manners, daughter of John and Dorothy, who married Sir Francis Fortescue of Salden, Buckinghamshire. When his wife Lucy Percy died in 1601, leaving him a widower with three small daughters, one still a babe in arms, he placed them with Grace's large family. Later **Sir Edward**'s daughter Frances married Sir John Fortescue, son of Sir Francis and Grace. This story is told in more detail in Chapter XXV. Sir Edward's children.

IVd. Haddon Hall with Dorothy's bridge

The bridge was built later than the elopement, but somehow acquired this name. Haddon Hall still belongs to the Manners family and is open to the public.

IVc. Dorothy Vernon of Haddon Hall

Poster for a production of the story of the elopement, 1906.

IVf. Dorothy Vernon

Griffiths's (1894) explanation of this (p. 177): 'The portrait of Dorothy is sketched by Miss Bredley, from a painting in the Porter's Lodge at Haddon, by kind permission given to me by the Duke of Rutland.' Followed immediately by this 'quaint' poem, origin undisclosed, but as it mentions Stanley along with Vernon and Rutland it is worth reproducing.

"Where are the high and stately dames
"Of princely Vernon's banner'd hall,
"And where the knights, and what their names,
"Who led them forth to festival?"
"Arise ye mighty dead arise!
"Can Vernon, Rutland, Stanley sleep?
"Whose gallant hearts, and eagle eyes,
"Disdain'd a[l]ike to crouch or weep."

IVe John Manners

Courtice Pounds as John Manners, performance in the early 19th century. Pounds (1862-1927) was an acclaimed actor and singer.

Chapter V
Two early recordings and lots of muddles

V-1. Introduction
V-2. The standard twentieth-century reproduction of recordings
V-3. A brief history of the two main seventeenth-century recordings
V-4. Four subsequently muddled aspects of the tomb and inscriptions
V-5. Muddles about the tomb itself and whose effigies are on it
V-6. Muddles about the effigies
V-7. Muddles about the MI
V-8. Muddles about the verse epitaphs — confusion with *The Phoenix and the Turtle*
V-9. Examples of more muddles in the eighteenth to twentieth centuries
V-10. Another muddle by Gough Nicholls
V-11. A sketch of the tomb
V-12. Authorship of the epitaphs

V-1. Introduction

The first recording of part of the MI ***including*** a transcription of the epitaphs and ***including*** their attribution to Shakespeare was by Sir William Dugdale (1605–86), possibly much earlier but in any case no later than the time of his Visitation of Shropshire in 1663 (we know from his Diaries that he visited Tong on 23 September 1663) when he was Norroy King of Arms. The text appears in his notes accompanying the Visitation (see illustration Va). The text immediately below became better known when his Diaries and some of his writings were printed in 1827: *The life, diary and correspondence of Sir William Dugdale,* London, 1827, 600 + pages. (This is now 'online'.) Dugdale's MS text is at the College of Arms and photographs of the original three relevant pages appear as illustrations Va, Vb and Vc. It has been transcribed many times, although more often than not as a copy of a copy of a copy, with few people going back to the original. The version used most frequently in the twentieth century reads as follows.

V–2. The standard twentieth-century reproduction of recordings

On the north side of the chancel of Tonge Church, in the county of Salop, stands a very stately tomb, supported with Corinthian columns. It hath two figures of men in armour thereon lying .... and this epitaph upon it: 'Thomas Stanley, Knight, second son of Edward, Earl of Derby,' etc. These following verses were made by William Shakespeare, the late famous tragedian.

Written upon the east end of the tomb

Ask who lies here, but do not weep;
He is not dead, he doth but sleep.
This stony register is for his bones,
His fame is more perpetual than these stones;
And his own goodness, with himself being gone,
Shall live when earthly monument is none.

Written upon the west end thereof

Not monumental stone preserves our fame,
Nor sky-aspiring pyramids our name;
The memory of him for whom this stands

Shall outlive marble and defacers' hands;
When all to Time's consumption shall be given,
Stanley, for whom this stands, shall stand in heaven.

(Sir William Dugdale, 1664)

(E. A. J. Honigmann, *Shakespeare, the 'lost years'* (Manchester UP, 1985; 2nd ed. 1998), p. 78,
with reference in an endnote: 'See Chambers, *Shakespeare*, II, pp. 268-9; I, 551 ff.;
and Schoenbaum, 'Shakespeare's Epitaphs' (in *Lives*, 1970, pp. 75-82).'

[E. K. Chambers, *William Shakespeare: A study of Facts and Problems*, 2 vols, 1930;
Samuel Schoenbaum, *Shakespeare's Lives*, Oxford, 1970.]

Professor Honigmann's book was my starting point, and his references in themselves provide a history of the epitaphs during the twentieth century. Sir Edmund Chambers (1866–1954) and Professor Samuel Schoenbaum (1927–96) were the two acknowledged 'Greats' in the field of Shakespeare Biography in the twentieth century. So Honigmann's quote from Schoenbaum, in turn from Chambers, represents the 'official' judgment of 'Stratfordians'. In the case of both Chambers and Schoenbaum, they were dubious, if not downright dismissive of any claims that the Tong epitaphs were from the pen of Shakespeare.

> According to E. K. Chambers, little reliance can be placed on ascriptions found in seventeenth-century manuscripts... Of (3) [the Dugdale inscription above] Chambers wrote, even more dismissively, that 'it is clear that one set of the verses cannot be Shakespeare's, if it relates to the Sir Edward who owned Tong [he died in 1632], and on internal evidence there is no temptation to accept either of them as his'.

(Honigmann, '*lost years*', p. 78)

Honigmann, however, presented a new aspect. He grouped together seven epitaphs: (1) to John Combe; (2) to Elias James; (3) the Stanley epitaphs in Tong; (4) to Ben Jo(h)nson; (5) to himself; (6) and (7) to un-named dedicatees. **The only one that concerns us here is (3):**

> I have grouped these epitaphs together because in each case new information has come to light, after the epitaphs were attributed to Shakespeare, some of it unknown to Chambers, confirming a 'special relationship' between the poet and those he allegedly wrote about...
>
> **(3)** Next, Sir Thomas and Sir Edward Stanley and Shakespeare's 'Lancashire connection'. The Stanley tomb at Tong, in Shropshire, carries the inscription 'Thomas Stanley, Knight, second son...' [omitted here is a minimal Stanley pedigree, which is given in Chapter VII. HM]. I agree with Chambers that the verse epitaphs were intended for the younger Sir Edward and for his father, but not entirely with his reservation that, since this Sir Edward died in 1632, 'his figure, if it is his, and the verses on him must have been added to the tomb after that date, and incidentally after Shakespeare's death'. The implication seems to be that Shakespeare, being dead, could not have been involved; and it is spelt out in the *Shakespeare Encyclopaedia*: if Sir Edward is Sir Thomas's son 'there can be no question that Shakespeare did not write the epitaphs, since Sir Edward died in 1632, 16 years after Shakespeare'.[1] At this time, however, tombs with all their accessories were not infrequently ordered by the living, for themselves — as in the case of Edmund Tilney, the Master of the Revels, who asked in his will (1 July 1610) 'that there be a monument erected and set upon the place where I with the consent of the parson and churchwarden there have appointed... if myself in my life-time do not finish the same'.[2] So, too, Bess of Hardwick arranged for her own burial 'in the place appointed', beneath her tomb, which was 'finished and wants nothing but setting up'.[3] As John Weever explained, 'It was usual in ancient times, and so it is in these our days, for persons of especial rank and quality to make their own tombs and monuments in their life-time; partly for that they might have a certain house to put their head in... and partly to please themselves, in the beholding of their dead countenance in marble.'[4] Since Shakespeare is said to have jokingly given John Combe his epitaph, and to have composed one for himself, there is no reason to believe that he could not have written, before 1616, the epitaph for Sir Edward Stanley.

That he actually did so seems much likelier now that we begin to understand the 'Lancashire connection'. Sir Thomas and Sir Edward cease to be two mere names, otherwise unconnected with Shakespeare; if the dramatist was one of Strange's Men early in his career (Sir Edward Stanley was Lord Strange's cousin), wrote verses (cf. Chapter IX [on *The Phoenix and the Turtle*]) for Sir John Salusbury and his wife (who was a niece of Sir Thomas, and likewise a cousin of Sir Edward Stanley), knew the Hoghtons, Heskeths, John Weever, etc., nothing would be more natural than that he would get to know Sir Edward Stanley of Winwick and Tong. Did Weever not dedicate *Faunus and Melliflora* (1600) 'to the right valorous and excellent accomplished gentleman, master Edward Stanley of Winwick, Esq.' (i.e. three years before Stanley was knighted)? Was not Sir Peter Leigh of Lyme, brother-in-law of Sir Richard Hoghton, a major figure in Winwick and a neighbour of the Stanleys?[5]

Chambers plausibly dated the inscription between 1603 (since Sir Edward is not referred to as a knight) and 1600 (when Sir Edward's daughter Venetia, named in the inscription, was born). Would not this be 'rather late to put up a monument to persons who died in 1576 and 1596 respectively, [i.e. Sir Edward's parents]?'[6] A good question, which can now be answered. We learn from inhabitants of Winwick v. Stanley (26 Elizabeth)[7] that Sir Thomas Stanley in his later years was in financial difficulties; one deponent, Thomas Heye, declared that most of the complainants gave a year's rent to Sir Thomas 'of their benevolences when he was in trouble' (9th interrogatory). There are no clues in Sir Thomas's will,[8] but his widow's[9] reveals another relevant fact: she married again, and might have wished to be buried with her second husband. In the event, however, she snubbed her second husband, leaving him no token of her love, decreeing 'my body to be buried in the Parish Church of Tong by my husband Sir Thomas Stanley'; her will states, cryptically, that it was 'made by the consent and agreement' of her second husband, William Mathe, Esq. The tomb, therefore could have been delayed because the family was short of funds and, later, because there would be doubt as to the figures to be represented.

1 *Shakespeare Encyclopaedia*, p. 821; so Schoenbaum, *Lives*, p. 78.
2 PPC (110 Wingfield).
3 D. N. Durant, *Bess of Hardwick* (1977), p. 200.
4 *Ancient Funeral Monuments*, p. 18.
5 According to the *Victoria County History*, there is a Leigh chapel in Winwick church, and Sir Peter Leigh re-founded Winwick Grammar School in 1619 (*Lancashire*, IV, 124, 130).
6 Chambers, *Shakespeare*, I, 553.
7 DL4 26 (18).
8 PCC (39 Carew). Sir Thomas was 'in trouble' in 1571 when he tried to rescue Mary Queen of Scots, and was imprisoned in the Tower for his pains.
9 PCC (92 Drake).

(Honigmann, *'lost years'*, pp. 78-81, from 'Chapter VII. The Shakespeare Epitaphs and the Stanleys'; footnotes, p. 160.)

V–3. A brief history of the two main seventeenth-century recordings

A perusal of these facts was followed by reading Honigmann's book on John Weever. Weever was another one who had made a much earlier note on the tomb and epitaphs, which is covered in full in the next chapter. His transcription was in c.1626, but he did not make any mention of Shakespeare.

Reading these epitaphs in Prof. Honigmann's books led to a rather remarkable paper-chase. By the end of the next chapter we will have read what other writers have written about the texts of the epitaphs, the MI on the tomb and read various versions and interpretations of the MI. The following details have been reproduced mainly with the aim of saving anyone else the need to follow the same paper-chase through an awful lot of muddles.

The basic story is that two eminent historians in the seventeenth century recorded the details on the tomb, or had people record them for them and deliver the results to them in London. The interests of both of these was in preserving details of 'ancient' church monuments, of which there are several in St Bartholomew's, Tong. While the informants were describing the 'ancient' tombs and recording the inscriptions, in one case also making sketches of some of them, they included details of one of the most recent tombs — the Stanley tomb, erected at the beginning of the century. The two historians/ antiquarians were:

1) John Weever (1575/6–1632), from Preston (or the near area), Lancashire, aspiring poet while at Cambridge University and later an antiquarian based in London, whose main and highly acclaimed work, the culmination of a life's work, was *Ancient Funeral Monuments within the United Monarchy of Great Britain* (1631). His biography is in the *DNB, Old and New* with much more detail in E. A. J. Honigmann, *John Weever: A biography of a literary associate of Shakespeare and Jonson, together with a photographic facsimile of Weever's Epigrammes (1599)*, Manchester UP, 1987.

2) Sir William Dugdale (1605–86), his father from Great Mitton, Lancashire. This is a few miles from Whalley and Clitheroe and, very interestingly for 'Shakespeare in Lancashire', only about eight miles from Hoghton Tower. His father moved to Oxford University with a group of students, with (Sir) William later acquiring his main seat at Blythe Hall near Shustoke in Warwickshire. Early in life he became an antiquarian, then herald at the College of Arms, rising to Norroy and later Garter. His main legacies of relevance to the subject of this book are the *Visitations of Shropshire* in 1663 and of *Lancashire and Cheshire* in 1664/5 (the latter published by the Chetham Society in the nineteenth century) during his period as Norroy; his main publications were *Antiquities of Warwickshire* (1656) (including the first recording of Shakespeare's epitaph for himself and a sketch of the Shakespeare tomb in Stratford Church); and *Antiquities of Shropshire* (1664). His biography is in the *DNB, Old and New*. We will return to him in more detail in Chapter VII. How reliable was Sir William Dugdale?

V–4. Four subsequently muddled aspects of the tomb and inscriptions

It is difficult to trace the exact journey of the original MSS containing details of the Stanley tomb, and in one sense, this does not matter. What does matter is that the tomb is still there today, with its MI and two verse epitaphs clearly legible and thus available for comparison with any later versions. It is also important that there are several different aspects of the tomb and inscriptions, and that neither of these antiquarians produced details of all of them. Anyone reporting in between, particularly anyone who had not actually visited the tomb, presented differing details in their transcriptions. These have all been muddled ever since, indeed several of them in very recent years. An attempt is made here to provide the sources of all the muddles. These can be listed as referring to:

1) The tomb itself
2) The effigies
3) The MI
4) The verse epitaphs, producing confusion between the Tong epitaphs and *The Phoenix and the Turtle*

V–5. Muddles about the tomb itself and whose effigies are on it

The tomb itself, with its two tiers, pillars and pyramids, etc. The fact that it has since been moved and some of its features placed in different places and positions is rather irrelevant for the early recordings. A facsimile of the 1664 sketch and photos of its appearance today appear together for the first time in this book. The Revd J.E. Auden's *Notes* give a full description at the time of the renovation of the church in 1892, which included entering the Stanley vault and renovating the tomb in its new place. To do justice to his enormous efforts, the whole relevant sections of his Notes dealing with the tomb and a few other relevant matters have been given a chapter to themselves.

The only early description of the tomb comes from Dugdale, as given above:

> On the north side of the chancel of Tonge Church, in the county of Salop, stands a very stately tomb, supported with Corinthian columns. It hath two figures of men in armour thereon lying, and this epitaph upon it: 'Thomas Stanley, Knight, second son of Edward, Earl of Derby,' etc.

In addition to giving the verse epitaphs, Weever gave no description of any architectural features of the tomb, but just a summary of the MI.

> [Tong here are many goodly monuments.] Sir Edward Stanley, Knight of the Bath, hath already made his own monument, whereon is the portraitures of himself, his wife, and his children, which were seven daughters and one son. She and her four daughters, Arbella, Mary, Alice and Priscilla, are interred under a monument in the church of Walthamstow in Essex; Thomas his son died in his infancy, and is buried in the church of Winwick in 'Lanchishyre'; Petronella, Frances and Venetia are yet living.
>
> (Honigmann, *Weever*, pp. 69-70; Weever, Society of Antiquaries, MS. 127, fo. 121a.)

Weever is erroneous is attributing the tomb at Tong as containing the 'portraitures of himself, his wife and his children'. Only an effigy of **Sir Edward** is on the tomb at Tong. His wife and four children (the ones that had just died) are in effigy on the tomb at Walthamstow, where **Sir Edward** does not appear. It seems that Weever did not actually visit either, but relied on reports by others, which he then muddled. It seems that his main source was Walthamstow, because he does not give the ages of the daughters, which only appear in the MI on the tomb at Tong.

~~~~~~~~~~

V–6. Muddles about the effigies

The effigies are of the two Stanley knights, father and son, and Margaret née Vernon, wife of one and mother of the other. Weever and Dugdale seem to have had no doubt about this, but this has not stopped others later from giving false details. One saw **Sir Thomas** buried at Walthamstow, another saw the Sir Edward on the tomb as **Sir Edward Sr**. Many have seen **Sir Edward Jr** as buried at Tong, when in fact he was buried at Eynsham. Also, wrong dates are given in some places. We will meet some of these reports later in this chapter. Let us establish brief details of the truth here, to pre-empt any erroneous versions encountered in future.

Sir Thomas, born c.1534 (probably at Lathom, Lancashire), died 21 December 1576 at Tong, buried in the Stanley vault at Tong. We know this because of the lead plate on his coffin, which gave this date, and which was rediscovered when the vault was re-opened in the 1890s (and the body found missing). It is confirmed by his last will and testament. (Chapter XVIII. Sir Thomas's (1576) and Lady Margaret's (1596) last wills and testaments.)

Margaret née Vernon, born c.1535 (at Haddon Hall, Derbyshire), died some time between the 'last day of August 1596', when she wrote her will and 4 December 1596, when probate was granted in London. She might have died somewhere other than Tong, but was definitely buried in the Stanley vault at Tong, according to her wishes. Her (empty) coffin was found there in the 1890s.

Sir Edward, born mid-late 1562 (probably at Winwick, in any case almost certainly in Lancashire), died 18 June 1632 at Eynsham Abbey, Oxfordshire, buried in St Leonard's Church, Eynsham. We know this because of a memorial in the church placed there by his daughter Petronella. It is confirmed by his will. (Chapter XXVII. Sir Edward Stanley's last will and testament.)

~~~~~~~~~~

V–7. Muddles about the MI

The MI detailed exactly who is commemorated by this tomb (text still there today, given in Chapter II. The Stanley tomb in Tong today), including not only those whose bodies were actually buried in the Stanley vault, but other immediate family members who died and were buried elsewhere. The latter include two infant deaths, one son each of both knights, Henry son of **Sir Thomas** (burial place unspecified, perhaps at Tong) and Thomas son of **Edward**, buried at Winwick, Lancashire. It also gives details of the monument in the parish church of Walthamstow, presumably already erected before the Tong tomb, for Lucy née Percy, wife of **Sir Edward Jr**, and four of their daughters, died at the same time, ages at death specified, with three daughters still living.

Neither John Weever nor Sir William Dugdale recorded the full text of the MI, which is one reason that so many muddles have occurred ever since. As far as I am aware no printed version of the full text appeared before that in the *Guidebook* in 2002; and almost certainly no photos of the three panels have appeared before the ones now in this book.

It was noted above that Dugdale referred to the MI very briefly, referring to it as an epitaph and the epitaphs as verses: '... and this epitaph upon it: "Thomas Stanley, Knight, second son of Edward, Earl of Derby" ', etc. and that Weever muddled the contents of the similar MIs at Tong and Walthamstow.

This is followed by Weever's transcriptions of the epitaphs, identical to those given by Dugdale above, apart from 'Time' being written with a small and not a capital 'T'. Discrepancies between Weever's muddled report and the tomb we see today are:

a) He does not mention the effigies of **Sir Thomas** and his wife.

b) '[...] whereon is the portraitures of himself, his wife, and his children' does not describe the tomb in Tong as we see it today, where **Sir Edward**'s effigy is there, but not that of his wife or any children.

c) His spelling of 'Lanchishyre' is not that on the tomb: 'Lanca:'

d) The four dead daughters are named on the tomb in Tong (presumably with their ages at death) as: '18 Arabella 16 Marie 15 Alice and 13 Priscilla'. Weever does not give the ages and spells 'Arbella' and 'Mary' differently.

e) The three daughters still living are recorded on the tomb as 'Ye other Three Petronella Francis and Venesie are yet living'; Weever records the last as 'Venetia', implying that he knew her, or knew about her and the more normal spelling of her name.

f) The MI in Tong gives the place of burial of **Sir Edward**'s wife as 'ye Churche of Waltham', which in itself has presented muddles, e.g. Katherine Esdaile (See Chapter IX. Contribution by Katherine Esdaile), who assumed that it was Waltham Abbey and that the monument had disappeared. Weever gives 'Walthamstow'. The latter is correct. The monument is still there in St Mary's, Walthamstow.

There could be several explanations for these, and one could be that Weever had received a copy of the epitaphs from **Sir Edward** himself (although not the text of the MI with all its muddles, which **Sir Edward** would presumably not have offered): we know that Weever knew him well enough to dedicate his poem *Faunus and Melliflora* to him in 1600 and he also knew that he was a Knight of the Bath, which was only true from mid-1603 at King James's coronation. We know that (at least later) he had in front of him the texts of the epitaphs, and yet did not record the authorship by Shakespeare, which Dugdale did later and so confidently. Why not? Moving in the circles he did, one might expect him to have heard this from someone, even if not from **Sir Edward** himself. One can attempt to explain this any way one wishes, but all would be pure speculation.

~~~~~~~~~~~~~~~

V-8. Muddles about the verse epitaphs–
confusion with *The Phoenix and the Turtle*

The main muddles that have arisen have come from what one defines as an epitaph. This is often applied indiscriminately to any text that appears on a tomb. Fair enough, but they do come in different forms and varieties. In the case of the tomb at Tong it seems that a different appellation should be given to the text explaining who is commemorated and the verse epitaphs, which are an 'added extra', as it were. This is easily done by always referring to them as such and the descriptive text as an MI, Memorial Inscription. This has by no means always been the case.

'Epitaph' is sometimes used also for a poem in praise of someone, often as an obituary, even if not destined for a gravestone. As an elegiac poem in praise of a couple, *The Phoenix and the Turtle* has sometimes been described as an epitaph. In principle, there is no way that this should ever have been confused with the verse epitaphs at Tong, but nevertheless it has. This has led to many more muddles, as we shall see on several future occasions.

~~~~~~~~~~~~~~~

V-9. Examples of more muddles in the eighteenth to twentieth centuries

Edmund Malone (1741–1812) was the great Shakespeare biography researcher at the end of the eighteenth century. His work has been admired ever since, but he never sorted out the Tong epitaphs.

His muddles were inherited by James Orchard Halliwell-Phillips (1820–89), the great and meticulous Shakespeare researcher in the mid-nineteenth century, who seems to have been among the next to take note of the Tong tomb and epitaphs, but concentrated on the epitaphs, never transcribed the MI and obviously never visited the tomb. Incidentally, his father was from Chorley, Lancashire, so James grew up with a strong sense of his native county and revisited it (Heyes, *History of Chorley*, Introduction), which makes it all the more surprising that he did not investigate the Lancashire links presented by these Shakespeare/ Stanley epitaphs.

E. K. Chambers, as has already been noted, was the first in the twentieth century to pay attention to the epitaphs, but expressed grave doubts over the authenticity of the Shakespeare attribution.

Oliver Baker's *In Shakespeare's Warwickshire* in 1937 provided a new impetus to the 'Shakespeare in Lancashire' theory, followed by Alan Keen, *The Annotator*, 1954. Citing Halliwell-Phillips, he gave his (Keen's) own synopsis of the information on the tomb, the MI and epitaphs and how they had come to the attention of Halliwell-Phillips. It is difficult to know how many mistakes came from Halliwell-Phillips and how many from Keen's own muddles.

Shropshire — TWO EPITAPHS
In Tong Church, Shropshire, are the tombs of Sir Thomas and Sir Edward Stanley, bearing poetical epitaphs engraved at their ends. Sir Thomas was of Winwick, Lancashire, and died in 1576. His widow, who died in 1596, had been Margaret Vernon, of the famous Shropshire family.[i] Sir Edward was a brother of Henry, fourth Earl of Derby,[ii] and his frequent visits to Knowsley and Lathom between the years 1561 and 1589 are recorded in the Household Books.[iii] He died in 1609.[iv] These epitaphs are described, and attributed to Shakespeare, in a MS. of *c*.1630. It is reproduced in facsimile by Halliwell-Phillips in his Folio of 1853, and more fully described by him in *Reliques*, p. 32. Later it was at Warwick Castle.[v]

This MS seems to be an earlier authority than Sir William Dugdale, who copied one epitaph with slightly different punctuation and spelling, in a collection appended to his *Visitation of Shropshire*, 1664.[vi] Thence Sir Isaac Heard, Garter, gave it to Malone, who printed it.

Halliday thinks the epitaph on Sir Edward sounds as if it might be by Shakespeare, but not that upon Sir Thomas. We agree with this, and of course hold that Shakespeare is likely to have met Sir Edward at Knowsley,[vii] either when the poet was there with Hesketh's Players, or when he first started work with Strange's Men. Sir Edward was Lord Strange's uncle.**[viii]** Here are the epitaphs, as quoted in the Halliwell-Phillips MS.:

Shakespeare. An epitaph on Sr. Edward Standly Ingraven on his Tombe in Tong Church.

> Not monumentall stones preserves our fame:
> Nor sky-aspiring Piramides our name:
> The memory of him for whom this standes
> Shall outlive marble and defacers hands
>   When all to times consumption shall be given
>   Standly for whom this stands shall stand in Heaven.

On Sir Thomas Standly.

> Idem, ibidem
> Ask who lies heere but doe not wheepe;
> Hee is not deade; hee doth but sleepe;
> This stony Register is for his bones,
> His Fame is more perpetuall, then these stones,
>   And his own goodnesse with him selfe being gone,
>   Shall live when Earthly monument is nonne.

(Keen, *The Annotator*, 1954, pp. 202-3.)

Notes by HM:

[i] '**Margaret Vernon, of the famous Shropshire family**'. This is a mere quibble, but with implications. Keen mistakenly called the Vernons a famous Shropshire family. They did indeed have many members in Shropshire, and Sir George Vernon owned Tong Castle in Shropshire, which is why it was inherited by his daughter Margaret, but Margaret's branch was from Derbyshire. Sir George Vernon of Haddon Hall, Nether Haddon was known as 'The King of the Peak', referring to the Peak District in Derbyshire, not Shropshire, and this was where Margaret was born, grew up and married. Had Keen realised this, his research might have been even more productive.

[ii] '**Sir Edward was a brother of Henry, fourth Earl of Derby**', He was indeed, but he is not the one on the tomb. This brother of Earl Henry and **Sir Thomas** was **Sir Edward Sr** (1535/40–1604). The one on the tomb is his nephew **Sir Edward Jr** (1562–1632).

[iii] '**his frequent visits to Knowsley and Lathom between the years 1561 and 1589 are recorded in the Household Books.**' Another quibble, but detailed records of visitors to Lathom and Knowsley have only survived from 1587–90. Although minimal records from 1561 onwards have survived, they do not include the extensive lists of visitors, as in 1587–90. We therefore have no records from this source of visitors before 1587. If we had, research into their biographies would have been somewhat easier, to say the least!

[iv] '**He died in 1609**'. This is a double muddle. Not only did Keen confuse the two **Sir Edwards, Sr** and **Jr**, but also confused them with at least one other Sir Edward Stanley, as so many others before and since. **Sir Edward Sr** very definitely died in 1604, buried in the Stanley vault at Ormskirk, with a record in the Parish Register. **Sir Edward Sr** was **Sir Thomas**'s brother and not the one on the tomb, who was his nephew. The Sir Edward Stanley who died in 1609 was a different one, not yet identified, place of burial unknown. Keen at least provides us with the correct date of death of **Sir Thomas**'s wife as 1596, subsequently confirmed by probate of her will. All these corrective details are thanks not least to Brian S(tanley) Roberts, webmaster of the Stanley Family Genealogy site.

[v] '**MS. of c.1630...Warwick Castle**'. Keen, researching in the 1940s and 1950s, was hampered by having knowledge of only two versions of the verse epitaphs. The MS of c.1630 was seen by Halliwell-Phillips, the great Shakespeare researcher in the middle of the nineteenth century. He combined this with Dugdale's version (which, we read, was passed by Sir Isaac Heard to Edmund Malone, and thence to H-P). H-P published both versions of the epitaphs in his Folio of 1853, then described them more fully in *Reliques* (1st ed. 1839, numerous later editions). The fact that the c.1630 MS ended up at Warwick Castle (at the latest by the 1950s) means we are talking about a different early version from the one in Weever's Notes. Because neither the author of this MS c.1630 nor later transcribers of Dugdale's 1663 MS had reproduced the MI with all the family details, various muddles were perpetuated post-Halliwell-Phillips. H-P had obviously not presented all details clearly enough to prevent a later enthusiastic sleuth such as Keen (re-)producing all his muddles. No one seems to have visited Tong to check on the texts from the tomb itself, and we read the subsequent main procession of recordings of the epitaphs, if not the MI, in the quote from Honigmann at the very beginning of this chapter. Chambers (1930) almost certainly copied the epitaphs from Halliwell-Phillips, and Schoenbaum (1975) copied them from one or both. When Keen was writing in the 1950s, Weever's even earlier transcription had not yet seen the light of day. This had to wait until Honigmann in his Shakespeare: the '*lost years*' (1985) and in his *Weever* (1987). The c.1630 MS is investigated further in the next Chapter VI. Seven seventeenth-century recordings, four attributing them to Shakespeare.

[vi] '**his *Visitation of Shropshire*, 1664**'. A minor quibble, but it was actually in 1663. We know from his Diaries that he also spent five days in Shrewsbury in 1664, ascertaining more details en route to Cheshire and Lancashire, but the bulk had been completed the previous year.

[vii] '**hold that Shakespeare is likely to have met Sir Edward at Knowsley**'. True, but again, Keen has muddled his Sir Edwards. The one he is talking about here is **Sir Edward Sr**, whereas Shakespeare wrote the epitaphs for **Sir Edward Jr**.

[viii] '**either when the poet was there with Hesketh's Players, or when he first started work with Strange's Men. Sir Edward was Lord Strange's uncle**'. Keen is still talking about **Sir Edward Sr**, and the years we are talking about are 1581–82. It could well be that **(Sir) Edward Jr** was at Lathom during these years, but he was a newly married man setting up a household with his wife and first children, so might well already have been living in Tong at this time. Both **Sir Edwards** were at Preston Guild in late August-mid-September, 1582, but this is a little late for '**when he first started work with Strange's Men**'.

~~~~~~~~~~~~~~~~~~

V–10. Another muddle by Gough Nichols

Just one more quote concerning the MI is provided here from 1863, by John Gough Nichols (ed), a highly respected Fellow of the Society of Antiquaries, and one presumes with Halliwell-Phillips's writings available to him. He was albeit quoting from Gough, publishing at the end of the eighteenth century, between the dates of Malone and H-P.

> ADDENDA
> p. 184. *Two monuments to the same Person*. – The two monuments to Thomas Lord Wharton are paralleled by those to **Sir Thomas Stanley** (ob. 1600), one at Tong, co. Salop, and the other at Walthamstow in Essex, with the same epitaph. Gough, *Sepulchral Monuments*, vol. ii. p. ccxxxvii.
> (*The Herald and Genealogist*, edited by John Gough Nichols, F.S.A., Volume the First, London: John Bowyer Nichols and Sons, Printers to the Society of Antiquaries, 1863, p. 570.)

In the paragraph immediately above Gough reported erroneously the following details:

a) A wrong date of death for **Sir Thomas Stanley**: he actually died in 1576 (not 1600) and his son **Edward** in 1632 — the latter's wife Lucy née Percy was the one who died closest to 1600, in 1601.
b) He ascribed the monument at Walthamstow as well that at Tong to **Sir Thomas**, having muddled **Sir Thomas** with his son **Sir Edward Jr**.
c) The tomb at Walthamstow contained the effigies only of Lucy Stanley and their daughters, NOT of **Sir Edward Jr**, and certainly not of **Sir Thomas**.

d) The MIs at Tong and Walthamstow, although similar, are not the same, e.g. the ages of the daughters are missing at Walthamstow.

It is difficult to imagine building more errors into one sentence! A little Google search produced the following dates of the author quoted by Gough Nichols: Richard Gough (1735–1809), *Sepulchral Monuments*, 3 vols (1786–99). He had obviously not visited either tomb. All details of the Walthamstow tomb are given in a later chapter. John Gough Nichols's dates were 1806–73.

V–11. A sketch of the tomb

As we have seen, a report from Tong appeared in notes made by the Revd J. E. Auden. This was the first time I had come across news of a sketch of the Tong tomb.

> In a volume of still unpublished M.S. by Sir Wm. Dugdale is a passage dealing with the Stanley monument. After quoting the prose epitaph in full Dugdale continues, "Shakespeare [in the margin]. These following verses were made by William Shakespeare, the late famous tragedian". Dugdale's text is followed by a series of drawings of Shropshire antiquities made by Francis Sandford, and in Sandford's sketch of the Stanley monument at Tong we see the pyramids with their finial balls and spikes in their original position; the allegorical figures, now sadly defaced and banished to the niches on the arch dividing the Vernon Chapel from the south aisle, standing on the canopy; and the whole composition from the side, a view which, wedged as the tomb now is between the earlier Vernon monument, it is today impossible to photograph.
>
> (*Auden's Notes on the History of Tong*, Vol. 2, 2005, p. 59.)

This report produced the first news (for me) about Francis Sandford's sketch of the Tong tomb. Why had this not been widely reported? What were Auden's sources? He had obviously not just read the Dugdale version repeated so often in other publications, but also seen a MS version of Dugdale's original notes on Shropshire antiquities, with sketches. Where had he seen this? Were there in fact two Dugdale texts?

All was revealed in due course after another paper-chase. The story was something like as follows. In September 1663 Sir William Dugdale conducted his Visitation of Shropshire. At the same time he was preparing his *Antiquities of Shropshire*. At some point he despatched Herald Francis Sandford to make sketches of multiple monuments, and one that Sandford executed was of the Stanley tomb. At the same time he transcribed the verse epitaphs again. This reached Dugdale in due course, but was not included in his *Antiquities of Shropshire*, presumably because it was not an antiquity. It remained unnoticed in his notes for more than a century before it was spotted, and most reports throughout the twentieth century gave the impression that there was only one transcription plus sketch, rather than two separate transcriptions, in a different hand, the second one including the sketch. Both transcriptions appear as illustrations in this book (Dugdale's as Va, Sandford's as Vb, Vc). As far as I am aware, this is the first time they have ever appeared together in a printed book.

V–12. Authorship of the epitaphs

As mentioned above, the main extant source for the authorship by Shakespeare is Sir William Dugdale. A discussion of his reliability and thus the potential authenticity seems too important to attempt to cover in a few paragraphs at the beginning of this book. First one should read what others have written and survey who has believed in the authenticity or dismissed it out of hand and why. It would also be useful to know as much as possible about **Sir Edward Stanley Jr**, the recipient of the epitaphs, whether they were by Shakespeare or not. The rest of this book presents explorations in all these areas. No attempt is made to conceal the fact that from the start I was prejudiced in favour of the authenticity (coming with considerable research behind me into Sir William Dugdale and the Stanleys, who were also vital in the background to sorting out the Lancashire ancestry of Pilgrim Father Captain Myles Standish), and had the hope that more details about the Stanleys concerned might in turn reveal another small part of Shakespeare's biography. The reader must judge whether or not the following account has been successful in coming to my conclusion that they were indeed by the Bard himself. If not, so be it. If so, then any future biographer of the Bard should include these epitaphs.

Sir Sidney Lee, in the first major biography for modern times in 1898, never even mentioned them. Chambers (1930) and Schoenbaum (1975) had certainly not paid a visit to Tong, and it is obvious (from their writings) that they did not consider the epitaphs to be worthy of further consideration in potentially providing any more details about Shakespeare's biography. For Chambers and Schoenbaum, the Tong epitaphs were at best a mildly interesting but unimportant sidestep, which would lead to nowhere, and they both thus rejected them as of little or no value, along with the 'Shakespeare in Lancashire' theory. Their voices were loud and important enough in Shakespeare biography in the twentieth century to completely bury the potential significance of the Tong epitaphs for quite some time. They remained almost buried until Professor Honigmann pursued the 'Shakespeare in Lancashire' theory (1985), with the Stanley epitaphs as part and parcel of this.

The only nodding recognition from Stratford since Honigmann's 1985 *'lost years'* came in the *Oxford Shakespeare*, eds. Stanley Wells and Gary Taylor, 2005 (pointed out to me personally by Professor Wells). However the few lines there are another reflection of various previous muddles. None of the Shakespeare 'popular' biographies which have appeared since then, with one almost annually since the Conference at Lancaster University 1999, have so much as mentioned them. They have all, without exception, included the 'Lancastrian Shakespeare theory' and the growing belief in Shakespeare's Catholicism, but none has mentioned **Sir Edward Stanley** and the epitaphs at Tong. This neglect is now redressed.

~~~~~~~~~~~~~~~~~~

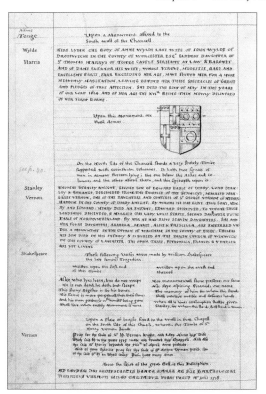

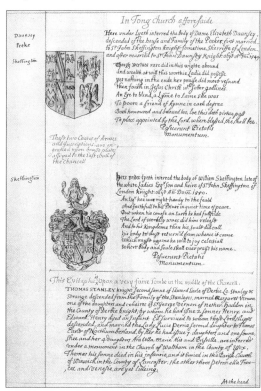

(Upper left)
Va. Dugdale's Diary from Notes in 1663
A copy of notes taken during his Heraldic Visitation of Shropshire; he was in Tong on 23 September 1663.
© College of Arms, Dugdale's Diary, C35, p. 20

(Upper right)
Vb. Sandford's Notes, 1664; Dugdale's Diary
© College of Arms, Dugdale's Diary, C35, p. 40

(Left)
Vc. Sandford's sketch of tomb, 1664; Dugdale's Diary
Francis Sandford, Rouge Dragon Poursuivant, was asked by Dugdale to produce this sketch, which was later added to a copy of his Diary notes. Although not included in the 1827 publication of Dugdale's Diary, these pages gradually became known to researchers of Shakespeare's biography. As far as is known, this is the first time that all three pages have been published together, which in itself is an explanation for many confused and confusing previous reports.
© College of Arms, Dugdale's Diary, C35, p. 41

(Full-page versions of Va, Vb, Vc appear in the Colour Section)

Chapter VI
Seven seventeenth-century recordings
of the Verse Epitaphs
(four attributing them to Shakespeare)

VI-1. Introduction
VI-2. Transcription 1– John Weever
VI-3. Transcription 2– Anon
VI-4. Transcription 3– Sir Francis Fane?
VI-5. Transcription 4– Sir Francis Fane?
VI-6. Transcription 5– Sir William Dugdale
VI-7. Transcription 6– Francis Sandford
VI-8. Transcription 7– Father Henry More
VI-9. Conclusions

VI–1. Introduction

So many versions of the Tong Verse Epitaphs have emerged that it seemed most sensible to gather them all together in one place. These are all verifiably seventeenth century. There must have been one original MS in Shakespeare's own handwriting, when he composed the verses and gave them to **Sir Edward Stanley**. There must have been another MS version provided by **Sir Edward** for the mason or artisan, to inscribe on the tomb in gold lettering. Neither of these has survived.

All of the subsequent transcriptions give more or less the same text, of course, but copying from one MS to another always provides the possibility of mistranscriptions or idiosyncratic interpretations of what the 'correct' punctuation ought to be. These very changes seem to provide clues as to who might have copied which MS, one after the other; or at least, which one came before another one. There may well have been other transcriptions, of course, which have not survived or not yet been detected. In addition there is always the possibility that a later transcriber in the nineteenth or twentieth century, preparing the text for publication, did not reproduce accurately the MS or printed copy (or text on the tomb itself) in front of him ('him', because all so far have been male).

The transcriptions provided below are all from the original MSS. One must mention one new name in praise: Professor Gordon Campbell of Leicester University. Until the late twentieth century, the 'standard' transcription was from a MS of 1663/4 at the College of Arms, written by Sir William Dugdale, Norroy King of Arms at the time. This was 'rediscovered' in the late eighteenth century, when research into Shakespeare's biography underwent a revival. Dugdale's transcription has appeared endlessly ever since, acquiring new spellings and punctuation all along the way.

Professor Campbell (in the late 1990s) seems to have been the first person for a long time to have actually gone back to the original MS at the College of Arms and identified two versions of the epitaphs in the same file, but in different handwriting (5c & 6 below), thus sorting out not a few previous muddles. In addition, he has re-detected three more seventeenth-century transcriptions (2, 3, 4 below), all of which seem to pre-date Dugdale's. Campbell was not particularly interested in whether the epitaphs were by Shakespeare or not; nor was he particularly interested in **Sir Thomas** and **Sir Edward**, whose effigies are on the tomb. His main interest, as an expert on Milton, was in detecting possible inspirations for 'young' Milton's Sonnet to Shakespeare, written 1630 and published 1632 in the Second Folio. His main reason for concluding that the Tong epitaphs might have been instrumental for Milton was in the 'sky aspiring pyramids'. He also noted the 'stones/bones' rhyme in both Shakespeare's epitaph for himself (on his tomb in Stratford) and the

Tong epitaphs. His two early publications (both meanwhile online), in which he gave transcriptions of the Tong epitaphs (and photos of St Bartholomew's, Tong, the tomb and the verse beginning 'Ask who lies here'), were:

> Campbell, 'Obelisks and Pyramids in Shakespeare, Milton and Alcalà', *Sederi*, 4, 1998, pp. 217-232.
> Campbell, 'Shakespeare and the Youth of Milton', *Milton Quarterly*, 33.4, 1999, Johns Hopkins University, pp. 95-105.

In the 1980s Professor Honigmann had already detected probably the earliest extant transcription (c.1626) by poet and antiquarian John Weever (1 below). This was during his research on the 'Shakespeare Lancashire connection' and the biography and works of John Weever. He was only peripherally interested in **Sir Thomas** and **Sir Edward Stanley**. Quotes below come from:

> Honigmann, *Shakespeare: the 'lost years'*, Manchester University Press, 1985 (2nd. ed.1998), Chapter VII. The Shakespeare Epitaphs, pp.77–89.
> Honigmann, *John Weever: A biography of a literary associate of Shakepeare and Jonson, together with a photographic facsimile of Weever's Epigrammes (1599)*, Manchester University Press, 1987.

My contribution has been to put these all together and try and make sense of what they tell us about:

a) how widespread was knowledge of the very existence of these epitaphs in the seventeenth century;
b) how reliable any of them are;
c) how much each transcription shows us about how many details of the members of the Stanley family concerned were known by the transcriber;
d) the probable order in which these transcriptions were written;
e) whether they were perceived at the time as two separate verses, or one divided into two;
f) if two, whether one was written for **Sir Thomas** and the other for **Sir Edward**;
g) whether one was written earlier and the other later, or both at the same time;
h) anything else they might reveal.

We are concerned here purely with the Verse Epitaphs. Without exception, not a single early seventeenth-century transcription (1–4) was accompanied by the complete MI at Tong. At best, there was a brief reference to it, the longest one being in No. 1. Some included a reference to Shakespeare's authorship; others did not. Most started with the verse at the foot, 'Ask who lies here', others reversed the order, with one (No. 2) getting into a complete muddle. Without exception the MS versions reproduced below changed or added to the punctuation on the tomb:

   i) Number assigned to transcription
   ii) Name of transcriber
   iii) (Approximate) date
   iv) Accuracy?
   v) Head-Foot, order
   vi) Shakespeare named?
   vii) Intimate, or at least some knowledge of the Stanley Family?
   viii) Evidence that the transcriber might actually have seen the tomb in Tong

NB. 7 does not qualify officially as a 'transcriber', but his obvious knowledge of the epitaphs and the Stanley family qualifies him as a 'participator' in the story and 'recorder' of the verses, which he must have seen or at least known about.

i)	ii)	iii)	iv)	v)	vi)	vii)	viii)
1	John Weever	1626?	++	H-F	-	+++	-
2	Anon	?	-	F-H	-	-	-
3	Sir Francis Fane?	1630? 1650?	++	F-H	Yes	+	+
4	Sir Francis Fane?	1630? 1650?	++	F-H	Yes	+	+
5	Sir William Dugdale	1663	+++	F-H	Yes	+++	+++
6	Francis Sandford	1664	+++	H-F	-	+++	+++
7	Father Henry More	Pre-1660			Yes	+++	+

VI–2. Transcription 1 — John Weever

1. John Weever (1576–1632); poet and antiquarian; from Lancashire; transcription c.1626; knew details from the MI; no attribution to Shakespeare. He 'muddled' the Stanley tombs in Tong and Walthamstow: **Sir Edward**'s effigy does not appear in Walthamstow and his wife's not in Tong. The MI in both places is more or less the same. It appears that Weever knew details of the Walthamstow tomb better, but also knew that **Sir Edward** had already prepared his own tomb. He obviously knew **Sir Edward**, because he dedicated a poem to him: *Faunus and Melliflora* in 1600. No mention of **Sir Thomas**. Weever's complete text was given in the preceding chapter of this book ('V. Two early recordings and lots of muddles'), quoted from Honigmann, *Weever*, 1987, 'VII, Ancient Funeral Monuments', pp. 68-70, (Society of Antiquaries, MS. 128, fo. 38).

VI-3. Transcription 2 - Anon

2. Anon; no date; no reference to MI; lines transposed; two lines missing; no attribution to Shakespeare. This, plus Nos. 3 and 4, seem to have been first discovered and transcribed all together by Professor Campbell in his hunt for possible inspirations for Milton's *Sonnet* to Shakespeare. [*Italics* indicate deviations from the text on the tomb. HM]

> Not monumental *stones* preserves *thy* fame
> Nor sky aspiring pyramids *thy* name
> The *monument* of him for whom this stands
> Shall outlive marble *or* defacers hands
> Ask who lies here but do not weep
> He is not dead he doth but sleep
> This *earthly* register his [*sic*] for his bones
> His fame is more perpetual than these stones
> *And* when to *time* consumption shall be given
> *Stanlye* for whom this stands shall stand in heaven.
>
> (Rawlinson MSS. Bodleian M32, fol 269v.)

This is clearly a corrupt text; it has no title, omits two lines, transposes two others and contains seven substantive variants from the other texts: in line 3, for example, it reads 'monument' for 'memory' and in line 7 it reads 'earthly' for 'stony'. The scribe assumes that it is a single poem, beginning with 'Not monumental stones', the quatrain at the foot of the effigy. That does not seem to me likely, because 'Ask who lies here' is surely a more appropriate opening, and the last line of that stanza, with its mention of the earthly monument, would seem to lead naturally on to 'nor [*sic*] monumental stone'.

(Campbell, 'Obelisks and Pyramids', p. 223.)

VI-4. Transcription 3 - Sir Francis Fane?

3. Anon; attribution to Shakespeare; confidently ascribes one verse each to father and son.

An Epitaph on Sir Edward Standly
Engraven on his Tomb
in Tong Church

Shakespeare

Not monumental stone preserves our fame
Nor sky-aspiring pyramids our name;
The memory of him for whom this stands,
Shall outlive marble, and defacers hands.
　　When all to times consumption shall be given
　　Standley for whom this stands shall stand in heaven.

Idem, ibidem　　　　On Sir Thomas Standley

Ask who lies here, but do not weep
He is not dead, he doth but sleep;
This stony register is for his bones
His fame is more perpetual than these stones:
　　And his own goodnes with himself being gone,
　　Shall live, when earthly monument is none.

'Collection of epitaphs in the Portland manuscripts at Nottingham University, MS 9, p. 12.'
(Campbell, 'Obelisks and Pyramids', pp. 223-4).

This and/or the next one may have been the one mentioned in the previous chapter, quoted by Halliwell-Phillips, as the MS of c.1630. One of c.1630 was also mentioned by the Revd J.E. Auden, quoting from Eyton, as Harleian MSS 5816 fol. So we may actually be concerned with three transcriptions here rather than two. Campbell gives a date of c.1650 for the one immediately above.

It has also been suggested that the collection was by Sir Francis Fane, but as there were three of this name in the seventeenth century, this makes it difficult to ascribe an accurate date to any of the transcriptions. Sir Francis Fane, 1st Earl of Westmorland (1580-1629), was related to many in the Stanley circle of relatives and friends. His third (but second surviving) son was also Sir Francis Fane (1611-81?), who also had a son Francis, who became a dramatist during the Restoration period. Biographies of all three appear in the expected places.

In summary, four references in MSS have been mentioned, but only the first two referred to by Campbell. The locations of these four MSS are:

Collection of epitaphs in the Portland manuscripts at Nottingham University, MS 9, p. 12.
Folger Library, MS 7, fol 8.
Folger MS Pw. V.37, p. 12 (the same or different?)
Harleian MS 5816 fol.

VI-5. Transcription 4 – Sir Francis Fane?

4. Ditto No. 3. Campbell introduces it as 'from a related collection [*to No. 3*] in the Folger Library'. [Slight differences from 3 are in italics. HM]

An Epitaph on Sir Edward Standly
Engraven on his Tomb
in Tong Church

Shakespeare

Not monumental *stones* preserves our fame,
Nor sky-aspiring pyramids our name;
The memory of him for whom this stands
Shall *out live* marble and defacers hands
  When all to times consumption shall be given,
  Standly for whom this stands shall stand in heaven.

Idem, ibidem   On Sir Thomas *Stanley*

Ask who lies here [*no comma*] but do not weep,
He is not dead he doth but sleep;
This stony register is for his bones,
His fame is more perpetual than these stones:
  And his own goodne*ss* with himself being gone,
  Shall live when earthly monument is none.

(Folger Library, MS 7, fol 8.)

(Campbell, 'Obelisks and Pyramids', p. 224)

VI-6. Transcription(s) 5 – Sir William Dugdale, 1663

5. Sir William Dugdale (1605–86); transcription most likely in September 1663 during his Visitation of Shropshire; MS at the College of Arms; attribution to Shakespeare. (For details of Dugdale see Chapter VII. How reliable was William Dugdale?) This is the transcription that has become ever more widely known since the end of the eighteenth century, and therefore has a longer entry than the others. Dugdale's transcription almost presents a potential monograph in itself.

Most transcriptions of the Tong epitaphs in the twentieth century are based on this, and quote and reference Dugdale. All writers, whether academic scholars or not, were well meaning, but most, in their own way and for their own purposes, reproduced Dugdale's transcription as a copy of a copy of a copy, with all the possibilities for changes in the spelling and punctuation. In one sense, this does not matter at all, because this transcription is dated accurately, but it is worth spending a little longer on this, for the sake of comparison with the original and later copies.

Transcription 5a (already given in last chapter)

On the north side of the chancel of Tonge Church, in the county of Salop, etc. stands a very stately tomb, supported with Corinthian columns. It hath two figures of men in armour thereon lying...and this epitaph upon it: "Thomas Stanley, Knight, second son of Edward, Earl of Derby," etc. These following verses were made by William Shakespeare, the late famous tragedian.

Written upon the east end of the tomb

Ask who lies here, but do not weep; etc.

Written upon the west end thereof

Not monumental stone preserves our fame, etc.

(E. A. J. Honigmann, *Shakespeare, the 'lost years'* (Manchester UP, 1985; 2nd ed. 1998), p. 78, with reference in an endnote: "See Chambers, *Shakespeare, [William Shakespeare: A study of Facts and Problems*, 2 vols, 1930] II, pp. 268-9; I, 551ff.; and Schoenbaum, 'Shakespeare's Epitaphs' (in *Lives*, 1970, pp. 75-82.)

This serves as the archetype of all twentieth-century transcriptions, going back at least to Chambers, who had already copied it from nineteenth-century transcriptions.

Transcription 5b

A more recent version of Dugdale's transcription appears in Peter Hyland, *An Introduction to Shakespeare's Poems*, Palgrave Macmillan, 2003 (online). Peter Hyland is Professor of English, Huron College, University of Western Ontario, Canada. His accompanying text sheds light on several surrounding matters, including the current position of many Shakespeare scholars about the Tong epitaphs, among other epitaphs.

Other brief scraps of verse have been attributed to Shakespeare over the years. Most of them are preserved in seventeenth-century manuscript miscellanies from about 1625 onwards.[i] These were essentially commonplace book collections of whatever took the fancy of their compilers; the generally haphazard method of collection meant that poems were often misattributed or left without attribution, and they are often in a corrupt state because of careless copying. The poems attributed to Shakespeare are connected in some way to people with whom he was acquainted,[ii] so they were eagerly taken up by early biographers. In no case has it been established that he was actually the author, but there is nothing either to suggest that he could not have been. Some contain a flash of wit, but most of them are epitaphs, and are rendered unremarkable by the conventions of the form. Wells and Taylor included some of the least improbable in their Oxford edition, and since then these have subsequently been included by Evans in his Penguin edition and by Greenblatt in the Norton edition, I shall briefly discuss them, as their inclusion in these editions affords them some legitimacy.[iii]

Epitaphs are not, of course, usually intended as works of literature, but to be engraved on marble or gilded monuments. The Stanley tomb at Tong, Shropshire, containing the remains of Sir Edward Stanley and Sir Thomas Stanley,[iv] is just such a monument, and boasts two epitaphs (or an epitaph in two stanzas). The epitaphs appear in a number of manuscripts in which Shakespeare is identified as the author, including the one appended to Sir William Dugdale's Visitation of Shropshire (College of Arms MS C.35, fol. 20D, 1664).[v] Shakespeare had a number of connections with this family and although the date of the tomb's construction is unknown[vi] it is certainly possible that he composed the epitaphs. On the east end[vii] of the tomb is the following:

Ask who lies here but do not weep.
He is not dead; he doth but sleep.
This stony register is for his bones;
His fame is more perpetual than these stones,
And his own goodness, with himself being gone,
Shall live when earthly monument is none.

On the west end[vii] is written
Not monumental stone preserves our fame,
Nor sky-aspiring pyramids our name.
The memory of him for whom this stands
Shall outlive marble and defacer's hands.
When all to time's consumption shall be given,
Stanley, for whom this stands, shall stand in heaven.

As epitaphs go these are not bad, in spite of the uneasy shift from tetrameter to pentameter in the third line of the first, and the lame, though understandable, play on 'Stanley/stand'.[viii]. There is a good image in this 'Stony register', and there appear to be clear echoes of the Sonnets, particularly sonnet 55, though this does not necessitate that Shakespeare himself wrote these lines. The 'bones/stones' rhyme comes, of course, within epitaph territory, and indeed it recurs in Shakespeare's own epitaph, carved on his tomb in Holy Trinity Church in Stratford.

A number of sources have claimed that Shakespeare wrote the epitaph, the earliest being Francis Fane in a seventeenth-century miscellany compiled around 1655-6 (Folger MS V.a.180, fol. 79).**[ix]**

(Peter Hyland, *An Introduction to Shakespeare's Poems*,
Palgrave Macmillan, 2003 (online), pp. 205-206)

Notes by HM:

[i] 'manuscript miscellanies from about 1625 onwards'. This date presumably/perhaps refers to Weever's MSS, which include a transcription of the Tong epitaphs.

[ii] 'people with whom he was acquainted'. In the case of the Stanley epitaphs in Tong, I argue that **Sir Edward** must have been more than a mere acquaintance of William Shakespeare, and more likely a long-standing friend from teenage days in Lancashire. **Sir Edward** was from an aristocratic family that had been of importance to his own Shakeshafte/ Shakespeare family since the days of both their 2-3x-great-grandfathers, who had fought together at Bosworth in 1485.

[iii] 'affords them some legitimacy' At this point in his text Hyland gives a superscript ref. [11] to a footnote, which unfortunately is not included in the pages online.

[iv] 'containing the remains of Sir Edward Stanley and Sir Thomas Stanley'. Professor Hyland is, alas, uninformed that **Sir Edward**'s remains, grave and MI are actually in Eynsham, Oxon, his funeral conducted by his unmarried daughter Petronella. **Sir Thomas**'s remains are, alas, no longer there, as discovered during the entry into the Stanley vault during the restoration of the church in 1891. (See Chapter IV. The Revd J.E. Auden's *History of Tong* re the Stanley tomb'.)

[v] 'Sir William Dugdale's *Visitation of Shropshire* (College of Arms MS C.35, fol. 20D, 1664)'. This reference was pursued at the College of Arms, who give their own reference as follows:

> To clarify the references first of all, they are all in our MS. C.35, in the church notes section or what could alternatively be called the second numeration:
> **1)** p.20 has the verses in Dugdale's hand
> **2)** p.41 has the verses and sketch of the tomb by Sandford; the entry relating to the tomb actually starts on p.40

(Email from College of Arms, 2011).

[vi] '. . . the date of the tomb's construction is unknown . . .'. It was unknown to Professor Hyland in 2003, but this book provides all the evidence that its construction must have been 1601–03.

[vii] 'On the east end' and **'on the west end'** is proof in itself that Hyland was copying from previous published versions of Dugdale's MS and had almost certainly not examined the text on the tomb. This is not a criticism, but Hyland's version of punctuation differs slightly from those in 5a (Honigmann via Chambers) and 5c (Campbell from the original), thus proving his own point about '**careless copying**'. Since the removal of the tomb in the 1760s, and the restoration at the end of the nineteenth century, the west and east references of the seventeenth century require clarification.

[viii] 'the lame, though understandable, play on "Stanley/stand".' Hyland here hits one nail on the head. I am not at all sure how many Stanley MSS he has read in archives, but their name appears in early MSS in Lancashire archives as 'Standley, Standly, Stanly, Stanley, Standleigh, Stanleigh', with other variations almost *ad inf*. By the time of Shakespeare (born 1564) and **Sir Edward Stanley** (1562) it had settled down in the Lancashire family to Stanley, but with distinct memories that it had recently been reproduced as Stan(d)l(e)y. At the risk of repetition, the origin of the name was in 'Stone-leigh' (stony meadow) in Staffordshire (see in all Stanley, Derby literature). The introduction of a 'd' was rather random, indiscriminate and idiosyncratic, but did provide Shakespeare with the opportunity for this **'lame, though understandable, play on "Stanley/stand".'**

[ix] 'Francis Fane in a seventeenth-century miscellany compiled around 1655-6 (Folger MS V.a.180, fol. 79)'. I assume that this refers to the Shakespeare epitaph to himself, and not to the Stanley epitaphs, but the following item (5c) also refers to a copy of the Stanley transcription at the Folger Library. This reference to Francis Fane and c.1655-6 seems to limit the collector in question to Sir Francis Fane II.

Transcription 5c

Campbell (op.cit), p. 224, gives a slightly different transcription of Dugdale's MS, particularly in the punctuation. Indeed he states that in all his transcriptions he has left the punctuation as in the original, but modernised the spelling: '[...] in Dugdale's "Visitation of Shropshire, 1663–1664 (MS c.35) [...] in the hand of the antiquarian Sir William Dugdale.".' This appears to be the first recent transcription from the original MS and not a copy of a copy of a copy.

These following verses were made by William Shakespeare the late famous tragedian.

Written upon the east end
  of this tomb

Ask who lies here, but do not weep
  He is not dead he doth but sleep
This stony register is for his bones
His fame is more perpetual than these stones.
And his own goodness with himself being gone,
Shall live when earthly monument is none.

Written upon the west end
  thereof

Not monumental stone preserves our fame,
Nor sky aspiring pyramids our name
The memory of him for whom this stands
Shall out-live marble and defacers hands.
  When all to times consumption shallbe given,
  Stanley, for whom this stands, shall stand in heaven.

An accompanying version of the verses in his article is indeed in another exact transcription, this time of the one on the tomb, which is all in capitals. This corresponds exactly with my own transcription, made directly from the tomb and photos, and double-checked by David Dixon of Tong, in St Bartholomew's, with my printed version and a pen in one hand and a torch in the other. The only significant difference is that the verses on the tomb are aligned left, and not centred. (See the photographs.) (For my transcription see Chapter II. The Stanley tomb in Tong today.)

ASK WHO LYES HEARE BVT DO NOT WEEP,
HE IS NOT DEAD, HE DOOTH BVT SLEEP
THIS STONY REGISTER, IS FOR HIS BONES
HIS FAME IS MORE PERPETVALL THÉ THEISE STONES
AND HIS OWNE GOODNES WT HIM SELF BEING GON
SHALL LYVE WHEN EARTHLIE MONAMENT IS NONE

NOT MONV(M)ENTALL STONE PRESERVES OVR FAME
NOR SKY ASPYRING PIRAMIDS OVR NAME
THE MEMORY OF HIM FOR WHOM THIS STANDS
SHALL OVTLYVE MARBL AND DEFACERS HANDS
WHEN ALL TO TYMES CONSVMPTION SHALL BE GEAVEN
STANDLEY FOR WHOM THIS STANDS SHALL STAND IN HEAVEN

VI-7. Transcription 6 — Francis Sandford

6. Francis Sandford (1630–94), herald and genealogist; in 1664 Lancaster Herald; MS at the College of Arms; in the same file as Dugdale's MS; includes a drawing of the Tong tomb, therefore he obviously visited Tong.

Campbell writes, 'In the same manuscript [*as 5 by Dugdale*] but in a different hand, is one that is unknown to Shakespeare scholars. It presents yet another text.' I am not sure that it is unknown, but it is certainly true that reports in the twentieth century completely muddled the two by Dugdale and Sandford.

My 'explanation' for the origin of these transcriptions of the epitaphs is as follows. We assume that Dugdale visited Tong and made his own transcription (5c) in the 1660s. This seems most likely to have been during his Visitation of Shropshire in 1663, because it appears among his notes for this Visitation. In the summer of 1664 he set off for his Visitations of Cheshire and Lancashire, but on the way stayed for a few days in Shrewsbury, adding more details to his notes about armigerous families. Towards the end of his Visitation of Lancashire in 1664, on his way back home he spent two days at Knowsley with the current Earl of Derby, when he may (or may not) have checked on details known in the family about **Sir Thomas** and **Sir Edward of Tong**. (Dates are from his *Diary*, published 1827, online). During the whole of this period he had been preparing his *Antiquities of Shropshire*, which was published in 1664. Some time during these peregrinations he realised that he did not have a sketch of the Stanley tomb, and dispatched Francis Sandford, Lancaster Herald, to Tong to produce this, with a completely accurate transcription. Dugdale did not include the sketch or any mention of the Stanley tomb in his *Antiquities of Shropshire*. This might have been because Sandford's sketch arrived too late for inclusion. Or Dugdale might, in any case, have decided that it did not qualify as an 'antiquity', given that **Sir Edward** had died in 1632, within Dugdale's own lifetime.

The inclusion of the drawing means that it is fairly certain that the MI was copied directly from the tomb.

Transcription 6a

This is the most accurate and most recent attempt at producing a copy from the Sandford MS at the College of Arms by Douglas Campbell (1998). This incorporates some modernisation of spelling.

At the head of the tomb are these verses

Not monumental stone preserves our fame
Nor sky aspiring pyramids our name
The memory of him for whom this stands
Shall out-live marble and defacers hands.
When all to times consumption shall be given
Standley for whom this stands shall stand in heaven.

A little lower on the verge

Beati mortui qui in Domino moriantur

[See illustration **Vc.** and colour section]

At the foot of the monument

Ask who lies here, but do not weep;
He is not dead, he doth but sleep.
This stony register is for his bones
His fame is more perpetual than these stones

And his own goodness with himself being gone
Shall live when earthly monument is none.

(Campbell, *op.cit.*, p. 225: College of Arms, MS 7, *op. cit.*)

Transcription 6b

Finally, after a long journey, we come to a definitive transcription of the Sandford MS from a photograph of the MS at the College of Arms (given as Illustration Vc), which allows any interested reader to check this for him/herself. This retains all 'idiosyncrasies', including the somewhat confusing use for modern eyes of an elongated version of 'f' for 's' in some cases, represented here as f; also the use of capitals as the first letter of some words. This is exactly as a learned herald in 1664 saw fit to transcribe it.

At the head of the Tombe are the fe Verfes

Not Monumentall Stone pre$f$erues our fame
Nor Sky aspireing piramides our name
The memorye of him for whom this $f$tands
Shall out-live marble, and defacers hands.
When all to times con$f$umption $f$hall be given
Standley for whome this $f$tands $f$hall $f$tand in Heaven.

    a little lower on the verge.

Beati mortui qui in Domino moriantur

    [See illustration **Vc.** and colour section]

    At the foote of the Monument

A$f$ke who lies here, but do not weepe,
He is not dead, he doth but sleepe.
This stonye Register is for his bones
His fame is more perpetuall than thefe $f$tones
And his owne goodne$f$s with him$f$elf being gone
Shall live when earthly Monument is none.

VI-8. Reference 7 — Father Henry Moore

7. Reference by Father Henry More, pre-1660. Strictly speaking this does not belong in this list because it does not provide a full transcription. However, in contrast to all the above renditions, he alone reveals a knowledge of the existence of these epitaphs PLUS a rather profound knowledge of relationships within the Stanley family.

> [...] for Father Henry More, telling a ghost-story in his History of the *English Province of the Society of Jesus*, written in 1660, says "Lord Stourton called his wife, a daughter of Edward, Earl of Derby, and sister to the Stanley whose epitaphs Shakespeare wrote [...]"

For a full treatment of this, see 'Appendix 8. Father Henry More'.

VI-9. Conclusions

1) Knowledge of the verse epitaphs written by Shakespeare for **Sir Edward Stanley** must have been fairly widespread in certain circles at the time, and remembered right throughout the seventeenth century until well after the Restoration. One might designate these circles as: literary, theatrical, antiquarian, aristocratic, upper gentry, recusant, Catholics in exile and Jesuit.
2) Knowledge of their inclusion on the Stanley tomb must have been fairly widespread.

3) Some of the transcribers seem to have had more than a passing knowledge of the Stanleys on the tomb.

4) The verse epitaphs were indeed composed by Shakespeare.

5) The most authentic seventeenth-century version of the verse epitaphs as they appear on the tomb is Transcription 6b by Francis Sandford.

It is perhaps irrelevant that he recorded them the other way round from Dugdale. He made it very clear which was at the head and which at the foot, whereas Dugdale recorded them as east and west. One might imagine that Sandford thought the head/foot assignation was more useful. He may or may not have had Dugdale's transcription with him, just to check it, but it seems more likely that he 'started from scratch'. However, the two are so similar that one might assume that Dugdale was very happy to have confirmation of his own transcription. One might assume that he had intended to include it in his *Antiquities of Shropshire*, but that by the time he received Sandford's transcription and sketch, the book was already at the printers. In any case Dugdale, during his Heraldic Visitation, was concerned mainly in recording the pedigrees of people still living in Shropshire, who wished to justify their coat of arms. Recording Antiquities was a separate project. He must have realised that the Stanleys of Tong did not qualify on either count:

1) They certainly did not qualify to be included under Shropshire Pedigrees, because **Sir Edward** had sold Tong Castle in 1603 and left no male heir;

2) The tomb hardly qualified as an 'antiquity', having been constructed in 1601–03 and **Sir Edward** having lived until 1632, overlapping with Sir William Dugdale's own lifetime (1605–86).

Chapter VII
How reliable was Sir William Dugdale?

The main source for Shakespeare's authorship is Sir William Dugdale (1605–86). His biography is in the *Old* and *New DNB*, with an adequate one on Wikipedia (part of which is reproduced below), but we are concerned here not so much with the facts of his life and details of his publications, but more with his reliability and his knowledge of and connections with the Stanleys and people who would have moved in their circles.

The surprise is that it took so long for a discussion on the authenticity of the Shakespeare epitaphs in Tong to be revived. For several centuries not much notice of the claim was taken by Shakespeare biography scholars (apart from Malone in the late eighteenth century), and particularly not after the great Shakespeare scholar in the first half of the twentieth century, E. K. Chambers, refused to accept these epitaphs as by the Bard because of the death dates of **Sir Thomas** (too early, in 1576) and **Sir Edward** (too late, in 1632). One of the greatest Shakespeare biography scholars towards the end of the twentieth century, Samuel Schoenbaum, was his usual amusing and cynical self, not believing anything that was not stamped and sealed, and dismissed Sir William Dugdale with a few anecdotes, which portrayed him as an unreliable source. I believe that both of them were wrong in their assessment of the reliability of Dugdale.

VIIa. (Sir) William Dugdale, 1656

Neither of them (Chambers & Schoenbaum) reported adequately on the superb reputation of Dugdale in the seventeenth century and for long afterwards. Neither of them knew much (or enough) about the laws of heraldry. Both of them reported negative rather than positive points. We can all laugh today about upstarts who pay large amounts of money for a 'new' coats of arms, but in the sixteenth and seventeenth centuries it was a different matter. Consult anything written about Dugdale at the time, and you will read that he was one of the most esteemed heralds and Kings of Arms (rising to Norroy 1660–77; Garter 1677–86), praised by all and sundry for his conscientiousness and historical accuracy. His word in most cases really cannot be doubted. He did make a few mistakes in other assumptions, but certainly not here. It is certain that he visited the tomb in Tong and made his own transcription of the epitaphs during his Visitation tour of Shropshire in 1663 (he recorded his visit in his diary on 23 September), presumably with insider knowledge.

However, he published *Antiquities of Shropshire* in 1664, which suggests that this book was already well on its way to publication. One must make a distinction between research on 'antiquities' and Visitations, the sole purpose of the latter being to establish any current family's claim to a coat of arms. By 1663, the Stanley family had been long gone from Shropshire and so could not present themselves there for verification of a coat of arms. Any interest shown by Dugdale must therefore have been because of his antiquarian pursuits, supplemented, presumably, by his knowledge of the genealogy of the Stanley family in Lancashire and Cheshire.

Dugdale had already started on his survey of 'antiquities' in the Midlands well before the Civil War and before he was appointed as a herald. As mentioned above, the main scholarly biography is in

In the fourth of King Edward VI. the Earl of Derby was one of the peers party to the articles of peace, made by King Edward with the Scots and French, wherein the emperor was also included.

In the sixth of this king, he made an exchange with his majesty of his house called Derby House, on St. Bennet's Hill, near Doctors' Commons, London, built by Thomas the first Earl of Derby, for certain lands adjoining to his park at Knowsley, in the county of Lancaster, of which he was lieutenant during this king's reign.

After the above exchange, he purchased a piece of land, in Channon Row, near Westminster, and thereon erected a new house, and called it Derby House, which being since sold by William Earl of Derby, elder brother to the late Earl James, is built into a court called Derby Court.

VIIb. Derby House,
the first home of the College of Arms
(Seacome, 1741) No image of the building has survived.

VIIc. The College of Arms today

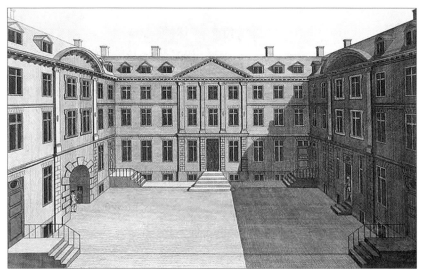

VIId. The College of Arms, 1756

The College of Arms, 1756

There are records of the heralds carrying out certain alterations to Derby Place over the years, but little of its appearance is now known except that it formed three sides of a quadrangle and was entered by a gate with a portcullis on the west side of the site. On the south range, where Queen Victoria Street now is, stood a large hall at the western end.

In 1666 the old Heralds College was swept away by the Great Fire. The College records were saved and taken to the Palace of Westminster where a temporary office was opened. It was probably a shortage of funds for rebuilding that delayed the planning of a new Heralds College until 1670. It was then that Francis Sandford, Rouge Dragon Pursuivant, and Morris Emmett, the King's bricklayer, seem to have proposed the new design, which was then followed. It was in this building that Dugdale worked during his last years.

(College of Arms website)

VIIe. First and Second College of Arms

the *Dictionary of National Biography* (*Old* and *New*), but the following synopsis is adequate for purposes here. I fully realise that many historians find Wikipedia dubious on many details, but whoever wrote this knew what (s)he was writing about.

> In 1638 Dugdale was created a pursuivant of arms extraordinary by the name of Blanch Lyon, and in 1639 he was promoted to the office of Rouge Croix Pursuivant of Arms in Ordinary. He now had a lodging in the College of Arms, and spent much of his time in London examining the records in the Tower and the Cottonian and other collections of manuscripts. In 1641 Sir Christopher Hatton, foreseeing the war and dreading the ruin and spoliation of the Church, commissioned him to make exact drafts of all the monuments in Westminster Abbey and the principal churches in England, including Peterborough Cathedral, Ely Cathedral, Norwich Cathedral, Lincoln Cathedral, Newark, Beverley Minster, Southwell Minster, Kingston-upon-Hull, York Minster, Selby Abbey, Chester Cathedral, Lichfield Cathedral, Tamworth and Warwick Cathedral.
>
> In June 1642 he was summoned to attend the king at York. When war broke out Charles deputed him to summon to surrender the castles of Banbury and Warwick, and other strongholds which were being rapidly filled with ammunition and rebels. He went with Charles to Oxford, remaining there till its surrender in 1646. He witnessed the Battle of Edgehill, where he made afterwards an exact survey of the field, noting how the armies were drawn up, and where and in what direction the various movements took place, and marking the graves of the slain. In November 1642 he was admitted MA of the University, and in 1644 the king created him Chester Herald of Arms in Ordinary.
>
> During his leisure at Oxford he collected material at the Bodleian Library and college libraries for his books. In 1646 Dugdale returned to London and compounded for his estates, which had been sequestrated, by a payment of £268. After a visit to France in 1648 he continued his antiquarian researches in London, collaborating with Roger Dodsworth in his *Monasticon Anglicanum*, which was published successively in single volumes in 1655, 1664 and 1673. At the Restoration Dugdale obtained the office of Norroy King of Arms. In 1677 he was knighted and promoted to the office of Garter Principal King of Arms, which he held until his death. He died "in his chair" at Blythe Hall in 1686.
>
> *(Wikipedia*, accessed 2010)

As we read, he was a very busy man, travelling much before the Civil War, but not (according to the list above) in Shropshire. However, we know that he was travelling around Warwickshire and visited Stratford in 1634, when he produced his sketch of Shakespeare's monument (date from <The Holloway Pages>: Shakespeare's Stratford Monument). He did not, however, publish anything around this time. Between 1642 and 1651 he spent most of his time researching in documents in Oxford and London and did not publish, understandably, during the Civil War.

His collaboration with Dodsworth during this period is particularly interesting in the context of 'Shakespeare in Lancashire', because Roger Dodsworth (1585–1654) was married to a Hesketh of Rufford in Lancashire, one family that preserved the oral tradition until the twentieth century that Shakespeare had spent a short time with them during his youth. This Dodsworth-Hesketh marriage is recorded in many Lancashire sources, including the genealogical tree in the well-researched official *Guidebook of Rufford Old Hall*, National Trust (1997): Holcroft Hesketh (d.1639), daughter of Robert Hesketh (1560-1620) and Mary (d. 1586), daughter and heiress of Sir George Stanley of Cross Hall, Lathom (m.1567) married (2) Roger Dodsworth (1585–1654), antiquary.

With Dugdale from an old Lancashire family from the Preston area (to be precise, Great Mitton, an hour or two by horse from Hoghton Tower), and Dodsworth married into a family in Rufford, not too far away, one might presume that they were both acquainted with details of Shakespeare's traditional stay in Lancashire, from people still living who were only one generation away from Shakespeare's stay. However, their main historical concern was to record as many antiquities as possible, particularly about the monasteries that had been affected by the Dissolution, many of which had already fallen into ruin, and churches that had been attacked and despoiled during the recent Civil War.

During the five years before the Restoration, Dugdale started publishing again: the first volume of *Monasticon Anglicanum* (1655), co-authored with Roger Dodsworth and later *Antiquities of Warwickshire* (1656) in just his own name. These were instant successes, which must have encouraged him to publish more, although most did not appear until after the Restoration. During the following decade Dugdale published *Antiquities of Shropshire* (1664) and the second volume of *Monasticon Anglicanum* (1665), just in his own name, even though it still drew on Dodsworth's research. In the meantime Dugdale had been appointed Norroy King of Arms, which required him to go on Visitation tours throughout the Northern counties, which included (for the relevance of this book) Shropshire, Cheshire and Lancashire. It was in a copy of his notebook/diary (still in the College of Arms, but not published in part until 1827) that details of the Tong tomb appeared.

> [...] visitation of the church on 23 September, 1663, probably in the hand of the antiquary William Dugdale or of a closely supervised amanuensis. (The original visitation notebook, which might provide clues to the origins of the attribution, has not been located.) The margin reads "Shakespeare", the text "These following verses were made by William Shakespeare the late famous tragedian". Another unascribed version is found in the same MS, p.41, along with an illustration of the tomb in its original state, surrounded by obelisks. The poem is also found ascribed in Folger MS Pw.V.37, p.12 and (unattributed and with many variants) in Bodleian MS Rawl.Poet, 117, fo.269v.
>
> (Quoted from C. Burrow, *Complete sonnets and poems, The Oxford Shakespeare*, (Oxford, 2002), p. 723, quoted by Watney, *op.cit.*, in note 4, p. 116.)

Dugdale omitted the publication of the sketch of the Stanley tomb at Tong by Francis Sandford in *Antiquities of Shropshire* (1664). One explanation, as suggested above, might be that this book was already well on the way to publication when he made a note of the MI and epitaphs, subsequently commissioned Sandford to produce a sketch, but it arrived too late for inclusion. We know that Dugdale made two Visitations of Lancashire in 1664 and 1665, which must have made this an extremely busy period for him. We know from his Diaries that on his return in 1664 he spent two days with the Earl of Derby at knowsley. This would have been another occasion to have received confirmation of the authorship of the verse epitaphs in Tong. In short, one must consider Sir William Dugdale as a historical pioneer, who was genuinely trying to preserve some of the history of England before, during and after the Civil War, when more than a few matters went awry.

We can forgive Dugdale for any mistakes he might have made, although many have never forgiven him for producing a sketch of the Shakespeare tomb that differs in many details from the monument in Stratford today. Even recently, in the early summer of 2006, a veritable 'war of words' was conducted on the letters page of the *Times Literary Supplement*. This revolved mainly around whether he had a woolsack or a cushion on his knee, but also the shape of his moustache, the gauntness of his face and other details. Another recent proposal is that it might have been a representation not of William but of his father John, who was a wool-dealer, among other activities. Dugdale's (and Sandford's) drawing skills might leave something to be desired, but not his desire to record history as accurately as possible. In the case of the Shakespeare monument, Dugdale certainly had no doubt that it contained an image of William and not his father John, just as he was certain that Shakespeare had composed the epitaphs on the Stanley tomb in Tong church. Anyone wishing to compare all details of the Shakespeare monument for themselves will find images of these and all subsequent relevant versions on <www.hollowaypages.com/Shakespearemonument>.

No Shakespeare scholar has ever forgiven Dugdale mainly, however, for not having written a biography of Shakespeare, however brief, nor recorded his genealogical pedigree, nor recorded his relationship to the Warwickshire Ardens. This is indeed regrettable. Dugdale must have known very well that Mary 'Arden' was not of the Warwickshire Ardens, but Mary Arderne descended from the Cheshire Ardernes of Arderne. A portion of the historical spadework by the author, proving this, is on a website, an offshoot of the Duxbury Family website (the proof coming via Robert Glover, *Ordinary of Arms*, another highly esteemed herald and antiquarian of the late sixteenth century). The full account will be presented in a forthcoming book *Shakespeare's Lancashire Links*.

Dugdale, as a herald, of necessity steeped in the laws of heraldry, would have known this instantly from the Cheshire Arderne coat of arms impaled into John Shakespeare's arms in 1599. The draft document was in the College of Arms at the time, as it still is today. He must also have known that the Shakespeares of Warwickshire were hardly ancient landed gentry; he must also have known whether or not William's branch had originated in the Shakeshaftes of Lancashire from the Preston area. Dugdale was in the best possible position to know, because his father was from Lancashire, not too far from Preston (the origin of the name is Dugdale in Great Mitton, Reaney & Wilson, *English Surnames*, 3rd ed. Oxford U.P., 1995) and moved to Oxford University with a group of students, subsequently settling in Warwickshire, where (Sir) William was born in 1605. There was also a Dugdale in the list of servants at Hoghton Tower in the 1581 Will of Alexander Hoghton, which also named William Shakeshafte.

As already mentioned several times previously, interest in the epitaphs at Tong was revived in 1985 by Honigmann's, *Shakespeare: the 'lost years'*. This was in the context of his exploration of the 'lost years' including the fairly reliable seventeenth-century report by Aubrey, from an actor whose father had acted with Shakespeare. He therefore reported that 'in his younger days he had been a schoolmaster in the country'. This can be combined with the old and persistent traditions in Lancashire, passed down from father to son over generations in the Hoghton and Hesketh families, that young Shakespeare had spent a couple of years at Hoghton Tower and a short time at Rufford Old Hall. There was also the tradition of the linking of his name, at least via performance of his early plays, with Strange's Players, Lord Strange being the title of the eldest son and heir of the Earls of Derby, from Lancashire.

These led Honigmann to view the potential authenticity of the epitaphs at Tong in a new light and, as mentioned frequently above, he devoted Chapter VII to them, 'The Shakespeare epitaphs and the Stanleys'. Here he established one of those on the tomb, **Sir Edward Stanley Jr**, as yet another of many connections between Shakespeare and the Earls of Derby, and put E. K. Chambers's quibbles about dates to rest by pointing out it was certainly not unknown at the time to commission one's tomb during one's own lifetime. [The following quote includes a repeat from a previous chapter, included here to keep it together with the family tree. HM]

> The Stanley tomb at Tong, in Shropshire, carries the inscription "Thomas Stanley, Knight, second son of Edward Earl of Derby...had issue two sons, Henry and Edward. Henry died an

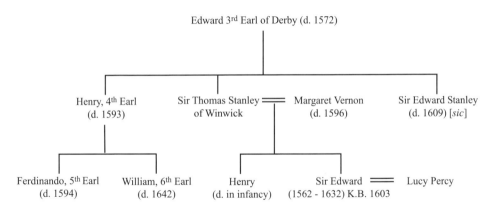

infant and Edward survived, to whom those lordships descended", and goes on to name Edward's wife and one son and seven daughters. The relevant part of the Stanley pedigree is as follows: [see bottom of previous page, HM]

I agree with Chambers that the verse epitaphs were intended for the younger Sir Edward and for his father, but not entirely with his reservation that, since this Sir Edward died in 1632, his figure, if it is his, and the verses on him must have been added to the tomb after that date, and incidentally after Shakespeare's death. The implication seems to be that Shakespeare, being dead, could not have been involved; and it is spelt out in the *Shakespeare Encyclopaedia*: if Sir Edward is Sir Thomas's son "there can be no question that Shakespeare did not write the epitaphs, since Sir Edward died in 1632, 16 years after Shakespeare". At this time, however, tombs with all their accessories were not infrequently ordered by the living, for themselves — as in the case of Edmund Tilney, the Master of the Revels, who asked in his will (1 July 1610) 'that there be a monument erected and set upon the place where I with the consent of the parson and churchwarden there have appointed... if myself in my life-time do not finish the same". So, too, Bess of Hardwick arranged for her own burial "in the place appointed", beneath her tomb, which was "finished and wants nothing but setting up". As John Weever explained, "It was usual in ancient times, and so it is in these our days, for persons of especial rank and quality to make their own tombs and monuments in their life-time; partly for that they might have a certain house to put their head in...and partly to please themselves in the beholding of their dead countenance in marble". Since Shakespeare is said to have jokingly given John Combe his epitaph, and to have composed one for himself, there is no reason to believe that he could not have written, before 1616, the epitaph for Sir Edward Stanley.

(Honigmann, *Shakespeare: the 'lost years'*, pp. 79-80.)

This was Honigmann's conclusion about the authenticity of authorship in 1985, and must be the conclusion today. Let us go one logical step further and deduce the following sequence of events. All evidence points to 1601–03 as the date of the commissioning of the complete tomb by **Sir Edward Jr** for his parents and himself, including his composition of the MI. When Shakespeare wrote the epitaphs he must have either seen the completed tomb or at least had details of the proposed form, including the pyramids. If the latter, this would date the composition of the epitaphs to any time 1601–03; if he had already seen the tomb, the composition of the epitaphs could probably be dated at the end rather than the beginning of this period. There happened, however, to be two suitable blank lengths of marble at the head and the foot, which allowed their inclusion there. Either these just happened to be available, or they were already planned in.

If the composition of the epitaphs was around 1603, then Shakespeare dashed them off after the success of *Hamlet*, and before *Othello*. In turn, one might venture to deduce that Shakespeare, at the height of his success, would not have taken the time to write epitaphs for a mere or recent acquaintance, which in turn implies that they had known each other rather well for some time.

It was suggested in a previous chapter that they might have met in 1599 in London, when **Edward Jr**'s cousin William Stanley, 6th Earl of Derby, was also writing plays there. One occasion on which they would have had every opportunity to meet was at the coronation of James I on 25 July 1603; and here we have documented facts. **Sir Edward Jr** was made a Knight of the Bath at the coronation; and Shakespeare's acting company was in the coronation procession (in every Shakespeare biography). These did not take place on the same day, for reasons explained below:

None of the troupes was playing when James entered the metropolis, for once again the plague gripped London. Such was the virulence of the epidemic that, when James was crowned in July 1603, the public was barred from the ceremony, and the royal procession through London cancelled. The triumphal arches erected for the occasion were dismantled, but they rose again when the processional entry belatedly took place on 15 March 1604. For that occasion each of the King's men named in the Patent [*for the formation of the group of players with royal patronage*] was entitled to receive, as a Groom of the Chamber and hence a member of the royal household, four and a half yards of scarlet-red cloth for his livery. This issue of cloth Sir George Home, Master of the Great Wardrobe, recorded in his account. Shakespeare's name, second in the Patent, this time heads the list. On such occasions the Crown lavishly distributed red cloth. Not all the recipients, however, joined in the solemn procession which, commencing at the Tower, wended its way — to the accompaniment of music, song, and orations — past symbolic pageants and through triumphal arches to Whitehall. Mainly the marchers consisted of noblemen and courtiers and government functionaries arranged in appropriate order by the heralds. No players receive mention in the elaborate accounts, some written by theatre men, of the Magnificent Entertainment of King James.

(Schoenbaum, *Compact Documentary Life*, 1987, pp. 251-2.)

It is difficult to believe that Shakespeare, as a member of the King's Men and the royal household, was at this time considered a mere 'member of the public', and so barred from the ceremony, but even if he was, one might assume that all the new knights would have wished to participate in the procession. Shakespeare might, of course, have declined to receive his 'four and a half yards of cloth' and participate in the procession, but this suspicion might seem rather perverse, given that he was in first place on the list of the King's Men. One might reasonably suppose that both he and **Sir Edward Jr** attended the coronation and that both were in the procession.

It is interesting to note that during this outbreak of plague there was a lull in theatre performances, and presumably a concomitant lack of pressure on playwrights to produce new plays. Although purely speculative, it is tempting to daydream and imagine that Shakespeare also took a short break and found time to dash off an epitaph or two for a newly created knight whose cousin had been his patron in the early years of his career. Daydream over. But the dates do match and fit together like the fingers of the proverbial glove.

Given that we are in 1603–04, it should perhaps be repeated that 1603 was when **Sir Edward Jr** sold several of his properties, including Tong Castle, and began a new life, as a knight, in Eynsham, Oxfordshire. So far there has been no documented hint as to his main motivation for this; nor will any hint appear in future chapters. Only the emergence of documentation undiscovered so far might resolve this particular mystery.

Conclusions drawn from details in this chapter with a large degree of certainty:

1) William Shakespeare did indeed write the epitaphs at Tong.
2) All dates point towards 1601–03, the same dates as for the commissioning of the tombs in Tong and Walthamstow and the composition of the MI.
3) William Shakespeare and (Sir) **Edward Stanley Jr** were not mere acquaintances, but knew each other rather better; they had almost certainly met via other close members of (Sir) **Edward**'s family.
4) One obvious opportunity for them to have met in London was 1599-1600, when William Stanley, (Sir) **Edward**'s cousin, was writing plays and (Sir) **Edward Jr** received a dedication from John Weever, an aspiring writer from Lancashire, who was making his name in Shakespeare circles.
5) Another obvious opportunity was during the events occasioned by the coronation of James I.
6) Sir Edward Jr might have planned the spaces on the tomb specifically to incorporate the MI and the epitaphs, or just fitted them in where space happened to be available.
7) It may or may not be a complete coincidence that, having completed most plans for the tomb in Tong, he decided to sell Tong Castle. If not a coincidence, then we are still in the dark about the circumstances that led him to this decision.
8) Sir William Dugdale, with all his Lancashire connections, most likely knew about Shakespeare's ancestry, and also his many connections with the Stanleys.
9) Sir William was certainly convinced that William Shakespeare had written the verse epitaphs at Tong.

~~~~~~~~~~~~~~~~~~

Chapter VIII
Weever, Middleton & Co., and dedications to Stanleys

VIII-1. John Weever's transcriptions, dedications and major work
VIII-2. Weever's Lancashire dedicatees and poets in his *Epigrammes*, 1599
VIII-3. Christopher Middleton's dedication
VIII-4. Other dedications to Stanleys

VIII-1. John Weever's transcriptions, dedications and major work

John Weever produced the earliest surviving transcription of the verse epitaphs in Tong in the early seventeenth century. Weever (1575/6–1632) was from the Preston area, Lancashire, poet, recent student at Cambridge and later antiquarian, author of the highly acclaimed *Ancient Funeral Monuments within the United Monarchy of Great Britain* (1631). Unfortunately he did not ascribe any authorship to the epitaphs; they just remained in his MS notes (Honigmann, *Weever*, pp.69–70). In 1987 Honigmann published *John Weever: A biography of a literary associate of Shakespeare and Jonson, together with a photographic facsimile of Weever's Epigrammes (1599)*. It is from this book that all details given below about Weever are taken.

Weever was very likely (one of) the first to transcribe the inscription on the Shakespeare monument at Stratford. Honigmann (p. 70) estimates Weever's recording as c.1626. Weever had also, immediately after his arrival in London, published a volume of direct relevance to 'Shakespeare's Lancashire Links' and the family of **Edward Stanley Jr**. In 1599 appeared *Epigrammes*, shortly after graduation from Cambridge University, which included epigrams to many gentry and aristocracy in Derby circles, plus to several literary figures in Shakespeare circles. One was to Shakespeare himself and another (as an obituary) to Ferdinando, 5th Earl of Derby, **Edward Jr**'s first cousin, who had died an agonising death (of suspected poisoning or witchcraft) in 1594:

> Week iv, *Epig. 22   Ad Gulielmum Shakespear*
>
> Honie-tong'd *Shakespeare* when I saw thine issue
> I swore *Apollo* got them and none other,
> Their rosie-tainted features cloth'd in tissue,
> Some heaven born goddess said to be their mother:
> Rose-ckeckt *Adonis* with his amber tresses,
> Faire sire-hot Venus charming him to love her,
> Chaste *Lucretia* virgine-like her dresses,
> Prowd lust-stung *Tarquine* seeking still to prove her:
> *Romea Richard*, more whose names I know not,
> Their sugred tongues, and power attractive beuty
> Say they are Saints although that Sts they shew not
> For thousands vowes to them subiective dutie:
> They burn in love thy childrê Shakespear het thê,
> Go, wo thy Muse more Nymphish brood beget them.
>
> Week vi, *Epig. 9   In tumulum Ferdinand. Darbie.*
>
> Be not so bould to ope this dead mans dore,
> Unlesse thou come from the'aerie house of woes,
> Ne dare thou once upon this Marble pore,
> Unlesse thou poure thy fight out on these roes,
> If to faire knighthoold thou bearst any zeale,
> Unrest, care, greife, sad discontent, and woe,

VIIIa. John Weever, 1631

On these five bells ring thou a dolefull peale,
Volies of sighes fast after them let goe:
Rest, in unrest, teares-spitting forge be burning,
Until some write *The Muses nine dayes mourning*.

However one judges the quality of these verses, the contents prove that Weever had read *Venus and Adonis* (1593) and *The Rape of Lucrece* (1594); and seen *Romeo and Juliet, Richard II* and/or *Richard III* and apparently several more plays whose names he could not remember. This does not, of course, prove that he had met Shakespeare, but one must presume that as an aspiring poet, newly arrived in London, he hoped to meet him. His inclusion of an obituary to Ferdinando, in the middle of so many epigrams to people still living, also indicates something more than just a passing knowledge of his reputation. He was certainly not seeking his patronage, because he was dead. He might, however, have been hoping for patronage from one of his family. In this case, though, why not include epigrams to any living Derbys? The most obvious one would have been Ferdinando's brother William, 6th Earl of Derby, currently writing plays in London. But perhaps he had just never met him? Weever had written his epigrams while at Cambridge University 1594–98. William Stanley had been abroad on his travels for several years until his return in 1593, when he was made Governor of the Isle of Man. With such a short or no overlap of both at the same time in Lancashire, it is possible that they never met.

Newly arrived in London, the first Stanley with whom Weever seems to have made contact was **Edward Stanley Jr**. One suspects this, at least, because the following year, 1600, Weever dedicated his next published poetical venture *Faunus and Melliflora* 'To the Right Valorous and excellent accomplished Gentleman, **Master Edward Stanley of Winwick**, Esquire....' He was still 'Master' because '**Stanley** was knighted in 1603'. (Honigmann, *Weever*, p. 69.) This is the only reference we have to **Edward Jr** as 'right valorous' and 'excellent accomplished', and these may well have been merely flattering formalities in a dedication, but it does seem that Weever might have actually known him and something about him. Weever referred to **Edward** as 'of Winwick', omitting any reference to Tong, where we know (or think we know) he was living at the time. One implication of this is that Weever perhaps had knowledge of his father as **Sir Thomas** of Winwick and perhaps knew that he had continued to keep on his father's rented property. We know that he knew that **Master Edward Esq**. had buried his infant son there. Perhaps they had met in the company of one or more of the Lancastrian dedicatees in his *Epigrammes*? As a fellow Lancastrian, Winwick would have meant more to Weever than anywhere else where **Edward** might have lived.

In 1600, as far as we know, **Edward** had not yet commissioned the tomb for his parents, nor his own effigy. His wife and all seven daughters were also still alive. As mentioned above, Honigmann estimated Weever's transcription as in c.1626. The implication is that Weever had stayed in touch with **Edward** until then since his dedication to him in 1600, followed his story, knew that the tomb was in Tong, although Edward himself was no longer living there, and he had perhaps heard about the Epitaphs from **Edward**'s own mouth (or a mutual acquaintance?). Given that he was busy collecting details of 'ancient' tombs, and that there are several in St Bartholomew's, it is possible that the Stanley tomb and inscriptions were just included by his informant who had visited the church. Perhaps the informant did not know that Shakespeare had written the epitaphs? Or perhaps the informant and/or Weever did know but did not bother to write it down. In any case it was inappropriate to include these inscriptions in a book on *Ancient Funeral Monuments*. A tomb erected only a couple of decades earlier by a man who was still living was hardly 'ancient'.

~~~~~~~~~~~~~~

VIII-2. Weever's Lancashire dedicatees and poets in his *Epigrammes*, 1599

A facsimile of the complete book is included in Honigmann, *Weever*, pp. 92ff., with this facsimile meanwhile online, although not the whole book. In this list below are included only the names of Lancashire (and some Cheshire) gentry and poets to whom he dedicated an epigram. They are divided into seven 'weeks', each 'week' containing a different number of epigrams. The primary/overall dedication is:

> ### To the right Worshipfull and
> worthie honoured Gentleman Sir Ri-
> chard Houghton of Houghton Tower,
> Knight : Justice of Peace, and Quorum: High
> *Sheriffe of Lancshire, &c. Adorned with all
> giftes, that valour may give, or
> vertue gaine.*

EPIGRAMMES
in the oldeſt cut, and
neweſt faſhion.

*A
twiſe ſeuen howres (in ſo many
weekes)ſtudie*

No longer (like the faſhion) not vn-
like to continue.

The firſt ſeuen.

Iohn Weeuer.

Sis voluiſſe, Sat valuiſſe.

At London
Printed by *V.S.* for *Thomas Baſtord*, and are to be
ſald at his ſhop at the great north doore
of *Paules* 1599

**VIIIb. Weever's *Epigrammes*,
1599, title page**

The numbers omitted below are mainly those to Weever's fellow Cambridge undergraduates or tutors; also to clerics; also those 'to the reader' or concerning abstract qualities, e.g. 'De Ingenio, Fortuna, Fama'. Honigmann gives tentative identifications of most names and autobiographical details of many (pp. 120–126). Details below about the Lancashire gentry are limited largely to their seat, usually a hall of the same name, and how well known they were to be included in the *Dictionary of National Biography* in c.1900 (given by Honigmann and below as *DNB*). All places are in Lancashire, unless specified otherwise. ***DHB*** means they appear in Chapter XVII. Sir Edward Sr and Jr in the *Derby*

Of the Author.

He Greeke Comœdian fitly doth compare
Poets to Swannes, for both delitious,
Both in requeſt, both white, both pretious are,
Both sing alike, and both melodious:
I but the swanne remaineth dumbe so long,
(As though her Muſike were too good to spend)
That so at last her soule-enchanting song,
Is but a funerall dirge to her end.
Weever, herein aboue the Swanne I praise,
Which freely spends his sweete melodious dittie,
Now in the budding of his youthful daies,
Delightsome, pleasant, full of Art, and wittie,
  Yet heavens forbid he should be neare his death,
  Though like the dying Swanne he sweetly breath.

M. D.

VIIIc. Sonnet in praise of Weever
by Michael Drayton from *Epigrammes*, 1599
In *Faunus and Melliflora*, 1600

TO THE RIGHT
Valorous and excellent accompliſht
*Gentleman , Maiſter Edward Stan-
ley* of Winwicke Eſquire , all fortunes, ſu-
table to the auncient woorth of the
Stanleyes.

Owſoeuer (moſt bounteous Sir) this
ſubiect which I preſent, may be either
diſagreeing to your diſpoſition, or being but a Shepheards lowly paſtorall,
farre vnworthie ſo worthie a Patron: yet the wil-
lingneſſe of my ſoule, to ſhew ſome ſigne of good
will to my countrymen, enforceth mee to conſe-
crate my cheefeſt ſtudies to the ſetting forth
of their admired vertues : which conſidered, I
doubt not but your Worſhip with curteſie, will
accept my ruſticke inciuilitie, and with fauoura-
ble Patronage, pardon my wood-borne imper-
fections.

Yours in all

Iohn Weeuer.

**VIIId. Weever, *Faunus and Melliflora*,
1600, dedication**

Week	No.	Name	Identification
1(23)	Gen.	To the readers	
	13	In Rogerum Manners Rutlandiæ Comitem.	Roger, 5th Earl of Rutland, *DNB*
	23	Ad Michaelem Drayton Poet	Poet
2 (25)	Gen.	Robert Dalton of Pilling, Esquier.	of Thurnham Hall near Lancaster
	1	Ad Robertum Dalton Armig.	Son of above
	23	Ad Robertum Dalton Armig.	
3 (23)	Gen.	Sir Richard Mollineux, knight, . . .	of Sefton, ***DHB***
	3	Ad D. Mounteagle	William Parker, 4th Lord Mounteagle of Hornby, *DNB*, ***DHB***
4 (23)	Gen.	Sir Edward Warren, knight . . .	of Poynton, Cheshire & Woodplumpton near Preston, ***DHB***
	1	Ad avunculum suum Henricum Butler Armig.	of Rawcliffe, Weever's uncle
	4	Ad Ro: Allott, & Chr. Middleton	Writer, poet; *DNB*
	20	Ad Dudleum North	*DNB*
	22	Ad Gulielmum Shakespear	Poet
	23	In Ed: Allen	Actor, mother a Towneley, Burnley
5 (24)	Gen.	Sir Thomas Gerrard, knight, Marshall & c . . .	of Ince near Wigan and Gerards Bromley, Staffs
	1	Ad Petrum Leigh de Vnderline Militem . . .	of Lyme, Cheshire & Winwick
	9	In Cumberlandiæ Comitem	George, 3rd Earl of Cumberland, Earl Henry's brother-in-law
	16	Ad Thomas Holcroft de Vaile Roiall. Armig.	of Vale Royal, Cheshire, ***DHB***
	23	Ad Johannem Egerton	(Later) 1st Earl of Bridgewater, son of Thomas Egerton, Master of the Rolls, later Lord Chancellor Ellesmere, *DNB*
6 (25)	Gen.	Sir Cuthbert Halsey, knight . . .	Earl Henry's son-in-law, ***DHB***
	1	Ad Richardum Houghton Militem	Main dedicatee of whole book, ***DHB***
	3	In tumulum Thomæ Houghton Armig.	Father of Sir Richard & William. d. 1589
	4	In Gulielmum Houghton.	Brother of Sir Richard, ***DHB***
	9	In tumulum Ferdinand. Darbie.	d. 1594, *DNB*, ***DHB***
	10	Ad Samuelem Daniel.	Poet
	11	Ad Io: Marston, & Ben Johnson.	Poets
	13	Ad Gulielmum Warner.	*DNB*
	22	In Gulielmum Rich: Cantabr:procu.	Word play on 'rich'
	23	In obitum Ed. Spencer Poeta prestantiss.	Poet, died 1599
	25	In Ed. Wrightington.	of Wrightington, ***DHB***
7 (17)	Gen.	Sir Peter Leigh of Vnderline, knight . . .	See 5.1
	1	Ad Thomem Gerard Militem	See 5. Gen.
	11	Ad Musam suam, de obitu fortissimi insignifq3 iuuenis Thome Egerton militis.	Brother of John, see 5.23; killed young 1599 in Ireland
	16	Ad Richardum Houghton Militem.	Overall dedicatee; also 6.1, ***DHB***

Household Books as visitors to the Earl of Derby in 1587-90 when **Sir Edward Sr** and **Jr** were also visitors, where more biographical details are given. Poets, writers and actors are all covered on numerous websites. The numbers in brackets are the number of epigrams in each 'week'.

~~~~~~~~~

VIII–3. Christopher Middleton's dedication

To the right worſhipfull Maſter Edward Stanley Eſquire.

The only other dedication known to have been received by **Edward Jr** was from Christopher Middleton, *The famous historie of Chinon of England* (prose, 1597), the dedication above appearing on page 3. Middleton was a student with Weever at Cambridge in the 1590s and received a joint epigram from him in 1599, 'Ad Ro. Allott, & Chr. Middleton, (iv.4)' (Honigmann, *Weever*, p.22, 123). Middleton was another aspiring writer and a friend of Michael Drayton's, the latter a friend of Shakespeare's, also from Warwickshire, and later with him and Ben Jonson in a drinking bout, by legend, shortly before Shakespeare died.

Chinon was printed by John Danter, proudly describing it as 'the first Booke of this kind I ever had power to dedicate'. This was in the same year that the abbreviated version of Shakespeare's *Romeo and Juliet*, in which Henry Chettle may well have had a hand, was printed by Danter. (*Shakespeare's Poems*, p. 445).

> **The Famous Historie of Chinon of England,**
> with his Strange Adventures for the love of
> **Celestina, daughter to Lewis, King of France;**
> with the worthy Atchievement of
> **Sir Lancelot du Lake, and Sir Tristram du Lions for faire Laura, daughter to Cadar, Earle of Cornewall, being all Knights of King Arthur's Round Table.**
> **By Chr. Middleton.**
> **At London,**
> printed by John Danter for Cuthbert Burbie, 1597

VIIIe. Full title of Middleton's *Chinon*, 1597
Dedicated to Master Edward Stanley Esquire

The juxtaposition of these names and dates seems to mean something, although it is not at all completely certain what. Middleton and Weever were students together at Cambridge (Weever 1594-98 at Queens'; Middleton a Sizar at St John's 1587, Bachelor c.1600); Middleton dedicated a work to **Edward Stanley** in 1597; some time around then or a little later Weever wrote an epigram to Middleton (jointly with Allott); Weever went to London in 1598 and published his *Epigrammes* in rather a hurry in 1599. As seen above Sir Richard Hoghton of Hoghton, Lancashire, was the main dedicatee and he included many other eminent gentry in Lancashire.

Then in 1600 Weever dedicated his next work to **Edward Stanley**. Another fact we know is that in 1599 William Stanley, 6th Earl of Derby, was writing plays in London (Greenstreet, 1891, reported the discovery of a report by George Fenners, a 'Jesuit spy', that in 1599 William was 'penning plays for the commoun players'). If Weever knew **Edward Stanley Jr** and knew so much about Ferdinando, it is rather difficult to believe that he did not also know about the play-writing activities and presence in London of William, **Edward Jr**'s first cousin. Middleton knew **Edward Stanley Jr**, Weever and Drayton, the last one becoming a great friend of Shakespeare's. All of them were in London in 1599 and/or 1600. Some in this little group must have introduced some to others. This is a possibility for at least one meeting between **Edward** and Shakespeare, and is rather close to the date of the commissioning of the tomb, with the epitaphs being written some time later, perhaps at the coronation of James I in 1603, when **Edward** was knighted and Shakespeare was in the procession.

Weever's descriptive text seems to confirm that the tomb was completed and in place well before **Sir Edward Jr**'s death in 1632, the same year as Weever died. It is surprising if **Sir Edward**'s effigy was already on the tomb while he was still alive, although it could be that it was completed, ready for inclusion, but not placed there until later. It will be noted that **Sir Edward Jr** being named 'Knight of the Bath' dates this to post-1603, the year he was knighted. It will also be noted that no details of the marriages of two of his daughters are given, whose later husbands were eminent enough to warrant another boast about family connections: Sir Kenelm Digby (married Venetia) and Sir John Fortescue (married Frances). This seems to date Weever's text perhaps to pre-1625 (marriage, although in secret, of Sir Kenelm and Venetia), a little earlier than the date c.1626 suggested by Honigmann, but close enough. We will remember that a previous conclusion was that all preparations were probably in place by 1603. That the monument was already completed before **Sir Edward Jr**'s death is proved by Weever's notes, and in any case certain because Weever died the same year.

~~~~~~~~~~~~~~~

VIII-4. Other dedications to Stanleys

Several more dedications to Stanleys are covered in *The Earls of Derby and the Verse Writers and Poets of the Sixteenth and Seventeenth Century* by Thomas Heywood, Chetham Society Old Series, 1853 (meanwhile online). None are of direct relevance to **Sir Thomas** and **Sir Edward**, but together provide a rich picture of the esteem in which the Stanleys were held by various circles.

~~~~~~~~~~~~~~~

VIIIf. Interior of Tong Church, 1841
From an etching by S.F. Every. It would have looked similar to this
when (Sir) Edward attended between 1570 and 1603.

Chapter IX
Katherine Esdaile's contribution (1929); also a time-line of recordings of the MI & epitaphs

IX-1. Introduction
IX-2. SHAKESPEARE'S VERSES IN TONG CHURCH, by Katherine Esdaile
IX-3. Time-line of recordings of the MI, epitaphs and sketches of the tomb until the mid-twentieth century

IX-1. Introduction

Dr Jeffery and I consider the following article so vital in sorting out the story of the Stanley tomb at Tong that most of it is reproduced below. We both consider that the main problems have now been solved with 99.99% certainty. We fully expect that others will continue to doubt on the basis of the remaining 0.01% uncertainty.

In chronological order in the twentieth century after Auden came next Mrs Katherine Esdaile, who was researching and writing in the 1920s and 1930s. She sorted out much of the story of the Tong tomb, which in theory ought to make this book redundant. She did, however, make a few mistakes: for one, she confused St Mary's Walthamstow with Waltham Abbey and thought that the Stanley tomb there had disappeared. It hasn't; it is still there, in St Mary's. She did, however, answer most of the questions raised in previous chapters about when the epitaphs with Dugdale's attribution first appeared with modern spelling, and the journey of them in the eighteenth century.

Her misfortune was that E. K. Chambers was writing with great erudition about Shakespeare's biography around the same time and he had serious doubts about the authenticity of the epitaphs. Shakespeare academia followed Chambers's judgment rather than Mrs Esdaile's. My tribute to Mrs Esdaile comes from retyping most of one of her articles and devoting adequate space to it. A Google search revealed that she was born on 14 December 1876 and baptised Katherine Mary Arundell, an interesting name in view of all the Arundells and Earls of Arundel that appear in the Stanley story. [*Any comments by myself within the article are in square brackets and italics*. HM]

IX–2. SHAKESPEARE'S VERSES IN TONG CHURCH
(Based on an article in *The Times* of 22 April 1929).
BY MRS ESDAILE

I. THE MONUMENT

In the year 1827 the publication of Dugdale's Diary added a valuable fact, that Shakespeare's monument was the work of Gerard Johnson, to our Shakespearean knowledge. It is Dugdale again who, in a serious official work, stated that the Stanley epitaph at Tong is Shakespeare's. Subsequent research into the history and the art of the Johnson Family has proved that Dugdale was right in the one case; much light has recently been thrown upon the close relationship existing between the College of Arms and the makers of monuments during the 17th century, and it is now possible to state that Dugdale, Chester Herald in 1644, Garter King of Arms in 1677, was most certainly right in the other.

In the year 1757 the Stanley monument was described by Horace Walpole's friend the antiquary Cole as "a monstrous large canopy tomb jostling the altar and before it". And in 1763 a writer in the Gentleman's Magazine more specifically notes that it stood on the north side of the choir, that one of the pyramids at the head was thrown down, "and the little figures at the top all broke". It was not until Malone was collecting the material for the great third Variorum Edition of Shakespeare that he received from his friend Joseph Harker, Garter Principal King at Arms, a transcript of the epitaph in modernized spelling, with the information that it was "preserved in a collection of epitaphs at the end of the Visitation of Shropshire, taken by Sir William Dugdale in 1664". Malone saw at once that the fact proved the authenticity of the epitaph, and perceived that "the last line, though the worst, bears very strong marks of the hand of Shakespeare." Others, as we shall see, were not so wise.

As Malone only knew the Visitation of Shropshire at second hand, and no one had apparently verified the statement from the original, it seemed worth while to examine the MS. itself, which proved to contain two transcripts of the prose and verse epitaphs, and an admirable drawing of the monument in its original condition. We quote the prose epitaph and description first, as given by Sandford on f.40, then Dugdale's on f.20:

"This epitaph is upon a very faire Tombe in the middle of the Chancell."

[There follows the text of the MI, not repeated here as already given so often. HM]

Sandford omits the ages of the daughters, 18,16,15, 13; quotes the balls, scale pattern bands on the sarcophagus and the armour, and washes of colour for the black and red marble of pyramids and columns, and adds:

[Here follows the verse epitaph beginning 'Not Monumentall Stone'. HM]

a little Lower on the verge
Beati mortui qui in Domino moriantur.

[Blessed are those who may die in the Lord. Mrs Esdaile follows this with the second verse beginning 'Aske who lies here'. HM]

(Esdaile, pp. 251-2)

Mrs Esdaile then describes the Sandford sketch. She continues:

Dugdale was a Warwickshire man, [*his father was from Great Mitton, Lancashire, near Whalley and Clitheroe, home, as far as one can deduce from meagre records, of all ancestors since the first one took the name Dugdale from the valley with this name. HM*] so much interested in Shakespeare that his pages on the subject in his Warwickshire are a locus classicus, and he took the trouble to note in his Diary the authorship of his monument and that of John à Combe, for whom Shakespeare wrote a sportive doggerel epitaph of which more presently. Moreover, it was an important part of a Herald's duties to check the designs, heraldry and inscriptions of all monuments. That the duty of sending in designs to be so checked was widely evaded is proved by a Proclamation of the Earl Marshal in November, 1618, that in consequence of the "sinister" activities of pretenders to the science of heraldry, all Carvers, Masons and Tomb-Makers were commanded henceforth to send in copies of all their monumental designs to the College of Arms, there to have the arms and epitaphs checked by the Heralds.

Dugdale therefore as a Herald would be officially cognizant of the authorship of the Stanley epitaph; that he took his duties seriously is proved by his note on the MS title-page prefixed to the series of drawings of Shropshire antiquities by Francis Sandford, subsequently himself a Herald, attached to the Visitation itself:

Haec etiam sequentia propria manu dicti Francisci Sandfordi exararata, delineata, et depicta, ego Willelmus Dugdale itidem addenda curavi. [*This may be paraphrased as: 'What follows I, William Dugdale, caused to be added with the addition of the sketch and transcriptions by the said Francis Sandford'. HM*]. Among them is the drawing here reproduced, which shows us the Stanley monument as the 17th century knew it [*illustration Vc*].

Now that we have established that Dugdale, Warwickshire interest apart, was in a position to be certain of the author of an epitaph, we may return to the history of the monument itself.

As we have seen, Cole and the *Gentleman's Magazine* took but a tepid interest in the work;

once the authorship of the inscription was stated by Malone, it could no longer be ignored. The Revd R.W. Eyton in his monumental *Antiquities of Shropshire* (1841) mentions the epitaph – that against which the name of Shakespeare actually stands in Dugdale's MS. – is "by an inferior hand" and "not worth transcribing", and reaches further depths of absurdity in his comment that, when **Sir Thomas Stanley**, to whom the monument is erected, died in 1576, "Shakespeare was not yet thirteen years of age"; that **Sir Thomas**'s son **Sir Edward** is shown as a man of mature age and the father of a family which includes a daughter born in 1600, and that **Sir Edward** was only knighted in 1603, went for nothing, apparently. The same year 1841 also saw the publication of Every's *Etchings of Tong Church*, where the monument is shown without the allegorical figures but with the pyramids in their original position at the four corners of the base; in the List of Plates he gives the year 1612 as the date of its erection. In 1885 Griffith's *History of Tong* shows that the monument had been moved, and that the "four square tapering columns of black marble, all damaged and standing apart," were each surmounted by a white marble figure; the original balls and spikes of the pyramids, that is, had gone, and the allegorical figures had been put in their place.

The author makes the unfortunate suggestion that **Sir Edward Stanley**'s son-in-law Sir Kenelm Digby, husband of the Venesie (Venetia) of the inscription, had a hand in the design; seeing that **Sir Edward** sold the Tong estates in 1623 [*sic, actually 1603 when he sold Tong Castle. Details of the settlement of the Manor, however, were protracted until 1607 and 1613 and perhaps until 1623.* HM] two years before the Digby marriage, the theory can be dismissed without further consideration. In 1892 a pamphlet dealing with the restoration of the church states that the monument had been repaired and re-erected parallel with the other tombs in the Vernon chapel, the pyramids being taken from floor level and placed at the corners of the upper slab where the allegorical figures once stood. Two years later a new edition states that these figures were all damaged and lying about the tomb, and that the 32 rosettes were missing from the canopy; it was after this, clearly, that they were set in spaces on the arch dividing the Vernon Chapel from the S. aisle. But it is here for the first time that we find an appreciation of the beauty of the low-relief decorations on the inner columns, the Antiques, as the 17th century called such arabesques, with their "Compasses, Spears, Greaves, books, censers, torches, drums, lances, body armour, helmets" and, we may add, their skulls, crossbones, and mattocks, emblems of death, flowers and fruit, emblems of Resurrection. Next comes Lady Victoria Manners' finely illustrated study of the Tong monuments in the Art Journal for March and September 1926, which deserves careful study: the disadvantages of the removal of the monument to its present position is forcibly seen in the fact that it is photographed from the end only, though a glimpse across its neighbours can be seen in another photograph. The fine prints specially taken by the kindness of Mr. Gerald Mander are a *tour de force* considering the conditions under which a photographer has to work.

Finally, the literature of the monument concludes with an article published in *The Times* of April 22, 1929, in which the statement as to Shakespeare's authorship given by Joseph Harker to Malone was traced to its source in the actual MS. of Dugdale's *Visitation of Shropshire* at the College of Arms, and attention was drawn to the contemporary drawing in the same volume ignored by Malone, whose concern was with the text of Shakespeare, but executed under Dugdale's supervision. Subsequent correspondence in the columns of *The Times* elicited further evidence: it could no longer be doubted that the Stanley epitaph is in fact, as Malone stated on the strength of evidence which he had not seen, by Shakespeare.

(Esdaile)

Mrs Esdaile continued with **II**. THE MONUMENT AS A WORK OF ART; **III**. THE EPITAPH; and **IV**. SHAKESPEARE AND THE STANLEYS.

Reproduced here are a few of her sentences from these sections.

II. THE MONUMENT AS A WORK OF ART

The effigy of **Sir Edward Stanley** in light armour lies on a low sarcophagus; above, on a great banded ledger, lie the parents, Sir Thomas Vernon and his wife [*sic, actually **Sir Thomas Stanley** and Margaret née Vernon*, HM], he in heavy plate armour with his head on a plumed helmet, she in black gown, cap and plaited ruff. At the corners, shorn of their spiked and gilded balls, are crowded the great pyramids, the little allegorical figures which once stood there, one holding a child, as the drawing clearly shows and therefore representing Charity, another with a skull, therefore Mortality, standing in the recesses of the arcade above; the other two figures are now so damaged that identification is difficult, but Immortality with a Crown of Life is likely to have been one. In the spandrels are armorial shields, and almost the whole surface of the arches inside the columns alluded to is covered with the arabesques already described. **Sir Thomas**'s sword is missing and the ends of his feet and his hands are broken off.

(Esdaile)

What I learned from this section was that **Sir Edward** was in light armour and **Sir Thomas** in heavy armour. Given that I know nothing about armour, other than recognising it as such, I had a few more thoughts about dates and why one should be in light and one in heavy armour? I still await enlightenment. It also made me aware that **Sir Thomas**'s sword was broken off. I had not realised until I read this that he ever had a sword on his tomb. This, and his feet and hands broken off are probably explained by the actions of Puritans during the Civil War, who went on a rampage through the church. Given the role of James Stanley, 7th Earl of Derby, during the Civil War, his presence at the Battle of Worcester, and his visit with Charles II to Boscobel and the famous oak tree in which the King hid (not far from Tong), it is explicable that any local Stanley tomb should have been desecrated.

III. THE EPITAPH

But, after all, it is the epitaph which is the glory of the Stanley tomb, and it is time to turn to what is known of Shakespeare's work in this field.

Of the doggerel rhymes on his own grave we can only say that Shakespeare may well have written them, as William Hall said in 1694 he did, "to suit the capacity of clerks and sextons, for the most part a very ignorant sort of people": the activities of the First Grave Digger are only too true a picture of what was going on all over England. They were engraved, says Dugdale, "Neare the wall where [the] monument is erected on a plaine knee stone, underneath wch his body is buried", and they served their purpose: Shakespeare's grave is still inviolate. He, like Sir Thomas Browne, clearly had a horror, in Browne's words, of being "knave'd out of his grave", and it is a remarkable fact that the lines do not seem to occur anywhere else in England before Shakespeare's death:

"Good friend, for Jesus' sake forbear
To dig the dust enclosed here.
Blest be the man that spares these stones,
And curst be he that moves my bones."

(Esdaile)

Shakespeare's grave has remained inviolate, but **Sir Thomas**'s and his wife Lady Margaret's bodies were dug up from their tomb in Tong, and we still have no idea when, why or where they went to. If the new burial place (if they were reburied?) were to be discovered and **Sir Thomas**'s body examined, it might be possible to establish how severely he was tortured during his spell in the Tower of London, which presumably contributed to his early death. Confirmation of his being put on the rack in 1571 has come from Brian S. Roberts, webmaster of the Stanley Family Genealogy Website.

To repeat, the information in Mrs Esdaile's article in *The Times* in 1929 was largely rejected by E. K Chambers in his books *William Shakespeare: A Study of Facts and Problems*, 2 vols (Oxford, 1930). To be fair to him, he had already written most of these two volumes before Mrs Esdaile published her information and his work still remains a classic on Shakespeare biography. Further research and publications by both (and others) in the 1940s were inevitably hampered by the Second World War.

~~~~~~~~~~~~~~~

IX-3. Time-line of reproductions of the MI,
epitaphs and sketches of the tomb until the mid-twentieth century

With Mrs Esdaile's information added to the information in previous chapters, it is now possible to construct a time-line of the main influential people who wrote and published what, where and when about the Stanley tomb in Tong.

Year	MS, Book, Article	Author, Finder, Recipient	Comments re authors, tomb, texts, publications, conclusions, etc.
1626?	MS	Weever	Antiquarian from Lancashire, in London.
1630? 1650?	MS MS	?Fane Anon	Three MS versions of the verse epitaphs copied in private collections of MSS. Two attributed them to Shakespeare.
1632	MS	Dugdale	Dugdale visited Tong during his tours as poursuivant and noted that Sir Edward had built a tomb for his parents, but didn't see his effigy. He didn't know that Sir Edward had died very recently. The effigy had presumably not yet been put in place. He didn't comment on the epitaphs until a return visit in 1663. (See Appendix 11. Epilogue)
1663, Sep.	MS	Dugdale	Visited the church during his Visitation of Shropshire and recorded it in his Diary.
1664	MS	Sandford	Francis Sandford visited Tong, presumably 'commissioned' by Dugdale, copied the text of MI & Epitaphs, and made a sketch of the tomb, when touring to make sketches of other tombs for Dugdale's projected *Antiquities of Shropshire*. Filed at College of Arms as f.20. (Esdaile)
1664	MS	Dugdale	Visitations of Shropshire, Lancashire and Cheshire. Publication of *Antiquities of Shropshire*; did not include the Stanley tomb, presumably because not ancient.
1757	Article	Cole	'In the year 1757 the Stanley monument was described by Horace Walpole's friend the antiquary Cole as "a monstrous large canopy tomb jostling the altar and before it".' (Esdaile)
1763	Article	Anon	'A writer in the *Gentleman's Magazine* more specifically notes that it stood on the north side of the choir, that one of the pyramids at the head was thrown down, and the little figures at the top all broke.' (Esdaile)
1780s?	MS copy of Dugdale's MS	Harker to Malone	'Malone was collecting the material for the great third Variorum Edition of Shakespeare . . . he received from his friend Joseph Harker, Garter Principal King at Arms, a transcript of the epitaph in modernized spelling, with the information that it was "preserved in a collection of epitaphs at the end of the Visitation of Shropshire, taken by Sir William Dugdale in 1664".' (Esdaile) One suspects that Malone only received one verse Epitaph and an abbreviated version of the MI. He immediately accepted the potential authenticity of the Epitaph beginning 'Not monumental stone', but did not pursue this further. However, 'once the authorship of the inscription was stated by Malone, it could no longer be ignored.' (Esdaile)
1817	Book	Drake	Nathan Drake (1766-1836), *Shakespeare and his Times* (1817), provided an influential account of Shakespeare's biography in its day. Included the Tong verse epitaphs. Gave wrong biographical details.
1827	Book	Dugdale	*Dugdale's Diaries* published, although not including his brief intro. to the MI and both verse Epitaphs. More attention was given to his notes on Shakespeare's own monument and epitaph in Stratford than those in Tong.
1841	Book	Eyton	'The Rev. R. W. Eyton in his monumental *Antiquities of Shropshire* (1841) mentions the epitaph that against which the name of Shakespeare actually stands in Dugdale's MS. - is "by an inferior hand" and "not worth transcribing", . . . "and reaches further depths of absurdity . . ."' (Esdaile)

continued....

Year	MS, Book, Article	Author, Finder, Recipient	Comments re authors, tomb, texts, publications, conclusions, etc.
1841	Article	Every	'1841 also saw the publication of Every's *Etchings of Tong Church*, where the monument is shown without the allegorical figures but with the pyramids in their original position at the four corners of the base; in the List of Plates he gives the year 1612 as the date of its erection.' (Esdaile)
1840s	Book	Halliwell-Phillips	*Reliques* Acknowledged the potential importance and authenticity of the verse epitaphs by Shakespeare.
1853	Book	Heywood	*Stanley Papers*, Part 1, Thomas Heywood, *The Earls of Derby and the Verse Writers and Poets of the Sixteenth and Seventeenth Centuries* (Chetham Society Old Series, Vol. 29, 1853). Heywood had actually written this in 1829 and quoted the version of the epitaphs from Nathan Drake (1817).
1885	Book	Griffiths	'In 1885 Griffith's History of Tong shows that the monument had been moved, and that the "four square tapering columns of black marble, all damaged and standing apart," were each surmounted by a white marble figure; the original balls and spikes of the pyramids, that is, had gone, and the allegorical figures had been put in their place.' (Esdaile)
1891/2			Church renovation; tomb moved. (Esdaile, Auden)
1898	Book	Lee	Sir Sidney Lee, magisterial authority, *Shakespeare: A Life*; no mention of the Epitaphs.
1900?	MS notes	Auden	Extensive report on renovations; useful genealogical details; first to mention the Vernon connection in some detail; expressed no opinion on authenticity of Shakespeare authorship claim. Notes remained unpublished until 2003-5.
1926	Article	Manners	'Lady Victoria Manners' finely illustrated study of the Tong monuments in the *Art Journal* for March and September 1926.' (Esdaile) Her very name suggests an interest in the Rutland connection.
1929	Article	Esdaile	Katherine Esdaile seems to have been the first and only person in the early 20th century to have looked at Dugdale's 1663/4 MS. Article in *The Times*. . . . it was 'preserved in a collection of epitaphs at the end of the Visitation of Shropshire, taken by Sir William Dugdale in 1664'. Malone had seen at once that the fact proved the authenticity of the epitaph, and perceived that 'the last line, though the worst, bears very strong marks of the hand of Shakespeare. Others, as we shall see, were not so wise.' Mrs Esdaile had no doubts.
1929ff	Articles, letters	(Esdaile)	'Subsequent correspondence in the columns of *The Times* elicited further evidence: it could no longer be doubted that the Stanley epitaph is in fact, as Malone stated on the strength of evidence which he had not seen, by Shakespeare.' (Esdaile)
1930	Book	Chambers	Chambers, THE current revered authority on Shakespeare's biography in the 1930s, had little time for the Tong Epitaphs and took little or no notice of Mrs Esdaile's conclusions, writing later: 'It is clear that one set of verses cannot be Shakespearean if it relates to Sir Edward Standish (*sic*, Stanley) who owned Tong (he died in 1632) and on internal evidence there is no temptation to accept either of them as his.' (Chambers.) Interesting that he got the name wrong.
1954	Book	Keen	'In Tong Church, Shropshire, are the tombs of **Sir Thomas** and **Sir Edward Stanley**, bearing poetical epitaphs engraved at their ends. **Sir Thomas** was of Winwick, Lancashire, and died in 1576. His widow, who died in 1596, had been Margaret Vernon, of the famous Shropshire family. **Sir Edward** was a brother of Henry, fourth Earl of Derby, and his frequent visits to Knowsley and Lathom between the years 1561 and 1589 are recorded in the Household Books. He died in 1609.1) These epitaphs are described, and attributed to Shakespeare, in a MS. of c. 1630. It is reproduced in facsimile by Halliwell-Phillips in his Folio of 1853, and more fully described by him in *Reliques*, p. 32. continued...

Year	MS, Book, Article	Author, Finder, Recipient	Comments re authors, tomb, texts, publications, conclusions, etc.
1954	Book	Keen	Later it was at Warwick Castle.' (Keen, *The Annotator*. H.M.) Presented as part of the "Shakespeare in Lancashire" theory. An enthusiastic "amateur", whose work was largely ignored by Shakespearean academia until Honigmann, between his first editions of 1985 and second edition of 1998. (See his Peface to the Second Edition.) 1) Keen had the wrong **Sir Edward** on the tomb, **Sr** instead of **Jr** and in any case with the wrong date of death. (HM)
1985, 1998	Book	Honigmann	Honigmann countered Chambers' position of rebuttal, devoted four pages to the Tong Stanley epitaphs (1985) and belatedly (1998) acknowledged the value of Keen incorporating the Tong epitaphs in the 'Shakespeare in Lancashire' theory.

I agree with Chambers that the verse epitaphs were intended for the younger Sir Edward and for his father, but not entirely with his reservation that, since this Sir Edward died in 1632, his figure, if it is his, and the verses on him must have been added to the tomb after that date, and incidentally after Shakespeare's death. The implication seems to be that Shakespeare, being dead, could not have been involved; and it is spelt out in the *Shakespeare Encyclopaedia*: if Sir Edward is Sir Thomas's son 'there can be no question that Shakespeare did not write the epitaphs, since Sir Edward died in 1632, 16 years after Shakespeare'.'

(Honigmann, *Shakespeare: the 'lost years'*, 1985.)

Honigmann was saying politely that Chambers came to his conclusions on the basis of far from adequate facts, but never pursued the missing ones. Chambers' conclusions, however, dominated the twentieth century until Honigmann in 1985 and beyond. Other relevant passages from Honigmann, *Shakespeare: the 'lost years'* have been quoted in previous chapters.

IXa. Tong Church in Dickens's *The Old Curiosity Shop* (1841), Cattermole

Very few of those named above actually visited the church, but Charles Dickens certainly did, describing it as 'a very aged, ghostly place.' Tong Church and its vault provided the setting of one of the scenes with Little Nell. 'A Mr Fletcher wrote: "I have several times heard him (Archdeacon Lloyd) say – once at the Archidiaconal Congress at Tong – that Charles Dickens told him personally that Tong Church was the church described in *The Old Curiosity Shop*." ' *(Auden's Notes)*The full story is given in Jeffery, *Discovering Tong*, Chapter 13. Some Victorian Curiosities.

IXb. Demolition of Tong Castle, 1954

'After 1913 no one lived in the castle, and it gradually fell into ruin. Understandably it became a tempting ruin for young explorers, and tragically one young man climbed a wall and fell almost from the top. He died in hospital six weeks later. The Territorial Army were brought in and in 1954 it was blown up. We are very gratful to the Shropshire Star for permission to use their pictures of that event. The top picture shows the shell that then remained; the centre the moment of the explosion and the bottom the debris that remained. Much later, in 1983, the M54 motorway was opened, and it now runs across the site of the former castle.'

(Ed.) Joyce Frost, *Auden's History of Tong*, Volume 1, Arima, 2005, pp. 201, 206.

Chapter X
1601: The Stanley tomb at Walthamstow, Essex; plus a few more tombs and inscriptions of relevance
by Simon Watney

X-1. Introduction

In this chapter we concentrate mainly on the Stanley tomb in St Mary's, Walthamstow, with its effigies and MIs.

The existence of the almost identical Stanley MIs in Walthamstow and Tong has been known and reported on for well over two centuries by antiquarians, local historians and, most recently, an expert on Church Monuments (Simon Watney in 2005, hence his appearance in the title of this chapter). There is little to no doubt that all the details given in these various independent reports produce the following fairly definitive conclusions about the date of commission and initial construction of the two monumental Stanley tombs in St Bartholomew's, Tong and St Mary's, Walthamstow.

It should perhaps be reiterated and emphasised that this chapter is mainly concerned with the establishment of all known details about the tombs themselves, the dates of commission and initial construction, the dates of completion, the dates of the MIs and any other texts on them, plus the fate of these tombs over the last four centuries, from their obvious appearance in marble and alabaster when first erected in the early seventeenth century through to their appearance today. Let us just be thankful that the Stanley tomb in St Mary's, Walthamstow, with all its effigies and MIs, has survived somewhat intact (although considerably modified), along with several other tombs with relevant details.

As a corollary to the previous paragraph, this means that for the moment we put aside any thoughts about whether or not Shakespeare wrote the Epitaphs on the tomb in Tong, and when. We are more concerned here as to why Lady Lucy was in Walthamstow in 1601, who she was visiting at the time, and why she and four of her daughters died there but not her other three daughters.

Xa. St Mary's Parish Church, Walthamstow, 1819
'Walthamstow Church from south-east
MS 1819— 6ins x 9ins, Essex Archives Online.

X-2. Latest conclusions concerning the two Stanley tombs and the MIs

1) The tomb was commissioned by **(Sir) Edward Stanley Jr** in late 1601 for his recently deceased beloved wife Lady Lucy and four of their daughters, also recently deceased.

2) The sculptors were different.

3) The biographical details in the MIs on both tombs were almost certainly written by **Edward** himself, or dictated by him, with a copy of this available to the two (presumably different) masons/artisans who added the texts onto the two tombs in Tong and Walthamstow.

4) The slight differences in spelling details in the MIs are accountable for by the amount of space available on the two tombs and decisions based on this, perhaps/probably made by the two artisans as they were working independently, just 'doing their job', one in Essex and one in Shropshire.

5) Perhaps the most relevant difference in the biographical MIs is that at Tong the ages of the deceased daughters are given, but not at Walthamstow.

6) Both tombs, which can still be seen today, are modified versions of the originals. Some differences are the results of the ravages of time (some damage possibly deliberate during the Civil War) and some because both tombs were removed and restored during nineteenth-century renovations, when various decisions needed to be taken.

~~~~~~~~~~~~~~~~~

X-3. The description by an expert in church monuments

In 2005 an article appeared about the tomb at Walthamstow, which corrected Mrs Esdaile's assumption (see Chapter IX. Katherine Esdaile) that the tomb of Lady Lucy had not survived. She had confused Waltham (Abbey) with (St Mary's) Walthamstow.

> Happily the monument to Lady Lucy Stanley and her four young daughters indeed survives in the parish church of St Mary at Walthamstow in Essex. It has been convincingly attributed by Adam White to William Cure II. Originally free-standing, it was, however, moved in 1819 and much altered in the process. It formerly consisted of a tomb chest carrying a substantial aedicule which contained the figure of Lady Stanley kneeling at a prie-dieu, in fashionable costume with her breasts daringly displayed, visible from both sides through a large central arch edged with a narrow frieze of guilloche on the front. The monument now stands against the north wall of the north aisle, and the former north side is thus no longer visible. Two daughters kneel in profile against the south side of the tomb chest, and the two daughters formerly on the north side are now placed on top of the aedicule, flanking a large framed escutcheon.
>
> Lady Stanley's monument does not appear to come from the same chisel as the monument to her husband and his parents at Tong, but it formerly included almost exactly the same epitaph as appears on the latter, although it is no longer complete. The epitaph is located on the north side of the prie-dieu at which Lady Stanley kneels, and was inexpertly repainted in the 1990s, except for the last few lines of the original Text. It may be noted that the epitaph at Tong elides 'Walthamstow' to 'Waltham', thus confusing Esdaile, but suggesting that the text at Walthamstow is the earlier of the two versions:
>
> (Simon Watney, 'Sky aspiring pyramids: Shakespeare and 'Shakespearean' epitaphs in early Stuart England'; Church Monuments, Vol. XX, 2005, pp. 105-6.)

There follows more or less the same MI text as at Tong, although with different spellings and abbreviations and no ages of the daughters. (The MI at Walthamstow appears in the next quote.)

Finally, from Watney, at the end of his article, after discussing other tombs (to which we return later), comes an earlier description of the tomb at Walthamstow. It is generally reported that the deaths were in c.1600, and the construction of the tomb c.1601. We now know that the deaths were early-mid 1601 (from Sir Kenelm Digby's memoir) and that Venetia, the last daughter, was born in December 1600. It is difficult to imagine that Lucy, the mother of her eighth baby in 1600, would undertake a considerable journey immediately after this birth. This makes the deaths more likely to have been later rather than earlier in the year and the construction of the tomb up to a year later.

~~~~~~~~~~~~~

X-4. APPENDIX 1 by Simon Watney
Antiquarian evidence on the epitaph on Lady Lucy Stanley's monument at St Mary's Church, Walthamstow

The church notes of William Holman of Halstead are housed in the Essex County Record Office in Chelmsford. Holman was helped in his research by various assistants. For clarification see anon, 'Holman's sources and his assistants', Essex County Records, T/P 195. Holman's notebook T/P 195/1 contains the following description, not in his usual clear hand:

"Under an arch of this monument is the effigy of a woman as large as life: on her head an early coronet. Kneeling on a cushion before a reading desk on it a book opened – on the south side of the monument an inscription on a table of black marble in golden capitals: "**Tho: Stanley Knight** Second Sonne of Edw Earl of Derbie Lo: Stanley & strange descended from ye family of ye Stanleys married Margaret Vernon ONE of ye daughters and coheirs of Sr George Vernon of NETHER Haddon in ye countie of Derby Knight by whom he had issue 2 Sonnes Henri and **Edw**. Henrie died an infant **Edw** survived by whome these lordships descended & married ye La Lucie Percie second daughter to the Earl of Northumberland by her he had issue 7 Daughters & One Sonne She & her 4 Daughters Arabella Marie Alis and Priscilla are interred under a monument in the church at Walthamstow in the countie Of Essex Thos his son died an infant & is buried in ye parishe church of Winwicke in ye countie of Lanc ye other three Petronella Francis & Venetia are yt living'. On the north side of this monument of the reading desk on a plate of marble in golden capitals on the square side of the reading desk '[**Sir Edw Stanley**] Erected this /Monument for a Testimonial of / His Love wch he bare to his wife / Ladie Lucie & his fore daughters / deceased'."

Holman's notes also identify a further inscription between two of the kneeling daughters: 'The Soules of Saintes / Live'. The text also describes (in largely indecipherable script) the two sides of the architrave of the monument, each with 'the sun setting on the one side: on the other a dyall', with two texts above them: 'Occident ut oriatur' and 'Qualibet expectes[?] Tamen'. These iconographically unusual features were perhaps formerly on the spandrels of the central arch, and may have been painted rather than carved, which might explain their total later disappearance. I am grateful to Julian Litten for drawing Holman and his assistants' unpublished notes to my attention.

(Left)
Xb. The Stanley tomb, Walthamstow, 1802
Print of a drawing, 1802. Engraved by W. P. Shenlock, London, published by Anthony Mateus, Printseller to Her Royal Highness the Duchess of York, No. 29, Pall Mall, Essex Archives Online. A comparison of this with Xc. shows some of the changes that have happened since then.

(Right)
Xc. The Stanley tomb today
Formerly free-standing but now placed against a wall with a railing, only one side can be seen. The effigies of two of the daughters have been moved onto the top. The hands of Lady Lucy and all four daughters, formerly clasped in prayer, have been knocked off at the wrist.

Writing in 1932, local historian S.J. Barns recorded the full inscription as it then appeared:

"**THO. STANLEY Knight** second sunne of Edwd / Earle of Derbie lo. Stanley & Strange / Descended from ye famili of ye Stanleis / Married Margaret Vernon one of ye Daughters / And coheirs of Sr George Vernon of Nether / Haddon in ye countie of Derbie Knight by / whom he had issue 2 Sonnes Henri and / **Edw**. Henri died an infant **Edw** survived / To whom this lordships descended & / Married La: Lucie Percie Second daugh- / ter to the Earle of Northymberland by her / he had issue 7 daughters & one sone she & / her daughters Arabella Mary Alis and / Priscilla interred under a Monument / in ye Church of Walthamstow in the countie of Essex Tho his son died an / infant & is buried in ye Parishe Church of Winkke in ye countie of Lanca ye other / three Petronella Frauncis & Venetia / are yt livinge.**(1)**"

On the same page Barns also stated that: ...there is a record of the following inscription: "**Sr Edw Stanley [i]** / effected this monu- / ment for a testi / monial of his love / Wch he bare to / his wife Ladie / Lucie & his foure / daughters deceased".' Barns did not provide the source of the 'record' in question, but it was presumably Holman. He added, p. 8, that 'in a panel immediately below Lady Lucy, and originally just above the faldstool: "The souls of saints / live. /" '. There is a small black rectangular inscription plate set into the tomb chest on the south side between the lower pair of kneeling daughters, which is now blank. It is not clear when or why Barns considered it was moved.

(1) S.J. Barns, 'St Mary the Virgin, Walthamstow: inscriptions in the church and churchyard, 2: memorials in the church', *Proceedings of the Walthamstow Antiquarian Society*, 27 (1932), p. 8.
(Watney, *ibid*, pp. 114-5).

[i] The naming of the widower as **Sir Edward Stanley** dates this text to 1603 ff, because before his knighthood at King James's coronation he was 'Mr' or 'Esq.'. The very least one can deduce from this later addition is that Sir Edward almost certainly visited the tomb, mourning his wife and four daughters *in situ*. Perhaps it was on one subsequent visit that he commissioned the additional sentence. **Sir Thomas** and **Sir Edward** appearing in **bold** above are my own additions.[HM].

X-5. Some intermediary facts and many more questions

A Google search produced the information that William Holman published a description of a local manor in Essex, the MS in Colchester Castle, in 1715. So he presumably wrote the notes above on the Stanley tomb around the same time, about half way between the erection in c.1601 and the changes made in 1819. The family history website of the Wyncolls of Essex and Suffolk provided a possible clue as to why Winwick in Lancashire was reproduced as 'Winkke' in Walthamstow. The painter of the MI was perhaps likely to have been more familiar with the rather more local family name 'Wyncoll' than the place 'Winwick' in distant Lancashire.

One significant feature of the Walthamstow tomb is that the Shakespeare verse epitaphs do not appear there, and one can only wonder why not. It could have been that this tomb was commissioned in c.1601 and completed before the one in Tong was started. This in itself would seem to date the composition of the MI in Walthamstow to earlier than the one in Tong. In any case, they must both predate 1603, the year when **Sir Edward** was knighted.

It seems clear that his and Lucy's marriage was a happy one and not, as I suspected at first during early research, that they might even have separated shortly before her death. It is still unclear why she and four of her daughters were in Walthamstow in 1601, and the cause of their deaths remains unknown. One might presume that they all died from the same contagious disease (the plague?) that had visited locally. More research in Walthamstow is needed. So far, no details have emerged from local historians reporting on parish registers that there was an epidemic in Walthamstow in 1601.

Meanwhile, no one seems to have asked the following questions until now:

1) Why was Lucy Stanley née Percy in Walthamstow in 1601?

2) Did she and four of her daughters really die of a contagious disease?

3) Why did her other three daughters, who survived, not also die of this same disease?

4) Were these three daughters, who survived, actually with her at Walthamstow?

5) Where was her husband **(Sir) Edward Stanley Jr** during Lucy's visit to Walthamstow in 1601?

6) Might these Stanleys have become caught up in various intrigues ongoing at the time?

7) Might Lucy and four of her daughters have actually died of poisoning?

8) How important was it in recent memory that Lucy's father, Thomas Percy, 7th Earl of Northumberland, had been executed for treason in 1582?

9) How important was it in recent memory that Lucy's father-in-law **Sir Thomas Stanley** had spent 2–3 years in the Tower of London for planning to 'rescue' Mary, Queen of Scots in 1570?

10) How important was it that so many of the rather immediate relatives of Lucy and her husband **Edward Stanley** were contenders as 'legitimate' successors to Queen Elizabeth's throne?

11) How close and often were the personal contacts between all Lucy's Percy/ Stanley/ Manners/ Spencer/ Seymour/ Devereux close relations?

These are all genuine and honest questions, totally open to criticism for even asking them in the first place. I fully accept that we might never find any answer to any of them in a contemporary and authenticated document, given how many of these documents have disappeared through the ravages of time.

They seemed worth asking, however, not least because in 1601 William Shakespeare was enjoying some of his greatest successes in the theatre in London and this date was not far from the various suggested dates of Shakespeare's composing the verse epitaphs for the Stanley tomb in Tong. (As a reminder, Professor Honigmann's suggested dates were 1601-1603, 'or earlier or later'.) In 1601 William Stanley, 6th Earl of Derby, **(Sir) Edward Jr**'s first cousin, was presumably still writing plays in London: he certainly had been in 1599 and soon afterwards was reported as being involved in the financing of some boys' troupes of actors. At the time he was still locked in legal battles with his sister-in-law Countess Alice over all the Derby estates. This battle had started in 1594, on the death of his brother Ferdinando, 5th Earl, and was to continue until 1609. **Sir Edward Sr** and his nephews **Edward Jr** and William were involved in at least some of these together, insisting on their legal and hereditary right to certain lands.

> (1600) Derby lands in reversion to William, 6th Earl of Derby, after the (future) death of Sir Edward Stanley Sr, brother of the 4th Earl of Derby: Thirsk & Kirkby Malzeard (Yorkshire).
>
> > (Coward, *Earls of Derby.*)
>
> (1600) Lands in reversion to "William, 6th Earl of Derby, after the death of Edward Stanley esq., son of Sir Thomas Stanley, younger brother of the 4th Earl of Derby: Eynsham (Oxon.)."
>
> > (Coward, *Earls of Derby.*)

In 1600/1 Countess Alice was still claiming pretty well all the estates for herself and her three daughters. On her side in her legal battle was her second husband (since 1600) Thomas Egerton, Viscount Brackley, Lord Chancellor, Lord Ellesmere. Her three daughters were all still rather young (Anne born in 1580, Frances in 1583 and Elizabeth in 1588), but she obviously wanted them to inherit as much as possible to allow them to make good matches. It is perhaps relevant that these three daughters were in line of succession to Elizabeth's throne, for the same reason that their father Ferdinando had been a potential successor (and been poisoned, presumably for this reason.) The first of the marriages of her daughters took place on 15 January 1601 between Elizabeth (aged only 13) and Henry Hastings, heir to his grandfather, the Earl of Huntingdon. This marriage might even provide one possibility for Lucy and her unmarried daughters being at Walthamstow around this time, only a few miles from central London. She and husband **(Sir) Edward Jr** were presumably looking around at this time for suitable husbands for their own daughters. We know from the MI at Tong that when they died in 1601 these were Arabella (18), Mary (16), Alice (15) and Priscilla (13).

It somehow seems rather relevant that in 1600/1 both Lady Lucy and Countess Alice were in a similar situation: both were Stanleys, married to first cousins; one was a Countess because the father of her children had been an Earl, the other 'only an honorary Lady', but her father had been an Earl; both had lost a loved one at a rather young age because of 'plots' to usurp Elizabeth's throne (Countess Alice had lost her husband, 'Lady' Lucy her father); both had no son but several daughters of (near-)marriageable age (Alice three, Lucy four). It seems possible that in letters they had agreed to meet in or near London on the occasion of the forthcoming marriage of one of Countess Alice's daughters. In the absence of any letters, this remains pure speculation.

We have no idea what position **(Sir) Edward Jr** felt himself in during the legal wrangle between his cousin and cousin-in-law over the Derby estates. We do know that during the two decades leading up to 1600/1 he had regularly revisited Lancashire and taken part in many Stanley affairs. (Documentary coverage of these lies in later chapters, and all specific documented dates are given in Chapter XXVIII. Time-line of Sir Thomas & Sir Edward Sr & Jr.)

X-6. Who did Lady Lucy stay with at Walthamstow in 1601?

We have no idea. However, it seems most likely that the reason for her and four of her daughters being there in the first place was that she was visiting some of her relatives, or planning to meet some of them in London, only a few miles down the road. A quick survey of these might reveal a few clues. We will remember that through her marriage to **(Sir) Edward Stanley Jr**, Lucy was very closely related to the Vernon and Manners families. These were scattered throughout various Midlands counties, which meant that any of their visits to London would have taken them down one of the main roads from the north and Walthamstow would have been only a minor detour.

To these we can easily add various de Vere-Cecil fairly close relatives, all of whom visited London regularly or were based there, with all their family seats north of London. At the risk of repetition: since 1595, the first cousin of Lucy's husband **Edward Stanley Jr**, Sir William Stanley, meanwhile 6th Earl of Derby had been married to Elizabeth de Vere (1575–1627), daughter of Edward de Vere, 17th Earl of Oxford (1550–1604) and Anne Cecil (1556–88) daughter of Sir William Cecil, Lord Burghley and therefore (half-)sister of Lords Thomas Cecil (soon afterwards 1st Earl of Exeter, creating this dynasty at Burghley House in Lincolnshire) and Robert Cecil (soon afterwards 1st Earl of Salisbury, creating this dynasty at Hatfield House in Middlesex). Walthamstow would have been a convenient place for them travelling from Burghley House or Hatfield to London. Elizabeth de Vere Stanley, as the eldest daughter of the Earl of Oxford, was his main heiress to the family estates at Hedingham, Essex. Although she spent much of her time in Lancashire with her husband William Stanley, Walthamstow would have been a convenient stopping place en route to London on any of her journeys to visit her Cecil relatives or her de Vere family's hereditary seat at Hedingham Castle.

In 1601 Thomas Cecil was Lord Burghley, a renowned politician, following on in his father's tradition, a leading figure at court, and a renowned soldier. Robert Cecil (unfortunately for him, hunchbacked and of rather small stature) was Secretary of State and Lord Privy Seal to the ageing Queen Elizabeth. He was also Chancellor of the Duchy of Lancaster (1590–1612), which presumably meant he was concerned on many occasions with the ongoing legal battle over hereditary lands of the Earl of Derby in the Duchy between William, 6th Earl of Derby and his sister-in-law Countess Alice née Spencer. She had recently (1600) re-married, as his third wife, Sir Thomas Egerton (c.1540–1617) of Cheshire, at various times Lord Keeper of the Great Seal, Privy Councillor, Viscount Brackley, Lord Chancellor Ellesmere, but most importantly in 1601 one of the most highly respected members in Elizabeth's government.

The following quote online about Chancellor Ellesmere is included as admirable in its succinctness. The details relevant to 1601 are in *italics*:

> He was thrice married. By his first wife, Elizabeth, daughter of Thomas Ravenscroft of Bretton, *Flintshire*, he had two sons and a daughter. The elder son, Thomas, predeceased him, leaving three daughters. The younger, John, succeeded his father as 2nd *Viscount Brackley*, was created *Earl of Bridgewater*, and, marrying *Lady Frances Stanley (daughter of his father's third wife, widow of the 5th Earl of Derby)*, was the ancestor of the earls and dukes of Bridgewater.

(Anon, online)

To see if any of these families occur in accounts of Lucy in Walthamstow, or of the ownership of property in Walthamstow, let us look at two accounts by historians of Essex, one earlier and one later.

~~~~~~~~~~~~~

X-7. 'Walthamstow', pp. 204-230, David Lysons, (1796) (Extract)
(*British History Online*)

This provides no information on who she might have been visiting and no information on the Stanley tomb other than its position and details already given above. However, quoting it here might save any interested reader the trouble of establishing this.

Monument of Lady Lucy Stanley.

On the north side of the chapel... Under the next arch is the monument of Lady Lucy, daughter and one of the coheirs of Thomas Earl of Northumberland, and wife of Sir Edward Stanley, K. B. (fn. 1), only surviving son of Sir Thomas Stanley (second son of Edward Earl of Derby) by Margaret, daughter and coheir of Sir George Vernon of Haddon in the county of Derby. The date of her death is not mentioned (fn. 2). She lies buried under this monument, together with four daughters, who died in their infancy. Three daughters survived her; Petronella, who died unmarried; Frances, married to John Fortescue, Esq. of Salden, Bucks; and Venetia, married to Sir Kenelm Digby the elder. The effigies [*sic*] of Lady Lucy Stanley is represented as large as the life, (with a viscountess's coronet,) kneeling under an open arch.

Footnote

(1) Arms—Stanley, with its Quarterings, as in vol. ii. p. 103. impaling Quarterly of 15.—1. Quarterly 1 and 4. O. a lion ramp. Az.—Brabant. 2 and 3. G. three fishes haurient Arg.—Lucy. 2. Az. a fesse lozengy O.—Percy. 3. Barry of six O. and V. a bend G.—Poynings. 4. G. three lions pass. Arg. a bend Az.—Fitzpain. 5. O. 3 piles meeting in base Az.—Bryan. 6. Sab. two bars nebuleé Erm.—Spencer. 7. The arms of England within a border gobony—Somerset. 8. G. a fesse between six cross crosslets O.—Beauchamp. 9. G. a chevron between ten crosses pateé Arg.—Berkley. 10. O. a fesse between two chevronels S.—Lisle. 11. G. a lion pass. regally crowned O.—Fitzgerald. 12. Az. three icicles in bend O.—Harbottle. 13. O. three escallops G.—Welwick. 14. Arg. three fleshpots G.—Monbocher. 15. S. three water-bougets Arg.—Charon.

[This footnote is useful mainly in providing Lady Lucy's arms, with those of many ancestors impaled in her own. It is particularly interesting in the context of this book to note the family connections, remembered and publicly acknowledged, with the families highlighted in **bold**: **Lucy** (a surname in this case), a contemporary member of which was Sir Thomas Lucy, from whose park near Stratford local legend tells us young Shakespeare had stolen a deer, been punished, and wrote a poem to hang on his door; **Percy**, Lucy's own family, of course, but with this an indication that there had been a previous marriage between two Percys; **Spencer**, indicating that she was a distant 'cousin' of Countess Alice Spencer Stanley, as well as an in-law; **Somerset**, another family closely connected to the monarchy; **Beauchamp**, early Earls of Warwick, also closely connected to the monarchy and whose six cross-crosslets echo the three cross-crosslets used by the Ardernes, Mary's family, wife of John Shakespeare. HM]

(2) It appears, by some parish records, that she died before 1630.

[We know, from other earlier and later accounts, that she actually died in 1601. HM]

~~~~~~~~~~~~~~~~~~~

<div align="center">

X-8. *Victoria County History*
A History of the County of Essex Volume 6
W. R. Powell (editor)
1973, pp. 253-263 (Extract)
Walthamstow Manors
(British History Online)

</div>

The following quote is presented as an example of an apparently impeccable piece of historical research. It still leaves us guessing as to why Lady Lucy Stanley was in Walthamstow and died there in 1601, but seems to present several clues. The families and individuals of most relevance to Lucy and **Sir Edward Stanley Jr** are shown in italics in the extract below. It will be remembered that his mother, Margaret Vernon, had a sister Dorothy, who married John Manners, second son of Thomas, 1st Earl of Rutland. John's elder brother was Henry Manners, who inherited the title of Earl of Rutland and Lord Ros, along with Belvoir Castle in Rutland, with John inheriting Haddon Hall via his wife Dorothy. This meant that the children of Margaret Vernon Stanley and Dorothy Vernon Manners were first cousins, with the children of Henry Manners, 2nd Earl of Rutland (the future Edward, 3rd Earl and John, 4th Earl) another set of first cousins of Sir George and Grace Manners at Haddon Hall. John and Dorothy's daughter Grace had meanwhile married Sir John Fortescue.

Edward Manners, 3rd Earl of Rutland, died without a son and heir in 1587, when the Earldom and Belvoir went to his younger brother John, now 4th Earl. Edward's daughter and heiress Elizabeth (as we read below) inherited at least one Manners family manor in Walthamstow, and she married William Cecil, Lord Burleigh/Burghley, grandson of the great Sir William, 1st Lord Burghley (1520-98), one of Queen Elizabeth's most trusted advisors, as her Principal Secretary and later Lord Treasurer. He had founded the dynasty and built the magnificent Burghley House at Stamford, Lincolnshire. His eldest son Thomas Cecil (1642-1622) inherited this, along with the title Lord Burghley, and was also later created 1st Earl of Exeter.

> The manor was once again kept in hand until 1554 when it was granted to Thomas, son of Giles Heron. (fn. 49) This grant probably never took effect, for in 1555 the manor was restored to the descendant of the Ros family in the person of *Henry Manners, Earl of Rutland and Lord Ros*, who was the *grandson* of *Eleanor, Lady Manners*, sister of Edmund, Lord Ros (d. 1508). (fn. 50) *Rutland (d.1563) was succeeded by his son Edward, Earl of Rutland.* (fn. 51) *The Rutlands'* title was apparently challenged in 1571 (fn. 52) and in 1583 the Crown actually granted the manor to Theophilus Adams, a "concealer", from whom, and from Robert Adams, *Rutland* had to purchase it in the same year. (fn. 53) This was described in 1612 as a purchase on a defective title. (fn. 54)
>
>   *Edward, Earl of Rutland* (d. 1587) was succeeded by his daughter *Elizabeth, who married William Cecil, son of Thomas Cecil, Lord Burleigh, later earl of Exeter.* (fn. 55) She died in 1591 leaving a son, *William Cecil*, Lord Ros, who came of age in 1611. (fn. 56) He immediately cut the entail on the Walthamstow portion of the Ros inheritance, apparently in order to mortgage it. (fn. 57) In 1616 he married Anne, daughter of Sir Thomas Lake, secretary of state. (fn. 58) In the same year he conveyed Walthamstow Tony to his father-in-law for £800, (fn. 59) and in 1617, for a further £500, to Arthur Lake, bishop of Bath and Wells, his wife's uncle, Arthur Lake, his brother-in-law, and Nicholas *Fortescue*. (fn. 60) Lady Ros later successfully claimed that the latter conveyance was a settlement in trust for her, (fn. 61) but Ros regarded it as a mortgage, and his grandfather, the earl of Exeter, refused his consent to the alienation of the manor. (fn. 62) The

manor was once again kept in hand until 1554 when it was granted to Thomas, son of Giles Heron. (fn. 49) This grant probably never took effect, for in 1555 the manor was restored to the descendant of the Ros family in the person of *Henry Manners, Earl of Rutland and Lord Ros*, who was the grandson of Eleanor, Lady *Manners*, sister of Edmund, Lord Ros (d. 1508). (fn. 50) *Rutland* (d. 1563) was succeeded by his son *Edward, Earl of Rutland*. (fn. 51) *The Rutlands'* title was apparently challenged in 1571 (fn. 52) and in 1583 the Crown actually granted the manor to Theophilus Adams, a 'concealer', from whom, and from Robert Adams, *Rutland* had to purchase it in the same year. (fn. 53) This was described in 1612 as a purchase on a defective title. (fn. 54)

Footnotes

49 Cal. Pat. 1553–4, 472. It was granted as the manor of 'High Hall or Walthamstow Tony or Walthamstow Francis or Low Hall', a multiple title adopted until 1639, although Thomas Heron and his successors never had or claimed Low Hall, which had descended independently since 1449: see below, p. 256.

50 Cal. Pat. 1554–5, 179; cf. *V.C.H. Essex*, v. 101. Eleanor married *Sir Robert Manners* (d. 1508): Morant, *Essex*, i. 56.

51 Barns, *Walthamstow Deeds, 1541–1862, 3; Complete Peerage*, xi. 257.

52 Hist. MSS. Com. 24, *12th Rep. IV, Rutland*, i, pp. 95–6 (letters to the *Earl of Rutland*).

53 Morant, *Essex*, i. 33; C 142/218/52; C 142/217/128.

54 Hist. MSS. Com. 24, *12th Rep. IV, Rutland*, i, p. 438.

55 C 142/217/28; C 142/218/52; *Complete Peerage*, xi. 109.

56 *Complete Peerage*, xi. 109; C 142/257/43.

57 E.R.O., D/DB T1102; Barns, *Walthamstow Deeds, 1595–1890*, 7; Hist. MSS. Com. 24, *12th Rep. IV, Rutland*, i, p. 438.

58 *Complete Peerage*, xi. 110; *D.N.B.*

59 C.P. 25(2)/295 Trin. 14 Jas. I.

60 Ibid. Eas. 15 Jas. I.

61 Barns, *Walthamstow Deeds, 1595–1890*, 8.

62 S. R. Gardiner, *Hist. England*, iii. 189–90. ('Walthamstow', The Environs of London: volume 4: Counties of Herts, Essex & Kent (1796), pp. 204-230. URL: www.british-history.ac.uk/reprt.aspx?compid=4547)

Although the tomb is briefly described in this account of Walthamstow from British History Online, no hints appear from local historians as to why Lady Lucy was there, nor of any disease raging at the time. However, the names in *italics* above imply that the close involvement of the Manners family in the manor might have provided a house there for them to stay in. And a Fortescue was later involved. After Lucy's death, **(Sir) Edward** placed his three surviving infant daughters in the care of Sir Francis Fortescue of Salden, Buckinghamshire, married to his first cousin Grace Manners of Haddon.

X-9. A few more inscriptions of relevance to Tong and Walthamstow

The article by Simon Watney in 2005 (above) made reference to two other highly relevant tombs: one in Bedfordshire containing the same first verse as at Tong and one in Chelsea on the tomb of one of **Sir Edward**'s close relatives.

Bedfordshire, 1st verse

It has not, however, hitherto been noticed that one of the verses on the Stanley monument at Tong is almost precisely duplicated on the free-standing marble and alabaster monument to Sir William Gostwick (d. 1615) in the parish church of St Laurence at Willington, Bedfordshire, which both Adam White and I have independently attributed to Maximilian Colt by comparison with other confirmed monuments.**(1)** Set up by his widow, with whom he had eleven children, Sir William's free-standing tomb consists of a recumbent effigy on top of an exuberantly decorated convex-sided sarcophagus above a narrow tomb chest with superbly carved emblems of death on the corner pilasters. The monument is crowned by an extremely rare wooden canopy of uncertain date. The chest carries a conventional epitaph on its north side.

Here Lieth The Bodie of Sr William Gostwick Baronett, Who / Had To Wife Jane Owen, the Daughter of Henry Owen Esquier, / By Whom He Had Issue Seaven Sonnes And Foure Daughters. / He (With Most Christian Resolution And Assured Hope Of A Joy= / Full Resurrection) Departed This Lyfe The 19th Of September 1615 / In The Fiftieth Yeare Of His Age. / The Ladie Jan Gostwick, His Widowe, To Perform Her Last / Duty And Love To The Sacred Memorie Of Her Dear Husband At Her / Own Cost And Charges Caused This Monument To Be Erected.

Meanwhile, on the south side appears a poem that is identical, save for the plural in the final line, to the verse on the east end of the Stanley monument at Tong:

Ask Who Lyeth Here And Doe Not Weepe / He Is Not Dead, He Doth But Sleepe. / This Stony Register Is For his Bones / His Fame Is More Perpetuall Then Theis Stones / And His Owne Goodness With Himself Being Gone / Shall Live When Earthly Monuments Are None.

(1) White, 'A biographical dictionary', p. 31.

(Watney, *ibid*, p. 107.)

It becomes boring to read this same verse yet again, although with more variations of spelling in other versions than perceived by Watney. What is fascinating is what the connection might have been between (1) Sir William Gostwick, married to Jane Owen; (2) **Sir Edward Stanley Jr**; and (3) Shakespeare. Research awaits, but a few clues are there already.

Watney continues:

The Gostwicks were an old gentry family which rose to prominence under Henry VIII and had no obvious close connection with the Stanleys beyond possible interactions at court. Sir William was made a baronet by James I in 1611. His mother Elizabeth came from the Catholic Petre family of Ingatesone in Essex, where the parish church contains an important sequence of family monuments by Cornelius Cure and his workshop, including the magnificent tomb of her father Sir William Petre (d. 1572) who had been Secretary of State to Henry VIII and a Privy Councillor to both him and to his three succeeding children. Such marriages across the religious divide were, however, hardly uncommon, and there seems to be no suggestion that the Gostwick family, unlike the Stanleys, was not Protestant.**(2)**

(2) See C. Isherwood, 'Willington Church, Bedfordshire', The Home Counties Magazine, 7 (1907), pp. 225-32.

(Watney, *ibid*, p. 108.)

As stated by Watney, there is no obvious connection between the Gostwicks and the Stanleys, but there is the Essex connection with Stanleys in Walthamstow; also the de Petre family of Essex in the form of Sir William's wife, who inherited through marriage the family properties of Walmesley of Dunkenhalgh, Lancashire. Sir Thomas Walmesley was a Justice of the Common Pleas and in this capacity travelled all over England. He was another Elizabethan Lancashire 'local boy made good'. He is the only one reported in Lancashire literature (perceived so far) with a poetic epitaph written during Shakespeare's lifetime, which appeared on his magnificent tomb in Blackburn (long since disappeared). There is not even the vaguest hint that this might have been written by Shakespeare, but we (think we) know that **Sir Edward Stanley Jr**'s epitaphs were written by Shakespeare around 1603, and we know that **Sir Edward Stanley Sr** and **Jr** and Sir Thomas Walmesley were together at Preston Guild in August 1582 and 1602 (Abram, *Preston Guild Rolls*). Could 'epitaphs and tombs' have been a topic of conversation between them on the second occasion?

Sir Thomas Walmesley, Knt., rebuilt the halls of Dunkenhalgh and Hacking – the latter in 1607. Sir Thomas died, aged 75, on the 26th Nov., 1612, and was buried in the south chapel of Blackburn Church, where an elaborate monument in alabaster was erected to him, destroyed during the Civil War, about 1642-4.

Lansdowne MS. 973, in the British Museum Library, contains a copy of Judge Walmesley's epitaph from the monument, which records that he was a Judge of the Common Pleas from the 31st Eliz., a space of 25 years, "during which time he went all the circuits of England, except that of Norfolk and Suffolk." The tomb also had inscribed upon it the elegy, the first and last lines of which are subjoined:

> Tombs have their periods, monuments decay,
> And age and rust wear epitaphs away:
> But neither rust, nor age, nor time shall wear
> Judge Walmesley's name, that lies entombed here,
> Who never did, for favour or for awe
> Of great men's frowns, quit or forsake the law.
>
> For when as old age, creeping on apace,
> Made him unable to supply his place,
> Yet he continued, by the King's permission,
> A judge until his death, still in commission;
> And still received, by his special grace,
> His fee, as full as when he served the place.

(Abram, *History of Blackburn*, 1877, p. 434.)

There is a brief article on Sir Thomas Walmesley, repeating some of the details above and giving others, on <cottontown.org>, devoted to the history of Blackburn and area. This also includes photographs of his two halls in Lancashire, Hacking Hall and Dunkenhalgh Hall (as they appear today) and the counterpart tomb of Anne, Duchess of Somerset (died 1587), in Westminster Abbey, complete with pyramids/obelisks as on the tomb at Tong. (Article and photographs by Gordon Hartley.)

> The statement about it being an exact counterpart I first found in a very early newspaper report about Judge Walmesley & have seen the same statement in more than one published book. If you read the book (*Rishton Parish Church and School*) by Carlton Noble page 60 you will see reference to it there.
>
> (Gordon Hartley, private communication.)

Maybe other details about the connection will be discovered in future? The following details do seem to present some interesting coincidences. Edward Seymour, 1st Duke of Somerset, was the one who built Somerset House in London, uncle of Edward VI, for whom he was Lord Protector, but executed in 1552. Edward and Anne were great-grandparents of William Seymour, who married Ar(a)bella Stuart (1575–1615), another claimant to Elizabeth's throne, whose rather unusual name Arbella was shared by one of **Sir Edward Jr**'s daughters. Ar(a)bella Stuart was brought up by her grandmother Bess of Hardwick, Countess of Shrewsbury, guardian at Chatsworth House in 1570 of Mary, Queen of Scots, from where **Sir Thomas** and **Sir Edward Sr** planned to rescue her (see Chapter XIII. 1570: Mary, Queen of Scots). Lady Joan Percy, Lucy's elder sister, was married to Lord Henry Seymour (1540–?), younger son of Edward Seymour, 1st Duke of Somerset and his wife Anne Stanhope. The latter 'died on 16 April 1587 and was buried in Westminster Abbey, London, where her tomb with its painted effigy can be viewed. Her memorial is in St. Peter and St. Paul's Church, Shelford [Nottinghamshire]'. (*Wikipedia*, biography, where an image of her tomb in Westminster Abbey can be seen.)

X-10. Sir Robert Stanley's tomb in Chelsea

Watney also reports on another tomb, this time with the relationship of the Stanleys involved well established from Lancashire history. Sir Robert Stanley, with a tomb in Chelsea, was born 9 February 1610, the younger surviving son of William, 6th Earl of Derby (**Sir Edward Jr**'s first cousin) and his wife Elizabeth née de Vere. Sir Robert married a daughter of Lord Witherington, had two children and he and both children died young, Sir Robert on 3 January 1622/3, i.e. 1623 new calendar, Sir Robert therefore aged just under twenty-three. We might remember that his father William has been proposed as a Shakespeare Alternative Authorship Candidate and that his mother Elizabeth was the daughter of another Candidate. His elder brother James, 7th of Derby, later fought for the Royalist cause and was wounded at the Battle of Wigan Lane in 1651, along with Lord Witherington (son of the one mentioned above?). These facts serve to implement Watney's details. Watney still expresses doubts about the authenticity of the Shakespeare epitaphs in Tong. Sir William Dugdale had none; Malone had none; Mrs Esdaile had none; Dr Jeffery has none; I have none. I do, however, share Watney's doubts about the origin of the epitaphs in Chelsea.

> It is, of course, possible that Shakespeare composed the verses at Tong for the cousin of his sometime patron Ferdinand, 5th Earl of Derby, and that one of these was duplicated at Willington. Yet the attribution to Shakespeare remains highly uncertain, not least because of the survival of a poem of two verses on another Stanley family monument at All Saints, Chelsea, which is also in several respects 'Shakespearean' in its imagery, though written some time after Shakespeare's death in 1616. Unconvincingly attributed to Edward Marshall by Esdaile, the remarkable monument at Chelsea commemorates Sir Robert Stanley (d. 1632) and his two children Ferdinando and Henrietta Maria. Like the second verse at Tong, its epitaph playfully puns on the Stanley name. The imagery of eagles derives directly from the family crest:
>
> *To say a Stanley lyes here that alone / Were Epitaph enough Noe Brass Noe Stone / No Glorious Tombe No Monumentall Hearse / Noe gilded Trophy or lamp labourd verse / Can dignify this grave or sett it forth / Like the Imortall fame of his own Worth / Then read fixe not here but quitt this Roome / And flye to Abram's bossome thers his Tombe / There rests his Soule & for his other parts / They are imbalm'd and lodg'd in good men's harts / A braver monument of Stone or Lyme / No Arte can rayse for this shall out last tympe. / To ye Lastinge Memories Of Two Of His Children / That is to say Fardinando Stanley His Sonne & / Henrite Maria Stanley His Daughter Who Lye / Buryed Within This Sepulcher.*
>
> This is followed by a second poem:
>
> *The Eagle Death greedie of some good prey / With nimble Eyes found where these infants laye / He truste them in his Tallents and conveyed / There Soules to Heaven & here their ashes layde / Lett no prophane Hand then these Reliques sever / But as they lye so lett them rest for ever.*
>
> It is not difficult to understand why early readers were tempted to attribute the verses at Tong to Shakespeare, given their close relation to the general imagery of monuments, death and resurrection which he employed so frequently throughout his career, and in particular the striking resemblances between the inscription at Tong and his Sonnet 55. Yet the poetic trope of the vulnerability of monuments was hardly exclusive to Shakespeare, however intensely and imaginatively he may have explored it, above all in his Sonnets.[1] Analogies between the decomposition of the body and the decay of monuments are frequently found in contemporary epitaphs. Indeed, given the raw physical evidence of recently vandalized and desecrated tombs in churches all around the country in this period, it is not surprising to find a widespread sceptical awareness in early-seventeenth-century epitaphs of the vulnerability of monuments, and a corresponding 'Shakespearean' sense of the greater potential durability of the written word.
>
> **[1]** There are also clear echoes of Sonnet 55 in the epitaph at Chelsea.

(Watney, *ibid*, pp. 108-9.)

Sir Robert Stanley did his best for posterity and establishing his ancestry by naming his son after his famous uncle Ferdinando, patron of Shakespeare, and his daughter after Henrietta Maria, the wife of Charles I, who (later) stayed for a couple of days with Susannah, Shakespeare's daughter, at New Place, Stratford, during the Civil War. Sir Robert lived his rather short life in the shadow of his father William, 6th Earl of Derby, a playwright in London at the same time as Shakespeare, and his elder brother James, later 7th Earl of Derby, who, along with his wife, Charlotte de Trémouille, performed in Jonson's Masques at court. One might assume that Sir Robert knew **Sir Edward Jr**, as their fathers were first cousins, their paternal grandfathers being brothers.

One final epitaph deserves a place here, written by John Milton for Shakespeare, given that it mentions 'a star-ypointing pyramid'. Whether it was inspired by the epitaph at Tong is not known; it seems significant, however, that no pyramid or obelisk appears on any version of Shakespeare's tomb at Stratford.

On *Shakespear*.

> WHAT needs my *Shakespear* for his honour'd Bones,
> The labour of an age in piled Stones,
> Or that his hallow'd reliques should be hid
> Under a Star-y pointing *Pyramid*?
> Dear son of memory, great heir of Fame,
> What need'st thou such weak witnes of thy name?
> Thou in our wonder and astonishment
> Hast built thy self a live-long Monument.
> For whilst to th'shame of slow-endeavouring art,
> Thy easie numbers flow, and that each heart
> Hath from the leaves of thy unvalu'd Book,
> Those Delphick lines with deep impression took,
> Then thou our fancy of it self bereaving,
> Dost make us Marble with too much conceaving;
> And so Sepulcher'd in such pomp dost lie,
> That Kings for such a Tomb would wish to die.

Notes: On *Shakespear*. *Reprinted 1632 in the second folio Shakespeare*: Title: An epitaph on the admirable dramaticke poet W. Shakespeare
Beeching, Revd H. C., ed. *The Poetical Works of John Milton*.
Oxford: Clarendon Press, 1900. 18.

www.luminarium.org/sevenlit/**milton**

N.B. Compare this rendition with the same poem on page 26. Rarely does one find two identical transcriptions of any poem of the sixteenth and seventeenth centuries.

~~~~~~~~~~~~~~~~

Chapter XI
Main Derby historians re Sir Thomas and Sir Edward Sr & Jr

XI-1. Introduction

Much research has been undertaken and many books published on the Earls of Derby by historians in Lancashire. Most publications in the late twentieth century (including Coward, 1983 and Bagley, 1985, both quoted from below rather extensively) give family trees, which more or less agree with each other, certainly on the Earls of Derby themselves. There are meanwhile biographies of all Earls of Derby in main recent encyclopedias and online, including all down to the current 19th Earl at Knowsley Hall, Merseyside. In this book our interest stops with the beheading of James, 7th Earl in 1651.

The side branches of the Stanley family present a different story. Bagley gives family trees of some of the main branches, but mainly those of immediate relevance to the Earls of Derby. The most ambitious project in the twenty-first century is The Stanley Genealogy Website run by Brian S. Roberts (S = Stanley, which explains his interest, and he is from Liverpool), the main aim of which is to include as many documented details as possible of all cadet branches and any record of any Stanley in any document, mainly for genealogical, but also for historical reasons. This was the result of a successful attempt to establish his own documented Stanley ancestry back to 1590 and a further attempt to link up to earlier branches. I am sure that all who have ever been interested in the Stanleys wish him good luck and fortitude in this project.

A previous attempt was by Peter Edmund Stanley, *The House of Stanley from the 12th century* (Pentland Press, 1998), the result of a lifetime of research, but unfortunately without any references. I do sympathise with him for not recording the source of every documented detail, but ultimately nothing will be accepted without precise references. It seems that investigations into the Stanley story will continue for many years and not a few people, whether academic or amateur historians of the period or people seeking their own ancestry, will contribute to this story.

XIa. Shields used by the 1st & 2nd Earls of Derby

Here, however and in this chapter, we concentrate on the main Derby line, as contributed by Derby historians and researchers in the eighteenth to twenty-first centuries. The Family Trees in Appendix 12 will be of use to the reader in sorting out many of the relationships.

XI-2. Stanley-Shakespeare connections

The following table might be helpful for the reader to explain how **Sir Thomas** and **Sir Edward Sr** fitted into their family history of a direct descent from the Earls of Derby, particularly those involved in plots and with Shakespeare connections. This is simplistic, and produced purely for the aims of this book; all details are ascertainable from documents; all below had the surname Stanley. A brief reminder of the origin of the title Earl of Derby is that all below were of the third creation, a title that had reverted to the crown, but was conveniently available as a reward for Lord Thomas, created 1st Earl by Henry VII after the Battle of Bosworth. Conveniently his main seats were in the hundred of West Derby in south-west Lancashire.

The title Lord Strange for the eldest son came to the family when Sir George, eldest son of Thomas, 1st Earl, married the heiress of Strange of Knockin, Shropshire.

		Dates of life & as Earl	Shakespeare connections	Plots, etc.
1st	Lord Thomas 2nd Baron Stanley	c. 1435-1504 Earl 1485>	Appears in *Richard III*; puts the crown on Henry VII after the Battle of Bosworth.	Main problem at Bosworth in deciding whether to support Richard III or Henry VII. He finally opted for his stepson Henry Tudor, son of his second wife Lady Margaret Beaufort.
	Sir George, eldest son of Thomas; 1st Lord Strange	c. 1460-1503 Never Earl; died before his father.	Has an off-stage role in *Richard III* as a hostage.	Died of suspected poisoning in London; why and by whom not known.
2nd	Thomas, eldest son of Sir George.	c. 1484-1521 Earl 1503>		
3rd	Edward, eldest son of Thomas, 2nd Earl.	1508/9-1572 Earl 1521>	His second son **Sir Thomas** and his grandson **Sir Edward Jr** have epitaphs by Shakespeare on their tomb in Tong.	Son **Sir Thomas** planned to rescue Mary, Queen of Scots from Chatsworth in 1570; ended up in the Tower of London, was tortured. Died aged c.42. His brother **Sir Edward Sr** was also involved and imprisoned.
4th	Henry, eldest son of Edward, 3rd Earl	1531-1593 Earl 1572>	Patron of Derby's Players, perhaps including young Shakespeare, before his son took over.	His marriage to Margaret Clifford, with her ancestry, put his sons in line of succession to the Tudor throne.
5th	Ferdinando, eldest son of Henry, 4th Earl	1568/9-94 Earl 1593>	Patron of Strange's Players, who performed Shakespeare's early plays.	Died by poisoning, aged c.35. A result of the proposal of the Catholic 'Hesketh plot' to put him on the throne as Elizabeth's successor.
6th	William, second son of Henry, 4th Earl.	1561-1642 Earl 1594>	Playwright in London in 1599. Proposed as an Alternative Shakespeare Authorship Candidate.	His marriage to Elizabeth de Vere, daughter of Edward, 17th Earl of Oxford, brings the latter as another Shakespeare Alternative Candidate into the family.
7th	James, eldest son of William, 6th Earl	1607-1651 Earl 1642>	Brother Sir Robert (d. 1632) has a Shakespearean epitaph on his tomb in Chelsea.	James supported Charles I & II during the Civil War. Beheaded in Bolton in 1651.

XI-3. John Seacome (1741)

The first serious attempt at a rather pious history of the Stanleys, Earls of Derby, was by John Seacome, Steward to the Earl of Derby, who had ready access to all papers remaining in the family. He published this as *Memoirs: containing a genealogical and historical account of the ancient and honourable house of Stanley; from the Conquest to the death of James late Earl of Derby, in the year 1735; as also a full description of the Isle of Man, etc.* (Liverpool, 1741). There were many updates and reprints during the following century and it remained the standard work. Other attempts during the eighteenth to early twentieth centuries at an account of the Earls of Derby relied heavily on Seacome. The main (although very brief) mention of **Sir Thomas** and **Sir Edward Sr** (without any mention of Tong) was in Seacome's account of Edward, 3rd Earl, their father, which is reproduced below in full.

Devoted as he was to the service of the Earl, we can forgive him for being over-pious and uncritical on occasion. Even having taken this into account, one must be critical of some of his interpretations and even his recounting of some events. To understand this, one must be aware of several circumstances beyond his control:

a) His was the first ever attempt at a 'full' history. He had no previous account to draw on, to complete and update. For many generations and events, he was 'starting from scratch' from unpublished MSS.

b) Although he had the Visitation Pedigrees and was fully aware of the repetition of so many names over the generations, he did not have the family papers of various side branches and thus on occasion confused various contemporaries with the same name.

c) Many of the family papers had gone up in flames during and after the second siege of Lathom House at the end of the Civil War, after which it was razed to the ground.

d) He had no access to State Papers in London.

e) Seacome's employer Lord James, 10th Earl until 1736, was the last direct male descendant in a long line and no doubt the recipient of many family traditions which needed to be built into the story (or rejected as non-historical). He was succeeded by a Stanley from a side-branch and a newcomer to the line of the Earls at Lathom House and Knowsley Hall, and so had not necessarily grown up hearing all the stories repeated at Lathom House. When Seacome was preparing his history, he was thus on occasion unable to call on the perhaps more reliable story handed down to James, 10th Earl.

Despite these limitations, Seacome performed a magnificent job, and his remained the standard version for nearly two and a half centuries. Not until the later twentieth century were some details challenged, first and foremost by Barry Coward, for his PhD thesis, which was adapted for publication by the Chetham Society and appeared in 1983 (see below).

We start on p .121 of an edition of Seacome of 1793, the one on my shelves. I took the precaution of checking this against an earlier edition in the Earl of Derby's library at Knowsley, which confirmed that the text was identical. All text in plain script and round brackets is by Seacome. Any additions by me are in italics in square brackets. I have occasionally included [*sic*] to indicate that this was either Seacome's or the printer's spelling. In bold are **Sir Thomas**, **Sir Edward Sr** and **Edward Jr**, plus those who are given in Chapter XXIII. Immediate ancestors and close relatives of Sir Thomas & Sir Edward and Chapter XXIV. Sir Edward's cousins and in-laws with Shakespeare connections. The relationship to **Sir Thomas** is given in square brackets and italics.

> Let us return to **Edward**, the younger son of **Thomas**, the second Earl of Derby, whom his father had supposed he had left under the care and ward of the most hopeful and promising trustees, being no less than nine ecclesiastics, and four lay-gentlemen, by which he judged sufficient security was provided for his son's right and the preservation of the immense estate he had left him. [Edward, 3rd Earl, was **Sir Thomas**'s father.]
>
> But such is the pride, avarice and depravity of human nature, that the greatest cautions

mankind can possibly take, oftentimes prove too slender to procure justice and equity when private interest and advantage compete.

And if he should refuse, his Supremacy in England would be in great danger: and that they could make no other construction of it, but that they were left to seek their remedy elsewhere.

And in the twenty-fourth of Henry VIII on the insurrection of the northern men, called the Pilgrimage of Grace, the King directed his letters to this Earl, to raise what forces he could, promising therein to repay all his charges; [*A muster roll of this army of 7000+ from Lancashire and Cheshire has survived and is reproduced in Coward, 1983.* HM] and, as Mr. Hollingshead observes, by the faithful diligence of the Earl of Derby, with the forces of Lancashire and Cheshire, they were kept back and brought to peace and quiet, though they were a very great number out of Cumberland, Westmoreland, and the north parts of Lancashire. [*'Mr. Hollingshead', from Cheshire, was one of the main historians in the sixteenth century, on whose works Shakespeare drew for his history plays.* HM]

The thirty-third year of that King he marched into Scotland with the Duke of Norfolk [*Earl Edward's father-in-law*], with an army of twenty thousand men, where meeting with little or no resistance, they burned several towns and villages, and so returned to England.

And in the thirty-eighth of that King, when the High Admiral of France, accompanied by the Bishop of Eureaux, the Earl of Nantville, the Earl of Villars, and others, came on a splendid embassy to England, the Earl of Derby, by the King's command, received them at Blackwall, and conducted them to his Majesty at Greenwich. And on the death of King Henry, and the accession of Prince Edward his son, by the title of King Edward VI, the Earl of Derby, and the Marquis of Dorset (afterwards Duke of Suffolk) were on the twenty-second of May 1547, elected Knights of the most nobly [*sic*] Order of the Garter. And in the fourth of King Edward VI the Earl of Derby was one of the Peers' party to the articles of peace, made by King Edward, with the Scots and French, wherein the Emperor was also included. And,

In the sixth of this King, he made an exchange with his Majesty of his house called Derby-house, on St Bennet's-hill, near Doctors-commons, London, built by Thomas, the first Earl of Derby, for certain lands adjoining to his park, at Knowsley, in the county of Lancaster, of which he was Lieutenant during this King's reign.

After the above exchange, he purchased a piece of land, in Channon-row, near Westminster, and thereon erected a new house, and called it Derby-house, which being since sold by William, Earl of Derby, elder brother to the late Earl James, is built into a court called Derby-court; and upon the death of King Edward, and Queen Mary's Accession to the throne, he was in the first year of that Queen, appointed (Sept. 29, 1553) by her, Lord High-Steward of England. From the day of her Majesty's coronation, which was performed on the fifth of October that year, with great solemnity. And upon advice of her Majesty's appointment, he set out from his seat of Latham, in the county of Lancaster, to wait on her Majesty, the eighteenth of August, most nobly attended; having upwards of eighty Esquires, all clad in velvet, and two hundred and eighteen Servants in liveries, with whom he arrived at his new house, in Channon-row, Westminster, in the greatest pomp and magnificence.

In the year 1557, he received orders from the Queen and council, to muster what forces he could raise to march against the Scots, then assisted by the French King, which he readily complied with; and was one of the noblemen that attended Philip, Prince of Spain, on his landing into England, to be married to Queen Mary, who before her marriage gave the house on St. Bennet's Hill, London, called Derby-house, and now in the crown, by virtue of the above exchange, to Gilbert Dethick, the then garter and principal king of arms: Thomas Hauley, clarenceiux, king of arms of the fourth parts; William Harvey, alias Norroy, king of arms of the north parts; and the other heralds and pursuivants of arms, and to their successors, all the capital messuage or house, called Derby-house, with the appurtenances, situate in the parish of St. Bennet and St. Peter, then being in the tenure of Sir Richard Sackville, Knight, and parcel of the lands of Edward, Earl of Derby; to the end, that the said kings, heralds and pursuivants of arms, and their successors, might dwell together, and meet, confer and agree among themselves, for the good government of their faculty. And that their records might be more safely kept, &c. dated the eighteenth of July, in the third year of Philip and Mary, 1555. [*This was the new home of the College of Arms.*]

Upon the above Queen Mary's death, and Queen Elizabeth's accession to the throne, although she knew the Earl of Derby, to have been one of the late Queen's Privy-council, yet she was so well apprized and satisfied of his justice, prudence and loyalty, that she appointed him one of her Privy-council; and in the first year of her reign, gave him, and others of that body, commission to take particular care that all persons enjoying any office or place of trust under her Majesty, should take the Oaths of Supremacy.

Likewise in the said first year of that gracious Queen, he had granted to him by patent, the high office of Chamberlain of Chester, for six years; and the next year was made one of her Majesty's most honourable Privy-council.

But at this time being aged, weak and infirm, he retired to his seat of Latham, and there gave up his life to the Almighty, Author of his being; and with humble resignation, submitted himself to his Divine will.

By his will, bearing date the twenty fourth of August, 1572, he bequeathed his body to be buried in the parish church of Ormskirk, Lancashire; and ordered, that a chapel should be there erected, and a tomb prepared for that purpose, agreeable to his dignity, which hath ever since been the common repository of his family and successors; the ancient monastery of Burscough, where his ancestors were laid, being totally demolished in the dissolution of abbeys and monastrys; and departing this life, on Friday the twenty-fourth of October next following, his body lay in state to the fourth of December after; during which time, all necessary preparations were made for his noble funeral, which will be related hereafter.

In which interval, give me leave to relate his marriages and issue, with his sumptuous and hospitable manner of living, which exceeded most, if not all, the noblemen in England at that time, and even since.

This noble Earl married three wives [*actually, four – Seacome did not know about his first wife, Katherine, niece of his second wife – see below, Bagley.*]: first [*second*], **Dorothy** [*T's mother*], one of the daughters of **Thomas Howard, Duke of Norfolk** [*T's maternal grandfather*], by whom he had issue three sons and four daughters, viz. **Henry**, his first son [*T's brother*]; **Thomas**, his second son [*'our' (Sir) Thomas*], and **Edward** his third son [*T's brother*], of all which in their order. [*These were the sons who subsequently became Henry, 4th Earl, Sir Thomas of Winwick and Tong and Sir Edward Sr.*]

Ann, his first daughter [*T's sister*], married **Charles, Lord Stourton** [*T's brother-in-law*], and he dying, she married **Sir John Arundel** [*T's brother-in-law*], of Lamborn, in the county of Cornwall. **Elizabeth**, his second daughter [*T's sister*], married **Henry, Lord Morley** [*T's brother-in-law*]. Mary, his third daughter [*T's sister*], Lord Stafford [*T's brother-in-law*]; and **Jane**, his fourth daughter [*T's sister*], **Edward, Lord Dudley**. [*These were, of course, sisters of Sir Thomas and Sir Edward, and their husbands were their in-laws; they were all, of course, aunts and uncles of Sir Edward Jr.*]

To his second [*third*] wife he married **Margaret** [*T's step-mother*], the daughter of Ellis Barlow, of Barlow, in the county of Lancaster, esq., and by her had issue one son and two daughters; George [*T's half-brother*], who died young and unmarried; **Margaret** his eldest daughter [*T's half-sister*], married **John Jermon** [*Jermyn/Jermin*], of Ruthbrook, in the county of Suffolk, Esq. [*T's brother-in-law*] and after his decease, **Sir Nich. Ponitz** [*Pointz*] [*T's brother-in-law*]; and **Catharine**, the youngest [*T's half sister*], to **Sir John Knivet** [*T's brother-in-law*].

To his third [*fourth*] wife he married Mary, the daughter of Sir George Cotton, of Combermere, in the county of Chester, by whom he had no issue. After his disease [*sic, decease*], Mary [*T's step-mother*], his widow, married **Henry, Earl of Kent**. [*T's step-father.*]

[Earl Henry, 4th Earl of Derby, and his brothers and sons]

Henry, his eldest son, succeeded him in honour and estate, of whom more hereafter. **Sir Thomas Stanley, his second son**, married **Margaret, one of the daughters and coheirs of Sir George Vernon, of Hadden**, in the county of Derby, by whom he had issue **a son, named Edward**, on which occasion he made the following settlement by deed, bearing date the fourth of Elizabeth [*1562/3*]; wherein it is declared, That the several manors and lands lying in the counties of Warwick, Devon and Oxford; also Dunham-massey, Bowden, Rungey, Hale, Aeton and

Darfield, in the county of Chester, now the estate of him the said Edward, Earl of Derby, shall appertain and belong to **Sir Thomas Stanley**, his said second son, for life [*Sir Thomas had been knighted in 1553 by Queen Mary*].

Remainder as a moiety to **Lady Margaret**, his wife, for life; remainder of all to the said **Edward Stanley, their son**, for life; remainder in fale-male [*sic*, fail-male] to **Henry**, the first son of him the said Earl; remainder to the heirs male of the said **Sir Thomas Stanley**, and remainder to the heirs male of the said **Edward Stanley, son of the said Sir Thomas**, and **dame Margaret**, his lady.

This **Edward Stanley**, the son, became (after the death of his father) **Sir Edward Stanley, of Ensham** [*Eynsham, actually Tong first, but Seacome apparently never knew this*], in the county of Oxford, and possessor of all the said manors and lands, by virtue of the said settlement; of whom more hereafter in due place.

But first proceed to Edward Stanley, the third son of the said Earl. He was a gentleman of the army in the service of Queen Elizabeth, under the command of the brave Earl of Leicester, in Holland; where at the siege of Zulphen [Zutphen], he acquired great reputation by a most uncommon action of valour and undaunted courage. In the attack of a fort of the said town, a Spaniard brandishing his lance at him, he caught hold of it, and held so fast, that he was drawn up by it into the fort; at which the garrison was so intimidated (supposing all the enemy were following him) that they fled, and left the fort to him; for which hardy and valiant action, the Earl of Leicester knighted him, and gave him forty pounds in hand, and a yearly pension of one hundred marks, payable in England, during his life. [*An eye-witness account of this action by the Earl of Leicester is given in full in Chapter XXII. Other (Sir) Edward Stanleys. It is highly doubtful - in fact well nigh impossible - that the Edward Stanley at Zutphen was one and the same as **Sir Edward Sr**, third son of Edward, 3rd Earl. It is interesting, however, that this Stanley story was well known in other branches of the family.*]

But so it is (as observed by the learned) that

> "The fortunate have whole years,
> And those they choose;
> But the unfortunate have only days,
> And those they lose."

For who could imagine that so gallant a man, and so well rewarded as he was, could forget his duty to his Sovereign, and take up arms against her in favour of Spain, whither he was obliged to fly, and die in exile and disgrace, either not knowing or forgetting the Spanish proverb, which they verified him by flight and contempt; "That they love the treason, but hate the traitor."

[*Seacome has confused two Edward Stanleys again. This other Edward appears in Chapter XXII. Other (Sir) Edward Stanleys.*]

This is followed by a lengthy description of the funeral, given in full in Chapter XIV. 1572: Earl Edward's funeral.

~~~~~~~~~~~~~~~~

XI-4. 19th to mid-20th centuries

As mentioned above, there were many new editions of Seacome throughout the eighteenth and nineteenth centuries, bringing the story up to date. Draper published *The House of Stanley* in 1894. Farrer (ed.) presented a solidly documented history of the various Stanley branches in Lancashire in the *Victoria County History of Lancashire* at the beginning of the twentieth century (now online courtesy of British History Online), but it was inevitably brief on each branch, because he was covering the whole of the county from the very earliest records. There is so little on **Sir Thomas** and **Sir Edward Sr** and **Jr** that it is not worth reproducing here. One had to wait until the 1980s until two scholars took on the task.

~~~~~~~~~~~~~~~~

XI-5. Barry Coward (1983)

(Later Professor) Barry Coward (from Lancashire) was the first to publish a scholarly history of the early Earls of Derby, as a revised version of his PhD thesis: *The Stanleys: Lords Stanley and Earls of Derby 1385-1672: The origins, wealth and power of a landowning family* (Chetham Society, 3rd Series, 1983). This set out to examine exactly what the title says, and was inevitably concerned more with the Earls of Derby themselves, rather than any younger brothers and nephews who disappeared off to other places. The following extracts from Coward are the only ones mentioning **Sir Thomas** and **Sir Edward Jr** of Tong, and **Sir Edward Sr**. Coward's references are given at the end of each of his chapters, therefore on different pages from the text quoted. Kind permission to reproduce these sections came from Professor Coward himself and from the current Head of Chetham's Library, Manchester, Dr Michael Powell, on behalf of the Chetham Society.

Chapter 9, THE STANLEY CONNECTION: THE TOWNS

Liverpool, like Chester, was allowed to send two representatives to the first parliament of Edward VI's reign for the first time since 1307. No record of the 1547 election survives, apart from the names of the men elected, Francis Cave and Thomas Stanley. But this is enough information to suggest the influences at work in the election. Cave was the younger brother of Sir Ambrose Cave, who represented Leicester in the same parliament and who was afterwards chancellor of the duchy of Lancaster (1558-68). **Stanley** was the second son of Edward, the third earl of Derby, who had probably agreed to share the nomination of the Liverpool members with the chancellor of the duchy.[5]

[5] *Return of Members of Parliament, J. A. Twenlow, ed., Liverpool Town Book: Proceedings of Assemblies, Common Councils, Portmoot Courts, etc., 1550-1862* (Liverpool, 1918), p. 375.

(Coward, p. 128.)

Rewarding as it would be to be able to add this to **Sir Thomas**'s *curriculum vitae*, it cannot have been him. He was born c.1534, so in 1547 was aged only about thirteen, hardly old enough to have been an MP. The Thomas Stanley who was MP for Liverpool in 1547 remains unidentified (although there are several contemporary candidates, because every son and grandson of Thomas, 1st Earl of Derby, named a son after him). It is easy to see why Coward might have assigned this role to him, because in 1568-9 'Sir Thomas Stanley, second son of Earl Edward' was the Mayor of Liverpool (Coward, p. 131). This would go a long way towards explaining why **Sir Thomas** did not move to Tong Castle in 1565, when he inherited this via his wife, Margaret Vernon, on the death of her father. One might assume that he had held other offices in Lancashire, or at least made his presence felt there politically, during the years leading up to his election as Mayor of Liverpool in 1568, and these duties would have required his presence in Lancashire. One might also extrapolate, because of his move to Tong in c.1574/5, that he did not intend to run for further office in Lancashire. One reason for the move away from Lancashire was presumably because he had just spent two (or three+?) years (1570-2/3/4) in the Tower of London after his participation in the attempt to free Mary, Queen of Scots from Chatsworth, had been tortured on the rack (Brian S. Roberts, Stanley Family Genealogy Website) and subsequently been fined heavily. A move away would at least have distanced him from his brother Henry, now 4th Earl of Derby, who was anxious to profess his total loyalty to Elizabeth. The continued presence in Lancashire of a brother with a recent history that threw this into doubt might have embarrassed him.

Coward also noted (p. 131) the presence at Preston Guild in 1582 and 1602 of **Edward**, the son of **Sir Thomas**, although he might have confused him with **Sir Edward Sr**, the brother. This is explored in more detail in Chapter XV. 1562, 1582, 1602: **Sir Thomas** and **Sir Edward** at Preston Guild.

More is given about the plot to free Mary, Queen of Scots from Chatsworth in 1570, and surrounding plots.

Chapter 10, THE STANLEYS AND THE CROWN

On 9 November 1571 John Lee, writing from Antwerp, told Sir William Cecil that Lords Seaton and Dacre were planning to set free the earl of Northumberland and that they counted on the support of the third earl of Derby 'affyrmynge playnely that he hath all redye refused to come uppe to the courte'.[11] It was Earl Edward's advanced age rather than any treasonable intentions that kept him at Lathom, but Cecil discovered that **the earl's youngest sons** were not so innocent. Many of Cecil's informants implicated **Sir Thomas** and **Sir Edward Stanley** in a plot to free Mary Queen of Scots from Chatsworth in 1570 and take her to the Isle of Man. [*A full account is given in Chapter XIII. 1570: Sir Thomas and Sr Edward Sr and Mary Queen of Scots.*] In November **the brothers** were ordered to go to court and by July 1571 Cecil had unravelled every detail of their part in the scheme. **Sir Thomas** played the principal role and in May 1572 he was still in the Tower along with the Bishop of Ross, the earl of Southampton, Lord Lumley and Thomas, the brother of Lord Cobham; all were suspected of being involved with the duke of Norfolk, who was executed in June.[12] Cecil also learned that both Norfolk and Ridolfi hoped that Earl Edward would support a Spanish invasion. In these circumstances Earl Edward inevitably came under suspicion, and the ever-careful Cecil instigated enquiries as to the earl's soundness in religion.[13] Although there is no evidence of the earl's sympathy for Norfolk, Ridolfi or **his own sons**, it was only his death in 1572 that ended the hopes of conspirators that he would raise Lancashire and Cheshire against the crown.

[11] P.R.O., SP 15/20/91.

[12] *H.M.C. Salisbury*, i, 509-10, examination of Francis Rolleston, 20 July, 1571; *C.S.P. Spain 1568-79*, p. 274; Williams, *Fourth Duke of Norfolk*, p. 209; A.P.C., vii, 398-9, privy council to the earl of Derby, 12 November 1570; *C.S.P. Spain 1568-79*, p. 393.

[13] *H.M.C. Salisbury*, i, Burghley to Sir Thomas Smith, 18 July 1571; *C.S.P. Rome 1572-78*, nos. 346, 698, 762.

(Coward, p. 145.)

The plan involving **Sir Thomas** rescuing Mary from Chatsworth was in May 1570. He was sent to the Tower towards the end of the year and he was still there in May 1572; also possibly/probably still there beyond the execution of the Duke of Norfolk. The date of his release has not been established, but he did not attend the funeral of his father, Earl Edward, on 4 December 1572, with the implication that he was still in the Tower. Although **Sir Thomas** is named above as playing 'the principal role', this was only as the principal of the two brothers; the main principal role among Lancashire knights was actually played by Sir Thomas Gerard of Bryn near Wigan, who was also imprisoned (for three years) and paid a hefty fine for his release. Other information about **Sir Thomas Stanley**:

> The men who worked with the lieutenants as special commissioners of muster were also chosen from the leading gentry. In 1569 the Cheshire commissioners were Sir Hugh Cholmondley, Sir John Savage, Sir Edward Fitton and Sir Lawrence Smythe. The Lancashire commissioners were Earl Edward, Lord Monteagle, **Sir Thomas Stanley**, Sir George Stanley, Sir John Atherton, Edward Holland and Edmund Ashton. The 1570 commissioners for Cheshire were Sir Hugh Cholmondley, Sir John Savage, Sir Lawrence Smythe, Sir Rowland Stanley of Hooton, Sir George Calveley, Sir Richard Bulkeley, Sir Edward Fitton, Thomas Stanley of Weaver and William Brereton. The Lancashire commissioners included Lord Monteagle, Sir Piers Leigh, Sir Richard Shireburn, Sir Thomas Hesketh, Sir John Radcliffe, Sir Edmund Trafford and Sir John Byron.[15]

[15] P.R.O., SP 12/238/160, statement of John Snowden to Burghley, 21 May 1591; SP 12/238/163, letter of Thomas Wilson, 22 May 1591; Handover, *the Second Cecil*, p. 108.

(Coward, pp. 154-5.)

These were, indeed, leading gentry, whose names crop up regularly in all Derby literature. Sir John Savage of Rock Savage was a direct descendant of his namesake, who had been in the vanguard of Henry Tudor's army at Bosworth Field. Sir Edward Fitton was of the family of Mary Fitton, maid of honour to Elizabeth and the first candidate in the nineteenth century for the Dark Lady of Shakespeare's Sonnets, although her candidature lapsed long ago. Lord Monteagle was a Stanley of the cadet branch at Hornby Castle near Lancaster, with this title created for an earlier Sir Edward after his victorious role at Flodden Field in 1513. The **Sir Thomas Stanley** in the list must have been the second son of Earl Edward, as he was the only Sir Thomas in the immediate family at the time. Sir George Stanley was of the Stanleys of Bickerstaffe, not far from Lathom. This cadet line inherited the Earldom of Derby in 1736 when James, the 10th Earl, died without a son and heir. Sir Rowland Stanley of Hooton in the Wirral was of the senior line of the Stanleys (knighted on the same day as **Sir Thomas**) and father of Sir William Stanley, who was already acquiring a name as a soldier in the wars in Ireland, and was to depart to the Netherlands in 1585 under Leicester, and desert to the Spanish the following year, surrendering Deventer. Thomas Stanley of Weaver/Weever was the current head of another cadet branch in Cheshire. Sir Piers/Peter Leigh/Legh/Leghe of Lyme was the seventh in line with this name, married to Margaret, daughter of Sir Thomas Gerard of Bryn, who was the leader of the plot in 1570 to free Mary, Queen of Scots. Sir Piers also owned an estate in Winwick almost next door to **Sir Thomas Stanley**. He might have been the 'Alde Legh' in Ben Jonson's eulogy to Venetia Stanley. Sir Richard Shireburne was later Treasurer for many years to Henry, 4th Earl of Derby. Sir Thomas Hesketh was the one who was asked, in Alexander Hoghton's will of 1581, to accept William Shakeshafte (Shakespeare?) into his household.

The most important deductions to be made from these lists concerning **Sir Thomas** are that a) he must have known all these rather well, and b) his appearance as a Lancashire commissioner in 1569 and not in 1570 was presumably connected with his participation in the plot to free Mary mid-1570. The month of appointment of the commissioners has not been ascertained, but if it was between July and November, he was already under suspicion by Cecil of treachery, and if later, he was already in the Tower.

Mentions by Coward of **Sir Edward Sr** and **Edward Jr** are in 1600, in the middle of the long drawn out legal battle between William, 6th Earl of Derby and Countess Alice, widow of his brother Ferdinando, as to the splitting of the Derby estates between the two of them. This list, of lands in reversion, is reproduced here in full, with **Sir Edward Sr** appearing under c) and **Edward Jr** under d).

APPENDIX B[5]

Lands in reversion to the earl

		£	s	d
a)	Hedingham and other estates in the right of Elizabeth countess of Derby	560	0	0
b)	Dower lands of Alice, widow of the fifth earl of Derby			
	Lancashire			
	Weeton	35	11	7
	Treales	62	11	4
	Bretherton	34	11	8 ½
	Liverpool, Toxteth and Smithdown	50	0	0
	Flintshire			
	Hawarden	74	11	11 ½
	Hope and Hopedale	39	7	0 ½
	Mold and Moldsdale	80	0	0
	Hawarden park and demesne	70	0	0
		£446	13	7 ½

continued

APPENDIX B[5] — *(continuation)*

Lands in reversion to the earl

		£	s	d
c)	Lands in reversion after the death of **Sir Edward Stanley**, brother of the fourth earl of Derby. **Thirsk (Yorkshire)** **Kirkby Malzeard (Yorkshire)**	105	1	2
d)	Lands in reversion after the death of **Edward Stanley esq.**, **son of Sir Thomas Stanley**, younger brother of the fourth earl of Derby. **Eynsham (Oxon)**	£600	0	0

[5]P.R.O., SP 12/278/18   *(Coward, p. 206.)*

This is the first clue as to where **Sir Edward Sr** might have been living until 1600 (Thirsk and/or Kirkby Malzeard in Yorkshire), and perhaps with one of these as his main seat until his death in 1604, although we know that he also spent considerable periods of time back at Lathom, visiting his brother Henry, 4ᵗʰ Earl until his death in 1593 and later, as the senior member of the family, with his nephews Ferdinando, 5ᵗʰ Earl and William, 6ᵗʰ Earl. He is also reported as being in Winwick and Eynsham on occasion, with Winwick Rectory leased and Eynsham Abbey owned by his nephew **(Sir) Edward Jr**, so **Sir Edward Sr** might well have spent considerable lengths of time with his nephew and family. He might also, of course, have acquired other lands in the meantime in his own right, but none have emerged in any lists. These 'in reversion' were Derby lands, to revert to the Earldom on his death without a male heir.

The 'reversion' of 'Eynsham (Oxon)' is clear. This was one of the estates in a scattered set of Derby lands in several counties (but none in the core lands in Lancashire) granted in a settlement in 1562/3 (the list of lands and list of reversions is given by Seacome, above). This is covered in detail in Chapter XIX. An excursion to Eynsham, Oxfordshire. One thing revealed by the list above is that the estate in Eynsham was of a considerable, indeed enormous, size, to be assessed at £600.

One final note about **Edward Jr** (from Coward) and the only mention of Tong, comes in another list during the assessment of his cousin Earl William's estates. This was for sales of the latter's estates from 1596 to 1599, where the following appears in the middle. Twenty-one estates, or groups of estates, are listed; this is in eleventh place. The prices range from £40 to £1820, with eleven of the estates, including the following, with no known price and, in this case, no comment. 'Bran Broughton' is a bit of a mystery, encountered in no other list or reference referring to Stanley properties. It was perhaps/presumably Brant Broughton in Lincolnshire. This is also the only reference encountered to Shifford in Oxfordshire, in the parish of Aston, not far from Eynsham.

Date	Estate	Purchaser	Price	Reference
12 March 1597	**Acton, Hurleston, Dorfold, Overmarsh (Ches.) Shifford (Oxon.)**	**Edward Stanley of Tonge Castle** and Bran Broughton	?	P.R.O. C54/1569

(Coward, p. 196.)

It is interesting to compare this with two other lists:

> Of the vast possessions of Sir Edward Stanley, Erdeswick writing circa 1596, speaks of him as "now Lord of Harlaston", and says of Cubleston "Edward Stanley is now owner thereof," and of West Bromwich, "now one of the Stanleys hath the seat of his house there." (Chapter IV. Auden's History.)

At **Edward Jr**'s birth in 1562, his grandfather, the 3rd Earl, made a Deed of Settlement on **Sir Thomas** as follows:

> ...he had issue a son, named **Edward**, on which occasion he made the following settlement by deed, bearing date the fourth of Elizabeth [*1562/3*]; wherein it is declared, That the several manors and lands lying in the counties of Warwick, Devon and Oxford; also Dunham-massey, Bowden, Rungey, Hale, Aeton and Darfield, in the county of Chester, now the estate of him the said Edward, Earl of Derby, shall appertain and belong to **Sir Thomas Stanley**, his said second son, for life.
>
> (Seacome, extract from the account of Earl Edward, above.)

If we add these three lists together we see **Sir Edward Jr** owning lands in the following places at various times between 1596 and 1600:

SHROPSHIRE: Tong Castle (inherited from mother).
CHESHIRE: Harleston (=Hurleston?) (Coward, 1600; Erdeswick, 1596); Acton (=Alton?), Dorfold (=Darfield?), Overmarsh (Coward, 1600); Dunham Massey, Bowden, Rungey Hall, Aeton (= Acton?), Darfield (= Dorfold?), (settlement of 1562/3).
OXFORDSHIRE: Eynsham, Shifford (Coward, 1600).
WARWICKSHIRE: West Bromwich (Erdeswick, 1596). If the Stanley there was indeed **Edward Jr**, but if it was **Sir Edward Sr**, this would perhaps/presumably have come to **Sir Edward Jr** anyway in 1604, if he was his heir. Or this might have been an Edward Stanley from a different branch.
STAFFORDSHIRE: Cubleston (Erdeswick, 1596). (Also belonging to **Sir Edward Sr**?)
DEVON: ??, no individual manors or places detected (settlement of 1562/3).
LINCOLNSHIRE: Brant Broughton.
WALES: ??. The only place in Wales detected is Stackpole (Pembrokeshire) (inherited from mother, sold; see in Chapter XXVIII. Time-line.)
LANCASHIRE: no ownership, just the 99-year lease of Winwick Rectory and glebe (details in Chapter XII. Winwick).

~~~~~~~~~~~~~~~~~

XI-6. J. J. Bagley (1985)

To coincide with the quincentenary of the Battle of Bosworth (which had led to the creation of Lord Thomas Stanley as 1st Earl of Derby), J. J. Bagley of the University of Liverpool published *The Earls of Derby 1485–1985* (Sidgwick and Jackson, London, 1985), a monumental task, which was inevitably brief on younger sons. The following extracts are the only ones of immediate relevance to **Sir Thomas, Sir Edward Jr**, and **Sir Edward Sr**. As with Coward, the most significant omission is of any mention of Tong (with the exception of the single appearance in the list in Coward immediately above). Bagley does, however, present interesting 'new' details, first of all, about Earl Edward, father of **Sir Thomas**, whose mother, Dorothy Howard, was Earl Edward's second wife. (Bagley gives no references but a bibliography for each chapter.)

> Only once in these early days at court did Edward ever appear to displease the King. Late in 1529 he married the daughter of Thomas Howard, third Duke of Norfolk, the son of the victor at

Flodden, without obtaining the King's licence – but apparently at the King's instigation! Henry was in no way affronted: that he granted a technical pardon for a technical offence can be taken as a sign of approval rather than of displeasure. The pardon names Edward's wife *Katherine*, but it was *Dorothy* Howard who later bore him children. It has usually been assumed that the name Katherine was a clerical error, but recently an American scholar, Dr Edward Zevin, has discovered from letters written by the Spanish ambassador at King Henry's court to Emperor Charles V that Katherine Howard was indeed Earl Edward's first wife. She died of the plague in March 1530, and later that year, to maintain the family alliance, Edward married Dorothy Howard, Katherine's young aunt, the daughter of the second Duke, the victor at Flodden, by his second wife, Agnes. From what the ambassador told the Emperor, it seems that it was Norfolk who feared losing the Stanley alliance 'as there is no other in the kingdom through which he could more strengthen himself'.

(Bagley, p. 37.)

Although the relationship between these various generations of Dukes of Norfolk and the Stanleys is extremely confusing, it means that the Norfolk in the Tower at the same time as **Sir Thomas** was a fairly close in-law. Another interesting reference is to Eynsham Abbey:

During the remaining ten years of Henry's reign, Edward did not face another situation as difficult as the Pilgrimage of Grace. He quickly reconciled himself to the Dissolution of the Monasteries both major and minor, and any lingering regrets he may have had did not prevent him from following fellow landowners into the scramble for monastic property. Among the church lands he bought were those of the Benedictine house at **Eynsham in Oxfordshire** and, as might have been expected, those of Burscough Priory. Later, after the dissolution of the chantries, he took over chantry property in Huyton and purchased the suppressed Manchester College.

(Bagley, p. 41.)

This explains how Eynsham Abbey first came into Derby hands and why it was subsequently available to be granted to his son **Sir Thomas**, to be inherited by his widow, and in turn by their son **Edward**, who died there. However, we will read in Chapter XIX. Eynsham that there were a couple of other owners before Earl Thomas bought the estate in Eynsham.

The Stanley family was by far the biggest burgage-holder in Liverpool, and the earliest extant freemen's roll, dated 1565, gives both Earl Edward and his eldest son, Henry, precedence over the mayor. **Sir Thomas Stanley**, Edward's second son, served as mayor in 1568-9. Henry followed him in office, and throughout the earldoms of Edward and Henry the burgesses habitually looked to the Earl to help them out of trouble. In return they usually voted his nominee into the Commons and treated him as royally as a king whenever he was in town.

(Bagley, p. 63.)

Coward had already given the date of **Sir Thomas** as Mayor of Liverpool, but this confirms, if confirmation were needed, that he achieved this office because he was nominated by his father. It is significant that Edward did not nominate him the following year, but his eldest son Henry. After 1570, it is doubtful whether the burgesses would have accepted someone who had 'plotted against' Queen Elizabeth, and in any case he would not have been considered when he was in the Tower for treason.

Bagley gives additional details in the lead up to the 1570 plot to free Mary, and the role Earl Edward played during this period.

In 1570, despite the early collapse of the Northern Rebellion, the tension increased even further. The publication of Pius V's excommunication of Elizabeth heightened the crisis. It forced Roman Catholics and 'church-papists' (those who attended the parish church but were Catholic in belief) to re-examine their consciences and loyalties. At least for a short period, even Earl Edward sheltered a Catholic priest or two and forbade his chaplains to use the English prayer book in household services. Yet, despite provoking some hostile reports which his enemies were ever ready to send to Cecil and the Council, and despite nourishing the hope in many recusants' hearts that he would soon openly take up their cause, Edward refused to encourage, still less to lead, rebellion against Elizabeth's government. Towards the end of 1570, he told Cecil that he found it comforting to know that the Queen herself was the judge of his conduct.

In that same year, however, two of his sons, **Sir Thomas** and **Sir Edward Stanley**, took part in a madcap plot to release Mary, Queen of Scots, from captivity in Sheffield [*sic*, actually Chatsworth]. Along with Francis Rolleston, a gentleman from the Midlands, and Sir Thomas Gerard of Bryn, they concocted a plan to seize the forewarned and willing Mary when she was walking 'to the height of the moors'. With an escort of two hundred armed horsemen they arranged to take 'the prisoner' to the Isle of Man, whence she would be free to go 'whither she best liked'. The hatching of this plot necessitated three or four clandestine meetings at Lathom, but in August 1570 the conspirators abandoned the whole scheme. Queen Mary and John Beton, the master of her meagre household, considered it too risky a plan, and when **Sir Thomas** received word at Lathom that Rolleston had confided in his son, George, he 'rent in pieces both letter and cipher saying that we were all undone.' He was right, for George Rolleston informed the Queen's ministers, and by November, Earl Edward was informing Cecil that he had sent **his two sons** to London 'according to the Queen's commandment'. They, with Rolleston and Gerard, were lodged in the Tower, and during the next two years suffered regular periods of inquisition. Gerard's son later reported that 'the payment of a large sum' secured his father's release, and it is probable that **the Stanley brothers** eventually had to purchase their liberty too. But there were no executions. The Queen probably considered it would be injudicious to alienate Stanley goodwill when Catholic opposition was gathering such strength in the north-west. She had already suspended the easy-going Bishop Downham and ordered Bishop Barnes of Carlisle to conduct a visitation of Chester diocese. Barnes's reports were alarming. From the Queen's government's point of view, Derby's loyalty was its chief guarantee against open revolt in Lancashire and Cheshire. And, despite his dislike of the hardening attitude of parliament and Council against recusants and traditionalists, Earl Edward maintained that loyalty until his death at Lathom on 24 October 1572.

(Bagley, pp. 48-9.)

A final note by Bagley on William Stanley, 6th Earl of Derby, shows that he was created Knight of the Bath in 1603, the same year as his cousin **Sir Edward Jr**; and gives his other main positions, activities and interests in the North West during the remaining years of his life, until the death of **Sir Edward Jr** in 1632 and his own in 1642.

Earl William might be one of the least ambitious of all the Earls of Derby, but he thought it both requisite and urgent to restore his family's prestige and political power. In 1598 he recovered the Earl's traditional seat on the Chester Ecclesiastical Commission, and five years later King James appointed him Knight of the Bath and, more importantly for William, Chamberlain of Chester, the post which his father and grandfather had valued so highly. To regain the Lieutenancy, however, was a bigger triumph still, and to retain the office for the rest of his life, as he did, fully re-established Stanley dominance.

(Bagley, p. 70)

~~~~~~~~~~~~~~~~~~~~~

XI-7. Peter Stanley (1998)

Peter Edmund Stanley, *The House of Stanley* (Pentland Press, 1998). His surname, perhaps, says it all. He was not an academic historian, but he did bear the name of the family. He traced his own line back as far as possible, at the same time gathering as much information as possible about the main line and its offshoots. He finally turned this labour of love, a project over many years, into a book, which presents an excellent overall (and often detailed) view of the development of the main original lines and some of the offshoots. His main sources were, of course, those named above, supplemented by extra details detected. Unfortunately, he gave no references. Not surprisingly (for me, at least), he also provided no additional details about **Sir Thomas, Sir Edward Sr** and **Jr** or the Stanley epitaphs in Tong. This therefore remains as a very readable history of the family, but has provided no quotes with references for this book on the epitaphs and the Stanleys involved.

~~~~~~~~~~~~~

XI-8. Brian S. Roberts (research ongoing in 2012)

The 'S' in his name stands for Stanley, which already explains much. He is the webmaster of the Stanley Genealogy Forum, which says even more. Brian has considerable genealogical expertise and has always provided details with sources. He has traced his own line back to 1590, in families that always lived in Stanley territory, he himself growing up in Liverpool (now and for many years living in New Jersey, US). Most importantly, his computer skills have allowed him to access anything available digitally, scan in numerous books from (often university) libraries and major repositories in Britain and the US, and present all clearly on a website. His research has been invaluable, and promises to continue to be so. I first became aware of his website in late 2007, and several details detected by him were highly interesting, to say the least. In a rather inverse but extremely productive way, his details served to delay the completion of this book for quite some time, but with the knowledge and regular confirmation that the delay was worthwhile by allowing the clarification of so many previous muddles by others. Just a few examples of documentary details he has provided, which were of inestimable value for this book:

a) All Stanley entries from the Lancashire Parish Records Society, thus coming reliably as close as possible to the original, transcribed by local enthusiasts with a knowledge of local names and idiosyncracies, and thus avoiding the sometimes dubious transcriptions on the IGI. One invaluable entry under burials at Ormskirk was that of **Sir Edward Stanley**, given as 'Sir' and 'Knight', on 4th September 1604. It simply could have been none other than a close member of the family of the Earls of Derby, and thus could have been none other than **Sir Edward Stanley Sr**. At one fell swoop this eliminated from the immediate picture all other contenders of Edward Stanleys who had died in Ireland, Spain, Portugal, elsewhere unknown, in 1594, 1597, 1609, 1636, etc., all of which details have been attributed to **Sir Edward Sr** in one previous account or another.

b) **Sir Edward Sr** was knighted in Ireland in 1560 by Queen Elizabeth. There seems no doubt that this was 'our' Sir Edward. This immediately eliminated him as a candidate for the Edward Stanley who heroically stormed the fort at Zutphen in 1586, as assumed by Seacome. This Mr Edward Stanley was knighted by Leicester after the battle.

c) All Stanley wills held in the National Archives, Kew. Thus before he knew of my research and interest in the Stanleys on the Tong tomb, he had already scanned in the wills of **Sir Thomas**, his widow Margaret Vernon Stanley Mather and **Sir Edward Jr**, which he kindly sent to me.

d) All Stanley Visitation Pedigrees of Lancashire and Cheshire. Just one gem that appeared on the Cheshire Stanley VP of 1580 was a Sir Edward Stanley 'knighted in Netherland, slaine in Ireland 1597', which is perhaps as close as we might come to identifying the heroic Edward Stanley who stormed the fort at Zutphen. (This is covered in detail in Chapter XXII. Other 'Sir' Edward Stanleys.) He was of the Elford, Staffordshire branch, which in itself presents a confusing picture of Stanleys of Lathom returning to close to the place of their origin in Stoneleigh, Staffordshire, but obviously staying in touch, which produced marriages between Lancashire, Cheshire and Staffordshire families. Brian and I are still puzzling over this line, suspecting that the Heralds (and the editors of the nineteenth-century publications of VPs) did not always record the various lines on the basis of documents, but perhaps sometimes by dubious 'hearsay'. One elusive knight in this muddled picture is Sir Humphrey Stanley, who was pretty obviously knighted after Bosworth, thus joining the ranks of thousands of other soldiers in the Stanley armies there.

One of the later lists accessed by Brian (in early 2010) was Stratford Parish Registers where, lo and behold, there were Stanley families in Shakespeare times! We are both still puzzling over these, jumping to no conclusions, but have just noted that there were Stanleys there at that time. As far as I am aware, no Shakespeare researcher has noted these Stanleys. They may or may not be significant, but they are at least worth a note.

With Brian's systematic trawl through all published collections containing Stanleys in the PRO, the National Archives and the British Library, this presents the best chance for the future in unearthing more details about 'our' Stanleys of Winwick and Tong. Let all interested in Stanleys thank him for all his work so far and wish him the very best of luck for the future

~~~~~~~~~~~~~~~

Chapter XII
An excursion to Winwick, Lancashire

XII-1. Introduction

As mentioned several times in previous chapters, **Sir Thomas** was on occasion referred to as **Sir Thomas of Winwick**, even after he had moved to Tong. It will also be remembered that his son **Sir Edward Jr** buried his only son infant Thomas not in Tong, but back in Winwick. Sooner or later, therefore, we must make an excursion to old Winwick to see what details might remain there of their lives. In **Sir Thomas**'s days Winwick was a township in Lancashire a few miles north of Warrington. This large town was on the north banks of the Mersey, which provided the boundary between Lancashire and Cheshire and earlier between the Kingdoms of Northumbria and Mercia. Warrington was the site of an ancient bridge, providing the first convenient crossing point of the river from its mouth, which Thomas Stanley, 1st Earl of Derby had caused to be rebuilt in stone in 1495 (third bridge on the site). Winwick, with Warrington, was very much in Stanley country. Since 1974, with the re-organisation of county boundaries, it became part of Warrington Unitary Authority, which stretched south of the Mersey, and with the whole area newly designated as within Cheshire. Many Warringtonians apparently still feel themselves to be from Lancashire rather than Cheshire. Winwickians in the sixteenth century certainly knew they were in Lancashire.

The obvious place to start searching for Sir Thomas was in Beaumont's *History of Winwick* (1897). A recent excursion via a Google search, which offered many websites on Winwick, revealed that Beaumont has been placed online on the Manx Notebook, courtesy of Dr Frances Coakley. After a first brief moment of surprise, this was in fact very logical. The Manx Notebook, an excellent compendium of many Manx matters, inevitably includes much valuable information on the dealings of the Earls of Derby with the island. They were virtual 'Kings of the Isle of Man' on and off for several centuries, and indeed, 'our' **Sir Thomas Stanley** was Governor of the Isle of Man 1562–66 and his nephew William, 6th Earl held this position in 1593. Through the Stanleys, Winwick did indeed enter the history of the Isle of Man and vice versa. It also transpired that Dr Coakley, a long-term resident of the Isle of Man, is one of the Warringtonians who grew up in Lancashire and is still rather 'miffed' that it is now in Cheshire (personal communication). Beaumont's *Winwick* offers perhaps most of what we might ever find out about 'our' **Sir Thomas** in Winwick, which is still not very much. It did, however, illuminate the cause of great confusion among three contemporary (Sir) Thomas Stanleys.

Sir Thomas of Winwick and Tong should not, in theory, have been confused with any other contemporary Thomas Stanley, because 'our' **Sir Thomas** was one of only two with this name knighted in the middle of the sixteenth century and the other was Lord Mo(u)nteagle, known more

The Old Rectory, Rectory Lane, Winwick, Warrington, WA2 8TD

The Old Rectory is located in the idyllic Cheshire village of Winwick approximately 3 miles to the north of Warrington town centre and immediately adjacent to Junction 9 of the M62. The Old Rectory is positioned in a striking setting surrounded by tree lined grounds. The period building has been modernised to provide excellent office space configured with a mixture of cellular and open plan areas. Many of the original features remain providing an attractive, efficient working environment.

Terms: Terms upon application

XIIa. The Old Rectory, Winwick

On sale in 2011. Leased with glebe lands in 1563 for 99 years to Sir Thomas Stanley by Thomas Stanley, Bishop of Sodor and Man, Rector of Winwick, Wigan, etc.. Lease continued by son (Sir) Edward Stanley Jr. Both used it as their base when re-visiting Lancashire. Winwick was always in Lancashire until the boundary reforms of 1974. It is now divorced from post-1974 Lancashire, between and below Merseyside and Greater Manchester and, somewhat confusingly, is a Civil Parish in the Borough of Warrington, a Unitary Authority in the Ceremonial County of Cheshire.

usually by this title. There has also been confusion, however, with Thomas Stanley (died 1568), who was Lord Bishop of Sodor and Man. As a clergyman he might have been referred to early in his career as 'Sir', a common honorary title given to clergymen who had no higher title, although I have not come across any mention of this one as 'Sir'. He did, however, have close contact with 'our' **Sir Thomas** when, as Bishop of Man and Rector of Wigan in 1563, he 'granted to **Sir Thomas Stanley, knight**, a lease of the rectory parish church and benefice [of Winwick], with the manor park and glebe lands for the term of 99 years, at the yearly rent of £120; which lease was confirmed by Edward, Earl of Derby and William Downham, Bishop of Chester'. We will read this below in the context in which it was written by historian Beaumont. The origin of the title of 'Bishop of Sodor and Man' is covered in detail on several Isle of Man websites; from now on only 'Man' is given.

The main feature of Thomas Stanley, Bishop of Man, is that he is far better documented than 'our' **Sir Thomas**, although this has not stopped him from being confused with his contemporary Sir Thomas Stanley, 2nd Lord Monteagle. It is generally agreed now that these two were half-brothers, both sons of Sir Edward Stanley, 1st Lord Monteagle of Hornby Castle (victor at Flodden in 1513): Sir Thomas was the eldest son of the first wife and Bishop Thomas was the illegitimate son of a mistress.

Quotes from the main relevant sources concerning all three contemporary Thomas Stanleys are included in full below:

(a) for the sake of completeness in bringing them all together on the printed page;

(b) for later cross-referencing to members of the Monteagle family, some of whom **Sir Thomas** and **Sir Edward** would almost certainly have known; indeed, one of them, the 4th Lord Monteagle mentioned below, attended Preston Guild with **Sir Edward Jr** and his uncle **Sir Edward Sr** in August 1602 (see Chapter XV. Preston Guild);

(c) for the sake of any reader of this book who does not have access to the internet;

(d) to allow readers to join in with another detective story with the aim of establishing how many (Sir) Thomas Stanleys were (and are still being) confused;

(e) in the hope that some reader in the region of Winwick might feel inspired to gather other relevant information;

(f) in the hope that the story of the Monteagle family might finally be sorted out to the satisfaction of all concerned.

XII-2. EXTRACT ONE (Seacome, 1741, 1793)

From John Seacome, *Memoirs: containing a genealogical and historical account of the ancient and honourable house of Stanley; from the Conquest to the death of James late Earl of Derby, in the year 1735; as also a full description of the Isle of Man, etc.,* (Liverpool, 1741). Reprints and new editions with updates (later ones sometimes under another title) at least Manchester 1767, Manchester 1783, Preston 1793, Liverpool 1801. The following is from the 1793 edition.

Seacome introduces us here, albeit briefly, to Thomas Stanley, Bishop of Man, and Thomas Stanley, 2nd Lord Monteagle, and his (con)fusion of the two probably lies at the root of later confusions. We know (from his other sections on Earl Edward) that Seacome knew about **Sir Thomas of Winwick and Tong**, but did not introduce him into this confusion.

This extract appears under Seacome's account of Sir Edward Stanley, created 1st Lord Mo(u)nteagle by Henry VIII for his role in the victory at Flodden Field in 1513. I use this opportunity to mention that the title in historical accounts is often given as 'Mounteagle', but today usually as 'Monteagle'. The name was derived from the 'mont/mount' of Hornby Castle in the Lune Valley near Lancaster and the eagle from the bird in the Stanley crest. The 'mont/mount' presumably derives from a Norman mount and bailey in a strategic situation on a hill on the route of many English armies *en route* to Scotland and vice versa. No one knows how it was pronounced in Tudor and Stuart times, because the line and title died out long ago. I happen to prefer 'Mounteagle', the version I heard when growing up in Lancashire, but bow to the current usage of 'Monteagle'. There is still a castle there, rebuilt much later and now owned privately. It appears on several websites.

[Comments by HM are in square brackets and italics.]

> This noble Lord married to his Lady, one of the daughters of Charles Brandon, Duke of Suffolk; by his second wife, a daughter of Sir Anthony Brown, Governor of Calais, and by her had issue a son, named Thomas, who was some time Bishop of Man, by the title of Thomas Stanley, son of Edward, the first Lord Monteagle. He sat as Bishop of that island, to the time of his father's death, and then becoming [*2nd*] Lord Monteagle, he resigned that Bishopric.

[Did he? Or were these two different Thomas Stanleys? They certainly were. Other sources provide the information that Sir Edward, 1st Lord Monteagle, had two sons named Thomas, from two different wives, or a wife and a mistress. One succeeded his father as 2nd Lord Monteagle and the other became Bishop of Man. Two sons with the same name was by no means uncommon at this time, often to ensure that this name would be perpetuated if one of them died young. In this case, there is little doubt that they were both named after Sir Edward's father Thomas, 1st Earl of Derby. HM]

> This Thomas, [*2nd*] Lord Monteagle married to Lady Ann, the daughter of Sir John Spencer, of Althorp, in the county of Northampton, and by her had issue a son, named William.

[Seacome was hopelessly muddled here. The correct marriages and descent of the Monteagles are as on the family trees in Appendices 12a and 12b. The Spencer family tree is available on an Althorp website, which also includes other accounts of the Monteagle family; see also Ann Spencer married to William Stanley, 3rd Baron Monteagle, Thomas's son, as his second wife. This Ann Spencer was a sister of Alice, wife of Ferdinando, 5th Earl of Derby.]

> who was the last male issue of this noble family. He left at his death, an only daughter and child, named Elizabeth, but by whom history is silent; but record informs us, that she married to Edward Parker, Lord Morley, and by him had issue a son, named William.

[William Parker was granted the title 4th Lord Monteagle by right of his mother. HM]

> This William [*Parker*] was by King James I. created [*4th*] Lord Monteagle, by the title of Lord Morley and Monteagle; and must be allowed by us, and all posterity, to have been born for the

good of the whole kingdom: for by an obscure letter sent to him, and by him produced to the King and Council, in the very nick of time, a discovery was made of the most detestable treason, that malice and wickedness could possibly contrive or project. For it being known that the King was to come to the House of Peers to pass some bills, this dark and aenigmatical letter insinuated, that the King and the whole House were to be destroyed in a moment.

www.isle-of-man.com/manxnotebook/fulltext/hs173x/pls03.htm#bp>

[*This refers to his role in the abortion of the Gunpowder Plot. Recent historians have not been so kind to this Monteagle, seeing him involved in a rather direct way at some point in the conspiracy but, becoming scared, betrayed his co-conspirators to save his own life. This is particularly interesting in the context of this book because of the involvement in the Gunpowder Plot of Sir Everard Digby, a close friend of* **Sir Edward Stanley Jr** *and father of Sir Kenelm Digby, the future husband of* **Edward's** *daughter Venetia.* HM]

XII-3. EXTRACT TWO from the Manx Notebook (Beaumont, *Winwick*, 1897)

www.isle-of-man/manxnotebook/fulltext/ww1897.htm#30. (Extracts 2–5 are on the same web page.)

From William Beaumont, *Winwick: Its History and Antiquities* (2nd ed. Warrington, 1897). This is extremely well documented. Some of the numbers for his footnotes have been used for my own comments [*these are shown in italics and square brackets* HM]. Other comments appear in the time-line of Thomas Stanley, Bishop of Man, see XII–5.

1552. — THOMAS STANLEY, Lord Bishop of Man, was presented to the living of Winwick by Edward, third Earl of Derby, on the 10th April, 1552, and paid his first fruits the same year. There had been four archdeacons and one bishop before him occupants of the living since the advowson became the property of Sir John Stanley. The bishop who now held the living had been consecrated to his see on the death of Hesketh, or Black-leach, in 1542; but in 1545 he was displaced from the see for refusing to comply with the Act of 33 Henry VIII, disconnecting the bishopric of Man from the province of Canterbury and attaching it to that of York. In 1553, when the royal commissioners came to Winwick to take an account of the bells and vestments they found at Winwick the following:

WINWICK.
iij bells wherof a clokke stikketh upon one. ij....sacrying bells ij little pixes of silu' th chalices. A vestment of ... wt .... belonging to the same. A olde vestmet of silke wt. brannchez .... fustean. And at the trinitie Church a vestmet of white .... An other vestemet of silke An other vestmet of crule wt. all things belonging .... coape white fusteanj belle called a sancts belle Wh. ij lyttill sacring belles belonging to the said Church."[1]

In 1556, however, the bishop was restored to his see, and on 5th August 5 and 6 Phil. and Mary, 1558, when he occurs in a deed with Thomas Lord Monteagle, he is expressly described as Thomas Lord Bishop of Man.[2] In 4 and 5 Phil. and Mary, 1557, and on the 9th August, 5 and 6 Phil. and Mary, 1558, he was first made Rector of Wigan, and then Rector of North Meols.[3] And as if this heap of preferments was not enough for one pluralist, he became also Rector of Badsworth and of Berwick-upon-Tweed, for all which it is said that he obtained the Pope's bull to hold them with the bishopric. If this were so, however, we see in it the last expiring glimmer of this once profitable part of the Pope's power in England. The Bishop was Rector of Winwick when the fall of the chantries took place in 1553, and William Stanley was returned as being the priest then serving the rector's, or perhaps more properly Lord Derby's chantry, as being founded under his will with an endowment of £3 0s. 9d.[4] In 1557 "dominus Ricardus Smith" is returned as the bishop's curate at Winwick. In 1559 Sir John Holcroft the elder, by his will of 2nd December, declared that if the tenants in Culcheth would purchase and make sure for ever lands of the value of £6 13s. 4d., and thereat to hire a priest at £5 13s. 4d. and a clerk at 20s. his best chain should be given towards the same - and this is believed to be the origin of the church at

Newchurch.[5] The testator had probably the founding of this chapel in his mind when he purchased the Culcheth tithes. By his same will he left xx-s. towards the glassinge of Winwick Church. In 1563 the parish registers commence, and the name of Andrew Rider, the curate, appears in them as having made the first, and a little later the bishop's monogram and autograph may be seen in some of them.[6] Not satisfied with the injury his absenteeism inflicted upon the parish and with living in forgetfulness of his responsibilities, of which we have a glimpse in a letter written by Pilkington, Bishop of Durham, to the Archbishop of Canterbury about this time, in which he says, "The Bishop of Man, Thomas Stanley, liveth here at his ease as merry as Pope Joan."[7] It would almost seem from this that to his other preferments he had added a stall at Durham, if not he was only imitating a number of the beneficed clergy of his time who absented themselves from their livings that they might be more free to enjoy themselves.[8] But pluralist as he was, the bishop was far eclipsed by Sir John Mansel, once Rector of Wigan, the next adjoining parish to Winwick, on the north, in the reign of Hen. III., who, besides being Lord Chancellor and occupying other offices in the State, presented himself to every living in his patronage which fell vacant while he was Chancellor.[9] But his absenteeism was not the worst evil which Bishop Stanley inflicted upon the living of Winwick; for on the 5th October, 1563, by an indenture in which he calls himself Thomas Stanley, Bishop of Man and rector of Winwick, he granted to Sir Thomas Stanley, knight, a lease of the rectory parish church and benefice, with the manor park and glebe lands for the term of 99 years, at the yearly rent of £120; which lease was confirmed by Edward Earl of Derby and William Bishop of Chester.

Hitherto we have seen no rector of Winwick appear as an author. Now, however, Bishop Stanley appears in that character among the first of the rectors of Winwick as the writer of the "Rhyming Chronicle," a sort of history in verse of the Stanley family continued to the year 1562. He is said to have had in his possession a very ancient painting of the face of our Blessed Lord, which was taken by him to Douglas in the Isle of Man, where it is still preserved.[10] The bishop died in 1568, but neither the place of his burial nor the exact nature of his origin has been ascertained. His name does not appear in the Knowsley pedigrees. It has been said that he was the son of the second Lord Monteagle,[11] but if so he is unnoticed in the pedigree of that family, and was probably illegitimate.[12] The first Lord Monteagle was Edward, who died in 1523; the second, Thomas, who died in 1560; and the third, William, who died without male heirs in 1557. [*The last date queried: other sources give 1581. HM*]

[1] From a copy in the Public Record Office obtained by J. E. Bailey, Esq. [*It is interesting that there was little of value in such an ancient church; most had presumably been confiscated by Commissioners of Henry VIII after the Dissolution of the Monasteries. HM*]

[2] Lanc. and Ches. Wills, Chetham So., part III. [*This is the main clue in the detective story: the two Thomases are obviously distinguished here, one already as 2nd Lord Monteagle and the other Bishop of Man, and not the latter becoming the former. This document alone precludes all previous assumptions that they were one and the same. HM*]

[3] Hist. Lanc.iii. 540, and iv. 277. [*North Meols is near Southport. HM*]

[4] Lancashire Chantries, Chet. Soc., i. 69, *in notis*.

[5] Lancashire and Cheshire Wills, Chet. So., i. 148.11

[6] Hist. Lanc. iii. 625. [*Probably referring to Baines, History of Lancashire, the latest edition at this time (1897) being the one revised by Croston, 5 vols, 1888-93. HM*]

[7] Hist. Lanc. iii, 100, and Parker Correspondence.

[8] Froude's Hist. Eng. ii. 416.

[9] Campbell's Lives of the Chancellors.

[10] Journal of the Royal Archaeological Institute, No. 107, p. 190 see also Manx Soc Vol XX

[11] [*Much more likely (from dates), son of the 1st Lord Monteagle. HM*]

[12] [*Or son of a second wife, who was thus not the son and heir and therefore quite likely to have been missed out of later Visitation Pedigrees. HM*]

XII-4. EXTRACT THREE from the Manx Notebook
(Beaumont, *Winwick*, 1897)

This follows on immediately from the one above, does not mention **Sir Thomas** by name, but is interesting in giving further details of the Rectorship of Winwick when **Sir Thomas** was still holding his lease of rectory property there. Beaumont implies that the Queen stepped into the picture to pre-empt **Sir Thomas** having any say in the appointment.

> 1569. — CHRISTOPHER THOMPSON was presented by the Queen on 19th March, 1569, and he paid his first fruits on the 31st of the same month. It does not appear under what circumstances the Queen claimed the right to present. It was not on account of the patron's minority, for he was of full age. If it was because his predecessor had been made a bishop, Her Majesty could hardly have claimed the presentation after suffering Thomas Stanley to hold it to the end of his life, notwithstanding that he had been made Bishop of Man.
>
> It is possible that the Queen disputed the right of the late bishop's lessee [*Sir Thomas*] to exercise the right of presentation.
>
> At all events, Christopher Thompson, of whom we have been unable to learn any particulars, held the living but a short time.

From all these details we can draw up a time-line for a brief biography of Thomas Stanley, Bishop of Sodor and Man, including some relevant dates for **Sir Thomas of Winwick**. All quotes, unless indicated otherwise, are from Beaumont, *Winwick*, from abstracts above or below.

XIIb. St Oswald's Parish Church, Winwick
Presumably attended by Sir Thomas and Sir Edward when resident in Winwick.
Sir Edward Jr's infant son Thomas was buried here.

~~~~~~~~~~~~~~~~~~~~~~~

XII-5. Time-line of Thomas Stanley, Bishop of Sodor and Man

??	Date and place of birth unknown; 'the exact nature of his origin has not been ascertained'; 'it has been said that he was the son of the second Lord Mounteagle, but if so he is unnoticed in the pedigree of that family, and was probably illegitimate' (Beaumont); much more likely a younger or illegitimate son of the 1st Lord Monteagle; mother unknown; best guess at a birth date of a minimum c. 25 years before his first known preferment as Bishop of Man, i.e. c.1517. One might assume, however, that he had had previous preferments before this lofty position, which would push his birth date back further. In any case, this makes him a generation earlier than Sir Thomas of Winwick and Tong (b. c.1534).
1542	Appointed Bishop of Man 'on the death of Hesketh or Black-leach'. (Beaumont.) This was during the Earldom of Edward, 3rd Earl (he succeeded on the death of his father Thomas, 2nd Earl, in 1521 and lived until 1572). Sir Edward, 1st Lord Monteagle had died in 1524, succeeded by his son and heir Thomas, 2nd Lord Monteagle. If the assumption is correct that Thomas Stanley, Bishop of Man, was a bastard son of the 1st Lord Monteagle, then he was a half-brother of Thomas Stanley, 2nd Lord Monteagle and first cousin of Thomas Stanley, 2nd Earl of Derby. For his preferment to the see of Man, one might presume that he showed some ability and that his close relationship to the Earls of Derby was recognised and acknowledged. It might also have been significant that Henry VIII had such a high opinion of his father Sir Edward, 1st Lord Monteagle, victor at Flodden in 1513, whom he apparently greeted in the corridors of power in London as 'Ho! my soldier!!' (Seacome, p. 111).
1545	'He was displaced from the see for refusing to comply with the Act of 33 Hen. VIII, disconnecting the bishopric of Man from the province of Canterbury and attaching it to that of York.' (Beaumont.) This must mean something about his position in relationship to the Crown and the higher echelons of the Church; further research might reveal more.
1547	Might he have been the elusive Thomas Stanley, Mayor of Liverpool (Coward, *op. cit.*), occupying this position while still debarred as Bishop of Man?
1552 10 April	'Presented to the living of Winwick by Edward, 3rd Earl of Derby.' (Beaumont.) Was this as compensation for losing his bishopric of Man?
1553	'The bishop was Rector of Winwick when the fall of the chantries took place in 1553, and William Stanley was returned as being the priest then serving the rector's, or perhaps more properly Lord Derby's chantry, as being founded under his will with an endowment of £3 0s 9d.' (Beaumont.) William Stanley remains unidentified, but was presumably a kinsman of the Earl of Derby and Thomas, Rector of Winwick, who (William) performed the duties during Thomas's absences.
1553 6 July	Edward VI died and after Lady Jane Grey's brief placement on the throne, Mary I became Queen. These constant changes of monarch with different religious adherences must have had some effect on Thomas, Bishop of Man.
1553 2 Oct.	**Sir Thomas of Winwick** knighted on the day after Queen Mary's coronation, in the presence of the Queen, by the Earl of Arundel. (Brian S. Roberts \<Stanley Family Genealogy>.)
1556	Thomas, Bishop of Man 'restored to his see.' (Beaumont.)
1557	Thomas, Bishop of Man, "first made Rector of Wigan." (Beaumont.)
1557	' "*Dominus Ricardus Smith*" is returned as the Bishop's curate at Winwick.' (Beaumont.)
1558 5 Aug.	'When he occurs in a deed with Thomas Stanley, Lord Mounteagle, he is expressly described as Thomas Lord Bishop of Man.' (Beaumont.) This document on its own, with the appearance of these two Thomas Stanleys, serves to distinguish them as two separate people.
1558 9 Aug.	Again (?) appointed 'Rector of Wigan' and first made 'Rector of North Meols'. (Beaumont.)
??	Some time later appointed 'Rector of Badsworth [near Pontefract in West Yorkshire?] and of Berwick-upon-Tweed, for all of which it is said that he obtained the Pope's bull to hold them with the bishopric. If this were so, however, we see in it the last expiring glimmer of this once profitable part of the Pope's power in England'. (Beaumont.) More research in these places is needed to establish dates.
1558 17 Nov.	Queen Mary died, succeeded by Elizabeth I.

Continued

Continuation

1558/9	Elizabeth confirmed Thomas, Bishop of Man, as Rector of Wigan for life.
1559 2 Dec.	'Sir John Holcroft, the elder, by his will of 2 Dec. . . . left xx-s. towards the glassinge of Winwick Church.' (Beaumont.) Sir John was an eminent local, whose family married into all the local gentry, one also marrying an Earl of Rutland, a family related to **Sir Thomas** by his wife Margaret Vernon. (See Chapter XIX. The Earls of Rutland.)
1562	'Hitherto we have seen no rector of Winwick appear as an author. Now, however, Bishop Stanley appears in that character among the first of the rectors of Winwick as the writer of the "Rhyming Chronicle", a sort of history in verse of the Stanley family continued to the year 1562.' (Beaumont.) This is referred to by Heywood, *Verse Writers* (Chetham Society, 1853), which was probably Beaumont's source.
1560s?	'He is said to have had in his possession a very ancient painting of the face of our Blessed Lord, which was taken by him to Douglas in the Isle of Man, where it is still preserved.' (Beaumont.) This is the only reference to an actual visit to the Isle of Man.
1562-66	**Sir Thomas Stanley** Governor of the Isle of Man (Beaumont, see Extract Four below).
1563	'The parish registers [of Winwick] commence, and the name of Andrew Rider, the curate, appears in them as having made the first, and a little later the Bishop's monogram and autograph may be seen in some of them.' (Beaumont.) This indicates that Thomas, Bishop of Man, at least paid the occasional visit to Winwick.
1563 5 Oct.	'By an indenture in which he calls himself Thomas Stanley, Bishop of Man and rector of Winwick, he granted to **Sir Thomas Stanley**, knight, a lease of the rectory parish church and benefice, with the manor park and glebe lands for the term of 99 years, at the yearly rent of £120; which lease was confirmed by Edward, Earl of Derby and William Downham, Bishop of Chester.' (Beaumont.) This is the first document (discovered so far) that places **Sir Thomas** fairly and squarely in **Winwick**, and presumably the reason for his being referred to from now on as **Sir Thomas of Winwick**. At this time **Sir Thomas** was still living elsewhere in Lancashire or on the Isle of Man. He obviously retained his interest in Winwick, however, proved by two known records: (1) his son **Edward** buried his infant son **Thomas** back at Winwick (date unknown) and (2) **Sir Thomas** enlisted the help of the parishioners of Winwick when in financial difficulties in the 1570s (Honigmann reference immediately below).
1561-8	'. . . a letter written by James Pilkington, Bishop of Durham, to Matthew Parker, Archbishop of Canterbury, in which he says, "The Bishop of Man, Thomas Stanley, liveth here at his ease as merry as Pope Joan". It would almost seem from this that to his other preferments he had added a stall at Durham, if not he was only imitating a number of the beneficed clergy of his time who absented themselves from their livings that they might be more free to enjoy themselves.' (Beaumont.) James Pilkington was from Rivington, Lancashire, went into exile in Mary's reign to escape persecution for his Protestant beliefs (along with later Archbishop of Canterbury Matthew 'Nosey Parker'), returned after her death, was appointed Bishop of Durham in 1561 by Elizabeth, founded Rivington Grammar School in 1566 and died in 1576. This letter must, therefore, have been written between 1561 (Pilkington's appointment as Bishop of Durham) and 1568 (death of Thomas, Bishop of Man).
1568	Thomas, Bishop of Man, died. 'The place of his burial . . . has [not] been ascertained.' (Beaumont.) With benefices in so many places, he might have died in any of these or anywhere en route.
P.S.	Query from Brian S. Roberts (private communication). 'Is he Thomas Stanley rector of Sutton Bonington; is he also Thomas Stanley of Shenstone, Staffordshire????' This certainly seems to fit into the general picture; a full biography still awaits.

~~~~~~~~~~

XII-6. EXTRACT FOUR from the Manx Notebook
(Beaumont, *Winwick*, 1897)

Beaumont, later in his book, also gives the following valuable brief biographies, including Sir Thomas's term as Governor of the Isle of Man 1562-66. The mistakes (?) Beaumont made (the corrections of which we think we know from other sources), and other intriguing items, are given in **bold** and commented on below.

Some Winwick Names and Personalities

XVII. — THOMAS STANLEY, afterwards **Sir Thomas Stanley, knight**, the second son of Edward, third Earl of Derby, following a then common but most reprehensible practice, in 3 Elizabeth, 1563, took from the rector, with the bishop's and patron's consent, a lease of the rectory, glebe and tithes of Winwick, for the term of ninety-nine years, at the yearly rent of £200. The lessee and not the rector seems then to have taken up his residence in the rectory, and he is mentioned in the Proceedings of the Lancashire Lieutenancy as still living there.[1] **Sir Thomas**, who married Margaret, the daughter of Sir George Vernon (*the King of the Peak*), **was probably the same person who from 1562 to 1566 was governor of the Isle of Man**, and who died on **15 Decr.,** 1576, at **Walthamstow, and was buried there.**

[1] Chet. Soc. 1., 36.

In the absence of further confirmation for or against, it does indeed seem that it was this **Sir Thomas** who was the Governor of the Isle of Man. Beaumont's reference to the date of death of **Sir Thomas** and his burial at Walthamstow is curious. When the Stanley vault at Tong was entered in 1891 the inscription on a lead plate beginning 'Hic jacet Thomas Stanley, Miles' gave his date of death as 21 December 1576; so where did Beaumont's date come from? We will remember that it was not given on the MI on his tomb at Tong.

Beaumont's assumption that **Sir Thomas** was buried at Walthamstow is even more curious. We know from the MIs at Tong and Walthamstow that only **Sir Edward Jr**'s wife and four daughters were buried there. The best explanation comes from a juxtaposition of dates. Beaumont's 2nd edition, we will remember, was in 1897. A note about the 'identical' MIs on Stanley tombs in Tong and Waltham appeared in 1863, in *The Herald and Genealogist*. It could be, therefore, that Beaumont had also seen this reference, or a similar one, and decided, for whatever reason, that it was more likely that **Sir Thomas** was buried at Walthamstow and not Tong. We know that he was wrong; but the source for the mistake still remains a mystery.

There is also still a mystery surrounding **Sir Thomas**'s coffin and body. *Auden's History* provided the details of a visitor to the Stanley vault commenting on the coffin: 'supposed to be Sir T. Stanley, but much broken, is in the shape of stone coffins, and Mr Christian considers it much older than the other lead coffins'. **Sir Thomas**'s body was not in the coffin, and as the coffin had been cut open, it almost seems that he was exhumed and reburied somewhere else, but Walthamstow seems an unlikely place. The only person known with a connection to Walthamstow was his daughter-in-law Lucy Percy, who was definitely buried there, along with four of their daughters. And yet when **Sir Thomas** died in 1576, his son **Edward** was only fourteen and not yet married to Lucy Percy. The main question until now has been why she was buried there, and it was assumed that it was because she and **Sir Edward** were living there at the time when she died, or at least visiting someone there. Why should his son **Sir Edward** commission such an elaborate tomb for his parents at Tong, and then dig up his parents and rebury them elsewhere? If **Sir Edward** had indeed moved his parents' bodies to Walthamstow, why did he not request to be buried there also, along with the whole family? He didn't, but was buried at Eynsham, Oxfordshire.

Meanwhile, Beaumont provided an invaluable brief biography of **Sir Edward Jr**, with some details unreported elsewhere.

~~~~~~~~~~~~~~~~~

XII-7. EXTRACT FIVE from the Manx Notebook (Beaumont, *Winwick*, 1897)

XVIII. — **SIR EDWARD STANLEY**, knight of the Bath, of Tonge Castle, in Shropshire, and of Eynsham, son and heir of **Sir Thomas**, seems like him to have made the rectory at Winwick his occasional residence.[1] **Sir Edward** married Lucy, daughter of Thomas Percy, Earl of

Northumberland, who for engaging in the northern insurrection, was attainted of high treason, and executed on 22 August, 1572. **Sir Edward** was made a knight of the Bath by James I. at Greenwich on Sunday, 24 July, 1603.[2] **He died 16 June, 1632, and was buried at Eynsham**. His wife died before him, and was buried at Walthamstow. Their only son Thomas, who had died an infant before them, was buried at Winwick, and their **four daughters** became the heirs. On the **29 June, 1586, another Sir Edward Stanley, uncle of the former, wrote a letter from his nephew's house at Winwick**, asking his brother, the Earl of Derby, to use his good offices with the Archbishop of Canterbury, to appoint his friend John Kine one of the proctors of the Court of Arches.[3] **Over the grave of the first Sir Edward** is the following inscription:-,-

Hic jacet corpus Edvardi Stanley, equitis balnei (filii Thomae, comitis Derby filii), obiit 18 June, 1632, aetatis suae 69. Petronilla Stanley, filia posuit.[4]

[1] Hist. Lan. iii., 540.
[2] Ibid 622.
[3] Brit. Lib. May, 1737.
[4] Collins' Peerage, iii., 78. [*Here lies the body of Edward Stanley, Knight of the Bath (son of Thomas, son of the Earl of Derby), died 18 June, 1632 aged 69. Petronilla Stanley, daughter, placed (this).* HM]

(www.isle-of-man/manxnotebook/fulltext/ww1897.htm#30)

In his text, Beaumont gives the date of death as '**16 June 1632**', but the inscription at Eynsham gives it as '**18 June**'. One of them was presumably correct, and the temptation is to accept the date on the inscription. '**The four daughters became the heirs**' is a confusion between the four daughters buried with their mother at Walthamstow, and the three surviving daughters. The letter written at Winwick '**by another Sir Edward Stanley, uncle of the former**' is given as 29 June 1586. This is the only letter discovered written by any of the three Stanleys central to this book.

'**Over the grave of the first Sir Edward**' is a confusion by Beaumont of the two Sir Edwards, unless he meant 'first-mentioned above'. It is a pity that Petronella did not mention the monuments at Tong and Walthamstow, but we can be grateful that she left this inscription. She was the unmarried one of the three surviving daughters.

XII-8. Other extracts concerning Winwick

Other references to **Sir Thomas Stanley** discovered (so far) re Winwick were detected by Professor Honigmann, in his investigations concerning the epitaphs in Tong.

We learn from *Inhabitants of Winwick v. Stanley* (26 Elizabeth)* that **Sir Thomas Stanley** in his later years was in financial difficulties; one deponent, Thomas Heye, declared that most of the complainants gave a year's rent to **Sir Thomas** 'of their benevolences when he was in trouble' (9th interrogatory).

*DL4 26 (18) = Duchy of Lancaster records in the Public Record Office.

(Honigmann, *Shakespeare: the 'lost years'*, p. 81.)

This 'trouble' 'in his later years', i.e. some time in the 1570s before his death in 1576, can only refer to his incarceration in the Tower, with regular inquisitions there from late 1570 onwards, with torture at least in 1571, to (perhaps) late 1572 or beyond (the date of his release has not yet been established). His financial troubles presumably lay in a heavy fine as a condition of his release.

1571, **Sir Thomas Stanley**. A confession on the rack brought about his arrest and committal to the Tower [Ridolfi plot]. From the library of the Public Record Office, *Prisoners of the Tower* by A .H. Cook, formerly Chief Warder H.M. Tower of London, 2 hand-written volumes.

(Brian S. Roberts, Stanley Family Genealogy website.)

We know that there were no executions of the main participants in this plan to free Mary, Queen of Scots, as **Sir Thomas Stanley**, his younger brother, **Sir Edward Sr** and Sir Thomas Gerard of Bryn, all lived on. We know that Sir Thomas Gerard was fined ruinously, we still do not know the punishment inflicted on **Sir Edward Sr**, but this court case and document seem to confirm that **Sir Thomas Stanley** was also fined heavily. The decision taken by the inhabitants of Winwick to support him in his 'trouble' by offering a whopping whole year's rent implies (1) his general popularity as a landlord in Winwick, (2) a general sympathy among the inhabitants for the plan to release Mary, Queen of Scots from her captivity, or (3) a mixture of both.

One problem comes from dates. *The Inhabitants of Winwick v. Stanley* was in 26 Elizabeth, i.e. 1584-5, but **Sir Thomas** had died in 1576, eight years earlier. Perhaps there has been a mistake in transcription of the date, or perhaps this was because of a later problem which occurred, and the inhabitants were reporting in retrospect? The answer seems to be related to a court case in 1584 involving William Stanley, son of Henry, 4th Earl (William later to become 6th Earl of Derby) and tied up with the entailment of the estates granted by Earl Edward to **Sir Thomas**. The article in Chapter XIX. Eynsham gives the following details, involving the succession of certain Stanley estates and the right of advowson:

> Therefore, after the 3rd Earl's death in 1572, the lands passed to **Sir Thomas Stanley**; but he died in 1576 and so Lady Margaret would have inherited. During her time we have the account of the 1584 quarrel between William Stanley and Thomas Peniston (see *Eynsham Record*, no. 1, p. 23, 1984). William was the younger son of Henry, the 4th Earl. In 1585 Thomas Peniston presented Thomas Secheverell to the Eynsham living.

Honigmann also provides details of **Sir Thomas**'s widow Margaret, who remarried:

> There are no clues in **Sir Thomas**'s will,* [*about his financial difficulties a few years before*] but his widow's** reveals another relevant fact: she married again, and might have wished to be buried with her second husband. In the event, however, she snubbed her second husband, leaving him no token of her love, decreeing 'my body to be buried in the Parish Church of Tong by my husband **Sir Thomas Stanley**'; her will states, cryptically, that it was 'made by the consent and agreement' of her second husband, William Mathe, Esq. The tomb, therefore could have been delayed because the family was short of funds and, later, because there would be some doubt as to the figures to be represented.
>
> *PCC (39 Carew). **Sir Thomas** was 'in trouble' in 1571 when he tried to rescue Mary Queen of Scots, and was imprisoned in the Tower for his pains.
> **PCC (92 Drake).
> PCC = Prerogative Court of Canterbury (all PCC wills are in the Public Record Office).
>   (Honigmann, *Shakespeare: the 'lost years'*, p. 81 + endnotes, p. 160.)

Only two further details have emerged so far about this second marriage: a note about (Sir) **Edward Stanley Jr** reveals his ownership of another property via his mother and provides a more likely alternative – Mather – as the surname of his stepfather on his mother's remarriage. The only Stackpole located is near Pembroke, on the Pembrokeshire coast.

Edward STANLEY (Sir)

Born: ABT 1563 [*sic*, actually mid-late 1562. HM]
Died: 1632

Notes: of Tong Castle. The Vernons held Stackpole until the death of **Sir George Vernon** in 1565. He too left two daughters, one of whom, **Margaret**, married **Thomas Stanley**, second son of **Edward, Earl of Derby**. After **Thomas'** death in 1576, Stackpole was divided between their son **Edward** and the widowed **Margaret**, who took a second husband, **William Mather**. It is doubtful whether **Edward**, whose main residence was Tong Castle in Shropshire, ever resided at Stackpole for any considerable period of time. In 1597 he demised his lands in Stackpole to **William Ingleby**, and there is every possibility that he was leasing them out before then. A family arrangement was made whereby **Edward** was to inherit half of the joint property of **William** and **Margaret Mather** upon his mother's death, and the other half after the death of his step-father, which occurred on 30 Nov 1607. As an outlying property situated far from his other estates Stackpole was of little interest to him, so a year later he disposed of it to **Roger Lort**, who had for some time been both an agent and a tenant of his mother in the Stackpole district.

(Tudorplace.com.ar/STANLEY)

[N.B. *There is no indication of the source of this note. In the above paragraph the names highlighted in bold are by the anonymous author.* HM]

One interesting name is William Ingleby, a Yorkshire recusant family. Sir William Ingleby pops up on the periphery of the Gunpowder Plot; further research might reveal whether they were one and the same.

The Wintours' mother was Jane Ingleby, daughter of Sir William Ingleby of Ripley Castle, near Knaresborough. Her brother Francis Ingleby was a priest: he had been hung, drawn and quartered in 1586.

(Fraser, *The Gunpowder Plot*, p. 58.)

Marple and Wybersley, which were also given to Margaret Vernon on her marriage to **Sir Thomas Stanley**, were also given at her death to her son **Edward**. (Brian S. Roberts, Stanley Family Genealogy website.)

~~~~~~~~~~~~~~~

XII-9. Chapels in Winwick Church

There was never a Stanley Chapel in Winwick Church, despite **Sir Thomas** and **Sir Edward Jr** leasing the Rectory there for so many decades and **Sir Edward Jr** burying his son there. There were (still are), however, Chapels endowed by two other families with property in Winwick and who enter **Sir Thomas** and **Sir Edward**'s stories at several points: the Leghs of Lyme Hall in Cheshire and the Gerards of Bryn Hall near Wigan, Lancashire. Although the Battle of Winwick was in 1648, too late for 'our' **Stanleys of Winwick**, the sentences referring to this are left in, as a reminder that Winwick was very much on the main route north-south over the Mersey.

All the stained glass in the Chancel was given in 1849 by Edward, 13th Earl of Derby, in memory of his family's service as Patrons of the Parish since 1433. The obituary window, above the memorial table has the family Coat of Arms and six small shields. The East window shows the writers of the New Testament; the other windows illustrate various Bible Stories. In the Gerard chapel, the East window depicting scenes from the life of St. Oswald was installed in 1938 as a memorial to the Stone family.**The Pugin Chancel** Cromwell had stationed his troops in the Church after the Battle of Red Bank 1648. Much damage was done to the church; from then onwards the mediaeval chancel decayed. It was reconstructed in 1849 by the famous architect A.W. Pugin who designed every detail – modelling it on the old chancel – from floor tiles to ceiling, and from stained glass to vestry cupboards. In 1970 the chancel was restored to Pugin's original design and is one of the glories of the church. In the Chancel can be seen memorials to more recent Rectors, and one dated 1689 to Rector Richard Sherlock who insisted on writing his own epitaph "tread under foot this worthless salt" – but his parishioners added "his life and merits exceed all praise".**The Gerard Chapel** On the floor of this chapel – the East end of the North aisle – is a magnificent, but damaged brass memorial to Sir Piers Gerard who died in 1495. Beneath the floor is the family vault. This has not been used since the Reformation. At the East end is a Communion Table dated 1725. This was the main Altar of the Church until the restoration of the Chancel. The Churchwardens Accounts record its purchase for £4.00. In the centre is an anagram of the initials of the Rector of the day – Rev. Dr. Francis Annesley, and in the corners are inlaid the initials of the Churchwardens. On the North wall is an aumbry containing the Reserved Sacrament.**The Legh Chapel** This chapel, the chantry chapel of the Legh family of Lyme Hall, contains several very fine marble monuments. It also contains an unusual brass – to Sir Peter Legh and his wife, dated 1527. Sir Peter is depicted wearing priests vestments over his armour – he was ordained after the death of his young wife. The fine Tudor roof with gilded carved angels. This chapel now houses the organ.

(Website of St Oswald's Parish Church, Winwick)

It is worth noting, before we leave Winwick, that there had been several other Stanleys involved in the advowson of the parish before and during the lifetimes of **Sir Thomas** and **Sir Edward Jr.**

Appointment	*Rectors of Winwick*	*Presented by*
1432/3	Thomas Bourchier	Sir John Stanley
1436	George Radcliffe, D. Decr.	--
1453	Edward Stanley	Sir Thomas Stanley
1462	James Stanley	Henry Byrom
1485	Robert Cliff	Lord Stanley
1493/4	Mr. James Stanley, D.Can.L.	Earl of Derby
1515	Mr. Thomas Larke	"
1525	Thomas Winter	The King
1529	William Boleyne	"
1552	Thomas Stanley	Earl of Derby
1568/9	Christopher Thompson, M.A.	Thomas Handford
1575/6	John Caldwell M.A.	Earl of Derby
1596/7	John Ryder, M.A.	-
1616	Josiah Horne	The King
27 June, 1626	Charles Herle, M.A.	**Sir Edward Stanley**

(*Victoria County History,* Vol. 4, 1911, Winwick, pp. 122-132.)

This **Sir Edward Stanley** in 1626 (table above) was presumably **Sir Edward Jr**, thus still showing an interest in Winwick during the last years of his life. He may or may not have known that there had previously been a Stanley Chantry in the church.

WINWICK'S CHANTRY CHAPELS AND EFFIGIES.
"Sephulchal stones appeared with Emblems graven, And foot-worn Epitaphs, and some with small and shining Effigies Of brass inlaid."

THE LOST CHANTRIES.
In the olden time, there were Chantry Altars and Chapels beneath our roof wherein prayers were offered for the souls of donors and their nominees. One chantry, in our Chapel of the Holy Trinity, was, in 1330, made by Gilbert de Haydock. "A fit and honest Chaplain was appointed to pray for the founder by name, every time a mass was sung.

A later foundation—Stanley's Chantry—in St. Oswald's, lay in what we named the Rector's Chapel.- It was duly endowed with the rents of certain houses and lands (burgages) in Lichfield and Chester and was worth about 66s. 8d. per annum.

All chantries in England were confiscated in 1548 under a law of King Edward the Sixth.

There is some indication that about six years before this confiscation, but in the time of King Henry the Eighth, Sir Peter Legh of Lyme, presented a chantry priest to St. Oswald's Church here at "Wynwych."

    The Registers of Christenings, Marriages and Burials commences with the year 1563. Of earlier records : — — - the first (paper) book is not known to be in existence to-day, but it has been suggested that the earliest entry therein was made in 1550 ?" One of our bells is thought to date from somewhere about the year 1600, it bears the initials which have been taken to stand for Peter Legh, Thomas Gerard, Edward Eccleston, **Edward Stanley, Thomas Stanley** and John Rider.

Joseph P. Leach, *The Church of Saint Oswald, Winwick in Legend and History* (1930s), on the website of Newton-le-Willows by Steven Dowd.

    The dates of the register explain why **(Sir) Edward Jr**'s baptismal record has not survived. We know he was born mid-late 1562 and the register only starts in 1563. It leaves another puzzle as to why the burial of his infant son Thomas is not recorded. We know that he was buried here from the inscription in Tong:

THO^s HIS SOON DIED IN HIS INFANCIE A IS BVRIED IN Y^e PARISHE CHVRCHE
OF WINWICKE IN Y^e COVNTIE OF LANCA:

    Presumably, if the interpretation of the initials on a bell is correct, he was somehow responsible for this. The guess that one of the bells is 'thought to date from somewhere about the year 1600' is interesting as being around the time when **Sir Edward Jr** commissioned the tomb for his wife Lucy in Walthamstow and for his parents and himself in Tong. We know that he was at Preston Guild in 1602, so this might have been the occasion for spending some time in Winwick and commissioning a bell.

<div align="center">~~~~~~~~~~~~~~</div>

XII-10. The location of the Rectory

Richard Kuerden (1623–90?), the Lancashire antiquary from Cuerden near Preston, who left so many invaluable notes on his research when planning to write a history of the county (now in Chetham's Library/Manchester Archives), passed through Winwick on one of his journeys. He left the following description, which, despite the intervening Civil Wars, cannot have been too much different from the route that **Sir Edward Jr** took on many occasions. The Rectory leased by him is the same as the Vicarage, 'a princely building equal to the revenue, call'd the Parsonage of Winwick'. The Leghs and Gerards mentioned were the grandsons of those **Sir Edward Jr** knew. The date below of 1695 conflicts with the date of death 1690? given by Chetham's, but this is a mere quibble.

    C. Coles, *History of Newton*, 1916 gives the following as the whole of the Kuerden Text:

> In a description of a journey made through the parish about the year **1695**, Dr. Kuerden, in his Lancashire Itinerary, under the heading of **"the Post Road from Warrington to Wigan"**, after describing the road from Warrington, goes on to say:
>
>   "A mile further stands a fair built church, called Winwick Church, a remarkable fabric dedicated to St. Wilfred (Oswald), a Christian Prince and King of Northumbria, slain by Panda, King of Mercia in Makerfield, when the said Panda invaded the Northumbrian Territories; in memory of which battle this Church was dedicated to St. Oswald.
>
>   Leaving the Church on the right, about a quarter of a mile westwards stands a princely building equal to the revenue, call'd the Parsonage of Winwick. And near the Church, on the right hand, stands a fair built School house. By the East end of the Church is another road, but less used, to the Borough of Wigan.
>
>   Having passed the school about half-a-mile you come to a sandy place call'd the Red Bank, where Hamilton and his army were beaten. Here, leaving Bradley Park and a good seat belonging to Mr. Brotherton, of Hey, a Member of Parliament for the Borough of Newton, on the left hand, and Newton Park on the right, you have a little Stone bridge over Newton Brook, three miles from Warrington, but on the left hand, close by a Water Mill, appear the ruins of the site of

129

the ancient Barony of Newton, where formerly was the Baron's Castle.

Having pass'd the bridge, you ascend a rock, where is a Pinfold cut out of the same, and upon the top of the rock was lately built a Court house for the Manor, and near to it a fair reedify'd Chapel of stone built by Rich: 'Legh, deceas'd, father to Mr. Legh, the present titular Baron of Newton. There stands a stately cross, near the Chapel, well adorn'd with the Arms belonging to the present Baron.

Having pass'd the Town of Newton you leave a cross road [Crow Lane] on the left, going to Liverpool by St. Ellen's Chapel. You pass in winter through a miry lane [Ashton Road] for half-a-mile. You leave another lane [Penny Lane] on the left, passing by Billing, the Hall of Winstanley, belonging to the Winstanleys, and so to Ormskirk.

Then passing on a sandy lane you leave Hadoc Park, and close by the road Hadoc Lodge, belonging to Mr. Legh, and going on for half-a-mile, you pass by the Chapel and through the town of Ashton, standing on a rocky ground which belongeth to Will Gerard, Bert., of Brin, but who resides at Garswood about a mile to the East."

(Blog of Steve Dowd re Newton-le-Willows)

XII-11. Conclusions

1. We are now in a position to write an outline of Sir Thomas's biography, as discovered up to this point, and the first one ever written: born c.1534; knighted 2 October 1553 on the day after Queen Mary's coronation; married Margaret Vernon 1558; son and heir Edward born mid-late 1562; son Henry perhaps born earlier than Edward, but died young and was probably buried at Tong; Governor of the Isle of Man 1562-66; leased the rectory in Winwick in 1563; Mayor of Liverpool 1568-69; Commissioner of muster for Lancashire 1569; involved in a plan to free Mary, Queen of Scots from Chatsworth May 1570; sent to the Tower November 1570; principal role established by July 1571 (before or after being put on the rack); still detained in May 1572, or perhaps considerably longer because he is not reported as attending his father's funeral on 4 December 1572; released (date unknown) on payment of a heavy fine; to pay this he was helped by his tenants in Winwick; moved to Tong Castle, his wife's property 1574/5; continued to meet Catholic gentlemen there; died at Tong 21 December 1576; buried in the newly created Stanley vault beneath the altar; succeeded by his only son and heir Edward, aged fourteen at his father's death. His widow remarried, William Mather; Margaret died in 1596 and Mather on 30 November 1607. Son Edward commissioned a tomb for his parents in St Bartholomew's Church, Tong, with effigies of both. Their bodies were later exhumed and perhaps buried elsewhere (place and reason unknown).

2. All the muddles and confusions among three contemporary Sir Thomas Stanleys seem to have been sorted out:

   i) **Sir Thomas Stanley** of Winwick and Tong (born c.1534, died 1576), second son of Edward, 3rd Earl of Derby.

   ii) Sir Thomas Stanley, 2nd Lord Monteagle (born 2 May 1507, died 25 August 1580, according to Stirnet.com), son and heir of Sir Edward, 1st Lord Monteagle.

   iii) Thomas Stanley, Bishop of Man and Rector of Winwick + many other places (born early sixteenth century?, died 1568), younger son of second wife or mistress of Sir Edward, 1st Lord Monteagle, and so half-brother of Thomas, 2nd Lord Monteagle.

3. The outline biography of Thomas Stanley, Bishop of Man, also now seems to be fairly clear.

4. We have taken a few steps forward following in **Sir Edward Jr**'s footsteps.

~~~~~~~~~~~~~~~~~~

XIIc. Liverpool waterfront in the 16th century

With the Stanley Tower and Molyneux Castle. Sir Thomas presumably saw this view whenever returning from the Isle of Man, and perhaps stayed at the family castle. An impression (rather imaginative!) by Jessica Lofthouse, a noted artist and writer on Lancashire history and the countryside in the 1960s–1980s. None of these buildings remain today, although there are still many roads, streets, avenues, etc. named Stanley, Derby and Molyneux.

Chapter XIII
1570: Sir Thomas & Sir Edward Sr and Mary, Queen of Scots

XIII-1. Introduction
XIII-2. Mary S. Lovell: the plot of 1570
XIII-3. The immediate consequences for the three Lancashire knights
XIII-4. Conclusion

XIII-1. Introduction

As already mentioned in previous chapters, in 1570 **Sir Thomas** and **Sir Edward Sr** were involved in a plan to 'kidnap' Mary, Queen of Scots from Chatsworth House in Derbyshire, one of the homes of the Earl of Shrewsbury and his recently married second wife Elizabeth née Hardwick, who is known in 'popular history' as Bess of Hardwick. (George Talbot, 6th Earl of Shrewsbury, with his family origins in Lancashire, was her fourth husband. Biographies of both are in the *DNB*, Old and New.) Brief accounts of this rescue attempt by Bagley and Coward were presented in previous chapters, but a more recent and much more comprehensive account reveals more details.

IIIa. Chatsworth House, 17th century

Painting of the west front of the Elizabethan house. One version was by Richard Wilson (1714-82) after a contemporary original by Jan Siberechts (1627-1703). The Wilson version is in the Devonshire collection at Chatsworth House. (Lovell, *Bess of Hardwick*)

Before embarking on this, it should be pointed out that George Talbot's first wife had been Gertrude Manners, daughter of Thomas Manners, 1st Earl of Rutland. She was a sister of John Manners, who had eloped with Dorothy Vernon, sister-in-law of **Sir Thomas Stanley**. George and Gertrude's eldest son Francis, Lord Talbot (who died before his father) had married Anne, daughter of William Herbert, 1st Earl of Pembroke. Their eldest son Henry had married as his second wife Katherine Talbot, a daughter of George, 6th Earl of Shrewsbury, and by his third wife Mary Sidney was father of William and Philip Herbert, the later Earls of Pembroke and Montgomery, to whom Shakespeare's First Folio in 1623 was dedicated. In 1570 many of these complicated relationships (even some of the births) still lay in the future, but already at this time George Talbot, 6th Earl of Shrewsbury was the brother-in-law of **Sir Thomas Stanley**'s sister-in-law Dorothy Manners née Vernon. Gilbert Talbot, son of George, 6th Earl of Shrewsbury, was also the godson of Sir George Vernon, 'King of the Peak', **Sir Thomas**'s father-in-law. To cope with these relationships (and other Stanley-Talbot links), about which they would almost certainly have known, the common practice at the time would have been to call each other 'cousins'.

XIII-2. Mary S. Lovell: the plot of 1570

Previous histories have seen this rescue attempt as from Sheffield Castle (e.g. Bagley, as given in a previous chapter), the main seat of the 6th Earl of Shrewsbury (1527–90), but the latest biography of

Bess of Hardwick, First Lady of Chatsworth by Mary S. Lovell (Little, Brown, 2005; pb. Abacus, 2006), which has been painstakingly and sympathetically researched, places the location unequivocally as Chatsworth House in Derbyshire. The events leading up to Mary Stuart's presence at Chatsworth are provided succinctly in this book (reproduced here with the kind permission of Ms Lovell).

> The marriage of Mary, Queen of Scots to the Earl of Bothwell (the suspected, though unproven, assassin of Lord Darnley) had evoked the wrath of Scottish nobles. Mary and Bothwell had been married only five weeks when her kingdom was threatened by revolt. After Bothwell left her to muster an army, Mary was taken into custody. He made several half-hearted attempts to rescue her, but the couple never saw each other again and later she miscarried twins. She was eventually required to abdicate in favour of her year-old-son James, on the evidence of the so-called 'Casket Letters', which, if genuine, linked her to the murder of her former husband. On 28 May 1568 the deposed Queen escaped from her island prison at the Castle of Lochleven and fled to Carlisle in England, where she begged asylum and placed herself under Elizabeth's protection.
>
> In a gesture of queenly solidarity, Elizabeth advised the Scottish government that she would refuse to acknowledge the infant James as King of Scotland while his mother lived. However, when the Privy Council met to discuss the matter of the refugee, Elizabeth was strongly counselled not to allow Mary to leave for France or Spain, nor, at present, to meet with her. Cecil was particularly concerned that Mary might become a rallying point for English Catholics. Since Mary could not be sent back to Scotland, and they could not let her travel to the mainland of Europe, it was decided for the time being to hold her in confinement, giving as a reason the fact that she was still under suspicion of being involved in the murder of Lord Darnley.
>
> It seems that the Queen had already worked out a new role for the Earl of Shrewsbury. If she had drawn up a specification for the Custodian of Mary, Queen of Scots, the Earl would have met every criterion for the position. Although a prisoner, Mary was still an anointed queen and needed to be treated as such – suitable accommodation was therefore required for her and for the members of her household, and Shrewsbury had a number of large properties, any one of which could house Mary and her retinue; he was a rich man and could afford to pay for the necessary additional servants and security required; he was happily married and therefore less likely to fall in love with Mary, as did many men who came into contact with her; his loyalty and sense of duty was unquestioned; and he and his wife were staunch Protestants.
>
> When Shrewsbury was summoned to Court he travelled to London with alacrity...By early December 1568 the Earl was stuck at Court, unable to leave without the Queen's permission....Ten days later the Earl was created a Privy Counsellor and made the custodian of the Scottish Queen. The Earl wrote to Bess the same day, 13 December, to advise her that it was 'now certain the Scots Queen comes to Tutbury, to my charge'.
>
> (Lovell, *Bess of Harwick*, pp. 201-5.)

A detailed account follows of the preparations at Tutbury, the decision that it was totally unsuitable as a long-term solution, and the preparation of Wingfield Manor, Sheffield Castle and Chatsworth House, all much more suitable for 'entertaining' a queen. And so it was that:

> in mid-May 1570 permission was granted for Mary to be transferred to Chatsworth, while Tutbury was 'cleansed and sweetened'.
>
> (Lovell, *Bess of Hardwick*, p. 225.)

The previous year had seen the Catholic pro-Mary 'Rising of the North'/ 'Northern Rising'/ 'Northern Rebellion', which was quelled without too much difficulty by forces faithful to Queen Elizabeth, but had profound consequences for many. These included Catholic Thomas Hoghton of Hoghton Tower, who almost immediately fled into exile in Flanders, never to return, and where he died in 1580. This was the Thomas Hoghton whose brother Alexander was later to name William Shakeshafte as a member of his household, associated with 'instruments of music and play-clothes', and one of the main bases for the 'Shakespeare in Lancashire' theory. (Honigmann, *Shakespeare: the 'lost years'*, II. Hoghton of Hoghton Tower, pp. 8–30.)

XIIIb. Bess of Hardwick, 1592

Second wife of Gilbert Talbot, 6th Earl of Shrewsbury (fourth husband), who was guardian of Mary, Queen of Scots in 1570 at Chatsworth, from where Sir Thomas planned to help her escape.

The Northern Rebellion of 1569 had also had serious consequences for Thomas Percy, 7th Earl of Northumberland (**Sir Edward Jr**'s future father-in-law), who was subsequently incarcerated and executed in York in 1572. (Biography in the *DNB*, with numerous biographies online.)

The main event that concerned **Sir Thomas** and **Sir Edward Sr** in 1570 was a scheme hatched by them and their Catholic friend Sir Thomas Gerard of Bryn to spirit Mary, Queen of Scots away from Chatsworth. Bryn was near Wigan, Lancashire, but his family also owned Etwall, Derbyshire, just a few miles north of Tutbury on the way to Chatsworth.

Prior to the northern rising there had been another plan to release Mary, concocted by a cousin of the Earl of Northumberland, Leonard Dacre... This plan had been squashed by Norfolk who, still hoping to marry Mary, thought that an escape would ruin all hope of ever gaining Elizabeth's approval to the match.

Now this old scheme was resurrected by a number of young men of the county under the leadership of Sir Thomas Gerard, a Catholic squire. Those involved were few: the brothers Francis and George Rolleston, John Hall (a former servant of the Earl of Shrewsbury) and two men from Lancashire, **Sir Thomas** and **Sir Edward Stanley**. The idea was that while riding out over the high moor, as she often did, Mary would be snatched. She would then be taken to the coast, and from there by boat to the Isle of Man, where she would be able to negotiate with Elizabeth from a position of strength. One morning at 5 a.m. the two Rolleston brothers met Mary's Master of Household, John Beaton, on the bleak and chilly 'high moor' above Chatsworth to coordinate the escape. Beaton was not convinced that the kidnap idea would work; the guards were too many and the plotters too few. He favoured Mary escaping at night by being let down on a rope from a window. Mary was still only in her twenties, and, despite her reported illnesses, she was strong. She had certainly endured worse, in her recent colourful career, than being lowered from a window on a rope.

Eventually, Bess got to hear of the plan and told Shrewsbury. The Rolleston brothers were arrested and sent to prison. Beaton died suddenly and was buried in the churchyard in the nearby village of Edensor before Cecil's men could question him. But it appears that the plan did not have Mary's approval anyway. When Beaton approached her about it, she turned it down, saying that she still had confidence that Elizabeth would restore her 'to her former dignity', following requests from the Kings of France and Spain.

(Lovell, *Bess of Hardwick*, pp. 226–7.)

An earlier account of the scheme to help Mary to escape from Chatsworth in 1570 had appeared in 1969 by Antonia Fraser, which also included an intriguing 'new' detail about **Sir Edward Sr**. How much truth there was in his excuse it is difficult to judge.

In May 1570 Mary was once more taken back to Chatsworth, and here a fantastic plan was hatched on the part of some romantic local squires to rescue her.

The fabric of the plot was revealed in the examinations of those involved after they had been arrested; it seemed the protagonists were Sir Thomas Gerard, a local Catholic squire (father of the future Jesuit missionary John Gerard), two brothers, Frances and George Rolleston, one John Hall and two Lancashire magnates, the brothers **Sir Thomas** and **Sir Edward Stanley**. But the most searching cross-examinations could never make the actual practical details of the plot amount to very much. **Sir Edward Stanley** strongly denied that he had had any effective part in it, giving the ingenious excuse that he had been away in the north at the time courting a Mrs

Strickland. Gerard's idea was that the Queen of Scots having escaped from Chatsworth should be shipped away to the Isle of Man by the good offices of **Thomas Stanley**; but he put his finger on the main trouble with any private rescue plot to do with Mary Stuart during all her years of captivity when he said that he had 'feared to make many privy thereof for danger of discovery, and unless many were made privy, the thing could not be done'.[26]

[26] Hat. Cal. I, p. 505. [Calendar of Manuscripts at Hatfield House.]

(Antonia Fraser, *Mary Queen of Scots*,
Weidenfeld and Nicolson, 1969, 1970; Phoenix, 2002, p. 524.)

The differing details in these two accounts seem to have appeared because Antonia Fraser was working mainly from manuscripts at Hatfield House, and Mary Lovell mainly from manuscripts at Chatsworth House.

**XIIIc. Mary, Queen of Scots
in captivity, c.1580**

Whether this was an 'ingenious excuse' or a genuine reason on the part of **Sir Edward Sr**, we will never know. The Stricklands were a prominent family in Westmorland and one Mary Strickland was intriguingly later 'one of the Maries', who gathered round Mary, Queen of Scots during the time leading up to her trial (www.stirnet.com). Whether she had anything directly to do with the Mrs Strickland being courted by **Sir Edward Sr** in 1570 is unknown. In any case, **Sir Edward Sr**'s courtship was obviously unsuccessful, because he never married.

There was one major Stanley link with Westmorland through the Clifford family, who, although Earls of Cumberland, also had extensive lands in Westmorland. **Sir Edward Sr**'s sister-in-law (wife of his elder brother Henry, Lord Strange, later 4th Earl of Derby) was Margaret Clifford, daughter of Henry Clifford, 2nd Earl of Cumberland, half-sister of George, 3rd Earl of Cumberland, another swashbuckling earl. At the very least it seems as good as certain that these would all have known each other as and when any of them were at court or otherwise in London, or when the Cliffords (and Stricklands?) were passing through Lancashire on their way south to London or north on their way back.

~~~~~~~~~~~~~~

XIII-3 . The immediate consequences for the three Lancashire knights

FIRST. SIR THOMAS GERARD. The Sir Thomas Gerard in question was of Bryn, near Wigan, Lancashire, an eminent local gentry family, many of whom remained staunchly Catholic and walked a tightrope on several occasions during Elizabeth's reign, often falling off the tightrope and into prison. For his participation in this plan to free Mary in 1570 Sir Thomas Gerard was sent to the Tower and fined heavily.

Gerard's son later reported that 'the payment of a large sum' secured his father's release, and it is probable that **the Stanley brothers** eventually had to purchase their liberty too.
<div align="right">(Bagley, quoted in Chapter IX. Main Derby Historians.)</div>

There may or may not have been confusion in reports of him being sent to the Tower the following year, 1571, for suspected involvement in the Ridolfi Plot. He could hardly have been sent there if he was there already. He was also incarcerated again later for suspicion of participation in the Babington Plot of 1586, which led directly to the execution of Mary, Queen of Scots. (Lists of Gerard Knights and Gerards in the Tower appear on the Stanley Genealogy website, courtesy of Brian S. Roberts, with all reference sources given.)

Given that this book is concerned with the Shakespeare Stanley Epitaphs in Tong, this is hardly the place to attempt to give the whole history of the Gerard Family, even in summary, although a few relevant points might be noted.

Sir Thomas Gerard had been knighted on 2 October 1553 by Queen Mary on the day after her coronation, the same occasion that had seen the knighting of **Sir Thomas Stanley** and two other Stanleys. This on its own, perhaps, is a good example to explain the intimate connections between Sir Thomas Gerard with **Sir Thomas Stanley** and other members of his family. Just two further lists where the two families appear together are those of *Preston Guild* and the *Derby Household Books*.

The Catholicism of the Gerards of Bryn was in contrast to the professed Protestantism of the Gerards of Ince, their near neighbours and close kinsmen. The latter family produced Sir Gilbert Gerard, Elizabeth's Attorney General and Master of the Rolls, and his brother William Gerard, an eminent Protestant lawyer in London. Sir Gilbert's son and heir Sir Thomas was equally eminent and became Elizabeth and James's Knight Marshall and Lord Gerard of Gerard's Bromley in Staffordshire, where the family also had property. We met all three of them when Sir Thomas of (Ince and) Staffordshire received a dedication from Weever in his *Epigrammes* in 1599 (Chapter VIII. Weever, Middleton & Co.)

The basic story of the Gerards of Bryn and Ince is in all standard sources of Lancashire History, including *Baines's History of Lancashire, the Victoria County History* (online), etc.. The biographies of Sir Gilbert and Sir Thomas Gerard of Ince and several other Gerards are in the *Dictionary of National Biography*. Biographies of many other minor contemporary Gerards still await the light of day.

Sir Thomas Gerard of Bryn's son and heir, also Thomas, was a close friend of the younger Earls of Derby, particularly Ferdinando, Lord Strange, the future 5th Earl. To leap ahead for a moment, Thomas Gerard Jr was knighted by James immediately after his succession in 1603, in York on his progression to London, for the help his (Thomas's) father had given to his (James's) mother, or at least had hoped to give her by helping her to escape from Chatsworth.

> Thomas was among the new knights created by James I at York. The King – not for the first or last time – chose to allude to his relationship with Mary Queen of Scots, identifying himself with her supporters. 'I am particularly bound to love your blood,' said the King to Sir Thomas Gerard, 'on account of the persecution you have borne for me.'
>
> (Fraser, *The Gunpowder Plot*, p. xxxiv.)

One can only suspect that **Sir Edward Stanley Jr** was dubbed Knight of the Bath by King James in 1603 for the same reasons. Sir Thomas Gerard Jr was created a baronet in 1611, but was excused the payment of £1000 because of the tribulations born by his father for Mary.

Another son of Sir Thomas Gerard Sr of Bryn was John Gerard, the Jesuit priest who wrote his autobiography, which included some gripping tales, not least the story of his escape from the Tower of London by swinging along a rope. (A few thousand references to numerous accounts of his story are online, just by googling John Gerard, priest.)

SECOND. SIR THOMAS STANLEY. This **Sir Thomas Stanley** is, of course, the one with his effigy on the tomb in Tong. From various reliable sources (given elsewhere in this book) we know that he was knighted by Queen Mary in 1553 and followed a fairly predictable and honourable career as the second son of the Earl of Derby, his father being Edward, 3rd Earl of Derby: he was Governor of the Isle of Man (1562-66), M.P. for Liverpool (1568-9) and Commissioner of Muster for Lancashire (1569). We also know that he was one of the main participants in the plan to free Mary Stuart from Chatsworth in 1570. When his role in this plan was discovered, he was ordered to go to London towards the end of this year to explain himself. We have no idea what explanations he might have given, but we know that he was incarcerated in the Tower. All the evidence indicates that he was there for two or more years, and that he was inquisitioned, with one report indicating that he was actually placed on the rack. He is not reported as attending his father Earl Edward's elaborate funeral ceremony in Ormskirk at the end of 1572 (Chapter XIV. Earl Edward's Funeral), with the implication that he might still have been in the Tower. No further reports have been detected of him in Lancashire or anywhere else in 1573 or 1574.

The next report after this discovered so far is in Shropshire, where he owned Tong Castle by right of his wife Margaret Vernon.

> AD 1575 Now latlie by credible report **Sir Thomas Stanley** is cum to dwell in this cuntrye, and many papists gentilmen resorte unto hym.

Taylor MSS in Shrewsbury School Library.
Quoted in Owen and Blakeway's *History of Shrewsbury*, p. 365.
Quoted in *Auden's History of Tong*, Vol. 1, p. 16, ed. Joyce Frost, 2004.

From this one may conclude (for the time being) that whenever he was released from the Tower, he decided not to return to Lancashire and not to resume any official duties there. The concomitant conclusion is that he decided to 'retire' and recuperate from his ordeal in the Tower in Shropshire at his wife's property Tong Castle, removed somewhat from the Court in London and the 'Northern Court' at the home of the Earl of Derby. **Sir Thomas**, via his wife Margaret, had come into possession of Tong in 1565 (*Auden's History*, Vol. 1, p. 16), but there is no record of his having lived there before the 1575 quote immediately above.

He survived only until the following year, dying on 21 December 1576 (*Auden's History*, p. 16). His death might, of course, have been from any disease imaginable, but we should remember that he was only 42. Although life expectancy was generally short at the time, it was rather higher for those of a privileged class, who lived in somewhat more hygienic conditions than others. Given that he was from an aristocratic and privileged family, many of whose male members lived into their 60s to 80s (unless they were poisoned at a relatively young age for devious political reasons), one must suspect that his death at 42 was affected by his stay and treatment in the Tower. If I am correct in concluding that he led a rather quiet and retired life at Tong Castle, apart from meeting various 'papists gentilmen', then it is logical also to conclude that this quiet period of retirement from public life might have benefited his health. It obviously did not, or at least did not prolong his life beyond the age of forty-two. He was buried in the newly created Stanley vault in St Bartholomew's, Tong. His wife survived him, with their only son, fourteen-year-old Edward. (The fullest possible biography at this stage is given in Chapter XXIX. Conclusion: biographies of Sir Thomas & Sir Edward Jr.)

With his death, his personal significance for William Shakespeare can be deemed rather irrelevant. We must wait for the story of his only son and heir **(Sir) Edward Stanley Jr**, born mid to late-1562, and therefore William Shakespeare's contemporary.

THIRD. SIR EDWARD STANLEY SR. He was also incarcerated in the Tower at the end of 1570, along with his brother **Sir Thomas Stanley** and Sir Thomas Gerard. We have read above his excuse that he was not actually involved, but courting a lady in Westmorland. The 'truth' will probably never be known. However, one indication that he was treated less severely than his elder brother **Sir Thomas** is that he lived on until 1604, aged 64-69 (his birth date was 1535-40), which allowed him to play father figure to his nephew and act as senior member of the family after the death of his elder brother Earl Henry in 1593. However, he, like his brother **Sir Thomas**, is not recorded as present at the funeral of father Edward, 3rd Earl in December 1572, which raises the possibility that he was still in the Tower at this time. There is silence for the next ten years, but he was fully functioning in his capacity as a senior member of the Derby family when he attended Preston Guild in 1582. His biography appears in more detail in Chapter XXI. Sir Edward Sr's first ever biography.

XIII-4. Conclusions

Although the above is the only mention of **Sir Thomas Stanley** in Lovell's biography of *Bess of Hardwick*, this book is rich in details of the network of relationships spreading out from the Earl of Shrewsbury's family and estates, and **Sir Thomas** must have known many of these and visited some of the country houses named. Apparently he never visited the Earl and Countess of Shrewsbury, or Lovell would have presumably uncovered his name among the hundreds of family papers and letters examined. However, we do learn that Sir George Vernon of Haddon Hall visited Bess at Chatsworth to congratulate her on the birth of her seventh child Mary by her second husband Sir William Cavendish, in January 1556 (Lovell, *Bess*, p. 93) and from other sources we know that Sir George's daughter Margaret Vernon married **Sir Thomas Stanley**, with their son (later Sir) **Edward** born in 1562. Maybe they all met (again) later at Haddon Hall, home of Margaret's sister Dorothy, **Sir Thomas**'s sister-in-law? Or those from Haddon Hall visited Tong? If so, this would have been in the period between his move to Tong in 1574/5 and his death in December 1576.

~~~~~~~~~~~~~~~~

XIIId. Fotheringay Great Hall

Contemporary drawing of the execution of Mary, Queen of Scots in 1587. Bess's husband (shown seated in right-hand chair at top) wept openly at the death of his former prisoner (Lovell, *Bess of Hardwick*). Henry Stanley, 4th Earl of Derby had been one of the jurors. His brothers Sir Thomas and Sir Edward had been incarcerated in the Tower for planning to help her escape from Chatsworth in 1570.

Chapter XIV
1572: Earl Edward's funeral

XIV-1. Introduction
XIV-2. Seacome's account of the funeral
XIV-3. Description of Ormskirk church and the Derby Chapel today
XIV-4. Conclusion

1. Introduction

Edward, 3rd Earl of Derby, was the father of Henry, Lord Strange (later 4th Earl), **Sir Thomas** and **Sir Edward Sr** by his second wife Dorothy Howard (his first wife Katherine Howard having died only three months after the marriage). Earl Edward died on 24 October 1572, after ailing for some time. **Sir Thomas** may or may not have been allowed to visit his ailing father and may or may not have attended his funeral on 4 December, but most probably not.

The reason for doubt is that at least until May 1572 **Sir Thomas** was still detained in the Tower, his detention extended until this time because of the suspicion that he had been involved in the plan of Thomas Howard, 4th Duke of Norfolk, to marry Mary, Queen of Scots; also the Ridolfi plot was still being investigated. Norfolk was a fairly close kinsman of **Sir Thomas**. **Sir Thomas**'s mother Dorothy Howard was daughter of Thomas Howard, 2nd Duke (1443-1524) and sister of Thomas Howard, 3rd Duke (1473-1554). The 4th Duke, also Thomas Howard (1536-72), the one in the Tower in 1572, was the grandson of the 3rd Duke, and so **Sir Thomas**'s first cousin once removed. He was executed on 2 June 1572. (Biographies and genealogies of all early Dukes of Norfolk are widely available in all major encyclopedias.) How long **Sir Thomas** was detained in the Tower after this is not known, but circumstantial evidence indicates until at least 1573 and possibly 1574.

Another reason for doubt is that **Sir Thomas**, **Sir Edward Sr** and young **Edward** are not named amongst the mourners at Earl Edward's funeral. The implication is, therefore, that none of them attended, and that **Sir Thomas**'s detention in the Tower had also prevented him from visiting his father during his final illness that led to his death in October 1572. As mentioned previously, Sir Thomas Gerard of Bryn, the chief initiator of the plan to free Mary from Chatsworth, is reported as having been in the Tower for three years, which makes it not unreasonable to assume that **Sir Thomas** was detained there for a similar period.

XIVa. Edward Stanley, 3rd Earl of Derby, drawing

The origin of this is the same as the drawings of his son Henry, 4th Earl and his grandson Ferdinando, 5th Earl. They were produced by Miss Farington of Worden Old Hall, the last descendant in the direct line in the nineteenth century, from portraits presented to her ancestor William ffarington of Worden, who had served as Comptroller of the Household to these three earls before his retirement on Ferdinando's death in 1594. In this capacity he was the compiler of the invaluable *Derby Household Books*; he had received the three portraits from his grateful employers. The drawings were produced for publication in Thomas Heywood, *The Earls of Derby and the Verse Writers and Poets of the sixteenth and seventeenth centuries, Stanley Papers Part I*, Chetham Society Old Series vol. 29, Manchester, 1853.

The account of the funeral procession presents a list of the most important male personages there (predictably, no females are mentioned), most of whom, one might assume, **Sir Thomas** would have known from his time in Lancashire in the 1560s. Earl Edward's magnificent funeral (which required six weeks of preparation) set a standard for later funerals among the aristocracy. For example, when planning the funeral of George Talbot, 6th Earl of Shrewsbury (guardian for many years of Mary, Queen of Scots), which took place on 10 January 1591, his son and heir...

> [...] Gilbert [Talbot] seems to have been determined that his funeral would be remembered in the area for centuries to come. With the assistance of the Heralds he drew on the records of funerals such as those of Mary, Queen of Scots and the Earls of Derby and Rutland when making the arrangements.
>
> (Lovell, *Bess of Hardwick*, p. 368, citing Hunter, *A History of Hallamshire*, pp. 97-8.)

XIV-2. Seacome's account of the funeral

This account from Seacome follows on immediately from the biographies of Earl Edward and Earl Henry given in Chapter XI. Main Derby historians. Comments by HM are in square brackets and *italics*.

[The funeral of Edward, 3rd Earl of Derby, on 4 December 1572]

[Although a rather tedious account, this is the one that has survived in Derby literature, and some of the names mentioned link to the story of 'Lancastrian Shakespeare' and the Stanleys in Shropshire and elsewhere. It also serves to illustrate the enormous amount of preparation and ceremony for the funeral of an earl in the sixteenth century. HM]

Having given the reader the marriages and issue of the noble Peer aforesaid, likewise of his sons and daughters, let us now attend his funeral obsequies, which was [sic] conducted with the greatest magnificence; a particular description whereof I met with in the hands of an obscure person near us, and may prove acceptable to all, as well as entertaining to the curious; a transcript whereof I shall give verbatim, viz.

XIVb. Earl Edward, portrait

By Sarah, Countess of Essex, *Memoirs of the Court of Queen Elizabeth*, published 1825.

First, after his decease, his body was wrapped in searcloth, then in lead, and afterwards chested. The chapel and the house, with the two courts, were hung with black cloth, garnished with escutcheons of his arms, and on Saturday before the funeral the body was brought into the chapel, where it was covered with a pall of black velvet, garnished with escutcheons of arms, and thereon was set his coat of arms, helmet and crest, sword and target; and about him was placed the standard, great banner and six bannerets.

On Thursday in the morning before the sermon, **Henry, then Earl of Derby, his son and successor**, being present, with the Esquires and Gentlemen his attendants, and the three chief officers of his house, viz. his Steward, Treasurer and Comptroller, standing about the body with white staves in their hands, clarencieux, king of arms, with his rich coat on, published this thanksgiving and stile of the defunct, in form following.

[Those officiating in 1572 are named below in the funeral procession as 'William Massey, Sir Richard Sherborne and Henry Stanley'. Sir Richard Shireburne of Stonyhurst was Treasurer to Earl Edward and Henry Stanley of Aughton, Earl Edward's first cousin, was Comptroller of

the Household along with William Farington. *'Clarencieux, king of arms', recorded above, who obviously presented the main speech as given below, was Robert Cooke, Clarenceux King of Arms 1567-9. He was one and the same who devised the Shakespeare coat of arms for Mr John Shakespeare in Stratford a few years later, c.1576, which for some inexplicable reason John only ratified twenty years later at the College of Arms in London, and which later appeared on his son William the Bard's tomb in Stratford.*

The two draft documents of 1596 and the further draft document of 1599, are all available at the College of Arms, with facsimiles and extracts from transcriptions appearing in much Shakespeare biography literature. (A list of the main Kings of Arms appears in Thomas Woodcock and John Martin Robinson, 'The Oxford Guide to Heraldry', OUP, 1988, Appendix B. This also reproduces on a colour plate between pp. 144-145 the 'catafalque of Edward (Stanley), 3rd Earl of Derby, from "Vincent's Precedents", showing heraldic display at a noble funeral including a standard, tabard with the deceased's arms, and banners of the family alliances' (Coll. Arms, Vincent 151, p. 366). This was by Augustine Vincent, who 'became Weever's closest friend and helper in his antiquarian labours' (Honigmann, Weever, 1987, p. 61). John Weever was the first to record the Shakespeare epitaphs in Tong.

We now continue with Clarenceux Robert Cooke's funeral oration and the procession.]

XIVc. Earl Edward, portrait from life
A b/w copy of the most reproduced portrait,
original in the Royal Collection.

All honour, laud and praise to Almighty God, who through his divine goodness, hath taken out of this transitory world, to his eternal joy and bliss, the Right Honourable Edward, Earl of Derby, Lord Stanley and Strange, and Lord of Man and the Isles, Chamberlain of Chester, one of the Lords of her Majesty's most honourable Privy council, and Knight Companion of the most noble Order of the Garter.

Next, of the manner and order of the hearse, wherein the body lay during the service. At Ormskirk in Lancashire, two miles from Latham, was erected a stately hearse, of five principals, thirty feet in height, twelve feet in length, and nine feet in breadth, double railed, and garnished in the order and manner following.

First, the top parts and the rails covered with black cloth, the valence and principals covered with velvet; to the valence a fringe of silk, the majesty being of taffety, lined with buckram, had thereon most curiously wrought in gold and silver; the atchievement [sic] of his arms, with helmet, crest, supporters and motto, and four buckram escutcheons in metal, the top garnished with escutcheons and jewels in metal, six great burian paste escutcheons at the four corners, and at the uppermost part, the valence set forth with small escutcheons of his arms, on buckram in metal, with the garter; the rails and posts also garnished with escutcheons, wrought in gold and silver, on paper royal.

The hearse was placed between the choir and the body of the church, which was also hung throughout with black cloth, with escutcheons thereon, not only of his own arms within the garter, but also impaled with the three Countesses his wives. [*Actually four, but as the first two were aunt and niece, they shared the same arms.*] Every thing being ready on Wednesday at night before the burial, the order of the procession on Thursday after (being the day appointed) was in manner following.

I.   Two Yeomen Conductors, with black Staves in their hands, to lead the way. Morgan ap-Roberts. Thomas Botel.

II.   Then all the Poor Men in gowns, two and two, to the number of one hundred.

III.   Then the Choir and Singing-men, to the number of forty in their surplices.

IV.   An Esquire bearing the Standard, with his Hood on his head, and horse trapped to the ground, garnished with a Shaffron of his Arms with the garter on his forehead, and four Escutcheons of Buckram Metal, on each side two. - Peter Stanley.

[This was almost certainly Peter Stanley of Moor Hall (1518-1592), whose later story enters that of the Hoghtons and Standishes of Duxbury, with both families near the centre of the stories of Pilgrim Father Captain Myles Standish and 'Lancastrian Shakespeare'. Peter's second son William married Bridget Hoghton, the only niece named in the 1622 will of Alexander Standish of Duxbury, the closest relative in Lancashire of Myles, who two years previously had sailed to America on The Mayflower. Bridget was also a niece of Alexander Hoghton, host of young William Shakeshafte/Shakespeare for 'a couple of years' a few years after this funeral.]

V.   Then the Defunct's Gentlemen, mounted on comely geldings, in their Gowns, and Hoods on their shoulders, to the number of eighty.

VI.   The Defunct's two Secretaries riding together, as the other gentlemen before. - Gilbert Moreton, Gabriel Mason.

VII.   Then the Knights and Esquires in like order, two and two, in number fifty.

VIII.   Then the Defunct's two Chaplains, with Hoods on their shoulders, according to their degrees. - Bachelor of Divinity, Master of Arts.

IX.   The Preacher, being the Dean of Chester, his horse trapped, and a Doctor's Hood on his shoulders. Doctor Longworth.

X.   The Defunct's three chief Officers of his Household, viz. the Steward, Treasurer and Comptroller, with white Staves in their hands, Hoods on the shoulder and their horses trapped. - William Massey, Sir Richard Sherborne, Henry Stanley.

XI.   Then an Esquire, bearing the great Banner of his Arms, with his Hood on his head, and his horse trapped and garnished with Escutcheons, as before. - Ed. Norris.

XII.   A Herald of Arms, with his Hood on his head, his horse trapped as aforesaid, wearing the Defunct's Coat of Arms of Damask, and bearing his Helmet of Steel, Pannel gilt, with Mantles of black Velvet, the knots gilt, and a wreath or torse of his Colours, stood his Crest, curiously carved, painted and wrought in Gold and Silver. - Lancaster Herald.

XIII.   Next a King of Arms, with his Hood on his head, wearing his Coat of Arms, richly embroidered with the Arms of England, his horse trapped and garnished as aforesaid, bearing the Shield of Arms of the Defunct, within the garter, and thereon a Coronet. - Norroy King of Arms.

[Norroy King of Arms in 1572 was William Flower, in this position 1562-88, who is of further great relevance to Lancashire gentry families because he had conducted a Visitation of Lancashire in 1567.]

XIV.   Then another King of Arms, riding in like order, bearing the Defunct's Sword, with the pummel upwards, the hilt and chape gilt, with a Scabbard of Velvet. - Clarencieux.

[As mentioned above, this was Robert Cooke.]

XV.   After them another King of Arms, riding in like order, bearing another of the Defunct's Coat of Arms, being wrought as before-mentioned. - Garter, George Leigh, Esqr.

XVI.   Then, on the left side of him, rode a Gentleman Usher, with a white Rod in his hand, his horse trapped, and Hood on his head. - Edward Scasebrick.

[Scaresbrick of Preese, Lancashire.]

XVII.   Then the Chariot, wherein the Body lay, was covered with black Velvet, garnished with
Escutcheons, and a Shaffron of his Arms, and on each horse sat a Page, in a black Coat, and
a Hood on his head; and on the fore seat of the chariot sat a Gentleman Usher, in his Gown,
his Hood on his head; and a white Rod in his hand; and next the body, rode four Esquires,
being assistants to the body, with Hoods on their heads, and horses trapped to the ground.
- Robert Baxter, Robert Dalton, R. Bradshaw, John Preston.

[Robert Dalton, perhaps the son of this, or another of the same name, received an epigram from John Weever, printed 1599, epigram ii.23. The Daltons of Pilling often appear amongst significant Lancashire gentry families.]

XVIII.   And on the outside of them, about the said chariot, six other Esquires, with Hoods on their
heads, and their horses trapped, each of them bearing a Banneret, not only of the Defunct's
Arms, but also the Arms of such noble houses whereof he was descended, viz. the Arms of
Thomas, the first Earl of Derby of that name, Lord Stanley and of Man, empaled with the
Arms of Eleanor his wife, daughter of Richard Nevill, Earl of Salisbury, and sister to
Richard Nevill, Earl of Warwick and Salisbury.

*[The latter was 'Warwick the Kingmaker', whose father could thus be counted amongst the direct ancestors of Earl Edward and **Sir Thomas**. (He is a major figure in Shakespeare's Henry VI trilogy.) The six bannerets mentioned here and following are depicted in colour in the 'Oxford Guide to Heraldry', Plate 32.]*

XIX.   The second Banneret was that of Geo. Lord Stanley and Strange, the son and heir of the said
Thomas, empaled with the Arms of Jane [*Joan*] his wife, daughter and heiress of John,
Lord Strange, of Knocking.

[Coward (1983) gives George's wife as 'Joan', hence the insertion of the alternative above. It is almost impossible to determine, in most cases, how anyone with a similar name in the sixteenth century was known to her contemporaries. More often than not, this name appears in documents in Latin as Jo(h)anna, which was a conglomerate for the Early Modern forms Joan and Jane.]

[Knockin in Shropshire. This was the first known entry of a Shropshire family into that of the Stanleys, who later became Earls of Derby, which brought the title Lord Strange (of Knockin) into the family for the eldest son and heir, a tradition that continues until today as the title of the eldest son and heir of the current 19th Earl of Derby. The three Lords Strange of most relevance to Shakespeare were:

(1) George, Lord Stanley and Strange, mentioned immediately above. He appears in an offstage role in Shakespeare's 'Richard III' as a hostage during the Battle of Bosworth. He never became Earl of Derby because he died before his father. His death in London was mysterious, suspected immediately at the time as resulting from poisoning, but nothing was ever proved.

(2) Henry, Lord Strange, eldest son of Earl Edward, and very much present at this funeral, because he organised it, along with all the Heralds, of course. He was also the patron of the Derby Players, perhaps the first troupe that young Shakespeare/Shakeshafte acted in, before they became Strange's Men/Players under the patronage of his son and heir Ferdinando, another later Lord Strange.

(3) Ferdinando, Lord Strange, eldest son and heir of Henry 4th Earl, and grandson of Edward, 3rd Earl, whose funeral we are in the middle of at the moment.]

XX.   The third Banneret was the Arms of the second Earl of Derby of that name, Lord Stanley
and Strange, and of Man, empaled with the Arms of Anne his wife, daughter of Edward,
Lord Hastings, and sister to George Hastings, the first Earl of Huntingdon, of that name.

XXI.	The fourth Banneret was the Arms of the Defunct, empaled with the Arms of Dorothy, his first [*second*] wife, and daughter of Thomas, Duke of Norfolk, Earl of Surry [*sic*] and Earl Marshal of England, Lord Mawbray, Seagrave and Bruce.
XXII.	On the fifth Banneret the Defunct's Arms, empaled with the Arms of Margaret, his second [*third*] wife, daughter of Ellis Barlow, of Barlow, Esqr.
XXIII.	And on the sixth Banneret, the Defunct's Arms, empaled with the Arms of Mary, his third [*fourth*] wife, daughter of Sir George Cotton, Knight, Vice-chamberlain to King Edward VI.
XXIV.	Next after the chariot, proceeded **the chief Mourner** in the Mourning-robes of an Earl, and on each side of him rode a Gentleman Usher, with white Rods in their hands, hoods on their heads, and their horses trapped. - Richard Ashton, Marmaduke Newton, Gentlemen Ushers. - **Henry**, **Earl of Derby**, **chief Mourner**.
XXV.	On the left side of him, and somewhat behind, rode the Gentleman of Horse, to the Defunct, his Hood on his head, his horse trapped, and leading in his hand the horse of estate, all covered and trapped with black Velvet. - John Ormston.
XXVI.	Next after rode eight other Mourners, being assistants to the chief mourners, their Hoods on their heads and shoulders, and their horses trapped with fine cloth to the ground. - **John, Lord Stourton, Sir Rowland Stanley, Sir Pierce Leigh**, - Butler, Esqur. - Ratcliff, Esqr., Alex Rigby, Alex. Barlow, Wm. Stopford, Esqur.

[*These men, or others in their families, were to play a large role in Earl Henry's council and those of his sons Ferdinando and William, and were almost certainly well known to* **Sir Thomas Stanley**.

John, Lord Stourton, *9th Baron Stourton of Stourton, was a Derby in-law. He was the son and heir of Charles, 8th Baron Stourton and Anne née Stanley (1531-1602), Earl Edward's eldest daughter. His parentage was known as such to Father Henry More SJ, who later wrote one of the attributions of the Tong Epitaphs to Shakespeare. (See Appendix 8. Father Henry More SJ.)*

Sir Rowland Stanley *was of the senior branch of the family of Hooton in the Wirral, father of Sir William, who was later to defect to the Spanish at Deventer. He had been knighted by Queen Mary on the same occasion as* **Sir Thomas** *on the day after her coronation in 1553. He was to live on until 1612. When he died, aged 96, he was 'the oldest knight in England'.*

Sir Piers Legh *was one of a long list with this name, of Lyme Park in North Cheshire, also with lands in Winwick, and one of the Derbys' chief supporters for centuries; his grandson, of the same name, received an epigram from Weever in 1599 (Chapter VIII. Weever, v.i; dedication of book vii).*

The Butler family had several branches in Lancashire, the most important at this time being those of Rawcliffe, related to many local gentry families, including the Standishes of Duxbury, with Henry Butler of Rawcliffe claimed as an uncle by Weever in his Epigrammes (iv.i).

The Ratcliffes/Radcliffes of Ordsall in Salford had produced the Earls of Sussex, with whom they were still in touch, and this John Ratcliffe, Esq. was almost certainly the father of John, killed in 1599 in Ireland, and his sister Margaret, maid-of-honour at Elizabeth's court, who died 'of a broken heart', according to family and doctors' reports, after her brother's death. Queen Elizabeth buried her in St Margaret's, Westminster and Ben Jonson wrote an acrostic poem in her honour. (She has recently been proposed as a mistress of William Shakespeare and the 'Dark Lady' of his Sonnets by Georges Bourbaki, Munich, 2011. This is of interest inasmuch as it provides yet another Dark Lady candidate with close connections to **Sir Thomas** *and* **Sir Edward**'*s family.)*

The Rigby family came to prominence during the Civil War, with members fighting on both sides, with and against the Derbys.

The Barlows were more in-laws.

Wm. Stopford subsequently became Steward of the Derby household until his death in 1584, with his widow Blanche of Shropshire marrying a Hesketh of Rufford. It was his Stopford family papers, 'buried' in DDHe, the Hesketh Papers in the Lancashire Record Office, which provided the main evidence for Pilgrim Father Myles Standish being a Standish of Duxbury, with nothing to do with the

Standish of Standish family of the Isle of Man.

In 1572, at Earl Edward's funeral, none of these had any idea that there would be future disputes about anything in the Stanley family. They all knew their role in Earl Edward's story. On that note, let us read the final items in Seacome's list of attendants.]

XXVII. Then a Yeoman bare-headed, in a black Coat, on foot.

XXVIII. Two sons of the principal Mourners in Gowns, and Hoods on their shoulders, each of them having a Gentleman to lead their horses. – **Wm. Stanley**, **Esqr**. **Franc. Stanley**, **Esqr**.

[*These were the second and third sons of Henry, 4th Earl, therefore grandsons of Edward, 3rd Earl, nephews of* **Sir Thomas**. *William was only eleven at this time and Francis a few years younger. The latter died a few years later, but William lived on to succeed as 6th Earl.* HM]

XXIX. Two Yeomen Ushers, with white Rods, on foot.

XXX. Then the Defunct's Yeomen, two and two, to the number of five hundred.

XXXI. Then all the Gentlemens' Servants, two and two; and thus being whiffled [*whissled/ whistled?*] all the way, by certain Yeomen in black coats, with black Staves in their hands, proceeded to the Church-door, where the servants attended to receive the horses. Being dismounted, those gentlemen that preceded the Corpse, entered into the Church, and received their places according to their degrees, leaving the hundred poor men without, on each side of the way.

Then the body was taken out of the chariot by eight gentlemen in gowns, with Hoods on their heads, assisted by four Yeomen in black Coats, and borne into the Hearse, where it was orderly placed upon a table three feet high, covered with black cloth, and upon him was not only laid a Pall of black Velvet, but also his Coat of Arms, Sword and Target, Helmet and Crest.

Taken out of the chariot, by William Oriel, Jasper North, Francis Banes, John Meare, Thomas Starkey, John Byron, Edmund Winstanley and James Bradshaw, Gentlemen.

And thus the body being placed, the principal Mourner entered the hearse, where was prepared for him at the head of the Defunct a Stool, with a Carpet and four Cushions of black Velvet, to kneel and lean upon.

Then entered the other eight Mourners, and took their places within the uttermost part of the hearse, on each side of the body, four on one side, and four on the other, each of them having a Cushion of black Velvet, to lean upon, and their Stools covered with black Cloth, and a Cushion of the same to kneel upon. At the feet of the Defunct, without the rails, stood the two Esquires, holding the Standard and great Banner; and on each side of the hearse, the other Esquires, with the Bannerets; and behind the principal Mourner stood three Kings of Arms, and the four Gentlemen Ushers; and between the Standard, and at the great Banner, stood the Lancaster Herald of Arms, wearing the Defunct's Coat of Arms.

And thus the body being placed, and every other estate according to their degree, Norroy, King of Arms, pronounced the Stile of the defunct as before-mentioned; which ended, the Dean of Chester began his Sermon, and after the Sermon, the Vicar began the Commemoration, and after the Epistle and Gospel, the Offering was commenced in Manner following.

First, **Henry, now Earl of Derby, being principal Mourner**, offered at the Altar for the Defunct, a Piece of Gold, having before him Garter, Clarencieux, and Norroy, King of Arms and Lancaster Herald of Arms; and on each side of Garter, a Gentleman Usher and Esquire, to bear the chief Mourner's Train.

After him proceeded the other eight Mourners, two and two, according to their Degrees; and in like order, he, with the other Mourners, repaired to their places, where he remaining a smale [*sic*] time, went to offer for himself, having Clarencieux and Lancaster Heralds only before him; and having thus offered, staid [*sic*] between the Vicar and Lancaster Heralds of Arms, to receive the Atchievements [*sic*] of his Father, offered up by the other eight Mourners, in manner and form following.

First, The **Lord Stourton** and Sir Rowland Stanley, offered up the Coat of Arms having before them Clarencieux King of Arms.

Secondly, **Sir Peter Leigh**, Knt. and Thomas Butler, Esq. offered the Sword, bearing the pommel forward, having before them Norroy, King of Arms.

Thirdly, John Radcliffe and Alexander Barlow, Esqrs. offered the Target of his Arms, and before them went Clarencieux.

Fourthly, Alexander Rigby and William Stopford, Esqrs. offered the Helmet and Crest, having before them Norroy, King of Arms.

Which ended, the principal Mourner repaired to his seat, and on each side of him a Gentleman Usher, with his Train borne by an Esquire; and before him Clarencieux, King of Arms, where he remained until the Offering was ended.

Then offered the other eight Mourners for themselves, viz.

The **Lord Stourton** and Sir Rowland Stanley, having before them Clarencieux, King of Arms.

Sir Peter Leigh, Knight, and Thomas Butler, esq; and before them Norroy, King of Arms.

John Ratcliffe and Alexander Barlow, Esquires, having before them Clarencieux, King of Arms.

Then Alexander Rigby and William Stopford, Esquires, having before them blue Mantle Pursuivant of Arms.

Thus when the principal Mourner and the eight Mourner's Assistants had offered and were placed again as aforesaid; then offered the four Esquires, assistants to the Defunct, having before them Lancaster Herald of Arms.

Then the Standard offered by the Esquire that bore it, and before him blue Mantle, Pursuivant of Arms.

Afterwards the great Banner offered by the Esquire that bore it, and before him blue Mantle, Pursuivant of Arms.

Which Standard and Banners being offered by them that bore them, they put off their Hoods, and took their places amongst the rest of the Mourners, being Gentlemen.

Then offered the Steward, Treasurer and Comptroller, with their white Staves in their hands, and Lancaster Herald of Arms before them.

Then all the other Knights, Esqrs. and Gentlemen, wearing black, proceeding in order two and two, according to their degrees.

The Offering being ended, the hundred poor men where [sic] placed to proceed homeward on foot, and Gentlemen, on horseback; then Garter, principal King of Arms, the principal Mourner, with the other eight Mourners, two and two; then the Yeomen on foot, two and two.

The Burial

After the whole departure presently the body was by the eight Gentlemen, and four Yeomen carried to the grave, and before it, Clarencieux and Norroy, King of Arms, and Lancaster Herald of Arms; and above the body, the four Assistants and the six Esquires, bearing the Bannerets.

After the body went the Steward, Treasurer and Comptroller, with two Gentlemen Ushers, and two Yeomen Ushers; who, when the body was buried, kneeling on their knees, with weeping and tears, broke their white Staves and Rods over their heads; and threw the shivers into the grave.

That done, the six Esquires delivered up the six Bannerets, which were presented with the rest of the Atchievements; orderly placed over, and about him; and departed to Latham-hall, where they received their offices and staves again of their new Earl, now their Lord and Master.

Having brought this great and honourable Earl to his last home (the Grave let us not bury him there in total oblivion; but with Sir William Dugdale, Mr. Cambden, Mr. Hollinshead, Mr. Stow, &c. lament his death [*four of the most eminent historians in the sixteenth and seventeenth centuries*], and not quite forget the memory of so eminent and noble a servant to his prince and country, but endeavour to transmit to posterity, for their example and admiration, his most renowned, steady, and faithful behaviour and conduct, under two Kings and two Queens, as well in peace, as in war.

[A final eulogy from Seacome]

It appears from all our Historians, that he lived in the greatest splendor [sic] and magnificence, without any dependance [*sic*] on the court. His greatness supported his goodness, and his goodness endeared his greatness. His height was looked upon with a double aspect; by himself, as an advantage of beneficence and others, of reverence. His great birth raised him above private respect, but his great soul never above public service.

He was kind to his tenants; liberal to his servants; generous to his friends; and hospitable to strangers; he was famous for house-keeping, and his extensive charity: insomuch, that Queen Elizabeth would jestingly say, that he and my Lord of Bedford made all beggars by their liberality.

His House was orderly and regular, a college of discipline, instruction and accomplishment, rather than a palace for entertainment; his and his lady's servants being so many young gentlemen and ladies, trained up to govern themselves by their example, who they knew understood themselves perfectly.

His provisions were natural, all necessaries, bred and provided of his own stock, rather plentiful than various, solid than dainty, that cost him less, and contented more. His table was constant where all were welcome and none invited. His hall was commonly full, his gates always; the one with the honest gentry and yeomen, who were his retainers in love and observance, bringing good stomachs to his table, and resolved hearts for his service; the other were the aged, decrepid, and industrious poor, whose cravings were prevented; the first being provided with meat, the second with money, and the third with labour.

In this northern insurrection against her Majesty Queen Elizabeth [*the Northern Rebellion in 1569*], he offered to raise Ten Thousand Men at his own charge for the suppressing thereof; but his appearance in the field was sufficient, the holding up of his hand being as effectual as the displaying of a banner. In a word, Mr. Cambden observes, that hospitality lieth buried in this Earl's grave, (1572 the time of his death) from whence may the Divine Power raise it and all mankind to everlasting bliss, when there will be no poor to be relieved, nor bounty wanted to relieve.

He had two hundred and twenty servants in a cheque roll for forty two years, and twice a day sixty old aged and decrepid poor, who were fed with meat; and on every Good-Friday for thirty-five years, he fed two thousand seven hundred persons with meat, drink, and money. Every gentleman in his service had a man and horse to attend him and his allowance for the expence of his house only, was four thousand pounds a year, besides the produce of his two large parks, and very great demesnes; insomuch, that his house was stiled the Northern Court. Neither was he munificient upon other men's charge; for once a month he looked into his income, and once a week into his disbursements, that none should wrong him, nor be wronged by him. The Earl of Derby (he would say) 'shall keep his own house, that frugality, justice and good management, might as well consist with greatness, as length with breadth.'

Therefore it was observed of him, and the second Duke of Norfolk [*his father-in-law*], that when they were dead, not a tradesman could demand the payment of a groat that they owed him; nor a neighbour the restitution of a penny that they had wronged him of.

It is a maxim that the grass groweth not where the Grand Signior's horse treads, nor do the people thrive where the noblemen inhabit; but here every tenant was a gentleman; and every gentleman my Lord's companion — such his civility toward the one, and his kind usage of the other.

Noblemen in those days esteemed the love of their neighbour more than their riches; and the service and fealty of their tenants, more than their money. They would commonly say, Let the underwood grow, the tenants are the support of a family; and the commonality are the strength of the kingdom. Improve thriftily, but force not violently.

XIV-3. Description of Ormskirk church and the Derby Chapel today

The following presents relevant extracts from the *Guidebook* to the church, i.e. the one revised in 1990, written by Canon Kenneth Thornton, B.A., Vicar of Ormskirk at that time.

The Parish Church of Ormskirk
dedicated to
St. Peter and St. Paul

TWO QUESTIONS

TWO QUESTIONS are usually asked by visitors to the church. The first is: How old is it? and the second: Why are there both tower and spire?

To the first is no simple answer. A church may have stood here for a thousand years or more, for the name of the town suggests a Scandinavian origin; but the oldest structural feature, the late Norman window on the north side of the chancel, is thought to have been built about 1170. Ormskirk Church with its endowments was bestowed on the Canons Regular of Burscough Priory (about two miles distant) by Robert, Lord of Lathom, in 1189. There have been many alterations and additions since then culminating in a major restoration towards the close of the 19th century including the re-construction of the nave pillars, the oak-timbered roof and most of the windows. The chancel arcade dates from about 1270, the base of the spire from 1430, and the great tower from 1540 or thereabouts; and other 15th- and 16th- century work remains.

This leads to the second question: Why tower and steeple? The answer is nothing to do with obstinate sisters. Henry VIII determined on the dissolution of the monasteries, and Burscough Priory had to go. Our tower was built apparently to house some of it bells, the existing steeple being inadequate for this. Masons' marks, we are told, suggest that they may have carted some of the stones from the Priory tower and used them here. One of the bells, older than Ormskirk's tower, stands in front of the Tower Screen today.

The Guide proceeds with a tour of the church including descriptions of The South Porch, The Tower, The Church Clock, The Font, The Organ, The Nave, The Chancel, The North Aisle, The Bickerstaffe Chapel and the Derby Chapel.

The Derby Chapel

Notice first the four effigies. They represent, on the far right, the first Earl of Derby and his first wife; and on the left, his second wife, and next to her, the great grandson of the first couple, who was the third Earl. The first three effigies were once in Burscough Priory; but following the dissolution the third Earl made provision by will for the construction of the chapel and a vault beneath, and for bringing the effigies here. The vault was the burial place of the Derby family until 1851. Thus here was buried the seventh Earl, who was beheaded during the Civil War, and his heroic wife Charlotte de la Tremouille, who with a scanty force sustained and repelled a three month siege of Lathom House.

The chapel incorporates the site of an earlier Lady Chapel. In 1536 this was endowed by public appeal, and a list of 476 subscribers forms the earliest directory of Ormskirk and its neighbourhood. Many names are those of families living here today.

The third Earl died in 1572. His body was embalmed, perhaps with the idea of postponing the funeral until the vault was ready. However, after six weeks he was buried in the high chancel after the most magnificently impressive funeral ever seen in Ormskirk. After all, his court at Lathom had rivalled in splendour that of the King himself. His son proceeded with the building of the chapel; and a study of heraldry gives the limiting dates for its completion. The arms of the fourth Earl (in the curved frame on the wall to your left) show him as a knight of the Garter, which he became in 1574. The arms on the opposite wall (not easily noticed) are of the Archdeacon of Richmond who consecrated the chapel. He became Bishop of Chester in 1579, after which his arms would have changed. So the chapel was finished between these two dates.

The new chairs in the Derby Chapel were provided in 1986 by the parishioners in memory of their relatives.

The Guide continues with sections on Lady Margaret Beaufort, The Scarisbrick Chapel, The South Aisle, The Spire, The Restoration of 1887-1891, Registers and Plate, Exterior Points of Interest and a list of Clergy since c.1190.

~~~~~~~~~~~~~~~~~~~~~

XIV-4. Conclusion

Earl Edward's funeral provides one of the most valuable accounts of details in the history of the Earls of Derby. It is valuable in the current context mainly because it includes many people and families of great interest to the biographies of **Sir Thomas, Sir Edward Sr** and **Sir Edward Jr**. Ormskirk Church is important as the burial place of so many Stanleys and Earls of Derby.

XIVd. The Derby Chapel in Ormskirk Parish Church

(Draper, *House of Stanley*, 1864)

XIVe. St Oswald's Parish Church, Ormskirk

St Oswald's with its distinctive tower and steeple.

(Draper, *House of Stanley*, 1864)

XIVf. Burscough Priory

Burial place of the Earls of Derby until the Dissolution of the Monasteries. Bought by Edward, 3rd Earl, but allowed to fall into a state of disrepair. A few walls can still be seen today.

(Draper, *House of Stanley*, 1864)

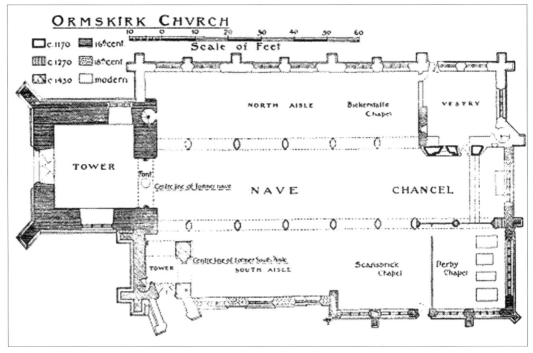

XIVg. Plan of Ormskirk Church

Indicating the four Derby tombs that have survived. These are of Baron Thomas Stanley, 1st Earl of Derby (victor at Bosworth, with a legless effigy – defaced during the Civil War?) and his two wives Eleanor Neville and Lady Margaret Beaufort. The latter, as the mother of Henry VII, also received a much more magnificent tomb in Westminster Abbey, still there today. The fourth has an effigy of Edward, 3rd Earl of Derby, father of Sir Thomas of Winwick & Tong.

Chapter XV
1562, 1582, 1602: Sir Thomas & Sir Edward Sr & Jr
at Preston Guild

XV-1. Introduction

At the end of August every twenty years during the second half of the sixteenth century and onwards the burgesses of Preston, Lancashire celebrated a Guild (they still do, with the latest one in 2012), which served various civic, commercial and social functions. (It had taken place since at least 1397, but only in 1542 was the twenty-year period inaugurated.) Preston was jealous of its status as a borough, one of only four in Lancashire in the sixteenth century, which meant that they returned MPs (the others being Wigan, Liverpool and Clitheroe). To be named a burgess of Preston was an honour which had to be upheld by following all civic rules and regulations. In return one was allowed to own a house and conduct trade there. To remain a burgess, registration was required at every Guild. Happily, many of the early lists survived and were transcribed and published:

> Abram, W. A., (ed.), *The rolls of the burgesses at the guilds merchant of the borough of Preston in the county of Lancaster, 1397-1682* (Lancashire and Cheshire Record Society, vol. 9, 1884). Often referred to as *Preston Guild Rolls*.

Because it took place only every twenty years, fathers were allowed to register all sons who would turn twenty-one before the next Guild, so that their status would be assured when they came of age and they would not need to wait until the next Guild. These lists therefore provide a superb and accurate account of all male burgesses over a long period. Not only that, but the precise relationship of each to the one named before was given, which allows the accurate reconstruction of family trees, at least of the males in each family.

This includes the Shakeshaftes during the lifetimes of John Shakespeare, Glover of Stratford and his son William. If it is accepted that John Shakeshafte, Glover, registered in 1562 and 1582, is one and the same as John Shakespeare, Glover of Stratford, then we have an accurate picture of the family back in the Preston area. A presentation of this family must wait until a future book, however, while we concentrate here on **Sir Thomas** and **Sir Edward Stanley** and their gentry friends.

Gradually registration was extended to permit inclusion of the gentry from the surrounding area, many of whom were not native burgesses, strictly speaking, but several of whom

XVa. Preston Market Place
At the beginning of industrialisation, in transition from a market town to a cotton town. It was completely rebuilt in the late Victorian era, with the Harris Museum & Art Gallery now having pride of place.

had town houses there and/or participated in affairs of the town in one way or the other. The doyen presiding over all was the Earl of Derby, who always attended from the mid-sixteenth century onwards, and in his wake came ever more of the county gentry from ever further afield. By 1602 it attracted others of Lancashire origin, living elsewhere but presumably still in touch with their families back in Preston. One interesting addition in 1602 was four merchants from Coventry, which confirms that there was regular trade and contact between Warwickshire and Lancashire up and down Watling Street (not uninteresting in the context of Shakespeare). In 1602 more than four thousand names were registered, way beyond the permanent male population of the borough.

Gradually it also assumed the role of a county social gathering for two weeks, with many performances, theatrical and musical. Unfortunately no list has survived of the precise events, so there is no way of knowing whether any of Shakespeare's plays were performed there in 1602; nor do we have a list of which groups of players or musicians attended. There was, however, always a 'ludimagister' present. The literal translation is 'master of the games' although one other meaning at the time was 'schoolmaster'. Perhaps he had a dual role? He would in any case have been a focal point for the organisation of certain theatrical events, and we know that in Elizabethan Grammar Schools drama (particularly Classical) played an increasingly important role. For much of Elizabeth's reign the schoolmasters at Preston Grammar School leaned towards Catholicism (Abram, *Preston Guild Rolls*, Introduction), along with the schoolmasters at Blackburn and Burnley Grammar Schools (Bennett, *History of Burnley*, pp. 144-5). Newly founded Protestant Grammar Schools in Lancashire seem to have been more the exception than the rule, e.g. Rivington, founded in 1566 by James Pilkington, Bishop of Durham (with a meticulously researched history by Margaret M. Kay, *The History of Rivington and Blackrod Grammar School*, 1931, Manchester UP, 2nd edition 1966).

By the 1570s all community performances of medieval 'mystery cycles' had been banned, which must have left a large lacuna in the number of dramatic offerings allowed to be performed at gatherings such as Preston Guild. One point in this context which might be of fairly immediate relevance to the 1582 Guild is that during the previous year Jesuit Edmund Campion had stayed for several weeks in the area, between Easter and Whitsuntide, dazzling everyone who attended his sermons with his oratory and charisma. He was also an ardent believer in the value of drama in education and wrote plays himself. Whether this had any influence on an increase in approved dramatic productions at Preston Grammar School or Preston Guild we will probably never know, but his oratorical skills were still being talked about in the area a century later. (Campion was captured later in the same year and, after torture and a mock trial, was hanged, drawn and quartered at Tyburn. Details appear in any biography of Campion, in all major encyclopedias and the *Dictionary of National Biography*.)

Sir Thomas and **Sir Edward Sr** and **Jr** were always at Preston Guild when possible. Attendance was by no means automatic for all Stanley brothers, nephews and in-laws, as can be seen from the lists below; in fact, **Sir Thomas** (as long as he was alive) and **Sir Edward Sr** and **Jr** were the only immediate members of the Derby family who consistently attended in 1562, 1582 and 1602. At the very least this seems to mean that they played a special role in the family, regularly returning to Lancashire from Tong or their various other estates and always keeping in touch. Although little has been written about **Sir Edward Sr** in the main Derby literature, he seems on occasion to have been one of the main representatives in Lancashire of Earl Henry during the latter's frequent absences in London and on missions abroad. (The two main missions were in early 1585 to France, ostensibly to award the Garter to Henri III, but presumably also to discuss any possible cooperation between England and France against the Spanish in the Netherlands; and in early 1588 to Flanders to negotiate with the Spanish in an attempt to avert the threatened invasion of England via the Spanish Armada. Details of both missions are given in Coward, *The Stanleys*.)

In the original lists all names appeared in (sometimes abbreviated) Latin and the Earl of Derby's immediate family has been left in this form. In the following lists (extracted for this book from Abram's full lists), only the first twenty or so gentry surnames are given (usually in English and with modern spelling), in order of first appearance, and not including the numerous family members who were also recorded. These were presumably the families with whom the Earls of Derby (and therefore **Sir Thomas** and **Sir Edward Sr** and **Jr**) consorted most frequently, along with the Mayor and members of the Borough Council. It is among extant papers of these families that further references to **Sir Thomas** and **Sir Edward Sr** and **Jr** might appear.

By word of explanation for any reader without Latin: 'Comes' = (Count)/Earl; 'Comiti' = of the County; 'Miles' = Knight; 'Ar' is an abbreviation for 'Armiger', meaning the right to bear a coat of arms, and therefore the head of the family normally labelled 'Esquire', with sons as 'Gentleman'; the rest are pretty obvious from English words.

[*Any comments by me within the lists are in italics in square brackets. Members of those families in **bold** were to play a significant role in 'Shakespeare in Lancashire' either around 1581, before the next Preston Guild in 1582, or later. HM*]

~~~~~~~~~~~~~~~~~~~

XV-2. 1562: Some present at Preston Guild

1562

Edwardus Comes Derbye [*3ʳᵈ Earl until his death in 1572*].

Henricus d'ñs Strange filius ~~dc~~'i Comiti et her' appar' [*Lord Strange, the Earl's eldest son and heir, aged 31.*]

fferdinandus filius et her' eius appar' [*Henry's eldest son and heir, b. 1558/9, so aged only 3-4 in this year. It appears that it was considered not worth registering son William, b. 1561, who would not turn 21 until after the next Preston Guild.*]

Thomas Stanley miles frater ~~pd~~ Henrici [*Henry's younger brother, **Sir Thomas** of the Tong epitaphs, b. c.1534, so still in his twenties in this year, still of Lancashire because he had not yet moved to Tong.*]

Edwardus Stanley miles fratur eius [***Sir Thomas***'s *younger brother, **Sir Edward Sr** (b. 1535-1540), also in his twenties in this year. His appearance here as **Sir Edward**, knight, seems to confirm in itself that he was the Edward Stanley knighted in 1560 in Ireland.*]

1. **Hoghton of Hoghton**, etc. [*In first place as the leading local gentry family. Head of the family in this year was Thomas Hoghton, later 'The Exile', from 1569 onwards. His younger brother Alexander was to be the reputed host of young William Shakespeare 'for a couple of years', presumably leading up to Alexander's will of 1581, in which he names William Shakeshafte three times.*]

2. **Langton of Walton-in-le-Dale** [*Baron Thomas Langton of Newton-in-Makerfield and Walton-le-Dale. Future uncle of poet and historian John Weever.*]

3. Southworth of Samlesbury [*Sir John Southworth was High Sheriff of Lancashire in this year.*]

4. **Hesketh of Rufford** [*Sir Thomas Hesketh was High Sheriff of Lancashire the following year. He was the later host of young William Shakespeare for 'a short time', by family tradition.*]

5. Osbaldeston of Osbaldeston

6. Crown of Alston, Armiger [*The only mention of this family.*]

7. Caterall of Little Mitton, Armiger [*Home of **Alexander Aspinall**, later teacher at Stratford Grammar School and a friend of the Shakespeares. William Shakespeare wrote a 'ditty' for him.*]

8. Talbot of Sailbury, [*Salesbury*] Armiger [*Kinsmen of the Talbots, Earls of Shrewsbury.*]

9. Fleetwood of Penwortham, Armiger

10. Clifton of Westby, Armiger

11. Barton of Barton, Armiger

12. Singleton of 'Shyngilhall' [*Chingle Hall*], Armiger

13. Skillicorne of Prees, Armiger

14. Farington of Worden [*formerly of Farington*], Armiger, Jur' [*William Farington of Worden kept the Derby Household Books as Comptroller of the household of three Earls of Derby. He was also the owner of the portraits of Earls Edward, Henry and Ferdinando, line-drawings from which are reproduced in this book.*]

15. Haydock of Cottam [*This family produced George Haydock, Catholic martyr in 1584.*]

16. Travers

17. Whittingham of Whittingham

18. Walton of Walton

19. Forshaw of Penwortham

20. Singleton of Staining, Halghton, Scale(s) juxta Kirkham and Ingolhead

etc.

The numbers above and in the lists below are the order in which these 'top twenty' families appear, regardless of the number of family members registered. It will be noted that the 1562 list includes only gentry in the fairly close area around Preston, as, indeed, does the next list. The second column below repeats the position in the 1562 list. The precise order in which these families were recorded was perhaps not as important as that they appeared somewhere towards the top. The absence of some gentry families is either an indication that the male line had died out in the meantime, or quite simply that the head of the family did or could not attend Preston Guild on registration day.

<hr />

XV-3. 1582: Some present at Preston Guild

XVb. Henry, 4ᵗʰ Earl of Derby
He presided over Preston Guild in 1582.

1582 [*This list is of particular interest, as it is the year when John Shakeshafte, Glover appears – was he one and the same as John Shakespeare, glover of Stratford, father of William? – with many of his family. They both certainly had the same dates and life span. John Shakeshafte had already appeared at Preston Guild in 1562, at a time when John Shakespeare was recorded as absent from Stratford. In 1562, however, not so many of John Shakeshafte's family were recorded. If they were one and the same, we have the names of several of William's uncles and cousins in Preston in this year. One 'uncle in Preston', intriguingly, was Anthony, the name of a Shakespeare who lived for a while near Stratford, and also a name used by the Bard in several of his plays.*

*The 1582 list also contains the names of some of the visitors of the Earl of Derby in 1587-90, as they appear in the 'Derby Household Books'. The head of the family is in **bold**, with a few* *biographical details appearing in Chapter XVII. Sir Edward Sr & Jr in the Derby Household Books, indicated by **DHB**. One might assume that these were amongst the closest with ties to the Earls of Derby, and those most likely to have met **Edward Stanley Jr** of Tong and Winwick when he was visiting Lancashire in 1589 and 1590. HM]*

Henricus Comes Derbie [*1531-93; 4th Earl since 1572*].

ffardinan~~d~~s D'ns Straunge [*1558/9-94; Lord Strange in 1582, later 5th Earl*].

Wi~~ll~~ms Stanley Ar' frater eius [*1561-1642; later 6th Earl*].

 ffranciscus Stanley Armig' frater eius [*Francis, fourth son of Earl Henry, in his teens in this year, died the following year, buried at Ormskirk 16 September, 1583. Third son Edward presumed dead before this year.*]

Edwar~~d~~z Stanley miles [***Sir Edward Sr**, b. 1535-40, d. 1604, Earl Henry's younger brother, unmarried, the other middle brother being **Sir Thomas** of Winwick and Tong, named immediately below and in the 1602 entry as deceased; he had died in 1576.*]

Edwar~~d~~z Stanley Ar, filius Thome Stanley miles defunct' [***Edward Jr** of Tong, (1562-1632) aged twenty in this year, not yet knighted, but already married to Lucy Percy.*]

'82 '62

1. (1) **Thomas Houghton de Lea Armiger** [*Family tradition had Shakespeare in their household for a couple of years in his youth. This Thomas was named as heir in brother Alexander's will of 1581, who requested him to accept William Shakeshafte (Shakespeare?) into his household; this Thomas was killed in November 1589 in the 'affray at Lea' over grazing rights with Baron Langton of Walton.*]

    Ri~~c~~us Houghton filius eius et heres appareñ [*Later son-in-law of Sir Gilbert Gerard, Master of the Rolls; later Sir Richard Houghton, Bt.,* **DHB**.]
    Wi~~ll~~ms Houghton frater eius [***DHB***]
    Thomas Houghton frater eius
    Adam Houghton frater eius

2. **Ri~~c~~us Shirburne miles Jur'** [*of Stonyhurst Hall. Treasurer to the Earl of Derby; biography in Brazendale, Lancashire's Historic Halls, 1994; tomb in Mitton Church. This was the place of origin of Alexander Aspinall, later teacher at Stratford Grammar School and friend of William Shakespeare, the latter writing a ditty for AA. (Schoenbaum, 1987, p. 67.),* **DHB**.]

    Ricus Shirburne Ar' filius eius et heres appareñ
    Hugo Shirburne frater eius
    Thomas Shirburne frater eius

3. (4) **Thomas Hesketh miles Jur'** [*of Rufford. Family tradition claims he was the host of young William Shakespeare for a short time. He spent several years in prison as a noted recusant.*]

    Ro~~b~~tus Hesketh Ar' filius eius et heres appar
    Thomas Hesketh filius ~~pd~~c'i Ro~~b~~ti
    Thomas Hesketh filius s~~e~~'dus ~~pd~~ Thome Hesketh mi~~l~~ Jur'
    Ri~~c~~us Hesketh frater eius

    Bartholomew Hesketh Ar' Jur' [*of Aughton. Brother of Alexander Hoghton's wife Elizabeth née Hesketh and Richard Hesketh. This Bartholomew was suspected of being involved in the 'Hesketh Plot' in 1593, when brother Richard brought a letter from some English Catholics in exile, proposing Ferdinando as the successor to Queen Elizabeth, which led to the poisoning of Ferdinando, 5th Earl of Derby in 1594.*]

    Gabriel Hesketh filius eius et heres appareñ

4. (3) **~~Johes~~ Southworth miles Jur'** [*Sir John Southworth of Samlesbury, **DHB**. A descendant was a later Catholic martyr, executed in 1654 at Tyburn, one of the 40 Martyrs of England and Wales canonised in 1970 by the Pope.*]

5. (2) **Thomas Langton Ar' Baron de Newton in Makerfield** [*Owner of the Manor of Walton-le-Dale; perpetrator of the 'affray at Lea' in 1589, in which Thomas Hoghton was killed. Uncle of poet and historian John Weever.*]

6. (5) **Osbaldeston** [*of Osbaldeston, **DHB**].

7. (8) **Talbot** of **Salisbury** [*Salesbury on the Ribble. Kinsmen of Talbots, Earls of Shrewsbury.*]

8. (9) **Fleetwood** of Penwortham

9. (14) **Farington** of Worden [*William Farington was Comptroller of the household of the Earl of Derby at this time and compiler of the **DHB**.*]

10. **Standish** of Duxbury [*Thomas Standish, stepfather of the Alexander whose biography is on the Duxbury website, who enters the 'Shakespeare in Lancashire' story at several points, **DHB**.*]

11. **Walmesley** [*of Dunkenhalgh. At this time an up and coming judge in London. The MI on his tomb in Blackburn appears in Chapter X. Other tombs of interest.*]

12. **Rigby** of Burgh [*in Duxbury. A neighbour of Standish of Duxbury. Members of this family in **DHB**.*]

13. **Anderton** of Clayton

14. (13) **Skillicorne** of Prees [***DHB***]

15. (10) Clifton of Westby

16. (11) Barton of Barton

17. (12) **Singleton** of Broughton (+20)

18. Westby of Mowbreck

19. (15) Haydock of Cottam

20. (17) Whittingham of Whittingham

etc.

~~~~~~~~~~~~~~~~~~~~

XV-4. 1602: Some present at Preston Guild

The next Guild in 1602 was three years after the publication of Weever's *Epigrammes* (1599), and those in the list who received an epigram are noted below, with names in **bold**. (Sir) **Edward Stanley Jr** had received the dedication from aspiring poet Christopher Middleton of *The famous history of Chinon of England* in 1597, and of *Faunus and Melliflora* from aspiring poet John Weever in 1600. Weever was a native of Preston (or somewhere rather close) and one might imagine that his work was one topic of conversation during the two weeks of Preston Guild. Several of those in the list below had appeared on Lord Burghley's map of 1590 as dangerous recusants (Gillow, *Lord Burghley's Map of Lancashire*, 1907). One other notable feature of participants in this list is the number of functionaries based in London and/or involved with the Duchy of Lancaster, with Queen Elizabeth I as the Duke of Lancaster (not Duchess, as, indeed, is true for Elizabeth II today). By 1602 presence at Preston Guild had also acquired much more prestige for a wider circle of gentry from ever further afield.

Another notable feature (not in the list below) is a number of participants from Warwickshire, particularly Coventry, not too far away from Stratford; these were presumably mainly Lancashire businessmen who had set up in Warwickshire because of the wool trade between the two counties. John Shakeshafte, glover and burgess of Preston, did not appear, but IF he was one and the same as John Shakespeare, glover of Stratford, one would not expect to find him here, because he had died in Stratford in 1601. The following are merely the first among more than four thousand names.

It will be noted that at the head are just three Stanleys: William, 6th Earl, his uncle **Sir Edward Sr** and his cousin **Edward Jr**. The latter must have attracted a certain amount of interest this year: admiration that he had recently received dedications from two poets, and commiseration on losing his wife Lucy Percy and four of his daughters the previous year. This was a period (one presumes) when the tomb in Tong was in preparation. We have no record as to whether he made Winwick his base for this return to Lancashire, nor how long he stayed; his three surviving daughters had been placed in the household of the Fortescue family of Salden, Buckinghamshire, cousins of **(Sir) Edward Jr**. Amongst topics of conversation between these three Stanleys must have been William's career in London as a playwright and the latest state of his long drawn out wranglings with his sister-in-law Countess Alice about which lands each was entitled to (these were to continue for several more years). Both **Edwards** were involved because of their own Derby inheritances with reversions.

They presumably also exchanged any news they had had of their various Stanley 'cousins' serving the Spanish King and the several brothers or cousins of their gentry neighbours who were Catholic priests in exile. Presumably they talked about the ageing Elizabeth and speculated about her successor, particularly relevant to the family because of the death of Ferdinando just eight years earlier and the recent confirmation of his eldest daughter Anne as officially in line of succession to the throne. Presumably they also exchanged their latest news of William's half-sisters Ursula and Dorothy, which brought Sir John Salusbury of Lleweni, into the conversation. He had married Ursula in 1586, and so was William's brother-in-law. He had been a regular visitor at Lathom in 1587-90 (*Derby Household Books*). Amidst their whole brood of children (eleven in all) they had named their nth child in 1599 Ferdinando, after Ursula's dead brother. Sir John (knighted by Elizabeth in 1601) had received several dedications from poets in the 1590s and was himself a dabbler. His friend Robert Chester had published these adulatory poems to Sir John (June 1601) in *Love's Martyr* or *Rosalin's Complaint*, a series of 'poetical essays', including contributions by Jonson, Chapman and Marston, and a poem beginning 'Let the bird of loudest lay' (usually known as *The Phoenix and (the) Turtle*), with the author's name printed as William Shake-speare.

(The most recent treatise on *The Phoenix and Turtle*, the dating, its authorship and a biography of Sir John Salusbury, is by John Idris Jones, 'William Shakespeare and John Salusbury: what was their relationship?', *Transactions of the Denbighshire Historical Society*, January, 2011. Following on from Honigmann, '*lost years*' (1985, 1998), Jones argues very persuasively that Shakespeare wrote it in celebration of Ursula and John's marriage in late 1586. 'Conventional' wisdom still places its composition as much later, not too long before publication, e.g. the latest biography of Shakespeare: Lois Potter, *The Life of William Shakespeare: A Critical Biography*, Blackwell, March, 2012, Chapter 12. 1599-1601, pp. 267-271. The book received an adulatory review in the *Times Literary Supplement* of 10 August, 2012 by Russ McDonald. For carefully explained reasons she gives a later than 'conventional' dating to other Shakespeare works, most particularly *Love's Labour's Lost*. Given the close association of this with William Stanley, 6th Earl of Derby, this is of great interest to his cousin **(Sir) Edward Jr**'s biography.)

One imagines that Shakespeare/Shakeshafte would have entered their conversations more than once, because of William, 6th Earl's active participation in the theatre and Shakespeare's recent string of great successes in London. (This would almost certainly have been the case if the 'Shakespeare in Lancashire'/'Lancastrian Shakespeare' theory is based on historical fact, and young William had spent time with the Hoghtons and Heskeths before joining Derby's/ Strange's Players). Might it have been on one of these occasions that William or **Sir Edward Stanley Sr** jokingly suggested to **Edward Jr** that next time he bumped into Shakespeare in London, he should ask him to write an epitaph for the Stanley 'tomb in the making' in Tong? A hypothetical and speculative question to which there will, alas, never be an answer.

1602 30 August

Will's Comes Derbei [*William, 6ᵗʰ Earl of Derby. Weever obituary to brother Ferdinando ('Epigrammes' 6.9), but no epigram for William.*]

Edw'us Stanley miles [*William's uncle, **Sir Edward Stanley Sr**; he would die in 1604 and be buried in the Stanley vault at Ormskirk. His presence here is proof enough on its own that he was NOT the Sir Edward who went into exile (and died in Spain in 1636), as reported by Seacome; nor the Edward Stanley who died in Portugal in 1590.*]

Edw'us Stanley armigʳ filius Thome defunct' [***Edward Stanley Esq**. son of **Thomas**, deceased. **Edward Jr**, was aged forty in this year. He would be created a Knight of the Bath by James I at his coronation the following year.*]

'02 '82 '62

1. (1) (1) **Hoghton of Hoghton** [*Weever epigrams to Sir Richard Hoghton (5.23 & 7.11), plus dedication of the whole book to him (1599). His brother William Hoghton also received an epigram (6.4) and there was an obituary to their father Thomas Hoghton, killed in 1589 in the 'affray at Lea' (6.3). Sir Richard Hoghton was a son-in-law of Sir Gilbert Gerard, Master of the Rolls.*]

2. **Parker, Lord Monteagle and Morley** [*Weever epigram (3.3). He was the one who 'exposed' the Gunpowder Plot three years later.*]

3. (11) Walmesley, J.P. [*Sir Thomas of Dunkenhalgh. An eminent lawyer in London, he was Justice of the Common Pleas. He too received an epitaph for his grave in Blackburn Church. Chapter X. Other tombs of relevance.*]

4. Savile, 3ʳᵈ Baron, lawyer at Westminster, Lancaster [*Sir John Savile of Howley, Yorkshire, a senior official in the Duchy of Lancaster. His daughter married into the Legh family of Lyme, Cheshire and Winwick, Lancashire.*]

5. **Gerard** [*Weever epigram section (5) dedicated to Sir Thomas Gerard, son of Sir Gilbert Gerard, Master of the Rolls, who had died in 1592. Sir Thomas was Knight Marshall to Elizabeth and James I. The other main branch of the family was of Bryn, which at this time had another Thomas Gerard as its head, who was to be knighted in 1603 by King James, as was (Sir) Edward Stanley Jr. Their fathers had 'plotted' together in 1570 to help Mary, Queen of Scots escape from Chatsworth House. The family owned the Bryn Chapel in Winwick church.*]

6. **Molyneux** [*of Sefton. Weever epigram section (3) dedicated to Sir Richard Molyneux, another son-in-law of Sir Gilbert Gerard. They owned the Molyneux Castle on the Liverpool waterfront.*]

7. **Warren** [*Weever epigram section (4) to Sir Edward Warren, of Poynton, Cheshire and Woodplumpton, Lancashire.*]

8. **Leigh** [*of Lyme and Winwick. Weever epigram to Sir Piers Legh of Lyme (5,1), plus a whole section (7) dedicated to him, another son-in-law of Sir Gilbert Gerard.*]

9.   **Halsall** [*High Sheriff of Lancashire the previous year. Weever section (6) dedicated to Sir Cuthbert Halsall, married to Dorothy Stanley, first cousin of* **Edward Jr**.]

10. (3) (4)   **Hesketh** [*of Rufford. Robert Hesketh now head of the family whose family tradition related that young William Shakespeare had spent a short time with them. Visitor in* **DHB**, *although not in Chapter XVII, because not there at the same time as* **Sir Edward Sr** *and* **Jr**. *His son or grandson (?) acquired a portrait of Sir Kenelm Digby, (Sir)* **Edward Stanley Jr**'s *later son-in-law, the portrait still hanging today in Rufford Old Hall.*]

11.   Brograve [*Attorney General of the Duchy of Lancaster.*]

12. (2)   **Sherborne** [*Shireburne of Stonyhurst. Sir Richard Shireburne had been Treasurer to Earl Henry,* **DHB**.]

13. (5) (2)   **Langton, Baron of Newton** [*Presumed uncle and patron of John Weever, poet (Honigmann, 'Weever', 1987), perpetrator of the 'affray at Lea' in 1589 and questioned by Sir William Cecil re the 'Hesketh Plot' in 1593. By 1602 at least partially rehabilitated by local Lancashire gentry.*]

14.   **Assheton** of London [*Alexander Standish of Duxbury's wife was an Assheton of Gt Lever, Bolton and Whalley Abbey. He knew John Weever in London. He later installed Countess Alice, Earl Ferdinando's widow, at Anglezarke, near Duxbury, during her second widowhood. See his biography online on the Duxbury Family Website.*]

15. (13)   Anderton of Lostock, Clayton

16. (8) (9)   Fleetwood [*of Penwortham. William Fleetwood was a lawyer in London, related to Cardinal Allen from Rossall, Lancashire, Spiritual Head of the English Catholics in Rome.*]

17.   Kirby of Rawcliffe

18. (9) (14) **Farington** [*of Worden. William Farington was Comptroller to the Earl of Derby and the compiler of the* **DHB**.]

19.   Charnock [*of Chorley*].

20.   **Rigby** [*of Burgh in Duxbury*].

etc. including Alexander Standish of Duxbury with young sons Thomas, Richard and Ralph. He receives several mentions above because he was my original 'smoking gun' to so many Shakespeare-Stanley contacts in 'Shakespeare's Lancashire Links'. Presumably he met **Edward Stanley Jr** at this Preston Guild. During the following years Alexander was involved in a series of court cases in London, at least one of them with John Weever, to sort out the estates of Baron Langton of Walton, who died in London without a son and heir in 1605. (*Standish of Duxbury Muniments*, Lancashire Record Office, Catalogue DP397, a chronological version on mylesstandish.info website.)

~~~~~~~~~~

XV-5. Conclusion

These lists are amongst the most valuable in reconstructing the biographies of **Sir Edward Sr** and **Sir Edward Jr**. They also shed light on the growing prestige attached to attendance at Preston Guild for an ever-widening group of gentry as well as regional and national functionaries.

~~~~~~~~~~

XVc. Glovers and skinners in the parade, Preston Guild, 1762

The parade of all guildsmen has long been an integral feature of Preston Guild, which has been held every twenty years since 1542 with only one break during World War II. The latest one was in 2012, when the Trades Procession was held on the first day, Saturday 1 September. At the front were the local British Aerospace and Leyland Motors. Needless to say, there were no glovers and skinners.

Chapter XVI
1587-90: the *Derby Household Books*: general

William Farington (usually spelt 'ffarington' in sixteenth-century manuscripts) of Worden Hall (near Leyland) was Comptroller (= Controller = Administrator) of the Household at Lathom and Knowsley for Earls of Derby Edward 3rd, Henry 4th and Ferdinando 5th. He retired in 1594 when William 6th began his long period as Earl (1594-1642). This is the explanation for Farington having portraits of Earls Edward, Henry and Ferdinando in his home, but not William. Other MS sources present attributions to William Farington as a much valued administrator. He has been proposed as the prototype of Shakespeare's Malvolio.

> "Ffarington as [Canon] Raines has shown us [writes Professor Alwin Thaler of the Department of English, Tennessee U in a published thesis, 'The Original Malvolio?' in the *Shakespeare Association Bulletin*, Vol. vii, no. 2] was born in 1537 and inherited from his father, Sir Henry Ffarington, a large property, an official connection with the Stanley family, an inordinate 'appetite for law' and nice conduct as a public official (and) an authoritative and unyielding manner which his inferiors and even 'the surrounding gentry . . . felt . . . sometimes to be inconvenient . . . and at other times oppressive.' He increased his property by a prudent marriage to a wealthy young daughter of the house of Stanley and by shrewd legal management. Meanwhile, he had become a Justice of the Peace of his home County and comptroller of the household to Edward, Earl of Derby."
> (Keen, 1954, pp. 190, 191) (Carol Curt Enos, *Shakespeare Encyclopedia* online)

We can only be thankful that he made these detailed accounts and that they have survived. All others, which he undoubtedly kept, have since disappeared, some no doubt in the razing of Lathom House after the Civil War. Old Worden Hall, home of Farington in the sixteenth-century, has recently been renovated. (Details of this are available on several websites.)

The origin of the line-drawings of the three Earls of Derby that appear in the *Derby Household Books* and are reproduced in this book are explained by Raines:

> The portraits of the three Earls of Derby in this book have been etched at the expense of Miss ffarington, and were reduced by her accurate pencil from the original pictures now at Worden Hall. There seems to be little doubt that these fine old portraits were presented to Mr. ffarington, the Comptroller, by the noble individuals whom they represent
>
> (Raines, p. lxv.)

The Revd (later Canon) F.R. Raines was the transcriber and editor of the *Derby Household Books*.

> F.R. Raines (ed.) *The Stanley Papers, pt.ii. The Derby household books; comprising an account of the household regulations and expenses of Edward and Henry, third and fourth Earls of Derby; together with a diary containing the names of the guests who visited the latter Earl at his houses in Lancashire, by William ffarington, esquire, the comptroller [1561-90]* (Chetham Society Old Series, vol. 31, 1853).

This is, of course, available in many Lancashire Libraries and has meanwhile appeared online during the Chetham Society's current programme to place most of their publications online.

Raines's transcription of the original manuscripts seems impeccable; in any case this is the only published version, has been referred to by everyone ever since who was concerned in any way with the history of the Earls of Derby, has been generally accepted as definitive and there has thus never been any need to check this or produce a later edition. His biographical notes are so extensive that it is easy to imagine that he explored every historical documentary source known to him — and anyone else in Lancashire at the time. Indeed, his list of references is truly impressive.

I had read Raines's lists and biographical notes several years before embarking on this book, and already produced a list of all visitors a few years ago, rearranged in alphabetical order, mainly as a reference point for myself. I recently re-read the *Derby Household Books* in the specific context of establishing the precise number of visits, with dates, of **Sir Edward Stanley Sr** and **Edward Stanley Jr** (who was not knighted until 1603, and so might appear as **Mr Edward Stanley**, etc.). There was no expectation of encountering **Sir Thomas** of Winwick and Tong as a visitor, because he had died in 1576. **Sir Edward Sr**, clearly identified as Earl Henry's brother on two occasions and **Mr Edward** (Jr), were certainly visitors.

Several entries also included the departure of Earl Henry or other prominent visitors from Lathom or Knowsley to Winwick. Also, there were frequent visits from the Parson of Winwick, sometimes on a Saturday, to preach a sermon on Sunday morning. This all seemed very logical, because the Earl of Derby was responsible for confirmation of any Rector/ Vicar/ Parson of Winwick and Earl Henry's brother had been known as **Sir Thomas** of Winwick, with Thomas's son **Edward Jr**, Henry's nephew, obviously returning to Winwick (we know he buried his only son Thomas there, from the inscription on the tomb at Tong). Any visit by Earl Henry to Winwick was also logical because two other visitors, kinsmen and prominent local gentry — Sir Piers Legh of Lyme and Sir John Holcroft of Holcroft — also had properties in Winwick. I fully expected that Raines, in his biographical notes, would provide a few details about **Sir Edward Sr** and **Edward Jr**, which could now be appraised and fitted in with all other known details of their lives from other sources.

My first surprise was that Raines, although naming both **Edwards** in his index, with reference to the pages where their visits had been recorded, had produced no biographical details of either **Edward**. My immediate tentative explanation was that so few records of either **Edward** had remained in Lancashire, because **Sir Edward Sr** seems to have lived mainly elsewhere (Yorkshire?) for much of his adult life when not visiting his close relatives in Lancashire and elsewhere; and **Edward Jr** had never lived permanently in Winwick, but only stayed there on his return visits to his Lancashire roots. Details about both of them were therefore rather thin on the ground in Lancashire and therefore not available to Raines.

I decided that an analysis of all names, references and details given might be in order, and thus set out on a count of names under various categories. This took a certain amount of time, as categories to be taken into account changed, but the results a third of the way through were already rather significant, and I stopped. As far as I am aware, no one before has undertaken such a count, and therefore relevant details are included below, in case they might be of interest to others contemplating (re)duplication of this analysis.

Contents of the *Derby Household Books*

Pages	Contents
i-lxvi	Introduction
1-22	1561 records
23-91	Lists of resident servants; weekly provisions, with costs; and visitors on a day to day basis 1587-90
93-219	Biographical and explanatory notes
221-247	Index

A few notes about the analysis of names in the index are appropriate. All names in the index are given page numbers. Any name mentioned only before p. 22 was ignored, because only mentioned in the Introduction or early text before the 1587-90 lists. If numbers do not add up to the same totals, this is because some names are duplicated in the index where they have different spellings in the lists 1587-90, even when they obviously refer to the same person, e.g. 'Allablaister, Sir Jhon, 87';

'Alleblaster, Sir John, clerk, an almoner, 26'; in which case they were counted as one rather than two people. Or with similar entries, which from the index might indicate several people of the same name, but which I happened to know from other sources were actually the same person. This was in the case of a few families that had almost become 'old friends', as I had researched them in some detail. Also omitted were names of historians to whom Raines made reference in his notes; monarchs; characters who lived much earlier or later; and a few other categories, but none of whom appeared as visitors in the lists (pp. 23-91). The differences in some of the numbers were so striking that these are the ones reproduced in the table immediately below. Anyone embarking on a future analysis might well come up with different numbers, but nothing significant as to the relative size of numbers.

Index, *Derby Household Books* pp. 221-229 (= a third of pp. 221-247); the figure in the final column in brackets is therefore x3, as an approximate number of all in this category.

Total number of names in index: of visitors and staff 1587-90, or others deemed relevant by Raines and mentioned in biographical notes	540	(c. 1600)
Number of names in index, with NO biographical notes given	408	(c. 1200)
Number of names in lists, with SOME biographical notes given	67	(c. 200)

(The c. 65 missing from the first column of numbers were for reasons indicated above.)

The immediate conclusion from these numbers is one that will come as no surprise to anyone who has read the *Derby Household Books*: his knowledge of Lancashire gentry was daunting. Canon Raines displayed a prodigious knowledge of the history of many local families, whose pedigrees and histories, as available in 1853, he had obviously consulted. He published transcriptions and annotations in over twenty volumes for the Chetham Society from 1845 until 1902. However, the numbers in the table immediately above speak for themselves. Of the 540 names counted in the first third of his index, only 67 received biographical notes. The other 408 appear just as names. So Raines's knowledge did not extend to all those mentioned, by any means. And among those under S appearing just as names in the lists were **Sir Edward Stanley Sr** and **Edward Jr**, albeit with a useful summary of **Sir Edward**'s activities in two of his personae, but splitting both Edwards into two people. Raines obviously knew no more about them and had not researched them further. This is surprising, particularly in the case of **Sir Edward Sr**, because he was named as Earl Henry's brother on two occasions. References to both of them in the index are:

Stanley, Sir Edward, 44, 66, 68, 69, 80, 82, 88, 89.
Stanley, Sir Edward, his annuity, 5; my Lord's brother, 27, 31; returns home from London, 40; goes towards Chester, 44, 59; to Preston, 62; at Knowsley 63, 65; accompanies the Earl to Winwick, 64; hunts with the Earl at Lathom, 65.
  [*Although helpful, the references are not always accurate, in content or page number.*]
Stanley, Mr. Edward, 57, 96 [*the one on p. 96 was a different Edward, of Cross Hall, in the bibliographical notes*].
Stanley, Mr. Edward, of Winwick, 58, 62, 65, 69, 79, 90.

The precise number of servants named in the lists and the index, with or without biographical notes, is irrelevant here. Suffice it to say that the several lists provide a fairly consistent number of up to 140 servants when the Earl was in residence; some names are duplicated in all lists, some had obviously departed since the year before and been replaced. Some were sons of local gentry, learning from the household of a great lord how they should manage their own households in future. Others were workers in the kitchens, gardens, stables, etc..

Similarly irrelevant here is the precise number of Preachers/Parsons/other clerics in the lists and the index. Those of most interest today are those who achieved a national reputation, e.g. the Revd William Leigh, Parson of Standish, later chaplain to Prince Henry (biography in Porteus, *History of Standish*, 1927 and the *Dictionary of National Biography*). This is not to say that the others were of any less interest to the Earl of Derby 1587-90, but their stories would require much more research before any conclusions could be reached about more widespread influence. The only one mentioned below and giving Raines's details is John Caldwall/Caldewell, Parson of Winwick, the rectory of which parish **Edward Jr** made his base when visiting his uncle Henry, and therefore almost certainly came into regular contact with the Parson. I assume, as just one example, that the following in the index all refer to same person:

> Caldewall, Mr., 30, 81, 118; some account of, 132.
> Caldewell, Mr., chaplain to Henry, Earl of Derby, 132, 188.
> Caldewell, Mr., parson of Winwick, 48; preached at Knowsley, 49; leaves there, 49; preached at
>   New Park, 55; at Lathom, 56.
> Caldwall, John, clerk, 133.

The note about him is as follows, which will give a flavour of the style and scope of Raines's biographical notes, as well as his meticulous references. (This makes it even more remarkable that he gave no biographical notes about **Sir Edward Sr** and **Edward Jr**.) The most important, perhaps, are those absent details, in that there is no mention of any of Caldwall's parishioners in Winwick (including **Edward Jr**). However, he was one of those responsible for raising troops in 1585-6 from the Diocese of Chester for the war in the Netherlands, and some of these were presumably from Winwick. The Diocese of Chester at that time included all of Cheshire, plus Lancashire between the Mersey and the Ribble, thus covering the vast majority of the Earl of Derby's lands in these two counties. It was in this war that an Edward Stanley fought, and performed a remarkable and heroic task at the Siege of Zutphen. Whoever he was, his identity was presumably known to 'our' Stanleys. Others have thought that it might have been **Sir Edward Sr**, but this is highly unlikely. At the outbreak of war in September 1585, **Sir Edward Sr** was in his late forties and unmarried and **Edward Jr** twenty-three and recently married, with a young family. Whether **Edward Jr** ever went off to this war, thus entitling him to wear armour in his effigy on his tomb, is not known, and perhaps never will be, but as a young married man with a young family, he would have had less incentive to volunteer than his middle-aged uncle. We have still not discovered why he decided to be depicted in armour on his tomb. In any case, **Sir Edward Sr** and **Edward Jr**, as residents in the Rectory of Winwick from time to time, would have known the Revd John Caldwall, which makes his biography worth repeating.

> 'Mr Caldewell.' John Caldwall B.A., was born in 1544 at Burton-upon-Trent in the co. of Stafford, and was probably a son of Richard Caldwall M.D., a learned man and a native of that county, who was elected student of Christ Church Oxon., and President of the College of Physicians, London, where he founded and endowed a Lecture, and died in 1585, æt. 72 (*Athen. Oxon.*) Mr. Caldwall was instituted to the Rectory of Mobberley in Cheshire in 1570, and held the living more than twenty-four years. He was also Rector of Winwick, to which he was instituted on the 7th Jan. 1575, on the presentation of his patron, Henry Earl of Derby, and about the same time appointed one of his Lordship's Domestic Chaplains. On the 29th September 1580, he, (with Edward Fleetwood Rector of Wigan, and John Asheton Rector of Middleton,) was one of the three Lancashire Clergy required by the Queen in Council to fit out each a Light Horseman by the 20th of October next following for the service of the Queen in Ireland, "to resiste certain foraine forces sent by the Pope and his confederates," and should these Ecclesiastics have had the temerity to disobey the royal mandate, they were to be summoned within four days afterwards to London to appear before the Council and "give an account of their so forgetting themselves." (*Peck's Desid. Cur.* vol. i. p. 95.) In January 1585-6 he was mentioned by name in the Queen's Letter to Bishop Chaderton for the purpose of raising soldiers for the defence of the Netherlands, being one of the two Clergymen in the Diocese of Chester required to contribute £50. (Nichols' *Prog. Qu. Eliz.*, vol. ii, p. 454.) Having been to visit his friends in Staffordshire, he fell sick on his return homewards at the Rectory House of Clifton Campville, near Tamworth, where he died on the 30th June 1595, and was buried in that Church on the day following, in the fifty-first year of his age. (Leycester's *Hist. Chesh.*) He appears to have been a

popular preacher, and more sermons are recorded by the Diarist [*Farington*] as having been delivered by him before his noble patron, than by any other of the Chaplains. He died intestate, and the following nuncupative Will was proved and registered at Chester: [*Raines gives details of his will, in which he bequeathed all to immediate members of his family, with no mention of the Earl of Derby or any parishioners in Winwick. He concludes the account:*] His cattle and husbandry for number and extent, were worthy of an old patriarch. "In his studdie-house" were his books, valued at xli, a very large sum. His maps, pedigrees and genealogies, iiis. Silver plate xxii iiis iiiid. In tankards, rings, piggins, viiili viiid; armour, as calivers, pistolate, haulbert, &c. iiili xiiis. In all £314 18s. 6d. (*Lanc. MSS.* Vol. *Wills.*)

(Raines, pp. 132-3.)

In case anyone with no access to the *Derby Household Books* has wondered what provisions had to be laid in every week for such a crowd of permanent residents and servants, plus constant visitors when the Earl was in residence, two from the last month are included as typical, the entries indicating that it was shortly after this when Farington stopped making this series of accounts. Maybe he just ran out of paper, or started a new notebook, since lost?

Knowsley 1590

A Wekely Bryffemt of the Expensis of the Howseholde of the Right Honorable Henry Earle of Derby in an howle yere begyning the xviiith of Jvlij 1590 et A° R. R. Eliz. xxxiido viz.

			The xxv of July 1590		The firste of Auguste 1590
Wheate for Howsholde	. . .	. . .	xix w. & x caste	. . .	xxi w. di. & x caste.
Wheate for Manchetts	. . .	. . .	i w. iii peckes & xviii cast	. . .	i w. di.
Wheate for Dredge	. . .	. . .	di. w.	. . .	i loffe di.
Wheate for Paste	. . .	. . .	iii w. & iii peckes	. . .	di. w.
Beare	. . .	. . .	xvii hog	. . .	xiiii hog.
Bieffes	. . .	. . .	i oxe I ꝗ & i tiell	. . .	i oxe ii tylle.
Vealles	. . .	. . .	viii	. . .	x.
Mottons	. . .	. . .	xiii	. . .	xii.
Lambes	. . .	. . .	i	. . .	iiii.
Lings	. . .	. . .	i	. . .	di.
Haberdaines	. . .	. . .	i	. . .	di.
White Lightes	. . .	. . .	xviiili	. . .	xxxli.
Waxe Lightes	. . .	. . .	nli	. . .	nli.
Sewett for the Kitchen	. . .	. . .	nli	. . .	viiili.
Accattes	. . .	. . . }		. . . }	
Pyllen	. . .	. . . }	vili viis id ob.	. . . }	vli iiis iid ob.
Freche fyshe	. . .	. . . }		. . . }	

(p. 88.)

Get out your Elizabethan cookery books and have a meal like a sixteenth-century Lord, with lots of beer and beef and, of course, by candlelight! Oxtail soup and veal, mutton or lamb, with or in several pastry dishes, would seem to be in order, with some 'freche fyshe'. The lists above are totally deficient in veggies and fruit, but presumably they grew their own, so these did not have to be bought, just the gardener-servants paid, and other agricultural tenants on their vast estates provided the rest. Lancashire Hotpot had not yet been invented because potatoes did not arrive until the early seventeenth-century (from a wreck, with a sack of potatoes washed up on the coast), and with no successful cultivation until much later. So cabbage, carrots, peas, turnips and beans would be in order — with lots of bread.

Let us now take a close look at the two **Edwards, Sr** and **Jr** in the *DHB* - in the next chapter.

XVIa. Lathom House 1   XVIb. Lathom House 2

Destroyed after the Siege of Lathom House at the end of the Civil War and later razed to the ground. No depiction of the original fortified house has survived. These two drawings are from the imagination of two later artists, working from a contemporary description. Most notable are the Eagle Tower and the turreted outer walls.

XVIc. Knowsley Hall, 18th century

Originally a hunting lodge in Knowsley Park, it became the main residence of the Earls of Derby
after the demolition of Lathom House after the Civil War.

XVId. Knowsley Hall, c.1880

Chapter XVII
Sir Edward Sr & Jr in the *Derby Household Books*

All quotes from the *DHB* are as in the transcription by Raines (Chetham Society OS, 1853) and here indented. Only entries including **Sir Edward Sr** and **Jr** are extracted and their names are in ***bold italics*** in the *DHB* texts. Other visitors commented on are in bold; these are restricted to those who are mentioned elsewhere in this book. Places of relevance to **Sir Edward Sr** and **Jr** are also given in bold, the most important one being **Winwick**, which saw many visits not least, one suspects, because the Rectory there was leased by **Edward Jr**, who used it as his base when in Lancashire, and seems to have been available for any other members of the immediate family passing through. Other places in bold are those they are recorded as visiting. All my comments are in square brackets and *italics*. These do not include any comments on the various 'plaiers' reported as performing for the Earl of Derby, which have been covered by several others, with David George, *Records of Early English Drama: Lancashire* (1991) for starters.

> A Checkerowle of my L. the Earle of Derbies Householde Servants the xiii^th daie of Maye A^o 1587 at wch tyme his L. didde begyne to sett uppe howse at Lathom after his retorne from the Courte, viz. (p. 23.)

[*There follows a list of the main members of the household who would remain in residence, with numbers of their personal servants, and a list of all other servants. It continues as follows.* HM]

> Besydes **Sr Edward Stanley**)
> **My L. brother** & his iiii Svants) iiii

> And so the totall of those his L. sv}antes &
> Househoulde for dailly attendans as affore-   } c^mi & xviiime psons.
> sayd doe amount vnto the nowmber of   (p. 27.)

[*118 servants, which in later lists would rise to 140: a large household indeed, and one administered by William Farington until the closure of the house on 17 February, 1588, by which time Earl Henry had already departed for London (1 September 1587) en route for Flanders to negotiate with the Spanish in an attempt to delay or cancel Philip II's Great Armada, with its threatened invasion of England. He left **Sir Edward Sr** in charge.*

***Sir Edward Sr** had four servants with him on this occasion. His specific presence mentioned during this period is given below, usually only when he departed to or returned from somewhere, in the middle of the entries of all the other comings and goings recorded for the whole of the relevant week. The account of each week always begins on the day when William Farington drew up his accounts for the purchase of victuals for the following week. This was not always on the same day, but normally at the beginning of the week.*]

> Week of 'the first of Juli' (1587)

> On Mondaye my L. came home, & Sr **Edward Stanley**; on Wednesdaye Sr **Jhon Sotheworth** & Mr Kilshaw, Mr Langton of the Low came & wente; on Thursdaye Mr **Ric. Molyenox** at dyner, Mr **Auditor Hoghton** came; on ffrydaye Mr **Skillycorne** came, & the same daye Mr Stewarde and M^r foxe came also. (p. 31.)

[*Several of these names are familiar from Preston Guild Rolls in 1582. The identity of many of the visitors is examined at length in the Introduction to the DHB. Those highlighted below are mainly those who play a role elsewhere in this book.*

'Sr John Sotheworth' was Sir John Southworth of Samlesbury Hall, one of the top gentry at Preston Guild. His family remained fairly resolutely Catholic.]

'Mr *Ric. Molyenox* was a near-neighbour, later **Sir Richard Molyneux (1st Baronet)** *of Sefton near Lathom. He was Lord of the Manor of Liverpool and his family built and owned Molyneux Castle in Liverpool, near the Stanley Tower on the waterfront. The following year (1588-89) he was Mayor of Liverpool. He was married to Frances Gerard, sister of Sir Thomas Gerard, Lord Marshal, son of Sir Gilbert Gerard of Ince near Wigan and Gerard's Bromley in Staffordshire.* **Sir Richard Molyneux** *was the dedicatee of one of Weever's seven sections (3) in his 'Epigrammes', 1599. This family was always up at the top of the rankings at Preston Guild.*

'Mr *Auditor Hoghton'* *was presumably one of the Hoghtons of Lea and Hoghton Tower, who were by family tradition hosts of young William Shakespeare/Shakeshafte 'for a couple of years', presumed to have been 1579-81, just six years before this entry in the DHB.* **Sir Richard Hoghton** *was the main dedicatee of Weever's 'Epigrammes' in 1599 and also received the last epigram in the book (7.16); this Mr Hoghton was perhaps his brother William, who also received an epigram (6.4). Their father* **Thomas Hoghton** *was still alive in 1587, but was destined to be killed in 1589 in the midnight 'affray at Lea'. He was to receive an obituary epigram (6.3). This family was always at the head of the gentry at Preston Guild.*

'Mr *Skillycorne'* *was presumably a Skillicorne of Prees, a family in the top twenty at Preston Guild.*]

Week of 'the xiiii of October' (1587)

On Fryday Sr **Edward Stanley** came home from London. (p. 40.)

[**Sir Edward Sr***'s arrival was presumably to deputise for Earl Henry during his absence, when many visitors continued to arrive at Lathom, including his nephew Ferdinando, Lord Strange, with his wife and daughters. Why* **Sir Edward** *should have gone to London in the period leading up to mid-October is not known. Perhaps to accompany his brother to London en route for the Netherlands? Or perhaps to prepare the London house for him? In any case* **Sir Edward Sr** *was back at Lathom in mid-October.*]

Week of 'the ii of December' (1587)

On Monday M^r **To. Gerrard & his wiffe** came & also Mr Skarsebrike & Mr **Nicolas Rigby** also; on Tvesday **my L. Bushoppe** & his wiffe came; on Wednesday Mr Skaresbrike & Mr **Rigby** depted, & the same daye one Mr Diconson a northern man came; on Fryday Mr **Osboston** & his ij sones came, & the same daye **Mr Gerrarde & his wiffe** wente awaye; on Saterday my L. Strandge & **his brother Sr Edwarde Stanley** Mr **Dudley** & Mr **Asheton wente towards Chester**, & Mr Skaresbrike came & also Mr **Salesbury**. (p. 44.)

[*In 1587* **'his brother Sr Edwarde Stanley'** *was almost certainly the brother of Earl Henry, Lord Strange for many years until the latter became 4th Earl of Derby in 1572 on the death of his father Earl Edward, and NOT the brother of Ferdinando, the current Lord Strange, as indicated by the above entry.* **Sir Edward Sr** *was the only Sir Edward Stanley in the immediate family at this time. Ferdinando had also had a younger brother Edward, but he had died young a few years earlier, buried at Ormskirk on 16 September 1583. One might presume that Farington just made a slip of the pen.*

'M^r **To. Gerrard'** *was a close friend of Ferdinando. His father Sir Thomas Gerard of Bryn was the one involved in the plan to free Mary, Queen of Scots from Chatsworth in 1570 along with* **Sir Edward Stanley Sr** *and his brother* **Sir Thomas**. *This* **Thomas Gerard Jr** *was destined to be knighted in 1603 by King James out of gratitude for his services to his mother. This was in York, on his way to London for his coronation, on the occasion of which he also knighted* **Sir Edward Stanley Jr**. *'his wiffe' was a Molyneux of Sefton, so he was thus the brother-in-law of* **Sir Richard Molyneux**. *The Gerards were always in the top twenty at Preston Guild.*

'Mr **Nicolas Rigby'** *was one of a family with several branches, the one at Burgh in Duxbury being the one that was always in the top twenty at Preston Guild.*

'M*r* *Osboston*' with his four sons was an **Osbaldeston of Osbaldeston**, *a family always in the top twenty at Preston Guild.*

'M*r* *Dudley*' was perhaps of the family of Lord Dudley, Earl Henry and **Sir Edward Sr**'s brother-in-law. Edward Sutton, 8*th* Lord Dudley, had married their sister Jane Stanley in 1566, but she had died in 1569.

'M*r* *Asheton*' might have been from one of several places, but the most influential at the time were the Asshetons of Great Lever near Bolton and Whalley Abbey, who were in the top twenty at Preston Guild. It was certainly one of this family who paid a later visit.

'M*r* *Salesbury*' was John Salesbury of Lleweni, married to Earl Henry's daughter Ursula since December 1586, an occasion which is seen by an increasing number of researchers as the inspiration for Shakespeare writing 'The Phoenix and Turtle'.

The next lengthy sojourn in Lancashire by Earl Henry was in September 1588, when he returned to great rejoicing after the defeat of the Armada, this time to New Park. The 'Imbassadge' in 'fflanders' referred to in the next quote was Earl Henry's mission on behalf of Elizabeth in an attempt to prevent by diplomacy the threatened invasion of England by the Spanish. Earl Henry was absent from Lathom for the whole of this period.]

At New P*j*ke 1588	A weekly brieffement of the Expensis of my L. the Earle of Derbye's Howsholde begyning the xxvi*th* daie of September 1588 et A*o* R. R. Eliz. XXX*o*, being his returne from his Jorneye & Imbassadge from fflanders viz. (p. 50.)

[*It is not known whether* **Sir Edward Sr** *was also in attendance for some or much of the time, but his presence seems to have been taken for granted by the family, and this year sees the beginning of the regular appearance of his nephew* **Edward Jr** *of Winwick and Tong; also several mentions of visits to* **Winwick***. The household moved to Lathom House on the 28 December 1588 and Earl Henry moved backwards and forwards to New Park on later occasions. However, the most important aspect of the records following is the proof that* **Sir Edward Sr** *and* **Edward Jr** *were regular visitors and must have met each other there. The frequent mention of* **Winwick** *in connection with* **Edward Jr** *seems proof enough in itself that he had maintained his father's property there, and stayed there on his returns to Lancashire.*]

SIR EDWARD Sr AND EDWARD Jr + WINWICK

[*We might remember yet again that* **Sir Thomas Stanley** *had died in 1576, when* **Edward Jr** *was only fourteen. In 1589* **Edward Jr** *was therefore twenty-seven. He had since married Lucy Percy in 1581 and they had had some of their children, who were all still rather little at this time. It is not known whether his family travelled to the North with him when he visited* **Winwick***, but if they did, this would have been a good reason for only making day visits to his uncles at Lathom or Knowsley. We know that his only son Thomas, who died very young, was buried at* **Winwick***.*]

Week of 'the vi of Januarii' (1589)

Sondaye **M*r* Caldewall** pretched, & that nyght the Plaiers plaied; Monday **my L. Bushoppe** pretched, & the same daye Mr Trafforth, **M*r* Edw. Stanley**, Mr Mydleton of Leighton came; on Tvsedaye **S*r* Ric. Shirborne**, M*r* Stewarde, **my L. Bushoppe**, S*r* Jhon Byron, & many others depted; Wednesdaye my L. removed to New Pke; on Frydaye M*r* Norres & M*r* Torbocke & M*r* Tildesley came & wente. (p. 57.)

['**M*r* Edw. Stanley**' might have been **Edward Stanley Jr** or a namesake from a local side branch.

'M*r* **Caldewall**' was John Caldewell, minister at Winwick, who one might expect to be well known to **(Sir) Edward Jr**. Raines's biography of him was given in the last chapter. He also merited an entry in the Victoria County History.]

Raines MSS. (Chet. Lib.), xxii, 52. It appears that the Bishop of Chester claimed the presentation, perhaps by lapse, John Shireburne, B.D., being nominated by him (see Brindle).

The Earl of Derby's nomination prevailed, and Caldwell paid his first-fruits on 20 Feb. 1575–6; Lancs. and Ches. Recs. ii, 410. He was also rector of Mobberley; Ormerod, *Ches.* (ed. Helsby), i, 412, 428. He was one of the earl's chaplains, and a favourite preacher; *Derby Household Bks.* (Chet. Soc.), 132, 133.

(*Victoria County History*, Vol. 4, Winwick, Note 57.)

['*My L. Bushoppe*' *was the Bishop of Chester, who was a regular visitor. It is interesting to see both a sermon and a theatrical performance on a Sunday. It has been generally assumed that when* 'the Plaiers' *are mentioned in the Derby Household Books, these were either a troupe kept by Earl Henry,* 'Derby's Players', *or by his son Ferdinando, elsewhere known as* 'Lord Strange's Players' *or* 'Strange's Men', *particularly when they performed in London or on tour.*

'*Sʳ Richard Shirborne*' *of Stonyhurst was a regular visitor because he was Treasurer to the Earl of Derby. He was the current one of four successive Sir Richard Shireburnes buried with magnificent tombs and effigies in the church at Mitton. His family's most notable legacy to history was that Stonyhurst Hall became the home of the first Catholic boarding school in 1794 – it still fulfils this function today as Stonyhurst College. On its website it claims a foundation in 1593 by Jesuit Robert Persons at the College at St Omer in Flanders; this almost coincides with the date of the original building of this Hall by the Sir Richard who appears here at Lathom House in 1589. It has always had strong Jesuit ties, with a statue of St Ignatius Loyola, the founder of the Jesuits, in the grounds.*]

Lathom	A Wekely Bryeffeᵗ of my L. expensis in his howsholde
1589	after his retorne from the Cowrte begyning Wednesdaye
	the xiᵗʰ of Jvne 1589 et Aᵒ xxxiᵒ Eliz. regni. (p. 59.)

Week of 'the viii of June' (1589)

My L. laid at the Lodge in Lathom Pke from Saturedaye the vᵗʰ of this Jvne vntill Wedesdaye the xᵗʰ of the same, where pte of the sayd chardges were spente, & the same Wednesdaye he & **Sʳ Edwarde Stanley**, Mʳ Dutton, & all my L. howsholde & many strandgers came to Lathom; on Tvsedaye Mʳ Dutton wente awayes, & **Mʳ Holcrofte, Sʳ Ric. Shirborne**, Mʳ Edwardes, **Mʳ Talbot of Bashall, my L. Bushoppe of Chester**, Mʳ To. Preston, & dyvers of the sayd **Sʳ Ryc. Shirborne** his children & sones in lawes, & also **Mʳ Jhon Osboston** came; on Fryday **Mʳ Holcrofte** wente awayes, & the same daye Mʳ Stewarde, Mʳ Scaresbryke, **Mʳ Robert Hesketh**, Mʳ Worsley, & Mr Sherington of Wigane, Mʳ Mollyneux of Hawkeliffe came; on Satterdaye they all depted. (pp. 59-60.)

['*Mʳ Holcrofte*' *was Thomas Holcroft of Vale Royal, Cheshire, who received an epigram from Weever in 1599 (5.16). His family was closely related by marriage to Manners, Earls of Rutland, the family of* **Edward Jr**'s *aunt Dorothy Manners née Vernon.*

'*Mʳ Talbot of Bashall*' *was from a family with several branches established near the River Ribble. They were always in the top twenty at Preston Guild. This family had also provided a branch that became the Earls of Shrewsbury, one of whom, George Talbot, the 6ᵗʰ Earl, had married Bess of Hardwick. They had been the custodians of Mary, Queen of Scots at Chatsworth House, from where* **Sir Edward Sr**, *with his brother* **Sir Thomas** *and their friend Sir Thomas Gerard had planned to rescue her in 1570.*

'*Mʳ Robert Hesketh*' *was the son and heir of Sir Thomas Hesketh of Rufford, whose family tradition was passed down for centuries that* 'young William Shakespeare had stayed with them for a short time in his youth'. *His first wife was Mary, daughter and heiress of Sir George Stanley of Cross Hall, Lathom, who had been knighted at Queen Mary's coronation at the same time as* **Sir Thomas**. *Mary died in 1586 and by 1589 he had married as his second wife Blanche née Twyford of Kenwick, Shropshire, widow of William Stopforth, a former Steward of Earl Henry for many years, who brought lands into her second marriage as her widow's third. Thus some Stopforth papers are still preserved* *in DDHe, The Hesketh Papers, at the Lancashire Record Office, which allowed the sorting out of the mysteries left behind by Captain Myles Standish's will of 1656. Portraits of Robert Hesketh and his two wives appear on the impressive illustrated 1594 pedigree of the Heskeths displayed at Rufford Old Hall (original in the British Library).]*

Week of 'the xxi of June' (1589)

On Sondaye Mr Skaresbryke, **Mr Cutbert Halsoll**, **Mr Nicalas Rigby** at dyner, wch daye there was a Sermon by **my L. Bushoppe**, & that nyghte came Mr Jhon Bradley from London; & **my L. Bushoppe** wente awayes vpon Mondaye & wth him also Mr Bradley; Tvsedaye my L. rydde to Pilkinton & **Sr Edwarde Stanley** wth him. (pp. 59-60.)

*[**Mr Cuthbert Halsall** was married to Earl Henry's daughter Dorothy by his mistress Jane Halsall, who were 'cousins' of some degree. By 1599 he had been knighted and received the dedication of Weever's sixth section of epigrams.*

In July the household moved to Knowsley, a week after the Queen's Players had 'plaied ii severall nights' at Lathom. (p. 62.)]

Week of 'the xviii of July' (1589)

Sondaye Mr Tatton came, & the same daye my L. wente towardes **Preston** & **Sr Edwarde Stanley** with him; Tvseday his L. returned home, & Mr Rec. & Mr ffoxe came also; on Wednesdaye my L. went to Wigan & retorned to the Lodge at Lathom; on Frydaye **Mr Edwarde Stanley of Winwicke** came. (p. 62.)

*[This visit to Preston of **Sir Edward Sr** with his brother is proof enough on its own that **Sir Edward** was involved in family business. Apparently he stayed away and was not there to receive **Edward Jr**, who arrived at the end of the week.]*

1589 Knowsley.	A Wekely Abrevemt of my L. the Earle of Derbys Howseholde for a howle yers expensis there beginning the xviiith daie of Jvly A^o dni 1589 et A^o R. R. Elizabethæ xxxij^{do} viz. (p. 62.)

Week of 'the seconde of Auguste' (1589)

Sondaie P^lson of Burrie preached, Mr Henry Stanley came, Mr Worsley junior; Mondaie my L. went to Mr Duttons, Mr Worsley went; Tuesdaie my L. came home, & **Sr Edw.**; Thursdaie my L. roowd to Lathome, **Sr Edw.** stayed; Frydaie **Mr Rigbie** came againe, my Lo. His Counsell were at the Declarac]on; this Saturdaie **my L. Bushoppe** came at nyght. (p. 63.)

Week of 'xxviii of August' (1589)

Sondaie Vicar of Rachdall preached; Mondaie my L. went to **Winwicke** & **Sr Edw. Stanley**, Mr Rogers, & Duchemel; Wednesdaie Mr Receiver & **Mr Ashton of Leiver** came & had supper; on Thursdaie they had breakfaste & went awaie & came againe to supper, & went awaie on Frydaie; this Saturdaie my Lo. came home and strangers with him. (p. 64.)

*[Lord Henry and **Sir Edward Sr** went to Winwick, The purpose is unknown, but they presumably made use of the Rectory to stay for several days, whether **Edward Jr** was there or not. The visit to **Winwick** with a gentleman with the very non-Lancashire name of Duchemel, and Lord Henry returning with 'strangers' is intriguing.]*

Week of 'August xxx' (1589)

Sondaie Mr Carter preached & great company, **Mr Cuthbart Halsall** & **M^r Jo. Bold** came; Mondaie in matter Deane of Chester & many others, **S^r Jo. Biron** came; Tuesdaie my L. & the rest went to Toxteth P[}]ke & so forth to Wirrall; **S^r Ed. Stanley** staied Wedensdaie, **my L. Dudley** & **Mr Edw. Stanley of Winwike** came; Thursdaie **M^r W^m** my Lo. sonne came; Frydaie he went to my Lo. in **Wirrall**; Saturdaie my Lo. came home wth Mr Bouthe of Dunhame. (p. 65.)

[*'Mr Jo. Bold'* was presumably one of the family of this name of North Meols, who were always in or close to the top twenty at Preston Guild.

'Sir Jo. Biron' was presumably the one who has an entry on Wikipedia: *'**Sir John Byron Junior** (c.1526–1600) was the son of Sir John Byron, Sr and lived at Clayton, Manchester and later Royton, both then in Lancashire, and later still at Newstead Abbey in Nottinghamshire. He was High Sheriff of Lancashire in 1572 and was knighted by Queen Elizabeth in 1579. His eldest son was John Byron, 1st Baron and he had several other sons. Their heirs inherited the title from the first baron.'* One of the heirs two hundred years later was the poet Lord Byron, 6th Baron Byron, who is irrelevant for the current story. Interestingly, however, the name 'Biron' is also that of one of the characters at the court of the Prince of Navarre in 'Love's Labour's Lost', a play that shows many links with William Stanley's recent travels in France with his tutor Richard Lloyd, author of a play called The Nine Worthies, which also appears in 'Love's Labour's Lost'. (See any Derbyite website for details about this.) As both Sir John Biron and Shakespeare were moving in Stanley circles in 1589 (according to the 'Lancastrian Shakespeare' theory), the former might have been amused to find his name being dramatised in a French setting. One wonders again who the French sounding Mr Duchemel was, who had visited Henry, Lord Strange the week before.

One might guess that the visit to the Wirral by 'my Lord and the rest' was primarily to see the Stanley family of Hooton, whose son Sir William had defected to the Spanish in 1587 when he surrendered Deventer. Sir Rowland, however, was still very much still residing at Hooton Hall. The Earls of Derby also owned Bidston Hall in the Wirral and had recently acquired New Park, presumed by some to be the site at the end of the Wirral where Leasowe Castle was built by 1593 at the latest. The horse races on the beach are one of the contenders for the origin of the word 'Derby', a term used worldwide for local contests.

William Stanley (**Mr Wm**), Earl Henry's younger son, arrived from somewhere (presumably from London, after his recent three year tour of Italy and the Middle East, including Egypt, Jerusalem and Constantinople, where he had had some allegedly hair-raising adventures) and immediately left for the Wirral to join his father. One might guess that one main topic of conversation at this time was William's recent travels.]

Week of 'September vi' (1589)

Sondaie P¹son of . . . . . . preached, great company; Mondaie **Mr Bolde** at diñer; Tuesdaie Mr Egerton, Mr Sherington, the Lawier & his brother came, Mr Bouth wente, my L., my **L. Dudley**, **Sr Edw. Stanley, Mr Wm** &c. went to Lathom to hunt, my **L. Dudley** his mê stayed; Saturdaie my L., my **L. Dudley**, & all the rest came home, **my L. Dudley brother in law** came; the Quene's Players came & played at nyght, my Lo. of Essex Players came. (p. 65.)

[*The Queen's Players and the Essex Players put on several more performances during the following week. It has often been suggested that Shakespeare might have been here at this time, acting with the Queen's Players, but the fact is that we do not know. Nor do we know which plays were performed. We do know, however, that **Sir Edward Stanley Sr** was staying at the time and that **Edward Jr** had been at Winwick the week before and visited his two uncles.*

*'My L. Dudley brother in law' was Edward Sutton, 4th Baron Dudley, one of Earl Henry's and **Sir Edward Sr**'s numerous brothers-in-law and therefore **Edward Jr**'s uncle. He had been married to sister Jane until her death twenty years earlier, but the brothers-in-law were obviously still in contact.*]

Week of 'Sept. viii' (1589)

Sondaie **Mr Leigh** preached & the Quenes Players played in the afternoone, & my L. of Essex at nyght; Mondaie my L. and all went away; Tuesdaie **Mr Townelay** came in the evening to have sene my L.; Wedensdaie he went home againe; Thursdaie ij stags were baked; Saturdaie my L. & **Sr Edw.** came home, my **L. Dudley** & **Mr Wm Stanley** went from my L. in Chester towards London. (pp. 65-6.)

[*'**Mr Leigh**' was the Revd William Leigh, Vicar of Standish. He was already gaining a national reputation for his sermons and was later to be appointed chaplain to Prince Henry, King James I's son. He was apparently much appreciated by Alice, Ferdinando's wife/widow, because in his will of 1639 he mentioned a bowl given to him by her (Porteus, History of Standish). He was also a close friend of Alexander Standish of Duxbury, which is why he appears in the 'Captain Myles Standish of Duxbury' story.*

*'**Mr Townelay**' was from Towneley Hall, Burnley. His family at this time were noted Catholics, who suffered much from imprisonment and hefty fines. This family produced several later notables, most importantly for this book the historian Christopher Towneley of the next generation, who worked closely with historian Roger Dodsworth, married to a Hesketh of Rufford, and historian Sir William Dugdale, whose father was from Mitton near Stonyhurst.*

*'**Mr Wm Stanley**''s departure for London with his uncle Lord Dudley is interesting when reviewing details of his travels around Europe.*]

Week of 'Sept. xx' (1589)

Mondaie my L. went to Asley & **S**ʳ **Ed. Stanley**, dyvers of my L. yomê stayed there; Wednesdaie they went to my Lo.; this Saturday the **P**ˡ**son of Winwicke** came. (pp. 65-6.)

Sondaie **P**ˡ**son of Winwicke** went to preach before my Lo. at Lathome, my L. Strange children dyned at Mʳ Suttons; Mondaie not any . . . . theme came home; Thursdaie my L. came not; this Saturdaie my L. came home, Mʳ Steward came & Mʳ ffoxe. (p. 66.)

Week of 'Oct. iiii. Apud New Pˡke' (1589)

Sondaie one Mʳ Byne preached, Mʳ Heston, **Mʳ Rigbie, Roger Rigbie, Nicolas Rigbie**; Tuesdaie Mʳ Steward went, my Lo. & Lady Strange came; Wedensdaie **Mʳ Bould** came & waent; Thursdaie my L. removed to New Pˡke, my L. Str. went to **Winwicke**; Sʳ John Biron, **Sʳ Richard Shearburne**, Mr Recˡ. came at nyght & John Bradley; Frydaie they went; Saturdaie Mʳ Maire of Chester & some of his brethrê came & went. (p. 66.)

Week of 'Octʳ the xxv New Pˡke' (1589)

Sondaie **Mʳ Leigh** preached, **Mʳ Tho. Standish**, Mʳ Skaresbrecke, Mʳ Adlintô & many of Standishe Pˡishe there; Tewsdaie my L. wente to Bideston, my La. Strange, **Sʳ Edw. Stanley**, my **L. Mounte-egle**'s mê & **Mr Pˡker stayed**; this Saturdaie my Lo. came home wth **Mr Salesburye** & Mʳ ffoxe. (p. 68.)

[*'**Mr Tho. Standish**' was the stepfather of young Alexander Standish, Lord of the Manor of Duxbury near Chorley, although by a historical quirk Duxbury was within the Parish of Standish. (Duxbury was in the 'far north' of the Parish and Standish in the 'deep south' near Wigan.) Their 'cousin' Catholic Edward Standish at Standish Hall had many disagreements with the Revd '**Mr Leigh**', Vicar at his Parish Church and a noted Protestant preacher, thus putting the latter more in sympathy with 'cousins' Thomas and Alexander Standish of Duxbury. One might imagine that this delegation from the north of the Parish at the same time as the **Revd William Leigh** was concerned in some way with the current religious situation.*]

Week of 'Novʳ the 1ˢᵗ' (1589)

Sondaie Mʳ Skaresbrecke, Mʳ H. Stanley, **Mʳ Barth. Hesketh** & many others at dinner, my L. Strange **my L. Montegle** are sˡved; Mondaie my Lo. went towards Pilkinton; **my Lo. Mountegle, Mʳ Salesbury** went, my L. & La. Strange & **Sʳ Edw.** stayed; Wedensdaie **Mʳ Halsall** junior came; Thursdaie he went to Pˡson of Wigâ & Mʳ Henry Stanley not at dinner; Fryday my L. Strange went to Pilkinton. (p. 68.)

[*'**Mr Barth. Hesketh**' was **Bartholomew Hesketh** of Aughton, brother-in-law of the Alexander Hoghton who had written his will in 1581 naming William Shakeshafte. Bartholomew was suspected* of sheltering Catholic priests and his brother Richard Hesketh was destined to arrive back from the Continent in September 1593 with the 'notorious' letter from Catholics in exile offering support for Ferdinando as heir to Elizabeth's throne.

It is not certain who **'my Lo. Mountegle'** was in 1589. William, 3rd Lord Mo(u)nteagle, of Hornby Castle near Lancaster, had died in 1581, leaving his second wife Anne Spencer (sister of Alice Spencer, wife of Ferdinando, who often appear with their daughters in the DHB) as his widow, and a daughter and heiress Elizabeth by his first wife Anne Leyburne. Elizabeth married Edward Parker, 12th Lord Morley, who was never actually Lord Mo(u)nteagle, although the head of the family at Hornby in 1589. Perhaps he was informally known locally as Lord Mo(u)nteagle because it was taken for granted that their son William Parker (born 1575) would be created Lord Mo(u)nteagle when he came of age? This did indeed happen later, when he became William Parker, 13th Lord Morley, 4th Baron Mo(u)nteagle. In 1599 he received an epigram 'Ad D. Mounteagle' from Weever (3.3). He was the one who was later to reveal the Gunpowder Plot to the authorities.]

Week of 'November the viii' (1589)

Mondaie my La. Str.[ange] rode to **Winwicke, Sr Edw**. stayed; Tuesdaie my L. came frô Pilkinton; Wednesdaie my Lo. Strange went ffrom **Winwicke**; Thursdaie my La. Strange came againe frô **Winwicke**; this Saturday Mr Anderton at dinner. (p. 69.)

Week of 'November the xv' (1589)

Sondaie Vicar of Ratchdale pᴵeched; Mondaie Mr ffoxe came; Tuesdaie my Lo. & also my La. Strange & **Sr Edw. Stanley** dyned at the Lodge in Lathome Pᴵke; Thursdaie **Mr Edw**. came, & on ffrydaie he wente againe; this Satturdaie . . . (p. 69.)

[*At last we have* **Edward Jr** *staying overnight! Or maybe it was another local namesake again? There is no further mention of either* **Sir Edward Sr** *or* **Edward Jr** *until 2 May 1590, when the latter stayed overnight. Between these dates various dramatic events are recorded: in the form of visits by more players and the 'dramatic' murder of Thomas Hoghton at the end of November 1589 by Baron Langton's men in the 'affray at Lea'. (A brief account of this is given in Honigmann, Shakespeare, the 'lost years', pp. 12-13, including a letter from Queen Elizabeth.) At this time there were a great many comings and goings between Lathom and Lancaster, where the trial was to be held under the supervision of Ferdinando. The trial never actually took place because it was impossible to assemble a jury prepared to convict anyone. The Earl departed for London, leaving Ferdinando and* **Sir Edward Sr** *in charge, and all gathered again in Lancashire the following May.*]

Week of 'the ii of Maye' at New Pᴵke (1590)

On Wednesday **Mr Petter Stanley** senioᴵ at dynner; Thursday **Mr Edward Stanley of Winwicke** came & my L. came home; on fryday **Mr Stanley** returned home & the same daye Mr Skaresbriyke came to dynner & also Mr Tunstall. (p. 79.)

[**'Mr Petter Stanley senioᴵ'** *was of Moor Hall, Aughton, who was the uncle of Sir Rowland Stanley of Hooton.*]

Week of 'the xxiii of Maye, at New Pᴵke' (1590)

Sondaye Mr Skaresbryke, **Mr Wrightington, Mr Nicolas Rigbie** came to dyñer, **Mr Hesketh** came and went also; Tewsdaye my L. went to Knowsley in his jorneye towards Hawrden, **Sr Edw. Stanley** & my L. Strandges children stayed behind. (p. 80.)

[**'Mr Wrightington'** *was Edward Wrightington of Wrightington, who received an epigram from Weever in 1599 (6.25).*

One presumes that this visit by Earl Henry to Hawarden was to see Jane Halsall, his mistress and mother of his second family, which included Ursula married to (Sir) **John Salesbury** and Dorothy married to (Sir) **Cuthbert Halsall**.

Sir Edward Sr seems to have been trusted enough to stay and look after his nieces.]

Week of 'the xx of June' (1590)

On Sonday Mr Steward & Mr Clerke Comptrowler came; on Monday my L. rydde to Knowsley; Tvseday Sr **Edwarde Stanley** & my L. Strandges children & all the Howseholde removed to **Knowsley**, & the same day Sr **Edward ffitton**, Mr Rec}., & Mr Orrell came; & on Wednesday they dep}ted; on Thursday Mr Norres, Mr Vrmeston, & Mr Blondell came & wente. (p. 82.)

[*'Sr Edward ffitton' was Sir Edward Fitton (1548-1606), an unsuccessful colonist of Munster. His sister Mary Fitton was Maid of Honour to Elizabeth I, who in the nineteenth century became the first candidate in the search for Shakespeare's 'Dark Lady' of the Sonnets.*

On 26 June comes another list of the whole household and a list of the almost permanently resident members of the Earl's family during the summer of 1590. This was the last mention of William, who departed soon afterwards for three years in Russia.]

My L. Stranges Children & S}vantes, viz.

1. M^ris Anne.

2. M^ris ffranses.

3. M^ris Elizabeth.

4. Margaret ffletcher.

5. M^ris Mawdeline.

6. Anne Cowp.

7. Mr Ryc. Lysster.

8. To. Gerrarde.

    Sr Edwarde Stanley iii

    Mr Wm Stanley my L. soñe . . . iii

Sum totall of the nowmber of all the severall p}sons in this Checkerowle contayned be	[Of the Family	5
	Servants	140
		145

(p. 88.)

Week of 'the firste of Auguste 1590'

On Tuesdaye Mr **Warren** came; Atherton came & wente; on Thursdaye my L. wente to the New P}ke to take the declaration of his Audytt, vnto whom all his Offysers & Cownsellers came; Sr **Edward Stanley** & my L. Stranges children remayned at Knowsley. (p. 89.)

Tvsedaye my L. wente to the New Parke, & Sr **Edwarde Stanley** stayed behinde; on Thursday the **Earle of Tyrone** came to my L., & on ffrydaye he dep}ted; and iiii Tayllyers were working all weke in making of a Teñte for my L. (p. 89.)

[*'**Mr Warren**' was (later Sir) **Edward Warren** (1563-1639) of Poynton, Cheshire and Woodplumpton, Lancashire. He received the dedication of Weever's fourth section of epigrams in 1599 as 'Sir Edward Warren knight'. His first wife was Margaret Fitton, daughter of **Sir Edward Fitton** (no issue); his second wife was Ann, daughter of Sir William Davenport of Bramall, Cheshire, a family connected by marriage to the Ardernes of (H)Arden, Cheshire, the family of Mary Arderne,*

John Shakespeare's second or third wife and William Shakespeare's stepmother.

*The 'Earle of Tyrone' was Hugh O'Neill, 'The Great O'Neill', who fought with his Irish forces first with and later against the English, with Spanish help. It seems that he probably met **Sir Edward Sr** at Lathom before joining Earl Henry at New Park. It was a pity that Tyrone did not stay on to enjoy whatever festivities were being planned for the near future in the tent that was being constructed. After his later defeat he returned to Lancashire, according to legend and an old tradition, not this time to Lathom house, but to hide out in a valley near Rochdale, still known as Tyrone's Bed, where a young lady helped to hide him and then to escape. Believe this or not, but the tradition is told in Harland and Wilkinson's 'Lancashire Legends', 1873, and a romanticised version is in 'Frank Hird's Lancashire Tales', selected by Cliff Hayes, 1998.*]

> Week of 'the xxii of Auguste' (1590)
>
> On Monday **Mr Stanley of Winwicke** came, & **Mr Edwarde Stanley**, my L. Strandges came also; Tvsedaye the[y] went awayes, & my L. retorned from New P[}]ke; Wednesdaye Sr Jhon Savadge & Mr Dvtton came & wente; Thursday the P[}]son of Walton & one Mr Gvdde a Sodjer came to dyñer & retorned; ffryday Mr Stewarde came; & on Saturday M^r P[}]son of **Winwicke** came. (p. 90.)

[*This is the first time another 'Mr Stanley of Winwicke' appears with what is obviously 'our' **Mr Edward Stanley**. The Stanley researcher Brian S. Roberts is fairly certain that 'Mr Stanley of Winwicke' is Gerard Stanley, an illegitimate son of **Sir Thomas** of Winwick and Tong. One wonders who 'Mr Gvdde' the soldier was and why he was there? A former comrade of Edward Stanley's at Zutphen or Sir William Stanley of Hooton's before he defected? Back from the Netherlands bearing messages? On his way to Ireland?*

This is the last entry in the Derby Household Books in the MS that has survived. We are lucky that this stayed with the Faringtons at Worden Hall; had it stayed at Lathom House, it would probably have disappeared along with many other family papers during the Civil War, when it was almost destroyed and demolished soon afterwards. HM]

My apologies in retrospect and RIP to all the gentlemen visitors – and the odd knight – who did not appear in bold. All were no doubt valued as visitors, but they happen not to have been among the top twenty at Preston Guild, nor received a dedication from Weever, nor played any evident role in **Sir Edward Sr** and **Jr**'s lives apart from visiting the Earl of Derby at the same time. This roll call is as follows, in alphabetical order and with modernised versions of place-names and their surnames, most of which are still common in Lancashire today, many of the names coming from fairly local place-names:

Mr Adlington (of Adlington?), Mr Anderton (of Anderton?), Mr Atherton (of Atherton?), Mr Booth of Dunham (Cheshire), Mr John Bradley (of Bradley?), Mr Dutton, Mr Edwards, Mr Egerton (which Cheshire branch?), Mr Kilshaw, Mr Langton of the Lowe, Mr Middleton of Lathom, Mr Molyneux of Hawcliffe, Mr Norris (of Speke?), Mr Orrel (of Orrell), Mr Thomas Preston, Mr Rogers, Sir John Savage (of Rock Savage, Cheshire), Mr Scarisbrick (a very regular visitor) (of Scarisbrick?), Mr Sherington of Wigan, Mr Sherington the Lawyer, Mr Henry Stanley (perhaps 'Mr Henry Stanley of Broughton', Earl Henry's second son from his second family; although attributed as this by Peter Stanley, *The House of Stanley*, nothing more is known about him), Mr Tarbuck, Mr Tatton (of Tatton?), Mr Trafford (of Trafford?), Mr Tyldesley (of Tyldesley?), Mr Urmeston (of Urmeston?), Mr Worsley (of Worsley?).

Then there were the rather non-Lancashire sounding names of Mr Blondell and Mr Duchamel. And last but not least, Mr Steward (steward of the household) and Mr Fox (on the staff at Lathom) were, quite naturally, nearly always there.

Chapter XVIII
Sir Thomas's (1576) and Lady Margaret Stanley's (1596) last wills and testaments

XVIII-1. Introduction

Images were obtained by Brian S. Roberts at the The National Archives (formerly the Public Record Office), Kew, with references given below. Following are transcriptions in modernised spelling of the English text and translations of the Latin texts.

It is worth mentioning that the only other precise references to these two wills that I have come across were by E. A. J. Honigmann, *Shakespeare: the 'lost years'* (1985, 1998) in his Chapter VII. 'The Shakespeare Epitaphs and the Stanleys'. He had obviously read the texts of both wills, but he had not explored the full biographies of the people concerned.

> There are no clues in Sir Thomas's will,[11] [*about the state of his finances*] but his widow's[12] reveals another relevant fact: she married again, and might have wished to be buried with her second husband. In the event, however, she snubbed her second husband, leaving him no token of her love, decreeing 'my body to be buried in the Parish Church of Tong by my husband Sir Thomas Stanley'; her will states, cryptically, that it was 'made by the consent and agreement' of her second husband, William Mathe, Esq. The tomb, therefore could have been delayed because the family was short of funds and, later, because there would be some doubt as to the figures to be represented.
>
> [11] PCC (39 Carew). Sir Thomas was 'in trouble' in 1571 when he tried to rescue Mary Queen of Scots, and was imprisoned in the Tower for his pains.
> [12] PCC (92 Drake). PCC - Prerogative Court of Canterbury
>
> (Honigmann, *op. cit.*, p. 81, End-notes, p. 160.)

We are now in a position to clarify some of Honigmann's comments. I interpret rather differently Lady Margaret's wish to be buried with her first husband. I find it quite natural, as the owner of Tong Castle and with a vault full of her Vernon ancestors in Tong Church, with effigies to many of them, that she would wish to be buried in Tong with all of them, along with her first husband, who was already there. Her second husband William Mather (not Mathe) seemed to be in good health when she was writing her will (indeed, he was destined to live on until 1607) and she had no idea whether he might marry again, nor where he would be buried. I cannot therefore consider that 'she snubbed her second husband'. Nor can I agree with Honigmann's suggestion that her statement was cryptic. All seems to have been quite open and above board and all the provisions in her will were, very sensibly, 'made by the consent and agreement of her second husband'.

As far as the financial situation was concerned, I agree that they were almost certainly 'short of funds' immediately after **Sir Thomas**'s release from the Tower, not least because he had almost certainly obtained his freedom by paying something perhaps approaching the huge fine of 5000 marks demanded from his fellow prisoner Henry Percy, 8th Earl of Northumberland, also imprisoned for 'treason' (see any biography of this Earl Henry Percy). **Sir Thomas** made no detailed financial provisions in his will, but, as we shall read, he seemed very happy to leave all to his widow and son, for them to do what they deemed necessary. We suspect that their financial difficulties had indeed continued until his death in 1576, indicated by Lady Margaret immediately selling half of her interest in Eynsham to Sir Thomas Harri(e)s (see Chapter XIX. An excursion to Eynsham). However, by the time she wrote her will twenty years had passed. These years had been full of dramatic and traumatic events in her husband's Stanley family and the family of her Percy in-laws, acquired when son Edward married Lucy Percy in c.1581 but, as far as we know, none of these events had been particularly detrimental financially to Lady Margaret. Also, as far as we know, her sister Dorothy Manners's family, the Earls of Rutland, had not suffered any great setbacks. Given that she was a joint heiress with Dorothy of their father's vast estates as the 'King of the Peak', she would have had plenty of advice close to hand on how best to deal with her own half of the inheritance. In any case, twenty years seems to have been ample time to allow Lady Margaret, with the help of her second and apparently understanding husband, to put her family affairs in order. Bearing all this in mind, let us read the wills through 'fresher' eyes than Professor Honigmann's in 1985.

XVIII-2. Sir Thomas's last will and testament (1576)

1576 - Sir Thomas Stanley -
TNA reference - PROB 11/58 - Name of Register: Carew
- Image Ref. 514/390

Thome   (in left margin)
Stanley mi[te]

In the name of god Amen. The 12th [?] day of December in the year of our Lord god 1576 and in the nineteenth year of the reign of our most gracious sovereign Lady Elizabeth by the grace of God Queen of England, France and Ireland, Defender of the Faith.[i] Sir Thomas Stanley of Tong in the County of Salop, knight,[ii] being sick in body but of good and perfect remembrance, thanks be given to god, before diverse witnesses made and 'derived' his last will and testament, [...]pative in mann~ and form following.[iii] Viz. After he had commended his soul to god and his body to Christian burial he gave and bequeathed all his goods moveable and irremoveable, chattels, credit and debt whatsoever unto his well beloved wife Dame Margaret Stanley and his son Edward Stanley, equally to be divided between them.

(From the Latin)

The [Diecesimo Secondo] of December, 1576, remitted [emanuit remissie] for Dame Margaret Stanley, widow of Sir Thomas Stanley, knight. Administration of the goods and debts in the testament vested in Thomas [....hew], notary, sworn [jurato in Debita].

[i] Although the precise date in Latin numerals in the English is difficult to decipher (?xmy[th]), some time around the twelfth can be assumed from the Latin text. As Elizabeth came to the throne on 17 November 1558, any date in December 1596 was in the nineteenth year of her reign. The date of death given on his coffin in the Stanley vault in St Bartholomew's, Tong is 21 December.

The Stanley vault contained:

(2) the lead coffin cut open of **Sir Thomas Stanley** with the inscription
 on a lead plate
'Hic jacet **Thomas Stanley, Miles**, filius secundus Edwardi comitis
Darbi, maritus Margarite filie et une heredum Georgii Vernon militis,
qui obiit vicessimo primo die decembris anno regni reginae Elizabeth –
decimo nono; anno Domini milesimo quingentessimo septuagessimo

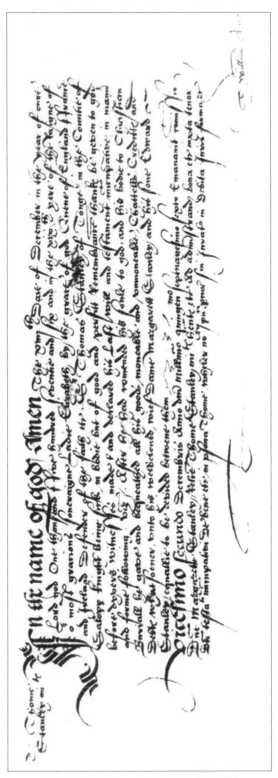

XVIIIa. Sir Thomas Stanley's will, 1576
TNA reference - PROB 11/58 - Name of Register: Carew – Image Ref. 514/390, accessed by Brian S. Roberts.

sexto.' Anima misereatur Deus.

Amen Per me Johannem in Lathomum.*

* [Here lies **Sir Thomas Stanley, Knight**, second son of Edward, Earl
of Derby, husband of Margaret, daughter and co-heir of George Vernon,
Knight, who died on the 21st December in the 19th year of the reign of
Queen Elizabeth AD 1576.

God have mercy on his soul. Amen. By me John Lathom.

(Translation from Griffiths, p. 65)]

(Footnote by Joyce Frost, transcriber of Auden's History.
See Chapter IV. Auden's History.)

[ii] '**Thomas Stanley of Tonge in the Countie of Salopp knight**'. It is interesting in that there is no mention of Winwick, a place with which he had been associated for so many years before 1570, and with which his son and heir **(Sir) Edward** was to continue to be associated. The most sensible explanation is that he did actually spend most of his last few years in Tong, where he died and was certainly buried. And Winwick Rectory was, after all, a property leased, not owned.

[iii] However, this does not read like a 'real will' in the conventional sense. Putting together the English and Latin texts, this reads more like the wishes of a dying man immediately before his expiry, without time to make any specific bequests and without time to call in a reliable scribe to record his dictation. It does mention that witnesses at his death 'made' and 'derived' his last will and testament, which is in the third person. These were apparently believed and accepted by the notary who was then called in. 'Administration of the goods and debts' was put in his hands for probate. No *Inquisition post mortem*, nor any inventory of his goods has survived.

Whatever the precise date of his 'will', it is perhaps worth noting one previous report of his death, in *Collins's Peerage of England*, Vol. 3 by Arthur Collins, Sir Egerton Brydges, 1812 (online on Google Books).

> Sir Thomas Stanley, of Winwick in Lancashire, Knight, who died December 18th, 1576, and was buried at Walthamstow in Essex. . .

Given that this makes no mention of Tong, and that we know that he was buried at Tong and not Walthamstow (the burial place of his future daughter-in-law), one must wonder where the writer obtained this date of death. Later sentences in this same text give his brother as **Sir Edward** of Eynsham, who died in '1609'. We know that the one of Eynsham was **Sir Edward Jr**, and that his uncle **Sir Edward Sr** was buried at Ormskirk in 1604. In brief, this report from *Collins's Peerage* is totally unreliable. However, the dates of his will and the later text in Latin confirm that he died in December 1576. This is further confirmed by the inscription on the coffin of **Sir Thomas** in the Stanley vault in St Bartholomew's, Tong (repeated above) where his date of death is given as 21 December.

The Stanley tomb today
A comparison with the 1664 sketch shows that the obelisks at each corner,
which were originally on the floor, are now on the upper tier.
© RJL Smith

The Stanley tomb today
Lady Margaret (d. 1596) and Sir Thomas Stanley (d. 1576) on the tomb built for them by their son Sir Edward Stanley in c.1601. These marble effigies are the only images of either of them to have survived. Many effigies and tombs in the church suffered damage during the Civil War, although their hands and feet might have been knocked off later. © RJL Smith

Sir Thomas and Lady Margaret were still alone on their tomb in late 1632 (written report by Dugdale). Sir Edward died on 18 June 1632 in Eynsham, Oxfordshire, where he was buried in the Parish Church by his daughter Petronella, with a memorial brass plaque on the wall. His alabaster effigy, in storage for many years, duly joined his parents' in Tong.

© RJL Smith

The Monumental Inscription is on three panels along the side of the tomb. A comparison with the 1664 sketch and Illustration IIb. Before the 1892 restoration shows that the tomb has been removed twice, each time turned by 90°. Either during the first (more likely) or second removal these panels were replaced on the opposite side of the tomb from originally, so that they were still visible.

NOT MONVENTALL STONE PRESERVES OVR FAME
NOR SKY ASPIRING PYRAMIDS OVR NAME,
THE MEMORY OF HIM OR WHOM THIS STANDS
SHALL OVTLYVE MARBL AND DEFACERS HANDS
WHEN ALL TO TYMES CONSVMPTION SHALL BE GEAVEN
STANDLY FOR WHOM THIS STANDS SHALL STAND IN HEAVEN

ASK WHO LYES HEARE BVT DO NOT WEEP
HE IS NOT DEAD HE DOOTH BVT SLEEP
THIS STONY REGISTER IS FOR HIS BONES
HIS FAME IS MORE PERPETVALL THEN THEISE STONES
AND HIS OWNE GOODNES W HIMSELF BEING GON
SHALL LYVE WHEN EARTHLIE MONAMENT IS NONE

The two Verse Epitaphs by Shakespeare, with 'Not monventall stone' at the head and 'Ask who lyes heare' at the foot, today as in the seventeenth century. According to one transcriber in the mid-seventeenth century, the one at the head was for Sir Edward and the one at the foot for Sir Thomas.

20

Adhuc
Tonge

Wylde

Harris

Upon a Monument affixed to the
South wall of the Chancell.

HERE LYETH THE BODY OF ANNE WYLDE LATE WIFE OF IOHN WYLDE OF
DROITWICHE IN THE COVNTY OF WORCESTER ESQ.ˢ ELDDEST DAVGHTER OF
Sᵗ THOMAS HARRYS OF TONGE CASTLE SERIEANT AT LAW & BARONET
AND OF DAME ELEANOR HIS WIFE; WHOSE VIRTVE, MODESTIE, RARE AND
EXCELLENT PARTS, FARR EXCEEDING HER AGE, HAVE FITTED HER FOR A MORE
HEAVENLY HABITATION, LEAVING BEHIND HER THESE SPECTACLES OF GREIFE
AND PLEDGES OF TRVE AFFECTION. SHE DIED THE SIXT OF MAY IN THE YEARE
OF OVR LORD 1624. AND OF HER AGE THE XVIᵗʰ BEING THEN NEWLY DELIVERED
OF HER FIRST BORNE.

Upon this Monument are
these Armes.

see p. 40.

Stanley.

Vernon

On the North side of the Chancell stands a very stately Tombe
supported with corinthian Columnes. It hath two figures of
men in armour thereon lying; the one below the Arches and columnes, and the other above them, and this Epitaph upon it.

THOMAS STANLEY KNIGHT, SECOND SON OF EDWARD EARLE OF DERBY, LORD STAN-
LEY & STRANGE, DESCENDED FROM THE FAMILIE OF THE STANLEYS, MARRIED MAR-
GARET VERNON, ONE OF THE DAVGHTERS AND COHEIRES OF Sᵗ GEORGE VERNON OF NETHER
HADDON IN THE COVNTY OF DERBY KNIGHT; BY WHOME HE HAD ISSVE TWO SONS, HEN-
RY AND EDWARD; HENRY DIED AN INFANT; EDWARD SVRVIVED; TO WHOME THOSE
LORDSHIPS DESCENDED, & MARRIED THE LADY LVCIE PERCIE, SECOND DAVGHTER TO THE
EARLE OF NORTHVMBERLAND; BY HER HE HAD ISSVE SEAVEN DAVGHTERS. SHE AND
HER FOVRE DAVGHTERS; ARABELLA, MARIE, ALICE & PRISCILLA, ARE INTERRED VN-
DER A MONVMENT IN THE CHVRCH OF WALTHAM IN THE COVNTY OF ESSEX; THOMAS
HIS SON DIED IN HIS INFANCY & IS BVRIED IN THE PARISH CHVRCH OF WINWICK
IN THE COVNTY OF LANCASTER. THE OTHER THREE, PETRONILLA, FRANCES & VENISIA
ARE YET LIVING.

Shakespeare

These following verses were made by William Shakespeare
the late famous Tragedian.

Written upon the East end
of this Tombe.

written upon the west end
thereof.

Aske who lyes here, but do not weepe
He is not dead, he doth but sleepe
This stony Register is for his bones
His Fame is more perpetuall than these stones
And his own goodnesse wᵗʰ himself being gone
Shall live when earthly Monument is none

Not monumentall stone preserves our Fame.
Nor skye aspiring Pizamids our name
The memory of him for whom this stands
Shall out-live marble and defacers hands.
When all to times consumption shallbe given
Stanley, for whom this stands, shall stand in Heaven.

Vernon

Upon a Plate of brasse fixed to the wall in that Chapell
on the South side of this Church, wherein the Tombe of Sᵗ
Henry Vernon stands.

Pray for the soule of Sᵗ H: Vernon knight, and Lady Anne his Wife.
Which said H: in the yeare 1515 made and founded this Chappell. And also
the said Sᵗ Henry departed the xiii ᵗʰ of Aprill anno predicto.
And of your charitie pray for the soule of Sᵗ Arthur Vernon priest, son
of the said Sᵗ H: on whose soules Jesu have mercy Amen.

About the skirt of the great Bell, is this Inscription.

AD LAVDEM DEI OMNIPOTANTIS BEATA MARIA AD Sᶜi BARTHOLOMAI
HANRICVS VERNON MILES CAMPANVM FIERI FECIT Aᵒ DñI 1518.

Va. Dugdale's Diary from Notes in 1663
A copy of notes taken during his Heraldic Visitation of Shropshire; he was in Tong on 23 September 1663.
© College of Arms, Dugdale's Diary, C35, p.20

In Tong church afforesaide

Daunsey
Peeke

Sheffington

Here vnder Lyeth interred the body of Dame Elizabeth Daunsey,
descended of the house and Family of the Peekes, first married
to Sr John Skeffington knight sometime Sherriffe of London
and after married to Sr John Daunsey Knight: obijt Ann: Dni: 1549.

Though vertues rare did in this wighte abound
and wealth at will this worthie Ladie did possesse
yet nothing in the ende her praise did more resound
then faith in Jesus Christ with sober godlines.
An Eye to blind, a Lyme to lame she was
To poore a friend of kynne in earth degree
Both honoured and beloued too, loe this doth virtue pass
To place appointed by the Lord, where blessed she shall bee.
Posuerunt Pietatis
Monumentum.

These two Coates of Armes
and Inscriptions, are in-
grailed vpon brasse plates
affixed to the East wall of
the chancell

Skeffington

Here vnder lyeth interred the body of William Skeffington late of
the white Ladies Esqr son and heire of Sr John Skeffington of
London knight: obijt An: Dom: 1550.
An Esqr hee was right hardy to the feald
And faithfull to his Prince in quiet time of peace.
But when his course on Earth he had fullfilde
The Lord of worldly woes did him release
And to his Kingdome then his soule did call
his body to dust return'd from whence it came
Which rayse againe he will to joy celestiall
Where Body and Soule shall euer praise his name.
Posuerunt Pietatis
Monumentum.

This Epitaphe is, Upon a very faire Tombe in the middle of the Chancell.

THOMAS STANLEY knight second sonne of Edward Earle of Derbie Lo. Stanley &
Strange descended from the Family of the Stanleyes, married Margaret Vernon
one of the daughters and coheires of Sr George Vernon of nether-haddon in
the County of Derbie knight, by whom he had issue 2. sonnes Henry, and
Edward. Henry dyed an Jnfant: Ed: suruiued to whom those Lordshipps
descended, and married the Lady Lucie Perrie second daughter to Thomas
Earle of Northumberland, by her he had issue 7. daughters, and one sonne,
Shee and her 4. daughters Arabella Marie Alis and Prisilla, are interred
vnder a monument in the Church of Waltham in the County of Essex,
Thomas his sonne died in his jnfanie, and is buried in the Parish Church
of Winwick in the County of Lancaster: the other three petronella Frances, and Venesie, are yet liueing.

At the head

At the head of the Tombe are these Verses

Not Monumentall Stone preserues our fame
nor sky aspireing Piramides our name
The memorye of him for whom this stands
Shall out-liue Marble, and defacers hands.
when all to times consumption shall be given
Standley for whome this stands shall stand in Heaven.

a little Lower on the verge.

Beati mortui qui in Domino moriantur.

At the foote of the Monument

Aske who lies here, but doe not weepe,
He is not dead, hee doth but sleepe.
This stonye Register is for his bones
His fame is more perpetuall then these stones
And his owne goodnesse with himselfe being gone
shall liue, when earthly Monument is none,.

A marble Tombe inlayd with brasse, in the middle of the church
contayning this Epitaph.

Hic iacent Dñus Willus Vernon miles quandam miles constabularius Anglie filius et
heres Ricardi Vernon militis, qui quondam erat Thesaurarius Calesie. Qui quidem
Dñus Willñs obijt, ultimo die mensis Junij Anno Domini Millessimo CCCC Lx. vij.
et Margaret vxor Dñi Willi filia et hereditar Dñi Roberti pypis et Spernores militis, que
quedam Margareta obijt —— die mensis—————aº Dñi millimo CCCC Lx, quorum animabus &c.

Vc. Sandford's sketch of tomb, 1664; Dugdale's Diary

Francis Sandford, Rouge Dragon Poursuivant, was asked by Dugdale to produce this sketch, which was later added to a copy of his Diary notes. Here we can clearly see the obelisks in their original position, surmounted by golden balls. The balls disappeared long ago, but the obelisks are still there, perhaps the inspiration for the 'sky-aspiring pyramids' in the epitaph at the head.

XVIII-3. Lady Margaret's last will and testament (1596)

1596 - Dame Margaret Stanley - TNA reference - PROB 11/88 - Name of Register: Drake
Quire Numbers: 53 - 92
- Image Ref. 426/3660

[HM's version in modernised spelling]

Dme Margaret   (in left margin)
Stanly[i]

The last Will and Testament of Dame[ii] Margaret Stanley, some time wife of Sir Thomas Stanley, knight deceased and late the wife of William Mathe[r][iii] Esquire, made by the consent and agreement of the said William her husband, as follows. The last day of August 1596.

In the name of the father and of the son and of the holy ghost Amen.

I ordain this my last will and testament, the last day of August, being in perfect memory of mind, thanks be to almighty god.

I wish and bequeath my soul to almighty god and the church of our Lord. And my body is to be buried in the parish church of Tonge by my husband Sir Thomas Stanley.[iv]

I do give to Tonge and Tonge Norton and Albrighton[v] ten pounds to be dealt there to poor folkes.

I do give two [??] to my burying and twenty sheep.

I do will and give unto John [??] four pounds in money and twenty of my sheep.

I do give also to my woman Margaret Nedeham[vi] all my best apparrel and six score [?] of my sheep.

I do give unto John Roder forty of my sheep.[vii]

And I do give unto Mr Lapworth my best hangings and to Mrs Lapworth my best .... ell.

Item I do give unto Mr Mather my two . . . . of old hangings and four featherbeds and two wrought tooles with silk.

I do also give to [. . . . .?] the best featherbed but one not all clothes to it [?].[viii]

I do also give and bequeath forty shillings to Elizabeth Blurton and forty shillings to Anne Barrett.

And to Johan [Joan?] my maide twenty shillings and four bowls of silver to be sold, and to be given to the poor by the di [?]of my woman Margaret Nedham.

I do make my executor Mr Edward Gifforde, and my cousin [*name indecipherable*] Corbett. And I do give unto Mr Gifforde one ring with five diamonds and three rubies, and to Mrs Gifforde I give one ring with a diamond. And I do give unto my cousin [??] Corbett one piece of gold called a double sovereign. And to John [??] forty shillings.

The Lady['s] mark in the presence of John Foder and John Fyeld [?].

Memorandum that this will was   after the death of my Lady Stanley,

Before Mr Lapworth, Parker Jo: Marston, Michael Lapworth.[ix]

Probatum fuit de testamentui superscriptum apud London
coram permorabili magio   Willmo   Pre=
rogative   sine   Quarto die mensis De=
sembries Anon Domini millesimo Quingentisimo Nonogesimo Sexto In vamento Thome
Lovell notari publici / Edwardi Gifford et   Corbett Executories
In huius   Testamenti nominal / Quibud comissa fuit administrario Bononi
et defuncte / Dobone et fedelitur die desember sebunt it fideliter administrandus Ad Samsa -
Dei Evangelia Jurat.

[Probate, from the Latin]

Probate of the above-written testament was at the prerogative court in London on the fourth of the month of December, 1596 in the presence of notary public Thomas Lovell, Edward Gifford and [. . . .?] Corbett, executors. In whose testament the commission was made for the administration of the goods of the defunct. Completed this day in December, faithfully administrated.

[i] 'Stanly'. Although the name was written with a variety of spellings, this spelling was not one used by someone who knew the family well. The identical handwriting in the English and Latin texts is a further indication that these were copies transcribed at some later date, perhaps even copies of copies.

[ii] 'Dame'/Lady. I am not sure what the distinction was in Elizabethan times, if any. She is called both in the body of the text, so presumably they were synonymous.

[iii] 'late the wife of William Mathe'. We know from other documents that he was William Mather. He and his family remain rather shadowy. I would be grateful to hear from anyone who has discovered any information about him or his family. We know that **Sir Thomas Stanley** died in December 1576 and that within the next year or so his widow Margaret married this gentleman, 'Esquire'. We also know that Margaret and William had a joint interest in a property in Pembrokeshire.

> 3 August 1578. Margaret and William Mather granted a lease to George Lort for the manor of Stackpole and other lands held by him in Pembrokeshire. (Tudorplace, online.)

The surname Mather. At the moment we have no idea who Margaret's second husband William Mather was, but the very name rang a few Lancashire bells, mainly because of my research on Myles Standish and the Pilgrim Fathers. I include a quote from the ever-sceptical Schoenbaum, when commenting on 'young Shakespeare in Lancashire'. His digression might even lead down a fruitful path.

> If there is something to the speculations respecting a Lancaster connection for Shakespeare, he would have been no more than fifteen or sixteen when he began to teach. There is precedent for such precocity. Richard Mather (1596-1669), who haled from Lowton, near Liverpool, and would win fame in the New World as a Congregational clergyman, taught at a grammar school in Lancashire at the age of fifteen. His grandson - the even more celebrated Cotton Mather - entered Harvard College at the age of twelve, and was teaching at fifteen.
> (Schoenbaum, *William Shakespeare: A Compact Documentary Life*, 1987, p. 324.)

It is certain that Lady Margaret and William Mather had no children from this marriage. We know from this 'will' that Margaret was already 'late the wife' when it was written in August 1596 (presumably therefore dictated by William, fully cognizant of her specific wishes) and so had presumably died shortly before. From other sources we know that William Mather survived her until 1607. We also know that

> Margaret at her death owned the manors of Marple and Wybersley, which she left to Sir Edward Stanley. He sold them in 1606. (Tudorplace, online; confirmed by a document on the Stanley Family History website of Brian S. Roberts.)

For lack of further identification, it might be assumed that these were the places of this name in North Cheshire/Derbyshire near Stockport. No indication is given of these in her will, nor of the other manors she had inherited from her father Sir George Vernon. So far, no documentary information has emerged to indicate where Lady Margaret and William Mather lived between 1576 and 1596, or where twice (?) widower William Mather lived for the following 11 years. Nor have we any documentary information as to where **Sir Thomas** and Margaret's only son **(Sir) Edward Jr** lived during the period of his mother's second marriage. We might remember that son Edward was only fourteen when his father died in 1576 and he married Lucy Percy about six years later in c.1582. Five

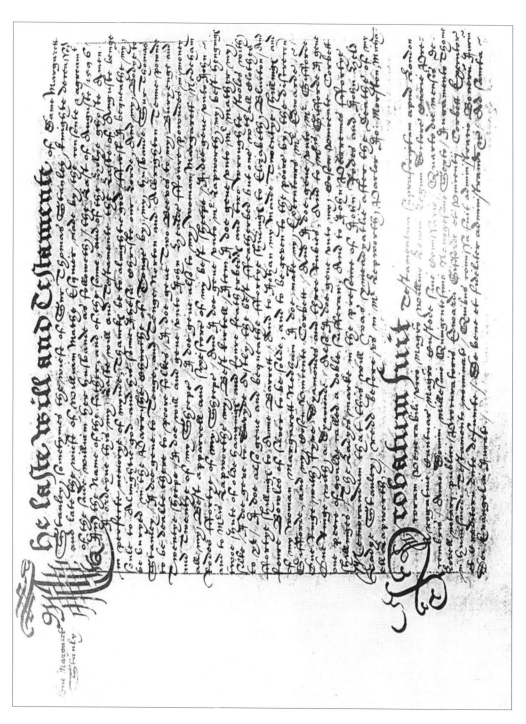

XVIIIb. Lady Margaret Stanley's will, 1596
TNA reference - PROB 11/88 - Name of Register: Drake Quire Numbers: 53 - 92 - Image Ref. 426/3660,
accessed by Brian S. Roberts.

years later he was known in Lancashire as 'Master Edward Stanley of Winwicke and Tong' (see Chapter XVII. Sir Edward Sr & Jr in the *Derby Household Books*), with the implication that he spent considerable periods of his married life in Tong, at the same time regularly returning to Lancashire and Winwick to visit his family.

[iv] 'my Bodye to be buryed in the parish churche of Tonge by my husbande Sir Thomas Stanley'. This is the only phrase in Lady Margaret's will to have been picked up by previous researchers. Honigmann (above) saw this as a sign that 'she snubbed her second husband, leaving him no token of her love', but the explanation might be different, as suggested in the Introduction above. She presumably did not know whether William would marry again, move away to another part of the country and be buried elsewhere. It seems quite natural (to me) that Tong would be her choice of place of burial. We (think we) know that she was indeed buried in the Stanley vault in St Bartholomew's, Tong, although there was the mystery of disappearing coffins and bodies. (Chapter IV. *Auden's History*)

[v] 'Tonge, and Tonge Norton and Albrighton'. The very listing of these villages implies that these were the places closest to Lady Margaret's heart on her deathbed. With this comes the implication that she might have lived in one of these places. One problem comes from the fact that there are two Albrightons in Shropshire, one next door to Tong Norton and one between Shrewsbury and Moreton Corbet. The proximity of the former makes it seem more likely to be the one meant by Lady Margaret, but the other one is close to the main seat of the family of 'my cousin Corbett' mentioned later.

[vi] 'my woman Margarett Nedeham'. She was obviously a very important person in Lady Margaret's life. She is mentioned again later in this will. Interestingly, there was a Corbett-Nedeham marriage, Sir Andrew Corbett-Jane Needham, so Margaret Ne(e)d(e)ham might have been a 'cousin' of some degree.

[vii] So many sheep! As Tong is in sheep-farming country, along with much of England, this is hardly surprising. What is perhaps surprising is that Lady Margaret took such an interest in them, in the middle of her featherbeds and jewellery. The number comes to over a hundred, and presumably these were from several flocks. I have no knowledge of the average size of a flock in the sixteenth century, but the implication seems to be that she owned several manors, each with a large flock of sheep. So far the only names of places directly associated with her are Tong, Tong Norton, Albrighton (Shropshire); Marple (Cheshire) and Wybersley (Derbyshire) near Stockport; and lands in Pembrokeshire including the manor of Stackpole (which might have come from her Vernon heritage or her marriage to William Mather). Let us hope that some as yet undetected documents will reveal the names of more of her manors - and therefore more of those inherited by **(Sir) Edward Jr**.

[viii] From the names alone we learn little. The bequests to men were John [??] and John Foder. Those to women were to Mrs Lapworth, Elizabeth Blurton and Anne Barrett. One can only presume that these were faithful servants and/or dear friends of long standing. She also remembered her maid 'Johan' [Joan/ Jane?]. The bequests were £4, £2; and 40, 40, 20 shillings. Together with the £10 for the poor of Tong and neighbourhood, this comes to £19. At first sight this might seem rather little - until one comes to compare amounts in other wills of the sixteenth and seventeenth centuries.

The list of bequests of featherbeds (including 'four featherbeds' and 'the best featherbed') is reminiscent of William Shakespeare's will, with the mystery in his case of his 'second best bed' bequeathed to his wife Anne Hathaway. Reams have been written about this, along with a comparison of other contemporary wills (one summary among many is in Schoenbaum, *Shakespeare: a Compact Documentary Life*, pp. 297-306). Maybe Lady Margaret's is just one more will to add to a list of those worth considering in this context. In any case, beds and bedding seem to have played an important role at the time.

The 'hangings' ('my best hangings' and 'my two olde hangings') are reminiscent of the will of Robert Arde(r)n(e), father of Mary Arde(r)n(e), John Shakespeare's wife. These seem to have been tapestries, much more easily transportable than paintings when residence was being taken up at another house.

Added together, these bequests by Lady Margaret leave the impression of a Lady of the Manor with considerable lands and wealth, and not the impression given by previous reporters of a Stanley family rather short of funds.

[ix] 'my executors Mr Edwarde Gifforde, and my cousin [?] Corbett'. Mr Gifforde received a ring with diamonds and rubies, Mrs Gifford a ring with diamonds and cousin Corbett a gold double sovereign. Mr and Mrs Edward Gifforde remain as just names, although descendants of this family, who have numerous genealogy sites, might be able to identify them.

Her 'cousin Corbett' can be identified as one of the family of Moreton Corbet, one of the largest landowning and most influential families in Shropshire. Tudorplace (online) provides enough details of this family to allow the identification of this Corbet(t) as a second cousin. Lady Margaret's grandfather, Sir Richard Vernon of Haddon Hall, had a sister Elizabeth Vernon (c.1479-1563), who married Sir Robert Corbet(t) (c.1477-1513). The latter was a son of Richard Corbet(t) (c.1448-1492) and Elizabeth Devereux (c.1454-1541), which brought the Vernons into the family of the Earls of Essex. Sir Robert Corbet(t) and Elizabeth Vernon Corbet(t) were the uncle and aunt of Lady Margaret's father Sir George Vernon, the 'King of the Peak'. Their children were therefore his first cousins, and their grandchildren second cousins of Lady Margaret Stanley. During her long life Dame Elizabeth Vernon Corbet(t) was godmother to many children, including a gt-gt-grandson on 8 June 1561, Robert Corbet son of Robert Corbet. His godfather was Sir Thomas Assheton, the famous founder of Shrewsbury School. One of the most famous pupils there was the courtier, soldier, diplomat and poet Sir Philip Sidney, whose death at Zutphen in 1586 in the army under his uncle Robert Dudley, Earl of Leicester was mourned by the whole country. His sister was Mary Sidney (1561-1621), a highly regarded poetess and patron of several poets. She married William Herbert, 2nd Earl of Pembroke, and they were parents of William and Philip Herbert, Earls of Pembroke and Montgomery, who were the dedicatees of Shakespeare's *First Folio* in 1623. All interesting grist for the millstone of circular connections of many characters in this book?

An eBook *History of the Corbet family* provides many details, particularly pp. 174-300.

> The family of Corbet; its life and times (Volume 2 ...
> Continues history of the Family of Corbet through the reigns of Queen .....
> www.ebooksread.com/...corbet/...family...corbet.../1-the-family-of-corbet-its-life-and-times-volume-2-bro.shtml

Maybe someone else will detect more relevant interesting connections?

~~~~~~~~~~~~~~~~~~~~

XVIII-4. Letter from Lady Margaret, 1594

This has been included in the same chapter as Lady Margaret's will as the only letter that has survived. It is from Griffiths, *History of Tong*, with no reference to his location of it. Pages 64 and 177 are where he gives details of the Stanley tomb and a few details of Lady Margaret's family.

A curious letter of Margaret, Lady Stanley (see pages 64 and 177), to her brother[-in-law], John Manners.

1594, Sept. 14, Tonge. I spoke to you before of a lease my father made of a tenement, at Harleston to Harry Vernon and Dorothy his wife and George their son for their lives, but [*sic*, by?] virtue of which they lived and died in that tenement. Now comes Maud Vernon and claims it by virtue of a prior lease granted by her father and mother and her, by my father. She can show no lease, but tries to prove it, by witnesses. As these witness fail, they want that Lady Vernon "will knocke yt deade, and that in her ye all there truste." It would be very bad if my lady should do so, as she cannot justify Maud Vernon's title, without [?beschmirching] my father's credit. I beg to be commended to my nephew George and his wife.

Signed

Why did Griffiths in 1885 call this letter 'curious'? As something belonging in a 'Cabinet of Curiosities', so popular in former times? It is not known who all the other Vernons in this letter were, but presumably all were 'cousins', however distant. Harlaston in Cheshire had seen Vernons living there for several centuries, so presumably Harry and Dorothy and their son George, tenants of Lady Margaret, were descendants of a side branch and Maud, who had come knocking at their door, was another 'cousin'. Who was the Lady Vernon in this letter in 1594, who "**will knocke yt deade, and that in her ye all there truste.**"? She ought to be easier to identify. Might she have been Elizabeth née Devereux, wife of Sir John Vernon of Hodnet, Shropshire? They were the parents of Elizabeth Vernon (1572-1655), a lady in waiting to Queen Elizabeth, who four years later, in 1598, was to marry Henry Wriothesley, 3rd Earl of Southampton, a favourite of Elizabeth I's, who in this same year as Lady Margaret's letter received the dedication of the poem *The Rape of Lucrece* from William Shakespeare, having received the dedication of the poem *Venus and Adonis* from the same poet the year before (1593). If we were to have identified this 'Lady Vernon' correctly, then in her daughter Elizabeth Vernon we have one of the early candidates for Shakespeare's 'Dark Lady' of the Sonnets, who was soon to marry one of the strongest candidates for the 'Fair Youth' of the Sonnets. Alas, if one checks dates (on any of many Tudor websites), Sir John had died in 1591 and his wife Lady Elizabeth already in 1583. However, their son and heir was Sir Robert Vernon (1577-1625), who is reported as having connections at Hodnet and Haddon (Family Search, Community Trees website), which sounds promising. Even more promising is that he is reported as being 'controller of the household of Queen Elizabeth', who knighted him. Even more promising is that he was married to Mary Needham, daughter of Sir Robert Needham of Shevington (whose pedigree was presented by his father to Robert Glover in the *Visitation of Cheshire*, 1580). Which brings us back to the name of 'Margarett Nedeham' in Lady Margaret's will, who was judged to be a very important person in Lady Margaret's life. One problem is that no Tudor site (found by HM) gives the date of Sir Robert Vernon's marriage, nor any further details about him. However, he was the brother of Elizabeth Vernon, the future Countess of Southampton, and both were close to known Shakespeare circles at court.

At least we know who John Manners the recipient was: Lady Margaret's brother-in-law, whom Griffiths implies she addressed as 'brother'. He had, of course, become the Lord of the Manor of Haddon when his wife Dorothy had inherited it in 1565 from father George. 'My nephew George', to whom Lady Margaret sends greetings, was their son George (1569-1623), named after his grandfather, Lady Margaret's father. 'His wife' was Grace Pierrepont, daughter of Sir Henry Pierrepont and Frances Cavendish. They had married on 1 August 1593 (just the year before Lady Margaret's letter) and he was to live until 23 April 1623. Their son (Sir) John Manners (1604-1679), not yet born when Lady Margaret died, became 8th Earl of Rutland in 1641 when all three male cousins at Belvoir Castle died *osp*. (See Chapter XXVI. The Earls of Rutland.) The eldest of these three brothers was Roger Manners, 5th Earl of Rutland since 1588, who had enough connections to Shakespeare that he would, over three hundred years later, be proposed as an Alternative Authorship Candidate. In 1594 he was married to Elizabeth Sidney, daughter and heiress of Sir Philip Sidney, who had written *Astrophel and Stella* in the 1580s (in which Stella is generally assumed to have been Penelope Devereux, another candidate for Shakespeare's 'Dark Lady'), who had been killed at Zutphen, the siege in which the hero was Edward Stanley, who was knighted by the Earl of Leicester (see Chapter XXII. Other (Sir) Edward Stanleys).

XVIII-5. Conclusion

The names in **Sir Thomas**'s and Lady Margaret's wills lead to many connections, which circle around each other, intersecting at many points, and many of the people in these spider's webs have been associated with Shakespeare in one way or another. These same people also lead to ever more detailed future biographies of **Sir Thomas** and Lady Margaret, and some leads may go down future fruitful paths, which might some day lead to someone stumbling over a real gem. Meanwhile, the most direct path from **Sir Thomas** and Lady Margaret to Shakespeare is that he wrote two verse epitaphs for their son (Sir) **Edward**, which he had inscribed on the tomb erected for them.

Chapter XIX
An excursion to Eynsham, Oxfordshire

XIX-1. Introduction
XIX-2. The Stanleys in Eynsham, by Lilian Wright
XIX-3. Footnote references HM
XIX-4. A time-line
XIX-5. Reference notes, continued

XIX-1. Introduction

At last we take an excursion to Eynsham in Oxfordshire, where **Sir Edward Jr** spent the last years of his life, died and was buried in 1632. It seems that one reason for the biographies of him and his father having been so neglected is because they lived in several different places, and details of their lives in these various places have never been put together. We already know how the estate at Eynsham came to **Sir Edward Jr** from his grandfather's grant of settlement in 1562/3 of a crop of estates, including Eynsham, on his second son **Sir Thomas**, with a series of reversions built in to ensure that it would stay with this family as long as there was a male heir. If the male line died out, it would then revert to the Earldom. (Chapter XI. Main Derby historians; Seacome; Coward.) Because Earl Edward and **Sir Thomas** made such little use of Eynsham Abbey, hardly any details appear in the Lancashire Stanley literature. The other side of the coin is that reports from Eynsham are rather scanty on details of the family back in Lancashire. This chapter is the first attempt to put together these two geographical ends of the story and develop a working theory as an explanation for the little that we do know about the Stanleys at Eynsham.

Most details known come from an article by Lilian Wright in the *Eynsham Record* no. 2, 1985 (sent to me, with so many others, by the Revd Dr Robert Jeffery). This is meanwhile online, and it appears that no more information has emerged since then, as indicated in the following reply in June 2010 to a query to Eynsham.

> Dear Mrs Moorwood,
>
> I have been asked by our church administrator to reply to your email.
> What is known about the Stanley family is collected in an article by Lilian Wright- "The Stanleys in Eynsham", Eynsham Record, vol. 2, page 32.
> The first twenty or so volumes of the Eynsham Record are now on line. Google "Eynsham On-line Eynsham Records" and follow the links. No one appears to have further information.
> One small point: the memorial with the coat of arms and the Latin inscription is on the floor (horizontal) to the right of the altar (looking east); not on the wall.
>
> Best wishes,
> Donald Richards

Since then Volume 27, 2012 of *Eynsham Record* has appeared online, which contains another article by Lilian Wright, 'Venetia Anastasia Stanley' (pp. 4-9). (See Chapter XXV. Sir Edward's children.)

Another valuable source on Eynsham is available on British History Online entitled *Eynsham Manor*, from *A History of the County of Oxford*: Volume 12, 1990. This gives basically the same Stanley information as in Lilian Wright's article and a long list of references. Not all details of the Lancashire end of the story of the Stanleys are correct, but those of relevance to the Stanleys who were connected with Eynsham have been given in previous chapters, and are corrected or commented on in footnotes below. Lilian Wright here gives the Eynsham end of the story. The footnote references are by HM, in the usual style.

XIX-2. THE STANLEYS IN EYNSHAM, by Lilian Wright
An outline of the Stanley connection, 1545-1653

After the Dissolution of the Monasteries and the surrender of Eynsham Abbey to the Crown in December 1539, the Eynsham lands passed from Sir George Darcy to Sir Edward North, and in 1545 to Edward, 3rd Earl of Derby.[i] Sir Henry Spelman (*History and Fate of Sacrilege*, 1698) specifically mentions Eynsham as an instance where the abbey lands passed quickly from one possessor to another and brought ruin to each![ii]

The 3rd Earl of Derby was a man of great wealth, owning vast lands in Lancashire, Cheshire and Shropshire (Richard Gough, *The History of Myddle*, 1701).[iii] He also inherited the Lordship of Man which had been granted to Sir John Stanley in 1406 by Henry IV, and remained with the Stanleys until 1736. He was a little younger than and marginally related to Henry VIII, Margaret Beaufort having been the grandmother of Henry VIII and the second wife of the first Earl of Derby. Edward, the 3rd Earl, went with Henry to the Field of the Cloth of Gold and helped in suppressing the Pilgrimage of Grace in 1536. He married as his first wife the daughter of Thomas Howard, 2nd Duke of Norfolk, and they had three sons and four daughters.[iv]

The 3rd Earl probably found Eynsham a convenient stopping place on the way from the north to London, but it would seem that this was not just an overnight resting place. Anthony Wood's ancestors came from Preston in Lancashire. His great grandfather had three daughters and a son. The daughters were menial servants of the household of the Earl of Derby (he thought at Latham House). And came with the rest of the household to 'Einsham' where the Earl had a seat on the site of 'Einsham abbey', and where they married tenants of the Earl! (A. Wood, *Life and Times*, 1, 1632-1663). Emma Wood married George Makyn of Eynsham in 1568 and was buried here in 1603. Alice Wood married John Beare of Eynsham, and Mary Wood married John Barncote of Eynsham in 1587. Her eldest son was Thomas Barncote and Anthony Wood often came to Eynsham to visit him. It is to these visits that we owe the drawing of the abbey remains, and the moving and graphic description of 1657. Thomas Barncote died in 1665 at the age of 77, and his burial was recorded in our Parish Registers on 4 June, 1665. The brother of the three sisters, Richard, married Elizabeth Jackson of Oxford, and they were the grandparents of Anthony Wood.[v]

William Camden recorded in his book *Britannia* (1586) that the 'Abby….. now is turned into a private dwelling house and acknowledgeth the Earl of Derby thereof' (translation by Richard Gough, 1789). The Earl seems to have kept servants permanently there, and presumably adapted the abbot's lodgings for his own use.' John Aubrey, writing in 1647 (sixty years later) said that he had been told by inhabitants of Cumnor that, within their remembrance there was still 'a worlde of painted Glasse, Stones, Coates of Armes, etc. There were curious buildings, excellent carved wainscot and wainscot ceilings guilded: a curious Chapelle'. He also adds as a footnote to his account of Venetia Stanley a further description of Eynsham Abbey 'At the west end of the church here were two towers as at Wells or Westminster Abbey, which were standing till about 1656. The rooms of the abbey were richly wainscoted, both sides and roof!' (J. Aubrey, *Brief Lives*, 1647). All this seems to indicate that, for the hundred years during which the Stanleys owned the abbey lands, they often lived in Eynsham and maintained at least some of the abbey buildings.[vi]

The vicar of Eynsham at the time of the Dissolution was John Gurle (d. 1552), and the Roman Catholic (Marian) priest was John Raynforth. The first Elizabethan vicar, John Nutlynge, would probably have been presented by the 3rd Earl, as would also William Emmot in 1568. Edward, the 3rd Earl, died in 1572, and his eldest son Henry inherited the Earldom, but not the Eynsham estates. There were two other sons, Thomas and Edward, and four daughters.

Sir Thomas Stanley, the second son, had married Margaret Vernon, whose father owned Haddon Hall in Derbyshire and Tong Castle in Shropshire. They had two sons, Henry (who died in infancy) and Edward, who eventually inherited the Eynsham estates. At this birth in 1562, his grandfather, the 3rd Earl, made a Deed of Settlement as follows:

[My] several manors and lands in the counties of Warwick, Devon and Oxford, also Dunham

Massey, Bowden, Rungy Hall, Alton and Darfield in Co. Chester shall appertain and belong to:-

    a) Sir Thomas Stanley [his second son] for life,

    b) his wife Lady Margaret for life,

    c) with remainder to Sir Edward [his third son] for life,

    d) with remainder to the Earl's first son [Henry],

    e) with remainder to heirs male of Sir Thomas,

    f) with remainder to heirs of Sir Edward.[vii]

Therefore, after the 3rd Earl's death in 1572, the lands passed to Sir Thomas Stanley; but he died in 1576 and so Lady Margaret would have inherited. During her time we have the account of the 1584 quarrel between William Stanley and Thomas Peniston (see *Eynsham Record*, no. 1, p. 23, 1984). William was the younger son of Henry, the 4th Earl.[viii] In 1585 Thomas Peniston presented Thomas Secheverell to the Eynsham living. He was here until 1591,[ix] and then followed three vicars where the Presentation Deeds are unrecorded, Hugh Lloyd, Robert Lloyd and Sampson West. After Lady Margaret's death in about 1595 the lands passed to Sir Edward (brother of Sir Thomas). He died in 1609 [*sic* 1604],[x] and they should then have gone to the 3rd Earl's first son, Henry.[xi]

However he had died in 1593, and so all the estates passed to the male heir of Sir Thomas, another Sir Edward, knighted in 1603. He had been born at Tong in Shropshire[xii] and had married Lady Lucy Percy, daughter of Thomas, Earl of Northumberland. (This Earl was executed at York in 1572 for conspiring against Elizabeth I, and his father was executed for his part in the Pilgrimage of Grace in 1536). Edward and Lucy had seven daughters, and one son who died in infancy: thus there was no surviving male heir to inherit the Eynsham estates. It is said that the youngest daughter Venetia, the famous beauty painted by Van Dyck, was born at Tong, so that they must still have been living there in 1600. Shortly after Venetia's birth, a family tragedy can be inferred from the inscription on the very fine tomb of Sir Thomas Stanley, his wife Lady Margaret, and his brother [*sic*, actually his son] Sir Edward at Tong, as noted by George Griffiths in his *History of Tong and Boscobel* (2nd edition, 1894).

[*Here follows the MI on the Tong tomb, already given so many times in this book, so not repeated here.* HM]

If I interpret this inscription correctly it would seem that the four older girls and their mother, Lady Lucy, all died at the same time, and away from home. This was while Venetia was still an infant. I think it has been assumed that Venetia was very young when she was sent to Eynsham; but Aubrey says 'She was a most beautiful, desirable creature and being <u>matura viro</u> [i.e. of mature age] was let by her father to live with a tenant and servants at Eynsham Abbey'. We are not sure when Sir Edward Stanley came to live in Eynsham, but he presented Thomas Longe to the living in 1617, and the map of 1615 shows the Park as belonging to Sir Edward Stanlake [cartographer's error for 'Stanley']. According to Griffiths, he sold Tong Castle to Sir Thomas Harries in 1623,[xiii] and so would have been in Eynsham during the great fire of 1629. Venetia had certainly left by then, for she was secretly married to Sir Kenelm Digby in 1625, although the marriage was not made known until after the birth of their second son in 1627. She died in 1633, only a year after her father, and was buried in the old church of Christ Church, Newgate Street, London, which was destroyed in the Great Fire.

Edward does not seem to have married again, and could well have lived here until his death in 1632. His tombstone is on the south side of the altar in St. Leonard's,[xiv] and the inscription when translated reads:-

Here lies Edward Stanley K.B. (son of Thomas, the son of Edward Earl of Derby). Died June 18th 1632, aged 69. His daughter Petronilla Stanley placed this here.

The quarterings on the shield are for the families of Stanley and Percy. No more is known about Petronilla, and she does not appear in our Parish registers.[xv]

When Edward died, the estates reverted to the Earldom. The reversion had been settled on Charlotte de Trémouille at her marriage in 1626 to James, son of William, 6th Earl of Derby. William died in 1642, and James succeeded as the 7th Earl. In 1643 Thomas Cordell, Vicar, and in 1644 John Piers, his successor, were presented to the Eynsham living by James, the 7th Earl. James was an ardent supporter of Charles I during the Civil War, and laid siege unsuccessfully to Manchester. After Marston Moor he went to live at Castle Rushen in the Isle of Man, and in 1651 supported Charles II in his efforts to regain the throne. He fought at Worcester and escorted Charles II to Boscobel. He was later captured and executed at Bolton in October 1651, becoming known as the Martyr Earl of Derby.

In an *Oxford Times* article of August 12th 1960, Mr. Bernard Green said that when he was a boy they still used to hang a branch of an oak tree from the church tower on Oak Apple Day, May 29th, even though the custom had died out in most places. I wonder if the practice continued in Eynsham because of this friendship between Charles II and James, the 7th Earl.[xvi]

During the Commonwealth the Eynsham lands were given to Sir Henry Marten, one of the regicides. Some briefly passed back to Charlotte, the Countess Dowager of Derby (she is one of the signatories for the sale of Twelve Acre Farm in February 1653/4). In 1652 a Parliamentary Committee, by a complicated series of transactions, transferred the Stanley interest; and in 1653 their interest and that of Sir Henry Marten were sold to a group of Eynsham men for the benefit of Thomas Jordan, (a Witney woolmerchant, and the Patron at the appointment of Edmund Meyricke as vicar in 1663).

So ended over a hundred years of Stanley influence in Eynsham.

(Lilian Wright, Eynsham Record No. 2, 1985, pp. 32-38.)

XIX-3. Footnote references HM

[i] These details concerning the purchase of Eynsham by two other people between the Dissolution of the Monasteries and Earl Edward acquiring it are mentioned nowhere in the standard Derby literature. For example, one of the latest accounts, albeit a summary, just gives:

> . . . did not prevent him [*Earl Edward*] from following fellow landowners into the scramble for monastic property. Among the church lands he bought were those of the Benedictine house at Eynsham in Oxfordshire and, as might have been expected, Burscough Priory."
>
> (Bagley, op. cit., 1985, p. 41.)

The implication is that the purchase of Eynsham was as soon as possible. We now know that it was two years later. Whether there was a distinction between Eynsham Abbey, Abbey lands and Eynsham Manor is not made clear, but *Eynsham Manor* provides the information that some or all was acquired 'as part of an exchange to settle debts of Sir Edward North'. One piece of information from the Lancashire end is that the part of Eynsham owned by the Earl of Derby, in a list of 'Lands in reversion to the earl' in 1600 was assessed as £600 (Chapter XI. Main Derby historians; Coward), an enormous sum. This implies a very large estate and many properties, which is of interest when wondering exactly where **Sir Edward Jr** lived when he moved there, and where he installed his daughter Venetia, apparently with her own household.

[ii] **'Sir Henry Spelman (*History and Fate of Sacrilege*, 1698) specifically mentions Eynsham as an instance where the abbey lands passed quickly from one possessor to another and brought ruin to each!'** It might have brought ruin to his two predecessors, but it certainly did not bring ruin to Edward, Earl of Derby – rather the opposite. It almost got lost on the periphery of the vast number of estates he owned in so many counties and was obviously considered as outside the main core of Derby lands and interests when it was chosen as suitable for granting to a younger son.

[iii] **'The 3rd Earl of Derby was a man of great wealth, owning vast lands in Lancashire, Cheshire and Shropshire. (Richard Gough, *The History of Myddle*, 1701).'** To these counties can be added Warwickshire, Devon and Oxfordshire (just Eynsham in this county, it is presumed) from the list in the settlement of 1562/3; and from the list of 'Lands in reversion to the Earl' in 1600, during negotiations between William, 6th Earl and Countess Alice, widow of Ferdinando (Chapter XI. Main

Derby historians; Coward) can be added Flintshire and Yorkshire. If Earl Edward owned lands in Shropshire, these were somewhere other than Tong - Tong Castle came to his son **Sir Thomas** from his wife Lady Margaret Vernon.

[iv] '**He married as his first wife the daughter of Thomas Howard, 2ⁿᵈ Duke of Norfolk, and they had three sons and four daughters.**' As late as 1985, Bagley published the recently discovered fact that Earl Edward's first wife had died very soon after marriage and before bearing any children, and his second wife was her aunt, although of a similar age. Until then it had been assumed that the use of 'Katherine Howard' and 'Dorothy Howard' as his first wife were clerical errors in copying. It was now established that they were two wives, niece and aunt, and the mother of the children was the second wife, Dorothy Howard. Details are given in Chapter XI. Main Derby historians; Bagley.

[v] Anthony Wood's account and his own ancestry with an Eynsham/ Stanley connection. This was a real bonus, so far undetected by the main Derby historians in Lancashire. Here was yet another seventeenth-century antiquarian of Lancashire origin, who was connected in some way to the families of **Sir Thomas** and **Sir Edward** of Winwick, Tong and Eynsham and/or others who appear in the forefront of the 'Shakespeare in Lancashire' theory. Anthony Wood (1632-95), *alias* Anthony à Wood, has a society in Oxford named after him, with most of his MS works in the Bodleian Library, Oxford. We now know that his grandfather was from Preston, Lancashire, moving as a boy with his family to Eynsham as servants of the Earls of Derby.

We can now add him to the list of noteworthy historians from Lancashire during the lifetime of William Shakespeare or the following generation: John Weever (born in the Preston area); Sir William Dugdale (father from the Preston area); Roger Dodsworth (married to a Hesketh of Rufford); Christopher Towneley (of Towneley Hall, Burnley); Richard Kuerden (Dugdale's assistant during his Visitations of Lancashire); and now Anthony Wood (with origins in Preston as given above by Lilian Wright). Plus four out of five teachers at Stratford Grammar School during John and William Shakespeare's lifetimes were from the general Preston area; plus Cardinal William Allen was also from Lancashire, who had been 'usher' for a while at Stratford Grammar School before fleeing into exile. They must all have known (of) the Shakespeares/Shakeshaftes and the Stanleys, but alas wrote nothing about them (that has survived), apart from the intriguing assertion by Sir William Dugdale in his Notes on the Stanley epitaphs at Tong: 'These following verses were made by William Shakespeare, the late famous tragedian.' And even this comment remained in a MS not attracting much attention until 1827, when his Diaries were published. Is there a faint glimmer of hope that other gems concerning Shakespeare/Stanley connections are still in MSS of the above historians, still waiting to be discovered? For example, many have despaired over Kuerden's MSS in Chetham's Library, which have often been found 'indecipherable'. (Private comment by Dr Michael Powell, Chief Librarian.) They have never been completely deciphered and published, although Farrer, the main writer and editor of the *Victoria County History* of Lancashire did his best. His papers are in Manchester Central Library, some still waiting to be published.

Anthony Wood was born in the year that **Sir Edward** died at Eynsham, but his later interests took him to many Stanley places. One of his collaborators in historical pursuits was John Aubrey, whose notes about Venetia appear in Chapter XXV. Sir Edward's children. What a pity that Wood gave no more information about the Stanleys at Eynsham.

[vi] '**William Camden recorded in his book *Britannia* (1586) that the "Abby..... now is turned into a private dwelling house and acknowledgeth the Earl of Derby thereof".**' The very date of 1586 is interesting, because this was in the middle of the period when it was under the ownership of **Sir Thomas**'s widow, Lady Margaret. This period extended from the death of **Sir Thomas** in 1576 until her own death in 1596. Perhaps it means no more than that Camden's informant was aware that the estate was part of a settlement with reversions, which would indeed revert to the Earl of Derby in the case of 'fail-male', or otherwise stay with an offshoot of the Earl's family. One implication, however, might be that neither Lady Margaret nor her son **Edward Jr** spent enough time there for it to have become associated with them in local consciousness. And yet we have the report that '**Edward Stanley esquire [Edward Jr]** was living with his wife at **Eynsham** in 1582. Also living there then was **Sir Edward Stanley [Sr]**.' (*Eynsham Manor.*) And then there was the visit by William Stanley in 1584 long enough to have his 'quarrel' with Thomas Peniston. It is surprising, perhaps, that Camden did not give a little more detail. Absentee landlords for much of the time, the 3rd and 4th Earls of Derby in office since 1545 – meanwhile for over forty years – seems to have been the accepted and adequate explanation for Camden in 1586.

[vii] Errata: The Sir Edward under c) (above) is the wrong Edward: it referred to **Edward Jr** and not **Sir Edward Sr**; and f) was actually given more specifically in the settlement grant as son of **Sir Thomas** and Margaret. We saw in Seacome's account in Chapter XI. Main Derby historians: Seacome that the succession of reversion of lands in the settlement was as follows, with **a), b), c)**, etc. added here, to match with the list above:

> . . . he had issue a son, named **Edward**, on which occasion he made the following settlement by deed, bearing date the fourth of Elizabeth [*1562/3*]; wherein it is declared, That the several manors and lands lying in the counties of Warwick, Devon and Oxford; also Dunham-massey, Bowden, Rungey, Hale, Aeton and Darfield, in the county of Chester, now the estate of him the said Edward, Earl of Derby, shall appertain and belong to **a) Sir Thomas Stanley**, his said second son, for life.
>
> **b)** Remainder as a moiety to **Lady Margaret**, his wife, for life; **c)** remainder of all to the said **Edward Stanley, their son**, for life; **d)** remainder in fale-male [*sic*, fail-male] to **Henry**, the first son of him the said Earl; **e)** remainder to the heirs male of the said **Sir Thomas Stanley**, and **f)** remainder to the heirs male of the said **Edward Stanley, son of the said Sir Thomas**, and **dame Margaret**, his lady.
>
> (Seacome, extract from quote given in Chapter XI. Main Derby historians.)

c) 'Edward' is definitely **Edward Jr**, son of **Sir Thomas** and Margaret Vernon, and NOT **Sir Edward Sr**, third son of Edward, 3rd Earl;, and **f)** is the same **Edward Jr** as in c). In brief, the intention of Earl Edward was for it to remain as long as possible in **Sir Thomas**'s family. As long as his son and heir **Edward Jr** survived, he would be the heir, but otherwise another son and heir would become the heir. If **Edward Jr** died before his father, then if he left his own son and heir, this grandson of Earl Edward's would inherit. Only in the case of 'fail-male' at any point would it revert to the Earldom. We know that **Edward Jr** did not leave a son and heir (his only son Thomas died as an infant and was buried in Winwick), which is why Eynsham stayed for such a relatively short time with the Stanleys. On **Sir Edward Jr**'s death in 1632 it reverted in theory to the Earldom in the person of his cousin William, 6th Earl, but he immediately passed it to his son and heir James, Lord Strange at that time, later the 7th Earl. When he was beheaded in 1651 for supporting the Royalist cause during the Civil War, it passed to his widow Charlotte de (la) Trémouille, who had been granted the reversion on their marriage in 1626, and who sold it in 1653, as given at the end of Lilian Wright's article.

[viii] '. . . the **1584 quarrel between William Stanley and Thomas Peniston (see *Eynsham Record*, no. 1, p. 23, 1984)**.' This reference provides the following quote, also by Lilian Wright:

> William Emmott was the Vicar of Eynsham at the time, and it is interesting to find that he helped another clergyman in trouble. By this we also know that he was alive in 1584, so must have died in February 1585 (his memorial is in our church). He features in another case in October where the Churchwardens exercised their duty of maintaining reverence and decency in Church. — Thomas Peniston said that:-
>
> "the Vicar of Eynsham, at the time specified in the bill of detection, was disturbed at divine service by means of William Stanley, gent. who would not suffer this respondent quietly to sit in

his seat which this respondent thinks belongs to his father, because he is half lord of the town, and whereas they have presented 2 seats to belong to the Earl of Derby, my Lord Strange having but half the right of Sir Thomas Stanley, knight (deceased), the other by all reason must appertain to this respondent's father who hath the other half interest."

So we may surmise that the Stanleys lived in Eynsham and worshipped in our church. William Stanley, who was 23 at this time, was the cousin of Sir Edward Stanley whose memorial is by the altar. His father was the patron of a group of actors who performed Shakespeare's plays. By 1595 he had become the 6th Earl of Derby and, in that year, he married Lady Elizabeth Vere. The Queen attended the wedding at Greenwich, and it is thought that *A Midsummer Night's Dream* was performed for this occasion. As for Thomas Peniston, perhaps he was 'half lord of the town' — He was the patron at the appointment of Thomas Secheverell, the vicar after William Emmott.

This can be put together with a statement from *Eynsham Manor*:

'**Sir Thomas**'s lands were divided between son **Edward [Jr]** and his widow **Margaret**, who remarried, William Mather'. . ., 'who sold her interest in Eynsham to Sir Thomas Peniston of Bampton, who insisted on a strict partition of the manor. The life interest continued until 1595 or later'.

Also to be considered is the quote already given above from *Eynsham Manor*:

'**Edward Stanley esquire [Edward Jr]** was living with his wife at **Eynsham** in 1582. Also living there then was **Sir Edward Stanley [Sr]**.' (*Eynsham Manor, online.*)

Several questions are raised before one can attempt to explain and reconcile these references. A little time-line may help.

XIXa. Eynsham Abbey before demolition
Bought by Edward Stanley, 3rd Earl of Derby in 1545 after the Dissolution of the Monasteries, it remained with the Stanley family until after the Civil War, when it was sold in 1653 by the widow of the 7th Earl.

XIXb. St Leonard's Parish Church, Eynsham
(English Heritage) Sir Edward Jr was buried here in 1632 with a brass memorial by his daughter Petronella.

XIX-4. A time-line

1576	**Sir Thomas** died and was buried in St Bartholomew's, Tong; reversion under the Derby settlement of 1562/3 gave Eynsham (and other lands in the settlement) to his widow Margaret, in her mid-30s (if born c.1540, as estimated).
1577 or later	'Sir Thomas's lands were divided between son **Edward [Jr]** and his widow **Margaret**. . .' This is not strictly true. Under the terms of the settlement of 1562/3, Eynsham, along with other lands, would have gone solely to widow Margaret. These would presumably in turn have gone to her son on her death so there was no need to give half to Edward, even if it were legally possible. Eynsham was obviously then divided into two when **Lady Margaret Stanley** sold half to Sir Thomas Peniston.
1577 or later	Margaret remarried, William Mather, Esquire. Could this marriage have been behind her sale of half of Eynsham? What reason might there have been? Might she have expected to have more children from this second marriage? (In fact, she had none.) Or might she still have been in financial difficulties because of **Sir Thomas**'s large fine for release from the Tower?
1582	**Edward Jr** and his wife Lucy Percy (married in c.1580) were living at Eynsham, with uncle **Sir Edward Sr** also living with them. How long did they live there, one wonders? Did they move there to set up their own establishment and leave Tong Castle to the sole occupancy of mother Margaret and her new husband? It does not matter at this point whether **Edward Jr** was a part owner of Eynsham, or living there as the future owner of the whole; quite simply, it was a family property and he was entitled to live there whenever he wanted.
1582 end of August	**Sir Edward Sr** and **Edward Jr** at Preston Guild, along with Earl Henry (brother and uncle of the two Edwards), and his sons Ferdinando, Lord Strange, William and Francis. (See Chapter XV. Preston Guild.) Did the two Edwards make Winwick their base during the visit to Lancashire? Did the two Edwards return together to Eynsham after this?
1583/4	From the events in 1584 it seems that **Edward Jr** was no longer living at Eynsham. Why not? Where did he and his wife go? They already had one daughter, Arabella. Where was she born?
1577-84	Some time between these two dates Margaret sold half her interest in Eynsham to Sir Thomas Peniston. 'The life interest continued until 1595 or later.' The date of '1595 or later' was perhaps/presumably related to Margaret's death in 1596. However, by 1584 Peniston was obviously fully in charge of his half of Eynsham.
1584	William Stanley had his 'quarrel' in Eynsham with Sir Thomas Peniston. William was the younger son of Henry, 4th Earl, aged 23 in this year. What was he doing here? Why was he the one to have the 'quarrel'? Wasn't **Edward Jr** (aged 22) capable of having his own quarrels? Did William, a son of an earl, as opposed to **Edward Jr**, a nephew, have more clout? In any case this is the only time William appears in records in Eynsham, and at the same time provides a valuable date for William's biography. The ballad 'Sir William Stanley's Garland' (numerous editions, early 19th century) sees him spending up to about eleven years travelling non-stop until after his father's death in September 1593. 'The Garland' takes him through France, Spain, (perhaps to North Africa), back through France, Italy, Egypt, Jerusalem, Constantinople, Russia and Greenland! Quite a journey! This appearance in Eynsham on its own means that the story of his travels needs drastic revision; as does his appearance at Knowsley with his father, brother Ferdinando, Uncle **Sir Edward Sr** and cousin **Edward Jr** in 1590 (see Chapter XVII. **Sir Edward Sr** and **Edward Jr** in the *Derby Household Books*). Being in Eynsham in October 1584 could easily be accounted for as during his period back in England after his first tour abroad, using Eynsham as a convenient stopping point on his way between London and Lathom. His first ever biography was written by Professor Leo Daugherty for the *New/Oxford Dictionary of National Bigraphy* (2004), where other relevant details can be found, although not this intriguing incident at Eynsham with Sir Thomas Peniston.
1585	See following note [viii].
1595	See following note [ix].

~~~~~~~~~~~~~~~~~~~

XIX-5. Reference notes, continued

[ix] 'In 1585 Thomas Peniston presented Thomas Secheverell to the Eynsham living. He was here until 1591...' Whatever the outcome of the quarrel with William Stanley, Peniston was the one who stayed in Eynsham, obviously with the right to present the living on this occasion. Another intriguing detail is that Secheverell replaced William Emmott, who was a native of Colne. 'William Emmot who was Vicar here in 1584 came from Colne in Lancashire. He was a prominent Oxford man but attempts to glean information on his early life at Colne came to nothing.' (Lilian Wright, private correspondence, July 2012.) Further research MIGHT reveal a connection between William Stanley and William Emmot via Oxford.

[x] 'After Lady Margaret's death in about 1595* the lands passed to Sir Edward (brother of Sir Thomas). He died in 1609 [*sic* 1604]...' Apart from being the wrong Edward in reference to Eynsham, **Sir Edward Sr**'s date of death has often been reported as 1609. He very definitely died in 1604 (presumably at Lathom or one of the other Derby properties close by) and was buried in the Stanley vault at Ormskirk church on 4 September 1604. The Sir Edward Stanley who died in 1609 has not yet been identified, nor the place of death. On Lady Margaret's death, under the provisions of reversion in the original settlement of 1562/3, Eynsham now reverted in full to her son **Edward Jr** for his life. As the inheritance was dependent on his having a son and heir, it must have been obvious in 1601, when his wife and four of his daughters died at Walthamstow, that unless he married again and produced a son, then on his death it would revert to the Earldom. We know that he never remarried.

* Her will and codicil give the date of death as definitely in 1596. (See Chapter XVIII. Lady Margaret's last will and testament.)

[xi] '... and they should then have gone to the 3rd Earl's first son, Henry.' An error dependent on muddling the two Edwards; see Note [vi]. After Margaret's death they went to her son **Edward Jr**, as provided for already in 1562/3.

[xii] 'He had been born at Tong in Shropshire.' Edward was born mid-late 1562, the year when his father **Sir Thomas** took up a four-year stint as Governor of the Isle of Man (1562-66); and the following year he took out a 99-year lease on the Rectory at Winwick near Warrington, which he made his base when returning to the mainland. Also, his wife Lady Margaret did not actually inherit Tong Castle until the death of her father in 1565. So it seems more likely that Edward was born in Lancashire or the Isle of Man, and the most likely place would have been at Lathom House, main seat of **Sir Thomas**'s father Earl Edward, where she would have had the best possible care and surroundings during the later stages of her pregnancy. Another possibility is that she might have returned to her parental home, Haddon Hall, Derbyshire, leaving **Sir Thomas** to do all the travelling and make all necessary arrangements for his new position on his own. In any case, it seems highly unlikely that **Edward** was born at Tong.

[xiii] 'We are not sure when Sir Edward Stanley came to live in Eynsham, but he presented Thomas Longe to the living in 1617, and the map of 1615 shows the Park as belonging to Sir Edward Stanlake [cartographer's error for 'Stanley']. According to Griffiths, he sold Tong Castle to Sir Thomas Harries in 1623.' Auden (Chapter IV. *Auden's History*) provides details that make it scertain that he sold Tong Castle in 1603, which was presumably about the same time as he moved to Eynsham. Dates of 1603, 1607-9, 1613 and 1623 have been proposed for the sale. He could, of course, still have held on to certain interests in Tong after he had taken up residence at Eynsham. The later dates at Tong seem to have been tied up with a settlement of the Manor, as opposed to the Castle. Later, we have the report from Aubrey about his installation of his youngest daughter Venetia at Eynsham Abbey.

> Venetia Stanley was daughter of Sir Edward Stanley. She was a most beautiful desirable creature; and being of a mature age was let by her father to live with a tenant and servants at Eynsham Abbey (his land, or the Earl of Derby's) in Oxfordshire; but as private as that place was, it seems her beauty could not lie hid. The young eagles had espied her, and she was sanguine and tractable, and of much suavity (which to abuse was great pity). (*Aubrey's Lives*)

Venetia being 'of a mature age' implies turned 18 (or 14? – marriageable age), which she turned at the end of 1618. However, we know from Sir Kenelm Digby's *Memoirs* that she had already been brought back to Eynsham before her father took her to London for the wedding of Princess Elizabeth to Frederick of the Palatinate in February 1613. She married Sir Kenelm Digby in c.1625, after which she lived elsewhere, so these are the outside dates of her residence at Eynsham with her own household. Venetia's story is told at more length in Chapter XXV. Sir Edward's children. It is not known where **Sir Edward** lived during this period and after Venetia's departure, but he would presumably have had many houses of relatives where he was welcome, and, indeed, many more properties which had come to him under the terms of the settlement of 1562/3. He may have felt spoilt for choice. All we know is that he wrote his will at Eynsham, died there and was buried in Eynsham Parish Church soon afterwards.

[xiv] '**His tombstone is on the south side of the altar in St. Leonard's.**' This has now been clarified for any first-time visitor looking for the memorial, by Donald Richards of Eynsham (letter above): 'the memorial with the coat of arms and the Latin inscription is on the floor (horizontal) to the right of the altar (looking east); not on the wall.'

[xv] '**No more is known about Petronilla, and she does not appear in our Parish registers.**' On her father's death, Petroni(/e)lla, unmarried, was alone. With no ageing father to take care of, and Eynsham reverting to William, 6th Earl of Derby, she might well have decided to live with one of her relatives. Her immediate relatives were her two married sisters, but there was also Earl William's son James, Lord Strange and his wife Charlotte at Lathom; and the families of all her second cousins on her mother's and both her grandmothers' sides; and the families of the grandchildren of the sisters of her grandfather **Sir Thomas**. Any or all of these, one might presume, would have offered her a home.

[xvi] '**. . . hang a branch of an oak tree from the church tower on Oak Apple Day, May 29th . . . wonder if the practice continued in Eynsham because of this friendship between Charles II and James, the 7th Earl.**' Lilian Wright was presumably referring to the fact that it was at Boscobel near Tong that Charles II eluded capture after the Battle of Worcester by hiding in an oak-tree. This Royal Oak was certainly venerated in the area, enough so that so many branches and twigs were cut from it that it had to be replaced. I believe the one to be seen today is the fourth generation.

And so ends our current exploration for all details of **Sir Thomas** and **Sir Edward** in the various places with which they were associated. It just remains to assemble all known and potentially relevant details in a time-line, from which their very first biographies can be written. But before this appears in Chapter XXVIII. Time-line, a few more relatives need to be covered.

~~~~~~~~~~~~~~~~~~~~

Chapter XX
Diaries of Sir Edward Sr & Jr 1587-90
& a few later events

Finally, an attempt at the diaries of **Sir Edward Sr** and **Edward Jr**, as they might have appeared in their own diaries (although still here in the third person). This is essentially the same information as in Chapter XVII. Sir Edward Sr & Jr in the *Derby Household Books*, but in a rather more readable form. It also emphasises the Winwick element. We also proceed beyond this period to the death of Ferdinando.

N.B. Only visitors mentioned elsewhere in this book, of potential significance for Shakespeare, and who were there on the same day, are given in this 'diary'.

1587, 13 May	**Sir Edward 'my Lords brother'**, with three servants, in the 'permanent' household at Lathom for the whole of the Earl's stay (*DHB*, p. 27).
1587, 1 July	Monday: **Sir Edward** came home to Lathom from somewhere with the Earl; visits that week from Richard Molyneux, Thomas Hoghton of Hoghton (*DHB*, p. 31).
1587, 14 Oct.	Friday: **Sir Edward** 'came home from London' to Lathom (*DHB*, p. 40).
1587, 2 Dec.	Saturday: **Sir Edward** went 'towards Chester' with his nephew Lord Strange and two others (*DHB*, p. 44).
1588, 16 Sep.	Earl Henry returned to New Parke, a new house built in Lathom Park, after his embassy to the Netherlands at the beginning of the year, and after the defeat of the Armada (*DHB*, p. 50).
1589, 6 Jan.	Sunday; the Parson of **Winwick** preached at Lathom, and 'that night the Plaiers plaied'. Monday: the Bishop of Chester preached; **Edward Stanley Jr** visited (*DHB*, p. 57).
1589, 5 June	Saturday 5, the Earl arrived from Court at New Parke; Wednesday 10 to Lathom for a gathering with **Sir Edward**, 'all my Lords' howsholde and many strandgers' (*DHB*, p. 59).
1589, 21 June	Tuesday: the Earl 'rydde to Pilkinton & **Sir Edward**' with him (*DHB*, p. 60).
1589, 18 July	Sunday: the Earl 'towards Preston & **Sir Edward**'with him; Tuesday: the Earl home; Friday:'**Mr Edward Stanley of Winwicke** came' (*DHB*, p. 62).
1589, 2 Aug.	Tuesday: the Earl 'came home, & **Sir Edward**', to Knowsley; Thursday the Earl to Lathom, **Sir Edward** stayed at Knowsley (*DHB*, p. 63).
1589, 28 Aug.	Monday: **Sir Edward** accompanied the Earl to **Winwick** (*DHB*, p. 64).
1589, 30 Aug.	Tuesday… the Earl and others went 'to Toxteth Park & so forth to Wirrall'; Wednesday: **Sir Edward** stayed at Knowsley; **Edward Jr of Winwick** came with Lord Dudley, Earl Henry's brother-in-law (*DHB*, p. 65).
1589, 6 Sep	Tuesday: the Earl, Lord Dudley, **Sir Edward**, William (Earl Henry's son) and others 'went to Lathom to hunt'; Saturday 6, all came back (to Lathom/Knowsley?); the Queen's Players played at night and the Essex Players came (*DHB*, p. 65).
1589, 8 Sep.	Sunday: Rev. William 'Leigh preached & the Quenes Players played in the afternoone, & my Lord of Essex at nyght'; Monday: the Earl and all (presumably including **Sir Edward**) 'went away', presumably to Chester; Saturday the Earl and **Sir Edward** came home; Lord Dudley and William went from Chester to London (*DHB*, p. 66).
1589, 20 Sep.	Monday: the Earl went to Astley (Chorley) & **Sir Edward** and several yeomen servants stayed there. (*DHB*, p. 66).
1589, 4 Oct.	Thursday: the Earl removed to New Park; Lord Strange went to **Winwick** (*DHB*, p. 66).
1589, 15 Oct.	Tuesday: the Earl went to Bidston (Cheshire); Lady Strange, **Sir Edward** and Lord Monteagle's men stayed (*DHB*, p. 68).

1589, 1 Nov.	Tuesday: Lord Monteagle and Mr Salesbury went; Lord and Lady Strange & **Sir Edward** stayed (*DHB*, p. 68).
1589, 8 Nov.	Monday: Lady Strange rode to **Winwick**, **Sir Edward** stayed; Wednesday: Lord Strange left **Winwick**; Thursday: Lady Strange 'came again from **Winwick**' (*DHB*, p. 69).
1589, 15 Nov.	Tuesday: the Earl, Lady Strange and **Sir Edward** 'dyned at the Lodge in Lathome Park'; Thursday **Edward Jr** 'came & on Friday he went again' (*DHB*, p. 69).
1590, 2 May	Thursday: **Edward Jr of Winwick** came to New Park, also the Earl came home; Friday: **Edward Jr** returned home. (*DHB*, p. 79).
1590, 23 May	Tuesday the Earl went from New Park to Knowsley on his journey towards Hawarden (Flintshire); **Sir Edward** and Lord Strange's children stayed behind (*DHB*, p. 80).
1590, 20 June	Tuesday: **Sir Edward**, Lord Strange's children and all the household moved to Knowsley (*DHB*, p. 82).
1590, 26 June	**Sir Edward** in a list of 5 members of the family in residence, with 3 servants; the other 4 were his nephew William and Lord Strange's 3 daughters (*DHB*, p. 88).
1590, 1 Aug.	Thursday: the Earl went to New Park to hold the audit with all his officers and Council; **Sir Edward** and Lord Strange's children stayed at Knowsley (*DHB*, p. 89).
1590, 14 Aug.	Tuesday: the Earl to New Park, **Sir Edward** stayed at Knowsley (*DHB*, p. 89).
1590, 22 Aug.	Monday: 'Mr Stanley of Winwick' came, also 'Mr Edward Stanley', and Lord Strange; Tuesday: they went away and the Earl returned from New Park (*DHB*, p. 90). Brian S. Roberts suspects, with much justification, that 'Mr Stanley of Winwick' was Gerard Stanley, an illegitimate son of **Sir Thomas**. More research is ongoing.

Three years later Earl Henry was on his deathbed and died on 25 September 1593. Much is known about this period because of the intended arrival at Lathom of Richard Hesketh on the day of his death, with a proposal from Jesuits on the continent that Ferdinando should accept the proposition of being their favourite candidate as Elizabeth's successor on the throne. He went to London with Richard Hesketh, went straight to the Queen at Windsor and turned Hesketh over to the authorities. After the inquisition of Hesketh and others close to him (including his brother Bartholomew and Baron Langton of Walton), he was executed on 29 November at St Albans. Ferdinando was exonerated by the Queen of any complicity and returned to Lathom, but died of poisoning the following April.

The story received considerable attention at the time, and several major accounts have been written during the last few decades, all sympathetic to the Catholic and Jesuit position and identifying Sir William Cecil, Lord Burghley and his son Sir Robert Cecil as the main members of the Council pulling the strings: Christopher Devlin, *Hamlet's divinity and other essays* (1963); Ian Wilson, *Shakespeare: The Evidence* (1993); Francis Edwards, *Plots and Plotters in the Reign of Elizabeth I* (2002); and Leo Daugherty, *The Assassination of Shakespeare's Patron: Investigating the Death of the Fifth Earl of Derby* (2011). The main reason for including the following extracts from Edwards, *Plots and Plotters* is because **Sir Edward Sr** was at Lathom at the time, and a few more details are revealed about him, namely that he was a known recusant who sheltered priests at his home in London (the reference for this is not given):

> The Hesketh plot of 1593 to 1594 was convincingly handled by Christopher Devlin and Ian Wilson. It comprised the usual mix. An eminent person taken to be inimical to the regime becomes tangled in a web of intrigue which brings him to the inevitably nasty end. There are agents provocateurs who flit on and off the scene, a fall-guy who likewise meets his doom, a recusant enclave which is clearly part of the target, and a dearth of reliable manuscript evidence of what really happened. Important documents have been 'lost' and others tampered with. The gods outside the machine seem to be – we will not be surprised – the Cecils, plural this time to include the rising star, son Robert. They preside over another scene of Walpurgisnacht weirdness. Leicester had left them by his death in 1588. Camden set out the basic details of the plot in his *Annals* as they were intended for popular acceptance. There were to be two versions of the story, both dictated, we may believe, by the demands of political correctness. . .
>
> (Edwards, *op. cit.*, p. 169.)

On 29 January 1587 William Stanley and his aide Sir Rowland Yorke, apparently disgusted with Leicester's conduct of the war and general incompetence, gave back Deventer to the Spaniards and defected with some 600 men out of a troop of 900 to the enemy. Meanwhile **Sir Edward Stanley in London harboured priests**, while the family in Lancashire looked benevolently on Catholic families and families with Catholic connections on their demesne – Hoghtons, Savages, Halsalls, Gerards and, of course, Heskeths. It all cried to Burghley and son for cleansing action. The need was emphasised by the fact that in 1590 over 700 Lancastrians had been indicted for recusancy.

(Edwards, *op. cit.*, p. 173.)

On Tuesday 25 September he [1593, *Hesketh*] set out for Lathom. . . This was the day the old earl died. It was not a time to disturb the household. Hesketh therefore turned aside to stay a short time at his brother Bartholomew's house at Aughton. On Thursday the 27th Richard went over to Lathom to hand in Hickman's letter and show his passport to **Sir Edward Stanley**. Ferdinando, the new earl, also saw his passport, as did the bishop of Chester who happened to be staying there. In the ordinary course of events, Hesketh would have returned home, as he was eager to do. But from this point the course of events for Hesketh was to be no longer ordinary. Earl Ferdinando had evidently read the letter and passed it to **Sir Edward, a recusant**, to deal immediately with Hesketh. **Sir Edward** assured him that the letter contained nothing important beyond news of plague deaths in London, which was experiencing one of its worst visitations at this time. As Devlin reasonably surmised, this was to try him out. It became apparent to **Sir Edward** that Hesketh knew nothing of the contents of the letter, but he kept him on at Lathom saying the earl wished to talk to him. The earl used further delaying tactics, time in which he could enquire further and make up his own mind. At last he declared he took so much pleasure in Hesketh's company that he must go with him to court.

(Edwards, *op. cit.*, pp. 179-80.)

They left the North West on 3 October, leaving Earl Henry apparently still unburied. With all the problems surrounding the Hesketh Plot, it seems that an elaborate burial, as for his father Edward, was not organised. One can only assume that **Sir Edward Sr** held the reins back at Lathom during Ferdinando's absence, anxiously awaiting news from London. One might also assume that most of the close family were gathered at Lathom during this disquieting period, including perhaps **Edward Jr**.

Ferdinando wasted no time in riding back to Lancashire, where, if the following report is correct, he appeared at Blackburn Grammar School on 9 October. One must, however, doubt whether he could have ridden to London, presented his report to Elizabeth, and been back in Lancashire six days later. This report was obviously produced later (Ferdinando's death is noted); also 'Sir Thomas Gerrarde junior' was not knighted until 1603. There is no reason, however, to disbelieve the composition of the governorship of the school, all duly elected by whoever was present on this day.

ANNALS OF THE GRAMMAR SCHOOL

The following Annals of the School, from 1593 onward, are compiled from the Record Books of the foundation:

An eleccion of Governors at Blackburne the 9th day October, 1593, made by the more p'te of the Governors then lyvynge, being then and theare p'sonally p'sent, so whosle names so elected are as followeth.

fferdinande Earle of Derby	-	-	20s.	[mortuus est 1594]
Randle Barton Esquier	-	-	20s.	
Thomas Soothworthe Esquier	-	-	20s.	
John Parker of Lovely gen.	-	-	20s.	(6s. 8d. pd.)
Henry Mawdysley	-	-	20s.	
James Astley of Plessington	-	-	20s.	

William Boulton and George Astley are appointed by all the Governors to collecte and gather the severall Somes above sett down.

(Abram, *History of Blackburn*, p. 328.)

From details in the *Derby Household Books* we can conclude with some confidence that **Sir Edward Sr**, by 1587, had been excused by all relevant authorities (most of all Queen Elizabeth's Council) for his participation in the plan to free Mary, Queen of Scots in 1570. One can only assume that it must have been considered that his imprisonment in the Tower had been punishment enough and that he presented no further threat to national security. We still know little about his life until his attendance at Preston Guild in August 1582 and that he wrote a letter from Winwick in June 1586. We now know that he was at Lathom in September 1593 with his dying brother Earl Henry and obviously still considered by new Earl Ferdinando as a wise counsellor. We also know (or do we?) that he was a known recusant who harboured Catholic priests in London. One might wonder where? Or has he been confused yet again with another Edward Stanley? A few summarising points can now usefully be made.

1. **Sir Edward Sr** was always an intimate of his brother Earl Henry. His long periods of residence at Henry's Lancashire properties must have been made easier because he was not married.
2. He was also an intimate of his nephew Ferdinando, Lord Strange, and his wife Lady Alice; their children were with him often enough in Lancashire for them to regard him as a trusted member of the family.
3. It seems that **Edward Jr** regarded his uncle **Sir Edward Sr** in a similar light; at least there is no evidence to the contrary: **Jr** visited **Sr** often enough at Lathom, with no indication of anything other than a normal family visit.
4. **Edward Jr** had still retained his father's lease for 99 years of the rectory of Winwick, which he used as his base on returns to Lancashire.
5. He was known locally as **Mr Edward Stanley of Winwick** and not of Tong. We cannot conclude from this that Winwick was his main residence and that he had 'abandoned' Tong, even for the period of three years of the *Derby Household Books*. His father **Sir Thomas** had been known as 'of Winwick', and this was naturally carried on to identify his son. One reason for this useful identification was to distinguish him from at least one other local Mr Edward Stanley of Cross Hall.
6. **Edward Jr** was in Winwick in January, July and August 1589. These might have been two or three separate visits to Lancashire, although those in July and August seem close enough to have taken place during the same stay.
7. **Edward Jr** stayed overnight with his uncles Earl Henry and/or **Sir Edward Sr** at Lathom or Knowsley in November 1589, May and August 1590. Three overnight stays in the same year, when previous visits had been within the day, suggest some change in circumstances. It would be pure speculation to guess what these might have been, but should be borne in mind in case any other evidence emerges.
8. Some of **Edward Jr**'s visits to Winwick were long enough to warrant taking his family of small children with him. There are two 'facts' that support this: a) his recorded visits in January, July and August 1589 were all within the day, when it would have been so easy to accommodate a nephew for the night, and yet he did not stay – in this case, because his wife and young children were waiting for him at Winwick?; b) we know that his only son Thomas, who died very young, was buried at Winwick. It is impossible to believe that, if Thomas had died at Tong, father **Edward Jr** would have gone to all the trouble to transport his body to Winwick for burial, when he could have been buried at Tong with his grandfather; *ergo*, infant Thomas was most likely at Winwick with his mother and sisters.
9. The Parson of Winwick was one of the favourite chaplains of Earl Henry, and given that **Edward Jr** held the lease on the rectory, it would seem more than plausible that they both stayed there together when at Winwick.

10. Earl Henry, Ferdinando and **Sir Edward Sr** visited Winwick on a few occasions recorded: in August 1589 Henry and **Sir Edward** went when **Edward Jr** was there; in October 1589 Ferdinando went there; in November Lady Alice went when **Edward Jr** was there, presumably to meet Ferdinando, who left from there before Alice, implying that Alice stayed on with **Edward Jr**. At least two others in Stanley circles also had property in Winwick: Sir John Holcroft of Holcroft (see his bequest to Winwick Parish Church in his will in Chapter XII. Winwick) and Sir Peter Leigh of Lyme, Cheshire, 'and of Winwick, Lancs.' (Honigmann, *Shakespeare, the 'lost years'*, p. 53). It could be, therefore, that Winwick was a highly convenient place for all of these to meet, particularly when the Stanleys were en route for Warrington, with its bridge over the River Mersey into Cheshire and North Wales.

11. The dates provided by the *Derby Household Books* are the only ones discovered so far for any event involving **Sir Edward Sr** and **Edward Jr** between mid-May 1587 and the end of August 1590.

12. From this time onwards we still know little about **Sir Edward Sr**'s activities until his death in 1604. The only certainty is that he was at Lathom again in September 1593, when his brother Henry died; he was still alive in 1600, when he owned lands in Yorkshire, subject to reversion to his nephew William Stanley, 6th Earl of Derby, on his (**Sir Edward Sr**'s) death (Coward); and in August 1602 he was at Preston Guild.

13. From this time onwards, there is also no record of **Edward Jr**'s activities in Lancashire, apart from his attendance at Preston Guild in 1602. In December 1600 Venetia, his last daughter, was born. We know (from the MI on the tomb) that he and his wife Lucy had eight children (son Thomas dying young), so just producing and nurturing his family, and administering his estates, would have kept him reasonably busy. After 1600 we must access all known details from records elsewhere, mainly in Tong, Eynsham and London.

We are now almost in a position to write the first-ever biographies of **Sir Edward Sr** and **Sir Edward Jr**.

~~~~~~~~~~~~~~~~~~~~~~~~~~~~~~~

Chapter XXI
Sir Edward Stanley Sr's first-ever biography

XXI-1. Introduction

I published two articles in 2008 on **Sir Edward Sr** in *Lancashire History Quarterly*:

'In search of Sir Edward Stanley Sr (c.1540-1604)', Vol. 11, No. 3, Winter/Spring 2008, pp. 27-38.
'In search of Sir Edward Stanley Sr (c.1540-1604) (part 2), Vol. 12, No. 1, Summer 2008, pp. 22-34.

At that time I was still genuinely in search of his 'true' biography and attempting to eliminate all the other Sir Edward Stanleys with whom he has been confused and rather hopelessly muddled in many previous accounts of the Stanley family. These muddles appeared not least in Shakespeare literature, where in any case no interest was shown in him other than confusing him with his nephew **Sir Edward Jr**, for whom Shakespeare wrote the epitaphs in Tong. Happily, most of these other contemporary Sir Edward Stanleys have now been eliminated from 'our' **Sir Edward Sr**'s biography and several of them accounted for, to a certain extent, although there is still a long way to go. It is now possible to produce this first-ever realistic biography, even though there are still many gaps. The articles given above have been made redundant.

Obviously he was a minor figure in the history of the Tudor period, or someone before me would have turned their attention to him. The main reason for this lack of attention, it seems, is that he never held any public office. This was perhaps normal for a third son. The eldest son inherited all of the family wealth, property and titles (in this case the eldest son was Henry, 4th Earl of Derby, Lord of Man), the second son was appointed to some of the family public offices (in this case **Sir Thomas Stanley** of Winwick and Tong, Governor of the Isle of Man 1562-66, Mayor of Liverpool in 1568, etc.), but the third son, unless he showed exceptional ability in some area, stayed in the background, in the shadow of his father and two elder brothers.

So why is he important now? It might have become obvious to any reader of earlier chapters of this book that **Sir Edward Stanley Sr**'s main importance was as the Senior Member in the immediate family of the Earls of Derby from the mid-1590s until his death in 1604, which is, of course, the cut off date for his immediate influence, if not that of his lingering importance for the family. Both his elder brothers were dead, **Sir Thomas** already in 1576 and Earl Henry in 1593. At this point he was the only surviving son of Edward, 3rd Earl of Derby. In this capacity alone, as senior head of the family, he deserves some belated attention. It seems almost certain that he was present at most of the important family events. He was so close to his namesake nephew **Sir Edward Jr** that he must have known about the Shakespeare epitaphs. One might even presume that he, too, had followed Shakespeare's career and knew all about his ancestry in the Shakeshaftes of Preston. He was the only one of the family to attend Preston Guild in 1562, 1582 and 1602. Maybe, just maybe, his own biography might shed a little light on the others at the centre of this book? Theirs certainly shed light on his.

Sir Edward Sr never married, but he had three surviving nephews for whom, it seems, he frequently played the valued role of supportive uncle. One specific role he played regularly was 'holding the fort' back at Lathom when his brother Earl Henry was in London or on diplomatic missions abroad for Queen Elizabeth. Another role appeared after 1576 when his brother **Sir Thomas Stanley** died, leaving an only child, fourteen-year-old son and heir **Edward Jr – Sir Edward Sr** stepped into his brother's family in the role of surrogate father figure. It seems that whenever there was a family crisis, **Sir Edward Sr** was always there, ready to step into the breach. He seemed to spend much of his time travelling round visiting his far flung relatives and thus played something like the role of a spider in the middle of the large Stanley web.

The most intriguing part of **Sir Edward Stanley Sr**'s biography for myself - and I presume a few others - is that all three Stanley nephews had strong associations with Shakespeare during the time when **Sir Edward** was the virtual head of the Stanley/Earl of Derby family. I still find it strange that these three nephews were rather remote from Shakespeare biographies for so long, but so it was. To repeat ad nauseam, but as a reminder in the context of **Sir Edward Sr**'s biography, the three nephews and their Shakespeare connections were:

1) Ferdinando, Lord Strange, briefly 5th Earl of Derby 1593-4, was the patron of Strange's Players, in which Shakespeare certainly acted in London during the early 1590s, at the beginning of his rather spectacular rise to fame in London as a dramatist and poet. It becomes ever more obvious that Shakespeare might well have been a member of this company since much earlier, quite possibly in its predecessor Derby's Men shortly after being named as William Shakeshafte in Alexander Hoghton's will in August, 1581.

2) William, 6th Earl of Derby 1594-1632, wrote plays and was involved with players in London at least from 1599-1602, at the time when Shakespeare was enjoying fame. Partly because they conveniently shared the same initials, William Stanley has even been proposed as an Alternative Shakespeare Authorship Candidate. This is nonsense, of course, but the very fact that some people have tried to 'prove' this claim has led to several connections between the two WSs emerging over the century since his candidacy was first proposed. Just one example is the proposition that *A Midsummer Night's Dream* was first performed at William Stanley's wedding in January 1595 in the presence of Queen Elizabeth. This appears to many Shakespeare scholars as the most cogent among three possible choices of weddings around this time.

3) **Sir Edward Jr**, although not actively involved in the theatre, nevertheless received two verse epitaphs from Shakespeare (apparently c.1603), which are still there today on the Stanley tomb in Tong, Shropshire.

During the last few decades, these nephews have all come rather more to the forefront of Shakespeare Studies, and with them now comes their longest-living Stanley uncle.

During the decade of trauma for the immediate family, starting in 1593, he obviously stepped into the breach again as a deeply valued uncle. In September 1593 the first disaster struck with the 'Hesketh Plot', as a result of which Ferdinando, 5th Earl died the following year, almost certainly poisoned. Brother William took over as 6th Earl, but was confronted with the beginning of what was to turn out to be a long drawn out acrimonious legal fight with his sister-in-law Countess Alice, Ferdinando's widow. The next disaster was with the third nephew **Sir Edward Jr**, when his wife and four daughters died in 1601 in Walthamstow, Essex, presumably of the plague or some other virulent disease. This part of the story has already been covered at length in previous chapters. The important point here is that uncle **Sir Edward Sr** obviously stepped into the breach once more as *pater familias*.

There are so many other contemporary Edward Stanleys in **Sir Edward Sr**'s biography following that it seems wise to continue with the convention adopted throughout this book to always call him this, in **bold**, with (Sir) in brackets until he was knighted in 1560. The same applies to **(Sir) Edward Jr.**

Apologies if this is often repetitive of details in previous chapters. It does have the virtue (?) of being in narrative form, bringing together chronologically all detected so far about **Sir Edward Sr**. References for the quotes and sources of facts and documents that appear in the following narrative are all given under the appropriate date in Chapter XXVIII. Time-line of Sir Thomas & Sir Edward Sr & Jr. The Family Tree Appendix 12b gives in pictorial form all the Stanley relatives who appear in **Sir Edward**'s so far untold story. All dates attributed to members of the immediate family have been in consultation with Brian S. Roberts, a Stanley family researcher.

XXI-2. Birth (1535-40) and early years

(Sir) **Edward Sr** was born some time between 1535 and 1540, the third (surviving) son of Edward, 3rd Earl of Derby and his second wife Dorothy, second daughter of Thomas Howard, 2nd Duke of Norfolk. Earl Edward's first wife Katherine Howard had died of the plague within a year of their marriage, but to cement the relationship between these two families, Earl Edward married Dorothy Howard, Katherine and Dorothy being aunt and niece. Dorothy was the mother of most of Earl Edward's children, and certainly of the three surviving sons. There were also numerous daughters, therefore (Sir) **Edward Sr**'s sisters.

His eldest brother Henry had been named in honour of Henry VIII, his second brother Thomas after both his grandfathers, who were both titled - paternal Thomas Stanley, 2nd Earl of Derby and maternal Thomas Howard, 2nd Duke of Norfolk. **Edward** was, of course, named after his father. There is no record of his birth or baptism, nor his age at death in 1604, so one can only calculate the date from other known dates. The most important date is that his elder brother Henry, the first (surviving) son, future 4th Earl of Derby, was born in 1531 (baptised 4 October). Numerous daughters were also born: Anne in 1531 and Isabel in 1533, followed by Jane in 1540, with Mary and Dorothy at unknown dates; also one further (surviving) son (Sir) **Thomas** and finally the third son (Sir) **Edward Sr**. The most realistic date of birth calculated before my articles in 2008 was c.1540. Since then, however, Brian S. Roberts has suggested an earlier date, based at least partly on *The House of Stanley*, an extremely interesting book by Peter Stanley, a result of lifelong research into the family, but one which unfortunately provides no references. Brian has been chasing the missing references and found many of the original documents. So, unless or until more relevant MSS emerge, **Sir Edward Stanley Sr** will now have a birthdate of between 1535 and 1540.

One assumes that (Sir) **Edward** was born at Lathom House, Lancashire, the main residence of his father. He certainly grew up in a large family, one hopes a happy family. Apart from his older brothers Henry, Lord Strange and **Sir Thomas**, he had five known sisters, the oldest being Anne (1531-1602) and Isabel (1533-1590), thus both older than **Edward**. Then came Jane (1540-1569) and Mary and Dorothy, one presumes in the late 1530s to 1540s and in any case before their mother Dorothy died. There are conflicting dates for her death reported by others, but some time shortly before 1547 seems the most logical, because this date is reported for Earl Edward's third marriage to Margaret Barlow, daughter of Ellis Barlow of Barlow (Lancashire) and Anne Redish. (Sir) **Edward** was thus very young when he lost his mother. He presumably grieved for her and was happy when his father married again. His stepmother Margaret bore two little half-sisters for him, Margaret and Catherine. Margaret Sr died on 19 January 1559 and was buried on 24 February in Ormskirk Church. Earl Edward married a fourth and last time in 1561, Mary Cotton, daughter of Sir George Cotton of Cumbermere, Cheshire and Mary Onley. Earl Edward and Mary had no children. She survived him (he died in 1572, she in 1580) and married again, Henry Grey, 6th Earl of Kent (1541-1615).

Edward's known sisters all survived to adulthood. Dorothy was the only one who remained unmarried, presumably spending most of her life at Lathom. Some of the marriages of the others provide interesting stories in themselves. Anne married first in 1649 Charles Stourton, 8th Baron Stourton (c.1520-1557) and second Sir John Arundel of Lamborn in Cornwall, with children from both marriages. These families remained devoutly Catholic, and it is interesting that the Stanley-Stourton connection was known about in the next century by Catholic-in-exile Father Henry More SJ, who also knew about the Shakespeare epitaphs in Tong (see Appendix 8. Father Henry More SJ). (In some reports Earl Edward is awarded another daughter Isabel, who married James Stanley. Brian S. Roberts is certain that Edward did not have a daughter named Isabel.) Jane (1540-1569) enjoyed only a short marriage from 1567 as the second wife of Edward Sutton, 4th Baron Dudley; she was buried on 4 September 1569 at Dudley, Worcestershire. During this short marriage she had two sons, Edward Sutton (born 17 September 1567), the later 5th Baron Dudley, and John (born 17 ?September /? November 1569), who later served briefly as MP for Staffordshire. The eagle-eyed reader will have detected an anomaly here in the dates: how could the second son have been born after his mother was already buried? Unfortunately, this problem is encountered all too often during historical research – so often a date is reported wrongly, and then repeated as fact without checking back to the original source. Whatever the true dates, one of these sons obviously remained close to his Stanley relatives, as Lord Dudley was a regular visitor at Lathom in the *Derby Household Books* 1587-90 when **Sir Edward Sr** was there. Sister Mary married on 23 November 1566 Edward Stafford, 3rd Baron Stafford (1535-1603), who served as MP for Stafford and also kept 'Lord Stafford's Company of Players'. **Edward**'s younger half-sister Margaret married first John Jermyn of Ruthbrook, Suffolk and second Sir Nicholas Poyntz (c.1537-85) from the family of Sutton Poyntz, Dorset. These were thus the members of his immediate family and in-laws, widespread throughout the country, whose fortunes he presumably followed and whose families he visited during his later peripatetic years. He also had numerous Stanley 'cousins', who were later to achieve local fame and in some cases national fame or notoriety.

In summary, he grew up in a large household in an aristocratic family, with a father who was a 'Magnate of the North' and thus regularly in London for political and diplomatic duties and services. Earl Edward's story obviously played the most important role in (Sir) **Edward Sr**'s early life. His mother Dorothy survived until c.1547, so at least he had this stability in his early years. After this his father married again twice. Earl Edward had been hereditary Earl of Derby since 1521, at the age of thirteen, when his father Thomas, 2nd Earl died. He had also been Lord of Man since the same date. Until he came of age he was under the wardship of Cardinal Wolsey. During (Sir) **Edward Sr**'s childhood his father was Lord Lieutenant of Lancashire (1552 onwards) and Lord High Steward of England in Mary's reign.

One might therefore presume that (Sir) **Edward Sr** knew the history of his own family and followed all these events, and was thus well aware of the roles that his various Stanley ancestors had played in national history and which roles current Stanley relatives were still playing.

No records have been discovered about his education. There is no record of his having attended a school or university. Schools during his youth were few and far between, so one can only presume that he received his education from tutors at home. Certain confirmation of a school at Lathom (in **bold** below) comes from the following report, with an amusing dedication by Furnivall (also in **bold**).

> Child Marriages, Divorces, and Ratifications, &c. in the Diocese of Chester, A.D. 1561-6.
> DEPOSITIONS IN TRIALS IN THE BISHOP'S COURT, CHESTER, CONCERNING
> 1. Child- Marriages, Divorce, and Ratifications. 2. Trothplights. 3. Adulteries. 4. Affiliations. 5.
> Libels. 6. Wills. 7. Miscellaneous Matters. 8. Clandestine Marriages.
> ALSO
> Entries from the Mayors' Books, Chester, A. D. 1558-1600.
> EDITED FROM THE MS. WRITTEN IN COURT WHILE THE WITNESSES

MADE THEIR DEPOSITIONS, AND FROM THE MAYORS' BOOKS,
by
FREDERICK J. FURNIVALL, M.A. TRINITY HALL, CAMBRIDGE; HON. DR. PHIL.
BERLIN, LONDON:
PUBLISHT FOR THE EARLY ENGLISH TEXT SOCIETY BY KEGAN PAUL, TRENCH,
TRÜBNER & CO., PATERNOSTER HOUSE, CHARING-CROSS ROAD. 1897.
**DEDICATED TO THE ANTIQUARIES OF CHESHIRE, IN THE HOPE THAT THEY
WILL AT ONCE HANG ONE OF THEIR NUMBER, TO ENCOURAGE THE REST
FORTHWITH TO PRINT ALL THE DEPOSITIONS AND OTHER VALUABLE
MATERIAL IN THE DIOCESAN REGISTRY AT CHESTER WHICH THEY HAVE SO
LONG AND SO CULPABLY LEFT IN MS. ONLY.**
    F. J. F.

This deponent sais, that the said William hath bene **at Schole at Lathum, with one Doctour
Standish**, and with therle of Derby in Service, for the most parte, sins tyme of the said Mariage;
and the said Anne hath helle separatid from the said William, in such places as her father hath
appointed her; . . .

The William Stanley in question here was the son of Sir Rowland Stanley of Hooton in the
Wirral, head of the senior branch of the family. (Sir Rowland had been knighted in 1533 at the same
time as **Sir Thomas**, (Sir) **Edward**'s older brother. We met him in Chapter XIV at Earl Edward's
funeral.) He was the future Sir William (1548-1630) who gained his spurs and was knighted in
Ireland, went to the Netherlands under the Earl of Leicester in 1585 and, for personal and religious
reasons, defected to the Spanish in 1587 when he surrendered Deventer to them. He lived in exile for
the rest of his life on a pension from Philip II, moving between the Spanish Netherlands and Spain
and dying at Ghent in Flanders. (Ghent had long had Lancastrian associations as the birthplace of
John of Gaunt [= Ghent], Duke of Lancaster, a Shakespeare character with a famous patriotic speech
in *Richard II*.) Sir William played the role of Military Leader of the English Catholics in exile, the
Spiritual Leader being Cardinal William Allen of Rossall, Lancashire.

One might safely assume that the three Stanley brothers at Lathom House and a few of their
'cousins' received their schooling at home from various Catholic clerics. The Dr Standish mentioned
above was Henry Standish from Standish Hall (the Standishes of Standish being devout Catholics),
who acted as chaplain to the Earl of Derby and was known as 'a passionate preacher'. (Sir) **Edward
Sr** therefore presumably had an equally 'passionate' Catholic education along with his 'cousin' Sir
William.

One assumes that Furnivall's call in 1897 for the immediate hanging of a Cheshire antiquary
triggered an upsurge in transcription activities. Unfortunately, no results in Cheshire detected so far
shed any more light on **Sir Edward**'s biography.

XXI-3. Young adulthood, up to the 1560s

And so we see him in the late 1550s, with nothing documented about his life before this date. We do
know, however, that his older brother **Sir Thomas** had been knighted by Lord Arundel on behalf of
Queen Mary on the day after her coronation in 1553, along with their 'cousin' Sir Rowland Stanley of
Hooton (schoolfriend 'cousin' William's father) and Sir Thomas Gerard, a close friend of the family.
Predictably, in the reign of Catholic Queen Mary, these new knights were Catholic.

During the reign of Mary his two older brothers married. Henry, Lord Strange married Margaret
Clifford, daughter of Henry, 2nd Earl of Cumberland on 7 February 1554/5 in the Royal Chapel,
Whitehall in the presence of Queen Mary and her husband Philip II, King of Spain. Incidentally, this
is one event behind the most sensible explanation for their naming their son and heir Ferdinando

(born 1558/9), his godfather and/or namesake being presumably one of several Ferdinand(o)s /Fernandos in King Philip's family. These included all the Spanish Fernandos and also several Ferdinands, leading members of the Austrian Habsburg dynasty in the Holy Roman Empire, Philip's father Charles V having been Holy Roman Emperor as well as King of Spain. Exactly which Fer(di)nand(o) was the most likely godfather has yet to be established. His mother Margaret Clifford, Lord Henry's wife, was the daughter of Lady Eleanor Brandon, who, because she was the daughter of Mary Tudor, Dowager Queen of France, sister of Henry VIII, was in the line of succession to Elizabeth's throne. Ferdinando thus inherited this right. (There had been two earlier children, son Edward and daughter Anne, both of whom died young.)

Brother **Sir Thomas** married Margaret Vernon of Haddon Hall in Derbyshire in c.1558, not quite so splendidly, but presumably in a suitable fashion for the son of an Earl and the daughter of Sir George Vernon, 'The King of the Peak'. One might assume that youngest brother (Sir) **Edward** was present at both these ceremonies. (**Sir Thomas** and his marriage is covered, of course, in his own biography in Chapter XXIX.)

Then Elizabeth came to the throne in November 1558 and father Earl Edward was received cordially. He joined her Privy Council and in 1559 she appointed him Chamberlain of Chester, to add to his titles and duties in the North West. Perhaps it was because of Earl Edward's position at court that on 2 January 1560 she knighted his youngest son **Sir Edward** by proxy in Ireland. He was presumably there during the first attempt at suppressing the Desmond Rebellion in Munster. On the same day were knighted Thomas Manners and James Fitzgerald (Shaw's *Book of Knights*, pp. 70-71). Whether or not he displayed heroism remains unknown, but this seems to have been the only time he ever served as a soldier. From now on we can leave out the brackets round Sir. A further exploration of other events in Ireland around this time might shed more light on his biography.

The only recorded event in 1561 of relevance is the baptism of nephew William on 20 July in London, the second son of brother Henry, Lord Strange. This was of importance to **Sir Edward** in the light of their future lives.

1562 turned out to be one of the years with most records relevant to **Sir Edward**. In August-September 1562 Earl Edward and all three sons attended Preston Guild. This was a long established part of the calendar of important events in Lancashire. It was held every twenty years (still today, the latest one in 2012). Attendance and registration was obligatory for every burgess and any merchant who wished to trade in the town, but increasingly it had also become an important social event, attended by many of the gentry from the surrounding area, with the Earl of Derby presiding over all. There were always several dramatic performances. Luckily the *Preston Guild Rolls* have survived, and so we know the names of all males who attended in 1562. We also therefore know where **Sir Edward** spent two weeks from the end of August of this year and the names of many of those he must have met. One of these names, interestingly, was 'John Shakeshafte, glover', whom I propose was one and the same as John Shakespeare, glover of Stratford-upon-Avon - a story which will be pursued elsewhere.

Around the time of Preston Guild brother **Sir Thomas**'s son **Edward** was born. The date can be calculated fairly accurately as mid-late 1562. Exactly where he was born is not known, but the most likely place was Lathom House, the main residence of Earl Edward. Lady Margaret must have been highly pregnant or a recent mother at the time of Preston Guild, so presumably did not attend the social events in Preston. Or maybe she did, and **Edward Jr** was actually born there? Alas we will never know. What we do know, from later events, is that **Sir Edward Sr** and (Sir) **Edward Jr** were bonded for life, through blood and by sharing the same name. From the MI on the Stanley tomb in Tong we know that **Sir Thomas** and Margaret had another son Henry, who died young. The text is 'by whom he had issue two sons Henry and Edward. Henry died an infant and Edward survived, to whom

Thomas's Lordships descended.' The implication is that Henry was the first son and Edward the second, which in turn implies that Henry had been born between the marriage in c.1558 and **Edward Jr**'s birth in 1562. Exactly when and where Henry 'died an infant' is not known. He might or might not have still been alive during Preston Guild in 1562, but other events indicate that he had probably died before this. **Edward Jr** must have therefore seemed all the more precious to his parents and his uncle **Sir Edward**.

1562 and the birth of **Edward Jr** also saw another significant event. Earl Edward obviously decided that he needed to start thinking about the future inheritance of his younger sons and his first grandson with the surname Stanley. One major event was a deed of settlement of many Derby manors and lands on **Sir Thomas** for life, then to his wife Margaret, passing to their son **Edward Jr** (this presents strong evidence for 'infant Henry' already having died). In the event of no further male heir, all properties were to revert to the Earldom of Derby. The terms were: 'a deed of settlement granting to **Sir Thomas** for life all his manors and land in the counties of Chester, Warwick, Oxford and Devon with remainder to his wife Margaret for life, with remainder to their son **Edward** for life.' The full list for Cheshire was 'Dunham-massey, Bowden, Rungey, Hale, Aeton and Darfield'.

At the same time he awarded a settlement of lands to his son **Sir Edward Sr**, presumably under the same conditions. These were at least in Thirsk and Kirkby Malzeard in Yorkshire. No one had any idea at the time that (Sir) **Edward Jr** would die in 1632 without a male heir, or that **Sir Edward Sr** would never marry and therefore also produce no male heir. However, all these lands were to play a part in the life of **Sir Edward Sr** during the following decades. He had his own lands in Yorkshire to administer and presumably often visited his brother **Sir Thomas** until the latter's death in 1576. When he adopted the role of father-figure to **Edward Jr**, he also kept an eye on all the lands that would come to his nephew in due course. But all this still lay in the future.

In 1562 **Sir Thomas** was appointed by father Earl Edward as Governor of the Isle of Man, a position he held for four years. Alas we have no record as to how much time he spent on the Isle of Man, nor any idea whether or not his wife and young son **Edward Jr** accompanied him, nor whether or not his brother **Sir Edward** visited him there.

1562 also saw the appearance of a poem, the 'Rhyming Chronicle(s)', a sort of history in verse of the Stanley family continued to the year 1562. This has generally been attributed to Thomas Stanley, Bishop of Man. This Thomas Stanley was almost certainly an illegitimate son of Sir Edward Stanley, hero at Flodden in 1513 and thus created 1st Lord Mounteagle of Hornby Castle near Lancaster. **Sir Edward Sr** must have known of this 'Rhyming Chronicle' and presumably read it. Bishop Stanley also happened to be Rector of Winwick, and as a cleric, was sometimes referred to as 'Sir Thomas Stanley'. His legitimate brother was also Sir Thomas Stanley, 2nd Lord Mo(u)nteagle. (Bishop Stanley's story appeared in Chapter XII. An excursion to Winwick.)

The importance of Winwick in the story is that in the following year **Sir Thomas** leased the Rectory of Winwick from Thomas, Bishop of Man, for 99 years. This led to his being known from then on as **Sir Thomas Stanley** of Winwick and his son later known as (Sir) **Edward** of Winwick. **Sir Edward Sr** visited his brother and later his nephew in Winwick regularly from then on, and so it becomes part of his own biography. In 1568-9 **Sir Thomas** was Mayor of Liverpool, another traditional Derby office, and in 1569 was a Commissioner of Muster for Lancashire, along with father 'Earl Edward, Lord Monteagle, Sir George Stanley, Sir John Atherton, Edward Holland and Edmund Ashton'.

The rest of the 1560s remains a blank for any records of **Sir Edward Sr**. His two older brothers continued to progress in their respective careers.

~~~~~~~~~~~~~~~~~~~~

XXI-4. The 1570s

In 1570 disaster struck. **Sir Thomas** and **Sir Edward**, along with their friend Sir Thomas Gerard of Bryn, dreamt up a scheme to rescue Mary, Queen of Scots from Chatsworth House, where she had just been placed under the custodianship of the 6th Earl of Shrewsbury, one of the richest men in England, and his second wife Elizabeth, known in popular history as Bess of Hardwick. This story has been told in great detail by Mary S. Lovell in *Bess of Hardwick* (2005), with relevant extracts appearing in Chapter XIII. 1570: Sir Thomas & Sir Edward Sr and Mary, Queen of Scots. Both were summoned to London to explain themselves and both ended up in the Tower of London. **Sir Thomas** was definitely tortured, confirmation coming from *Prisoners in the Tower* by A. H. Cook, formerly Chief Warder at H.M. Tower of London (two handwritten volumes, 1959): 'A confession on the rack brought about his arrest and committal to the Tower (Ridolfi Plot)'. **Sir Thomas** seems to have been kept there for up to three years along with Sir Thomas Gerard, and maybe even longer. **Sir Edward Sr** seems to have got off more lightly and been released rather sooner. One story is:

> **Sir Edward Stanley** strongly denied that he had had any effective part in it, giving the ingenious excuse that he had been away in the north at the time courting a Mrs Strickland.
>
> (Antonia Fraser, *Mary, Queen of Scots*, 1970.)

If he did court her, he was unsuccessful, because he never married. Strickland was a fairly common name in Cumberland, which matches with **Sir Edward**'s admired lady being 'in the north'. Meanwhile he must have been very well aware what was happening to his brother. In May 1572 **Sir Thomas** was still in the Tower along with the Bishop of Ross, the Earl of Southampton, Lord Lumley and Thomas, the brother of Lord Cobham; all were suspected of being involved with the Duke of Norfolk's plots and plans. On 2 June the Duke of Norfolk was executed in the Tower. He was an in-law of all the Stanleys, Earls of Derby. His half-sister Dorothy née Howard was Earl Edward Stanley's second wife and mother of **Sir Thomas** and **Sir Edward**.

Then on the 22 August Thomas Percy, 7th Earl of Northumberland was executed at York for his role in the Northern Rebellion of 1569-70. He left four daughters, the second one Lucy, who later married (Sir) **Edward Jr**. It is tempting to imagine that uncle **Sir Edward Sr** might have played a role in arranging this match.

The next major family event was the death of Earl Edward, with the elaborate funeral taking place on 4 December 1572 at Ormskirk, the Stanley church. **Sir Thomas** was still in the Tower, but the whereabouts of **Sir Edward Sr** is not known. He is not listed amongst the mourners in the procession. (Chapter XIV. 1572: Earl Edward's funeral.)

During the following year or later **Sir Thomas** was released from the Tower and went to live at Tong Castle, his wife's property, where he was certainly living in 1575, 'now latlie by credible report **Sir Thomas Stanley** is come to dwell in this cuntrie, and many papists gentilmen resorte unto him.' Whether **Sir Edward Sr** was classed as one of these 'papists gentilmen' is not known, but his life was about to change when his brother died the following year. In his will he mentioned only his wife Lady Margaret and his son **Edward Jr**.

Whether he was present at his brother's death and funeral in Tong in December 1576 is not known, but from then on he seems to have adopted the role of surrogate father to his nephew **Edward Jr**, fourteen years old at the time and an only child. Whether this was by moving into Tong Castle or taking him to live at Lathom or elsewhere to receive tuition is not known. There would have been other possibilities, of course. Within the next year or so Lady Margaret married again, William Mather, who, of course, became young **Edward Jr**'s stepfather. As far as is known this was a happy marriage, but there is a hint in Lady Margaret's later will that she and her second husband might have been happy to allow his uncle to act in loco parentis. Although an only child and her son and heir, he is not mentioned at all. In any case there is no doubt that the two **Edwards**, uncle and nephew, continued to have a close relationship. **Sir Edward Sr** also seems to have taken an active interest in his other nephews Ferdinando and William (and Francis), who were a little older than **Edward Jr**.

In c.1579 Ferdinando, aged twenty, married Alice Spencer (born 4 May 1559), the youngest of eight daughters of Sir John Spencer (d. 1586) of Althorp, Northamptonshire, and Katherine Kytson, eldest daughter and heiress of Sir Thomas Kytson of London. The marriage took place secretly. 'Since he and his mother, Margaret, Countess of Derby, were potential successors to Elizabeth I, the marriage caused considerable suspicion, especially as it had been promoted by the Earl of Leicester.' (*ODNB*) Given the 'secrecy', it will never be known where the wedding took place, nor whether **Sir Edward Sr** was present. There is little doubt, however, that he followed all news from this marriage, and the birth of their daughters, with great interest. Their first daughter Anne was born in 1580 and she, of course, inherited Ferdinando's place in line of succession to Elizabeth's throne.

XXI-5. The 1580s

In 1581/2 his second nephew **Edward Jr** married. This was to Lucy Percy, second daughter of Thomas Percy, 7th Earl of Northumberland and Anne née Somerset, daughter of Henry Somerset, 2nd Earl of Worcester. Lucy's father had been executed in 1572 for his role in the Northern Rebellion in support of Mary, Queen of Scots, and her mother Anne, also one of the instigators, had fled into exile among the English Catholics in the Spanish Netherlands, never to return to England. It was speculated above that **Sir Edward** might have had a hand in organizing this match. Lucy had been brought up by her uncle Henry Percy, 8th Earl of Northumberland, who inherited the title from her father. She had thus lived from an early age at Petworth House, Sussex. No record has survived of the date or place of the marriage, but a date of late 1581 to mid-1582 is indicated by their entertainment of uncle **Sir Edward Sr** at Eynsham in 1582. Indeed, **Sir Edward Sr** is reported as actually living at Eynsham in 1582 with his nephew **Edward Jr** and his wife. The approximate date of marriage is confirmed by the fact that their first daughter Arabella was born in 1582/3. (We know this because she was aged 18 when she died at Walthamstow in early-mid 1601.) The very fact that **Edward Jr** and Lucy were living at Eynsham and not at Tong at the beginning of their married life raises several questions, which may never find an answer, but one thing is certain – uncle **Sir Edward Sr** wasted no time in visiting the newly-married couple, perhaps even living with them for some time.

It may well have been from Eynsham that they set off for the North West for a family reunion. At the end of August 1582 several of the Stanleys were at Preston Guild together: Earl Henry, his sons Ferdinando, William and Francis (the latter to die not too long afterwards), **Sir Edward Sr** and **Edward Jr**. Also there in first place among the gentry was Thomas Hoghton of Lea and Hoghton Tower with four of his sons. This was the brother of Alexander Hoghton, who the previous year had written his will naming William Shakeshafte three times in combination with musical instruments and playclothes. He had asked brother Thomas to accept him and Fulke Gyllom into his service, if he wished, and if not, to send them to their friend Thomas Hesketh of Rufford. The latter was indeed their destination 'for a short time', according to family tradition, and Thomas Hesketh was at Preston Guild, in third place in the gentry list. But by now William Shakeshafte/Shakespeare had almost certainly passed on again into Derby's Men, later renamed Strange's Players when Ferdinando took over as their patron. It is difficult to imagine that Strange's Players did not turn up at Preston Guild to perform. One can thus fondly imagine that young William Shakespeare might have performed there in front of **Sir Edward Sr** and his family, with his father John Shakeshafte/Shakespeare and many of his family also in the audience.

On 16 September 1583 his young nephew Francis was buried at Ormskirk, and one might imagine that **Sir Edward** attended the funeral. As well as this loss, there had been two recent new additions to the family in the form of second daughter, Frances to nephew Ferdinando and Alice, and Arabella - the first of many daughters - to nephew **Edward Jr** and his wife Lucy née Percy. Her name was a rather unusual one, but reasonably common in the aristocracy, particularly those with Scottish connections. One of her distant relatives had the same name, Ar(a)bella Stuart (born 1575), a first cousin of James VI of Scotland. This may or may not be a coincidence. She had a similar claim to the throne of England as Ferdinando and his daughter, with one descended from Margaret Tudor and the other from Mary Tudor, sisters of Henry VIII. Arbella Stuart at this time was orphaned and had been put under the guardianship of her grandmother Bess of Hardwick, married to Gilbert Talbot, 6th Earl of Shrewsbury. It was from their 'guardianship' at Chatsworth that **Sir Edward**'s brother **Sir Thomas** (and **Sir Edward Sr** himself?) had planned to rescue Mary, Queen of Scots back in 1570. Another granddaughter of Bess was Grace Pierrepoint, who was later to marry Sir George Manners, **Sir Thomas**'s nephew and **Edward Jr**'s first cousin.

In 1584 another Stanley popped up at Eynsham, **Sir Edward Sr**'s nephew William, although it is not obvious that **Sir Edwards Sr** and **Jr** were there at the same time. William was back in England for a while between his travels on the continent, and took the opportunity while in Eynsham to establish the family rights to the manorial pew, denying them to Thomas Peniston. As the latter had bought half of the manor, it is difficult to see the reason for this. Perhaps there had been some other dispute? It at least shows that William as well as his uncle **Sir Edward Sr** used Eynsham as a convenient stopping-off place on their journeys between London and Lancashire.

From January to March 1585 **Sir Edward** was perhaps called upon again to hold the fort back at Lathom while his brother Earl Henry was on a mission to France for Queen Elizabeth. This was ostensibly to invest Henri III as Knight of the Garter, but is generally presumed to have also involved secret negotiations and discussions on how France and England should act together against the Spanish in the Low Countries. The result of these talks was that Elizabeth decided to send an English army to the Netherlands under the command of her 'favourite', Robert Dudley, Earl of Leicester, who had many interests in Stanley territory in Cheshire and North Wales. At this time he was Chamberlain of Chester, having succeeded Earl Edward to this position, a post he held from 1565 until his death in 1588.

At least two Stanleys accompanied Leicester to the Netherlands. One was another Edward Stanley, who was to become a hero when he stormed the walls at Zutphen in October 1586 almost single-handed and was promptly knighted by Leicester. (See Chapter XXII. Other (Sir) Edward Stanleys.) He has often been confused with **Sir Edward Stanley Sr** (e.g. by Seacome, the pious first Derby biographer in 1741), but it was definitely not 'our' **Sir Edward**, who had already been a knight for twenty-six years. The Edward at Zutphen might well have been Sir Edward Stanley of Elford 'knighted in Netherland, slaine in Ireland in 1597' (Stanley, *Visitation of Cheshire*, 1580). The other was Sir William Stanley of Hooton, the one who was at school at Lathom with Dr Henry Standish, presumably with his young Stanley 'cousins' **Sir Thomas** and **Sir Edward**, and in Ireland when the latter was knighted there in 1560. In January 1587 Sir William surrendered Deventer to the Spanish and never returned to England. He became the military commander of the English troops in exile, the spiritual leader of the English Catholic exiles being (later Cardinal) William Allen, from Rossall in Lancashire, who had founded the English College at Douai in 1562. During one report on Sir William Stanley, now known as 'the exile' and 'the traitor', and other Stanleys, it was stated that 'meanwhile **Sir Edward Stanley** in London harboured priests'.

During this period **Sir Edward** seemed to pursue his usual activity of visiting his relatives. On 29 June, 1586 he was at Winwick, from where he 'wrote a letter from his nephew's house at Winwick, asking his brother, the Earl of Derby, to use his good offices with the Archbishop of Canterbury, to appoint his friend John Kine one of the proctors of the court of Arches.' From this alone one might suspect that **Sir Edward Sr** often visited his nephew **Edward Jr** in Winwick when both were visiting Earl Henry and other relatives at Lathom.

December 1586 saw the wedding of Ursula Stanley (**Sir Edward Sr**'s niece) and John Salusbury at Lleweni, Denbigh. This is presumed by some as the event that inspired Shakespeare's poem *The Phoenix and the Turtle*. Ursula was an illegitimate, but fully recognised daughter of Henry, 4th Earl of Derby; John Salusbury was another descendant of Henry VII via an illegitimate son and Catherine of Berain. His brother Thomas Salusbury had been executed earlier this year (21 September) as one of the conspirators in the Babington Plot. Again, we do not know whether **Sir Edward** attended this wedding, but he and John Salusbury were regular guests at Lathom during the following years. Brother Earl Henry was absent from home again in 1587 when he was on the 'jury' at the 'trial' at Fotheringay of Mary, Queen of Scots.

From now until 1590 all details come from the *Derby Household Books*, with **Sir Edward**'s visits given in full in Chapter XVII. Sir Edward Sr & Jr in the *Derby Household Books*, and repeated to a certain extent in Chapter XX. Sir Edward Sr and Jr's diaries 1586-90. They are thus not repeated here. In brief, **Sir Edward Sr** was a frequent visitor at his brother Earl Henry's seats in Lancashire and the Wirral, frequently overlapping with visits by his nephews and on occasion arriving there from London. We take up the story again in the 1590s.

XXI-6. The 1590s

'A tenement called the church house in Northchurch in the tenure of ------Axhill was granted in 1590/1 to **Sir Edward Stanley**.' (*VCH Hertford*, Vol. 2) This seems to have been **Sir Edward Sr**, because **Edward Jr** had not yet been knighted. It might, of course, have been the Sir Edward who was destined to be killed in Ireland in 1597 or a different Sir Edward Stanley, as yet unidentified. If it was 'our' **Sir Edward Sr**, this provides the mystery as to why he should have acquired this tenement in Hertfordshire. Around the same time he is reporting as owning lands in other parts of the country: 'Of the vast possessions of **Sir Edward Stanley**, Erdeswick writing circa 1596, speaks of him as "now Lord of **Harlaston**", and says of **Cubleston** "**Edward Stanley** is now owner thereof," and of **West Bromwich**, "now **one of the Stanleys** hath the seat of his house there."' These are the only references detected to the potential inheritance of Derby lands back in the settlement of 1562/3, when his brother **Sir Thomas** had been awarded a set of lands, subsequently inherited by Lady Margaret and their son (Sir) **Edward Jr**. If all indeed refer to **Sir Edward Sr**, then they present a lead as to where he might well have spent time during the long periods when otherwise no record of him has remained. At the very least the seat of a Stanley in West Bromwich in the Midlands in the 1590s is very interesting, given the proximity to Meriden, where the Earl of Derby held lands, and the estate in North Warwickshire inherited by John Shakespeare's ancestors. Other near neighbours were the Ardens of Park Hall in Castle Bromwich, long presumed (falsely) to be the immediate family of Mary Arde(r)n(e), John Shakespeare's wife.

Meanwhile, in 1592 **Sir Edward** was mentioned as a recusant and 'a dangerous person'. Again, one can only presume that this was 'our' **Sir Edward**, but if he was 'a dangerous person' he managed to steer clear of any direct confrontation with the authorities. It was still a time of great suspicion and fear that there might be another attempt at Spanish invasion via Ireland and 'whispers that predominantly Catholic Lancashire might be the invasion bridge had raised suspicions about the local magnate, the Earl of Derby'. It was natural that his brother should also come under suspicion.

From now until the end of the 1590s, alas, all that remains of his story comes from events involving his close relatives, all of whose biographies have been told elsewhere. His elder brother Henry, 4th Earl of Derby, after a protracted illness, died on 25 September, 1593 at Lathom. This left

Sir Edward Sr as the sole survivor of the three sons of Earl Edward, and the senior member of the family. In this capacity, one can only presume that he was present on many family occasions and that his advice was sought on many matters.

His nephew Ferdinando became 5th Earl of Derby and was immediately involved in the 'Hesketh Plot', which was an attempt by English Catholics in Exile to put forward Ferdinando as their favourite successor to Queen Elizabeth. We know that **Sir Edward** was present at Lathom from a report: 'On Thursday the 27th (September, 1593) Richard (Hesketh) went over to Lathom to hand in Hickman's letter and show his passport to **Sir Edward Stanley**. Ferdinando, the new earl, also saw his passport, as did the bishop of Chester who happened to be staying there.' Interestingly, there is no mention of William. This letter led to Ferdinando departing to London to 'defend' himself against any prior knowledge of or participation in this 'plot'. **Sir Edward Sr** presumably took over all the reins at Lathom and organised the funeral of his brother, which duly took place in Ormskirk Church on 4 December. The investigation of the 'plot' by the authorities in London led to the execution of Richard Hesketh. It also led to the poisoning of Ferdinando, back at Lathom, resulting in two agonising weeks for him before his death on 16 April, 1594. He left his widow Countess Alice and three young daughters. (This story has been explored in depth – and re-interpreted – most recently by Leo Daugherty, *The Assassination of Shakespeare's Patron: Investigating the Death of the Fifth Earl of Derby*, 2011. He was also the author of the first-ever biography of William Stanley, 6th Earl of Derby, for the *ODNB*, 2004. The full story still awaits clarification on some points.)

Nephew William was in a strange position. As the younger son he had never expected to inherit the earldom. He had spent many of the years since 1582 on three 'grand tours' travelling in Europe and as far as Jerusalem, Constantinople and Moscow, returning to England in between for only short periods. When he finally returned in 1593 he was immediately appointed Governor of the Isle of Man, and was thus absent at his father's death. From the quote above about 'the Hickman letter' we know that it was **Sir Edward** who was now considered as the head of the family after his brother Henry's death, followed by Ferdinando, with William not mentioned. On brother Ferdinando's death, having himself been abroad for so long, it must indeed have been an enormous leap to suddenly take on all the responsibilities of being an earl without any of the normal preparations for this. It was not at all certain that his succession as 6th Earl would be approved by the authorities. One suspects that **Sir Edward** might well have been instrumental in obtaining this approval and, after some doubt, William did indeed become the 6th Earl. He must have been grateful for the presence and experience of uncle **Sir Edward** in coping with all his new responsibilities. These must have been aggravated by the retirement of the long-standing Comptroller of the Household for the last three earls, William Farington.

After surmounting various other problems, he married Elizabeth de Vere in January, 1595 at Greenwich in the presence of Queen Elizabeth, an occasion which is a strong contender for the first performance of *A Midsummer Night's Dream*. At the end of the decade he was writing plays in London. During these early years of his marriage there were not a few problems and disagreements and the only child to appear was a daughter, who died soon after birth. There were also the disagreeable legal battles with Countess Alice, who was fighting to retain as much as possible of her husband's inheritance for her daughters.

Sir Edward Sr presumably felt divided in his loyalties between two of his closest relatives in the younger generation. One suspects, because of his obvious regular presence in the bosom of the family, that he felt a strong commitment to the welfare of all, and it is easy to imagine him trying to play the role of mediator. The scanty evidence that remains indicates that he sided more with his nephew William than his niece-in-law Countess Alice. Both he and William were very concerned about the succession of the earldom of Derby. **Sir Edward Sr** had never married, and therefore had no son. Nephew William had no son – yet. And meanwhile nephew **Edward Jr** and his wife Lucy kept producing daughters, the sixth one in c.1598, but no son. It must have been an extremely worrying time for all. At least one worry had been removed - that of another poisoning in the family because of the line of succession to the throne. In 1596 Countess Alice had achieved one of her aims – to have her eldest daughter Anne officially declared in line of succession, following her father Ferdinando. This news must have been greeted with some relief by nephew William, who was thus placed one step further away from the line of fire.

There is one other area of activity during this period about which **Sir Edward** must have been well informed, although here again the story is murky. This revolves around the activities of Dr John Dee, named 'The Arch Conjuror of England' in the title of his latest biography (Glyn Parry, 2011). In 1596 he was appointed Warden of Manchester College, with his official residence in what is today Chetham's Library, the oldest public library in England (since 1653). The building was owned by William, 6th Earl of Derby and the appointment was largely because of William's intervention. In this post of Warden Dr Dee replaced William Chaderton, Bishop of Chester, who had meanwhile become Bishop of Lincoln. We met him briefly above as present at Lathom with **Sir Edward** when the 'Hickman letter' from Richard Hesketh was delivered. The precise identity of 'Hickman' is unknown, there being three of this name involved in spying at the time. One of these was Bartholomew Hickman, who appears in many entries in Dr John Dee's Diaries, acting in the role of his 'skryer' or medium during his spiritualist activities. Richard Hesketh had also appeared in his diary in 1581. (Daugherty's recent research *op.cit.* goes far in this identification and a new interpretation of events and people involved.) We know from this diary that William and his entourage visited him in Manchester on at least one occasion. One can only presume that **Sir Edward** was with him in his entourage or that, yet again, he was holding the fort back at Lathom.

None of them had any idea at the time that William Stanley, during the following two centuries, would have a ballad written about his travels, which involved him with Dr Dee in Moscow (a muddle of Dr John in Bohemia and his son Dr Arthur later in Moscow). Nor that three hundred years later William would be proposed as an Alternative Authorship Candidate for some of Shakespeare's plays, along with his father-in-law Edward de Vere, 17th Earl of Oxford and his nephew **Edward Jr**'s 'cousin' Roger Manners, 5th Earl of Rutland. Nor did they have any idea that Dr John Dee would be proposed as the prototype for Prospero in *The Tempest*. They might have had an idea that Shakespeare revealed his acquaintance with them in some 'secret' way, such as naming the King of Navarre in *Love's Labour's Lost* Ferdinand, and they must have known that he had given roles to many of their ancestors in his Lancastrian king plays. They might have known that John Shakespeare in 1599 had successfully applied for impalement of his wife Mary's arms – those of the Ardernes of Harden near Stockport, just down the road from Manchester, who claimed kinship with the Stanleys. Although William Shakespeare had not yet written the two verse epitaphs for **Edward Jr**, their 'friendship' or at least acquaintance must have been known about by **Sir Edward**. He must also have known whether or not Shakespeare had written the poem *The Phoenix and the Turtle* on the occasion of the wedding of his niece Ursula and her husband John Salusbury.

In brief, **Sir Edward Sr** must have known all these people - his brothers and nieces and nephews and their in-laws, of course, and also Dr John Dee, Hickman and John and William Shakeshafte/speare. What a pity he left no diary. If he had, it might have nipped in the bud so many later muddles and wild speculations. There were enough of these at the time, but not as many as a few centuries later when trying to disentangle them all.

XXI-7. The end

In 1600 he appeared in a list of lands in reversion to the Earldom, as part of the long drawn-out dispute between Countess Alice, Ferdinando's widow and William, 6th Earl. These were in Thirsk and Kirkby Malzeard in Yorkshire. In 1601 he presumably grieved along with his nephew (Sir) **Edward Jr**, who lost his wife and four daughters when staying at Walthamstow in Essex. In late August 1602 **Sir Edward Sr**, cousin William, 6th Earl and nephew **Edward Jr** were all together again at Preston Guild. One wonders whether he was at King James's coronation in 1603 when nephew **Edward Jr** was knighted. If so, and if at the procession, postponed because of an outbreak of the plague until 15 March of the following year, he would have met William Shakespeare again. Wherever he spent the beginning of 1604, in the summer he was back at Lathom, the house where he was born, had spent so much of his life and which was now presumably where he died. On 4 September, 1604 he was buried in the Derby Chapel in Ormskirk Church. The entry in the Parish Register on this date reads 'S*ere Edward Stanley bur. in my Lords Chapl'. He was united there with many of his close relatives. Depending on when he was born between 1535 and 1540, he had attained 64-69 years of age.

And so ends the very first biography of this minor yet seminal figure - but his story is not yet quite at an end. His death has been reported as in 1609 in several places, although there is no doubt that it was in 1604. The namesake who died in 1609 remains elusive – or this date was a mistranscription somewhere along the line. The false date was first given by Seacome (1741), which is surprising, because living at Knowsley Hall he presumably had access to Ormskirk Parish Records. However, he gave 1609 as his date of death and it has been repeated ever since. Also, the lands he owned still had to be sorted out after his death. As seen, these were in reversion to the Earldom on his death without an immediate heir. No last will and testament has survived, so we have no idea of his dying wishes. But his two nephews survived him by many years, **Sir Edward Jr** until 1632 and William, 6th Earl until 1642, so many memories of **Sir Edward Sr** must have lived on.

Ormskirk church suffered much damage during the Civil War, so there might have been a memorial plaque, which has not survived. Lathom House, where he had spent so much of his life, was razed to the ground after the Civil War. Many of his papers might well have gone up in flames at this time.

In the index for the early Parish Records of Ormskirk appear twenty-three Edward Stanleys. This covers albeit a longer period than **Sir Edward Sr**'s lifetime and includes baptisms, marriages and burials, so some refer to the same person. Most of the family of the Earl of Derby married elsewhere and christened their babies in their own private chapel, so do not appear in the Parish Registers. Of course it will never be known how many of those in the Parish Register were named after **Sir Edward Sr**, or just because it was a family name. The name has lived on in the 11th-19th Earls of Derby, descendants of Sir James Stanley of Cross Hall, Lathom, younger brother of **Sir Edward Sr**'s grandfather Thomas, 2nd Earl of Derby.

One is fortunate to have been able to separate this **Sir Edward Sr** from all his other contemporary namesakes. More details about him might yet emerge.

XXIa. St Mary's Church, Thirsk, Yorkshire

Over 500 years old, having been built on the site of a previous Norman Church. Sir Edward Stanley Sr inherited lands here under reversion to the Earls of Derby, similarly to Sir Edward Jr with Eynsham.

XXIb. Kirkby Malzeard, Yorkshire

Postcard from the 1940s, looking perhaps similar to in 1600, when Sir Edward Sr was named as holding lands here. (www.kirkbymalzeard.com)

Chapter XXII
Other (Sir) Edward Stanleys

XXII-1. Introduction

Given that there were so many Edward Stanleys living at the same time as **Sir Edward Stanley Sr** and **Jr**, and that all have fairly frequently been confused with each other, it seemed appropriate to give an account of at least two, whose story has been well documented, at least at the scene of battle. The best hope of identifying these and all the other Edward Stanleys lies with the research of Brian S. Roberts in his constant pursuance of all Stanley references for his Stanley Family Genealogy site.

It has been mentioned elsewhere why there were so many Edward Stanleys, but it bears repeating here. It goes back partly to Sir Edward Stanley, 1st Lord Monteagle (c.1463-1523/4), victor at Flodden in 1513, younger son of Baron Thomas, 1st Earl of Derby (c.1435-1504), victor at Bosworth in 1485. Another main source for the name was Edward, 3rd Earl of Derby (1509-1572), great-grandson of Thomas, 1st Earl. The absolutely standard practice in naming habits was to call the first son after the paternal grandfather, the second son after the maternal grandfather and the third son after the father. So with any of these fathers named Edward, one could expect an Edward in the next generation and possibly two or three in the generation after that. Thus it is hardly surprising that there were so many with this name during **Sir Edward Jr**'s lifetime (1562-1632), which encompassed Shakespeare's lifetime (1564-1616).

There are several examples of other contemporary families in Lancashire and Cheshire in the entourage of the Stanleys who produced similar endless muddles. One can mention two prime examples, Legh and Gerard. In both of these families they managed to keep the eldest son and heir alive generation after generation, who was therefore given the same name as his father AND paternal grandfather. Sir Piers Leigh of Lyme had nine generations with this name, one after the other; and the Gerards of Bryn managed several Sir Thomases, with even more in the family of their kinsmen Gerard of Ince. This wreaks havoc on occasion in trying to identify which one is under scrutiny. This was the main reason I had to assign a Generation Number to all the nine generations of (Sir) William Stanley of Hooton (see Family Trees in Appendix 12a and 12b).

Perhaps surprisingly, there was no long line of surviving (Sir) Edward Stanleys within any one family. The problem is that there were so many Stanley families at the time of 'our' **Sir Edward Sr** and **Jr**, and all of them had a few Edwards. There was a crop in North Cheshire from the original Stanley line there and another crop around Lathom and elsewhere from the Derby line. To complicate matters there was another crop in Staffordshire from the ur-original line at 'Stanleigh' before migration to Cheshire, with a marriage into a later line, one of whom had returned to Staffordshire on a Stanley-Arderne marriage to found the Stanleys of Elford and Pipe.

As mentioned in the last chapter, in the index for early Ormskirk Parish Registers alone there are 23 Edward Stanleys, albeit covering baptisms, marriages and burials. This list does not include all the baptisms and marriages that took place in private chapels, whose records have not survived.

XXII-2. Edward Stanley at the Great Siege of Malta, 1565

A day-by-day and eye-witness account was written by Francisco Balbi di Correggio, an Italian serving in the Spanish corps of the Knights of St John as an arquebusier during the whole time of the siege. This attack was authorised by Suleiman (Soleyman) the Magnificent, who had conquered and subjugated much of the Middle East and Eastern Europe from his capital in Constantinople. The intended capture of Malta, with its strategic position and superb harbours, was with the aim of securing domination of the central and eastern Mediterranean. To achieve this, however, he needed to defeat the Knights of St John, who had been awarded the Maltese Islands in 1530 by Charles V of Spain, Holy Roman Emperor, as their permanent home base after expulsion from Rhodes. In this attempt he failed, with a staggering number of Suleiman's soldiers killed (an estimated 25,000 out of an estimated 30,000 to 40,000). The Knights of St John put up a valiant defence with only a few hundred knights and an estimated 9,000 supporting troops from the countries still supporting the community; plus the heroic support of virtually the whole of the Maltese population, who cannot be praised enough by any commentators for their unstinting efforts.

Balbi's account was published in Spanish in 1568, which received great recognition in many quarters, but was largely neglected by the English-speaking world. It was finally translated almost complete (with a few lists left out) into English by Ernle Bradford, *The Siege of Malta, 1565; Francisco Balbi di Correggio; translated by Ernle Bradford* (The Folio Society Limited, 1965; Penguin, 2003). This was a follow-up to the same author's *The Great Siege, Malta 1565* (Hodder and Stoughton, 1961), with a second revised edition (Penguin, 1964, with whom it has been in print ever since). These are the two paperback accounts on widest offer in all bookshops on Malta. There have been other publications, of course, in various languages, and Bradford gives quotes and references from many, but these two Penguins together conveniently provide perhaps the most complete and accurate account for English-speaking readers, as a main starting point. Ernle Bradford's interest was that he was in the British Navy during WWII, based in Malta, with no time to pursue its history at the time, but returned and lived there until his death in 1986. Several articles have since appeared (some online), but none revealing any more information on the identity of Edward Stanley.

No attempt is made here to present details of the early months (May 1565 onwards), when the fatal mistake (in retrospect) on the Turkish side was the award of dual responsibility by Sultan Suleiman to two people: Mustapha, Pasha of his army and Piali, admiral of his navy, both subject to the advice of a third, the corsair Dragut. Piali insisted throughout on keeping his ships in the harbour of Marsamusetto, and for their protection this necessitated first the reduction of Fort St Elmo, attacking from the heights of Mount Sciberras (today Floriana). This plan was followed disregarding the opinion of Mustapha and later Dragut that the most common sense strategy was to attack Gozo and take the islands from the north, thus cutting off any contact with or reinforcement from Sicily. The island forces were led by la Vallette, Grand Master of the Knights of St John, whose iron will and strategy throughout proved to be the most important facts that led to the final expulsion of the Ottoman forces and the building and naming of the future capital, Valletta, after him. In the context of this book, the main interest comes in July 1565 with the arrival of the 'piccolo soccorso', the 'small relief' of c.700 soldiers from Sicily. These were knights of St John or their supporters from all over Europe, who had congregated in Naples, then Sicily, with a desire to help the defendants of Malta.

One of these was Edward Stanley (Eduardo Stamle, Bradford, 1964, p. 151; Eduardo Stample, *ibid*, index). I first hoped to identify him as **Sir Edward Stanley Sr** but soon abandoned this notion completely. For a while it was tempting, because an intensive study of the Stanley family based on the Earls of Derby in Lancashire produced no other obvious contemporary Edward Stanley who was as well qualified as 'our' **Sir Edward**, who was:

a) unmarried;

b) a soldier in Ireland in 1560;

c) with no obvious record in England at this period;

d) held in high standing as substitute 'head of the family' by the family of the Earls of Derby during their own later troubles; and

e) perhaps the inspiration for his young nephew William Stanley to set off later on his travels, which included France, Spain, Italy, the Holy Land and Turkey, if not Malta.

However, it was definitely not him. If it had been, one might reasonably expect at least a whiff of a mention in Lancashire - there was none. Also, he had already been knighted in 1560, five years before the Siege of Malta. We will just have to keep on hunting for this Edward Stanley.

Any English reader might be initially surprised that so few Englishmen were involved in the Great Siege of Malta: three or four to be precise. At the outbreak of war in May 1565 there was only one in Malta: Sir Oliver Starkey, Latin Secretary and close confidant of Grand Master la Vallette. (He appears several times in Bradford's books.) Little to nothing is known of his early life, but Starkey was/is very much a common name in North West England and all records indicate that he was from Cheshire. As the Stanleys had many lands and several branches of the family in Cheshire in the sixteenth century, there is therefore a strong possibility that Starkey was known personally to some Stanleys. Bradford gives an interesting list of those present in Malta at the beginning of the Great Siege, which highlights the paucity of the presence from England. The main reason for this was that Henry VIII had just one generation earlier (in the 1530s) severed relations with the Pope, therefore at the same time with the Knights of St John and the Holy Roman Empire, and had dissolved the Monasteries in England. The story of Henry VIII's three children who subsequently ascended the throne of England (Eward VI, Mary I and Elizabeth I) is too well known to require repetition, but the consequences of these for some of the main protagonists in this book still demand further investigation. One area of enquiry must be to investigate further the wars in Europe in the sixteenth century, and what role **Sir Edward Sr** might have played; and if not him, then the various other contemporary Edward Stanleys.

541 Knights and servants-at-arms who were present in Malta in the spring of 1565 were divided among the various Langues [geographical sections] as follows:

	Knights	Servants-at-arms
Provence	61	15
Auvergne	25	14
France	57	24
Italy	164	5
England	1	-
Germany	13	1
Castile	68	6
Aragon	85	1

(Bradford, *The Great Siege, Malta 1565*, Penguin, 1964, p. 233.)

At the beginning of July Sir Oliver was joined by two other Englishmen in the 'piccolo soccorso', a relief force of 700 men sent by Don Garcia de Toledo from Sicily. They were under orders not to land if the Fort of St Elmo had been taken. It had already fallen, in fact, but the man sent ashore to obtain the news concealed the information and the force was landed nevertheless.

The post of England, which up to then had been held by Sir Oliver Starkey's mixed corps of foreign soldiers, had received two English volunteers in the relief force led by the Chevalier de Robles. Balbi records their names - Juan Smilt (John Smith?) and Eduardo Stamle (Edward Stanley). These two soldiers of fortune were probably Catholic exiles, a number of whom had taken up residence in Rome rather than return to the England of Queen Elizabeth.

(Bradford, *The Great Siege*, p. 151.)

XXIIa. The Great Siege of Malta, 1565
27 May, 1565. In fort St Elmo were two English soldiers, one of them Edward Stanley,
as yet unidentified. (Bradford, *Siege of Malta*)

This was a good surmise by Bradford, but he did not pursue them. Whether the identity of John Smith (?) and Edward Stanley, who arrived in Malta in early July, 1565, will ever be established beyond all doubt, remains to be seen. The most famous soldier and adventurer in the sixteenth century with the name was Captain John Smith, of Pocahontas fame, who mapped much of New England, but as he was not born until 1580, it cannot have been him. There might well have been a few dozen or hundred John Smiths living in 1565, but as soldiers of fortune often tended to run in families, the John Smith on Malta MIGHT have been related in some way to the later Captain.

Edward Stanley should be easy to account for in the family that achieved dominance mainly in Lancashire and Cheshire, not least for military prowess, with their regular support of and by the Tudors throughout all the religious vicissitudes. So far, however, he has remained elusive. Whichever Edward Stanley it was, he arrived under the command of French Chevalier Marshall de Robles, who was initially attached to the anachronistically named 'English' force defending St Michael's Fort at the southern inland end of Senglea peninsula and later withdrew for the final stand at Fort St Angelo, at the northern seaward end of the peninsula containing the fortified fishing village Birgu, subsequently rebuilt and renamed Vittoriosa, after the victorious outcome of the siege.

Back to Edward Stanley and Chevalier de Robles: the presence of the latter at various scenes of fighting was largely identified by Balbi, but there is no further mention of Stanley. Grand Master La Vallette, Sir Oliver Starkey, Chevalier de Robles and many others almost miraculously survived at

Fort St Angelo. At long last Don Garcia sent a large relieving force in September from Sicily, and the remaining Ottoman forces, meanwhile decimated, retreated back to Constantinople.

Another English knight recorded is not mentioned by name by Balbi and appears only at the very end of the siege, in a report written from eye-witness accounts by others.

> When Mustapha Pasha saw that his vanguard was fleeing in disorder before a handful of men, he detailed a good number of arquebusiers from his squadron to cover the Turkish retreat. They were fresh and untried, and did their job well, forcing our exhausted men to retreat to a height near St Paul's Bay. Two or three of our men were killed by the enemy, and many more would have been but for the fact that on this high ground stood Captain Marcos de Toledo and an English knight, as well as others armed with swords and shields.
>
> (Bradford, *Balbi*, p. 185.)

Who was this English knight, one wonders? Sir Oliver Starkey? Only three Englishmen are mentioned in a report on Elizabeth's reaction, in which Bradford assumes they were indeed the three mentioned earlier.

> The heroic defence had aroused the admiration of all Europe. Even that great Protestant Queen, Elizabeth I of England, whose country was only represented by Sir Oliver Starkey and those two gentlemen adventurers 'Mr John Evan Smith and Mr Edward Stanley', was moved by this siege. It recalled the great days of medieval chivalry. Queen Elizabeth was too astute a ruler not to be aware of what might happen if this island were conquered. '. . . If the Turks,' she wrote, 'should prevail against the Isle of Malta, it is uncertain what further peril might follow to the rest of Christendom.'
>
> (Bradford, *The Great Siege*, p. 190.)

On this note we leave 'gentleman adventurer' Edward Stanley in Malta and proceed to the Spanish Netherlands over twenty years later, with another heroic Edward Stanley.

XXII-3. (Sir) Edward Stanley at the storming of Zutphen, 1586

XXIIb. Plan of Zutphen in the 16th century

Assault on Zutphen, by
Robert Dudley, Earl of Leicester

6 October 1586

I thank God he hath given us this day a very happy success of the two principal forts here. We have taken one by a gallant and a thorough-fought assault, and for a quarter of an hour we did look for a very furious resistance, yet so it pleased God to daunt heir hearts, and to animate those worthy soldiers who attempt it, as it was entered, and the enemy, as many as did abide, killed, the rest fled to the other fort.

There was one gentleman whom we all present did behold, that had the leading of all the rest that went to the assault, which was Mr Edward Stanley, Lieutenant to Sir William Stanley.* Since I was born I did never see any man to behave himself as he did. First climb the breach, a pike-length before and above any person that followed him, so did he alone maintain the fight, first with his pike, and afterward his sword, against at the least nine or ten, and every man either brake his pike upon his breast, or hit him with the shot of their musket, yet would he not back a foot, but kept himself in this sort without any one man to get up to him; we all gave him for lost if he had a hundred lives.

When he had long thus dealt most valiently and worthily, and none of his company easily could come to him, at length they all came so fast together as one bare up another even to the op of the breach, where that gentleman got a halberd and leapt among the enemies, and then the rest with him, in so resolute manner as they speedily despatched the enemy, and in the sight of all the town both placed their ensigns and made this fight…. This gentleman shall I never forget if I live a hundred year, for so worthily he did by God's goodness, as was the chief cause of all the honour of this day, and he shall have part of my living for it as long as he lives.

(Assault on Zutphen; Camden Society, XXVII:427.)

(www.hillsdale.edu/Personal/Stewart/war/16e/1586-Zutphen.htm)

* Leicester refers to him unequivocally as 'Mr Edward Stanley', with the implication that he was not yet knighted (borne out by his being knighted by Leicester immediately afterwards) and thus eliminating **Sir Edward Stanley Sr** as a candidate. Leicester also refers to him as 'Lieutenant to Sir William Stanley', and not as brother to this Sir William (who may or may not have had a brother Edward – another area of muddles). For this feat Edward was knighted by Leicester, which produced a third contemporary knight named Sir Edward Stanley. The Sir William Stanley mentioned was the one from Hooton (son of Sir Rowland, who was knighted in 1553 with **Sir Thomas**), at school in Lathom with 'our' **Sir Edward Stanley Sr**, with Dr Henry Standish as their teacher. Sir William was a hero of the Irish campaigns, who had also fought at Zutphen the previous year but, for personal and religious reasons, surrendered Deventer and defected to the Spanish in January 1587. (*ODNB*)

The identification of this Sir Edward Stanley is perhaps/probably the one given on the 1580 *Visitation of Cheshire* as 'Sir Edward Stanley, knighted in Netherland, slain in Ireland 1597'. The

XXIIc. Part of the walls of Zutphen today

The town walls were stormed in 1586 with Edward Stanley in the vanguard, knighted by the Earl of Leicester, who wrote an eye-witness account. He was perhaps the Sir Edward Stanley from Elford, Staffordshire killed in Ireland in 1597 (according to the nineteenth-century editor of the *Cheshire Visitation* Stanley Pedigree, 1580).

1597 date must, however, have come from a different and later source than the Visitation of 1580, and been added by the compiler in the nineteenth century, so may not be accurate. He appears in one branch of the Cheshire Stanleys, the ancestor of whom had moved to Staffordshire to become the Stanleys of Elford and Pipe.

XXIId. Robert Dudley,
1st Earl of Leicester, c.1564

He knighted Sir Edward Stanley at Zutphen. In the background can be seen the arms of Knights of the Garter. Leicester was created KG in 1559 at the same time as two of Sir Thomas Stanley's relatives: Thomas Howard, 4th Duke of Norfolk, his mother Dorothy Howard's 'cousin', and Henry Manners, 2nd Earl of Rutland, the brother of his brother-in-law John Manners of Haddon Hall.

XXII-4. More (Sir) Edward Stanleys

Another Edward Stanley has a published embryo biography, as follows. Unfortunately, in the book given below, no source references are given, so we must take these details on trust until or unless there is any reason to doubt them.

> Sir Rowland Stanley (1518-1613) succeeded in 1547. [*As Lord of the Manor of Hooton.*] He was knighted in 1553[i] and made Sheriff of Chester in 1575, and a Justice of the Peace. In 1579 he was Special Commissioner for Musters . . . a staunch Catholic . . . he opened his private chapel to all Catholics in the surrounding district as a place of worship. His home, Hooton Hall, became a refuge for all the hunted priests of Lancashire, Cheshire and North Wales. . . Sir Rowland had three sons:
>
> 1   William (1548-1630)
>
> 2   John liv. in 1575 and 1591.
>
> 3   Edward (1564-1639).[ii] Born in Staffordshire.[iii] He served with distinction in the Spanish Army for 23 years, under his brother Sir William Stanley. He entered the English College in Rome on 19 March 1609, under the name of Francis Bretherton, and was ordained a priest in 1611 . . . He left Rome the following Lent on route for England where he served as a mission priest for seven years. He entered the Society of Jesus in 1620 . . . In 1632 he was Minister at Ghent, and again in 1636 at Watton, where he died on 9 January 1639, aged seventy-five years. He was described as a man of great virtue and prudence.

> (Peter Stanley, *The House of Stanley from the 12th century* (Pentland Press, 1998), pp. 71-2.
> Pedigree Chart, Stanleys of Hooton, pp. 88-91.)
> (Reference to Harleian MS 6063, Brian S. Roberts.)

Notes by HM:

[i] Sir Rowland was one of three Stanleys knighted on the day after Queen Mary's coronation in 1553, all becoming Knights Bachelor. The other two were 'our' **Sir Thomas** of Lathom and Sir George Stanley of Cross Hall, Lathom.

[ii] This Edward Stanley was an exact contemporary of (**Sir**) **Edward Jr** (1562-1632).

[iii] Staffordshire was the original home of the Stanleys before one of them migrated to Cheshire and founded the Hooton branch. One part of the original family still stayed on in Staffordshire, later reinforced by a Stanley-Arderne marriage to become the Stanleys of Elford and Pipe. One of its most prominent members at the time of Bosworth was Sir Humphrey Stanley. Whether the Edward Stanley above in the biography by Peter Stanley really was a son of Sir Rowland of Hooton, or from the Staffordshire branch, with therefore two separate Edwards involved, must remain queried until or unless further evidence emerges. Brian S. Roberts and I strongly suspect that these were two separate Edward Stanleys.

Then there was another (Sir) Edward Stanley in Portugal, who apparently died in 1590. Another one died in 1609, an erroneous date of death often given for 'our' **Sir Edward Sr**, who we now know was buried at Ormskirk in 1604. Perhaps there were even more, who might be distinguished from each other and all (Sir) Edwards above satisfactorily some day?

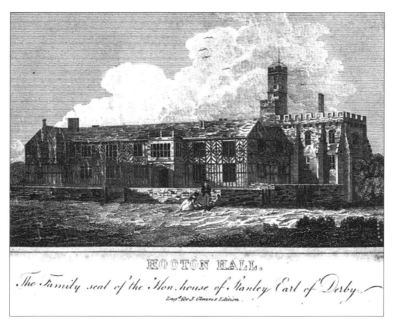

XXIIe. Hooton Hall in the Wirral, Cheshire

Home of the Senior Stanley branch from the early fourteenth century, including Sir Rowland and Sir William Stanley at Zutphen and Deventer. The later Tudor version survived until 1788, replaced in c.1800 by a larger hall, demolished in 1932. The site is covered today by a Vauxhall Motors Plant.

Chapter XXIII
Immediate ancestors and close relatives of
Sir Thomas & Sir Edward

XXIII-1. Introduction
XXIII-2. Stanley ancestors and close relatives
XXIII-3. Manners and Vernon close relatives
XXIII-4. Percy close relatives
XXIII-5. A few more interesting contemporaries
XXIII-6. Conclusion

XXIII-1. Introduction

The following Stanley details are an amalgamation of those given by the three main historians and authors on the history of the 1st-7th Earls of Derby of the fifteenth-seventeenth centuries: Seacome (1741), Coward (1983) and Bagley (1985). They all agree on the main details, but some give additional members of the family and sort out a few more details. There have been many other authors, but on the whole, those in the nineteenth century just repeated details from Seacome, with a few newly discovered facts from archives, without incorporating them fully into the known details; or they were too concerned with the local picture. The latest authoritative book is by Peter Stanley, *The House of Stanley* (1998), which gives the latest version down to Ferdinando's children in a Pedigree Chart (pp. 167-8), with precise years of birth and marriage in many cases. These are taken on trust, as he gives no references, but are accepted when they are very close to previous estimates.

Tudorplace online also gives several dates, often with no reference. Although valuable as a large survey in general, in the case of the Stanleys there are several mistakes and many omissions, but also a few valuable details correcting dates from other accounts. *Wikipedia* gives brief biographies of all Earls mentioned below, and some of their offspring. On the whole the details there come from the latest generally accepted scholarly biographies of the earls in the *New/Oxford Dictionary of National Biography* and thus provide the same reliability.

Where no dates are given below, these do not appear in the main Stanley literature and have not yet been researched. I fully realize that many details here are repetitious. The sole aim is that this chapter should stand on its own, with the most important close relatives grouped together. The Family Trees in Appendix 12 should serve as helpful in seeing the relationships in a diagrammatic form. All dates have been checked by Brian S. Roberts, a Stanley family researcher.

XXIII-2. Stanley ancestors and close relatives

Sir Thomas's paternal grandparents were Thomas, 2nd Earl of Derby (1485-1521) and (married 1506) Ann, daughter of Edward, Baron Hungerford, Lord Hastings, sister of George Hastings, 1st Earl of Huntingdon (seventh creation) (1488-1544). They had four children:

1. George, died young of 'sweating sickness'
2. Edward (1509-72), Lord Strange, later Knight of the Garter, 3rd Earl of Derby.
3. Henry (d. 1528). Died of 'sweating sickness'. Buried at Hillingdon, Middx.
4. Margaret, married Robert Ratcliffe/Radcliffe, 1st Earl of Sussex (c.1483-1542).

Sir Thomas's father was Edward Stanley, 3rd Earl of Derby (1509-1572), details of whose stately funeral were given in Chapter XIV. He held many offices under Henry VIII, Edward VI, Mary and Elizabeth. He was married to:

1   Katherine Howard, daughter of Thomas Howard, 3rd Duke of Norfolk (1473-1554), the son of the victor at Flodden in 1513, together with Sir Edward Stanley, 1st Lord Monteagle. The marriage was in late 1529 and Katherine died in March 1530 of the plague *osp*. (Bagley, 1985, was the first in Lancashire to discover details of this marriage and her early death, reporting on a recent finding by American Dr Edward Zedin. See Chapter XI. Main Derby historians.)

2   Dorothy Howard (marriage late 1530 – another report gives 21 February 1530, which would bring forward the death of first wife Katherine or make this date of marriage wrong). Dorothy was the young aunt of first wife Katherine Howard, because the daughter of the 2nd Duke of Norfolk (1443-1524), the victor at Flodden, by his second wife, Agnes (Tilney). Dorothy was mother of the following children, all therefore brothers and sisters of **Sir Thomas** and uncles and aunts of **Sir Edward Jr**. It is not known when all the daughters were born in relation to the sons, but Peter Stanley (1998) gives the following order, with dates of marriage for the daughters and dates of death for some husbands, but no references. Many dates of the daughters still remain elusive.

   1   Anne (1531*-1602), married (1) 10 Feb. 1549, Derbyshire, Charles, Lord Stourton, 8th Baron Stourton of Stourton (c.1520-57); (2) 1567, Sir John Arundel of Lamborn (Leaherne/ Lanherne), Cornwall (d. 1591).
        * It seems unlikely, although not totally impossible, that she was born in the same year as brother Henry; Tudorplace gives born c.1542, which is impossible because of her marriage date; died 22 Sep. 1602, buried St Colomb Major, Cornwall (*The Complete Peerage* vol. IV, p. 210, note e)...

   2   Henry (1531, bap. 4 Oct. 1531-93, d. 25 Sep., bur. 4 Dec.), Lord Strange, later 4th Earl of Derby. Buried Ormskirk...

   3   Dorothy (1533-57), unmarried.

   4   (Later **Sir**) **Thomas of Winwick** (c.1534-1576, ~~12~~ 21 December). Buried Tong...

   5   Elizabeth (d. 1590), married Henry Parker, Lord Morley, 2nd Baron Morley.
        I BELIEVE THAT THIS IS WRONG. The Family Tree in Appendix 12b shows that the relevant (Edward) Parker was actually 12th Baron Morley, who married Elizabeth, daughter of William Stanley, 3rd Lord Monteagle. If I am correct, Elizabeth does not belong in this list, unless two different Elizabeth Stanleys married two different Lord Morleys.
        [It is worth including the comment from Brian S. Roberts, when asked about this problem, as an example of the difficulties in ascertaining the historical truth. Many errors crept in by well-meaning nineteenth-century editors of sixteenth-century manuscripts.
        "Visitation of the County Palatine of Lancaster, made in the year 1567 by William Flower, Esq., Norroy king of arms. Published by the Chetham Society, 1870, Volume 81, page 78. The Earls of Derby pedigree shows – Elizabeth married Lord Morley – no first name or surname given. This volume contains errors and omissions. *House of Stanley* has the following – Elizabeth Stanley daughter of William Stanley (3rd Lord Monteagle) married Edward Parker, son and heir of Henry, Lord Morley (by Elizabeth daughter of Edward Stanley, 3rd Earl of Derby). Now I need to find a pedigree for the Parkers for validation." So be it – for the moment. HM]

   6   Mary, married 1566, 23 Nov. Edward Stafford, 3rd Baron Stafford (1535-1603).

   7   (Later **Sir**) **Edward** (1535/40-1604). Peter Stanley in *House of Stanley* gives his dates as 1535-90, 'of Eynsham co. Oxford, died unmarried in Portugal', which is clearly a confusion among **Sir Edward Sr**, his nephew **Sir Edward Jr** (of Eynsham) and some other Edward Stanley, of Hooton or elsewhere (who died in Portugal, one might presume as a Catholic priest or at least a Catholic exile). This is, of course, **Sir Edward Sr**, who was buried at Ormskirk in 1604. His birth was established in Chapter XXI. Sir Edward Stanley Sr's first-ever biography, as between 1535 and 1540.

   8   Jane (1540-69), married 1566 [1566/7], Edward Sutton, 8th [*sic*, 4th] Lord Dudley (1525-86) as his second wife.

9   Margaret (Coward gives no dates or further details. She is almost certainly Margaret, daughter of
     Earl Edward's third wife, as below).
     N.B. Isabel (1533-90) is missing from the list above. She married James Stanley. Or she does not
     belong here at all as a daughter of Earl Edward. This Isabel Stanley and her husband still await
     identification and correct placement.

Edward, 3rd Earl, married

3   Margaret, daughter of Ellis Barlow of Barlow, Lancs., by whom he had the following issue
     (half-brother and sisters of **Sir Thomas** of Tong):

10   George, died young.

11   Margaret (died 1585), married (1) John Jermin/Jermyn of Rushbrook, Suffolk, (2) Sir Nicholas
     Poyntz/Ponitz/Pointz/Poyntey (c.1537-85).

12   Catherine married Sir John Knivet [P. Stanley and Tudorplace give Sir Thomas Knyvett], 4 March
     (?November) 1565, marriage settlement.

Edward, 3rd Earl, married

4   1559, Mary, daughter of Sir George Cotton of Combermere Abbey, Cheshire. She died in 1580
     after marrying 2) Henry Grey, 6th Earl of Kent. Edward, 3rd Earl and Mary had no issue.

Henry, 4th Earl of Derby (1531-93) married 7 February, 1555 at Whitehall Palace Margaret (died
1596), daughter and heiress of Henry Clifford, 2nd Earl of Cumberland, by whom he had the
following issue (first cousins of **Sir Edward Jr**):

1   Ferdinando (1558/9-1594) Lord Strange, later 5th Earl of Derby, married c.1579 Alice Spencer,
     youngest daughter of Sir John Spencer of Althorp, Northamptonshire (1559-1637). More about
     Ferdinando and Alice in the next chapter.

2   William (1561-1642), later 6th Earl of Derby, married 26 January 1595 at Greenwich, Elizabeth,
     daughter of Edward de Vere, 17th Earl of Oxford. More about William and Elizabeth in the next
     chapter.

3   Edward, died before 1582. He might well have been the first son, named after his grandfather, born a
     year or two after the marriage in 1555.

4   Francis, died 1583, buried at Ormskirk, 16 September, 1583. Birthdate unknown, but presumed after
     William in 1561.

5   Anne, died young. No dates or details known beyond her name. She might well have been born
     between the marriage in 1555 and Ferdinando's birth in 1588/9.

Earl Henry separated from, but never divorced his wife Margaret née Clifford; he had a mistress,
Jane Halsall of Knowsley, whose children were illegitimate but all fully acknowledged and known
variously as Halsall, Stanley or Halsall/Stanley (also first cousins of **Sir Edward Jr**). He installed
them in Hawarden Castle, Flintshire. [Remembered today as the country home of Prime Minister
William Ewart Gladstone, where he died in 1898.]

6   Thomas Stanley of Eccleston, Lancashire.

7   Henry Stanley of Broughton, Lancashire. He, or another Henry Stanley, was a frequent visitor at
     Lathom 1587-90 in the *Derby Household Books*.

8   Dorothy Stanley, married Sir Cuthbert Halsall of Halsall, Lancashire, a relative of Jane. More in next
     chapter.

9   Ursula Stanley, married 1586 Sir John Salusbury of Sterney, Derbs. & Lleweni, Denbigh. More in
     next chapter.

~~~~~~~~~~~~~~~~~~~~~~~~~~~~

XXIII-3. Manners and Vernon close relatives

Sir Thomas Stanley married (1558) Margaret VERNON, daughter of Sir George VERNON of Haddon and Tong, which brought all her relatives into the family. Some of these were given in *Auden's History*, including **Sir Thomas**'s sister-in-law Dorothy, married to John MANNERS, second son of the 1st Earl of Rutland. His family appears in Chapter XXVI. The Earls of Rutland. The VERNON family included Elizabeth VERNON, one of the candidates for Shakespeare's Dark Lady in the Sonnets. Grace MANNERS, daughter of Dorothy and John, married a FORTESCUE, which brings all of this name into **Sir Edward**'s family, most importantly when Grace took widower **Sir Edward Jr**'s three infant daughters into her household in 1601. He was also related not too distantly to the DEVEREUX, SIDNEY and CECIL families.

XXIII-4. Percy close relatives

Edward Jr (born mid-late 1562) married (early 1580s) Lucy Percy, second daughter of Thomas, 7th Earl of Northumberland. Thomas Percy had married (1558) Lady Anne Somerset, daughter of Henry Somerset, 2nd Earl of Worcester and either his first wife Margaret Courtenay or second wife Elizabeth Browne. All details following on the Percy family come from entries in the *Catholic Encyclopedia* (online), *DNB*, and Tudorplace, with no further research undertaken. These details are thus taken on trust, but with a certain amount of confidence about the Earls of Northumberland of this period, who have been the subject of much research, not least because of their alarming habit of being involved in activities that sent them to the Tower of London, often to be executed or otherwise die there. [*Relevant corrections/additions are, as usual, in brackets and italics.* HM]

The issue of Thomas Percy, 7th Earl and Anne Somerset was as follows. These were, of course, Lucy's sisters and brothers-in-law and their stories therefore presumably well known to **Sir Edward Jr** of Tong:

1 Thomas Percy (d. 1560).

2 Elizabeth Percy, married Richard Woodroffe of Wolley.

3 Joan Percy, married Henry Seymour. He was a younger son of Edward Seymour, 1st Duke of Somerset and his wife Anne Stanhope.

4 Lucy Percy, married **Sir Edward Stanley**. He was a younger son [*sic, actually son of a younger son*] of Edward Stanley, 3rd Earl of Derby and Dorothy Howard. Dorothy was a daughter of Thomas Howard, 2nd Duke of Norfolk and his second wife Agnes Tilney. [*We know from the MI at Tong that Lucy was the second daughter, so the order of Elizabeth, Joan, Lucy must have been different.* HM]

5 Mary Percy (11 June 1570-1643). A nun. Founder of the Benedictine Dames in Brussels.

Thomas Percy, Lucy's father, fits into his family as the 7th Earl, as follows (from standard sources given above):

5th Earl   Henry Percy (1477-1527) had 5 children, including Henry 6th Earl and Sir Thomas, executed in 1537 after the Pilgrimage of Grace. Sir Thomas was father of Thomas 7th and Henry 8th Earl. [*Sir Thomas was Lucy's grandfather, although she never knew him.* HM]

6th Earl   Henry Percy (1502-37), son of Henry 5th Earl. Anne Boleyn's lover before King Henry VIII. He had no issue, so was succeeded by his nephew Thomas. [*This Henry was Lucy's great-uncle; she never knew him.* HM]

7th Earl   Thomas Percy (1528-72) [*Lucy's father*], heir of his uncle when a young boy, and granted the title of Earl of Northumberland in 1557. Executed for his role in the Northern Uprising of 1569-70. He left no sons, so his brother Henry succeeded to the title.

8th Earl   Henry Percy (1532-85), brother of Thomas 7th Earl. [*This Henry was Lucy's uncle, into whose care she and her two sisters were entrusted when their mother went into exile.* HM] Although a Protestant and fought against his brother and the northern rebels, he too ended up dying in the Tower on 21 June 1585 under suspicious circumstances. The idea of suicide was propagated at the time, but it was widely suspected that it was possibly murder. His son Henry succeeded him as 9th Earl.

9th Earl   Henry Percy (1564-1632), son of Henry 8th Earl; known as 'The Wizard Earl' because of his interest in scientific experiments and his library. [*This Henry was Lucy's first cousin and her contemporary. She grew up with him at Petworth, Sussex.* HM] A younger brother was Sir Charles Percy, who commissioned a performance of Shakespeare's *Richard II* at the Globe on the eve of the Essex insurrection in 1601. For this both he and Essex were sent to the Tower and subsequently lost their heads. [*Sir Charles was therefore also a first cousin of Lucy, but she died before he lost his head and before Henry 'The Wizard Earl' was sent to the Tower in due course because attainted as a result of his kinsman Thomas Percy's complicity in the Gunpowder Plot.* HM]

Lucy Percy (born in the early-mid 1560s) must have grown up and spent her childhood and early adulthood with a rather distressing view of what happened to so many of her close male relatives – to say the least. Her paternal grandfather Sir Thomas Percy had been executed in 1537 for his participation in the Catholic Pilgrimage of Grace: her father Thomas the 7th Earl was executed in 1572 for his participation in the Catholic Northern Uprising, when she was still a young girl; her father-in-law **Sir Thomas Stanley** (whom she probably never knew, but might well have known of as a girl) had spent several years in the Tower of London because of his Catholic plan to free Mary, Queen of Scots, was tortured and died in 1576 within a few years after his release; and her uncle Henry the 8th Earl, her 'guardian', died in the Tower under suspicious circumstances not too long after her marriage in c.1580. Ten years earlier he too had been in the Tower at the same time as **Sir Thomas**, also suspected of being involved in plans to free Mary, Queen of Scots. Through great pleading and promises of future loyalty, Queen Elizabeth agreed to his release on a payment of 5000 marks. It was this fine, and the release after a fine of fellow-conspirator from Lancashire Sir Thomas Gerard of Bryn, which makes it highly likely that **Sir Thomas**, too, had been released only on the payment of a large fine. In turn it is logical that this fine was one cause of his financial difficulties during the final years of his life. It is easy to speculate that the presence in the Tower at the same time and for the same reason of **Sir Thomas Stanley** and Henry Percy, 8th Earl of Northumberland, and the later marriage of **Sir Thomas**'s son **(Sir) Edward** and Henry Percy's niece Lucy, was not unrelated. Indeed, it is easy to suspect that this future marriage might well have been first mooted in the Tower.

The member of the Percy family that both Lucy and her husband **Edward Stanley** would have known best was, therefore, her cousin Henry, 'The Wizard Earl'; also his brothers, including Sir Charles Percy. She grew up with them at Petworth House, West Sussex, placed there when her Catholic mother went into exile. This Earl Henry of Northumberland would have provided an introduction for Lucy and her husband to an interesting group of people, which in turn suggests endless potential occasions in the 1590s when **Edward Jr** might have met Shakespeare. Later exploits of her cousins 9th Earl Henry and Sir Charles Percy occurred during the Essex insurrection in 1601 and after the Gunpowder Plot in 1605, by which time Lucy was dead and buried. Her husband **Edward**, however, lived on until 1632 and must have been very much aware of all events concerning his Percy in-laws.

Henry, 'The Wizard Earl'

Although his title was from the north of England, Percy's estates were in the south at Petworth House and at Syon House, a few miles north of Richmond-upon-Thames, acquired by his marriage to Dorothy Devereux (sister of Robert Devereux, 2nd Earl of Essex) in 1594. . . The marriage was not successful, and the couple separated after a time.

The Percy family was still largely Catholic, while Henry was at least nominally Protestant. When it became clear that the Protestant James VI of Scotland was likely to succeed Elizabeth,

Henry sent Thomas Percy, a recent Catholic convert, on a secret mission to James's court three times in 1602. He said that English Catholics would accept James as king if he reduced the persecution of Catholics. Henry employed Thomas Percy [*a young kinsman*] as a rent-collector at Syon House. . . Thomas Percy went on to become one of the five [*sic, there were actually more*] conspirators in the Gunpowder Plot of 1605. When the plot was discovered Thomas Percy fled and was besieged at Holbeache House in Warwickshire. On November 8, 1605, a marksman shot dead both Robert Catesby and Thomas Percy with a single bullet. As a result, the Earl of Northumberland was suspected of being part of the plot and spent the next 16 years as a prisoner in the Tower of London.

Henry Percy met friends while in the Tower; these included Thomas Harriot and Sir Walter Raleigh. They discussed advanced scientific ideas and smoked tobacco. Harriot had been a navigational tutor to Sir Walter Raleigh and his captains. From 1598 (or possibly from 1607) Harriot lived in Syon House, Henry's estate near Richmond. There he used a telescope to make a map of the moon several months before Galileo did the same. He may have been the first person to observe sunspots.

The School of Night

In William Shakespeare's "Love's Labour's Lost" (1594), there is a mention of the "School of Night". It is now usually accepted that this refers to a circle of scientific investigators which met at Syon House. Thomas Harriot and Christopher Marlowe were members. Because of his interest in scientific experiments and his library, Henry acquired the nickname "The Wizard Earl". The astrologer John Dee was also a friend of Henry. There is no evidence that William Shakespeare was involved, but it is possible he was.

(*Wikipedia*, 'Henry Percy, 9th Earl of Northumberland', downloaded 2010, additions from *ODNB* and other reliable Tudor sources by HM.)

It will be interesting to see if any mention of **Sir Edward Stanley Sr** or **Jr** crops up in the large body of historiographical literature about 'The School of Night' (although none has so far been detected). The name of their nephew/cousin Ferdinando certainly does (see the section on him in the next chapter). And *Love's Labour's Lost* is the strongest contestant in the Shakespeare Folio for his brother William Stanley, the playwright, to have had some contact with Shakespeare. It was set at the court in Navarre, which (it is presumed) William visited on his tour of France and Spain in the early 1580s. The 'Academy' set up by Henri, King of Navarre, where he required the pledge of his courtiers to forsake contact with young women for three years for the sake of learning, has been considered as a model for the 'School of Night'. Intriguingly, Shakespeare did not call the King in *Love's Labour's Lost* Henry – but Ferdinand, the name of **(Sir) Edward**'s first cousin.

XXIII-5. A few more interesting contemporaries

The mention in the quotation above of 'Thomas Harriot' and 'the astrologer John Dee' opens up vast fields of enquiry and research, which seemed worth a few paragraphs here, not least because they must have been known to **Sir Edward Jr**. They were both rather colourful and controversial characters – at the time and ever since. Thomas Har(r)iot (1560-1621) was known (to me) many years ago as the writer of a dictionary of Algonquin, the language of the local American Indians that he had lived with on his visit to Virginia. My main interest when I first read about this was when researching Captain Myles Standish (of Lancashire), on the Mayflower in 1620, whose colony in Plymouth, Massachusetts succeeded in establishing itself. My main query was how much Standish and his companions knew about Native American languages before they set sail from Plymouth, Devon. The answer turned out to be 'not much, if anything at all', but as they went off their intended course over the Atlantic and landed in Massachusetts instead of Virginia, Hariot's dictionary would probably not have been of too much use anyway. This was apart from the fact that they almost immediately met a friendly local Native American who spoke English! This is in no way a denigration of the exploits of the Pilgrim Fathers, as they have since come to be known. Returning to England, Hariot went on to later scientific pursuits at Syon House, his astronomical discoveries overshadowed by Galileo. There is a large amount online about Hariot, whose reputation seems to have gradually risen during the last century.

Dr John Dee (1527-1608) had entered the Stanley story on several occasions. By tradition, via a ballad still being sung in the nineteenth century, William Stanley, 6th Earl of Derby, had met him in Russia. It turned out that Dr John never went to Russia (although he travelled widely and at length in Poland and Bohemia) and it was his son Dr Arthur Dee (1579-1651), born in Manchester, who was personal physician to the Tsar, whose undying gratitude he received when he succeeded in healing his foot. By this time William Stanley had been long back in England, 6th Earl of Derby since 1594, where he certainly met Dr John Dee when the latter was appointed, 1595-1605, as Warden of Manchester College. This was owned by William because his grandfather Edward, 3rd Earl, had bought it after the Dissolution of the Monasteries. (Dee's diary provides 19 August, 1597 as the date of one visit to him in Manchester by William, 6th Earl, his wife and entourage.)

I intimated in my Introduction above that, as soon as possible, I intend to publish a monograph, *The Travels of William Stanley, 6th Earl of Derby*. I came to certain conclusions quite some time ago, on the basis of documentary evidence in the sixteenth and seventeenth centuries and the juxtaposition of recorded dates. The main conclusion was that there were almost certainly kernels of truth in all the wild and Romanticised (mainly nineteenth century) stories emanating from Lancashire surrounding William's travels. He almost certainly went on three two to three-year tours (the normal period granted by Queen Elizabeth): the first to France and Spain, the second to the Mediterranean, including Italy, Egypt, the Holy Land and Constantinople, and the third to Russia. Back home his story became entangled with Dr John Dee's alchemy and astrology; his association with Edward Kelley in Prague, another alchemist, who happened to have done a little previous necromancing in the churchyard at Walton-le-Dale, a manor owned by Baron Langton of Walton, who had provoked the 'affray at Lea' in 1589; his brother Ferdinando's involvement in the 'Hesketh Plot' in 1593; the tradition that Shakespeare spent time in Lancashire in his youth; etc. etc. The main problem was trying to separate the kernels of historical 'truth' from the later accretions.

The most recent serious and scholarly attempt at William Stanley's biography was by Professor Leo Daugherty in the *Oxford Dictionary of National Biography* (2004). Although authoritative, details of William's travels still require clarification. The most recent biography of Dr John Dee is by Professor Glyn Parry, *The Arch-Conjurer of England: John Dee*, Yale University Press (December 2011). Several reviews from early 2012 are online. One interim conclusion is that much Tudor history is being rewritten at the moment, and that the Stanleys were involved much more centrally in many issues than those with which they have so far been credited.

XXIII-6. Conclusion

The main conclusion to be drawn from details in this chapter is quite simple: **Sir Edward Jr** was surrounded by close relatives, friends and acquaintances who have hit headlines in history, while he has remained in relative obscurity. At least he has one distinction not shared by anyone else: Shakespeare wrote two verse epitaphs for him, both of which have survived on solid stone. There are few doubts that it was **Sir Edward**'s own efforts and his long-standing acquaintance/ friendship with the poet that led to them appearing on his tomb at Tong. He was also related, closely or more distantly, to pretty well every aristocrat who has ever entered the 'Shakespeare story', including several of the Alternative Authorship Candidates and most of the aristocratic candidates as the Dark Lady of his Sonnets.

Chapter XXIV
Sir Edward's Derby cousins and in-laws
with Shakespeare connections

XXIV-1. Introduction

The main reason for grouping together the following details about some of Earl Henry's children (and their wives and husbands and children) from scattered references elsewhere is because these first cousins of **Sir Edward Jr**'s all had direct or otherwise very close contacts with Shakespeare and others in his circle, and any one of them could have (re-)introduced Shakespeare to **Sir Edward Jr** on any number of occasions. They were all, of course, nephews and nieces of **Sir Edward Sr**. Details of some have already been dealt with in previous chapters, but here the concentration is on the connections to Shakespeare.

XXIV-2. Ferdinando Stanley, Lord Strange, 5th Earl of Derby

Ferdinando, Lord Strange (1558/9-1594) until he became 5th Earl of Derby on the death of his father in September 1593, has long been associated with Shakespeare, and he presents the most obvious person with close links to both him and his cousin **(Sir) Edward**. For much of the twentieth century he appeared in Shakespeare biographies mainly as the patron of Lord Strange's Men, who were the earliest troupe on record as having performed Shakespeare's plays in London in the early 1590s. Only with the reawakening of interest in the Lancashire end of his story, in the context of explorations into 'Shakespeare in Lancashire', mainly after Honigmann's *Shakespeare, the 'lost years'* in 1985, was more interest shown in him. The following is a fair summary of the current evaluation among some Shakespeare scholars of his character and status in various circles, particularly those sympathetic to the acceptance of the 'Catholic Shakespeare' theory.

XXIVa. Ferdinando Stanley, Lord Strange, 5th Earl of Derby

Sir Edward Jr's first cousin. The origin of this line drawing is the same as that of his grandfather Earl Edward and father Earl Henry.

> In the late 1580s, Shakespeare was a member of the acting company Lord Strange's Men,[i] and Ferdinando Stanley, Lord Strange, was a man as enigmatic and intriguing as his name suggests.[ii] The great-nephew of the outspoken Magdalen Montague,[iii] he was strongly suspected of Catholicism. 'All the Stanleys are traitors' growled one of the hit men of the regime, Richard Topcliffe.[iv] But most of the Stanleys were also cautious

characters who played their cards close to their chest. Strange's understated portrait[v] gives little away, yet he was clearly an attractive and highly intelligent man. The future Earl of Derby, he was the unwilling focus of hopes for a Catholic succession, and he kept his religious and political allegiance carefully secret, adopting instead the harmless role of a scholarly dilettante. Of the same generation as Shakespeare and Southwell,[vi] he was the leading light of a group of intellectual noblemen that included the equally suspect Henry Percy, a scientist and necromancer known as the 'Wizard Earl' of Northumberland.[vii] Strange's own plays and poetry were widely admired, and his patronage was courted on all sides. Many of the leading writers of the day were on his payroll – among them Kyd, Marlowe,[viii] Lodge and Nashe. Unlike their rivals, the Queen's Men, who could be trusted to stage patriotic propaganda while touring the country,[ix] Lord Strange's Men were a seditious group, sailing perilously close to the wind with daringly subversive plays and responding in 'very Contemptuous manner' to an order to cease playing in 1589.*

* (Endnote) Thomas Merriam, 'The Misunderstanding of Munday as Author of Sir Thomas More', *Review of English Studies*, New Series, vol. 51, no. 204 (2000) p. 562. The article traces Shakespeare's involvement with the company and with Lord Strange in great detail.

(Clare Asquith, Shadowplay, 2006, pp. 51-2.)

Notes by HM:

[i] 'In the late 1580s, Shakespeare was a member of the acting company Lord Strange's Men.' As far as I am aware this has never been proved, although it seems highly likely, and he was certainly with them in London in the early 1590s when the company performed some of his early successes. Over the past few decades Shakespeare's association with Lord Strange's Men and their predecessors, Derby's Players, has gradually been moved earlier. 'The plaiers', presumably Lord Strange's Men, performed for the household and friends of his father Henry, 4th Earl of Derby, on several occasions at his main houses in Lancashire between 1587 and 1590, the only years for which records of visitors remain. **Edward Jr** was also a frequent visitor there. (*Derby Household Books*.) REED (Records of Early English Drama) has an ever-growing website covering touring companies. On this site the possibility that Shakespeare started his acting career with the Hoghtons in Lancashire is still (early 2013) offered only as a tenuous possibility. It remains to be seen whether this is accepted in future as highly plausible and more than just tenuous.

[ii] '**Lord Strange**' was the name given to the son and heir of the Earl of Derby since Sir George Stanley (c.1460-1503), son and heir of Thomas, 1st Earl of Derby, married (26 February 1481) Joan, daughter and heiress of John Lord Strange of Knockin near Shrewsbury. This courtesy title has continued until today for the son and heir, with no connotation at all that they were 'strange' other than by name and title. Its origins lie in a 'stranger' in Knockin in the twelfth century.

[iii] '. . . the outspoken **Magdalen Montague**.' Asquith gives a brief biography of this lady earlier in the book, including the following details, interesting for this book, of her relationship to Ferdinando, his relationship to Henry Wriothesley, and her public Catholicism and connections to a Gunpowder Plotter, a group which included **Sir Edward Jr**'s friend Sir Everard Digby:

> She was Magdalen Browne, Viscountess Montague, second wife of the Viscount Montague who had spoken out against the Oath of Supremacy at the beginning of Elizabeth's reign. . . Her great-nephew Ferdinando Stanley, Lord Strange, was Shakespeare's first patron; her grandson Henry Wriothesley, Earl of Southampton, was his second. . . Lady Magdalen's public Catholicism remained resolutely unaltered from her early years spent in the pious household of Anne, Countess of Bedford, until her death, three reigns later at the age of seventy-two. . . A tall, majestic figure, ever conscious of her descent from the earls of Shrewsbury . . . The Queen overlooked the fact that the three Montague houses were not only storehouses where statues, chalices, relics and altar stones awaited the restoration to England of the old religion (there is a story of one precariously balanced altar stone falling on a visitor) but were well known centres of refuge for priests where Mass was celebrated openly and with ceremony. . . Towards the end of

Magdalen Montague's life, it looked as if the Montagues might founder at last, for Guy Fawkes, a member of the 1605 conspiracy to blow up the Houses of Parliament known as the Gunpowder Plot, had once served as a retainer in their household.

(Asquith, *Shadowplay*, 2006, pp. 36-9.)

[iv] Richard Topcliffe (1532-1604) was a notorious Protestant torturer, who specialised in tormenting Catholic sympathisers. He might well have been the one who put **Sir Thomas** on the rack in the Tower in 1571. On one occasion he apparently growled, 'All the Stanleys are traitors', frequently quoted (without a reference).

[v] '**Strange's understated portrait**' (no portraits appear in her book) is presumably referring to the one at Knowsley Hall. A black and white photograph is in Honigmann, *Shakespeare, the 'lost years'*, between pp. 30-31, with other photographic plates of relevant portraits: his wife Countess Alice, his brother William (both also at Knowsley Hall) and Alexander Hoghton (in the Banqueting Hall at Hoghton Tower). Colour reproductions of details from the Knowsley portraits of Earl Edward, Earl Henry and Earl Ferdinando can be seen online at an Isle of Man website <castlerushen.pdf>, © Manx National Heritage 2003, with a warning that these 'may be reproduced for free educational use only'. A slightly modified copy of the Knowsley portrait (with curly, as opposed to wavy hair, and looking slightly to his right rather than straight ahead) appears on www.thepeerage.com, also the website Images of portraits of Ferdinando Stanley, Lord Strange, and in b/w on the website tudorplace. The line-drawing of Ferdinando which appears in this book, on which he is shown in armour for jousting, is from another portrait in the possession of the descendants of the Faringtons of Worden in the middle of the nineteenth century. It seems that William Farington of Worden, Comptroller for many years of the household of Earls Edward, Henry and Ferdinando, commissioned the paintings, or received them as gifts from his grateful masters. The current location of these portraits remains slightly mysterious (Leo Daugherty, private communication). Another detective hunt might track them down.

Since writing the above paragraph I received notification of a forthcoming book, which has since appeared. On the cover of this is the original of the Worden portrait: Leo Daugherty, The *Assassination of Shakespeare's Patron: Investigating the Death of the Fifth Earl of Derby*, Cambria, 2011 (the cover with the portrait is online). Professor Daugherty wrote (private correspondence) that there is indeed something of a mystery and the current owner is remaining anonymous. Ferdinando continues to exude mystery!

[vi] Robert Southwell, Catholic priest and poet, martyr, executed in 1595 at Tyburn, one of the 40 Martyrs of England and Wales canonised in 1970 by the Pope. Biography in all main encyclopedias.

[vii] '**the 'Wizard Earl' of Northumberland**' was Henry, 9th Earl of Northumberland, a cousin of **Sir Edward Jr**'s wife Lucy Percy, with whom she grew up. A brief biography was given in the last chapter.

[viii] The inclusion of Marlowe in this list is particularly interesting in the context of the 'tradition' that he was at Tong. See 'Appendix 2. Was Christopher Marlowe ever in Shropshire?'

[ix] There is a record in the *Derby Household Books* of the Queen's Players visiting the Earl of Derby at Lathom in September 1589. Other troupes regularly performed there; unfortunately no titles of plays appear.

Ferdinando, after two weeks of suffering, died a horrible death in April 1594. As **Sir Edward Sr** was such a regular visitor to Lancashire, he might well have rushed there to visit Ferdinando on his deathbed, or, one might presume, at least to attend his funeral. At the time witchcraft was suspected, but it is now generally accepted that he was poisoned. This was almost certainly as a result of the Hesketh Plot in 1593, when Richard Hesketh of Aughton, brother of Elizabeth, widow of Alexander

Hoghton of Hoghton and Lea, returned from Flanders to Lancashire with a Catholic proposal to place Ferdinando on the throne in the case of Queen Elizabeth's death. He had been adopted as the best candidate, amongst all the potential claimants who were direct descendants of Henry VII, by Robert Persons, leader of the English Jesuits in Rome, and Cardinal William Allen, spiritual leader of English Catholics in exile. An account of the development of this 'plot', very sympathetic towards the Catholic position, appeared in Francis Edwards, *Plots and Plotters in the Reign of Elizabeth* (2002). In 1594 Persons (under the name Doleman) wrote a pamphlet, *A Conference about the Next Succession to the Crown of England*, in which he proposed Ferdinando's eldest daughter Ann. It is significant that he did not propose Ferdinando's brother William, now 6th Earl of Derby, who had exactly the same claim to the throne. The jury is still out on reasons for this.

Weever published an obituary in verse to Ferdinand(o) in 1599, the text given in Chapter V. Two early recordings.

XXIV-3. Countess Alice Stanley née Spencer (and her claimed relationship to Edmund Spenser)

XXIVb. Althorp Hall, Northamptonshire
Home of the Spencers, including Alice Spencer, wife of Ferdinando, Lord Strange, therefore Sir Edward Jr's cousin-in-law. Her liaison in Lancashire during her second widowhood (1617-22) with Alexander Standish of Duxbury was one of the keys that unlocked doors to 'Lancastrian Shakespeare'.

Ferdinando's wife and widow (c.1560-1637) has been widely reported as a patron of the arts. The following details are the contents list of notes for her biography, on The Duxbury Family History website since 2004.

> Baroness Ellesmere and Viscountess Brackley (via her second husband Sir Thomas Egerton of Cheshire);
> patroness and dedicatee of many Tudor and Stuart poets and playwrights (including Spenser, Shakespeare, Donne and Milton);
> sister-in-law of Barons William Stanley, 3rd Lord Monteagle (from Lancashire) and George Carey, 2nd Lord Hundson (patron of Shakespeare in the Chamberlain's Men) plus Robert Sackville, 2nd Earl of Dorset, son of Queen Elizabeth's treasurer and father of the 3rd Earl of Dorset, who married Lady Anne Clifford, first cousin of Countess Alice's first husband Ferdinando, etc., etc

> Materials for a future Biography
> Basic dates & details about Countess Alice
> [*Amidst details in this file are comments about my puzzlement at all the confusing reports about various Sir Thomas, Sir Edward and Sir William Stanleys, all contemporaries of Countess Alice. Such was the situation in early 2004; I hope that these are now all sorted out in this book.*]

Countess Alice at Harefield and Haydon Hall, Eastcote, Middlesex

Articles by others (with links to the texts, which include several references to Shakespeare connections):

(1) 'The Lady of Harefield Place' by Iva Howard, Middlesex Quarterly, Winter 1953.

(2) 'Harefield's Place in History' by Morris W. Hughes, New Middlesex County Pictorial, June/July 1962.

(3) 'The bed ain't what it used to be' by Christine Sheppard, Hillingdon Mirror, 2 December 1969.

(4) 'Countess Alice at Haydon Hall, Eastcote'. From a talk given by Mr. L. E. Morris at Eastcote Residents Association Meeting on 1/3/1955.

(5) *The Kings of England – London North of the Thames* by Arthur Mee, Hodder and Stoughton Ltd., 1972, pp. 228-9.

(6) 'St Mary's Church, Harefield' by Eileen Bowlte, Hillingdon Family History Society Magazine Journal No. 64, December 2003.

(7) Inscriptions on the tomb

THIS IS Y E MONU=
=MENT OF ALICE CUVNTESSE
DOWAGER OF DERBY, ONE OF
Y E DAVGHT RS OF S: R JOHN SPENCER
OF ALLTHROP IN Y E COUNTY OF NORTHÂP
TON KN T , & WIFE OF Y E RIGHT HONO: BLE
FERDENA N DO EARLE OF DERBY, BY
WHOME SHE HAD ISSUE 3 DAVGHT: RS ,
HIS DAVGHT RS (??????) ANN Y E ELDST
MARIED TO GRAY L D CHAND OS FRAVNCES
Y E SECOND TO JOHN EARLE OF BRIDGEWA TER
ELIZABETH Y E 3 TO HENRY EARLE OF
HVNTINGDÕ. THIS COVNTESS DIED Y E
26 OF IAN, 1636. & HER AFORESAID HONO BLE
LORD & HUSBAND (WHO DIED BEFORE HER)
LIETH BVRIED IN Y E PARISH CHURCHE
OF ORMESKERKE W TH HIS AVNCESTO RS WHOS E
SOULES REMAINE IN EVERLASTING JOY.

(Added later, behind Alice's head)

This Noble Ladys Second
husband was my Lord Chan.
cellor Eggerton: whose
only Daughter, was Mother
to JULIAN Lady
NEWDIGATE.

Edmund Spenser claimed kinship with Countess Alice, although the exact connection has never been discovered. The kinship was claimed in his dedication to her of his poem *Teares of the Muses* in 1591. He obviously knew her and her family well enough to include them in a poem in 1594, *Colin Clouts come home again*, under allegorical names: 'Amyntas' is Ferdinando, recently died; 'Amarillis' is his mourning widow Alice; and 'Aetion' is Ferdinando's brother William. He also groups together 'Amarillis', 'Phyllis' and 'Charillis', the three daughters of Sir John Spencer (died 1586); in 1594 Alice's sister Anne was the widow of William Stanley, 3rd Lord Monteagle (died 1581), a kinsman of Ferdinando; and Elizabeth was still married to George Carey, 2nd Lord Hunsdon (died 1603), patron of 'the Lord Chamberlain's Men', which took over 'Strange's Men' and performed Shakespeare's plays. Elsewhere in the same poem he names Samuel Daniel openly and it is generally agreed that 'the shepheard of the Ocean' is Sir Walter Raleigh, 'Astrofell' is Sir Philip Sidney and 'Cynthia' Queen Elizabeth. Sir Philip Sidney had been Spenser's patron and both were inspirations for Shakespeare's poems. Shakespeare, therefore, seems to have been an important figure for all of these in one way or another, and all seem to have been important in Spenser's eyes, when he named them all together in one poem. He did not, one must hastily add, mention Shakespeare in this poem by any name – his own or allegorical - but must have known of him because of the publication of his two long poems in 1593 and 1594, both of which were successes.

We will remember that **Sir Edward Stanley Sr**, in the *Derby Household Books*, was a regular companion at Lathom of Ferdinando, Alice and William; also of his nephew **Edward Stanley Jr**. It is difficult to believe that some or all of them did not also meet in London as well as Lancashire during the 1590s. Spenser's claimed relationship to Countess Alice makes him another person, therefore, in 'Shakespeare's Lancashire Links', particularly in view of the tradition that he came from the Lancashire branch of the Spensers/Spencers. A summary of the pros and cons is:

> For many years there has been a tradition that Edmund Spenser, the famous Elizabethan poet, lived at Hurstwood [*near Burnley*] for a time even if he were not born there; one authority has however connected him with the Spensers of Filly Close [*also near Burnley*]. The main arguments for the claim of Spenser's connection with Hurstwood may be briefly summarised: (1) the name "Edmund Spenser" is very common in the neighbourhood, (2) the poet was connected with the noble family of the Spensers of Althorpe and their coat of arms is almost the same as that of the Hurstwood Spensers, (3) Spenser is known to have resided for a time in the North of England and he used Lancashire words and phrases and describes mountainous country such as may be found between Lancashire and Yorkshire, (4) he is known to have been helped by Dean Nowell of Read [*near Whalley*] who took a special interest in all who came from Lancashire, (5) Anne Clifford, Lady of Skipton castle, erected the poet's tomb and the printer of his works was of a Lancashire family. There is little known about Spenser's early life and other localities have been suggested for Spenser's stay in the North. Critics of the theory that Hurstwood was Spenser's home in the North point out that the name "Spenser" is a fairly common one in other parts of Lancashire, and that the Lancashire phrases and words which the poet uses are common in other parts of England, that his descriptions of mountainous country is equally applicable to many counties, that he does not mention "Pendle" and that the only river to which he refers is "the Lune"; they also point out that Dean Nowell helped many boys who did not come from Lancashire.
>
> (Bennett, *History of Burnley*, vol. 2, 1947, p. 248.)

XXIV-4. William Stanley, 6th Earl of Derby

William Stanley's reputation was rather overshadowed by his brother Ferdinando's for a long time, but he received considerable attention from professors of English Literature during the twentieth century because of Shakespeare. He was proposed as a 'Shakespeare Authorship Candidate' by French/Belgian Professor Abel Lefranc in 1918 in *Sous le masque de William Shakespeare, VIe conte de Derby* and this cause was adopted enthusiastically by a few others. (For an excellent objective account of the candidacy of William Stanley and dozens of others, see John Michell, *Who Wrote Shakespeare?*, 1999, although beware of some of the false details claimed by proponents, e.g. he was actually born and baptised in London in 1561, and there is no evidence that he spent any time in his youth at the family estate at Meriden in Warwickshire.) Stanley's candidacy was helped along by the fact that the initials of both are conveniently the same, making it easy to attribute a few W.S. poems to William Stanley. He certainly wrote plays: in 1599 a report from a Jesuit 'spy' stated that 'he was busy penning plays for the common players'. Unfortunately not a single one of his plays has survived.

Despite this lacuna, William Stanley has gained a new champion for his role as Shakespeare author on the internet, 'Was the sixth Earl of Derby Really Shakespeare?, a Derbyite website', also amusingly called 'The URL of Derby', run by John Raithel, with (in my opinion, and he knows this) little chance of winning (m)any converts, but very interesting and useful nevertheless in providing many now easily accessible details about William Stanley, including the full text of the quote re 'penning plays' (Greenstreet, 1891, 1892). It also provided the trail to Father Henry More's knowledge of the Tong epitaphs (see Appendix 8. *Historia* by Father Henry More).

XXIVc. William Stanley, 6th Earl of Derby
Sir Edward Jr's first cousin, younger brother of Ferdinando. He married Elizabeth de Vere, eldest daughter of Edward de Vere, 17th Earl of Oxford. Both of these earls are Alternative Authorship Candidates for Shakespeare's works.
(© Knowsley Hall)

Professor E. A. J. Honigmann (*Shakespeare: the 'lost years'*, Appendix C, 1985, 1998) saw William Stanley's main significance for Shakespeare as the potential reason for the writing and first performance of *A Midsummer Night's Dream* at his wedding to Elizabeth de Vere, eldest daughter of Edward, 17th Earl of Oxford. This wedding took place at the Royal Palace in Greenwich in the presence of Queen Elizabeth in January 1595. Two other weddings have been proposed for the first performance of *Dream*, but William's marriage to Elizabeth seems to be winning in some quarters (see the long quote from Asquith below).

The first-ever dedicated biography of Earl William was commissioned from Professor Leo Daugherty for the *New/Oxford Dictionary of National Biography* (2004), which duly appeared and which saw no role for William Stanley as the author of Shakespeare's plays. (Nor did it claim that *Dream* was written for this wedding.) However, his research for this biography led to his proposal of William Stanley as Shakespeare's 'Fair Youth' in his Sonnets in *William Shakespeare, Richard Barnfield and the Sixth Earl of Derby*, 2010, which also sees Richard Barnfield as the 'Rival Poet', also dedicating Sonnets to William Stanley. Acceptance or rejection of these proposals is still being debated. The 'conventional' candidate for the 'Fair Youth' for a long time has been Henry Wriothesley, 3rd Earl of Southampton, the dedicatee of the two poems *Venus and Adonis* in 1593 and *The Rape of Lucrece* in 1594. He already entered William Stanley's story because he happens to have earlier rejected Elizabeth de Vere as his wife, paying £1000 for the privilege of rejection. In any case, they were 'cousins', because Henry's maternal great-grandmother Margaret Stanley was the sister of William's paternal grandfather Edward, 3rd Earl of Derby. (See any biography of Henry Wriothesley for the facts and his 'Fair Youth' candidacy.) Young William presumably knew this connection as a youth, born in 1561 and his grandfather living until 1572, although Henry Wriothesley was not born until 1573.

Whatever the historical truth in these various claims, William Stanley has belatedly come in from the wings and threatens to enter centre stage in The Bard's biography as certainly an acquaintance and more than likely a friend since they were both young men in Lancashire. This close connection is certainly not weakened by his first cousin **Sir Edward Stanley Jr** later receiving two Verse Epitaphs from Shakespeare.

The recent upsurge in literature on Catholic Shakespeare has produced the following summary of the events around the death of William Stanley's brother Ferdinando, his own succession to the earldom and his marriage.

> A ruthless contemporary comment survives on the role played by the Lord Treasurer, William Cecil, in Strange's death. 'It is no marvel', wrote Sir Richard Yorke in 1594 to Strange's exiled cousin, Sir William Stanley,[i] 'when Machiavellian policies govern England. I durst pawn my life that the Lord Treasurer caused him to be poisoned that he being dead he might marry the young Lady Vere unto the brother of the said Earl of Derby.'* Yorke's suspicions were shared by many others. Among the benefits Strange's murder brought the Cecils was the chance to drive a wedge into a bastion of Northern English Catholicism by marrying into one of the wealthiest earldoms in the country. Elizabeth de Vere, the granddaughter of William Cecil, whom Southampton[ii] had paid so much not to marry, was known to be again on offer, and this time accepted by the new Earl. But there was a hitch. Ferdinando's widow vigorously contested the whole settlement, refusing to give up the earldom and claiming that she was pregnant with a Stanley heir. A ruinous lawsuit followed. In the end it became clear that the distraught dowager had simply made up the story of the pregnancy,[iii] and nine months later the path was cleared for the wedding to go ahead; it was celebrated at Greenwich Palace in the presence of the Queen on 26 January 1595. It appears that the Queen herself commissioned the evening's entertainment from the Lord Chamberlain's new company for her beloved 'spirit', the seventy-five-year-old William Cecil. Few tasks could have been less congenial to a writer who owed so much to the murdered Earl of Derby; few plays could have had a more intimidating first-night audience. Their reaction was critical to Shakespeare's future. . .
>
> Shakespeare's response to this test of loyalty and skill was one of his most brilliant achievements: *A Midsummer Night's Dream*.
>
> * (Endnote) Ian Wilson, *Shakespeare: The Evidence: Unlocking the Mysteries of the Man and His Work* (London, 1993), p. 176.

(Clare Asquith, Shadowplay, 2005, pp. 106-7.)

Notes by HM:

[i] 'Cousin' can only be applied here in the loosest of possible senses. This was Sir William Stanley of Hooton in the Wirral, Cheshire, the original senior line of the Stanleys before the junior line became Earls of Derby. The two distinct families always stayed in close contact and certainly considered each other to be close kinsmen, but would have to go back seven generations to find first cousins in the ancestors of the two Sir William Stanleys living at the end of the sixteenth century. (Ormerod's *Cheshire* and the Family Trees in Appendix 12a and 12b make this very clear.) These two William Stanleys have often been confused in previous accounts, but their careers could not have been more different. This Sir William of Hooton, although Catholic at heart, had been a stalwart soldier and loyal to Queen Elizabeth throughout several Irish campaigns and at the beginning of the campaign in the Netherlands against the Spanish. He finally became disillusioned with many aspects of his own situation and the Protestant machinations of Elizabeth's regime and in 1587 surrendered Deventer to the Spanish, along with his regiment. (For a Catholic apologia, see Heywood (ed.), *Cardinal Allen's defence of Sir William Stanley's surrender of Deventer, January 29, 1586-7* (1851).) From then on he was the military leader of the English Catholic exiles, with Cardinal Allen (from Lancashire) the spiritual leader. William Allen had taught as an usher at Stratford Grammar School 1563-5, paid for by John Shakespeare when Chamberlain of the borough (Savage and Fripp, *Minutes and Accounts of Stratford-upon-Avon*, vol. 1, p. 128) and must have taken a keen interest in the success of a pupil at his former school. Biographies of this Sir William Stanley and Cardinal William Allen are in all main encyclopedias.

[ii] Henry Wriothesley, 3rd Earl of Southampton, was the dedicatee of Shakespeare's two long poems, *Venus and Adonis* published in 1593 and *The Rape of Lucrece* in 1594. His relationship to William Stanley was given above.

[iii] I beg to differ. It might have been a phantom pregnancy, but Alice almost certainly believed that it was real. As she had already borne three healthy children, she presumably recognised the normal symptoms. In this case, the more likely explanation is that she had a miscarriage and a still-born child. Her grief would be understandable, not only at losing a child but also her hope dashed that it would be a healthy boy who would inherit her late husband's title and all his estates. Having been thwarted of this hope, it is hardly surprising that she was resentful of her brother-in-law William, who had spent most of his twenties and early thirties 'gallivanting' around Europe, the Middle East and Russia, showing no interest in family responsibilities at home, unlike his brother Ferdinando.

Further comments:

After his marriage to Elizabeth de Vere, which presented certain problems and disagreements, William settled down to his responsibilities and divided his time mainly between his estates in Lancashire and the family home in Canon Row, London. As a Knight of the Garter he was expected to make regular appearances at court and he used his time in London to act as patron for one or more of the boys' companies then in fashion, also 'penning plays' for them. The 'Countess of Derby' was frequently mentioned as performing at masques at James's court, but as there were two Countesses of Derby at this time – Elizabeth, wife of the 6th Earl and Alice, widow of the 5th Earl (a title she continued to use during her second marriage to Lord Chancellor Thomas Egerton) – it is not always obvious which one was being referred to.

William Stanley's interest in the theatre was put to another use when he had a theatre built at Prescot, near Knowsley, or at least was involved with this in some way. This had the distinction of being the first indoor purpose-built theatre in England. How much use was made of it is not, alas, on record. It was not used as a theatre for long and it disappeared during the Civil War, along with all other theatres. A recent attempt was made to raise funds to build a replica for Shakespeare North, but sadly (predictably?) the money was not forthcoming. The 'vision' faded away, as had a previous attempt around 2000 to re-create an Elizabethan theatre at Hoghton Tower, the traditional home for a while of young William Shakespeare. This was in the enthusiasm created for 'Lancastrian Shakespeare' by a conference at Lancaster University in the summer of 1999.

William and Elizabeth had a mainly happy marriage, although with a few early notable disputes on record. Elizabeth died in 1627, after which William handed over all his public responsibilities to his son and heir James, Lord Strange, and retired to his house in Watergate, Chester on an annual 'pension' of £1000, where he enjoyed a life of entertaining and musical activities. One might imagine that his widowhood would have led to him seeing more of his long-widowed cousin **Sir Edward Jr**. Maybe they did spend time together in Chester or Eynsham, but no record has survived. By this time, of course, Shakespeare was well and truly dead, but William's second surviving son Robert provided another interesting possible Shakespearean connection with the epitaph on his tomb (Chapter X). The following paragraphs are thus more relevant to **Sir Edward** than to Shakespeare.

William and Elizabeth had six children, three boys (only two surviving to adulthood) and three girls (one surviving), although it is not known in which order the daughters were born. There were two daughters Elizabeth, both of whom died young. The first one might have been the one who died shortly after birth within the year after their marriage. One daughter Ann survived and married (1) Sir Henry Portman of Orchard, Somerset and (2) Sir Robert Carr, Earl of Ancram. William's son and heir James, Lord Strange, was born in 1607 and named after King James (his godfather?). **Sir Edward Jr** would have met him when James returned to England as a married man. James had been sent abroad by his father (who presumably believed he himself had benefited from his travels abroad) and when staying at the court in The Hague, met (by arrangement) and married in 1626 Charlotte de (la) Trémouille, a French Huguenot related to the French royal family.

Son James, although a staunch Protestant with a Puritan tinge, was also a staunch Royalist, and commanded an army throughout the Civil Wars. Charlotte has gone down in history mainly as the undaunted and indomitable lady who held out during the Siege of Lathom in 1644 with a small force against a besieging Parliamentarian army of over 2,000. This dissolved, however, at the approach of Prince Rupert of the Rhine, first cousin of Charles I. Rupert's mother was Elizabeth, sister of James I, the Winter Queen, wife of Frederick of the Palatinate, King of Bohemia for a short time. After the defeat of his forces at the Battle of the White Mountain outside Prague in 1621, which was one of the early major events in the Thirty Years War, Elizabeth and Frederick had escaped to The Hague, which was where James, Lord Strange had met them and his wife Charlotte. It is from letters by Charlotte to an aunt in France that we know that William continued to speak fluent French all his life. After the death of William in September 1642, James, as 7th Earl of Derby, fought many battles for Charles I, helped Charles II to hide in the oak tree at Boscobel near Tong after the Battle of Worcester and paid for his allegiance to the crown by losing his head in Bolton in 1651. His father William did not live long enough to see this, and nor did his cousin **Sir Edward Jr**, who had died in 1632.

Sir Edward Jr would also have known William's second surviving son, Sir Robert, born 9 February 1610, who married a daughter of Lord Witherington and had issue (to repeat, details of his tomb with its Shakespearean epitaph appeared in Chapter X-10); and the last son Charles Henry, who died in 1629. One might imagine that **Sir Edward Jr**, whose only son Thomas had died in infancy, took great interest in his cousin's sons, his closest male relatives in the next generation of Stanleys. One might also imagine that he commiserated, at least in writing, with his cousin William on the death of his wife Elizabeth in 1627: two ageing widowers, neither of whom remarried. No letter has survived.

The devotion of four pages here to William Stanley is a hint that more is on the way from the pen of this author, which will include a reassessment of the extent of his travels, and a much-expanded version of his biography from the only existing one so far in the *ODNB*. But the main person to whom this book is devoted is his cousin **Sir Edward Jr**, who must remain in the limelight as far as possible, with others still in the shadows. This seems an appropriate place, however, to take a little sidestep into the Shakespeare Authorship Controversy, in which William Stanley has played a role during the whole of the 20th century, and indeed still does.

XXIV-5. Other contenders
as Shakespeare Alternative Authorship Candidates

William Stanley's father-in-law Edward de Vere, 17th Earl of Oxford, happens to be the current favourite 'Shakespeare Alternative Authorship Candidate' – or at least the one with the most vociferous following by members of the Shakespeare Oxford Society. Their website www.shakespeare-oxford.com provides the arguments for; the most damning argument against is that de Vere died in 1604, before the first performance of Shakespeare's late masterpieces. Whatever one believes about this issue, no one can deny that research in this area has uncovered many valuable insights into de Vere's life and therefore also of his daughters. His most recent biographer, Alan H. Nelson, *Monstrous Adversary: The Life of Edward de Vere, 17th Earl of Oxford* (Liverpool UP, 2003), depicts him as a rather unsavoury character. The recent film *Anonymous* (2011) depicts him as a romantic character and the author of all of Shakespeare's plays. Neither his daughter Elizabeth de Vere nor his son-in-law William Stanley get a look in. Oxford was, of course, portrayed as the author of *Dream*, having played Puck in the version he had written forty years earlier as a precocious nine-year-old! Enough said. We can all have our dreams, but the Oxfordian one does not stand up in the face of known facts.

I wrote a review of Roland Emmerich's film *Anonymous*, first screened in many countries September-November 2011, also giving an overview of the Authorship Controversy. This was written in German for German readers in the magazine *Synesis* Nr. 2/2012. In no uncertain terms I rejected the Oxfordian theory, although quite enjoyed the film, if taken in the spirit of the film *Shakespeare in Love*, admiring the cinematography, although being confused by frequent flashbacks to five or even forty years earlier. However, it was presented as 'historically accurate', which was untenable. There were so many historical inaccuracies, which on their own led to a rejection of most of the rest. The film attracted many reviews in German papers, not least because producer/director Emmerich is German and it was filmed in the Babelsberg Studios, Berlin. Also, a recent book by a German author advocates Oxford as Shakespeare: Kurt Kreiler, *Der Mann, der Shakespeare erfand* (Insel Verlag, 2009). An English translation has appeared, *Anonymous Shake-speare: the Man Behind* (Doeling und Galitz Verlag, 2011). Interestingly, two Munich authors are supporting Christopher Marlowe: Georges Bourbaki, *Der Nachruf oder: Es war doch dieser Schlawiner Marlowe*, Eigenverlag (published privately), Munich, 2003. And Bastian Conrad, *Christopher Marlowe: Der wahre Shakespeare*, Buch & Media, Munich, 2011. My article in German went online soon after publication. This and the English version are on my website.

The best recent publication dealing with the Authorship Controversy is by James Shapiro, *Contested Will: Who Wrote Shakespeare?* (2010). Probably the best result of the film *Anonymous* is that it caused the Shakespeare Birthplace Trust to actively enter the fray in the autumn of 2011, first and foremost with an ebook (available free for downloading) *Shakespeare Bites Back: not so anonymous* by Paul Edmondson and Stanley Wells.

Having made my position clear that I do not believe for one moment that Shakespeare did not write his own works, it has often become glaringly obvious during the course of researching and writing this book that the Stanley family very obviously played some Shakespearean role(s) – not as authors, but certainly as patrons and perhaps as the provider of contacts, welcoming houses, libraries and some ideas which he later included in his plays. I believe that their role in Shakespeare's life has been previously overlooked or rather neglected. If one looks at a list, such as that given by Wikipedia in a 'List of Shakespeare Authorship Candidates' (79 of them in mid 2012! - with links to the biographies of many), it is not difficult to find family relationships and other close connections between several of the 'main' ones and the Stanley family. They obviously all knew each other, and through them Shakespeare would have known them. But a full account must await a future publication.

~~~~~~~~~~~~~~~~~~~~~~

XXIV-6. Countess Elizabeth Stanley née de Vere

One Stanley connection to Shakespeare, Jonson and theatrical activities at court was Countess Elizabeth's performance in some of Jonson's masques, although, as mentioned above, it is sometimes difficult to distinguish between two Countesses of Derby: Elizabeth and her sister-in-law Alice. Both provide several interesting Shakespeare connections, but here we are concerned with Elizabeth's, who serves as another spider in the Stanley-Shakespeare web.

Before her marriage to William Stanley in January 1595 she had been engaged to Henry Wriothesley, Earl of Southampton during the time when he was Shakespeare's dedicatee, but he refused to marry her. Later he married Elizabeth Vernon, a 'cousin' of **Sir Edward Jr** via his mother Margaret née Vernon, and so yet another 'cousin' who became a candidate for Shakespeare's 'Dark Lady'.

Her youngest sister Susan de Vere (1587-1628/9) married Philip Herbert, 1st Earl of Montgomery, 4th Earl of Pembroke, one of the dedicatees of the *First Folio* in 1623. He married, secondly in 1630, Lady Anne Clifford (1590-1676), another first cousin of William, 6th Earl of Derby (via his mother Margaret Clifford and her brother Sir George Clifford, Anne's father). Although too young to have been directly connected with Shakespeare, her resident tutor in childhood had been poet Samuel Daniel, who was closely connected to him, and she too performed in Ben Jonson's Masques at court. Unfortunately her published diary only begins in 1617, the year after Shakespeare's death. This is doubly unfortunate, because her first husband had been Richard Sackville, 3rd Earl of Dorset (1589-1624), the alleged (by Aubrey's informant) admirer of Venetia Stanley, **Sir Edward Jr**'s youngest daughter.

Elizabeth's middle sister was Bridget de Vere, who was first engaged to William Herbert, 3rd Earl of Pembroke, the brother of Philip and co-dedicatee of the *First Folio*, who had also had Samuel Daniel as a tutor. He continued his bachelor life with an affair with Mary Fitton (one of the early candidates for Shakespeare's 'Dark Lady') and married Mary Talbot, a granddaughter of Bess of Hardwick. However, Bridget's marriage produced no Shakespeare connections:

> On 28 April 1599, shortly after her 15th birthday, she married Francis Norris of Rycote, the son of Sir William Norris of Rycote and Elizabeth Morrison, and heir apparent to his grandfather Henry Norris, 1st Baron Norreys. On 17 October 1601, Norris succeeded to the title of 2nd Baron Norris, and Bridget was henceforth styled as Lady Norris.

> (Wikipedia)

XXIV-7. Dorothy Halsall née Stanley/Halsall

Ferdinando and William's half-sister Dorothy Stanley married Sir Cuthbert Halsall of Halsall. She was one of two daughters of Earl Henry by his mistress Jane Halsall of Knowsley after his separation from his wife Margaret Clifford. Dorothy was thus a Halsall via her mother and also her husband, but always completely acknowledged as a Stanley by her father. The only indirect connection to Shakespeare (discovered to date) is that both Sir Cuthbert and William Shakespeare received epigrams from John Weever in 1599 (Honigmann, *Weever*, 1987). (Sir) Cuthbert and (Sir) **Edward Stanley Jr** were both frequent visitors at Lathom when Earl Henry was in residence (*Derby Household Books*) and they almost certainly met on 30 August 1602 when the presence of both was registered at Preston Guild (*Preston Guild Rolls*). Dorothy seems to have been a beloved sister-in-law of Sir John Salusbury, who wrote poems with acrostics of her name.

XXIV-8. Ursula Salusbury née Stanley/Halsall

Ursula Stanley was the other daughter of Earl Henry and Jane Halsall. She married (Sir) John Salusbury at Lleweni, Denbigh, in December 1586. Honigmann, in *Shakespeare: the 'lost years'*, Chapter IX, 'The Phoenix and the Turtle', argued cogently for their wedding as the setting and inspiration for Shakespeare's allegorical and enigmatic poem of this name, with one possible explanation for his presence being his participation in the wedding festivities with Lord Strange's Men. In his 'Preface to the second edition' of 1998 he reported on the scepticism that greeted this proposal, the main objection being that it was 'much too early for Shakespeare to have written this in 1586'. 'Why too early?', one might ask, as did Honigmann. He was twenty-two, 1586 was within only a few years of his taking the London theatre scene by storm with his early plays; and only seven and eight years later he published his two long poems, *Venus and Adonis* and *The Rape of Lucrece*. Were all these produced without an 'apprenticeship' period? How many poets have ever written their first poem aged nearly thirty? The debate continues, with several other candidates proposed. Time will tell whether any consensus of opinion will ever be reached or whether those concerned will agree to disagree. Whatever the outcome, the proof of some fairly direct connection between Shakespeare and Sir John Salusbury comes from the publication in 1601 by Robert Chester, *Love's Martyr*, a series of poems dedicated to Sir John, including offerings by Jonson and Marston and the first publication of *The Phoenix and the Turtle* in an Appendix. This might well have been written several years previously, as was the case with his *Sonnets*, which were first published in 1609, with many of them recorded as circulating in manuscript form before 1598.

An unpublished book by John Idris Jones explores the lives of Sir John and Ursula Salusbury in detail and comes to the conclusion (confirming that of Honigmann's in 1985) that *The Phoenix and the Turtle* does indeed refer to the occasion of this marriage, even though it might have been written later (private communication). He has also established that Ursula and Dorothy grew up at Hawarden in Flintshire, one of Earl Henry's estates in North Wales, where he installed his mistress Jane Halsall. Evidence for this and much more appear in his book, *Where was Shakespeare? The Lancashire Theory with New Additions* (so far unpublished). Meanwhile, as announced elsewhere, he has published an article: 'William Shakespeare and John Salusbury: what was their relationship?', *Transactions of the Denbighshire Historical Society*, January 2011, with an earlier version on his website.

XXIV-9. Conclusion

The list could go on and on by moving just slightly further away from the Stanley family. Various other in-laws were connected to the Devereux and Sidneys, families with strong Shakespeare connections. The only conclusion to be drawn from details in this chapter is that these first cousins of **Sir Edward Jr**'s were amongst the most likely people to have provided a setting for several meetings between him and Shakespeare. His writing the verse epitaphs for **Sir Edward Jr** was just a logical conclusion of a life-long friendship, or at least acquaintance. The surprise is that he did not write any epitaphs for any other aristocrat. Or maybe he did and no manuscripts have survived? Certainly none ever made their way onto a tomb other than those for **Sir Edward**'s in Tong.

XXIV-10. Postscript. A connection via a book?

In August 2011 my attention was drawn to a copy of Plutarch's *Lives* at the Shakespeare Birthplace Trust, which contains several signatures of Stanleys. The query had been raised by a reader of Sylvia Morris's Shakespeare Blog, in which she related her interest and a visit to Tong in pursuit of Sir Edward Stanley's tomb.

> http://theshakespeareblog.com/2011/08/living-monuments-shakespeares-epitaphs/
> One copy of the book Plutarch's *Lives of the noble Grecians and Romans*, published in 1579, now owned by the Shakespeare Birthplace Trust, has a fascinating history. On publication it was given to Henry Stanley, 4th Earl of Derby and from him it passed to his son Ferdinando, 5th Earl of Derby, who died in 1594. Shakespeare based his Roman plays, including *Antony and Cleopatra* and *Julius Caesar*, on the stories in this book, and because Ferdinando and Shakespeare knew each other there is a strong possibility that this could be the copy he used.
>
> (Image of the effigy of **Sir Edward Jr**)
>
> There is a signature in the book indicating that in 1611 it became the property of Edward Stanley, probably the man whose effigy is on the lower deck of the monument and a real Shakespeare connection.
>
> Sylvia Morris

She directed my attention to the relevant website of the Shakespeare Birthplace Trust.

Plutarch's *Lives of the noble Grecians and Romanes*

Written originally in the late 1st century this English translation by Thomas North was published in 1579 and is the major source used by William Shakespeare for his Roman and Greek plays, including *Antony and Cleopatra*, *Julius Caesar*, *Coriolanus* and *Timon of Athens*.

This particular copy of the first edition has an intriguing provenance or history. The title page inscriptions record that the book was given to Henry Stanley, 4th Earl of Derby by William Chaderton, who became Bishop of Chester in 1579;[i] the book passed to the 5th Earl, Ferdinando, Lord Strange, whose company of players presented some of Shakespeare's first plays, including *Titus Andronicus*. A second inscription, later deleted and obscured, but which can be read by ultra-violet light, is by Ferdinando's widow, Alice, who presents the volume to 'William'. A third inscription 'Edw:Stanley 1611' indicates that the book later came back to the Stanley family.[ii]

One can speculate whether or not the 'William' referred to was Shakespeare himself.[iii] What we do know is that the printer Thomas Vautrollier took another boy from Stratford-upon-Avon, Richard Field (1561-1624), as an apprentice shortly before the Plutarch was published. Richard Field was Shakespeare's life-long friend and it is possible that the young Field shared proof-reading the work with the future playwright, and this introduction led to his extensive use of the book in later years. Field went on to print the first four editions of *Venus and Adonis* and the first quarto of *The Rape of Lucrece*, possibly with Shakespeare's direct involvement.

(Shakespeare Birthplace Trust website)

Notes by HM:

[i] We met William Chaderton, Bishop of Chester at Lathom House, when Richard Hesketh presented the 'Hickman letter' concerning the 'Hesketh Plot' to **Sir Edward Stanley Sr** in September 1593.

[ii] If this was **Sir Edward Jr**, as seems likely, then the book did not come back to the Stanley family – it never left it.

[iii] One can indeed speculate whether the William who received the book from widow Alice was William Shakespeare, but it seems highly unlikely. Far more likely and logical is that Alice, when sorting through her husband's belongings, including his library, was asked by her brother-in-law William, now the 6th Earl of Derby and himself an aspiring playwright, if he could take the book, which had come to Ferdinando from their father presumably because he was the elder son. The most logical next owner would have been the second son, William. Given what we know about the tense situation over the coming decade between William and Alice, with the latter fighting to the bitter end to retain all of Ferdinando's property for their three daughters, it is more likely that William received the book earlier rather than later during Alice's widowhood.

If William Stanley in turn passed it on, then in due course it would most likely have been to someone in the immediate family. In 1611 William's own sons were very small and his cousin **Edward** might well have been on a visit to Lathom House and expressed interest in a book that had provided historical material for Shakespeare, who had written two Verse Epitaphs for his family tomb a few years earlier. This would certainly explain the fact that there were no titles and no surnames for Ferdinando, Alice and William: if this were indeed to have been the journey of the book, then it did not 'come back to the Stanley family', but never left it between the dates in question.

If it did go to and stayed in **Sir Edward**'s library at Eynsham Abbey until his death in 1632, one must wonder what its future path was and how it came to the Shakespeare Birthplace Trust. No details of its provenance appear on its website. One might be grateful that it did not stay in the Stanley library at Lathom House, because it would have gone up in flames with all the rest when it was razed to the ground.

XXIVd. Hornby Castle, near Lancaster
Home of the 4th Baron Monteagle, Sir Edward Jr's kinsman and revealer of the Gunpowder Plot,
which is assumed to have been a direct 'inspiration' for *Macbeth*.
An artist's impression. Hornby Castle still exists, in private ownership.

XXIVe. Lleweni Hall, Denbighshire, 1792
Home of Sir John Salusbury, married to Ursula Halsall/Stanley, first cousin of Sir Edward Jr.
Their marriage in 1586 is assumed by some to have been the inspiration for Shakespeare's poem
The Phoenix and the Turtle (Honigmann, 1985; Jones, 2011).
It has since been largely dismantled and the art treasures dispersed.

Chapter XXV
Sir Edward's children

XXV-1. Names and dates
XXV-2. Petronella
XXV-3. Frances
XXV-4. Venetia

XXV-1. Names and dates

Sir Edward's children have been mentioned so often throughout this book. However, it still seemed sensible to bring them all together one last time, with everything we know about all of them. We know from the MI on his tomb at Tong (and the tomb at Walthamstow) that **Sir Edward Jr** had one son and seven daughters by his wife Lucy, second daughter of Thomas, 7th Earl of Northumberland. We do not know exactly when they were born as no relevant Parish Registers from this time have survived. From the MI, however, we do have the ages at death of four of his daughters, and know that his only son died in infancy.

> Thomas his soone died in infancie and is Buried in Ye parishe Church of Winwick in Ye Countie of Lanca:

This was Winwick parish, in which the Rectory was leased by father and son. It was concluded, in Chapter XVII. Sir Edward Sr and Jr in the *Derby Household Books*, that **Edward Jr** returned to Lancashire with his whole family on occasion, when visiting his Stanley relatives at Lathom; and that it was during one of these visits that young Thomas died and was buried there. As there is no intimation of this event in 1587-90 (*Derby Household Books*), one might assume it was at the earliest during the mid-1580s, during a previous unrecorded visit to Lancashire, or in the 1590s, during a similarly unrecorded visit. In any case young Thomas's death and burial occurred before four of his sisters were buried and commemorated at Walthamstow and Tong in 1601.

> 18 Arabella 16 Marie 15 Alice 13 Priscilla (from the tomb at Tong)

It is assumed that these numbers, as given in the MI on the tomb at Tong, were their ages at death. They had been buried with their mother at Walthamstow, without giving ages of death. Three daughters survived.

> Petronella Francis and Venesie are still living

These were recorded in this order in the MIs, presumably in order of seniority. The only date of birth known is of Venetia, on 19 December 1600 (according to her husband Sir Kenelm Digby in his *Memoirs*). One might extrapolate the following approximate dates and sequence of births, on the assumption of a marriage in 1581.

	Born ? c.	*Died ? c.*	*Buried*	*Age at death*
Arabella	1582	1601	Walthamstow	18
Mary	1584	1601	Walthamstow	16
Alice	1585	1601	Walthamstow	15
Priscilla	1587	1601	Walthamstow	13
Thomas	1582-90s	1582-90s	Winwick	Infant
Petronella	1595?	1632>	?	?
Frances	1598?	1657	Salden, Bucks?	59+
Venetia	1600, Dec.	1633	London	33

These estimates cannot be wildly wrong and the burial of the first four daughters with their mother all at the same time implies a virulent disease (the plague?). The mystery and miracle is that the father and the three other daughters survived.

One other little mystery is the origin of all the names. Had they followed traditional naming habits, the first daughter would have been named Anne (maternal grandmother), the second Margaret (paternal grandmother) and the third Lucy (her own mother); but none of these names were used. Unless, that is, there were more daughters born and given these names, who did not survive until 1601. But even then, one might have expected a later one to bear one of these names. Looking around their aunts, **Edward Jr**'s Stanley aunts were Anne, Jane, Mary, Dorothy, Margaret and Catherine, with his Vernon aunt Dorothy. His Stanley first cousins were Anne, Ursula and Dorothy. Lucy's sisters were Elizabeth, Joan and Mary. Of all of these names, only Mary was used by **Edward** and Lucy. It is strange that they did not use Anne, with three Annes in the immediate family.

Arabella is striking as the name of a claimant to the throne, Ar(a)bella Stuart (1575-1615), granddaughter of Bess of Hardwick, Countess of Shrewsbury and doyenne at Chatsworth House. This name might have been given in honour of her, although she was rather young to be a godmother. Arabella was apparently a fairly common name in Scotland, but Edward and Lucy had no obvious Scottish connections. The only Alice in sight is Ferdinando's wife, so maybe she was godmother of the third daughter? Priscilla and Petronella are also mysteries. Although Frances was a common enough name, there were no immediate relatives with this name.

Venetia, the last daughter, is a real puzzler. I have read somewhere the suggestion that it might have been a derivation of Gwyneth, but this seems rather dubious, even spurious. It was spelt Venesie in the MI at Tong, which seems rather strange, if father Edward had written the text to be copied onto the tomb. It seems most likely to have been a derivation of Venice, although there is no known direct connection of either family with the city. But Shakespeare is believed to have written *The Merchant of Venice* between 1596 and 1598, so maybe this is a clue? Had Edward and Lucy seen a performance somewhere and been so enamoured with the play and the idea of Venice itself that they chose this name? Alas, we will never know. In some recent biographies she is awarded the double name of Venetia Anastasia, but it seems that this was a later accretion rather than a baptismal name. It would seem rather odd to give two names to only one child and for the second name not to be used by her father or her husband. Another little puzzle. The only clue detected so far is a footnote by Nicolas in his edition of *Sir Kenelm Digby's Memoirs* (1827, 2nd ed. 1828) where he gives his source for 'Anastatia' as Hutchins, *History of Dorset* (1747). Another clue here for a future sleuth?

XXV-2. Petronella

Petronella/Petronilla never married, but 'inherited' Eynsham in Oxfordshire from **Sir Edward** when he died in 1632 (*Auden's History*). She did not actually inherit, because the property was in reversion to the Earldom of Derby in the case of 'fail-male', i.e. no son and heir, which was indeed the case. But one can hardly imagine the family throwing her out of her home for so many years. Nothing more is known of her life, but the very fact that she buried her father and commissioned a memorial for his grave seems to present a strong hint that she lived with her father for several years until his death. After that, there would have been several households where she would presumably have been welcome: those of her two sisters and multiple cousins, for starters.

Interestingly, she does appear in one document in 1617, 'Earl of Worcester, Petronella Stanley, John Fortescue and Frances his wife v Ryder Bishop of Killake and Josiah Herne: Winwick: DL4/65/39 – Ref. 10', located by Brian S. Roberts (on his Stanley Family History website, Doc. 112).

'John Fortescue and Frances' were her sister and brother-in-law, with both of whom Petronella had spent her early years. More research might or might not produce interesting details to expand on her bare biography. At the very least she seems to have been in Winwick, or somehow concerned with Winwick, in 1617.

The Earl of Worcester in this year was Edward Somerset, 4th Earl of Worcester (>1568-1628), a fellow Knight of the Garter with William Stanley, 6th Earl of Derby and advisor to King James. Spenser had written his *Protholamion* in 1596 on the occasion of the joint marriage of two of Worcester's daughters. Worcester had served as Lord Privy Seal 1614-1616, and was thus an impressive personage to have on one's side in a court case in 1617. The most important connection, however, seems to have been blood relationship. Worcester was a first cousin of Lucy, Petronella's mother. Lucy's mother was Anne née Somerset, sister of William Somerset, 3rd Earl of Worcester, father of Edward in the 1617 document. Lucy's Catholic mother had died in exile in 1596, but her cousin Edward Somerset was still very much alive and active. Lucy herself had died in 1601, but the family links still seem to have been maintained. It is very interesting that Edward Somerset was very much an openly practising Catholic, who nevertheless evaded punishment because he was so highly regarded by King James. We (think we) know that **Sir Edward Jr** had been knighted by James at his coronation because of his father **Sir Thomas**'s suffering on behalf of his mother Mary, Queen of Scots, planning to help her escape from Chatsworth back in 1570. Given that Anne née Somerset's husband Thomas Percy, 7th Earl of Northumberland, had been executed because of his role in the pro-Catholic Mary Northern Rebellion of 1569, and Anne herself had fled into exile for the same reason, it seems that James's forgiveness was extended to all her Somerset family.

Perhaps the biggest mystery Petronella poses is her birthdate. This remains unknown, but the very fact that her four older sisters died together with their mother far away from home, and that she was the eldest of the three surviving daughters, including baby Venetia, provides thoughts for speculation. If the three youngest children were left behind at Tong when the rest of the family was visiting Walthamstow, one reason might well have been that they were deemed rather young to benefit from a visit to London – if that was where they were going. This would give a tentative birthdate for Frances about two years before Venetia, i.e, in c.1598, and Petronella two or three years before that, i.e. c.1595. This, however, still leaves the best part of a decade between this year and Priscilla's presumed birth date, the youngest of the other group. Could this be a hint that **(Sir) Edward** and Lucy had a long separation? This possibility is explored further in Appendix 10, by taking a close look at all Sir Kenelm Digby's memories of his father-in-law.

XXV-3. Frances

Frances married (Sir) John Fortescue (Bt), about whom Tudorplace and www.fortescue.org combined provide the following details:

John FORTESCUE of Salden (1st Baronet of Nova Scotia)
Born: 1592
Baptised: Mursley
Died: Sep 1656, Mursley, Buckinghamshire, England
Father: **Francis FORTESCUE of Salden (Sir)**
Mother: **Grace MANNERS**
Married: **Frances STANLEY of Eynsham, Oxon,** died in 1657. Married before 1614.
She was buried on 4 May 1657. Parents: Sir Edward STANLEY KB of Eynsham, Oxon
Children:
Sir John FORTESCUE 2nd Baronet of Nova Scotia

Sir Edward FORTESCUE of Salden
Frances FORTESCUE
Grace FORTESCUE

It seems that son Edward Fortescue might have been named after **Sir Edward**, which provided at least one grandchild in the next generation with his name. Sir John's mother, Grace Manners, was the daughter of Sir John Manners and Dorothy Vernon of Haddon Hall, which meant that Grace and **Sir Edward** were first cousins and their children therefore second cousins. This was presumably the reason why . . .

> ...when her [Venetia's] mother died young, her father sent her to be brought up by his friends, Francis and Grace Fortescue of Selden, [*sic*] Buckinghamshire. It was as a young girl that she first came into contact with her future husband, Kenelm Digby, for he lived nearby at Gothurst [*aka Gayhurst*] with his formidable widowed mother, Mary Mulscho.
> (Ann Sumner, 'Venetia Digby on her deathbed', *History Today*, October 1995, p. 21.)

Frances also went there with Venetia and thus knew her future husband from childhood. A slight modification to the above statement is that Francis and Grace Fortescue were not just 'his friends', but **Sir Edward**'s first cousin and husband. Francis and Grace had a large family (thirteen children are given on Tudorplace), so three more would not have made much difference. Mary, one of Sir John's sisters, married John Talbot, 10th Earl of Shrewsbury, which brings this family into the local Stanley picture yet again. An interesting Shakespearean link is that a John Fortescue was involved in the Blackfriars Gatehouse, of which Shakespeare was a co-owner. (More on this appears in 'Appendix 7. Shakespeare Encyclopedia' and 'Appendix 8. Father Henry More'.) The website www.fortescue.org gives further intriguing information, particularly on Sir John Fortescue, grandfather of Frances's husband, most of which details **Sir Edward Jr** would presumably have known:

> 'Queen Elizabeth possibly visited Salden' in 1602, and on 24th March 1603 she died. Her funeral at Westminster on April 28th was arranged largely by Sir John.
> 'On 24 May 1603 James confirmed John as Chancellor of the Duchy of Lancaster, and of the County Palatine of Lancaster and as Master of the Great Wardrobe, but he did not confirm him as Chancellor and Under-Treasurer of the Exchequer. On 27th June King James visited Salden, and made many knights there, and at the homes of Sir Francis, son of Sir John; also at the home of Mr George Fortescue. A Baronry was offered to Sir John but he declined.
> 'Sir John died on 23rd December 1607 at Westminster, aged 74. A monument to him and his wife Cecilia was placed at Murseley Church, Buckinghamshire, by their sons Francis and William. The funeral was deferred until 6th July 1608.
>
> (www.fortescue.org)

In St Mary the Virgin, Murseley, Bucks are two Fortescue tombs/memorials, with the following descriptions:

> 1. Here lies Sir John Fortesque Master of the Great Wardrobe, Chancellor and Under treasurer of the Exchequer and a member of the Privy Council of Queen Elizabeth. Later in the First year of King James's reign he became Chancellor of the Duchy of Lancaster.
>
> He lived for 76 years and died on the 23rd December in the year of our Lord 1607. He was survived by his sons Francis Knight of the Most Noble Order of the Bath and William Knight who placed this Memorial in Memory of their Dead Father.
>
> 2. The second memorial shows Sir Frances [*sic*, Francis] Fortesque and his wife Grace with their children those carrying skulls denote they died in childhood.
> (Website: Waymarking.com/Fortesque – St Mary the Virgin, Murseley, Bucks)

It seems that the Fortescue family requires further research. John Fortescue, Esquire (1592-1656), one of the surviving sons of Sir Francis and Grace, and **Sir Edward**'s son-in-law, was named by **Sir Edward** as one of the executors of his will in June 1632. One of the witnesses was Anthony Fortescue, who has not so far been identified. John Fortescue was also named as an executor in London in December 1632 when the administration of the will took place 'emanating from the home of Kenelm Digby, knight, husband of Venetie Digby'. John was later created 1st Baronet Fortescue of Nova Scotia by King Charles in 1636 during the King's enthusiasm for developing trading links with North America. His later life has been researched, but his earlier life during the lifetime of his father-in-law **Sir Edward** remains a blank, apart from his marriage to Frances Stanley. The minimal details about this family that appear in *Sir Kenelm Digby's Memoirs* are included in Appendix 10.

A Fortescue was also involved in the lease of the Blackfriars Theatre in London. In August 1608 the King's Men assumed the lease of the Blackfriars theatre, in which William Shakespeare was closely involved. The Blackfriars Theatre is being reconstructed as a 'winter partner home' of The New Globe, although will be named The Sam Wanamaker Theatre in honour of the inspirer of The New Globe, and will be close by. (Details appear on many websites; the expected opening will be in 2014.) Professor Andrew Gurr has been a consultant for both theatres. In his account of 'London's Blackfriars Playhouse and the Chamberlain's Men' in *Essays on the Blackfriars Stage* (2006) there is no mention of any Stanley or Fortescue. Maybe their names will appear in future research into the earlier history of Blackfriars Playhouse and add a few details about **Sir Edward**'s close family, even if not for his own biography?

XXV-4. Venetia

The other daughter who married was Venetia. Her short and colourful life must have compensated to some extent for all those children who had died, and enough to keep **Sir Edward** interested in her affairs during the last decade of his life. A short biography is in *Wikipedia*, which names her as Venetia Anastasia, but perhaps the best known account of her life, as detected still within living memory later in the century, was by John Aubrey (1626-97). If some details given by him are correct, then after living with the Fortescues for some years, she lived at Eynsham for some time before departing for London. Her story has been told so often, but for the record, for any reader who might have missed it, here is Aubrey's account.

Venetia Digby (1600-33)

Venetia Stanley was daughter of **Sir Edward Stanley**. She was a most beautiful desirable creature; and being of a mature age was let by her father to live with a tenant and servants at Eynsham Abbey* (his land, or the Earl of Derby's) in Oxfordshire; but as private as that place was, it seems her beauty could not lie hid. The young eagles had espied her, and she was sanguine and tractable, and of much suavity (which to abuse was great pity).

In those days Richard Earl of Dorset (grandson and heir to the Lord Treasurer) lived in the greatest splendour of any nobleman of England. Among other pleasures that he enjoyed, Venus was not the least.† This pretty creature's fame quickly came to his lordship's ears, who made no delay to catch at such an opportunity.

I have now forgotten who first brought her to town, but I have heard my uncle Danvers say (who was her contemporary) that she was so commonly courted, and that by grandees, that it was written over her lodging one night in uncial letters,

Pray come not near,
for Dame Venetia lodgeth here.

The Earl of Dorset, aforesaid, was her greatest gallant, who was extremely enamoured of her, and had one if not more children by her. He settled on her an annuity of £500 per annum.‡

Among other young sparks of that time, Sir Kenelm Digby grew acquainted with her, and fell so much in love with her that he married her, much against the good will of his mother; he would say that 'a wise man, and lusty, could make an honest woman out of a brothel house'. Sir Edmund Wyld had her picture (and you may imagine was very familiar with her), which picture is now at Droitwich in Worcestershire, at an inn, where now the town keep their meetings. Also at Mr Rose's, a jeweller in Henrietta Street in Covent Garden, is an excellent piece of her, drawn after she was newly dead.

She had a most lovely and sweet-turned face, delicate dark brown hair. She had a perfect healthy constitution; strong; good skin; well proportioned; much inclining to a wanton (near altogether). Her face, a short oval; dark brown eyebrow, about which much sweetness, as also in the opening of her eyelids. The colour of her cheeks was just that of the damask rose, which is neither too hot nor too pale. She was of a just stature, not very tall.

Sir Kenelm had several pictures of her by Vandyke, etc. He had her hands cast in plaster, and her feet and her face. See Ben Jonson's second volume, where he made her live in poetry, in his drawing of her, both body and mind:

'Sitting, and ready to be drawn,
What makes these tiffany, silks, and lawn,
Embroideries, feathers, fringes, lace,
When every limb takes like a face!' - etc.

When these verses were made she had three children by Sir Kenelm, who are there mentioned, viz Kenelm, George and John.

Her picture drawn by Sir Anthony Vandyke hangs in the queen's drawing room, at Windsor Castle, over the chimney.

She died in her bed suddenly. Some suspected that she was poisoned. When her head was opened there was found but little brain, which her husband imputed to her drinking of viper wine; but spiteful women would say it was a viper-husband who was jealous of her, that she would steal a leap. I have heard some say, - e.g. my cousin Elizabeth Faulkner – that after her marriage she redeemed her honour by her strict living. Once a year the Earl of Dorset invited her and Sir Kenelm to dinner, where the earl would behold her with such passion, and only kiss her hand.

Sir Kenelm erected to her memory a sumptuous and stately monument at Christ Church (near Newgate Street) in the east end of the south aisle, where her body lies in a vault of brickwork, over which are three steps of black marble, on which was a stately altar of black marble with four inscriptions in copper gilt affixed to it: upon this altar her bust of copper gilt, all which (except only the vault, which was only opened a little by the fall) is utterly destroyed by the great conflagration. Among the monuments in the book mentioned in Sir Kenelm Digby's life is to be seen a curious drawing of this monument, with copies of the several inscriptions.

About 1676 or 5, as I was walking through Newgate Street, I saw Dame Venetia's bust standing at a stall at the Golden Cross, a brazier's shop. I perfected it, but the fire had got off the gilding: but taking notice of it to one that was with me, I could never see it afterwards exposed to the street. They melted it down. How these curiosities would be quite forgotten, did not such idle fellows as I am put them down!

*At the west end of the church here were two towers as at Wells or Westminster Abbey, which were standing till about 1656. The rooms of the abbey were richly wainscotted, both sides and roof.
†Samual [*sic*] Daniel: 'Cheeks of roses, locks of amber, To b'enprisoned in a chamber etc.
‡In fact probably his brother Edward, who succeeded him in the earldom in 1624.
(*John Aubrey: Brief Lives*, ed. Richard Barber, Boydell, 1975, 1982, pp. 105-6.)

The account is immediately preceded in this edition by Aubrey's biography of Sir Kenelm. He also left his own *Memoirs*, which give many more details. Venetia must have been quite a lady! The portrait of her on her deathbed is now in Dulwich Picture Gallery, associated with Dulwich College, founded by the actor Edward Alleyn (whose mother, incidentally, was a Towneley of Towneley near Burnley, providing another Lancashire connection).

After Venetia's death Sir Kenelm went into mourning, suitably dressed in a long black cloak, and devoted himself to studies at Gresham College. One of his activities was writing his *Memoirs*, which give his personal account of Venetia as his childhood playmate, later sweetheart and finally wife, after many vicissitudes. This is now available online. Sections which include details directly relevant to **Sir Edward** are included in Appendix 10.

As seen above in Aubrey's account, Ben Jonson wrote a poem about her (another one appears below), as did Samuel Daniel, which leads to another interesting connection. Daniel was tutor to Lady Anne Clifford (whom we met briefly above), another first cousin of William Stanley, 6th Earl of Derby. She was the daughter of George Clifford, 3rd Earl of Cumberland, half-brother of Margaret Clifford, wife of Henry, 4th Earl of Derby. In 1600 Lady Anne was ten and Venetia had only just been born, but later their lives were to become connected, because Lady Anne married in 1609 Richard Sackville, 3rd Earl of Dorset, who maintained Venetia as his mistress (according to Aubrey). His brother Edward Sackville, 4th Earl of Dorset has since been offered as an alternative suitor, but it is generally judged that there is no historical foundation to support Aubrey's claim. Lady Anne's biography has been told several times; the one on my shelf is by Martin Holmes, *Proud Northern Lady*, (1975, 1984 and still in print in 2006). She was another formidable lady, who enters Shakespeare's posthumous story inasmuch as her second husband (1630) was Philip Herbert, 1st Earl of Montgomery, 4th Earl of Pembroke, one of the brothers to whom Shakespeare's *First Folio* was dedicated in 1623. His first wife had been Susan de Vere, sister-in-law of William Stanley, 6th Earl of Derby.

XXVa. Venetia Stanley, Lady Digby
Not too long before her death. A copy of an unidentified portrait. Numerous portraits were painted of her, many appearing on a multitude of websites, most of them in art galleries and under copyright. Maybe, when her next biography is written, all will appear together in chronological order and with a full history of each one? Salden House in Mursley, Bucks, where she grew up, built in the late sixteenth century for Sir John Fortescue, was mostly demolished in 1738-43. (British Listed Buildings)

Sir Edward must have known his son-in-law Sir Kenelm, one suspects rather better than in the general picture that has come down to us. He was responsible, with his wife Venetia and others, for the administration of **Sir Edward**'s will in London in December 1632, and mentions him several times in his *Memoirs*, albeit rather sparing in details. **Sir Edward** also almost certainly knew his father Sir Everard Digby, one of the Gunpowder Plotters, executed for his role in this plot. Ben Jonson certainly knew (of) Sir Everard, as he (Ben) was known to have been supping with Gunpowder Plotters at the Mermaid Tavern shortly before the event, and he certainly knew Venetia, for him to have written such a complimentary poem about her. Jonson proved again and again that he was on close terms with the Derbys and various Stanley relations. Apart from other writings dedicated to or performed by members of the family, he started a history of the family of the Earls of Derby in a poem dedicated to Venetia Stanley (reproduced in Thomas Heywood, *The Earls of Derby and the Verse Writers and Poets of the sixteenth and seventeenth centuries*, Chetham Society, 1853):

> Footnote, p. 16
>
> Jonson began the pedigree of the Stanleys in verse, but soon abandoned the attempt. The lines occur in the poem entitled "Eupheme, or the fair fame of Lady Venetia Digby."

> > I sing the just and uncontroul'd descent
> > Of Dame Venetia Digby, stil'd the Fair,
> > For Mind and Body the most excellent
> > That ever Nature, or the later Air,
> > Gave two such Houses as Northumberland
> > And Stanley, to which she was co-heir.
> > Speak it you bold Penates, you that stand
> > At either stern, and know the veins of good

Run from your roots; Tell, testifie the grand
Meeting of graces, that so swell
The flood of vertues in her, as in short she grew
The wonder of her sex, and of your blood.
And tell thou Alde Legh, none can tell more true
Thy Nieces line, than thou that gav'st thy name
Into the kindred whence thy Adam drew
Meschines honour, with the Cestrian fame
Of the first Lupus in the family
By Ranulph   (*The rest of this Song is lost.*)

Jonson also, according to tradition, supped with Shakespeare and Michael Drayton in Stratford, after which the Bard caught a fever and died. That was in 1616, when Venetia was still a teenager. Sir Edward was to live until 1632 and Venetia until 1633. It is difficult to imagine that, before and between these dates, Sir Edward did not encounter all the poets and members of the aristocracy and upper gentry mentioned in this chapter.

~~~~~~~~~~~~~~~~~~~~~~~~~~~

XXVb. Sir Kenelm Digby
Venetia's childhood sweetheart. After a long separation they married. Their fathers were friends and Sir Kenelm wrote about Sir Edward Stanley, his father-in-law, in his *Memoirs*. His father Sir Everard Digby was executed as a Gunpowder Plotter.

XXVc. Thomas Percy
One of the plotters in XXVe and a 'cousin' of
Lady Lucy Percy Stanley.

XXVd. Gayhurst House, Bucks

In more recent times than when it was the home of Sir Everard Digby, where his son Sir Kenelm grew up.
It was previously known as Gothurst. In the 1970s it was converted to multiple flats.

XXVe. Gunpowder Plotters

The well-known depiction of the plotters, not including Sir Everard Digby, who joined in later.

Chapter XXVI
The Earls of Rutland, Sir Thomas & Sir Edward Jr and Shakespeare

At some point one should try to sort out the Earls of Rutland, the son of one of whom, John Manners, was the brother-in-law of **Sir Thomas Stanley** of Tong and a later one received an epigram from Weever. This same later one, Roger the 5th Earl, has also been proposed as an Alternative Authorship Candidate for some or all of Shakespeare's works. They have certainly confused many before me, as they are so often referred to just as the Earl of Rutland, without a forename or which number earl. A request to the Leicestershire Record Office (which covers Rutland) for a pedigree chart of the Earls of Rutland produced sections VIII and IX of *The History and Antiquities of the County of Rutland* by James Wright (L914.2 RUT) (dates mentioned in the text indicate its publication in the mid-eighteenth century.) The following dates and details were thus gleaned from a source that appeared to be rather reliably close to the horse's mouth (geographically, at least) and in any case long before the Earls of Rutland were perceived to have any relevance to Shakespeare's biography. These details revealed the source of many confusions (so many of them were brothers rather than son and heir) and also made it very clear why they had so much contact in the sixteenth century with the Earls of Derby. Some were Knights of the Garter (as were all relevant Earls of Derby) and one was involved in the defence of the North against the Scots (along with the Earl of Derby). They also married into families of relevance to the Stanleys. Those details and names of individuals of most relevance in the context of this book are given in **bold** in the table. All Earls of Rutland appear on the Family Tree in Appendix 12c: MANNERS, VERNON, PERCY, FORTESCUE.

1st–8th Earls of Rutland (2nd creation, surname Manners)
(from the text by Wright, *Rutland*). [Dates and other details in square brackets are from Tudorplace, with no source references given and so taken on trust.]

1st Earl of Rutland (of Belvoir)	Thomas Manners = Alianore, daughter of Sir William Paston d. 35 Henry Sep. 20 [Born bef. 1488, Etal, Northumberland; acceded 18 June 1523/5; died 20 Sep. 1543; buried St Mary the Virgin Church, Bottesford, Leics.] Thomas had five sons: 1) Henry, 2nd Earl; 2) **John Esquire**, who married **Dorothy Vernon**, daughter and co-heir of **Sir George Vernon of Haddon**, Co. Derby; 3) Roger; 4) Thomas; 5) Oliver.
2nd Earl Henry	d. 1563 Sep. 17; 2 Ed. VI Constable of Nottingham Castle; 3/4 Ph. & M. Capt. Gen. of forces in France; 1 Eliz. Lieutenant of Co. Nottingham & Rutland; 3 Eliz. Lord President of the Council of the North, Knight of the Garter. [Born c. 23 Sep 1526, Haddon Hall, Derbys.; bap. Enfield; d. 17 Sep. 1563; m. Margaret Neville, 3 July 1536, Holywell, Shoreditch, Middlesex.] Henry had two sons: Edward, 3rd Earl and John, 4th Earl.
3rd Earl Edward	d. 1587 April 14; 1582 Lieutenant of Co. Lincoln; 1584 Knight of the Garter; o.s.p., so the Earldom went to his brother John. [Born 12 July 1549; d. 14 Apr. 1587 Puddle Wharf, London; bur. St Mary the Virgin Church, Bottesford, Leics.; m. **Isabel Holcroft** (d. 16 Jan 1605) 6 June 1573.] (She was from Cheshire, Derby territory.)
4th Earl John	d. 1587 Feb. 21; 29 Eliz. Constable of Nottingham Castle, Lieutenant of Co. Nottingham. [Born bef. 1552; d. 24 Feb. 1587/8 Nottingham; bur. St Mary the Virgin Church, Bottesford; m. 1574 Elizabeth Charlton.]

continued

	3rd Earl Edward and 4th Earl John had a cousin, **Sir George, son of John Esquire**, 2nd son of 1st Earl Thomas. Sir George's son & heir was John, who became 8th Earl John (of Haddon – see below) when the 3 brothers of the senior line (Roger 5th, Francis 6th and George 7th – see below) died without leaving a single male heir. Sir George's sister was **Grace, who married Sir Francis Fortescue.**
5th Earl Roger	d. 1612 Jun 26 without a son & heir, so the Earldom went to his brother Francis. 1 James 1: Lieutenant of Co. Lincoln; **ambassador to Denmark**. [Born 6 Oct. 1576; d. 26 June 1612; bur. St Mary the Virgin, Bottesford, Leics.; m. **Elizabeth Sidney** 5 Mar. 1598.] **He is the Russian Alternative Authorship Candidate for Shakespeare**.
6th Earl Francis	d. 1632 Dec 17 without a son & heir, so the Earldom went to his brother George. [B. 1578; d. 17 Dec. 1632 Bishops Stortford, Herts.; bur. St Mary the Virgin, Bottesford; m. Frances Knyvett 6 May 1602.] **He is the one who received the Impresa from 'Mr Shakespeare'**.
7th Earl George	d. 1641 Mar 29 without a son & heir, so the Earldom went to his half-cousin John, descendant of the **Vernon heiress of Haddon**, son of Sir George, son of John, etc., as above. [Born 1580; d. 29 Mar. 1641; bur. St Mary's Bottesford; m. **Frances Carey** 3 Mar 1605.]
8th Earl John (of Haddon)	d. 1679 Sep 29. After this they became Dukes of Rutland, with their main seat at Belvoir Castle, Rutland

So far, so clear, but it seems that the Earls of Rutland and their wives deserve more attention. When Wright was writing his history he was mainly concerned with documenting the line of descent, and as four of the first seven earls died without leaving a son and heir, their wives received rather short shrift.

My main interest in the Earls of Rutland came because during reading around 'Shakespeare in Lancashire' they had popped up at so many steps along the way as kinsmen or neighbours of the Earls of Derby (through marriage to a Holcroft). Roger the 5th was a dedicatee of an epigram by Weever (1599), from Preston, and was also a friend of the Earls of Essex and Southampton (he went to the Tower with them after the Essex Rebellion in 1601); Roger was also an Alternative Authorship Candidate for some or all of Shakespeare's works (nonsense, of course, but there did seem to have been some personal connection); he also married Elizabeth Sidney, daughter of Sir Philip Sidney, who had fought at Zutphen with (Sir) Edward Stanley and Sir William Stanley of Hooton, who (one presumes) was at school at Lathom with **Sir Thomas Stanley**. The junior Manners branch at Haddon Hall, Derbyshire had close connections with the junior branch of the Stanleys of Tong. Further delving produced the following (most) relevant details about Roger.

Roger, the 5th Earl, has often been associated with Shakespeare circles as a very good friend of Henry Wriothesley, 3rd Earl of Southampton and dedicatee of Shakespeare's two long poems *Venus and Adonis* and *The Rape of Lucrece*. Roger went to Queens' College, Cambridge in 1587; Wriothesley was at St John's at the same time. They both joined Essex on some of his campaigns, with Rutland on the expedition to the Azores in 1597 and Ireland in 1599. Rutland also accompanied the Earl of Northumberland to the Netherlands in 1600 in the war against the Spanish, and joined in with Essex's Rebellion in 1601, for which he was imprisoned but escaped with a hefty fine. He also happened to marry the only daughter of Sir Philip Sidney, who had died of his wounds in that war in

1586 and who had attended Shrewsbury Grammar School along with his friend Sir Fulke Greville, Recorder of Stratford-upon-Avon. Roger Manners had estates in Cheshire, which took him there quite often. His uncle Edward, 3rd Earl of Rutland, had married a daughter of Thomas Holcroft of Vale Royal, Cheshire; Lady Elizabeth Manners had married Sir John Savage of Rock Savage, Cheshire; and one of their daughters married Baron Langton (of the 'affray at Lea' in 1589, where Thomas Hoghton was killed, whose family was host, by tradition, of young William Shakespeare). This takes us straight into the whole circle of those who had received epigrams from the poet John Weever in 1599, including Roger the 5th Earl and Shakespeare. Another notable fact seemed to be that Rutland received James I at Belvoir in 1603, where he was entertained with a Ben Jonson play, and in December joined the king at Wilton House at the same time as Shakespeare is reported as having been there. One suspects they must all have known each other rather well.

5th Earl Roger is the one who is the Russian Shakespeare Alternative Authorship candidate, based mainly, it seems, on the fact that he visited Denmark and might thus have heard the Hamlet story; he also visited Padua when two German (Danish?) students Rosencrantz and Guildenstern were there; plus some of the other connections mentioned above. John Michell, *Who Wrote Shakespeare?* gives a good brief biography of Roger, pointing out the many Shakespeare connections claimed by his supporters.

(Michell did not for one minute believe that Rutland was Shakespeare in disguise; nor any of the other sixty or so other candidates proposed (private communication). When I contacted him about his and my research on William Stanley, 6th Earl of Derby, he was delighted to hear that the latter had so many associations with Shakespeare – even more than he had detected in Derbyite literature - because he was always secretly his favourite, after Shakespeare being himself, of course. Sadly, John Michell died in 2009. Whilst we are in brackets, may I take the liberty of relating a couple of anecdotes? Several years ago I visited Belvoir Castle, main seat of the Earls and Dukes of Rutland. I talked to several guides there, who, one might have thought, would be amongst the first to be enthusiastic Rutlanders. Not a bit of it – none of them believed in his candidature, although they had been interested a few weeks previously that a Russian film crew had been there pursuing the theory yet again. My main disappointment was that we were not allowed into the library because Merchant

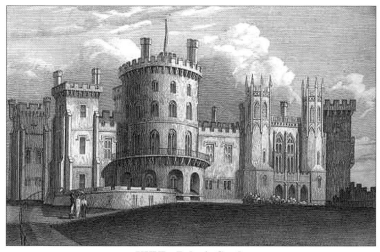

XXVIa. Belvoir Castle

Etching, 1819. Seat of the Manners family, Earls of Rutland. Sir Edward's Aunt Dorothy Vernon of Haddon Hall married John Manners, brother of the 1st Earl of Rutland of Belvoir, and their great-grandson became the 8th Earl, inheriting Belvoir when the main line died out. Still in existence, open to the public.

and Ivory were filming a scene there for *The Golden Bowl* by Henry James that very day – this dates my visit to 2000. I didn't have time to hang around in the hope of seeing them or any of the stars – or the library, so had to wait for the film to see the library. Not long afterwards I met Russian Professor Rashid Sunyaev – although not of English Literature but astrophysics – and asked him if the Rutland candidacy for Shakespeare was well known in Russia. 'Not to me,' he said with a twinkle in his eye and a big grin, 'but the Russians ONLY believe in conspiracy theories!' So much for Roger as William Shakespeare.)

One final reference here to the Earl of Rutland and Shakespeare. In the accounts of the Earl of Rutland at Belvoir Castle is a record on 24 March 1613 of '44s' paid to 'Mr Shakespeare in gold about my Lord's *impresa*', and the same amount to 'Richard Burbadge for painting and making it'. The *impresa* is a term from heraldry, meaning an emblem or device, usually a motto, as on a coat of arms, to be worn at a tournament or other notable occasion. It is generally accepted that the 'Richard Burbadge' named was Shakespeare's fellow-actor, who was a talented amateur painter. Schoenbaum believed that 'the linking of his name with Shakespeare's effectively eliminates any doubt that it was the poet rather than some other Shakespeare – John Shakespeare, the royal bit-maker, for example – who created the Earl's *impresa*.' (Schoenbaum, *Compact Documentary Life*, p. 272). On the same page, in a footnote, 'The Rutland papers record payment to Burbage for another *impresa* on 25 March 1616'.

This statement by Schoenbaum was a refutal of the findings of Charlotte Stopes at the beginning of the twentieth century (*Shakespeare's Family*, 1901). She located several references to a John Shakespeare, bit-maker at court, involving the production of scenery for masques at James's court, which were regularly staged by Ben Jonson and others. Mrs Stopes was sure that this was the 'Mr Shakespeare' in the accounts of the Earl of Rutland, not William. (Michell, *Who Wrote Shakespeare?*, p. 50, repeats this point.) John Shakespeare the bit-maker also appears in the wardrobe account of Charles I, as prince and king, when he made 'full bosses charged with the arms of England', so must still have been around for some time after 1625, and painting 'bosses' sounds awfully similar to painting *impresas*. As all major tournaments and masques were staged in London, it is more than possible that the paintings of bosses occurred here, with payment also made here, with the amount recorded in the family accounts later. It does not necessarily require the presence of 'Mr Shakespeare' at Belvoir. Incidentally, the Earl of Rutland in 1613 was not the Alternative Authorship Candidate but Roger's brother Francis, 6th Earl, because the former had died the year before leaving no male heir. This also applies to the other *impresa* in 1616.

I would argue that, on a balance of probabilities, it is more likely that Stopes was right and Schoenbaum wrong, i.e. that 'Mr Shakespeare' on 24 March 1613 was much more likely to have been 'Mr John the bit-maker' than William the actor, poet and playwright. Furthermore, I would argue that 'Mr John' was almost certainly an older brother of William, who had followed him to the capital and also ended up at court. This is part of another long story, which involves an analysis of other Shakespeares in London, including one family that continued to bear the Shakespeare coat of arms acquired by William's father John in 1596. This family has been overlooked or ignored by all Shakespeare scholars and will lead to a complete reassessment of William's Shakespeare relatives, thanks to the sterling research conducted by Stephen Pearson and associates, webmaster of The Shakespeare Family History website, and local historian Peter Lee, who has an authoritative article there: 'Shakespeare's Hidden Family?'. Pearson's most relevant article, among many other relevant details, is 'Wherefore Art Thou, Grandfather?'

Another relevant point seems to be the date of recording of the payment for the *impresa*: 24 March 1613. One does not need to search very far for celebrations in London early in this year organised to celebrate the marriage of Princess Elizabeth (King James's daughter) to Frederick V of the Palatinate of the Rhine, later King of Bohemia, among other festivities.

Frederick traveled to London to retrieve his bride, landing on English soil on 6 October 1612. Frederick and Elizabeth, who had previously corresponded in French, now met each other for the first time, and got on well together. They were formally engaged in January 1613. They were subsequently married on 24 February 1613 at the royal chapel at the Palace of Whitehall. Shortly before the ceremony, Frederick was inducted into the Order of the Garter and he wore the Order's chain during the wedding ceremony. Elaborate celebrations, organized by Francis Bacon, followed the ceremony; these included a performance of The Masque of the Inner Temple and Gray's Inn by Francis Beaumont and The Memorable Masque of the Middle Temple and Lincoln's Inn by George Chapman.

(Wikipedia)

Sir Edward Stanley Jr was called to court to attend this marriage, and we know from his later son-in-law *Sir Kenelm Digby's Memoirs* that he did indeed go. One might presume that when he was there he met Francis Manners, 6th Earl of Rutland, a close kinsman of his Vernon/Manners relatives. One might also presume that his cousin William Stanley, 6th Earl of Derby and Knight of the Garter since 1601, was also summoned and attended. Indeed, it must have presented an admirable occasion for many of the people mentioned previously in this book to meet again. Perhaps William Shakespeare in semi-retirement in Stratford also travelled to London for this splendid occasion and participated in some of the events in 1613, admiring his brother John's work?

XXVIb. Roger Manners, 5th Earl of Rutland
(1576-1612) Sir Edward Jr's and Shakespeare's
contemporary

Chapter XXVII
Sir Edward Jr's last will and testament, 1632

XXIVII-1. Introduction

Following is a transcription of the MS in the National Archives at Kew. I acknowledge with gratitude the receipt of a scanned copy of the original MS at Kew from Brian S. Roberts, webmaster of the main Stanley Family History website. Brian's conclusion on reading this in c.2008 was that it was not very revealing. I accepted his judgment at the time, but my reading of this MS two years later provided a somewhat different conclusion. We obviously both needed two more years of research.

As far as I am aware the following transcription is the first one ever undertaken and published. Any criticisms/corrections of this [HM's] transcription will be most gratefully received. No doubt some expert will decipher all the missing words, but I doubt very much whether these will contribute more to the interpretation, as given in footnotes.

First and foremost, it is obvious that the MS at Kew is actually a later copy of two separate MSS. The first half (in English) was the Last Will and Testament of **Sir Edward**, dictated by him on his deathbed in Eynsham, Oxon (presumably at Eynsham Abbey) on 10 June 1632. He died eight days later and was buried in the Parish Church of St Leonard, Eynsham. The second half, Administration for Probate (in Latin), was written in London in December 1632. One can only presume that the originals have not survived, and we are confronted with subsequent copies onto one and the same page, all in the same hand. However, one can presume that the MS which has survived comes as close as possible to the original.

Sir Edward Jr's will was obviously a testament dictated a few days before the end of his life; for me [HM], reading this rather belatedly in late 2010, it was the end of a documentary journey through **Sir Edward Jr**'s life, nearly four centuries later. Many/most of his secrets went with him to his grave in Eynsham, Oxon. However, his last will reveals, via a scribe, the thoughts uppermost in his mind when he dictated this. The Latin text reveals that his son-in-law Sir Kenelm Digby was involved in the aftermath of sorting out the estate. I have taken the liberty of adding a few commas and full stops in the transcription.

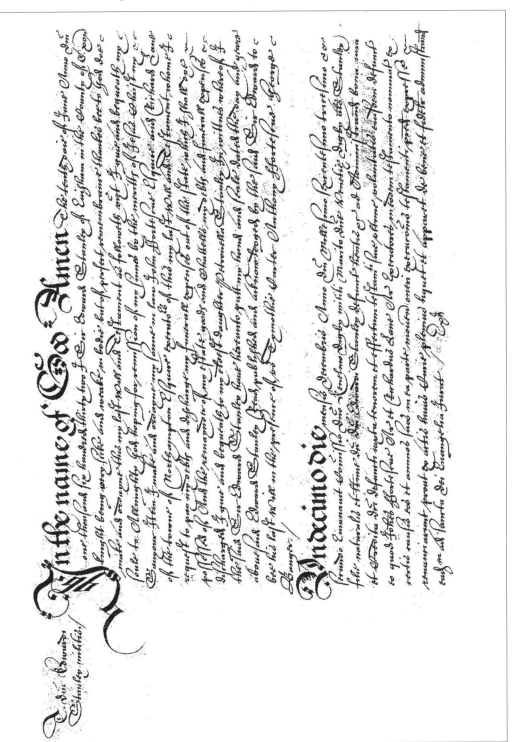

XXVIIa. Sir Edward Stanley Jr's will, 1632

Sir Edward Jr's last will and testament in June + Admin. for probate in December, 1632.
National Archives, PROB 11/162/Records of the Prerogative Court of Canterbury, Audley Quire Numbers 66-126,
Image ref. 695/609, accessed by Brian S. Roberts.

XXVII-2. Sir Edward's last will and testament 10 June 1632

Reference for Sir Edward Stanley's will - NATIONAL ARCHIVES, KEW

Date	11 December 1632
Catalogue reference	PROB 11/162
Dept	Records of the Prerogative Court of Canterbury
Series	Prerogative Court of Canterbury and related Probate Jurisdictions: Will Registers
Piece	Name of Register: Audley Quire Numbers: 66 - 126
Image reference	695/609

Transcription of the last will and testament [*with notes*]

Testm Edwards Stanley militis [*in the left margin*] [*Testament of Edward Stanley, knight*]

In the name of God Amen The tenth daie of June Anno dm [*domini*] / one thousand six hundred thirty two.[ii] I Sir Edward Stanley of Enisham in the County of Oxon / knight[iii] being very sicke and weake in bodie but of perfect remembrance thankes bee to God doe / make and ordayne this my last Will and Testament as followeth viz. I give and bequeath my / soule to Allmighty God hoping for remission of my sinnes by the meritts of Jesus Christ my / Savyour.[iiii] Item I make and ordayne my Sonne in law John ffortescue Esquire[iv] and Richard Lane / of the towne of Northampton Esquire[v] executo^rs of this my last will and Testament, whome I / request to pay my debts and dyscharge my funerall expenses out of the estate which I shall [?*doe*] / possession of. And the remainder of my estate goods and chattells, my debts and funerall expenses discharged, I grant [?] and bequeath to my eldest daughter Petronella Stanley.[vi] In witness whereof I the said Sir Edward Stanley have hereunto putt my hand and seale dated the day and year / abovesaid.

Edward Stanley [??], published and acknowledged by the said Sir Edward to / bee his last Will in the presence of Tymothie [?*Daxter*] Anthony ffortescue George / [?*Banger*][vii]

Notes by HM:

[i] This dates **Sir Edward**'s will very precisely to 10 June 1632. We know that he died eight days later, from the memorial in Eynsham church, with the following inscription:

> Here lies Edward Stanley K.B. (son of Thomas, the son of Edward Earl of Derby). Died June 18th 1632, aged 69. His daughter Petronilla Stanley placed this here
>
> > (Reproduced from Lilian Wright's article given in full in Chapter XIX. An excursion to Eynsham, Oxfordshire.)

We have no idea what he died of, but reaching the age of nearly seventy was an achievement in itself at that time.

[ii] It is interesting that **Sir Edward**, when writing his will on his deathbed, considered himself as 'of Eynsham in Oxfordshire'. No mention is made of Winwick in Lancashire or Tong in Shropshire or anywhere else he might have lived or been associated with. The main fact that seems to emerge from his will is that he had spent long enough in Eynsham for him to regard himself as associated with this place more than any other during the last years of his life, since selling Tong Castle in 1603. Perhaps the most glaring omission, with hindsight, is that there is no mention of any of his Derby relatives in his will. The main candidates would have been:

- His first cousin and fellow-widower William Stanley, 6th Earl of Derby since 1594, who was still very much alive (he was destined to live until 1642). We know that William had visited Eynsham on at least one occasion in 1584 and played an active role there. (See Chapter XIX. Eynsham.) However, in 1632 William had been living in Chester for several years, rather withdrawn from public life, having handed over all his public responsibilities to his son and heir James, Lord Strange.

- James, Lord Strange, William's elder son, who had been busy during the years leading up to 1632. He had travelled to The Hague, Holland in 1626 to marry Charlotte de la Trémouille, from an aristocratic French Huguenot family, and was very busy from then on back in Lathom and Knowsley, Lancashire administering the family properties, serving as MP for Liverpool on occasion, fathering several children, etc.. Perhaps he was just too busy in 1632 to pay much attention to the estates of his father's cousin in distant Eynsham. It is nevertheless a slight surprise that he does not appear in **Sir Edward**'s will, given that Eynsham was one of the properties in reversion to the Earldom of Derby if **Sir Edward** were to die without a male heir. It did indeed revert later, after the Civil War, to Earl James's widow Countess Charlotte. (See Chapter XIX. Eynsham.)

- Sir Robert, Earl William's younger son, who was living in London in 1632 with his second wife. However, he died just six months after **Sir Edward**, on 3 January 1633. (We know this because it is recorded on his tomb in Chelsea.) Whether **Sir Edward** knew or not that this 'cousin' was about to die will probably remain unknown. It is, however, worth repeating that Sir Robert has a Shakespearean epitaph on his tomb, with whatever implications this might offer. (See Chapter XIX. Other tombs, by Simon Watney.)

[iii] This preamble reads (for me) like a Catholic will. It will no doubt be interpreted as this or otherwise by others.

[iv] The very fact that **Sir Edward** named his son-in-law '**John Fortescue Esquire**' as one of his executors seems to imply that he held him in esteem above all other close relatives. We will remember that John Fortescue married **Sir Edward**'s daughter Frances, both of them having grown up together in the large Fortescue household in Salden, Buckinghamshire, where **Sir Edward** placed his three surviving little daughters some time after his wife Lucy and four of their daughters had died in Walthamstow, Essex in 1601. The mother of John Fortescue, the executor, was Grace née Manners, daughter of John Manners and Dorothy née Vernon of Haddon Hall. Dorothy was **Sir Edward**'s aunt, sister of his mother Margaret née Vernon. **Sir Edward**'s will tells us that John Fortescue was still 'Esquire' in 1632; his baronetcy came later. Most commentators agree that he was Catholic and his children certainly were; he later fought on the Royalist side in the Civil War. **Sir Edward**'s other married daughter Venetia had been married for several years to Sir Kenelm Digby (since c.1625). Why did **Sir Edward** not designate Sir Kenelm as an executor? We will never know, but it seemed worth asking this question. Interestingly, Sir Kenelm appears in the later paragraph concerning the administration and thus was very obviously involved in the aftermath and probate of **Sir Edward**'s will six months after his death.

[v] '**Richard Lane Esquire of Northampton**.' It seems strange that someone in Eynsham, Oxon should designate someone in Northampton as one of two executors of his will. Maybe this is a clue to something else - maybe another important part of **Sir Edward**'s biography, as yet undetected? One might reasonably assume that 'Richard Lane of Northampton' had played a rather important role in **Sir Edward**'s life during the years since **Sir Edward** sold Tong Castle and Manor, thus moving away from Tong and settling in Eynsham. Perhaps he had been one of the lawyers responsible for these transactions?

There seems to be one prime candidate for this Richard Lane. In the online *A History of the*

Church of St Peter Northampton, including neighbouring parishes, by R. M. Sergeantson (1904), appears the following information.

> The Monuments.
>
> The monuments in the church are not very numerous, nor are there any now remaining of special beauty. In Bridges' time [1720], however, there was to be seen "near the steps of the communion table," a slab of considerable interest, which was thus inscribed: —
>
> Here lieth body of the Lady Margaret Lane, late wife to the right honourable Sir Richard Lane, Lord Keeper of the Great Seale of England to K. Charles the first and K. Charles the second, who dyed in banishment for his loyalty to the Crown. She departed the 22 of April, 1669.1
>
> Sir Richard Lane was the son of Richard Lane, of Courteenhall, Northamptonshire, by his wife Elizabeth, daughter of Clement Vincent, of Harpole, and was baptized at Harpole, November 12th, 1584.
>
> 1 The Lady Margaret Lane buried April 24th, 1669.—Kingsthorpe Parish Registers.
>
> 18 KINGSTHORPE CHURCH.
>
> [. . .] though of good family, was poor, and it was entirely by his own industry and talents that young Lane raised himself from obscurity. He was called to the bar as a member of the Middle Temple, and practised in the Court of Exchequer. In 1630 he was elected reader, and in 1637 treasurer to his Inn. In 1634 he was appointed Attorney General to the Prince of Wales, and in 1638 was nominated by Lord Holland, as his deputy in the Forest Courts.
>
> When Strafford was impeached for high treason by the House of Commons in 1641, Lane was retained as his leading counsel, and defended him with such marked ability that his acquittal appeared certain. The Commons thereupon put an end to the trial, and on the motion of Sir Arthur Hesilrige, brought in a Bill "for the attainder of the Earl of Strafford of high treason."
>
> After the condemnation of his client, Lane remained for two years in London, quietly pursuing his profession, but in 1643, King Charles, by proclamation under the Great Seal, moved all the law courts to Oxford, and though the Parliament issued a counter order, the Royalist lawyers considered it their duty to obey the king. Lane accordingly proceeded to Oxford, and as a reward for his loyalty, was knighted January 4th, 1643-4. A few weeks later (January 25th) he was made Lord Chief Baron of the Exchequer, having two days previously been invested with the coif as a serjeant-at-law. For some years before the outbreak of hostilities, Lane had acted as Recorder of Northampton, but at an Assembly held December 14th, 1642, it was resolved that [...]
>
> Whereas Richard Lane esquier Recorder of the Towne of Northampton is altogether absent in these tymes of danger from this Corporation, soe as the Corporation cannot have his Countenance and Counsel in this tyme of need, that as well for this cause as for other causes knowen to this assemblie. It is ordered that he shalbe noe longer Recorder of this towne. And therefore by consent of the whole assemblie Edward, Earl of Manchester is elected and chosen Recorder of this towne.*
>
> In January, 1645, Lane acted as chief of the Royal Commissioners in the negotiations at Uxbridge, and with other lawyers, strenuously resisted the demands [...]
>
> * Northampton Borough Records, ii, 106.

So if they were one and the same, Richard Lane, executor of **Sir Edward**'s Will in 1632, was already an established lawyer, at the beginning of an impressive career which led to his appointment as Lord Keeper of the Great Seal to Charles I and II. We still have no idea where **Sir Edward** might have met him, nor what legal work, if any, he might have performed for **Sir Edward** during the previous years. Lane's later career seems to indicate a similar crisis of Catholic/Royalist sympathies to those encountered by others in **Sir Edward**'s family, most notably his sons-in-law John Fortescue and Sir Kenelm Digby and his nephew James, Lord Strange, although in the early 1630s these were still compatible with public and parliamentary service.

The very presence of 'Richard Lane of Northampton' in this Stuart context also conjures up a memory of the Spencers of Althorp, Northamptonshire, just a few miles from Kingsthorpe. The major Spencer figure in **Sir Edward**'s story on his deathbed in 1632 was Countess Alice née Spencer of Althorp, widow since 1594 of Ferdinando Stanley, 5th Earl of Derby, **Sir Edward**'s first cousin. Countess Alice had been widowed again since 1617 on the death of her second husband Thomas Egerton of Cheshire, 1st Viscount Brackley, Lord Ellesmere, Lord Chancellor. During the early years of her second widowhood (1622-23) she was back in Lancashire under the auspices of her 'friend' Alexander Standish of Duxbury, widower. (See Notes for the biography of Alexander Standish of Duxbury online on the Duxbury Family Website and the website mylesstandish.info, by HM.) In 1632 she was living at Harefield, Middlesex, still apparently active in many areas, as a patroness of the arts and actors and involved in much scheming until her death and burial at Harefield in 1637, celebrated by a magnificent tomb, still there today. (See Notes for the biography of Countess Alice on same websites.) She had been taking her brother-in-law William Stanley, 6th Earl of Derby to court from 1594-1609, fighting for Derby lands to be awarded in perpetuity to her three daughters. There must be a suspicion that 'Richard Lane Esquire of Northampton' in 1632 might have been a lawyer involved in the aftermath of some of these previous disputes. Any confirmation (or not) of this suspicion might come from local historians in Northamptonshire. In any case, Sir Edward was obviously well aware that lawyers would be involved in the aftermath of his death, when all his Derby estates, including Eynsham, would revert in tail-male to the earldom, in the persons of his Cousin William or nephew James.

Other intriguing links around this time emerge between Countess Alice and John Milton, whose *Comus* was dedicated to her and performed in her honour in 1634. Current research suggests that this may have been based on the recent scandals in her family, including the 'Castlehaven Scandal' in 1631. Milton also (or his father) 'wrote a poem to a versifier called John Lane'. Who was John Lane? A relative of Richard Lane, executor of Sir Edward's will? These details emerge from previous studies, meanwhile online, which eerily seem to cover the same area as **Sir Edward**'s tomb in Tong with its 'sky aspiring pyramids' and even reproduce photos of the Stanley tomb. See two articles online by Gordon Campbell of the University of Leicester:

> 'Obelisks and Pyramids in Shakespeare, Milton and Alcalá' (1998).
> 'Shakespeare and the Youth of Milton' (*Milton Quarterly* 33.4, Johns Hopkins UP, 1999, pp. 95-105.)

Embedded in the second article is the similarly intriguing information:

> [John] Lane's enormous and equally dreadful "Triton's Trumpet to the Twelve Months husbanded and moralised", date 1621, also remains unpublished. Milton's father was a trustee of the Blackfriars Playhouse.

So here we have John Milton's father associated with a Lane, and a trustee of the Playhouse in which a Fortescue was involved. William Shakespeare had also had an interest in the Blackfriars Playhouse and Gatehouse (see any Shakespeare biography), as did a Fortescue. Which brings us back to the two executors of **Sir Edward**'s will being a Fortescue and a Lane, who both reappear in the Administration document in London in December 1632. The Stanley links with Milton seem to be fairly strong, and in 1630 John Milton Jr wrote his Sonnet to Shakespeare, which appeared in the 1632 *Second Folio* edition of Shakespeare's Works. Are all these connections mere coincidences?

[vi] Petronella was **Sir Edward**'s eldest surviving daughter, who had remained unmarried. As she was recorded as the first of the three surviving daughters on the Stanley MIs on the tombs in Tong and Walthamstow, one might presume she was the oldest, and has thus consistently been given a birthdate in this book in the mid-1590s. One might assume that she was at Eynsham with her father for much of the time when Eynsham Abbey was the main residence of **Sir Edward**. She duly buried her father in

St Leonard's Church, Eynsham with a memorial, still to be seen today, albeit moved from its original place. Why did she not import his effigy from Tong to Eynsham? We know (or think we know) that **Sir Edward** had commissioned this several decades earlier, when he was aged around forty. We also know that this was shortly after the death of his wife and four of Petronella's older sisters at Walthamstow, Essex in 1601. We have no idea where his effigy had been stored in the meantime. We will probably never know the reason for none of them being reunited in death by at least their effigies, but presumably Petronella had her reasons. It is perhaps strange that he made no provision for this in his will. Perhaps he had already made his wishes absolutely clear to all concerned? In theory, on her father's death in 1632 without a male Stanley heir, Eynsham should have immediately reverted to the Earldom of Derby in the person of William, 6th Earl or his son James, Lord Strange, which in fact duly happened. So Petronella knew that, although her father's death signalled the end of her automatic entitlement to live there, it still belonged to the family. No record has been discovered as to where Petronella lived after her father's death, nor when or where she died. IF she survived to a good old age, she MIGHT have lived through the Civil War and into the Restoration. What stories she might have been able to tell! Alas, she left no records (discovered so far).

[vii] The (difficult to decipher) surnames of Timothy and George are presumably/perhaps those of two of **Sir Edward**'s tenants or servants in Eynsham. The presence of Anthony Fortescue as a witness is interesting inasmuch as he was perhaps a representative of **Sir Edward**'s son-in-law John Fortescue, one of the executors. The website Tudorplace gives a couple of Anthony Fortescues, but with the wrong dates to be the Anthony in **Sir Edward**'s will. However, it was obviously a name used in the Fortescue family. All we can deduce from his presence as a witness is that **Sir Edward** had at least one Fortescue visitor when he was ailing in old age at Eynsham and at his death bed on 10 June 1632.

~~~~~~~~~~

XXVII-3. Admin. in Latin, six months after Sir Edward's death[viii]

In decimo die mensis Decembris Anno dm millesimo sesentisimo treresimo
Secundo[ix] Emenauit domisso duo Kenelme Digby militi marito ——Venetie Digby als [*alias*] Stanley
filia naturalie[x] et——— de Sir Edward Stanley defunct———ad Domine——————
bona iure
et heredita dei defuncti mo——— mortum et offertum————voluntatis eodem defunct
eo quod Johes ffortescue Ar[xi] et Richardus Lane Ar Executores[xii] in eodem testamento
nommat eo —— —— eod et ammos suos in ea parte montendoneri ———— ————————
————testamenti pred ———— remunerierunt prout eo artis huius ——— plerrid
—— et appart de bene fideli administrand
eodem——— dei Enanysham Jurat[xiii] / Egh[xiv]

Very rough (*mea culpa*) translation of the main points

On the tenth day of December in the year of our Lord sixteen hundred and thirty two, emanating from the home of Kenelm Digby, knight, husband of Venetie Digby alias [*née*] Stanley, natural daughter of Sir Edward Stanley deceased . . . . . heiress of the deceased . . . death and offered . . . . . .
to whom John Fortescue, Esquire and Richard Lane, Esquire were named in the testament of the deceased will remunerate . . . . and in good faith administrate the same . . . Eynsham.

[viii] The very fact that this Admin. (letter of administration, i.e. instructions for complying with the clauses of the will prior to an *Inquisition post mortem* and probate) appears on the same page in the MS in the National Archives, along with the will, seems to prove that the MS will and Admin. together were a copy from some previous recording of the will. The will had obviously appeared in

London some time between June and December, and come to the attention of his son-in-law Sir Kenelm Digby.

[ix] 10 December 1632. Exactly six months after **Sir Edward**'s death at Eynsham.

[x] These very names appearing here are enough to prove that Sir Kenelm and his wife Venetia, Sir **Edward**'s youngest daughter, were involved in the winding up of **Sir Edward**'s estate. 'Emanuit domisso' implies that the original document was actually written at the house of Sir Kenelm and Venetia in London. Given that this couple were minor celebrities in London at the time, and have been ever since, this glimpse into their whereabouts on 10 December 1632 might be of interest. Venetia died not too long afterwards, on 1 May 1633. Their stories have been told at length in many places. A few details about **Sir Edward** emerge from a re-examination of Sir Kenelm's *Memoirs*. One abbreviated version online is as follows below. I have taken the liberty of putting in *italics* those details of relevance to **Sir Edward**'s biography, with notes below. A rather closer analysis appears in Appendix 10. *Sir Kenelm Digby's Memoirs*.

[xi] John Fortescue Armiger appears again. We know that he was appointed an executor of **Sir Edward**'s will in June 1632, as his son-in-law. Might his appearance here in December 1632, apparently/perhaps in London, contribute to a future biography of him? The Fortescue family seems to be crying out for more research. It was, of course, in this household that **Sir Edward**'s three little daughters were placed after the death of their mother.

[xii] Richard Lane Armiger appears again. We know from **Sir Edward**'s will in June 1632 that Richard was from Northampton, and from his biography that at the end of 1632 he was a member of the Middle Temple, and practising in the Court of Exchequer, so ideally placed to sort out any legal or testamentary problems.

[xiii] This rigmarole refers to the last will and testament written and signed at Eynsham.

[xiv] This is presumably/perhaps an abbreviation of the signature of the scribe. Enlightenment from an erudite reader?

~~~~~~~~~~~~~~~~~~~~~~

XXVII-4. Sir Edward in a Deed, 1613

Following is the text of a Deed transcribed by Griffiths in *A History of Tong and Boscobel* (2nd ed. 1894), p. 218. It is worthy of inclusion here because it is the only Deed detected (so far) in which **Sir Edward** appears as a participant in a court case, with his signature and seal. It is also interesting because his partner in court was Sir Baptist Hicks, whose entry on Wikipedia reveals much interesting information, including the detail that he was knighted at the same time as **Sir Edward**, at the coronation of James I.

218   DEEDS RELATING TO TONG

Richard Barbour, of Stone, gent.; George Bennett, the elder, of London, and George Bennett the younger ; and John Daintry, of Spott Grange, yeoman of the other part. A.D. 1613.
(L. F. C. xi., 30, Brit. Mus.)

This Indenture made the three and twentieth daye of June in the yeres of the Raigne of our Soueraigne lord James by the grace of God king of England Scotland ffraunce and Ireland Defender of the ffaith etc. That is to saye of England ffraunce and Ireland the Eleuenth, and of Scotland the Sixe and ffouretieth, Betweene Sir Edward Stanley of Ensham in the Countie of Oxon Knight of the Honorable order of the Bath Sir Baptist Hickes of the City of London Knight and Dame Elizabeth his wife of the one partie, And Thomas Crompton of Stone in the Countie of Stafford Esquire, Robert Challenor and Richard Barbour of Stone aforesaid gent. George Bennett the elder Citizen and Salter of London, and George Bennett the younger Sonne of the saide George Bennett the elder. And John Daintry of Spott grange in the said Countie of Stafford yeoman on the other partie, Whereas the saide Sir Edward Stanley and Sir Baptist Hickes, by diverse and sundry deedes Indented bearing date the second day of November last past before the date of these presents, and enrolled in his Majesties High Court of Chancery, as also by diverse and sundry other deeds bearing date the Tenth day of November last past before the date of these presents, Have for the Consideracions in the said Deeds expressed graunted bargained sold assured Conveighed vnto them the aforesaid Thomas Crompton Robert Challenor Richard Barbour and John Daintry theire heires and assignees, And vnto the said George Bennett the elder and George Bennett the yonger and the heires and assignees of the saide George Bennett the elder diverse Messuages Cottages ffarmes lands Tenements Commons and Hereditaments situate lying and being or to be had Received or taken within the Manor or Lordshipp of Cublaston *alias* Kibbulstan *alias* Kobleston, *alias* kebulston *alias* Cubleston, and in Stone in the aforesaid Countie of Stafford; as by the said severall deeds more at larger appeareth, And whereas also the saide Sir Edward Stanley, Sir Baptist Hickes and Dame Elizabeth his wife have in the Octaves of Saint Martin last past before the date of these presents leased and acknowledged one ffine before his Majesties Justices of the Common Pleas at Westminster vnto the aforesaid Thomas Crompton and Robert Challenor and to the heires of the saide Thomas of Thirty Messuages, Tenne Cottages, ffourety gardens three hundred acres of land, two hundred acres of ffures and Heath, and one Hundred acres of Moore with the appurtenaunces in Cublaston *alias* Kibbulston *alias* Kubleston *alias* Cubleston Meyford *alias* Meyforth Outonne *alias* oulton Cotwalton Woodhouses *alias* Woodhousen Spott and Stone, and of Common of pasture for all manner of Cattle in Outone *alias* Oulton and Meyford *alias* Meyforth as by the Record of the saide ffine more at large appeareth : Now these present witnesse that the entent and true meaning of the parties to the said ffine at the tyme of the acknowledging thereof was, That the Messuages Cottages lands Tenements Commons and other the hereditaments in the saide ffines Conteyned were, And it was ment and entended they should be the Messuages Cottages lands, Tenements and hereditaments by the aforesaid deeds enrolled and other the Conveiances aforesaide graunted bargained sold assured and Conveighed, or thereby menetoned to be graunted bargained sold assured and Conveighed, And all and every the parties to these presents doe further by these presents declaire, And for them and every of them theire and every of theire heires and assignes doe Covenent graunt and agree that the saide ffine shall be an envre, and shall be deemed and taken to be an envure. And that the saide Thomas Crompton and Robert Challenor theire heires and assignes shall stand and be seized of the premisses in the saide ffin mencioned and Conteyned vnto the uses entents and purpose hereafter followinge. That is to say that as to the Messuages [etc., etc.,] . . . . . .

In witness whereof the parties above said to these presents have interchangeably put their hands and seales the day and yere above written. [A.D. 1613.]

Seals of the arms of

Sir Edward Stanley and
Sir Baptist Hickes.

Edward Stanley.   Baptiste Hickes.

Sealed and delivered in the presence of } Sealed and delivered) Sealed and delivered
    John Lathom, **(a)**   per Sir Baptist Hickes

Simon Smith.   In the presents of vz.

                Robt. Grigg.
                Ælcocke.

(a) It will be remembered that this man wrote the coffin plate recently found in the vault in Tong Church. See page 65.

(Griffiths, *Tong*, p. 218.)

[**Note by HM**. **(a)** refers to the plate on **Sir Thomas**'s coffin in the vault at Tong Church, giving his date of death; full text in Chapter IV. Auden's *History*, Section IV-5.]

This, of course, deals with a minor dispute in Cubleston, Staffordshire, one place in this county where **Sir Edward** owned lands. It is worth reminding ourselves that this was one of the places where he owned lands which were not part of the entailed inheritance from his grandfather Edward, 3rd Earl.

> Of the vast possessions of Sir Edward Stanley, Erdeswick writing circa 1596, speaks of him as "now Lord of Harlaston", and says of Cubleston "Edward Stanley is now owner thereof," and of West Bromwich, "now one of the Stanleys hath the seat of his house there." (Quoted in Chapter IV-5. Auden's *History*.)

When first coming across this list, the query was raised whether or not the Sir Edward in question might have been **Sir Edward Sr**. That possibility still remains. However, with him dying in 1604, it is clear that the owner of Cubleston in 1613 was **Sir Edward Jr**. The Stanley at West Bromwich remains to be identified. This would be interesting to know, not least because this was in North Warwickshire, not far from John Shakespeare's 'cousins' mentioned in his application for the impalement of his wife Mary Arderne's arms in 1599. Her distant Arden kinsmen also lived nearby at Park Hall, Castle Bromwich.

Disputes such as this were rather common, particularly in the case of absentee landlords, as was the case here. One might imagine that **Sir Edward** was involved with many more such cases during the period of his ownership of lands in Shropshire, Oxfordshire, Warwickshire and Cheshire. Maybe other deeds concerning transactions in other places where he owned lands will yet come to light? This at least provides us with evidence that he was personally involved with affairs in Cubleston in 1613, later in the same year when he had been in London in February for the wedding of Princess Mary. It also reveals that he had the best possible connections in London for dealing with legal matters.

> **Baptist Hicks, 1st Viscount Campden** (1551-18 October 1629) was an English merchant and politician who sat in the House of Commons between 1621 and 1628 when he was raised to the peerage as Viscount Campden.
>
> Hicks was the son of Robert Hicks, a wealthy mercer of Cheapside, London and grandson of John Hicks of Tortworth. He was brought up in father's business and imported rich silks from Italy and other foreign places. Through the influence of his brother Michael he contracted a large amount of business with the court and amassed a large fortune. He was sworn in as servant to James I in 1603, knighted on 23 July 1603 and became the King's financial agent. He was in dispute with Court of Aldermen of the City of London, firstly in 1607 because he was one of first citizens who kept shop to receive the honour of financial agent, and secondly concerning the precedency of his knighthood. He purchased the manor of Campden soon after 1608 and built house there. (The house was burnt down by Royalists in the civil war).[1] In 1612 he founded and endowed an almshouse for 6 poor men and 6 poor women in Campden and performed other charitable acts. In his life, he gave £100,000 for charity. He was created a baronet on 1 July 1620.[2]
>
> In 1621, Hicks was elected Member of Parliament for Tavistock. In 1624 he was elected MP for Tewkesbury. He was re-elected MP for Tewkesbury in 1625.[3] Hicks became a JP for Gloucestershire in 1625 and a Deputy Lieutenant for Middlesex on 23 March 1625.[2] He was re-elected MP for Tewkesbury in 1626 and 1628.[3] He sat until May 1628 when he was created Viscount Campden with remainder to his son in law Edward Lord Noel.[2]
>
> Hicks died at the age of 78.
>
> Hicks married on 6 March 1612 Elizabeth May daughter of Richard May of London and sister of Sir Humphrey May Alderman of London. His elder daughter Julian married Edward Lord Noel. His younger daughter Mary married firstly Sir Charles Morrison, 1st Baronet of Cashiobury, secondly Sir John Cooper, 1st Baronet and thirdly Sir Edward Alford.[2]
>
> **References**
> 1. 'Sir Baptist Hickes'. *Cotsworld Famous Peopl*e. Retrieved 7 December 2011.
> 2. W R Williams *Parliamentary History of the County of Gloucester*

3. Willis, Browne (1750). *Notitia Parliamentaria, Part II: A Series or Lists of the Representatives in the several Parliaments held from the Reformation 1541, to the Restoration 1660 …* London. pp. 229-239.

> (Wikipedia. Copied verbatim, but with all indications of links removed.
> For these, see online.)

~~~~~~~~~~~~~~~~~~~~~~~~

XXVII-5. Sir Kenelm Digby's *Memoirs* re Sir Edward

This has been included in the chapter with **Sir Edward**'s will because, having known him all his life, and as his son-in-law from c.1625 onwards, Sir Kenelm was in the best possible position to provide information on **Sir Edward**'s last years. His memoirs were first transcribed by Nicholas Harris Nicolas, published in 1827 in London. Nicolas provided an extremely useful introduction, which cut through some of the layers of ambiguity introduced by Sir Kenelm himself in recounting his *Memoirs* peopled by allegorical figures with names such as *Theagenes* for himself, *Stelliana* for his wife Venetia and *Nearchus* for his father-in-law **Sir Edward**. Several copies of this edition have been digitised and appear online. Given Sir Kenelm's reputation during his lifetime and ever since, the whole book is well worth reading. Below are abstracted only a few paragraphs of relevance to **Sir Edward**'s biography. The liberty has been taken of italicizing those phrases which call for comment in the context of the book in the reader's hand.

<div align="center">

PRIVATE MEMOIRS

OF

SIR KENELM DIGBY,

GENTLEMAN OF THE BEDCHAMBER

TO

KING CHARLES THE FIRST.

WRITTEN BY HIMSELF.

NOW FIRST PUBLISHED FROM THE ORIGINAL MANUSCRIPT
WITH
AN INTRODUCTORY MEMOIR

</div>

(p. x) Venetia Stanley, *to whose names one writer has also added that of Anastatia,** [i] was one of the daughters, and, eventually, co-heirs of Sir Edward Stanley, of Tonge Castle in Shropshire, Knight of the Bath, eldest son of Sir Thomas Stanley, Knt. a younger son of Edward, third Earl of Derby, K.G. and *was born on the 19th of December, 1600.*[ii] Her mother was Lucy, daughter and co-heiress of Thomas Percy, seventh Earl of Northumberland, who, we

* Hutchin's History of Dorset.

(p. xi) learn from this memoir, *died when she was but a few months old.**[iii] Truly, indeed, might Digby boast that his Venetia was 'born of parents that, in the antiquity and lustre of their houses and in the goods of fortune, were inferior to none in Great Britain,'† and that *some of her ancestors had exalted and pulled down Kings in England,*[iv] and that their successors still have right to wear a regal crown upon their princely temples,‡ an allusion to the sovereignty of the Isle of Man, which was then possessed by the Earls of Derby. Her beauty and accomplishments equaled the lustre of her birth, but her character has been impeached in the most unqualified terms, and it must be confessed that there are many causes for believing in the accusations. This delicate subject cannot be passed over in silence, for as Digby himself alludes to rumours against her fame, the question demands that some attention should be given to it; but it is first necessary to notice what he previously says of her.

* P. 13.
† Ibid.
‡ p. 272.

(p. xii) *Sir Edward Stanley, he informs us, though a negligent husband, was so much afflicted at the loss of his wife, that he resolved on passing his life in absolute seclusion;*[v] *and therefore committed Venetia to the care of the wife of one of his relations, whose house was situated near to that of Lady Digby, This naturally produced frequent visits between the two families, and Kenelm became known to Venetia in his childhood, when a mutual attachment arose, and which 'grew with their growth. '*[vi]

After a few years had thus passed away, Sir Edward Stanley sent for his daughter to his own house;[vii] *but upon the marriage of the Princess Elizabeth with the Count Palatine, which soon afterward took place, he was summoned to the Court;*[viii] *and, being desirous of shewing her 'the magnificent entertainments that are usual at such times, and also being glad to let the world now see that fame was nothing too lavish in setting out her perfections,' took Venetia with him to London;*[ix] *where 'her beauty and discretion did soon draw*
(p. xiii) the eyes and thoughts of all men to admiration.'*

The royal alliance alluded to, occurred in February, 1613, when she was but little more than thirteen years of age.[x] *To Aubrey, her detractor, we are indebted for the little which is known about her; and some parts of his statement agree with Digby's, for he says, 'She was a most beautiful desirable creature, and, being* matura viro *was left by her father to live with a tenant at Enston Abbey, in Oxfordshire; but, as private as that place was, it seems her beauty could not lie hid.'†* [xi] *Enston is not more than thirty miles from Gothurst, the seat of Lady Digby;*[xii] *and the only difference between the Memoir and Aubrey on the subject of Venetia's residence is, that in the former* the individual to whose care she was intrusted, is called her father's kinsman.[xiii]

* P. 21. † Aubrey's Letters by Eminent Persons, vol. ii. p. 330, note.

Notes on this Introduction by HM:

[i] '*to whose names one writer has also added that of Anastatia,*' It has often puzzled me why Venetia was the only one of seven daughters to be given two names. This puzzle still remains unsolved, but one explanation might be hinted at here: the second name was awarded her as a 'nickname' at some later date, in recognition of her beauty. Whether her father accepted this, and used the name himself, is open to question. For him she was always Venetia. She was born on 19 December, not the 2 December, a day associated with Anastasia, mentioned in the following quote, but this might have played a role in her subsequently acquiring this 'nickname'.

> Anastasia (Greek Αναστασία) is a personal name and the female form of the Greek male name Anastasius/Anastasios (Koine Greek: Αναστασία) meaning "resurrection." The name, and its male counterpart, were often given to Greek children born around December 2 or around Easter during the early days of Christianity.
>
> (Wikipedia)

[ii] '*was born on the 19th of December, 1600.*' This seems fairly definite. It presumably comes straight from the mouth of Sir Kenelm. It still sheds no light on where she was born and baptised, although the strongest contestant must be Tong Castle, with perhaps a baptism at St Bartholomew's or in a private chapel, the records of neither of which have survived.

[iii] 'Her mother was Lucy, . . who, we learn from this memoir, *died when she was but a few months old.*' This dates the deaths at Walthamstow rather precisely to early-mid 1601.

[iv] '*some of her ancestors had exalted and pulled down Kings in England.*' True, but the most recent Stanley who had 'pulled down a King' had been Venetia's 4xgt-grandfather Lord Thomas Stanley, whose Lancastrian armies defeated Richard III's Yorkist armies at the Battle of Bosworth, as a result of which Henry VII created him 1st Earl of Derby. He had died in 1504, nearly a hundred years before Venetia's birth, but it seems that many family stories had been passed down by all concerned. One might perhaps assume that **Sir Edward** and his daughter had seen a performance of Shakespeare's *Richard III* in London during the years he took her there. Many of her mother's Percy, Earls of Northumberland earlier ancestors had indeed 'exalted' Kings and Queens, but all the recent ones had been on the losing side.

[v] '*Sir Edward Stanley, he informs us, though a negligent husband, was so much afflicted at the loss of his wife, that he resolved on passing his life in absolute seclusion;*' Now this is interesting. 'A negligent husband'? In what way, one wonders? Perhaps Sir Kenelm had heard no evidence about **Sir Edward** and Lucy experiencing the passion in their marriage that obviously existed between himself and Venetia? Or could it be a hint that Edward and Lucy had had problems during one period, which might even have led to a separation? At the very least this seems to provide confirmation that **Sir Edward** made no great efforts at self-publicity at court, in society or in politics - or to find a new wife.

[vi] '*and therefore committed Venetia to the care of the wife of one of his relations, whose house was situated near to that of Lady Digby, This naturally produced frequent visits between the two families, and Kenelm became known to Venetia in his childhood, when a mutual attachment arose, and which "grew with their growth."*' All this has been known for a long time. We now know the identity of the 'wife of one of his relations': his first cousin Grace née Manners of Haddon Hall, Derbyshire, who had married Sir John Fortescue of Salden, Bucks and had a large family. Sir Kenelm was not born until 1603, so this limits the years when 'Kenelm became known to Venetia in his childhood' to c.1604-c.1612.

[vii] '*After a few years had thus passed away. Sir Edward Stanley sent for his daughter to his own house;*' This house can safely be named as Eynsham Abbey. We can also fairly safely date his calling for his daughters - and perhaps all three and not just Venetia - to c.1612.

[viii] '*but upon the marriage of the Princess Elizabeth with the Count Palatine, which soon afterward took place, he was summoned to the Court;*' One might expect this 'summons' in 1613 was because he was a Knight of the Bath and his first cousin William, 6th Earl of Derby, was a Knight of the Garter. It could be that he had been to court several times in the previous years, but no record has survived. It could be that another Manners cousin, Sir George of Haddon Hall, was trying to bring him out of his 'seclusion'. Chapter XXVI. Earls of Rutland provides details of all their cousins, the Earls of Rutland, at this time. The most recent one had been Roger Manners, 5th Earl (died 1612), who had been Elizabeth's ambassador to Denmark in 1602, with the family of James's Queen Anne of Denmark. Queen Anne was a great patron of the arts. Roger Manners, when still 'Esquire', had also been the guardian of Sir Everard Digby after he lost his father at a young age. (See any biography of Roger Manners, 5th Earl of Rutland and/or Sir Everard Digby.)

[ix] '*the magnificent entertainments that are usual at such times, and also being glad to let the world now see that fame was nothing too lavish in setting out her perfections,*' took Venetia with him to London; where '*her beauty and discretion did soon draw the eyes and thoughts of all men to admiration*'. 'The magnificent entertainments' were due in no small part to Queen Anne, who patronised many authors writing masques at the time, including Ben Jonson, Shakespeare's friend and admirer.

[x] '*The royal alliance alluded to, occurred in February, 1613, when she was but little more than thirteen years of age.*' At least this gives us another firm date for **Sir Edward**'s time-line.

[xi] '*She was a most beautiful desirable creature, and, being matura viro was left by her father to live with a tenant at Enston Abbey, in Oxfordshire; but, as private as that place was, it seems her beauty could not lie hid.*' This part of Venetia's story is well known, but we still do not know whether her sisters or **Sir Edward** himself were living at Eynsham at the same time, nor in which year he installed her with one of his tenants. Might the tenant referred to have been one of the witnesses of his will? '*matura viro*' indicates that Venetia was fourteen and thus eligible for marriage. This places the event at the earliest in c.1614.

[xii] '*Enston*' [which is, of course, Eynsham] is not more than thirty miles from Gothurst, the seat of

Lady Digby;' Presumably (Sir) Kenelm and Venetia saw each other as children during periods of several days when the families visited each other. Despite the mobility at that time, thirty miles seems rather a long way to pay a short visit.

[xiii] '*and the only difference between the Memoir and Aubrey on the subject of Venetians residence is, that in the former the individual to whose care she was intrusted, is called her father's kinsman.*' The identity was covered under Note **[vi]**.

Nicolas continues with Sir Kenelm's biography in his Introduction but, alas, Sir Kenelm's Private Memoirs stop in 1628 after his adventure at Scanderoon, a Turkish harbour. We therefore learn nothing more from him about **Sir Edward**. The latter was, however, commemorated in a Memorial Inscription on Venetia's tomb in London, along with his father and grandfather and Lucy and her father. All had disappeared by the end of the seventeenth century. (Nicolas, p. li.)

Mem. Sacrum.
Venetiæ
Edwardi Stanley Equitis Honoratiss. Ord.
Balnei (Filii Thomæ, Edwardi comitis Derbiæ
Filii) Filiæ ac cohaeredi, ex Luciâ Thomæ
Comitis Northumbriæ Filiâ et Cohaerede,
Posuit
Kenelmus Digby Eques Auratus
Cui quatuor Peperit Filios
Kenelmum Nat. VI. Octob. MDCXXV.
Joannem Nat. XXIX. Decemb. MDCXXVII.
Everardum (in cunis Mortuum) Nat. XII. Jan.
MXCXIX.
Georgium Nat. XVII. Jan. MDCXXXII.
Nata est Decemb. XIX. MDC
Denata Maii. I. MDCXXXIII.

To the sacred memory of Venetia, daughter and co-heiress of Edward Stanley,
Knight of the Honourable Order of the Bath
(son of Thomas, son of Edward Earl of Derby)
and Lucy, daughter and co-heiress of Thomas Earl of Northumberland,
This was placed by
Kenelm Digby Knight Bachelor
To whom she bore four sons
Kenelm born 6 October 1625
John born 29 December 1627
Everard (died in his cradle) born 12 January 1629 (=1630, New Calendar)
George born 17 January 1632 (=1633, New Calendar)
She was born December 19 1600
She died May 1 1633

[N.B. There is no mention of a daughter Margery, who is given in other accounts. One might expect that Sir Kenelm knew who his own children were. HM]

Readers who might wish to read the relevant sections in Sir Kenelm's original text in his *Memoirs* are directed to Appendix 10. *Sir Kenelm Digby's Memoirs.*

Chapter XXVIII
Time-line of Sir Thomas & Sir Edward Sr & Jr

This has been several years 'in the making' and probably still presents many lacunae, with many relevant documents lying as yet undetected in various MS collections, but at least it presents a start. It also presents a chronological skeleton summary of this book. The ultimate aim is to provide the basis for narrative biographies as complete as possible of the three Stanleys named in the title. All three are mentioned on various online sites, but in all cases with minimal information and sometimes with 'just plain wrong' details of exploits and dates attached to them, having been muddled with other contemporary namesakes. The main reason for there being so many namesakes is because the first two Earls of Derby were both Thomas and the third Earl of Derby was Edward. Most sons and grandsons, several of whom had meanwhile established various junior lines, named sons after these two eminent ancestors, and several of these (gt-)grandsons were living at the same time as the three Stanleys in the title of this Time-line.

To make it absolutely clear, the only Thomas and Edward Stanleys in **bold** below are without doubt the ones in the title: **Sir Thomas** (c.1534-76) and **Sir Edward Sr** (1535/40-1604), the second and third sons of Edward Stanley, 3rd Earl of Derby (d. 1572) and therefore younger brothers of Henry, 4th Earl of Derby (1531-93). **Sir Thomas** had only one legitimate surviving son, **Sir Edward Jr**. **Sir Edward Sr** never married and therefore had no Stanley children - nor any illegitimate ones, it seems, unlike elder brother Henry, 4th Earl, who had a whole family by his mistress Jane Halsall (including another Thomas as well as a legitimate Edward), who were, of course, cousins of **Sir Edward Jr**. None of these sons, of course, was knighted at birth and so in principle one should not award them this title before the date of dubbing. On the whole, I have tried to stick to this self-imposed rule by putting **(Sir)** in brackets until they were actually knighted. They are usually not in bold in direct quotes by others.

At the same time it is hoped to be able to match these dates in future with William Shakespeare's time-line. This is given in the most detail found anywhere (by HM) in Eric Sams (d. 2004), *The Real Shakespeare I* (1995) & *II*, an ebook put posthumously online by his son. Through a comparison of these two time-lines it might thus be possible to establish the most likely times and places when and where Shakespeare and **Sir Edward Jr** might well have met before James I's coronation, and indeed during the following few years. A juxtaposition of all known dates in the lives of Ferdinando and William Stanley might also be fruitful.

My position is made clear throughout this book that I am convinced of the authenticity of the 'Shakespeare in Lancashire'/'Lancastrian Shakespeare' theory, as so ably presented by Professor E.A.J. Honigmann in Shakespeare: the 'lost years' (1985, 1998), and am also convinced of the authenticity of the authorship of (one or) both of the verse epitaphs on the Stanley tomb in Tong by William Shakespeare, as recorded in writing by Sir William Dugdale in September 1663. Some dates relating to the writings or findings of both of these are therefore also included.

Roman numerals in square brackets at the bottom right of cells in the first column refer to the chapters in this book where these and further details are presented. In bold in the text are the names of the three Stanleys above, plus the wives of **Sir Thomas (Margaret Vernon)** and **Sir Edward Jr (Lucy Percy)**, and the three surviving daughters of **Sr Edward Jr (Petronella, Frances and Venetia)**. Also in bold are the places where they lived at various times: **Lathom** House, Lancashire, main residence of the Earls of Derby; **Winwick** Rectory, Lancashire (since 1974 within the Borough of Warrington, Cheshire), leased by **Sir Thomas** in 1563 for 99 years and used as his and his son's main Lancashire base when returning there; **Tong** Castle, Shropshire, inheritance of **Margaret Vernon** as a co-heiress of her father; and **Eynsham** Abbey, Oxfordshire, a Derby estate which passed under a settlement in 1562/3 to **Sir Thomas**, his widow **Margaret** for her life, then to their son **Sir Edward Jr**, and on his death without a male heir by reversion back to the Earl of Derby. Also in bold are the names of places/manors/estates in other counties owned by one of the three Stanleys in the title.

c.1534 (This year of birth is estimated from 1531, the known year of birth of elder brother Earl Henry.) [III], [IX	**(Sir) Thomas Stanley** born (probably at **Lathom**), second son of Edward, 3rd Earl of Derby and Dorothy, second daughter of Thomas Howard, 2nd Duke of Norfolk. (Bagley) Previous accounts have confused Katherine (married 1529, died 3 months later) and Dorothy Howard, Earl Edward's first two wives, who were aunt and niece. Dorothy (married 1530) was the mother of his early children. (Bagley) His future wife was '**Margaret Vernon**, daughter of Sir George Vernon of **Tong** and Haddon, "the King of the Peak", (?1514-65), and Margaret, daughter and heiress of Sir Gilbert Talboys'. (*Auden's History*) **Margaret** was probably born several years after the marriage, judging from later events, and so in this book is given a birthdate of c.1540, when her father was 26. Sir George Vernon's biography appears on several sites online. 'George Vernon married (2ndly) Matilda daughter of Ralph Longford, knight, but by her had no issue. He died in 1565 and was buried at Bakewell.' (*Auden's History*)
1535 [XI], [XIX]	Edward, 3rd Earl of Derby, acquired **Eynsham Abbey** after the Dissolution of the Monasteries 'as part of an exchange to settle debts of Sir Edward North' (*Eynsham Manor*); later bequeathed it to son **Sir Thomas** for his son **Edward Jr**, along with other properties. (Seacome, Coward)
1535-40 [XXI]	**(Sir) Edward Stanley Sr** born (probably at **Lathom**), third son of Earl Edward and Dorothy Howard. He never married, d. 1604, buried at Ormskirk. His birth date has been calculated on the same basis as his brother **Thomas**'s and is given in this book as 1535-40.
c.1545 [IV]	Dorothy Vernon born, second daughter and co-heiress of Sir George Vernon of **Tong** and Haddon (d. 1565) and Margaret, daughter and heiress of Sir Gilbert Talboys. (*Auden's History*) Dorothy's date of birth has been reported in wildly different years, even as late as 1569! She was the younger sister of **Margaret Vernon** who married **Sir Thomas Stanley** in c.1558. Because of surrounding events, particularly her elopement and marriage to John Manners before the death of her father and the birth of her first (surviving) child, daughter Grace (sometimes given as born in c.1563, but this seems to be a complete guess), her birth has been calculated as probably earlier rather than later in this period. It is given in this book as c.1545 (at the very latest), which would still make her only 13 when she eloped. Dorothy died 24 June 1584; John Manners died 4 June 1611. This in-law link to the Manners family introduces other later Shakespeare elements into the Stanley story via Manners, Earls of Rutland.
?1540s [XXI]	Dr Henry Standish, 'a passionate Catholic preacher' was schoolmaster at Lathom for the Stanley boys, including (Sir) William Stanley of Hooton (1548-1630). More research needed on precise dates, if details have survived.
1553, 2 Oct.	**Sir Thomas** dubbed Knight Bachelor – 'made the day after the Coronation of Queen Mary, in the presence of the Queen, by the Earl of Arundel, lord steward of the Household'. (Shaw, *The Knights of England*) At the same time two other Stanleys were knighted: Sir Rowland Stanley of Hooton and Sir George Stanley of Cross Hall, Lathom. Also knighted that day were Sir Thomas Gerard of Bryn, a friend of the family, and Sir Thomas Hesketh of Rufford, the future host of young William Shakeshafte/Shakespeare (the last-named noted importantly by Oliver Baker, 1937, Alan Keen, 1954, p. 45 ff., as a clue to 'Shakespeare in Lancashire').

1554, 25 July	'In July 1554, Earl Edward was one of the noblemen who greeted King Philip II of Spain at Southampton and accompanied him to Winchester for his marriage to Queen Mary.' (Bagley) 'Their marriage at Winchester Cathedral on 25 July 1554 took place just days after their first meeting. Philip could not speak English, and so they spoke in a mixture of Spanish, French, and Latin.' (Wikipedia) 'In July 1554 when Mary married Philip of Spain, Henry regained his old court office of gentleman of the King's privy chamber.' (Bagley, p. 54.)
1555, 7 Feb	Brother Henry, Lord Strange, 'married Lady Margaret Clifford. She was the only surviving child of Henry Clifford, 2nd Earl of Cumberland and Lady Eleanor Brandon. The marriage took place in a chapel of the Palace of Whitehall and was attended by Queen Mary I of England and her consort Philip of Spain. They were relatives of the bride through her maternal grandmother Mary Tudor, former queen consort of France.' (Wikipedia)
1553-5 [XI]	Earl Edward served in many positions during Queen Mary and Philip's reign. This, along with other facts, provides a background to his family's later frequent involvements in French and Spanish affairs and the family's unwavering sympathy for English Catholics. There are no reports during this period of the whereabouts or activities of **Sir Thomas**, until his marriage. However, this period is one of the most likely for the birth of an illegitimate son Gerard Stanley, later of Winwick/Ashton-in-Makerfield.
1555-58	W. A. Carrington in the June 1900 issue of *The Journal of the British Archaeological Association* notes 'That the betrothal and marriage of Margaret had no element of romance, whatever may have been the case with regard to her sister Dorothy, is abundantly evident from the entries in an early volume of Household Accounts [of Haddon Hall]: "1555 - Spent by me Mr. [George Vernon] at Newcastle-under-Lyme upon Thursday the fifth of September at the talks of the marriage between Sir Thomas Stanley and Miss Margaret [age 15], five shillings. 1556 - At London, paid for the copying of the articles between the Earl of Derby and my Mr. for the marriage that should be had between the said Earl's son and his daughter, three shillings, four pence. The marriage of Sir Thomas Stanley with Margaret Vernon took place between January and May 1558, when Margaret was about eighteen years of age".' This is the first reference that places the Vernon - Stanley marriage in 1558, making it unlikely that Dorothy, at thirteen, would elope at the same time. There are no indications that household accounts were preserved for the period leading up to the Vernon - Manners marriage in 1563. (David Trutt, *Haddon Hall's Dorothy Vernon*, p. 40.)
1558 between January and May [IV], [XXIII], [XXIV]	**Margaret Vernon** married Sir Thomas Stanley. (*Auden's History*) Their betrothal celebration at Haddon Hall may have been the setting for the elopement of **Margaret**'s sister Dorothy with John Manners, second son of the 1st Earl of Rutland. There are doubts about several dates around this time, but **Sir Thomas** and **Margaret** were definitely married at the latest soon after this, because their (second?) son **Edward** was definitely born in mid to late-1562. Dorothy Vernon's, Sir George's younger daughter and heiress, and John Manners's eldest son George was born in 1569, which makes the elopement in 1558 rather dubious, although there might have been several other unrecorded previous children.

1558, 17 Nov.	Queen Mary died; Elizabeth acceded to the throne. This marked the beginning of another delicate balancing act for all the Stanleys (and many others, of course), often concerning their religious allegiance. The most notable feature of the Stanleys, Earls of Derby, in this context, was how many plots they and their in-laws were associated with.
1558-9	Ferdinando born, son and heir of Henry, Lord Strange, elder brother of **Sir Thomas** and **Sir Edward Sr**. Henry became 4th Earl in 1572, Ferdinando 5th Earl in 1593. Ferdinando's name can best be accounted for by a godfather Ferdinand(o) of the Austrian-Spanish Holy Roman Empire. This name was given to many sons in Lancashire in the next generation and, intriguingly, to later Shakespeares. (Steve Pearson, webmaster of the Shakespeare Family History website, and I, are still puzzling over this fact.) Ferdinando, Lord Strange, future 5th Earl, was a nephew of **Sir Thomas** and **Sir Edward Stanley Sr** and first cousin of **Edward Stanley Jr**.
1560, 2 Jan.	**Sir Edward Sr** knighted, aged c.20(-24?), in Ireland on behalf of Queen Elizabeth. (Roberts, Stanley Family Genealogy website.) This was right at the beginning of the English-Irish wars. Whether or not he had already won his spurs in battle is not known, but from now on he appears as an influential member of the family of the Earls of Derby.
c.1560? [IV]	**Sir Thomas**'s son Henry born, who died as an infant. This date was calculated as half way between **Sir Thomas**'s assumed marriage in 1558 and the birth of **Edward Jr** in mid- to late-1562. It could be, however, that there were miscarriages before **Edward**'s birth, to account for the gap, and that Henry was born after **Edward Jr**. His place of death is unknown; he might have been buried in a small coffin found in the Stanley vault in Tong during restoration work in 1891. (*Auden's History*)
1561, 20 July [XXIII], [XXIV]	William Stanley born and baptised in London (bap. 20 July, 1561 at St Martin, Ludgate), second surviving son of Henry, Lord Strange, later 4th Earl of Derby. William became 6th Earl of Derby in 1594, on the death of his brother Ferdinando. At the beginning of the 20th century he entered the ranks of Shakespeare Alternative Authorship Candidates. Rubbish, of course. He enters the documented story of **Sir Edward Sr** and **Jr** on several occasions, as their nephew and cousin. The first scholarly biography of William was not written, surprisingly, until the *New/Oxford DNB* (2004) by Professor Leo Daugherty. This can be regarded as authoritative, although the most likely dates of his extensive travels abroad still need to be re-examined.
1562 [XII]	Thomas Stanley, Bishop of Man, wrote the 'Rhyming Chronicles', a sort of history in verse of the Stanley family continued to the year 1562. (Beaumont, *Winwick*; Heywood, *Stanley Verses*) (Brian Roberts suspects a later date for the writing of this.)
1562, end Aug. [XV]	**Sir Thomas** attended Preston Guild with his father Earl Edward and his two brothers Sir Henry, Lord Strange (older brother) and **Sir Edward Sr** (younger brother). (*Preston Guild Rolls*) John Shakeshafte, glover, was also present as a burgess. If this was one and the same as John Shakespeare, glover of Stratford, this is his first appearance in records in Lancashire. He was already married (although not to Mary Arderne), with children (Pearson, Shakespeare Family History website); and son William was born less than two years later.

1562, mid-late [IV], [XXVII]	**Sir Thomas**'s son **(Sir) Edward Jr** born. 'His son and heir Edward Stanley was born in 1562, and on his birth Thomas' father, the Earl of Derby, made a deed of settlement granting to Sir Thomas for life all his manors and lands in the counties of Chester, Warwick, Oxford and Devon with remainder to his wife Margaret for life, with remainder to their son Edward for life.' (*Auden's History*)
1562/3 [XI], [XIX]	To repeat this settlement in more detail: Earl Edward made a settlement of 'the several manors and lands lying in the counties of Warwick, Devon and Oxford; also **Dunham-massey, Bowden, Rungey, Hale, Aeton** and **Darfield**, in the county of Chester, now the estate of him the said Edward, Earl of Derby, shall appertain and belong to **Sir Thomas Stanley**, his said second son, for life.' After his death, to his **widow**; after her death to their son **Edward**; if no son and heir, then reversion to the Earl of Derby (Seacome). The 'manors and lands' in Oxfordshire included **Eynsham**, with no other lands in this county known. No mention appears at a later date of any these estates in connection with **Sir Edward Jr**; nor the lands in Warwickshire and Devon. Any possible role of 'manors and lands' in the latter counties in the life of **Sir Thomas** and **Sir Edward Jr** remains a mystery. Ownership of lands in Warwickshire is, of course, intriguing in the Shakespeare/Stanley context. Cousin William, when 6th Earl of Derby, had lands in Meriden, Warwickshire, which is one of the bases for Derbyites claiming him as an Alternative Authorship Candidate. No later report of the history of Meriden (at least none online) makes any mention of previous Stanley ownership.
1562-66 [XI], [XII]	**Sir Thomas** Governor of the Isle of Man (Beaumont, *Winwick*). The Earls of Derby were hereditary Lords of Man and the governors were all their appointees until 1594, when the Crown took over after the death of Ferdinando, 5th Earl. The Lordship of Man was later restored to William, 6th Earl.
1563, 5 Oct. [XII]	**Sir Thomas** was granted the lease for 99 years of the **rectory of Winwick with the manor park** by Thomas Stanley, Bishop of Man and Rector of **Winwick**, at a yearly rent of £120 (elsewhere £200 is given). Lease confirmed by Earl Edward and William Durham, Bishop of Chester (Beaumont, *Winwick*). The Stanleys had long been patrons of **Winwick** Church. Brief biographies appear in this book of this (Sir) Thomas Stanley, Bishop of Man, illegitimate son of the 1st Lord Monteagle, hero at Flodden, and his elder (legitimate) half-brother, yet another Sir Thomas Stanley, who became 2nd Lord Monteagle. All three contemporary Sir Thomas Stanleys have been confused in previous accounts in one way or another. The only one that concerns us from now on in this Time-line is **Sir Thomas**, the one with his tomb in **Tong**. Other (Sir) Edward Stanleys still remain to be dispensed with as DEFINITELY NOT 'our' **Sir Edward** Sr & **Jr**.
1564	William Shakespeare baptised in Stratford and Christopher Marlowe in Canterbury. These are only included here only because it makes them contemporaries of **Edward Jr**, b. 1562. They have both been seen by various previous writers to have played a somewhat significant role a couple of decades or so later in the Stanley story. At the time, of course, no one had any inkling of this.
1565	Sir George Vernon's will. From *The History of Parliament - The House of Commons*: 'His [George Vernon's] wife, his son-in-law John Manners, his brother-in-law Nicholas Longford and his "loving neighbours and faithful friends" Thomas Sutton and Richard Wennesley were each to receive £20 for their services as executors.' (David Trutt, *Haddon Hall's Dorothy Vernon*, p. 55.)

1565, 31 Aug. [IV]	Sir George Vernon, 'the King of the Peak' died and was buried at Bakewell, Derbyshire. **Sir Thomas Stanley** subsequently inherited **Tong Castle**, via the inheritance of his wife **Margaret Vernon**, co-heiress of father Sir George. (*Auden's History*) We might assume they visited **Tong** around this time and this MIGHT have been the occasion of the death and burial of son Henry. However, at this time **Sir Thomas** was still Governor of the Isle of Man.
1565	Muddock writes on the subject of Dorothy's Age and Appearance. 'There is one point which on the first blush seems to support the contention that Dorothy did not elope at the time stated [1558], and that is her age. Sir George Vernon died in August 1565. Both his daughters were then married, and a post-mortem Inquisition was held to prove the heirship of Margaret and Dorothy to their father's immense property. Margaret was 25 years old, and Dorothy 20 years. It is known that Margaret was married to Sir Thomas Stanley about May of 1558, when she would be 18 years of age. If Dorothy was 20 when her father died, she could only have been thirteen when she eloped [at her sister's wedding ball]. These old Inquisitions often erred, however, with regard to the ages of people concerned in them ... At the time of her marriage she would be between 14 and 15 years of age. Although so youthful she would not have been considered an unmarriageable age at that period.' Muddock still insists on Dorothy's elopement at the time of her sister's wedding, even though he moves the date to 1558 from the 1567 of his earlier stories. The actual date of her planned marriage or elopement is 1563, when she was 18. <div align="right">(David Trutt, *Haddon Hall's Dorothy Vernon*, pp. 50-51.)</div>
1565, June-Sep. [XXII]	An Edward Stanley was at the Siege of Malta as one of only two Englishmen in the 'piccolo socorso' dispatched by the Sicilians. The siege succeeded in evicting the Turks from Malta. Potential eye-witness account later by Edward Stanley possibly gave details to Christopher Marlowe for *The Jew of Malta (Millersville)*. This was NOT **Sir Edward Sr**, but one of several namesakes.
1568 [XII]	Thomas Stanley, Bishop of Man, died, place and date unknown. (Beaumont, *Winwick*) The only reason for including this is that it removes him from any later confusions with **Sir Thomas** of **Winwick** and **Tong**.
1568-9 [XI]	**Sir Thomas** Mayor of Liverpool. (Coward, Bagley)
1569 [XI]	Commissioners of muster for Lancashire: Earl Edward, Lord Monteagle, **Sir Thomas Stanley**, Sir George Stanley, Sir John Atherton, Edward Holland and Edmund Ashton. (Bagley)
1569-70 [XI]	Elder brother Henry, Lord Strange, followed **Sir Thomas** as Mayor of Liverpool. (Coward)
1569 [XXIX]	From the entry for Anne Somerset on the website Tudor Women. Anne Percy née Somerset, Countess of Northumberland, was the mother of **Lucy Percy**. 'In 1569, together with Jane Howard, countess of Westmorland, Anne was an instigator of the Northern Rebellion. Her husband was hesitant, but when, in the dead of night, his servants came to tell him that his enemies were surrounding him, the earl and countess fled to Branspeth, Westmorland's house, and from there began their uprising against Queen Elizabeth. Lord Hunsdon, at the head of the Queen's troops, reported that Lady Northumberland was "stouter" than her husband and rode "up and down with the army." <div align="right">*continued*</div>

continuation 1569 [XXIX]	When the rebellion failed, Northumberland sought refuge with Hector Graham, a borderlands robber, but Graham betrayed Northumberland to the earl of Moray. Anne was pregnant during the uprising. She gave birth on June 11, 1570 in Old Aberdeen, Scotland. On August 23, she and her baby fled to the Continent, arriving in Bruges on August 31,1570. Anne hoped to raise enough money to ransom her husband. She persuaded both King Philip II and the Pope to contribute to her cause, but her effort was in vain.'
1570, May [XI], [XIII]	**Sir Thomas** and brother **Sir Edward Sr** planned to free Mary, Queen of Scots from Chatsworth and spirit her to the Isle of Man, from where she would be in a strong position to negotiate with Elizabeth, or escape to France or Spain. (Coward, Bagley, Lovell)
1570, Aug. [XIII]	In August the conspirators abandoned the whole scheme (Bagley), not least because Mary had declined, still believing that French and Spanish requests for her release to Elizabeth might be successful. (Lovell)
1570 [XI]	Commissioners of muster for Lancashire did not include **Sir Thomas**. (Coward)
1570, Nov.	Earl Edward sent his **two younger sons** to court; both sent to the Tower. (Bagley)
1571 beginning? [XIII]	I had long suspected that **Sir Thomas** might have been tortured, and confirmation came from Brian Roberts, quoting from *Prisoners of the Tower* by A.H. Cook, formerly Chief Warder at H.M. Tower of London, 2 hand-written volumes. 'A confession on the rack brought about his arrest and committal to the Tower (Ridolfi Plot)'.
1571, mid [XI], [XIII]	**Sir Thomas** still being inquisitioned in the Tower. By July all details of **the brothers**' involvement had been established. **Sir Thomas** was deemed the principal 'plotter' of the two brothers. (Bagley)
1571, 7 Oct.	Sea battle of Lepanto between the Ottoman Turks and the Venetian coalition, which included support from the Knights of Malta; the 'Holy League' forces were under the command of Don Juan de Austria, an illegitimate son of Emperor Charles V. (He was born in Regensburg and was also a key candidate of the Spanish to marry Mary, Queen of Scots and become king of England. Unfortunately for him, he died of typhus in 1578.) Lists have survived of the Turkish and Venetian naval commanders, but no lists so far discovered (by me) of any English participants in the 20,000 strong military force. This is included here purely as a 'history marker', of an event that fired the imagination of all Europe and produced the background for *Othello*.
1572	Ferdinando and William matriculated at St John's, Oxford.
1572, May [XI]	**Sir Thomas** still in the Tower along with the Bishop of Ross, the Earl of Southampton, Lord Lumley and Thomas, the brother of Lord Cobham; all were suspected of being involved with the Duke of Norfolk in his 'plotting'. (Coward)
1572, 2 June	Duke of Norfolk executed in the Tower. He was an in-law of all the Stanleys, Earls of Derby.
1572, 22 Aug. [App. 7]	Thomas Percy, 7th Earl of Northumberland executed at York for his role in the Northern Rebellion of 1569-70. Left four daughters, the second one **Lucy**, who later married **(Sir) Edward Stanley Jr**. 'After the earl's flight to Scotland his wife remained on the borders, so that she might the better be able to render him assistance. She made every effort to raise money for his ransom. *continued*

continuation 1572, 22 Aug. [App. 7]	In Aug. 1570 she arrived at Antwerp with her newly born child, Mary, and obtained funds and devised a plan by which her husband might be sent into Flanders. But her energetic endeavours to purchase his liberty failed. For a time she resided at Liège, and in 1573 she was at Mechlin, and subsequently removed to Brussels. In 1576, at Queen Elizabeth's request, she was temporarily expelled from Spanish territory. She died of smallpox in a convent at Namur, Oct. 17, 1596.' (Carol Curt Enos, *Shakespeare Encyclopedia*)
1572, 24 Oct.	Edward, 3rd Earl of Derby, died at Lathom.
1572, 4 Dec. [XIV]	Elaborate state funeral of Edward, 3rd Earl of Derby at Ormskirk (Seacome). Sons **Sir Thomas** and **Sir Edward Sr** not listed among the mourners; **Sir Thomas** assumed still in the Tower; we are still hunting for **Sir Edward Sr**'s whereabouts around this time.
c.1572-3	**Sir Thomas**'s tenants in **Winwick** reported later (1584), that most of the complainants gave a year's rent to **Sir Thomas** 'of their benevolences when he was in trouble'. (Honigmann, *'lost years'*, p. 81.) One assumes that the 'trouble' that required money was payment of a heavy fine for his release. The following entry shows that within the next year or so he was released.
c.1574-5 [IV]	**Sir Thomas** moved to **Tong** Castle. 'A.D. 1575 Now latlie by credible report **Sir Thomas Stanley** is cum to dwell in this cuntrie, and many papists gentilmen resorte unto hym.' (*Auden's History*)
1576, 21 Dec. [XVIII]	'**Sir Thomas Stanley** died 21 December 1576, being succeeded by his only son, **Edward**, then aged 14.' (*Auden's History*) He was buried in the Stanley vault in **Tong** Church. His lands were divided between son **Edward Jr** and his widow **Margaret**, who remarried, William Mather. It was she 'who sold her interest in **Eynsham** to Sir Thomas Peniston of Bampton, who insisted on a strict partition of the manor. The life interest continued until 1595 or later'. (*Eynsham Manor*) From other sources we know that **Margaret** died in 1596. Sir Thomas's will PRO Prob. 11/58 sig 39. (National Archives, Brian Roberts)
1578, 3 Aug. [XVIII]	Widow **Margaret** definitely married to William Mather by this time: 'Margaret Vernon and William Mather granted a lease to George Fort for the manor of Stackpole and other lands held by him in Pembrokeshire'. (*Tudorplace*)
1579, mid	The assumed date (by HM at least) for William Shakespeare arriving in Lancashire, aged 15, to take up duties as 'a schoolmaster in the country' in the Hoghton household.
1579	Assumed year of the secret marriage of cousin Ferdinando Stanley and Alice Spencer, whose first daughter Ann was born in May 1580.
1581 [II]	**Edward Stanley Jr** married **Lucy Percy**, second daughter of Thomas, 7th Earl of Northumberland. '**Sir Edward Stanley**, their son, was married to **Lady Lucy Percy** whose father was executed by Elizabeth I in 1572 for plotting against her. Her grandfather had been executed by Henry VIII.' (Jeffery, *Guidebook Tong Church*)
1581	This is probably the very earliest date for the painting of a miniature of **Lady Lucy Percy** by Isaac Oliver (c.1565-1617). A black and white stipple engraving by A. Birrell, published in 1802, is in the National Portrait Gallery. (© NPG D7676.) *continued*

continuation 1581	This might, however, have been of a later Lady Lucy Percy, by a different artist. The only known image definitely of her is the effigy on her tomb in Walthamstow Church.
1581, Easter to Whit.	Jesuit Edmund Campion in Lancashire, in the Preston area; among his hosts were a Hoghton and a Hesketh, families closely linked by status and friendship with the Stanleys, Earls of Derby. If Campion, via his works & oratory, had any influence on young Shakespeare, it would have manifested itself at this time. If his father John received his copy of the Spiritual Testament by Carlo Borromeo (found in the 18th century hidden in the rafters of the house in Henley Street) during this Catholic Mission, it would most likely have been from Campion on his way through Warwickshire to Yorkshire and Lancashire.
1581, 3 Aug.	William Shakeshafte named in the will of Alexander Hoghton. This is the main piece of documentary evidence for William Shakespeare's traditional stay for a couple of years in his youth with the Hoghtons in Lancashire. (Transcript of will in Honigmann, *'lost years'*, App. A.) I believe that this William Shakeshafte was young William Shakespeare, but the documentary evidence behind this belief will have to await my forthcoming book *Shakespeare's Lancashire Links*. My best attempt at a summary in one sentence (with a few semi-colons) is that John Shakespeare, William's father, was a great-grandson of a Shakeshafte at Bosworth, who was rewarded by Henry VII with lands in North Warwickshire; John was son of a younger son, so with no expectation of inheriting property; he was a rather successful local entrepreneur as a glover in Stratford, among other activities, but kept up all his Lancashire links; his wife Mary Arderne became his third wife in c.1575/6 and was therefore not the natural mother of William the Bard; she was a great-granddaughter of Arderne of Cheshire, similarly awarded lands in Leicestershire after Bosworth, and it was her upper gentry relatives, among others, who afforded William access to libraries, etc..
1582 [XIX]	'**Edward Stanley esquire [Edward Jr]** was living with his wife at **Eynsham** in 1582. Also living there then was **Sir Edward Stanley [Sr].**' (*Eynsham Manor.*) One might presume that at this time they were moving between **Eynsham** and **Tong**, spending equal time at both - or not.
1582, end Aug. [XV]	Earl Henry, sons Ferdinando, Lord Strange, William & Francis; + **Sir Edward Sr** and (Sir) **Edward Jr** at Preston Guild. (*Preston Guild Rolls*) John Shakeshafte, glover and burgess, was also there with many male relatives. If he was one and the same as John Shakespeare, glover of Stratford, then we have the names of many of the Bard's uncles and cousins. One might assume that **Edward Jr** stayed in **Winwick** during this visit. It may even have been during this visit (if his wife was with him) that his infant son Thomas died and was buried here. If so, he must have been aware of a previous Stanley connection and burial here. 'Peter Gerard had married Margaret, daughter of Sir William Stanley of Hooton [Gen. 5] and Margaret Bromley. Peter died in 1494 and is buried in the Gerard chapel in Winwick.' (Brian S. Roberts, personal communication.)
1582	Summer-Autumn William Stanley, younger son of Henry, future 4th Earl of Derby, set off on the first of his extended tours, this one to France and Spain. All details will appear in my future monograph on his travels. His suspected stay in Navarre is assumed by some to have inspired *Love's Labour's Lost*. He certainly managed to insult a Spanish nobleman in Madrid, fought a duel, and had to flee.

1582, 28 Nov.	William Shakespeare married Anne Hathaway when she was three months pregnant. So much has been speculated and written about this. My contribution is the theory that he was on tour with Strange's Men when word reached him that she was pregnant (the result of a 'one-night-stand' on a previous visit?); he returned (not quite post-haste) and did his duty by taking out a marriage-licence in a hurry, under threat from her neighbours, thus making an honest woman of her.
1583, 16 Sep	Burial of Francis Stanley at Ormskirk. Earl Henry's son, **Edward Jr**'s first cousin.
1583	Eldest daughter Arabella born. In early-mid 1601, when she died at Walthamstow, she was aged 18.
1584 [XIII]	*Inhabitants of Winwick v.* **Stanley** (26 Elizabeth), reported that they had helped **Sir Thomas** in his 'trouble' in his later years, i.e. between 1571 and 1576; the reason for this court case is not known. (Honigmann, *'lost years'*, p. 81.) (Brian Roberts, Records of the Duchy of Lancaster, PRO, DL 4/26/18.)
1576-84 [XIX]	Some time between these two dates **Margaret** sold half her interest in **Eynsham** to Sir Thomas Peniston. 'The life interest continued until 1595 or later.' The date of '1595 or later' was perhaps/presumably related to **Margaret**'s death in 1596. However, by 1584 Peniston was obviously fully in charge of his half of **Eynsham**.
1584	'William Emmot who was Vicar here in 1584 came from Colne in Lancashire. He was a prominent Oxford man but attempts to glean information on his early life at Colne came to nothing.' (Lilian Wright of **Eynsham**, July 2012.) 'William Emmot, vicar 1569-85, a Lancastrian and former fellow of Brasenose College, Oxford, was described as "one of the superior types of Elizabethan clergy"; he was resident, taught children and bequeathed Bibles and other books to neighbouring clergy and pupils. Robert Lloyd, vicar c.1593-1608, also bequeathed books.' (*Victoria County History, County of Oxford*, Eynsham, 1990.)
1584-6 [XIX]	'Other Stanleys were also concerned in **Eynsham**: in 1584 William Stanley, younger son of Henry, earl of Derby (d. 1593), caused a disturbance in **Eynsham** church by seeking to prevent Sir Thomas Peniston's son from using the manorial pew; he was still in **Eynsham** in 1586.' (*Eynsham Manor*.) (We met Thomas Peniston back in 1576.) William was almost certainly not living permanently there on either of these dates, because he was in the middle of his travels around Europe again. The best explanation (at the moment) is that he used **Eynsham** as a convenient stopover between Lancashire and London, thus renewing his friendship with his cousin **Edward Jr**, who, we know from later events, retained his parents' interest in **Eynsham** until his death in 1632.
1585, Jan.- March [IX]	Earl Henry's mission to France, ostensibly to invest Roi Henri III as Knight of the Garter, but presumed also to investigate how France and England should act together against the Spanish in the Low Countries (Bagley, Coward). Son William might have accompanied him, in the company of John Donne (Denis Flynne, Donne biographer).
1585	Second daughter Marie born. In early-mid 1601, when she died at Walthamstow, she was aged 16.
1585-6	Ferdinando Mayor of Liverpool.

1585, Sep.	Queen Elizabeth agreed to send an English army to the Netherlands, under the command of Robert Dudley, Earl of Leicester. He was accompanied by Sir William Stanley of Hooton, hero in the Irish wars, a distant 'cousin' of **Edward Jr**.
1586, Jan.	'Mr Stanleyes Boyes played at court.' (URL of Derby website.) It is not obvious which 'Mr Stanley' this was, but the strongest candidate is Ferdinando, Lord Strange.
1586 XIX]	'William Camden recorded in his book *Britannia* (1586) that Eynsham "Abby….. now is turned into a private dwelling house and acknowledgeth the Earl of Derby thereof" (translation by Richard Gough, 1789). The Earl seems to have kept servants permanently there, and presumably adapted the abbot's lodgings for his own use.' (Lilian Wright) The earl in 1586 was Henry, 4th Earl, which reflects the knowledge of locals that, although the widow of his brother **Sir Thomas** now owned **Eynsham**, it was in tail-male to the Earldom. The implication is that son **Edward Jr** was not there very often and certainly not at the time of Camden's visit.
1586	According to the reputable *Victoria County History* of Oxfordshire (*Eynsham Manor*) 'he [*William*] was still in **Eynsham** in 1586'. It is impossible to believe that William stayed for two years in **Eynsham** and this was presumably a return visit. It seems most likely that it was him, as there were no other Williams in the immediate family. The date and original source need to be checked.
1586, 29 June [X]	**Sir Edward Sr** 'wrote a letter from his nephew's house at **Winwick**, asking his brother, the Earl of Derby, to use his good offices with the Archbishop of Canterbury, to appoint his friend John Kine one of the proctors of the court of Arches.' (Beaumont, *Winwick*.)
1586	Fourth daughter Alice born. In early-mid 1601, when she died at Walthamstow, she was aged 15.
1586, 4 Oct. [XXII]	An Edward Stanley fought heroically at Zutphen, during the siege of which Sir Philip Sidney was mortally wounded. Knighted by the Earl of Leicester in Holland, who wrote an eye-witness account (*Camden Society*, XXVII: 427). He has often been confused with **Sir Edward Stanley Sr**. He might have been the Sir Edward Stanley of Elford 'knighted in Netherland, slaine in Ireland in 1597'. (Stanley, *Visitation of Cheshire*, 1580.)
1586, Dec.	Wedding of Ursula Stanley (**Edward Jr**'s cousin) and John Salusbury at Lleweni, Denbigh. Presumed event that inspired Shakespeare's poem *The Phoenix and the Turtle*. Ursula was an illegitimate, but fully recognised, daughter of Henry, 4th Earl of Derby; John Salusbury was a descendant of Henry VII via an illegitimate son and Catherine of Berain. His brother Thomas Salusbury had been executed earlier this year (21 Sep.) as one of the conspirators in the Babington Plot. (Honigmann, *'lost years'*; Jones, article in *Transactions of the Denbighshire Historical Society*, January, 2011; book *Where was Shakespeare?*, lodged with Shakespeare Birthplace Trust.)
1587, Jan	Sir William Stanley of Hooton surrendered Deventer to the Spanish and never returned to England, spending most of his time in the Spanish Netherlands and Spain. He became the military commander of English and Irish troops in exile. *continued*

continuation 1587, Jan.	The spiritual leader of the English Catholic exiles was (later Cardinal) William Allen, from Lancashire, who had spent a short time as a schoolmaster in Stratford and later founded the English School/College at Douai, to which many young English Catholics were sent for their education. In a subsequent investigation of all the Stanleys: 'Meanwhile Sir Edward Stanley in London harboured priests'. (Edwards, *Plots and Plotters*, p. 173) Was this **Sir Edward Sr**?
1587, 8 Feb. [XIII]	Execution of Mary, Queen of Scots at Fotheringay. Henry, 4th Earl of Derby had been one of the peers at her trial. As a reminder, **Sir Thomas** and **Sir Edward Sr** had planned to free her from Chatsworth in May, 1570.
1587, 13 May- beg. Dec. [XV]	**Sir Edward Sr** visited brother Earl Henry at **Lathom** with 4 servants; on 14 October he returned to Lathom from London; at the beginning of December he went 'towards Chester' with Ferdinando. (*Derby Household Books, DHB*)
1587-88 [IX]	Earl Henry went to the Netherlands to negotiate with the Spanish leaders, in an attempt to prevent the launching of the Spanish Armada. (Coward)
1588, 6 Jan.	**Edward Jr** visited Earl Henry at **Lathom**. *(DHB)*
1588 [XXIII]	Roger Manners became 5th Earl of Rutland when the three sons of his uncle Edward, 4th Earl, died *osp*. Roger was a second cousin of John, the grandson of John Manners and Dorothy Vernon, sister of Margaret Vernon, **Sir Edward Jr**'s mother. This brings the Earls of Rutland into the Stanley story.
1588	Fourth daughter Priscilla born. In early-mid 1601, when she died at Walthamstow, she was aged 13.
1588, 14 Dec.	**Sir Edward Sr** at **Lathom**. (*DHB*)
1589, 10 June	Earl Henry returned to Lancashire again; **Sir Edward Sr** in residence. (*DHB*)
1589, 23 July	'Mr Edward Stanley of Winwicke' visited Earl Henry and **Sir Edward Sr** at Lathom. (*DHB*) **Sir Thomas**'s illegitimate son?
1589, 28 Aug.	**Sir Edward Sr** and Earl Henry to **Winwick**. (*DHB*) On 30 Henry to the Wirral; **Sir Edward Sr** stayed at Knowsley, where **Edward Jr** arrived with his uncle Lord Dudley. (*DHB*)
1589, 6 Sep.	On Tuesday Earl Henry, Lord Dudley, **Sir Edward Sr**, William 'went to **Lathom** to hunt'; all back at Knowsley on Saturday 6, when the Queen's Players performed at night and the Essex Players arrived. On Sunday the Revd William Leigh (Parson of Standish, a vital figure in this context) preached in the morning, the Queen's Players performed in the afternoon and the Essex Players in the evening. More coming and going before Lord Dudley and William Stanley went to London. (*DHB*) William was off on the last of his 'grand tours', this time to Russia.
1589, 4 Oct.	Thursday Earl Henry to New Park, Ferdinando to **Winwick**. (*DHB*)
1589, 15 Oct.	Earl Henry to Bidston, Cheshire; **Sir Edward Sr** stayed at Lathom with Lady Strange. (*DHB*)
1589, 1 Nov.	Lord Monteagle and Mr Salusbury left. (Future Sir John Salusbury, already husband of Henry's daughter Ursula, see *Phoenix and Turtle* in 1586.) **Sir Edward Sr** stayed with Ferdinando and Alice. (*DHB*)
1589, 8 Nov.	Monday, Lady Strange to **Winwick**; **Sir Edward Sr** stayed; Wed. Lord and Lady Strange met at **Winwick**; Thurs. Lady Strange back. (*DHB*)

1589, 15 Nov.	Thursday **Edward Jr** came and stayed overnight. (*DHB*)
1589, 20 Nov.	'The affray at Lea', when Thomas Hoghton was killed in an affray close to midnight by a band under the leadership of Baron Langton of Walton. This has loomed large in many accounts of Lancashire history, given that it involved so many local notables and came to the ears of Queen Elizabeth. For the moment it is just here as a date. Honigmann gives a brief account and an extract from Elizabeth's letter. (*'lost years'*, pp. 12-13.) Carol Enos has read the relevant MSS in the John Rylands Library, Manchester, and reported the list of those involved (all relevant quotes in my forthcoming book *Shakespeare's Lancashire Links*). Many have suspected that it had more to do than with just cattle stealing, but no one, so far, has provided a satisfactory explanation. I suspect that this was just one more mystery that MIGHT provide a clue to several other mysteries.
1580s, late	Precise date and occasion yet to be established. '"All the Stanleys are traitors" growled one of the hit men of the regime, Richard Topcliffe.' (Asquith, *Shadowplay*, p. 51.)
1590, 2 May	Thursday **Edward Jr** came to New Park to uncle Henry's and stayed overnight. Earl Henry left, the rest of the family stayed, including **Sir Edward Sr**, on and off until the middle of August, by when Henry was back. (*DHB*)
1590, 22 Aug.	'**Mr Edwarde Stanley**', who must have been **Edward Jr**, visited **Lathom** and stayed overnight. (*DHB*) With him was his cousin Ferdinando and a 'Mr Stanley of Winwicke'. It seems more than likely that this was Gerard Stanley of Ashton-in-Makerfield, an illegitimate son of **Sir Thomas** and therefore **Sir Edward Jr**'s half-brother. More research is pending by Brian S. Roberts.
1590	Lord Burghley commissioned a map of Lancashire, with all known recusants marked with an ominous cross. This has also loomed large in Lancashire history, with little consensus of opinion in the 20th-21st centuries as to what happened to some individuals after 1590. All recusant events were of necessity cloaked in secrecy.
1590/1	'A tenement called the church house in **Northchurch** in the tenure of — Axhill was granted in 1590–1 to **Sir Edward Stanley**. (fn. 97) (*Victoria County History of Hertford*, Vol. 2, pp. 245-250, british-history.ac.uk) (fn. 97 - Pat. 33 Eliz. pt. 16, m. 2.) This seems to have been **Sir Edward Sr** or a namesake, because **Edward Jr** had not yet been knighted.
Early 1590s	Possible date of death of infant Thomas, only son of **Edward Jr** and **Lady Lucy**, buried at **Winwick**.
1592	**Sir Edward Sr** mentioned as a recusant and 'a dangerous person'. (*Millersville*, quote from Nicholl, *The Reckoning*.) Or a different Sir Edward Stanley?
1592	(Fears of Spanish invasion) 'Whispers that predominantly Catholic Lancashire might be the invasion bridge had raised suspicions about the local magnate, the Earl of Derby.'[67] [67] BL MS Royal 18. D.III, fos. 82v-83r; TNA SP 12/242/116, 121, and APC, xxiii, pp. 163-4 (Parry, *Dr John Dee*, 2011, p. 229.)
1592, early	All agree that William Shakespeare had arrived in London by this time at the latest. It is also on record that Christopher Marlowe's *The Jew of Malta* was performed at the Rose Theatre at this time. *continued*

continuation 1592, early [App. 2]	One source suggested for Maltese details was an Edward Stanley's participation at the Siege of Malta in 1565. Edward Alleyn played the main role; Alleyn's mother was a Towneley of Towneley, Burnley, Lancashire. (Keen, Conlan)
1593, 1 June [App. 2]	Christopher Marlowe killed at Deptford during an incident that was explained satisfactorily for all – but not for the first Marlovians 300 years later! There is a tradition that he visited **Tong** and wrote some of his works there, although there is no evidence that dates this tradition back to his lifetime.
1593	William Stanley, Ferdinando's brother, back in Lancashire after three years in Russia; appointed Governor of the Isle of Man. The ballad sees him still abroad when his father died, having been with Dr John Dee in Russia. This was a confusion with his son Dr Arthur Dee, who *was* in Russia as physician to the Tsar, but later, in the reign of James I. (See his biography, *DNB*)
1593, 25 Sep. [IX], [XXI]	Earl Henry died, buried 4 December. The delay was presumably partly because of the necessary preparations (no record of these has survived) and partly because of the following: **Sir Edward Sr** was at Lathom with Ferdinando, now the 5th Earl, at the death of Henry; they received a letter via Richard Hesketh (of Aughton), from Catholic exiles, offering the throne to Ferdinando in the event of Elizabeth's death without naming an heir. It was reported that he was at Lathom when 'On Thursday the 27th (September, 1593) Richard (Hesketh) went over to Lathom to hand in Hickman's letter and show his passport to **Sir Edward Stanley**. Ferdinando, the new earl, also saw his passport, as did the bishop of Chester who happened to be staying there.' (Edwards, *Plots and Plotters*, p. 179.) **Sir Edward Sr** was known as a recusant who harboured Catholic priests in London. (Edwards, *Plots and Plotters*, p. 173.) The 'Hickman letter' perhaps brings Bartholomew Hickman, a 'skryer' or medium for Dr John Dee, and thus Dr Dee into the story.
1593, 3 Oct. [IX]	Soon afterwards Ferdinando left the North West for London with Hesketh, went straight to Queen Elizabeth at Windsor, who exonerated him from any suspicion of complicity. Richard Hesketh was turned over to the regime and suffered the (by now) predictable fate of torture and execution. (Edwards, *Plots and Plotters*) As a minor footnote here (and yet very important for Lancashire connections), Richard Hesketh was the brother of Bartholomew Hesketh of Aughton, and their sister was Elizabeth, the wife of Alexander Hoghton, who wrote his will in 1581 mentioning William Shakeshafte. Bartholomew had also been one of the alleged hosts of Edmund Campion in Lancashire in 1581.
1593, 9 Oct. [XX]	Ferdinando, now 5th Earl of Derby, at Blackburn Grammar School? Named at the head of a list of Governors (Abram, *History of Blackburn*). If really present, he must have returned to Lancashire post-haste, not least because his father's funeral still needed to be organised and many in his family were still waiting back in Lancashire, no doubt wondering about the outcome of this latest 'plot'. 'Deceased' was added after his name on the list at Blackburn Grammar School, but this may have been added later.
1593, 4 Dec.	Henry, 4th Earl buried in the Derby chapel at Ormskirk. (*Parish Register*) One suspects that **Sir Edward Sr** had been in charge of the arrangements. 'In the funeral oration, his friend Bishop Chadderton praised him for his fidelity, justice and generosity.' (Bagley, p. 62.)

1594	Henry Percy, 9th Earl of Northumberland, **Lucy**'s cousin and childhood companion, married Dorothy Devereux, sister of Penelope Devereux (candidate for Shakespeare's 'Dark Lady') and Robert Devereux, 2nd Earl of Essex.
1594, 16 April	Ferdinando died at Lathom after two weeks in agonising pain. Witchcraft was suspected, but poisoning more likely. It was presumed to part of the aftermath of the failed 'Hesketh Plot'. One could imagine that first cousin **Edward Jr** hurried to Lancashire when he heard of the illness, or at least would have made every effort to attend the funeral. One might also presume that uncle **Sir Edward Sr** was there too, as he seemed to be in residence most of the time when the family was in Lancashire. Contemporary reports of Ferdinando's death are conflicting as to who organised the poisoning. A horseman was considered suspect, when he rode off immediately afterwards. Various members of his household were suspected and questioned. Various close relatives, politicians of the time and historians a few years later recorded their opinions as to the cause of his death, whether by poisoning or witchcraft, and initiated by whom. Some accused the Cecils, Sir William (Lord Burghley) and his son Sir Robert (later Earl of Salisbury), of organising this; some accused the Jesuits on the continent; some accused Catholic sympathisers in England. The only fact everyone agrees on is that Ferdinando died after a couple of pretty horrible weeks of suffering. He left a widow, Countess Alice née Spencer, and three daughters, plus younger brother William, who almost immediately became the 6th Earl; these two battled on for a dozen years trying to solve the future of the vast estates of the Earl of Derby. Their stories linger on during many future dates, as potentially relevant to **Sir Edward Stanley Sr** and **Jr**, but details for the next few months are still lacking. (Latest account in Daugherty, *The Assassination of Shakespeare's Patron: Investigating the Death of the Fifth Earl of Derby*, 2011.)
1594, 28 May	Burial of Ferdinando, 5th Earl of Derby, at Ormskirk. (*Parish register*)
1594, Sep. [XVIII]	Lady **Margaret** Stanley wrote a letter to her brother-in-law John Manners at Haddon Hall about tenants of her property at Harleston, greeting her nephew George and wife.
1595, 26 Jan.	William Stanley, 6th Earl of Derby, married Elizabeth de Vere, daughter of Edward, 17th Earl of Oxford, at Greenwich, in the presence of Queen Elizabeth. Strong contestant for the wedding at which the premiere of *A Midsummer Night's Dream* was performed. (Honigmann, *'lost years'*, App. C.) This wedding among three contestants is a matter of 'you pays your money and you takes your choice', but William and Elizabeth's marriage has strong support (e.g. Asquith, *Shadowplay*, 2005, pp. 106-7).
c.1595	Theatre built at Prescot near Lathom by/for William, 6th Earl. This has the distinction of being the first purpose-built theatre in the North. (It did not survive the Civil War.) As such, Prescot was the proposed site for a new theatre for 'Shakespeare North' in the mid-Noughties, but sufficient funds were not forthcoming.
?c.1595/6	**Petronella** born. This date calculated as the oldest of the three surviving daughters, with **Venetia** born in December 1600.
c.1596	'Of the vast possessions of **Sir Edward Stanley**, Erdeswick writing circa 1596, speaks of him as "now Lord of **Harlaston**", *continued*

continuation c.1596 [IV], [XVII], [XXI]	and says of **Cubleston** "**Edward Stanley** is now owner thereof," and of **West Bromwich**, "now **one of the Stanleys** hath the seat of his house there."' (*Auden's History*)
1596 [XVIII]	**Edward Jr**'s mother **Margaret née Vernon** died. In her will she requested to be buried with her first husband **Sir Thomas**. This might have been one impetus for their son to think about commissioning a tomb for them and himself at Tong, although this did not happen until a few years later. She left **Marple** and **Wybersley** to son **Edward**. PRO Prob. 11/58 sig 39 (Brian Roberts, Stanley Family Genealogy). Her ownership of the Derby lands under the settlement of 1562/3 (including **Eynsham**) passed automatically to her son.
1596, 17 Oct. [App. 7]	'[**Lucy**'s mother] died of smallpox at a convent near Namur.' (Enos, *Shakespeare Encyclopedia*.) Her daughter Mary, **Lucy**'s sister, had founded a Benedictine Convent. Their two other sisters had married into titled families. Extract from Anne Somerset on website Tudor Women. 'Anne Somerset's daughters had to be abandoned in England when the rebellion failed. Two of them were found at Wressel, the family seat, in a pitiful state, nearly frozen, half starved, and terrified. The servants with whom they'd been left had been murdered and the house ransacked. Their uncle, Henry Percy, who subsequently was granted their father's title, took his brother's daughters into his own household and they were raised at Petworth. Meanwhile, their mother was at Liège, living on a pension from Philip II. There she wrote "Discours des troubles du Comte de Northumberland" and involved herself in Catholic plots. She spent the next decade moving from place to place in the Spanish Netherlands, staying in contact with other exiles. She was living at Malines in 1572, in Mechlin in 1573, in Brussels in 1574 and again in 1576, and was back in Liège in 1575. In 1576 she was briefly expelled from the territory in an attempt to placate Queen Elizabeth, but she returned almost immediately. In September 1591, Charles Paget, an English exile in Antwerp, wrote to the Percy family in London to say that Anne had died and to request that her youngest daughter, Jane, come to Flanders to claim her mother's belongings. This appears to have been a ruse to allow Jane to visit her mother. Anne died of smallpox while living in the convent at Namur, but not until five years later.'
1596	Dr John Dee appointed Warden of Manchester College, the building owned by William, 6th Earl of Derby. Dee succeeded William Chaderton, former Bishop of Chester and Lincoln; Dee was there until 1603. While there he was visited by Earl William and entourage. (Dee's *Diary*) He had entered the Stanley story several times previously and has been proposed as a model for Prospero in *The Tempest*.
1597, 12 March [IX]	**Edward Jr** bought the following estates from his cousin William Stanley, 6th Earl of Derby: **Acton, Hurleston, Dorfold, Overmarsh (Ches.); Shifford (Oxon)**. Price unknown. (Coward, *The Stanleys*, p. 196.) This was during the legal battles between William and his sister-in-law Countess Alice.
1597 [App.7]	**Edward Jr** demised his lands in **Stackpole** (Pembrokeshire?) to William Ingleby. (Tudorplace website) One of this name was later involved on the periphery of the Gunpowder Plot (*Fraser*), and one of his brothers was Ven. Francis Ingleby, a martyr in York in 1586 for being a priest. (*Catholic Encyclopedia* website) Both were sons of Sir William Ingleby of Ripley, Yorkshire. It is not known whether the William Ingleby who acquired Stackpole was the same, but it seems likely that they were related.

1597 [V]	Christopher Middleton dedicated *Chinon* to **Edward Jr**. (Honigmann, *Weever*, p. 22.)
1597 [XIX]	Sir Edward Stanley 'knight in Netherland, slain in Ireland 1597'. (*Visitation of Cheshire*, 1580, pub. 1882.) NOT our **Sir Edward Sr**; possibly the one knighted at Zutphen by Leicester in 1586. Possibly/probably of Elford, Staffordshire.
?c.1598	Daughter **Frances** born.
1599 [VIII]	John Weever published *Epigrammes*, including many dedicated to **Edward Jr**'s kinsmen, friends and acquaintances and one 'ad Gulielmum Shakespeare'. (Honigmann, *Weever*)
1599	Shakespeare, with others, re-built The Globe theatre on the south bank. One trustee was Thomas Savage, an in-law of the Heskeths of Rufford. (Honigmann, *'lost years'*) Another was William Leveson, of a family with large holdings in Staffordshire and Shropshire. (Keen) It is more than possible that **Edward Jr** knew this family.
1599	Other events around this time led Prof. James Shapiro to write *1599: A Year in the Life of William Shakespeare* (2005). He does not mention **Sir Edward Sr** or **Edward Jr**.
1599, 30 June	1599, June 30, London. *George Fenner to his partner Baltazar Gybels, Antwerp.* "Therle of Darby is busyed only in penning comedies for the commoun players." [*State Papers, Domestic, Elizabeth, vol. 271, No. 34.*] 1599, June 30, London. *George Fenner to Sire Humfredo Galdelli or Guiseppe Tusinga, Venice.* "Our Earle of Darby is busye in penning commodyes for the commoun players." [*Ibid., No. 35.*] (James H. Greenstreet, 'A Hitherto Unknown Noble Writer of Elizabethan Comedies', *The Genealogist*, July 1891. Quoted on website The URL of Derby.) This record is the main reason for the proposal that he actually wrote (some of) Shakespeare's plays. Nonsense, but it does make him a fellow-playwright.
1599-1601	In 1599 William Stanley, 6th Earl 'is also reported as financing one of London's two children's drama companies, the Paul's Boys, and for roughly the period 1599-1601, his playing company, Derby's Men, was active, and very successfully so, at the Boar's Head, just outside London. In addition the company played multiple times at court in 1600 and 1601. (URL of Derby website, ref. Gurr, Andrew. *The Shakesperian Playing Companies*. 'My Lord Darby hath put up the playes of the children in Pawles to his great paines and charge.' Gurr's source is: *Historical Manuscripts Commission, Report on the manuscripts of Lord de L'Isle and Dudley* ed. C. L. Kingsford.) 'In 1599 he financed the revival of the Children of Paul's company, in apparent partnership with John Marston and others, and one of more of this troupe's extant unattributed plays cold be his. As Thomas Middleton and the earl's friend William Percy (younger brother of the ninth earl of Northumberland, another friend) also wrote for the Paul's boys at this time. Derby would necessarily have worked in association with them.' (Leo Daugherty, biography of William Stanley, *ODNB*, 2004.)
1600 [IX], [XIX], [XXI]	Derby lands in reversion to William, 6th Earl of Derby, after the (future) death of **Sir Edward Stanley Sr**, brother of the 4th Earl of Derby: **Thirsk & Kirkby Malzeard** (Yorkshire). (Coward) *continued*

continuation 1600 [IX], [XIX], [XXI]	Lands in reversion to 'William, 6th Earl of Derby, after the death of **Edward Stanley esq.**, son of **Sir Thomas Stanley**, younger brother of the 4th Earl of Derby: **Eynsham** (Oxon.).' (Coward) These were in the middle of the long drawn out dispute of Derby lands between William and Countess Alice.
1600 [V]	'**Master Edward Stanley**' was the dedicatee of John Weever's *Faunus and Melliflora*. (Honigmann, *Weever*, p. 22.)
1600, 19 Dec. [II]	**Venetia Stanley** born, daughter of **Edward Jr** and his last child. The choice of Venetia's name must surely have been inspired by Venice. (*The Merchant of Venice* assumed written c. 1597.) Other direct or indirect Stanley connections with Venice not established, unless cousin William had visited it on his 'grand tour' to Italy in the late 1580s.
1601, 5 or 6 Feb.	Sir Charles Percy, first cousin of **Lucy**, **Edward Jr**'s wife, paid forty shillings for a specially commissioned performance of Shakespeare's Richard II, on the eve of the Essex insurrection.
1601, 25 Feb. [App. 3]	Robert Devereux, 2nd Earl of Essex, and Sir Charles Percy executed on Tower Hill (with others). The Devereux family was intricately related to **Edward Jr** via many routes. Just one main example here: Dorothy Devereux, sister of Robert, 2nd Earl, was married to Henry Percy, 9th Earl of Northumberland, the 'Wizard Earl', a first cousin of **Lucy**'s, with whom she grew up. Another sister, Penelope, is one of the main contestants for Shakespeare's 'Dark Lady' of the Sonnets, IF the latter was indeed a real life lady and not an imagined composite.
1601, early-mid [X]	Lady **Lucy**, **Sir Edward Jr**'s wife died along with four of their daughters and were buried at Walthamstow. A tomb was commissioned for them, date of completion and erection unknown, but assumed within a year after the deaths. **Lucy**'s near life-size effigy is on the tomb, along with the four daughters in miniature.
1601 ff. [XXIV]	**Sir Edward Jr** placed his infant daughter **Venetia** (and his two other surviving daughters **Frances** and **Petronella**) with a cousin 'to be brought up by his friends, Francis and Grace Fortescue of Selden, Buckinghamshire' not far from the Digby home (Sir Everard and son Kenelm, future husband of Venetia). (*Aubrey*) They were not only friends but Grace was a first cousin; and as they had 13 children, 3 more would not have made much difference (one presumes!). Grace Manners was daughter of John Manners and Dorothy Vernon of Haddon Hall (sister of **Edward Jr**'s mother Margaret Vernon), which meant that Grace and **Edward Jr** were first cousins and their children therefore second cousins. Daughter **Frances** Stanley later married son (Sir) John Fortescue Bt, 'from whose nephew another John Shakespeare acquired the London Gatehouse replete with Catholic associations (as discussed by Ian Wilson in *Shakespeare, The Evidence* (1993).' (Milward)
1601	'Footnote 14. Pal. of Lanc. Feet of F. bdle. 63, no. 281. William, Earl of Derby, and **Edward Stanley, esq.**, were the deforciants, the property being described as the manor of Halliwell, with twenty messuages, &c., 300 acres of land, &c., and 2s. rent in Halliwell and Smithills. This was land confiscated from Robert Hulton, Esq. Lord of the Manor of Hulton, who had taken part in the Simnel rising, and was attainted after the battle of Stoke; Rolls of Parl. vi, 397. Early in 1489 his manors of Halliwell and Smithills and various lands were granted to the Earl of Derby; Pat 4 Hen. VII, 25 Feb.' (*Victoria County History*, Vol. 5, Halliwell.) 'In 1601 it was held by Edward Stanley. (fn. 14) [**Edward Jr?**] *continued*

1601	About that time it seems to have been sold, part going to Robert Marsh of Halliwell, (fn. 15) whose son-in-law Samuel Shipton, clerk, was in possession in 1638; (fn. 16) afterwards it descended to Samuel Aspinall, (fn. 17) and then disappears from notice. (fn. 18). (*VCH*, Halliwell, including all footnotes.)
c.1601-03/4 [II], [III], [IV], [X]	Shakespeare wrote two epitaphs (or one?) for **Edward Jr**. At the beginning of this period **Edward Jr**, after burying his wife and four daughters at Walthamstow, commissioned a tomb for his parents and himself at **Tong**. It must also have been at this time that he (or someone close to him) wrote the text of the MI on both tombs, almost identical, but with significant differences. The fact that the verse epitaphs appear only on the **Tong** tomb seems to present certain implications, one being that the Walthamstow tomb might have been completed before the epitaphs were even written. Or it might be that **Edward Jr** considered them only relevant for the tomb for his father and himself. The effigies of his parents and himself on the tomb are the only known images, his own presumably from life as a c. 40-year-old, his parents' presumably from portraits or sketches from memory.
1601	John Shakespeare buried at Stratford. Whether son William was there for the funeral is unknown. The place of his grave is unknown and no epitaph for him has survived, nor indeed for any of William Shakespeare's immediate family except the one for himself. However, the Shakespeare arms granted to John in 1596 do appear on other memorials. (Pearson, 'Wherefore art thou, Grandfather?', Shakespeare Family History Site.)
1601	Sir John Salusbury's poems published in *Love's Martyr* by Robert Chester, including the first publication of *The Phoenix and the Turtle*, with Shakespeare as the poet. Sir John's wife was Ursula Stanley, **Edward Jr**'s first cousin. (Honigmann, *'lost years'*, Ch. IX. The Phoenix and the Turtle.)
1602, end Aug. [XV]	William, 6th Earl of Derby, with uncle **Sir Edward Sr** & cousin **Edward Jr** at Preston Guild. Lord Monteagle also there. (*Preston Guild Rolls*) John Shakeshafte, glover, was not there, which implies that he had died around the same time as John Shakespeare, glover, of Stratford. One and the same?
c.1600-1602? [XII]	A bell was commissioned c.1600 for St Oswald's, Winwick with initials of various people, possibly including TS and ES for **Sir Thomas** and **Edward Stanley**.
1601-1602	Around this time **Sir Edward Jr** 'was so much afflicted at the loss of his wife, that he resolved on passing his life in absolute seclusion.' (*Memoir of Sir Kenelm Digby*) This was according to the report of his later son-in-law, but the facts do not bear out the 'absolute seclusion'. We see him commissioning two tombs, visiting Preston Guild, visiting London for the coronation and to receive his knighthood. It was also at the time when his cousin William had interests in the Blackfriars Playhouse, along with a Fortescue relative. It must, however, have been at this time that he starting thinking about selling **Tong** Castle and moving to **Eynsham**.
1603, 24 March [XI], [XXIII], [XXVI]	Elizabeth died and King James, on his progression from Edinburgh to London, and after his arrival, created about 230 knights. One of these, in York, was Sir Thomas Gerard, whose father had been the leader of the plan in May 1570 to free Mary, Queen of Scots from Chatsworth. Other participants had been **Sir Thomas** and **Sir Edward Stanley Sr**, father and uncle of **Edward Jr**, which presumably explains the next entry. On his way towards London James stayed at Belvoir with Roger Manners, 5th Earl of Rutland, *continued*

continuation 1603, 24 Mar. [XI], [XXIII], [XXVI]	a close relative of the Manners family of Haddon Hall, descended from John Manners and Dorothy Vernon, sister of **Margare**t Vernon, mother of **Edward Jr**. While there they were entertained with a play by Ben Jonson.
1603, 25 July	**Sir Edward Jr** dubbed Knight of the Bath by James I at his coronation. As Shakespeare was at the head of the list of the newly re-formed King's Men, there seems a strong probability that **Edward Jr** and Shakespeare could have renewed their acquaintance on this occasion. Also, again, at the procession and festivities the next year, postponed because of an outbreak of plague. This period must be a strong contestant for the composition of the Tong epitaphs.
1603 [III], [XVI]	**Sir Edward Jr**: 'In 1603 he sold **Harlaston** to Sir Edward Brabazon, and about the same time, the manor of **West Bromwich** to his cousin Sir Richard Sheldon, and **Tong** to Sir Thomas Harris.' (*Auden's History*.) It seems that soon after this he moved to **Eynsham**, Oxon. Certainly his daughter Venetia was living here when she later started to be courted by many suitors. '**Sir Edward Sr** alleged to have lived at **Eynsham**, but the evidence is conflicting.' (*Eynsham Manor*.) Whichever report this came from, it might have been a straight confusion between the two **Sir Edwards**. The history of **Sir Edward Jr**'s other properties (as given under 1562/3) in Cheshire and Devon is not (yet) known.
1603 ff. [X]	**Sir Edward Jr**, already a knight, had another text written on the tomb at Walthamstow: he 'effected this monument for a testimonial of his love which he bare to his wife Lady **Lucy** & his four daughters deceased.'
1603-4	William Stanley, 6th Earl of Derby, was Lord Mayor of Liverpool.
1604, 15 Mar.	Belated festivities and procession for the coronation of King James, after the outbreak of plague had died down. This would be another occasion on which **Edward Jr** might have met Shakespeare.
1604, June	Edward de Vere, 17th Earl of Oxford, died in Hackney, London. He was the father-in-law of William Stanley, 6th Earl of Derby. This date puts him out of the running as the writer of any of Shakespeare's later plays.
1604, 4 Sep.	Burial of **Sir Edward Sr** in 'my lord's chapel' at Ormskirk. No tomb. (*Parish Register*)
1605, 5 Nov.	Exposure of the Gunpowder Plot by Edward Parker, 4th Lord Monteagle, a Lancashire kinsman of the Earls of Derby. There is no suggestion that **Sir Edward Sr** or **Jr** had been involved, directly or indirectly, but they must have known many of their rather close relatives, who *were* involved in some way. Henry Percy the 'Wizard Earl', **Lucy**'s first cousin and **Sir Edward Jr**'s cousin-in-law, was sent to the Tower for 15 years, where he renewed his friendship with Sir Walter Raleigh. Thomas Percy, a kinsman who worked for Henry, the 'Wizard Earl', who was definitely involved in the Gunpowder Plot, was killed at Holbeach in Warwickshire in a shootout, brought down by the same bullet that killed Robert Catesby. Sir Everard Digby, friend of **Sir Edward Jr** and father of future son-in-law Sir Kenelm Digby, was executed for his role. The main element missing so far (for me) is a consideration of all the Lancashire connections. Just one is mentioned here, from the 'confession' of Father Henry Garnet, later executed, who reported that Catesby 'had been close to the Earl of Rutland, yet did not try to spare him from the explosion. *continued*

continuation 1605, 5 Nov.	Even if Catesby had had some idea of disabling the (Catholic) Earl of Arundel to keep him from Parliament, he had avoided the company of Lady Derby and Lady Strange "though he loved them above all others because it pitied him to think that they must also die".' (Fraser, *Gunpowder Plot*, p. 252.) It is difficult to know who is being referred to here. Lady Derby was Elizabeth née de Vere, wife of **Sir Edward Jr**'s first cousin William Stanley, 6th Earl of Derby, but there was no Lady Strange at this time. Earl William's son and heir James, Lord Strange was not yet born and was not to marry until 1625. Perhaps a confusion with Alice, Ferdinando's widow, who was still sometimes referred to as Countess of Derby and had been Lady Strange.
1606 [XI]	An Act of Parliament finally established the division of lands between William, 6th Earl of Derby, and Countess Alice, Ferdinando's widow, meanwhile married to Sir Thomas Egerton, 1st Viscount Brackley, Baron Ellesmere, Lord Chancellor (from Cheshire, married in 1600). (*Coward.*) **Eynsham** to revert to the earldom on the death of **Sir Edward**, if without a son and heir. Confusingly, 1607 and 1609 come into various reports. Perhaps errors, or perhaps tidying up a few dangling ends?
1606	**Sir Edward Jr** sold **Marple** and **Wybersley**. 'The last of the Vernons to possess Marple and Wybersley was Sir George Vernon of Haddon Hall, better known as the King of the Peak. He died without male heirs and his estates were divided between his two daughters, Margaret who married Sir Thomas Stanley and the more famous Dorothy who married Sir John Manners. On the death of Lady Margaret Stanley in 1596 the area came into the possession of Sir Edward Stanley of Tonge. Sir Edward, the last of the Feudal Lords, having no male heirs, sold the manors of Marple and Wybersley off in small lots in 1606. Henry Bradshawe (I), grandfather of the famous John Bradshawe, purchased the Halls of Marple and Wybersley, together with 1000 acres of land for the sum of £270.' (Marple website).
1607	Birth of James, Lord Strange, son and heir of William Stanley, 6th Earl of Derby, **Sir Edward Jr**'s cousin.
1607, 30 Nov.	Death of William Mather, **Sir Edward**'s stepfather, with **Sir Edward** inheriting the joint property held by Mather and Lady Margaret, Sir Edward's mother, including **Stackpole**.
1608	**Sir Edward** 'disposed of' the property in **Stackpole** 'to Roger Lort, who had for some time been both an agent and a tenant of his mother in the Stackpole district.' (Tudorplace website)
1607-9 [IV]	'The king gave licence to **Sir Edward Stanley** to alienate the manor of **Tong** to Thomas Harris, Sergeant-at–Law, afterwards knight and baronet, which Harris had one son and three daughters. The son died in his youth.' (*Originalia*, 6 & 7 Jas. 1. 1st 9 1607-9) (*Auden's History*, vol. 1, p. 18.) This date and comment seem to be more confusing than enlightening, as Auden also reported that Sir Thomas Harris had bought **Tong Castle** in 1603. It might have been an oversight by Auden, or it might have been a legal technicality concerning the Manor, rather than the Castle.
1609 [XXI], [XXII]	Sir Edward Stanley died, 'uncle of **Sir Edward [Jr]** of Tong'. (Coward, p. 206.) This must be a different Sir Edward Stanley. **Sir Edward Stanley Sr** was buried at Ormskirk in 1604. This is one of several Sir Edward Stanleys still awaiting identification.

1609	Shakespeare's *Sonnets* published.
1611	'Edw:Stanley, 1611' inscribed in Earl Henry's copy of Plutarch's *Lives*. Previous owners (in reverse order) had been William, Alice, Ferdinando, Henry 4th Earl, who received it 1579 (year of publication of English translation) from William Chaderton, Bishop of Chester, later Warden of Manchester College, succeeded by John Dee. (Stratford Birthplace Trust)
1611, 4 June [XXVI]	John Manners of Haddon died, brother-in-law of **Sir Thomas Stanley** and uncle of **Sir Edward Jr**. His descendant Sir George Manners later became 8th Earl of Rutland when the senior male line at Belvoir Castle, Rutland, died out. At this time the 5th Earl of Rutland, Roger Manners, another Shakespeare Alternative Authorship Candidate, was still living, although died the following year.
c.1611-12	Assumed date when **Sir Edward** sent for his daughters to come and live with him at Eynsham. Also the assumed date of the marriage of daughter **Frances** to (Sir) John Fortescue of Salden, the two of them having grown up together. These two events might not be unconnected.
1612	Sir Rowland Stanley of Hooton (knighted with **Sir Thomas** in 1533) died in 1612 at the age of 96, the oldest knight in England.
1613, 24 Feb.	Marriage of Princess Elizabeth and Frederick, Elector of the Palatinate, when Sir Edward 'was summoned to the court' and took **Venetia** with him, 'being desirous of shewing her "the magnificent entertainments that are usual at such times"'. (*Memoir of Sir Kenelm Digby*)
1613	'The steward of the Earl of Rutland recorded in 1613, "to Mr Shakespeare in gold about my Lord's 'impreso', xliijs; to Richard Burbage for painting and making it, in gold, xliiijs."' (Honigmann, *'lost years'*, p. 83.) No one can deny this payment, but I will argue that this was not William, but his brother Mr John, the bit-maker at court. This presumably had something to do with all the 'magnificent entertainments' surrounding the wedding celebrations.
1613	Another year reported as the date of the sale of **Tong** Castle by **Sir Edward**. Presumably something to do with **Tong** did actually take place, but it might have been another step in clarifying ownership of the manor.
1613, 23 June [XXVII]	**Sir Edward** in a court case in London, partner eminent lawyer Sir Baptist Hicks, concerning property in Cubleston, Staffordshire. Signatures and seals of both.
1614	John Fortescue born, son & heir of Sir John and **Frances** Fortescue; **Sir Edward**'s first grandson. He was one of six sons and four daughters born to **Sir Edward**'s daughter **Frances**, the precise order of birth and the birthdates unknown.
1615 [XIX]	**Sir Edward** appeared as the owner of the Park at **Eynsham** on a map. (Lilian Wright)
1616, 23 April	William Shakespeare died in Stratford. The date conveniently coincided with his presumed birthdate and St George's Day.
1617 [XIX]	**Sir Edward Jr** 'presented Thomas Longe to the living in 1617' (as vicar of **Eynsham**). (Lilian Wright) This proves that he still retained the advowson.
1617 [XXV]	'Earl of Worcester, **Petronella** Stanley, John Fortescue and **Frances** his wife v Ryder, Bishop of Killake and Josiah Horne: Winwick: DL4/65/39. Ref. 10.'

continued

continuation 1617 [XXV]	(Brian S. Roberts, Stanley Family History, No. 112 Documents.) The only appearance (so far) of **Petronella** in a document, apart from in her father's will. With her sister **Frances** and her husband. The 4th Earl of Worcester in 1617 was Edward Somerset, KG, Lord Privy Seal. **Sir Edward**'s daughters appearing re **Winwick** suggests they were acting on his behalf. For a biography of John Ryder, Rector of **Winwick**, Bishop of Killaloe, see Wikipedia.
?1614-24 [XXV], App. 10]	**Venetia** 'courted' at **Eynsham** by several gentlemen, and at some point moved to London. (*Aubrey*) Not known where **Sir Edward** was living at this time, but presumably **Eynsham**.
1623	Shakespeare's *First Folio* published.
c.1625 [XXV], [App. 10]	**Sir Edward Jr**'s daughter **Venetia** married Sir Kenelm Digby in secret and on 6 October gave birth to their first son Kenelm in **Eynsham**. The main sources for their romance are *Sir Kenelm Digby's Memoirs* and the notes (normally known as *Brief Lives*) left by the antiquarian John Aubrey, both unpublished until the 19th century. A rumour reported by Aubrey claimed that one of **Venetia**'s lovers was Richard Sackville, 3rd Earl of Dorset. Although historically unsubstantiated, it is interesting that he was the first husband of Lady Anne Clifford, first cousin of Ferdinando and William, Earls of Derby. Among the Earl of Dorset's several mistresses was Martha Penistone, the wife of Sir Thomas Penistone, one of the Earl's retinue. Although from a Kent family, it is intriguing that he later moved to a family seat in Cornwell, Oxfordshire and that he shared his name with the owner of half of **Eynsham** Manor.
1625	James, Lord Strange appointed MP for Liverpool. (Stanley history repeating itself. **Sir Thomas** and William had previously held this post. I happen to have known this date for a long time because the other MP for Liverpool in this year was Thomas Standish of Duxbury, whose family history needed to be sorted out to explain Pilgrim Father Myles Standish's ancestry.)
1626, 26 June [XI], [XIX], [XXIV]	James, Lord Strange, married Charlotte de la Trémouille in The Hague. (*Seacome, Coward, Bagley*) They were there when Princess Elizabeth and Frederick of the Palatinate, the 'Winter King and Queen', were living there in exile. The reversion of **Eynsham** was later settled on Charlotte. (*Eynsham Manor*)
1626, 27 June [XII]	**Sir Edward Stanley** appointed Charles Herle, M.A. as Rector of Winwick. (*VCH*, 4, Winwick, pp. 122-132.)
c.1626 [V]	Estimated date of recording of MI and verse epitaphs by John Weever, although he was rather muddled about the **Tong** and Walthamstow texts. (Honigmann, *Weever*) It may have been earlier. In any case, this seems to have been the earliest surviving recording.
1627 [XI], [XXIV]	Elizabeth née de Vere, Earl William's wife, died. (*Derby history*) One might imagine **Sir Edward Jr** commiserating with him at the earliest possible opportunity, as one aging widower to another, his first cousin
1627, 29 Dec.	John Digby born, second son of Sir Kenelm & **Venetia**; **Sir Edward**'s grandson.
1629 [XIX]	We do not know whether he was at 'Eynsham during the great fire of 1629.' (Lilian Wright, *Eynsham Record*, Vol. 2, 1985.)
1630, 12 Jan.	Everard Digby born, third son of Sir Kenelm & **Venetia**; died in his cradle.

1630 [VI]	The date attached to Milton's eulogy of Shakespeare in the publication in 1645 of some of Milton's poems. The most significant detail is that he includes 'pyramids' in one line, a feature in the **Tong** epitaphs and on the tomb, but not on Shakespeare's tomb in Stratford. (Campbell)
1632 [VIII]	John Weever died in London: will 16 February 1632; proved 29 March 1632. (Honigmann, *'lost years'*, App. A.)
1632, 10 June [XXV]	**Sir Edward** wrote his last will and testament at **Eynsham**. Executors his son-in-law John Fortescue, Esq. and Richard Lane, Esquire of Northampton. All was left to **Petronella**. He had presumably already accommodated his two married daughters.
1632, 18 June [XII], [XIX]	**Sir Edward Jr** died at **Eynsham**, Oxon, aged 69, and was buried there by his unmarried daughter **Petronella**, who placed a memorial with MI over his grave. (Beaumont, *Winwick*; Wright, *Eynsham*) No further details have been discovered about **Petronella**'s life after this.
1632, 10 Dec. [XXVII]	Admin. granted in London of **Sir Edward**'s will, naming the two executors and also daughter **Venetia** and son-in-law Sir Kenelm Digby as administrator. The admin. was conducted 'from Sir Kenelm's house' in London. Executor Richard Lane at this time was a member of the Middle Temple and practised in the Court of the Exchequer.

Posthumous details of potential retrospective significance

1632, Dec. [App. 10]	'in December 1632, the church was visited by the antiquary William Dugdale, who later recorded in a manuscript collection of church notes (Bod3, fol. 159ʳ) that at **Tong** 'On the North side of the chancel is there a goodly monument lately erected by Sir Edward Stanley KB for his father'. Dugdale copied the prose and the verse inscriptions in the east-west order ('Vpon the east end of the monument this Epitaph . . . Vpon the west end this Epitaph').' (*Shakespeare's Poems*, Duncan-Jones and Woudhuysen, p. 438 – see Appendix 10. Epilogue.) Dugdale, living and touring in the Midlands, must have been unaware that **Sir Edward** had died six months earlier. This proves, however, that his effigy was not yet on the tomb at **Tong**.
1633, 3 Jan. [X]	Sir Robert Stanley died and was buried in All Saints, Chelsea, London. He was the younger son of William, 6ᵗʰ Earl of Derby. His tomb contains Shakespearean epitaphs.
1633, 1 May [XXV], [XXVII], [App. 10]	Daughter **Venetia** died in London leaving sons Kenelm (b. 1625) and John (b. 1627). Everard (b. 1630) and George (b. early 1633) had both died as infants. (No Edward; why not?) **Venetia** had several portraits painted. Her husband Sir Kenelm Digby mourned her intensely and wrote his Memoirs. He also left several portraits of himself, including one, intriguingly, hanging in Rufford Old Hall, Lancashire, home of the Heskeths, alleged hosts of young Shakespeare for a short time.
1634 [XVI]	Manor of **Eynsham** confirmed to James, Lord Strange (*Eynsham Manor*).
1634	Milton wrote *Comus* for Countess Alice and her family, performed at Ludlow. In a roundabout way this brings Milton again into the **Tong**/Shakespeare epitaph/Derby story; he had already written a eulogy on Shakespeare in 1630, which included 'pyramids' (echo of the tomb and epitaphs at **Tong**?).

1637, 26 Jan.	Countess Alice died and was buried at Harefield, Middlesex, aged about 77, the longest living of **Sir Edward Jr**'s female Derby relatives and contemporaries. She had also had her effigy for her tomb carved long before her death, on which she was depicted as a beautiful young woman.
1642, 25 Sep	Earl William died, aged 81, in Chester, the longest living of **Sir Edward Jr**'s Derby relatives and contemporaries. This was just before the outbreak of Civil War in Lancashire, in which his son James, now 7th Earl, was active for King Charles. Earl William was buried in Cheshire, his body moved for reburial in the Stanley vault in Ormskirk in 1662. (Roberts, Stanley Genealogy Forum.)
1642-44	Several Stanley properties attacked during the early years of the Civil War, including **Tong Castle** and **Lathom House**, with Prince Rupert involved in the Civil War in Lancashire at this time. His story has been written many times, but so far lacking (for me) several Lancashire, particularly Stanley (and posthumous Shakespeare) connections. His parents were Frederick of the Palatinate and Elizabeth, sister of Charles I, the 'Winter King and Queen' who had escaped from Prague to The Hague at the beginning of the Thirty Years War after defeat at the Battle of the White Mountain. It was at the Protestant court in the Hague that James, Lord Strange married Huguenot Charlotte de Trémouille in 1625. Rupert was in Warwickshire at the same time as Queen Henrietta Maria, the latter staying a couple of nights at New Place in Stratford with Susannah, Shakespeare's daughter. From there he advanced via Shropshire (passing through **Tong**?) to relieve the siege of Liverpool and then in theory to aid Charlotte, Countess of Derby, who was holding the fort at Lathom House, while James, Lord Strange was in the Isle of Man. Among the leaders on both sides were the sons of many whose fathers had moved in Stanley (and Shakespeare) circles.
1644, 2 July	The Battle of Marston Moor near York. This was a resounding victory for the Parliamentarians, which effectively lost the North for Charles.
1648, 17 Aug.	The Battle of Preston, the next step towards the end of the Civil War.
1649, 30 Jan	Charles I beheaded.
1649 [XVI]	"Earl James forfeited all his estates as a delinquent and parliament granted **Eynsham** to Col. Henry Marten, the regicide." (*Eynsham Manor*)
1651, 3 Sep.	Battle of Worcester. James, Earl of Derby, had led his last army against Cromwell's forces in Lancashire; the Parliamentarians won a running battle from Preston to Wigan; James fled south to join Charles II; they lost the Battle of Worcester; James escaped with Charles, leading to the Boscobel story of Charles in the oak tree (not far from **Tong**). Shortly afterwards James surrendered himself and was beheaded on 15 October 1651 in Bolton (it so happens by one of my Whewell ancestors – my mother was a Whewell - whose skull is still on display in a local pub!).
1651 [XVI]	"In 1651 Marten sold **Eynsham** to Orlando Bridgeman and others acting for Charlotte, countess of Derby, who a year later was appealing for discharge from the sequestration on her **Eynsham** estate." (*Eynsham Manor*.) Bridgeman was eminent in Lancashire in the Civil War.
1653-7 [III], [XVI]	"In 1653 the estate was granted to her son-in-law Henry Pierrepont, earl of Kingston-upon-Hull, and in that year he and Charlotte *continued*

continuation 1653-7 [III], [XVI]	sold the furze and bushes on **Eynsham** heath to Thomas Jordan, a Witney clothier; in 1657 Jordan purchased the rest of **Eynsham**." (*Eynsham Manor*.) This helps to explain the arrival of the Pierreponts at **Tong**, and the burial of one of them in the Stanley tomb there. He was "The Right Hon. Gervas Lord Pierrepont died May 22 1715" buried in the Stanley vault at **Tong**. (*Auden's History*)

Landmarks in events and publications relevant to the Tong Epitaphs

1660 [App. 8]	Father Henry More SJ published his *History of the English Jesuits* in Latin. Included a reference to epitaphs to Stanleys by Shakespeare.
1663, Sep. [V]	Sir William Dugdale recorded the **Tong** epitaphs during his Visitation of Shropshire, noting authorship by Shakespeare.
1664 [VII]	Dugdale published *Antiquities of Shropshire* (1664), not including the **Tong** epitaphs. These remained in his notebook, undetected until the late 18th century.
1760s	Stanley tomb moved by the Durants to make place for the Durant tombs.
1790s [App. 10]	Isaac Hearne forwarded the verse epitaphs recorded by Dugdale to Edmund Malone, who published them.
1827	Dugdale's diaries published, which led to more widespread knowledge about his recording of the **Tong** epitaphs by William Shakespeare
1840s ??	Halliwell-Phillips published one of the recordings of the epitaphs. He believed they were by Shakespeare.
1891 [IV]	Stanley vault at **Tong** opened; coffins of **Sir Thomas** and his wife were found cut open and no bodies. It is still a mystery when this happened, why, and what happened to them.
1892 [IV]	Stanley tomb at **Tong** moved; and some ornamentation removed.
1898	Sir Sidney Lee did not even mention the **Tong** Epitaphs is his *A Life of William Shakespeare*.
c.1900 [IV]	Rev. Auden produced all his valuable historical notes and articles. His notes, including those concerning the Stanley tomb and epitaphs, remained unpublished until 2003-2005.
1929 [IX]	Katherine Esdaile studied the **Tong** tomb and her article in *The Times* created a flurry of interest. She also reproduced the Sandford sketch.
1930	E.K. Chambers rejected the **Tong** epitaphs as not from Shakespeare's hand, mainly because of Stanley dates: **Sir Thomas** died too early and **Sir Edward Jr** too late. This quashed scholarly interest for the next fifty years.
1954	Following on from Oliver Baker (1937), Alan Keen and Roger Lubbock published their invaluable book *The Annotator*. The jury is still out on whether or not a particular copy of Halle's *Chronicles* was ever in the possession of Shakespeare, but Keen opened up a new field of enquiry about 'Shakespeare in Lancashire', which led to the discovery of a swathe of family connections from Warwickshire through Shropshire to Lancashire.
1970s	Professor Sidney Schoenbaum continued to pour cold water on the authenticity of the epitaphs.

1973	Profess Peter Milward SJ published *Shakespeare's Religious Background*, which opened up a new field of studies on Shakespeare's Catholicism.
1985	Professor E. A. J. Honigmann published Shakespeare: the 'lost years', which has since become a classic in opening up new studies of Shakespeare biography, including 'Shakespeare in Lancashire', the **Tong** Epitaphs and *The Phoenix and the Turtle*.
1987	Honigmann published *John Weever*, including an updated biography, a facsimile of the *Epigrammes* of 1599, and the revelation that Weever was the first to write down a copy of the text of the **Tong** Epitaphs (1620s [?]) in his notes, the relevant section unpublished until 1987.
1990s	'When they did a large excavation at the [Eynsham]Abbey site in the 90s they found a layer in one of the cess pits corresponding to the time of the Stanleys here which contained bones of swans and other rather superior foods indicating much more sophisticated living at that time. There is also John Aubrey's account of a fairly magnificent building so I think the Stanleys did use Eynsham for some time.' (Personal communication, Lilian Wright, August 2012.)
1998	2nd edition of Honigmann, *Shakespeare: the 'lost years'*, which at long last had received enough attention and sparked enough interest to inspire the organisation of a conference.
1999, July [App. 5]	Conference on 'Shakespeare in Lancashire' at Lancaster University and Hoghton Tower, papers published 2004, eds. Professors Richard Dutton, Alison Findlay & Richard Wilson, organisers of the Conference and 'converts' to 'Shakespeare in Lancashire'. Unleashed the next series of Shakespeare biographies, all accepting (to varying degrees) the 'Catholic Shakespeare' and the 'Shakespeare in Lancashire' theories, incorporating the 'new' information, but still ignoring the **Tong** epitaphs.
2004, Aug.	Three day residential course on 'Shakespeare's Lancashire Links' at Alston Hall, Adult Education Programme of Lancashire County Council, led by Helen Moorwood, papers by Carol Curt Enos and Peter Milward (read on his behalf). En route to this, HM visited **Tong** and inspected the tomb. Interest was awakened
2003-5	Rev. Auden's *Notes on the History of Tong* published, 2 Volumes, edited by Joyce Frost, wife of the Vicar of **Tong**.
2005-12	Helen Moorwood focussed her attention on the **Tong** Epitaphs and the relevant Stanleys, and intermittently researched and wrote this book (juggling this all the way with researching Captain Myles Standish). Her hope is that it leads to the acceptance that the **Tong** Epitaphs are by Shakespeare. Although doing nothing to enhance his reputation as a poet, it nevertheless contributes to his biography and an appreciation of some of his aristocratic and upper gentry contacts (including via his own Shakeshafte ancestors).

Chapter XXIX
Conclusion: biographies of
Sir Thomas and Sir Edward Jr

XXIX-1. Introduction: Stanley, Shakespeare, Shakeshafte, Lancashire, Lancastrian

The Tong Verse Epitaphs were the result of just one of a whole series of personal contacts between Stanleys and Shakespeares/Shakeshaftes during Tudor times, starting with a Shakeshafte soldier from the Preston area (William Shakespeare's gt-gt-grandfather) fighting at the Battle of Bosworth in 1485 in the victorious Lancashire and Cheshire Stanley army under Baron Thomas Stanley, 1st Earl of Derby (who has a role in *Richard III*) and being rewarded by his stepson Lancastrian Henry VII with a small estate in North Warwickshire, with lands forfeited by Yorkist supporters. William's father John Shakespeare told us this in almost these words (although not quite as many) when applying for the impalement of his wife's Arderne arms at the College of Arms in London in 1599.

This, and similar grants of lands to many others, were followed by a mini-exodus from the North West to the Midlands, with the migrants still maintaining contacts back in Lancashire and Cheshire with their own immediate ancestors and their patrons, the Earls of Derby and other Stanleys. John Shakespeare's sending of young William for service in an upper gentry family in the Preston area in Lancashire was one direct result of this. This was not least because of John's (re-)conversion to Catholicism after his third marriage in c.1575 to Mary née Arderne, of the Catholic family of Harden Hall in Cheshire, just over the River Tame from historical Lancashire (today in Greater Manchester) and NOT the Catholic Ardens of Warwickshire, although they were historically distantly related. (The evidence behind this claim will appear asap in articles on my website and in the forthcoming *Shakespeare's Lancashire Links/Lancastrian Shakespeare proved* or similar title.) At that time Stanley patronage in remote and still predominantly Catholic Lancashire provided the safest available protection from religious persecution. When William Shakespeare wrote the two Verse Epitaphs for Sir Edward Stanley (probably in London) in 1601-4, it was one natural outcome of all these Shakespeare/Shakeshafte/Arderne/Stanley contacts, which had started back in 1485 and continued through to Sir Edward Stanley and William Shakespeare's lifetimes.

It seemed that a study leading to the biographies of the recipients of these Verse Epitaphs by Shakespeare might shed some light on Shakespeare's own biography. The following biographies have emerged, to be set against what little we know of the Bard's own. Few references are given below, but every last statement is completely documented and referenced during previous chapters of this book and many of them are on the time-line in Chapter XXVIII. In other words, references in footnotes in these biographies would merely refer back to almost every page in this book.

XXIX-2. Biographies of those Stanleys on the Tong tomb, and other relatives

It has been possible to reconstruct the basic 'new' biographies of several of the Stanleys involved. In first place, of course, are Sir Thomas of Winwick and Tong, whose effigy is on the upper tier with his wife Lady Margaret née Vernon, and their only surviving son Sir Edward Jr, effigy on the lower tier. He is given this appellation to distinguish him from Sir Edward Sr, younger brother of Sir Thomas and therefore uncle of Sir Edward Jr, with all three of them playing a vital role in the wider story, each in their own way.

Other Stanleys who entered their stories were Edward, 3rd Earl of Derby (*Oxford Dictionary of National Biography, ODNB*), after whom Sir Edwards Sr and Jr were named; Henry, 4th Earl of Derby (*ODNB*), elder brother of Sir Thomas and Sir Edward Sr; then in the next generation brothers Ferdinando, 5th Earl of Derby (*ODNB*) and William, 6th Earl of Derby (*ODNB*), both first cousins of Sir Edward Jr. All their wives, of course, also enter the story. The biographies of many of these have already been written, several of them in the *ODNB* (as indicated above), but although a few extra details about several have emerged, the biographies of only two are told below, those of Sir Thomas and his son Sir Edward Jr. These are envisioned as a first step towards providing more lengthy biographies in future, on the assumption that more details might yet emerge. Their names are not in bold, as it is obvious who they are in their own (first-ever) biographies.

XXIX-3. Sir Thomas's biography
Childhood in the 1530s & 1540s

He was born in c.1534, second son of Edward Stanley, 3rd Earl of Derby (1509-1572) and his second wife Dorothy Howard, daughter of Thomas Howard, 2nd Duke of Norfolk, the victor at Flodden in 1513, with vital support by Sir Edward Stanley, 1st Lord Monteagle, providing a previous martial family link. The Norfolk-Derby relationship is slightly complicated because Edward had first married Katherine, daughter of Thomas, 3rd Duke of Norfolk, son of the 2nd Duke, in 1529, but she died three months later in an outbreak of the plague. To keep the link with this family, Earl Edward married soon afterwards in 1530 Dorothy, who, although of a similar age, was in fact the young aunt of Katherine. Dorothy was the mother of Earl Edward's three sons and his first five daughters.

Thomas's elder brother Henry (born 1531) was named after Henry VIII, and Thomas after both his grandfathers, Thomas Howard and Thomas Stanley, 2nd Earl of Derby. No records survive of the place of birth of himself or his younger brother Edward in 1535-40, but they were probably born at Lathom House, the main family seat of the Earls of Derby, and brought up there, educated to play a future role suitable for their rank, with the three brothers Henry, Thomas and Edward dividing responsibilities until ready to take over duties in Lancashire and elsewhere from their father Edward, 3rd Earl of Derby. After a childhood as a ward of Henry VIII, their father had held various high positions at the courts of Henry VIII, Edward VI, Mary and Elizabeth. One report in 1530 from the Spanish ambassador in London to the Holy Roman Emperor Charles V gave Norfolk's opinion of Earl Edward that 'there is no other in the kingdom through which he could more strengthen himself'. It was thus in the shadow of his eminent father that Sir Thomas grew up.

Eldest son and heir Henry, Lord Strange, was destined to become the 4th Earl of Derby, which was not to happen, however, until 1572. The three boys were educated at a 'school' in Lathom, probably within Lathom House itself, by local clerics, one of whom was Dr Henry Standish of Standish, known as 'a passionate Catholic preacher'. This was during the reign of Henry VIII. The further education of all three boys during the reign of Protestant Edward VI (1547-53) remains unknown, but there is no record of any of them attending university and one presumes that they mainly stayed at Lathom in the bosom of their Catholic household, with perhaps occasional forays to London with their father. Their four sisters Anne, Jane, Mary and Dorothy (with a possible, but dubious fifth sister Isabel) were born between 1531 and c.1547, by which year their mother Dorothy had died. Soon afterwards father Edward married a local young woman, Margaret Barlow, daughter of Ellis Barlow, who produced two more daughters, Margaret and Catherine, before herself dying in 1559. His fourth wife was Mary Cotton, daughter of Sir George Cotton and Mary Onley, the marriage in 1561 producing no children. She outlived Earl Edward, who died in 1572, and as a widow married Henry Grey, 6th Earl of Kent, Mary dying in 1580. No records have survived of the influence on young Thomas of his mother and two later stepmothers.

Knighthood in the 1550s

It was presumably with great relief for the family when Catholic Mary, the daughter of Henry VIII and Catherine of Aragon, came to the throne in 1553, and at last Sir Thomas's life started to become public. He was knighted in London on 2 October 1553 in the presence of Queen Mary on the day after her coronation by Lord Arundel, Lord Steward of the Household. At the same time two other Stanleys were knighted: Sir Rowland Stanley (c.1516-1612) of Hooton (the senior branch of the family) and Sir George, grandson of Sir James Stanley of Cross Hall in Lathom, Marshal of Ireland, Sir George being a second cousin of Sir Thomas. Also knighted at the same time were two other Sir Thomases: Sir Thomas Gerard of Bryn near Wigan, a Catholic close friend of the family, who was to play an important role in Sir Thomas Stanley's life, and Sir Thomas Hesketh of Rufford, also Catholic, who, although it was of course unpredictable at this time, was destined to become the host for a short time of young William Shakespeare before he joined Derby's Men in 1582.

The recently knighted Sir Thomas Stanley was presumably at court again on 7 February 1554 when his brother Henry, Lord Strange married Lady Margaret Clifford (born 1540). She was the only surviving child of Henry Clifford, 2nd Earl of Cumberland and Lady Eleanor Brandon, a niece of Henry VIII. Because of her mother's Tudor ancestry, Margaret was in the line of succession to the English throne. The marriage took place in a chapel of the Palace of Whitehall and was attended by Queen Mary and her husband King Philip II of Spain, son of Holy Roman Emperor Charles V. Henry and Margaret's (eldest surviving) son Ferdinando (born c.1559) was presumably named after one of the several Spanish Ferdinand(o)s or Habsburg relatives of King Philip. Because of his royal blood through his mother, Ferdinando was also in the line of succession to the English throne.

Sir Thomas's activities as a young knight remain unknown. Presumably he followed with interest the lives of his sisters, the eldest of whom, Anne had married in 1548/9 Charles Stourton, 8th Baron Stourton. His sister Jane did not marry until 1567, Edward Sutton, 4th Baron Dudley. His sister Mary later married Edward, 3rd Baron Stafford and the youngest sister Dorothy never married. His two younger half-sisters married, Margaret first to John Jermin and secondly to Sir Nicholas Poyntz, and Catherine to Thomas Knivet.

Marriage in 1558 and career in the 1560s

Between January and May 1558 Sir Thomas married Margaret Vernon (b. c.1535), daughter and co-heiress of Sir George Vernon of Haddon Hall, Derbyshire, 'the King of the Peak', who brought Tong Castle to the marriage as part of her inheritance on the death of her father in 1565. They did not move there immediately, however, but only in the 1570s. Margaret was one of two heiresses, her five-year-younger sister being Dorothy, around whom the romantic legend of an elopement has been woven. This was with John Manners, second son of the 1st Earl of Rutland. Dorothy inherited Haddon Hall on the death of Sir George Vernon in 1565, and their family was to play an important role later in the life of Sir Thomas's son Edward.

Sir Thomas's marriage to Lady Margaret Vernon had been arranged by their parents and the wedding celebrations, according to tradition, took place at Haddon Hall with a great feast. They had just two sons: Henry and Edward, the latter born mid-late 1562. It is not known whether Henry was the first or second, but he died an infant, with the place unknown. Nor is it known where he was buried, but a small coffin with a body disintegrated in lime found during the opening of the Stanley tomb in Tong in 1891 might have contained his body. This could, however, have been transported there from anywhere else, just to be in the new family vault.

Sir Thomas and his brothers Henry, Lord Strange and Sir Edward were in attendance on their father Earl Edward at Preston Guild in August/September 1562, and from 1562-66 Sir Thomas was Governor of the Isle of Man. This was a hereditary family position ever since their ancestor Sir John Stanley had been created Lord of Man in 1405. As son Edward was born in mid-late 1562, this was most likely when his parents were living fairly permanently in the North West or on the Isle of Man. It is not known how seriously Sir Thomas undertook his gubernatorial responsibilities, nor how long he spent on the island, but the very fact that he occupied this post for four years indicates an active period of service *in situ* rather than a passive period *in absentia.*

In 1563 he leased the rectory and glebe lands in Winwick near Warrington for 99 years (not too far from the Stanley family home of Lathom House). 'On the 5th October, 1563, by an indenture in which he calls himself Thomas Stanley, Bishop of Man and rector of Winwick, he granted to Sir Thomas Stanley, knight, a lease of the rectory parish church and benefice, with the manor park and glebe lands for the term of 99 years, at the yearly rent of £120; which lease was confirmed by Edward Earl of Derby and William Bishop of Chester.' From now on Sir Thomas was often called 'of Winwick' to distinguish him from other (Sir) Thomas Stanleys. One Thomas Stanley from whom he needs to be distinguished was a 'cousin' of the same name, the one in the quote immediately above, who was Bishop of Sodor and Man at the same time as Sir Thomas was Governor of the Isle of Man, as well as being Rector of Winwick, Wigan, and several other places, including holding a stall in Durham Cathedral. 'We have a glimpse [of his reputation] in a letter written by Pilkington, Bishop of Durham, [James Pilkington, another Lancashire man, who had founded Rivington Grammar School in 1566] to the Archbishop of Canterbury about this time, in which he says, "The Bishop of Man, Thomas Stanley, liveth here at his ease as merry as Pope Joan."' He was from the Stanley family, Lords Monteagle of Hornby Castle near Lancaster, an illegitimate son of Sir Edward Stanley, 1st Lord Monteagle, the hero at Flodden. Bishop Thomas Stanley might have had a dubious reputation during his life-time, but he earned the gratitude of later historians by writing a history of the Stanley family in the *Rhyming Chronicles* in 1562 or soon after, before dying in 1568. The Stanleys had long been patrons of the church at Winwick. 'Bishop Stanley had been Rector of Winwick since before the fall of the chantries in 1553, and William Stanley [from a side-branch] was returned as being the priest then serving the rector's, or perhaps more properly Lord Derby's chantry, as being founded under his will with an endowment of £3 0s. 9d.'

Winwick Rectory was to remain the main residence of Sir Thomas in the North West, available for his use on frequent returns from the Isle of Man and London. Several local gentry families also had property and interests here, most relevantly Sir Peter Legh of Lyme, just over the border in Cheshire, and Sir Thomas Gerard of Bryn near Wigan, both of whom had family chapels in Winwick Church. This was the same Sir Thomas Gerard of Bryn who had been knighted at the same time as Sir Thomas Stanley at court. These two Sir Thomases were kinsmen because of at least one previous Stanley-Gerard marriage. (Peter/Sir Piers Gerard, d. 1494, married Margaret, daughter of Sir William Stanley of Hooton [Gen. 5]. His brass memorial is still in the Gerard Chapel). Winwick was just a few miles north of Warrington, the site of the main bridge over the Mersey and the route from much of the North West when travelling to Cheshire and North Wales, where there were several Stanley 'cousins'. His elder brother Henry, Lord Strange, after he had separated from his wife Margaret née Clifford, installed his mistress Jane Halsall and his second family in Hawarden Castle in Flintshire. Their four children, all first cousins of Sir Thomas and fully acknowledged as Stanleys, were Ursula (b. c.1568), Dorothy, Thomas (later of Eccleston) and Henry (later of Broughton). One imagines that Sir Thomas might thus have had many visitors when he was in residence in Winwick, not least his elder brother Henry on his journeys between Lathom and Hawarden and his younger brother Sir Edward. The latter had been a soldier and knighted in Ireland in 1560, remained unmarried and seemed to spend most of his time travelling round the country, including frequent visits back to Lathom, where he later took on the role of Senior Figure in the family.

Winwick would also have been a convenient base for Sir Thomas from which to visit his own extensive properties. These had been settled on him by his father Earl Edward in a grant of 1562/3 after the birth of Sir Thomas's son Edward. The settlement included a large number of peripheral and far flung Stanley lands in Cheshire (Dunham Massey, Bowden, Rungey, Hale, Acton and Darfield), Warwickshire, Oxfordshire (Eynsham) and Devon. These had been granted to him by his father in reversion in tail-male, i.e. as long as there was a son and heir to inherit, and in the absence of such they would revert to the Earldom. In the case of Sir Thomas's early death, they would pass to his widow Margaret and on her death to their son and heir Edward. Brother Sir Edward had similarly been granted lands in tail-male in at least Thirsk and Kirkby Malzeard in Yorkshire.

Sir Thomas's whereabouts and activities for the two years after 1566, the end of his period as Governor of the Isle of Man, remain unknown, but it might be presumed that he stayed in the North West, because he was one of the two MPs returned for Liverpool in 1568-9. This was another virtual Stanley appointment, with the citizens of Liverpool usually happily accepting the nominees of the Earl of Derby, who owned the Stanley Tower on the waterfront. One assumes that during this period he needed to spend a considerable length of time in Liverpool and London, and might well have used the opportunity to visit some of his properties en route, although the only one that was to play a considerable role in the immediate family was Eynsham Abbey in Oxfordshire. When in London one presumes that he stayed in Derby House in Canon Row, the permanent residence of the Earls of Derby in London ever since they had granted away, via an exchange deal for lands, their previous house near St Paul's, which became the home of the College of Arms (still on the same site today).

In 1569 he was presumably still using Liverpool and Winwick as his base when he was appointed as one of the Commissioners of Muster for Lancashire. This was a particularly dramatic year, which saw the Rising of the North/Northern Rebellion, when at any moment Earl Edward expected to be called upon by Elizabeth to quell the revolt. The Rising was led by a group of Northern Catholic noblemen, including Thomas Percy, 7th Earl of Northumberland, in protest at some of Queen Elizabeth's policies and in support of the claim of Catholic Mary, Queen of Scots to the English throne. As it turned out, it was suppressed and more or less died out in the North East before it required the Stanley army from the North West. If the Stanley army produced in 1536 to quell the Pilgrimage of Grace is an accurate model (for which a complete list has survived), Earl Edward could easily have summoned up an army of 7,000+, with his son Sir Thomas as one of the Commissioners and presumably his soldier son Sir Edward as one of the commanders.

This period when Sir Thomas was in his twenties until 1569, in his mid-thirties, seems to be the most likely one when he had an illegitimate son, who was obviously acknowledged, because he bore the name of Gerard Stanley. In turn this leaves little doubt that his mother was from, or closely connected to the Gerards. These had meanwhile split into two major branches: the Gerards of Bryn, who remained staunchly Catholic, producing John Gerard the Jesuit Priest, and whose members were constantly under suspicion; and the Gerards of Ince, who were Protestant and produced several who achieved high rank under Elizabeth, the most eminent at this time being Sir Gilbert Gerard, Elizabeth's Master of the Rolls. Gerard Stanley's mother seems to have had Staffordshire links, which in itself does not identify her, because both branches of the Gerards had lands there. However, it does mean that Sir Thomas's son and heir Edward grew up knowing that he had an illegitimate half-brother. What effect this had on Sir Thomas's marriage to Lady Margaret remains unknown. The most relevant fact is that they had no more children after son and heir Edward in 1562.

Disaster and death in the 1570s

The next few years, after serving in his public positions, were to prove disastrous for Sir Thomas and presumably led to his early death. In 1570 his world was blown apart by his participation in a scheme to rescue Mary, Queen of Scots from Chatsworth House in Derbyshire and spirit her away to the Isle of Man, from where it would be easy for her to escape to France or Spain, and be in a much stronger position to negotiate with Queen Elizabeth. The three Lancashire knights involved were the brothers Sir Thomas and Sir Edward Stanley Sr, and their friend Sir Thomas Gerard of Bryn, a staunch Catholic. The Chatsworth Plan and the involvement of Sir Thomas Stanley were perhaps not unrelated to his wife Margaret née Vernon also coming from Derbyshire. Mary was at Chatsworth because Elizabeth had placed her under the 'guardianship' of George Talbot, 6th Earl of Shrewsbury (1528-90), one of the richest men in England, and his second wife Elizabeth, who has gone down in popular history as Bess of Hardwick (she owned Hardwick Hall in Derbyshire, her ancestral home). As magnates in Derbyshire, Staffordshire (Tutbury) and Yorkshire (Sheffield Castle), among other estates in the Midlands, they had been in regular contact with the Vernons of Haddon Hall, Lady Margaret Stanley's ancestral home, where her married sister Dorothy was now living. Their father Sir George Vernon, the 'King of the Peak' had been godfather to Gilbert Talbot, son and heir of George, 6th Earl of Shrewsbury. Mary was reluctant to go along with the plan, however, as at that time, very soon after her flight from Scotland, she still had hopes that she could come to some sort of accommodation with Elizabeth. By August the plan was also abandoned as impractical for other reasons, but rumours reached government circles and in November the three Lancashire knights were ordered to appear in London. There they were arrested and imprisoned in the Tower of London. By July 1571 Sir Thomas Gerard's and Sir Thomas Stanley's principal roles had been established through inquisition, including being put on the rack. Brother Sir Edward Stanley seemed to get off rather more lightly. He claimed that at the time he had actually been in the North courting a Mrs Strickland. (Whether true or not, he never married.)

It was a time when Thomas Howard, 4th Duke of Norfolk was also imprisoned in the Tower because of his intentions to marry Mary, Queen of Scots and this was also at the height of investigations into the Ridolfi Plot. Sir Thomases Stanley and Gerard were suspected of also being involved in this plot. Sir Thomas was still detained in May 1572, or perhaps considerably longer, because neither he nor his brother Sir Edward were on the list of mourners at their father's magnificent funeral at Ormskirk on 4 December 1572. Their retention for this length of time may or may not have been connected with the intrigues of the Duke of Norfolk, who had been executed in June 1572. This was Thomas Howard, the 4th Duke, grandson of the 3rd Duke, and gt-grandson of Sir Thomas's grandfather, so a cousin of some degree. At the same time the main leaders of the Rising of the North were still being dealt with, which led to the execution in York on 22 August 1572 of Thomas Percy, 7th Earl of Northumberland, for high treason. Given that his daughter Lucy Percy later married Sir Thomas Stanley's only son Edward, it almost seems as if this marriage might have been planned when both fathers were in prison. In the Tower with Sir Thomas Stanley was also Henry Percy, younger brother of Thomas Percy, 7th Earl. Henry managed to escape execution and was released in 1572 after paying a huge fine of 5000 marks, after which he was granted the title of 8th Earl, succeeding his brother. He then became the guardian of his nieces, including Lucy, who were brought up with his own children at Petworth House, Sussex.

The Stanleys, Earls of Derby were far too valuable to the Crown for the 'Defence of the North' against the Scots to risk alienating them by an execution in this family. Sir Thomas was released from the Tower (date unknown, but presumed 1573/4). Given that his fellow prisoners Henry Percy and Sir Thomas Gerard of Bryn are documented as being released on payment of a heavy fine, one might assume that this was also the case with Sir Thomas. Certainly he needed to raise a large sum of money around this time, for which he was helped by his tenants in Winwick, some of whom gave a year's rent 'of their benevolences when he was in trouble'. One implication is that he had been a popular landlord, with his Catholicism and championing of Mary, Queen of Scots producing great sympathy in his tenants. One suspects that he came out of the Tower with his health broken. It seems that he never returned to Lancashire and he held no further public offices. By 1575 he had moved to Tong Castle, his wife's inheritance, when it was reported that 'many papists gentilmen resorte unto hym'.

He wrote his will on 12 December 1576, leaving everything to his wife and son Edward, to be divided equally between them, and died there on 21 December 1576 in his early forties. He was buried in the newly created Stanley vault beneath the altar in St Bartholomew's, Tong, above which his son was later to erect a tomb with effigies of his parents. If these were life-size, his height was 1.69 m (5' 61/2") and Lady Margaret's 1.58 m (5' 2"). His death left his widow Lady Margaret and their son Edward aged fourteen.

Widow Lady Margaret

Very little is known about the biography of his wife/widow from the day they married (1558) until the day he died (1576), other than through her husband's biography. She had inherited Tong Castle when her father died in 1565 and had just two children, Henry dying as an infant and Edward surviving. One can imagine that she spent several years in distress whilst her husband was in the Tower. It is not known where she spent these years (although presumably with Tong Castle as her main base), nor what provision she made for the education of son Edward. She stayed in close contact with her younger sister Dorothy, married to John Manners at Haddon Hall, and knew their children as they were growing up.

By 1578 she had remarried, William Mather, Esquire. This is known because in this year both were involved in granting the lease of a property of hers at Stackpole, Pembrokeshire. There are hints in her will that she might have lived at Tong or fairly locally with her second husband. Indeed, there is no reason to believe that they lived anywhere other than at Tong Castle, although she had inherited all her husband Sir Thomas's Derby lands in tail-male on his death.

She must have been in contact with her Stanley in-laws during this period, as well as meeting the Percy family, the latter resulting in the marriage in c.1581 of son Edward to Lucy Percy, who had been in the care of her uncle since her father had been executed in 1572. Her mother Countess Anne née Somerset had gone into exile with the English Catholic community in the Spanish Netherlands. Presumably Lady Margaret shared in her son and daughter-in-law's joy at the birth of their daughters and their grief at the death of their only son Thomas as an infant. Edward and Lucy lived at Eynsham for at least a short period during the early years of marriage, but Edward was regularly in Lancashire, having continued his father's lease of Winwick Rectory, from where he attended Preston Guild in 1582. He was frequently at Lathom with his uncle Henry, 4th Earl of Derby and cousins Ferdinando and William during the late 1580s.

As mentioned, on her husband's death Lady Margaret had inherited all his lands under the terms of the 1562/3 settlement, but also all his debts. It seems that she was still suffering financially from her husband's fine, because by 1584 (perhaps as early as 1577) she had sold half her interest in Eynsham to Sir Thomas Peniston. Her nephew William Stanley of Lathom was involved in a dispute with him over church pews in St Leonard's, Eynsham in 1584. Nothing is known (yet) about her management of all the other properties in the settlement, nor indeed about any of the properties in addition to Tong that she had inherited from her father, apart from Harleston (in Cheshire). A surviving letter from September 1594 shows her still in contact with her brother-in-law John Manners at Haddon Hall about her property at Harleston, in which she greeted her nephew George (b. 1569) and wife.

She wrote her will on the last day of August 1596, leaving many bequests to servants, the poor and friends. Among these were many sheep, several sums of money and also 'all my best apparel', 'my best hangings', 'old hangings', 'four featherbeds', 'the best featherbed but one not all clothes to it','two wrought tooles with silk' and 'four bowls of silver'. To her two executors she left: to 'Mr Edward Gifforde''one ring with five diamonds and three rubies, and to Mrs Gifforde I give one ring with a diamond'; to her cousin Corbett 'one piece of gold called a double sovereign'.

One presumes that all her own property went to son Edward, although the only ones on record are those mentioned above, plus Marple and Wybersley in Cheshire. Probate was granted in London on 4 December 1596. She stated in her will that she wished to be buried next to her first husband at Tong, with the consent of her second husband. This was understandable, given that she owned Tong Castle and there was a family vault available in Tong Church. This was also the resting place of so many of her Vernon ancestors.

The only image of her that has survived is her effigy, which her son later commissioned for the family tomb in Tong Church. When the vault was opened in 1891 only the coffin of Sir Thomas was found, although with no body. It was speculated at the time that a small box might have held Lady Margaret's heart. What happened to her coffin remains a mystery.

~~~~~~~~~~~~~~~~~~~~~~~~~~~

XXIX-4. Sir Edward Stanley Jr's biography
Childhood in the 1560s

Edward was born in mid-late 1562, one presumes in Lancashire or maybe on the Isle of Man, where his father was Governor 1562-66 and took out a 99-year lease on Winwick Rectory in 1563, using this as his Lancashire base. His only brother Henry died as an infant. Edward thus grew up as an only child, almost certainly with the Rectory as his main home. Given that his grandfather Earl Edward and his Stanley first cousins, the four sons of his uncle Henry, Lord Strange, lived not too far away at the palatial Lathom House, it seems likely that his parents took him to visit them for shorter or longer periods and that the young cousins spent more than a little time together. Cousins Edward and Ferdinando were a few years older than Edward, and William was just one year older, with the last son, cousin Francis born during the following years. 'Our' Edward would have known them all as young children in Lancashire.

It is not known how often his father visited the Isle of Man or whether his mother ever accompanied him, but the family was obviously committed to the North West for the whole of Edward's childhood. We know from his later frequent return visits that he must have regarded Lathom as a second home. One might wonder today whether young Edward himself wondered at the time why his parents produced no more brothers or sisters for him. Perhaps four years with his father spending much time on the Isle of Man was one reason? Perhaps this was one reason for his father deciding to vacate this post? After a break from public office for a year, in 1568-9 Sir Thomas was MP for Liverpool, which must have involved one or more trips to Parliament in London. He was certainly still living in the North West in 1569 when he served as a Commissioner of Muster for Lancashire along with his father Earl Edward and 'cousins' William Stanley, 3rd Lord Monteagle and Sir George Stanley of Cross Hall, Lathom. One might thus also assume that young Edward grew up knowing these 'uncles', and that he was used to having an absentee father. The latter was soon to be become a permanent state, caused rather dramatically.

Fatherless youth in the 1570s

In May 1570 when Edward was in his eighth year his father Sir Thomas and uncle Sir Edward Sr, along with their friend Sir Thomas Gerard, were involved in a plan to free Mary, Queen of Scots from Chatsworth House. This was revealed to the authorities and by the end of the year Gerard and the two

Stanley brothers were sent to the Tower of London. Sir Edward Sr was released but Sir Thomas was kept in for interrogation under torture and detained for two to four years. During this period his father, Earl Edward, young Edward's namesake grandfather, died at Lathom, but neither of the younger brothers attended the magnificent funeral in December 1572. Presumably grandson Edward was also absent. We have no idea where Edward and his mother spent the time during Sir Thomas's imprisonment.

When Sir Thomas was released, and certainly by 1575, his parents moved to Tong Castle, his mother's inheritance, where his father died in December 1576. Young Edward must have felt that he had hardly known his father. It is a matter of pure conjecture how he much he was affected by and reacted to the absence of his father in the Tower of London, the knowledge of his torture and the subsequent financial problems in raising money for the huge fine for release. This conjecture also applies to his mother. Rather than staying in Winwick or Tong Castle on her own with son Edward or with her Stanley in-laws at Lathom, it is easy to imagine that Lady Margaret sought solace with her relatives, with the most obvious comforter being her sister Dorothy Manners at Haddon Hall, with her young and growing family.

Nothing is known about young Edward's education up to this point. He might have been tutored privately at home with other local children, or sent to the family of one of his numerous first cousins from either side of the family at Lathom House or Haddon Hall, to be tutored privately with them. Hints that the latter might well have been the case come from some later events in his life.

All we know is that Edward was left fatherless, aged fourteen, with no siblings, but destined to own large estates as the only son and heir. As we have seen from his father's biography, soon after Edward was born in 1562, many Derby manors and lands in the counties of Chester, Warwickshire, Oxfordshire and Devon had been granted to his father Sir Thomas by his grandfather Edward, 3rd Earl of Derby, to stay in the family via Sir Thomas's wife and their son. In the event of Edward dying without male heirs, they would return to the Earl of Derby. One imagines that, even at this tender age, Edward knew that he would be expected to marry as soon as possible and produce a son to keep this inheritance in his own family.

His mother had married again within a year or two of Sir Thomas's death, certainly by 1576, her new husband being William Mather, Esquire, about whom nothing is known. Mather was a rather frequent name in both Lancashire and Derbyshire at the time. Very few records have survived for the following years. Maybe Edward stayed alone with his mother and stepfather at Tong, with the companionship of local children? Or maybe he spent time with his Stanley cousins of about the same age with his two uncles, Earl Henry and Sir Edward Sr providing the senior figures. Ferdinando and William both attended St John's, Oxford University, having matriculated in 1572, but no evidence has emerged to indicate that Edward accompanied them. He also had his Manners cousins at Haddon Hall, which had been inherited by his aunt Dorothy when his mother had inherited Tong Castle. They had several children including (later Sir) George (b. 1569) and Grace (birth date unknown), who was to play a large role in Edward's life after 1601. It has not been discovered whether, as a teenager, Edward visited any of these or any of the properties in his inheritance.

If he visited his Stanley cousins at Lathom House in the period 1579-1581/2 he might well have been aware of troupes of players in Lancashire. It was at this time that young William Shakeshafte/Shakespeare was in the Hoghton household, moving to the Heskeths at Rufford in 1581 for a short time and soon afterwards to Derby's Players, with Edward's uncle Earl Henry as their patron, soon to be renamed Strange's Players when cousin Ferdinando took over the patronage. It might well have been during this period that Edward first met young William Shakespeare.

Marriage and the 1580s

In about 1581 Edward married. Neither the place nor the exact date is known. His bride was Lucy Percy, second daughter of Thomas Percy, 7th Earl of Northumberland, who had been executed at York in 1572 for his role in the Northern Uprising of 1569 when Edward's father Sir Thomas was in the Tower. Given their contemporaneous imprisonment, it is difficult not to imagine that both families saw this union of their children as somehow logical and desirable. Lucy's mother was Anne née Somerset, daughter of Henry, 2nd Earl of Worcester. They were devout Catholics. Anne, during the imprisonment of her husband, had gone into exile with her youngest daughter Mary to join other English Catholics in the Low Countries, later received a pension from Philip II of Spain, wrote a treatise in defence of her husband and died at a convent at Namur in 1596. Earl Thomas was much later (1895) beatified by the Catholic Church as the martyr Blessed Thomas Percy. Lucy's youngest sister Mary (1570-1643) later became a nun and was the founder of the Benedictine Dames in Brussels.

Lucy and the other two older Percy sisters had not accompanied their mother into exile. After a traumatic period during their childhood after the execution of their father and flight of their mother, they were brought up at Petworth House in Sussex by their uncle Henry, 8th Earl of Northumberland, who had inherited the title after the execution of his brother in 1572. Lucy thus grew up with her cousin Henry Percy, the future 9th Earl of Northumberland, who was later known as the 'Wizard Earl' because of his interest in scientific and alchemical experiments. Lucy's elder sister Elizabeth married Richard Woodroffe of Woolley, son of Sir Francis; and younger sister Joan married Lord Henry Seymour, younger son of Edward Seymour, 1st Duke of Somerset and Anne Stanhope. Joan's father-in-law (d. 1560) was the brother of Jane Seymour, King Henry VIII's third wife and mother of Edward VI. Edward Stanley thus acquired more royal connections through his bride.

In the summer of 1582 Edward and Lucy were living at Eynsham Abbey, where they were visited by his uncle Sir Edward Sr, who lived with them for a while. They all went together at the end of August to Preston Guild. Presumably their first port of call in Lancashire was Winwick, where Edward had retained the lease of the Rectory taken out for 99 years by his father Sir Thomas in 1563. Edward and Lucy had just one son Thomas, named after both grandfathers, who died as an infant at Winwick, where he was buried. It is not known where Thomas came in the order of their children, only that he was the only son amongst seven daughters. If he was their first child, then the death and burial might well have been during their stay in Winwick en route to or from Preston Guild in August-September 1582, where Edward was registered along with his two uncles, Earl Henry and Sir Edward Sr, and his cousins Ferdinando (Lord Strange), William, and Francis (the last was to die the following year, buried at Ormskirk alongside his father and grandfather in September 1583). The following paragraph on Preston Guild is included in Edward's biography because attendance there was obviously firmly in his diary for 1582 and again in 1602.

Preston Guild took place every twenty years (it has done ever since 1542, and still does), and was a highlight in the business and social life of the town, a manufacturing centre, which had become the de facto administrative county town of Lancashire because Lancaster lay so far to the north. All citizens and anyone who wished to conduct trade there ('In-burgesses and Out-burgesses') were obliged to attend the Guild Merchant and register. All the local gentry also registered, with the Earl of Derby at their head, to re-affirm their prestigious position in the county community. On registration all family relationships were given, including underage sons who would reach maturity before the next Guild. And so we have a rather complete and invaluable picture of (the males in) many local families. Also present in 1582 as an 'In-burgess' was 'John Shakeshafte, Glover', with many of his family. On a balance of probabilities, the scales come down heavily in favour of him being one and the same as John Shakespeare, glover of Stratford, who had also attended the previous Preston Guild in 1562 along with his father, also John Shakeshafte, Glover. If this assumption is correct, then we have a composite picture of the Shakeshafte family based on Preston, with their offshoot Shakespeare branch in Warwickshire and John in Stratford. Given that Preston Guild was noted for its social events, including dramatic performances by strolling players, this presents one occasion when everyone involved in the 'Shakespeare in Lancashire' story, including Edward Stanley Jr, might well have renewed acquaintance with William Shakespeare/Shakeshafte, actor in Strange's Players and budding poet and dramatist.

It is worth repeating that 1579-82 is the period when (also following the 'Shakespeare in Lancashire' theory) young William Shakespeare/Shakeshafte was with the Hoghtons and Heskeths, and is presumed to have joined Derby's Players around 1581/2, turning into Strange's Players when Ferdinando took over the patronage of the company which was to present Shakespeare's early successes in London a decade later. There could have been several occasions when Edward might have seen the budding actor and dramatist in action. I have a fond picture in my imagination of Strange's Players performing at Preston Guild in front of a mixed audience of Stanleys and other local gentry, and the whole Shakeshafte clan. Immediately afterwards William must have passed through Stratford (with Strange's Men?) to impregnate Anne Hathaway. News of her pregnancy took some time to reach him on tour, which forced him to return for a 'shotgun wedding'.

Edward and Lucy were to have seven daughters when their main residence was Tong Castle during the 1580s and 1590s (the last one Venetia born on 19 December, 1600), although they might also have spent time at Eynsham, where we have fleeting glimpses of visits by members of his family. Cousin William was in the church at Eynsham in 1584 protesting about rights to seats in the manorial pew against the son of Sir Thomas Peniston, who had bought half the manor from Lady Margaret. The Vicar of Eynsham at this time was William Emmot from Colne in Lancashire, an Oxford man and known more widely as 'one of the superior types of Elizabethan clergy; he was resident, taught children and bequeathed Bibles and other books to neighbouring clergy and pupils'. Whether Emmott's Lancashire origin was a mere co-incidence, or connected with Stanley patronage is not known. Edward presumably knew him and perhaps considered him as a future tutor for his daughters, but Emmott retired from Eynsham in 1585. Cousin William was presumably en route to or from Lancashire. According to the reputable *Victoria County History* of Oxfordshire (*Eynsham Manor*) 'he was still in Eynsham in 1586'. It is impossible to believe that William stayed for two years in Eynsham and one must assume this was a return visit. It seems most likely that it was one and the same, as there were no other Williams in the immediate family. This also means that the dates of his early extensive travels require a rewrite. These travels in themselves do not affect cousin Edward's biography, but it is easy to suppose that around the time of this visit to Eynsham in 1586 he called in on Edward (wherever he was living at the time) to give his report.

In brief, members of Edward's family seem to have valued their association with Eynsham, but more as a stopover point than as a (semi-)permanent residence. 'William Camden recorded in his book *Britannia* (1586) that the "Abby..... now is turned into a private dwelling house and acknowledgeth the Earl of Derby thereof". The Earl seems to have kept servants permanently there, and presumably adapted the abbot's lodgings for his own use.' Among the Stanley tenants and servants were the ancestors (from Preston, Lancashire) of the seventeenth-century Oxford historian Anthony (à) Wood. So reports a local historian (Lilian Wright), researching for many years the history of the Stanley period of ownership of Eynsham. The earl in 1586 was Henry, 4th Earl, which reflects the knowledge of locals that, although the widow of his brother Sir Thomas now owned (half of) the manor, it was in tail-male to the earldom. The implication is that son Edward was not there very often and certainly not at the time of Camden's visit. However, the local historian also reports: 'John Aubrey, writing in 1647 (sixty years later) said that he had been told by inhabitants of Cumnor that, within their remembrance there was still "a worlde of painted Glasse, Stones, Coates of Armes, etc. There were curious buildings, excellent carved wainscot and wainscot ceilings guilded: a curious

Chapelle". He also adds as a footnote to his account of Venetia Stanley a further description of Eynsham Abbey "At the west end of the church here were two towers as at Wells or Westminster Abbey, which were standing till about 1656. The rooms of the abbey were richly wainscoted, both sides and roof!" (J. Aubrey, *Brief Lives*, 1647).' All this seems to indicate that, for the hundred years during which the Stanleys owned the abbey lands, they often lived in Eynsham and maintained at least some of the abbey buildings. This is further confirmed by another report: 'When they did a large excavation at the [Eynsham] Abbey site in the 90s they found a layer in one of the cess pits corresponding to the time of the Stanleys here which contained bones of swans and other rather superior foods indicating much more sophisticated living at that time.'

In October of 1586 Edward must have been interested to hear about a namesake Mr Edward Stanley fighting in the Anglo-Spanish War in the English contingent under the Earl of Leicester. He scaled the walls and captured the town of Zutphen almost single-handed, for which feat he was knighted on the spot by the Earl of Leicester, who left an eye-witness account. He has frequently been confused with uncle Sir Edward Sr, but this one seems to have been from Elford, Staffordshire, so a namesake cousin of a rather distant degree, one of the Stanley-Ardernes, who may have been the Sir Edward Stanley killed in Ireland in 1597. Another Stanley 'cousin' fighting in the war in the Spanish Netherlands was Sir William Stanley of Hooton, who had been taught at Lathom, along with Edward's father Sir Thomas and his brothers, by Dr Henry Standish, 'a passionate Catholic preacher'. His father Sir Rowland Stanley had been knighted by Queen Mary on the same day as Sir Thomas, Edward's father. This Sir William Stanley went down immediately in history as 'The Traitor' after capturing the town of Deventer and then surrendering it to the Spanish in January 1587. His continuing Catholicism, among other factors, had led to his dissatisfaction with the English cause. He spent the rest of his life in exile in Spain and Spanish Flanders, where it is more than likely that he was aware of Edward's Percy in-laws - Lucy's mother Anne remained active there as a rather outspoken nun until her death in 1596. Sir William became the de facto civilian leader of the English Catholic Exiles until his death in 1630, while Cardinal William Allen (from Lancashire) was the spiritual leader until his death in 1594.

Edward and Lucy's only son Thomas might well have been born and died during this later period and not immediately after the marriage as suggested above, but that would have required at least one visit back to Winwick, where we know infant Thomas was buried (from the MIs at Tong and Walthamstow). There were certainly several visits to Winwick during the late 1580s, when Edward regularly turned up at Lathom House and members of his family visited Winwick several times. Uncle Sir Edward Sr was in Winwick on 29 June 1586 writing a letter, but Edward Jr was not necessarily also in residence. Records of visitors to Henry, 4th Earl of Derby have only survived from 1587-90 (*Derby Household Books*), and in each case Edward was there on his own. He might have left Lucy and the girls back in Tong, or taken them as far as Winwick, but during the years in question his wife and children did not visit Uncle Earl Henry at Lathom. It would not have been easy transporting a whole bevy of little girls around. Uncle Henry was absent from Lathom for a while at the beginning of 1587 when he was on the 'jury' at the 'trial' of Mary Queen of Scots at Fotheringay and later in the year when he went on a diplomatic mission to the Spanish Netherlands in an attempt to avert the threatened invasion of England by the Spanish. We all know that he was unsuccessful and the outcome was the arrival and defeat of the Spanish Armada the following year. Earl Henry returned to great scenes of jubilation in Lancashire and Cheshire. Maybe he stayed with nephew Edward in Tong on his frequent journeys to and from his missions? It would certainly have been a convenient stopping off place en route to Fotheringay as well as London.

The turbulent 1590s

On one of Edward's visits to Lathom from Winwick in August 1590 he arrived on the same day as his cousin Ferdinando and another Stanley, all of whom stayed overnight. The precise record is for Monday of the week of 'the xxii of Auguste', with the visitors recorded as 'Mr Stanley of Winwicke came & Mr Edwarde Stanley, my L. Strandges came also; Tvesdaye the[y] went awayes.' Brian S. Roberts (a Stanley Family researcher) is of the opinion that 'Mr Edwarde Stanley' was 'our' Edward of Winwick and Tong, and that 'Mr Stanley of Winwicke' was most plausibly Gerard Stanley, an illegitimate son of Sir Thomas and therefore (Sir) Edward Jr's half-brother. Gerard Stanley married Elizabeth (surname unknown) and had four children, and appears in records in Harleston in Staffordshire (among other places), along with Sir Edward (after his knighthood in 1603). Harleston/ Hurleston appears in several other scattered Stanley documents, although sometimes apparently in Cheshire and Shropshire. If further research were to sort out all the Harleston and Hurleston references and make this Stanley relationship more certain, then father Sir Thomas's biography would need to be modified. It already includes this putative illegitimate son, although rather tentatively. This would at least fill in one detail during his 'lost years', perhaps as a young knight before his marriage in 1558 or during the period leading up to his incarceration in 1570. The two half-brothers certainly met at Lathom House in 1590, which implies an acceptance of Gerard Stanley as a member of the family.

Edward and Lucy may or may not have been directly involved in various dramatic events in Lancashire in the early 1590s, which involved Edward's immediate relatives, but they must have heard much about them. 1593 saw the return of cousin William from the last of his travels, the latest one (in the light of current research) for up to three years in Russia, almost immediately to disappear off as Governor of the Isle of Man. Soon afterwards came the death of his father Earl Henry in September 1593, with the succession by brother Ferdinando as 5th Earl of Derby, at the same time as the 'Hesketh Plot'. Richard Hesketh of Aughton, a brother of Alexander Hoghton's widow (hosts of William Shakeshafte in 1581), brought a letter to Lathom from Cardinal William Allen (of Lancashire origin), the head of the English Catholic Church in Exile, offering support for Ferdinando as Elizabeth's successor on the throne of England. Although always very aware of this right, acquired from the descent from Henry VII of his mother Margaret Clifford, he was also cognizant of the extreme danger that this presented for his own life. Ferdinando took Hesketh with him to London (which resulted in the latter's execution) and established his own innocence in this plan. This did not prevent his subsequent poisoning in April 1594, a story that has been told many times. He left widow Countess Alice née Spencer of Althorp and three daughters, but no son. It also left without their patron the former Strange's Players, the company which performed Shakespeare's early successes in London in the early 1590s. This became Derby's Players during Ferdinando's brief tenure as Earl and for a short time afterwards (under the patronage of widow Countess Alice?), but then re-amalgamated as the Lord Chamberlain's Players under Lord Hunsdon.

Cousin William was now 6th Earl of Derby and Edward automatically became next in line of succession to the earldom. These were now the only two surviving legitimate Stanley grandsons of Edward, 3rd Earl. William soon fulfilled a family obligation to attempt to produce a son and heir by marrying Elizabeth de Vere, eldest daughter of Edward, 17th Earl of Oxford. Interestingly, she had previously been offered as a bride to Henry, 3rd Earl of Southampton, the dedicatee of Shakespeare's two recently published poems *Venus and Adonis* in 1593 and *The Rape of Lucrece* in 1594. He had turned this offer down and paid £5000 as a fine. The Stanley-de Vere wedding was on 26 January 1595 at Greenwich Palace in the presence of Queen Elizabeth.This is a strong contender for the wedding which was celebrated with the first performance of *A Midsummer Night's Dream*. One presumes that Edward and Lucy made every effort to attend, and although full of 'ifs', this would have been another occasion for a Shakespeare-Stanley meeting. As it turned out, William and

Elizabeth's first child born at the end of this year was a daughter, who died at birth.

Before continuing with Edward's biography via the albeit sparse documentation discovered so far, it seems appropriate to pause here for a reflection on various missing events between c.1587 and c.1595. First and foremost is the apparent lack of births to Edward and Lucy during this period. The ages of their first four daughters at death are given on the MI at Tong, which provides the approximate birth dates of Arabella in 1582, Marie 1584, Alice 1586 and Priscilla 1587. This last date coincides with the beginning of the *Derby Household Books* records, which see Edward visiting Lathom without Lucy on several occasions until 1590. As suggested above, the reason for this might have been quite innocent, with Lucy just staying at home with the daughters, wherever their home was during these years. Maybe it was considered too inconvenient to transport four little girls round the country? And yet cousin Ferdinando's wife Lady Alice visited Lathom with their three little daughters at this time (Anne, b. 1580, Frances, b. 1583, Elizabeth, b. 1588), when they might well have been living somewhere else. Surely this would have been an incentive for Edward and Lucy to allow their daughters to spend time with their half-cousins?

Then we have the fact that Edward and Lucy's three youngest daughters survived whatever pestilence struck Lucy and the four oldest ones in early-mid 1601. It is almost as if there were two separate families here, albeit with the same parents. We know that the seventh and last daughter Venetia was born on 19 December 1600 (her later husband Sir Kenelm Digby provided this information). By extrapolation, and assuming a normal pattern of pregnancy, this would place the births of the preceding daughters as Frances in c.1597/8/9 and Petronella in c.1595/6/7. If these estimates are correct, then we are left with the gap between 1587 and 1595. If the date of birth of c.1595/6/7 for their fifth daughter Petronella is correct, then the rather long gap between the first four and the last three daughters must somehow be taken into account. Had Edward and Lucy had marital problems during the previous decade, which had led to their separation? Or had Lucy had several miscarriages, which were never recorded? There are hints in their future son-in-law *Sir Kenelm Digby's Memoirs* that Edward was 'too negligent a husband' and that he 'formerly' lived in an 'unhappy state', although it is not clear which period 'formerly' referred to. This could in any case only have been from hearsay via others and long after the time in question, but the hint is there. To this we can add Sir Kenelm's account that it was only after Lucy's death that Edward realized what a treasure he had lost, consoled mainly by the blossoming of Venetia as a 'phoenix' rising from Lucy's ashes.

We also have the story at the end of this period of his cousin William, as given above. He had returned from his travels to find himself losing in rapid succession his father Henry in 1593 and his brother Ferdinando in early 1594, which left him, totally unexpectedly, as heir presumptive to the Earldom of Derby. This had needed to be established by a higher authority, however, because widow Countess Alice was claiming everything, including the earldom and all the estates, for her three daughters, as well as establishing her daughter Anne's inheritance via Ferdinando as one of the heiresses presumptive to Queen Elizabeth's throne. The long drawn out legal battle between Countess Alice and Earl William has been told many times, with the information that her brother-in-law in a letter to Alice on one occasion called William a 'nidicock', almost as if it was her opinion too. There was certainly no love lost between them. However, not too long after Ferdinando's death, brother William was indeed confirmed as the 6th Earl of Derby and in 1596 Alice's eldest daughter Anne was confirmed as 'heiress presumptive' to the throne, which at least put William one or several steps down this ladder. He now had his title as Earl, but still needed to fight to regain as many as possible of the hereditary lands to allow him to maintain a style of life commensurate to his position. He also needed to produce an heir, and we have seen above that he married as soon as possible.

Meanwhile, as also mentioned above, cousin Edward, after Ferdinando's death without a son and heir, was the next legitimate male in line of succession to the earldom, and he had no son and heir either. Could it have been that Edward and Lucy had had several years of separation, and that the need for a son and heir brought them together again? This would certainly explain the long gap between births, Lucy's non-appearance at Lathom and also, perhaps, their non-appearance in mother Lady Margaret's will in 1596.

At the end of August 1596 Edward's mother Lady Margaret expressed her dying wishes, recorded by her second husband William Mather in her will, leaving several bequests to retainers and friends. She requested, with the consent of her husband, to be buried in the Stanley vault at Tong next to her first husband Sir Thomas, which duly happened. However, it is interesting that she mentioned no property and did not even mention son Edward. She did not need to make provision for the lands from the settlement of 1562/3, because on her death all these Derby lands would come to him automatically. She had presumably already settled many property matters beforehand with her second husband (who survived until 1607). And yet it is strange that she made no mention of her only daughter-in-law Lucy, and left no bequests to any of her granddaughters.

Somehow, during or after probate, some of her lands did come to Edward, including Marple and Wybersley (Cheshire/Staffordshire). These were presumably other properties in Margaret's inheritance from her father back in 1565, along with Tong Castle. Other lands were reported by Erdeswick in c.1596 as owned by Edward, lands whose history is not yet accounted for: he was 'now Lord of Harlaston' (this place again), and says of Cubleston 'Edward Stanley is now owner thereof', and of West Bromwich, 'now one of the Stanleys hath the seat of his house there.' West Bromwich is interesting not least because this was near Park Hall in Aston, the seat of the Ardens of Warwickshire, who, according to the 'conventional biography' of William Shakespeare, was the family of Mary Arden, William's mother. This turns out to be a false assumption, and is yet one more muddle that needs to be sorted out before Edward Stanley's and William Shakespeare's biographies come as close as possible to the historical truth. Also living in the vicinity in North Warwickshire in 1599 were John Shakespeare's 'cousins', who had moved there from Lancashire after the Battle of Bosworth in 1485.

On 17 October, 1596 Countess Anne Percy, Lucy's mother, died of smallpox in a convent near Namur in the Spanish Netherlands. She had made an attempt a few years previously to call her daughter Joan, Lucy's sister, to visit her in Flanders, but this apparently did not take place. There is no record of Lucy's involvement in any way with her mother's predicament during the whole of her period in exile. One can only presume, however, that Edward and Lucy were deeply affected by both losing their mothers within a few months. Might this have been one more reason for bringing them back together? Or at least bringing them closer together in their sorrow.

They were now the sole owners of their Stanley-Vernon-Percy inheritances, with their main seats at Tong Castle and Eynsham Abbey, and the lease on the Rectory at Winwick. It must have been a time for taking stock of their possessions and making a few decisions about their plans for the next few years, including planning for the future of their daughters. In 1596 they already had daughters Arabella aged about 14, Marie about 12, Alice about 10 and Priscilla about 8, so all of these were rapidly approaching an age when future marriage prospects must have been being considered. Despite the speculation of a longish separation, it is fact that they must have lived together during the last few years of the 1590s, when their last three daughters were born.

Edward was meanwhile very much involved throughout the second half of the 1590s with his cousin William's legal battle against his sister-in-law Countess Alice. On her side was the fact that her eldest daughter Anne was confirmed as 'heiress presumptive' to Elizabeth's throne in 1596. Brother-in-law William, now 6th Earl, was equally strongly of the opinion that as many Derby lands as possible should stay with the earldom. Edward must have felt torn between these two positions. On the one hand, with four daughters of his own, he must have felt empathy with widow Alice and her three daughters. On the other hand, his own daughters' Derby inheritance, should he have no son, were completely dependent on the tail-male reversion to the earldom on his own death. The future of both William's and Edward's Derby inheritances, and indeed the future of the earldom, seemed to depend on both, or at least one of them, producing a son. This might even have been the main motivation for Edward and Lucy continuing (or resuming) their attempt to produce this elusive son.

Cousin William was having no luck in this area. Indeed, his marriage went through a rocky period. In the words of his recent biographer: 'The early years of the marriage were stormy, particularly during the stressful period of the lawsuit, marked by rumours of Elizabeth's infidelity with both Essex and Ralegh, Elizabeth's alarming bouts of sickness, much bitter quarrelling, and periods of separation.' (Daugherty, *ODNB*) We know with hindsight that, although William and Elizabeth were subsequently reconciled and lived in harmony, they did not produce a son, James, until 1607, and Edward and Lucy never produced another son. Back in the late 1590s, of course, they could not yet predict this and must have lived in constant hope. It must have been a rather frustrating period in many respects. William, certainly, was deeply affected by his financial situation after 1594, which 'would all but consume him for the next five years and not reach final settlement until 1610'. This was not helped by knowing that sister-in-law Alice's family regarded him as a 'nidicock'. It is not known whether or not this judgment was extended to include cousin Edward, who seems to have taken William's side. In any case William's fortunes must have been of considerable interest for Edward, given that he was his heir to the earldom. 'Earl William might be one of the least ambitious of all the Earls of Derby, but he thought it both requisite and urgent to restore his family's prestige and political power. In 1598 he recovered the Earl's traditional seat on the Chester Ecclesiastical Commission, and five years later King James appointed him Knight of the Bath and, more importantly for William, Chamberlain of Chester, the post which his father and grandfather had valued so highly. To regain the Lieutenancy, however, was a bigger triumph still, and to retain the office for the rest of his life, as he did, fully re-established Stanley dominance.' Were William to suffer an untimely early death, one potential heir to these positions would be first cousin Edward.

Many financial transactions from these years have survived, but it is still difficult to obtain a clear picture, particularly from Edward's end. William sold lands to Edward on 12 March 1597 in Cheshire (Acton, Hurleston, Dorfold, Overmarsh) and Oxfordshire (Shifford), along with other lands to others. Whether this was a genuine sale or a legal manœuvre to deprive Alice from acquiring these lands is difficult to judge. In 1597 Edward 'demised his lands in Stackpole, Pembrokeshire to William Ingleby'. These lands had previously appeared in a transaction with his mother Margaret and stepfather William Mather. There is no evidence that any of them ever visited South Wales, and this must have been a property that Edward was quite happy to have administered by someone else until he decided what to do with it. In 1600 it was confirmed that Derby lands in Thirsk and Malzeard (Yorkshire) were in reversion to William, 6th Earl of Derby after the death of Sir Edward Stanley Sr, William and Edward's only surviving uncle, who was to live until 1604.

After all the family tragedies in the mid-1590s, and despite the continuing financial struggles, life at the end of the decade must have seemed rather rosier for the family, particular in the literary field. Edward received the dedication in 1597 of *The Famous History of Chinon* in England from budding writer Christopher Middleton (just finished his studies at Cambridge) and in 1600 the dedication of the poem *Faunus and Melliflora* from another budding writer John Weever (from the Preston area and a fellow student with Middleton). Maybe hoped for patronage from Edward was connected with his cousin William writing plays in London at the time? Edward was certainly affluent enough to be a patron. The full dedication from Weever reads 'To the right valorous and excellent accomplisht Gentleman, Maister Edward Stanley of Winwicke Esquire, all fortunes, suitable to the ancient woorth of the Stanleys'. In 1599 Weever had published his *Epigrammes*, with poems dedicated to all and sundry in the circle associated with 'Shakespeare in Lancashire', including a sonnet to Shakespeare and an obituary poem in memory of Ferdinando. He had not included Edward, so maybe the dedication of *Faunus and Melliflora* was by way of compensation? It is interesting that he calls him 'of Winwick' with no mention of Tong or Eynsham, but then his property in Winwick was presumably better known to someone from Lancashire than a property in Shropshire or Oxfordshire.

At the same time as Edward was receiving dedications from poets, cousin William was reported by a 'Jesuit spy' George Fenner, in a letter written on 30 June 1599, that he was 'busye in penning comedyes for the common players'. He 'is also reported as financing one of London's two children's drama companies, the Paul's boys, and for roughly the period 1599-1601, his playing company, Derby's Men, was active, and very successfully so, at the Boar's Head, just outside London'. The company played multiple times at court in 1600 and 1601 and 'my Lord Darby hath put up the playes of the children in Pawles to his great paines and charge.' (Gurr, 1996) His recent biographer points to some interesting associations: 'In 1599 he financed the revival of the Children of Paul's company, in apparent partnership with John Marston and others, and one or more of this troupe's extant unattributed plays could be his. As Thomas Middleton and the earl's friend William Percy (younger brother of the ninth earl of Northumberland, another friend) also wrote for the Paul's boys at this time. Derby would necessarily have worked in association with them.' (Daugherty, 2004) William Percy and his brother Henry, 9th Earl of Northumberland had, of course, been Lucy's childhood companions, brought up together at Petworth in Sussex. One might assume that Edward Stanley was well informed of these activities.

Disasters in the early 1600s

On 19 December 1600 Edward and Lucy's seventh daughter Venetia was born, so one might assume they stayed quietly at home in Tong for Christmas. This turned out to be the calm before the storm of 1601. Various dramatic events involving their relatives were unfolding in London. On 5 or 6 February, 1601 Sir Charles Percy, Lucy's first cousin, paid forty shillings for a specially commissioned performance of Shakespeare's *Richard II*, on the eve of the Essex insurrection. Robert Devereux, 2nd Earl of Essex, was intricately related to Edward and Lucy Stanley via many routes. Just one main example here: Dorothy Devereux, sister of Robert, 2nd Earl, was married to Henry Percy, 9th Earl of Northumberland, the 'Wizard Earl', a first cousin of Lucy's, with whom she had grown up. Robert and Dorothy's sister Penelope Rich née Devereux is a candidate for the Dark Lady of Shakespeare's Sonnets. This might be nonsense, but it presents an attractive additional Shakespeare-Devereux-Percy-Stanley link. Sir Charles Percy and Robert Devereux, Earl of Essex were executed on Tower Hill on 25 February 1601. 'Ironically, Derby was one of the peers who served on the court during the 1601 Essex trial but then took Essex's place three months later, on 23 April, as knight of the Garter (invested on 26 May).' 'Derby' was, of course, William, 6th Earl of Derby, Edward's cousin.

Within a few months Lucy and their four eldest daughters travelled to Walthamstow, a few miles north-east and just an hour on horseback or by coach from the centre of London. Presumably they travelled from Tong, with a stopover at Walthamstow on the way. Whether or not Edward and the three younger daughters were also with them is not known, but it is hardly likely that Lucy abandoned her baby daughter, other than perhaps to the charge of a wet-nurse. One can only guess at the reason for this expedition. To visit friends or relatives? To attend some events in London? To assess the marriage market for their four eldest daughters? Whatever the reasons and circumstances, disaster struck when Lucy and the four eldest daughters died in or near Walthamstow. Given that they all seem to have died at the same time, one can only suppose that it was from the plague or some other virulent disease. That Edward was heartbroken and felt that his life was about to change dramatically is not only to be suspected, but also on record in the later memoirs of his son-in-law. They were all buried there and soon received a tomb with effigies of Lucy and the four daughters and a memorial inscription. The (more or less the same) MI on the tomb at Tong gives

18 Arabella 16 Marie 15 Alice 13 Priscilla

One presumes that these were their ages at death. In any case this left Edward a grieving widower with three young daughters.

Petronella Francis and Venesie are yet living

Quite naturally, this tragic loss of his wife and four daughters at one fell swoop proved to be a turning point for Edward. There are several indications that he commissioned the tomb in St Mary's, Walthamstow before the tomb in St Bartholomew's, Tong for his parents. The latter was a two-tier tomb, with his parents' effigies on the upper tier, leaving space for an effigy of himself on the lower tier. He also very thoughtfully arranged for enough space for two verse epitaphs to be included at the head and foot as well as a memorial inscription along the side – almost the same as the MI at Walthamstow. This may or may not indicate that he had already received the Verse Epitaphs from Shakespeare. His parents' effigies are in marble and were presumably placed there on completion of the tomb. His own effigy is in alabaster and, following the customs of the time, was put in storage until it should be erected after his own death. His effigy depicts him as a c. forty-year-old, which on its own dates the tomb to around 1601-3. No portrait has survived (nor of his parents), so this is the only pictorial record. He was a handsome man, which one might have assumed from the later renowned beauty of his daughter Venetia. He was also rather tall, 1.85 m (6' 1").

His future son-in-law Sir Kenelm Digby later reported that after the death of his wife Edward was 'melancholic' and was resolved to live rather withdrawn from the world. For a time he lived alone at home with his three daughters. The implication is that Edward kept them in his own care, presumably at Tong Castle, for some time after Lucy's death and as long as Venetia was still in swaddling clothes, which in Tudor times would be until about eight or nine months. Then, 'as soon as she had attained to such strength as that her remove might be without danger, he sent her to a kinsman of his, whose wife being a grave and virtuous lady, had given him assurance that no care of diligence should be wanting on her part to cultivate those natural endowments which did already shine through her tender age.' It is anyone's guess whether this was within a year after Venetia's birth or within the next couple of years, but cannot have been later than 1603.

Meanwhile, wherever his daughters were at the time, Edward made it again to Preston Guild in August 1602, along with cousin William and uncle Sir Edward Sr. These were the only surviving males in the immediate family. Presumably he used Winwick as his base and it might have been at this time that he, with others, commissioned a bell for Winwick church bearing several initials. 'One of our bells is thought to date from somewhere about the year 1600; it bears the initials which have been taken to stand for Peter Legh, Thomas Gerard, Edward Eccleston, Edward Stanley, Thomas Stanley and John Rider.'

Amongst topics of conversation between the three Stanleys at Preston Guild must have been William's career in London as a playwright and the latest state of his long drawn out wranglings with his sister-in-law Countess Alice about which lands each was entitled to. The situation had been complicated two years previously when she had married Thomas Egerton from Cheshire, 1st Viscount Brackley, (later) Lord Ellesmere and Elizabeth's Lord Chancellor. This very year (1602) her daughter Frances married his son John Egerton, 2nd Viscount Brackley. This marital alliance with the Lord Chancellor put Alice in an even stronger position to pursue her claims and, indeed, all was to drag on for several more years until a final agreement was reached. Lord Ellesmere had in 1598 re-established his base in the North West with the purchase of the Old Hall at Tatton Park in Cheshire and in 1601 had bought Harefield House in Middlesex for Alice, where she set up her own little 'court', entertaining Queen Elizabeth in 1602 and garnering many dedications from poets. These had already been flowing in for a decade, and were to continue. Edmund Spenser claimed kinship with Countess Alice, although the exact connection has never been discovered. (There is a a long-standing tradition in Hurstwood near Burnley in Lancashire that the 'Spencer House' there was his home for some time.) The kinship was claimed in his dedication to her of his poem *Teares of the Muses* in 1591. He obviously knew her and her family well enough to include them in a poem in 1594, *Colin Clouts come home again*, under allegorical names: 'Amyntas' is Ferdinando, recently died; 'Amarillis' is his mourning widow Alice; and 'Aetion' is Ferdinando's brother William. He also groups together 'Amarillis', 'Phyllis' and 'Charillis', the three daughters of Sir John Spencer (died 1586); in 1594 Alice's sister Anne was the widow of William Stanley, 3rd Lord Monteagle (died 1581), a kinsman of Ferdinando; and Elizabeth was still married to George Carey, 2nd Lord Hunsdon (died 1603), patron of 'the Lord Chamberlain's Men', which took over 'Strange's Men' and performed Shakespeare's plays. Elsewhere in the same poem he names Samuel Daniel openly and it is generally agreed that 'the shepheard of the Ocean' is Sir Walter Raleigh, 'Astrofell' is Sir Philip Sidney and 'Cynthia' Queen Elizabeth. Although none of this belongs directly in Edward Stanley's biography, it is difficult to believe that all these publications and family connections did not affect him in some way. One direct result around this time was his receiving the two Verse Epitaphs from Shakespeare for his parents' and his own tomb in Tong.

Meanwhile cousin William had re-established himself in the North West, where he was now spending most of his time. His marriage had now entered a happier phase, and he was again more hopeful of producing a male heir. He had also consolidated the traditional roles of the Earls of Derby in many positions in Lancashire and Cheshire, and the following year (1603-4) was to serve as Lord Mayor of Liverpool. He had also constructed (or at least known and approved of) a theatre at Prescot, near Knowsley, the first purpose built indoor theatre in Lancashire and, indeed, in the whole of England. He had also had contact with Dr John Dee, whom he had been instrumental in appointing as Warden of Manchester College in 1595, in a building owned by William (today Chetham's Library). Dr Dee was one of the most noted scholars of the day, who had spent many years in Poland, Bohemia and Prague, acquiring a reputation in science and alchemy. He had also acquired a more notorious reputation as a necromancer by his association with Edward Kelly, a companion in Prague, who had performed a locally famous necromancing act in the churchyard of Walton-le-Dale near Preston. Dr Dee's son Arthur was born in Manchester during his father's period as Warden, and his own story as a physician to the Tsar of Russia (where he healed his foot) was later to be muddled with his father's story, and even more muddled during the next century when convolutedly introduced into the story and ballad of Sir William Stanley's extensive and adventurous travels of 1582-92/3. Again, these events do not strictly belong to Edward's biography, but with his frequent meetings with cousin William, he must have been very aware of all the people mentioned.

William and the two Edwards Sr and Jr presumably also exchanged any news they had of their various Stanley 'cousins' serving the Spanish King and the several brothers or cousins of their gentry neighbours who were Catholic priests in exile. (One of the most famous, largely because he left his autobiography, was John Gerard, younger brother of Sir Thomas Gerard Jr, who was knighted along with Sir Edward Jr by King James as soon as he came to the throne of England.) Presumably they talked about the ageing Elizabeth and speculated about her successor, particularly relevant to the family because just eight years earlier their niece Anne had been confirmed as an 'heiress presumptive'. Presumably they also exchanged their latest news of William's half-sisters Ursula and Dorothy, which brought Sir John Salusbury of Lleweni into the conversation. He had married Ursula in 1586, and so was William's brother-in-law. Amidst their whole brood of children (eleven in all) they had named their nth child in 1599 Ferdinando, after Ursula's dead half-brother. Sir John (knighted by Elizabeth in 1601) had received several dedications from poets in the 1590s and was himself a dabbler. His friend Robert Chester had published some adulatory poems to Sir John (June

1601) in *Love's Martyr*, a series of 'poetical essays', including contributions by Jonson, Chapman and Marston, and a poem beginning 'Let the bird of loudest lay' (usually known as *The Phoenix and the Turtle*), with the author's name printed as William Shake-speare. There are compelling arguments for this having been composed on the occasion of the marriage of Sir John to Ursula back in 1586.

One imagines that Shake-speare/Shakeshafte would have entered their conversations more than once, because of William, 6th Earl's active participation in the theatre and Shakespeare's recent string of great successes in London. (This would almost certainly have been the case if the 'Shakespeare in Lancashire' theory is based on historical fact, and young William had spent time with the Hoghtons and Heskeths, several of whom were also present at Preston Guild in 1602.) Might it have been on one of these occasions that William or Sir Edward Stanley Sr jokingly suggested to Edward Jr that next time he bumped into Shakespeare in London, he should ask him to write an epitaph for the Stanley 'tomb in the making' in Tong? A hypothetical and speculative question to which there will, alas, never be an answer.

Knighthood in 1603 and great changes in his life

One might presume that two major events of 1603 – his knighthood by James I at his coronation and his sale of Tong Castle – were not unconnected with the decision to place his young daughters in a household which would provide a more suitable environment for them than just the company of their father and his household servants. Eynsham Abbey, Oxfordshire was much closer to Salden in Mursely, Buckinghamshire, which was where he placed his daughters. The 'grave and virtuous lady' whose family Edward's daughters joined was his first cousin Grace Fortescue née Manners, daughter of his aunt Dorothy and uncle John of Haddon Hall, his mother Lady Margaret's sister. Grace had married (Sir) Francis Fortescue of Salden in 1589 and by 1601-3 they already had several of the final quota of twelve or thirteen children. Three more, one suspects, would have been easily accommodated! In 1603 Sir Francis was dubbed a Knight of the Bath on the occasion of James's coronation, at the same time as Sir Edward. Maybe this was when the offer came to take in the three motherless little Stanley girls? Sir Francis, following on from his father Sir John Fortescue, held many public posts, as MP for Buckingham and later (1608) High Sheriff of Buckinghamshire, the year when he succeeded to the estates of his father. The latter had also held many high positions, including Chancellor of the Duchy of Lancaster for several years until his death. Sir Francis was apparently a committed Catholic all his life and in 1618 appeared on a recusancy list for Oxfordshire. It was in this household that many of the events of the next few years of relevance to Sir Edward were to unfold.

The most complete lists of Sir Francis and Grace Fortescue's children include (although not always given in the same order): Mary, John, Robert, Gilbert, William, Adrian, Francis, Roger, Frances, Dorothy, Catherine, one unnamed son and one unnamed daughter, who presumably died at birth. This comes to 13. On their tomb in Mursley Church are small effigies of 6 sons and 4 daughters, some holding skulls. As the tomb was erected by their surviving children, one might presume that the number on the tomb is correct. The brief biographies, or at least a few details, appear in local history publications and on websites of at least (Sir) John, the son and heir, Mary (who married John Talbot, 10th Earl of Shrewsbury, thus bringing Chatsworth in Derbyshire into the family picture again), Francis and William. None of them appears in Sir Kenelm's *Memoirs*, which is slightly surprising, because he obviously knew them all during his own childhood and they played such an important role in Venetia's upbringing. Edward must have stayed in close touch with the family because John Fortescue, Esquire was named by him as one of the executors of his will in 1632. John was later (1636) created 1st Baronet Fortescue of Nova Scotia, a reflection of King Charles's enthusiasm for the new trading-links with North America. Among the friends of the Fortescues were the Digbys at Gayhurst in Bedfordshire. Kenelm Digby reports that the two families came together quite often with the children. There is no reference to how often Sir Edward visited them. One interesting point is that a Fortescue relative was very much involved with the Blackfriars Gatehouse in London, which William Shakespeare was to purchase in 1613, along with two others, for use as an indoors winter theatre. This was a labyrinthine building known as a hiding place for Catholics. It seems that much is still waiting to be learnt about the history and circumstances surrounding this purchase, which would no doubt be of interest to those currently planning a reconstruction next to The New Globe in Southwark. This is due to open on 9 January 2014 as the Sam Wanamaker Playhouse.

In 1603, as already mentioned, Edward was in London for King James's coronation, where he was made a Knight of the Bath at Greenwich on Sunday, 24 July 1603. There is no record as to why he was knighted, but one potential reason immediately presents itself. Another who had been knighted in York by James on his progress from Scotland to London was Sir Thomas Gerard Jr, for the troubles his father had borne in the cause of his mother. We will remember that Sir Thomas Gerard Sr and Sir Thomas Stanley had been the Lancashire leaders in the plan in 1570 to free Mary, Queen of Scots from Chatsworth, and both had been imprisoned and inquisitioned in the Tower. As Sir Thomas Gerard Jr was obviously knighted in recognition of his father's participation, it is logical to assume that the same reason provided Sir Edward Stanley Jr's knighthood. Another in this trio in 1570 had been Sir Edward Sr, who was released before the other two and, until his death at Lathom in 1604, was the Senior Member of the Family, holding the fort back in Lancashire on several occasions. He might therefore have been in Lancashire during the time of the coronation, the festivities for which in any case were postponed until 1604 because of an outbreak of the plague. Later that year Sir Edward Sr died and was buried in 'my lord's chapel' Ormskirk on 4 September 1604. Whether Sir Edward Jr was able to see his dear uncle again and be with him at his death or attend his funeral remains, alas, unrecorded.

Another who played a role in the coronation procession was William Shakespeare. We know that the King's Men, of which he was a member, joined in, wearing the red cloth granted to them for their livery. This seems to be one obvious occasion when he might have thought about penning the epitaphs for Sir Edward, perhaps later when having a merry drink together, with Sir Edward receiving commiserations on the loss of his wife and four children all at once and now the death of his only remaining uncle. Sir Edward would also have commiserated on Shakespeare's loss of his son Hamnet in 1596 and his father in 1601, if he not already commiserated on a previous occasion.

Life goes on at Eynsham after 1604, but quietly

By 1604 Sir Edward had definitely sold Tong Castle and retired to Eynsham Abbey. One can only speculate on the reasons for Sir Edward's move. One already suggested is because it was considerably closer to Salden, where his three daughters were growing up. At the same time as selling Tong to Sir Thomas Harris, he had also sold Harlaston to Sir Edward Brabazon and the manor of West Bromwich to his 'cousin' Sir Richard Sheldon. He certainly did not need the money, so it presumably had something to do with wishing to pare down his ownership of property and responsibilities. The Tong sale apparently still left a few dangling ends, because in 1607-9 the king stepped in to authorise the alienation of the manor to Sir Thomas Harris. The dates of 1613 and 1623 have also occurred in various accounts until the new ownership of Tong Castle and Manor was well and truly settled.

Meanwhile in 1606 Edward sold Marple and Wybersley and in 1608 sold the property in Stackpole, Pembrokeshire to Roger Lort, who had been a tenant and the agent there. This saw the end of Sir Edward's Stackpole story, which had also involved his stepfather William Mather. It was presumably connected to the death of Mather in 1607, which saw the end of another period of Sir Edward's life. He had now divested himself of many of his possessions and withdrew himself to Eynsham Abbey.

Little has been discovered about his life at Eynsham other than via the biography of daughter Venetia, which will be recounted below. Maybe he returned to Lancashire on occasion to visit his cousin William and family? Maybe he travelled to London for some periods and saw Shakespeare's latest plays? Maybe Eynsham was a stopping off point for relatives and friends en route from London to Lancashire or Derbyshire? One might assume that he was aware of various events that involved his family and friends. One had been the Gunpowder Plot in 1605, in which Sir Everard Digby, a friend of the Fortescues, was tragically involved and which his 'cousin' Lord Monteagle was instrumental in revealing to the authorities.

One hint of a possible visit back to Lancashire in 1611 comes from the inscription of 'Edw: Stanley 1611' as the latest owner of a copy of Thomas North's English translation of Plutarch's *Lives of the Noble Greeks and Romans*, a book generally accepted as the source of many details in Shakespeare's Greek and Roman plays. In the copy owned by the Shakespeare Birthplace Trust the previous owners had signed their names (in reverse order) as William, Alice, Ferdinando and Henry, 4th Earl of Derby, who had received it in 1579, the year of its publication, from William Chaderton, Bishop of Chester. If the last named owner in 1611, Edward Stanley, was indeed William's cousin, which seems to be the most logical explanation, then the book had stayed within the family for two generations, spanning exactly the time of William Shakespeare's career. Into this one can read what one will.

1613-1626 and a new life via his daughters

Several events during the following years happened as a result of his visit to London in February 1613, summoned to court to attend the wedding celebrations of Princess Elizabeth to Frederick V of the Palatinate, his main seat in Heidelberg, later King of Bohemia. Frederick and Elizabeth were to go down in history as The Winter King and Queen after the disastrous defeat of their troops at the Battle of the White Mountain outside Prague in November 1620 at the beginning of the Thirty Years War. They escaped to The Hague, where in 1626 James, son and heir of Sir Edward's cousin William, 6th Earl, arrived to marry Charlotte de la Trémouille, a French Huguenot related to the French royal family. These were among several Stanleys travelling up and down the country, and it may well be that some of them stopped off at Eynsham to stay with Sir Edward. It must certainly have seemed a convenient place to stay, as Tong Castle had previously been, on the (normally four to six day) journey from London to Lancashire. It was well known to James that, because Sir Edward had no son and heir, Eynsham would revert to the earldom after Sir Edward's death, and therefore to James after his father William's death. It would certainly be ironically appropriate if Charlotte did stay at Eynsham with Sir Edward in 1626, because thirty years later she would in fact inherit it herself, as the widow of Earl James, executed after the Civil War.

Apart from possibly receiving these and other visitors, Sir Edward seems to have lived this period of his life at least partly through his two married daughters. Frances was the first to marry. In about 1612/13, aged (estimated) about seventeen or eighteen, she married (Sir) John Fortescue (Bt) (1592-1656), son and heir of her 'guardians' at Salden. They soon had a family, providing several grandchildren for Sir Edward. The first was John in 1614, followed by at least Edward, Frances and Grace. There was obviously continuing contact, because John Fortescue was later appointed one of the executors of Sir Edward's will.

The story of his daughter Venetia, a noted beauty, has been told many times, most notoriously by John Aubrey in the 1660s and most movingly by her husband, childhood sweetheart Sir Kenelm Digby in his *Memoirs*, who was heartbroken when she died in 1633. In about 1612/13 Sir Edward brought his daughter Venetia from Salden back to his own home at Eynsham. From the memoir we know that she had had some 'tutors' while at Salden, as well as 'loving care'. Did she really 'exceed all others of her age'? Was Venetia intellectually precocious? She seems to have been, at least in Sir Kenelm's eyes and memory.

Whatever problems Edward and Lucy might have had during their marriage, she seems to have become ever more saintly in death – at least in his memory of her. We know that he never married again and we have at least one reason, in the eulogy to Lucy, whether from Sir Kenelm's pen alone, or repeating words that he had heard from Sir Edward. Did Sir Edward really become more and more 'melancholic'? Or was bringing Venetia back to his home a sign that he wanted to participate more in society for her sake? Did he really see Venetia as a phœnix rising from the ashes of her mother?

Surprisingly, Sir Kenelm never mentions sisters Petronella or Frances, neither during the childhood scenes nor later. This is rather surprising, not least because (as mentioned above) John Fortescue and Frances Stanley married about this time, which might have affected Sir Edward's decision to take Venetia with him to London for the royal wedding, to give her a first glimpse of the 'marriage market'. At this point we turn to Sir Kenelm's account, for a flavour of his somewhat abstruse language, peppered with classical pseudonyms.

> . . . when the marriage of the King of Morea's daughter with one of the greatest princes of Achaya, invited all men of eminence to the court, to contribute their particular joys to the great and public solemnities. Wherefore Nearchus being desirous to give his daughter the content of seeing the magnificent entertainments that are usual at such times, and also being glad to let the world now see that fame was nothing too lavish in setting out her perfections, took this occasion to bring her to Corinth the metropolitan city, where her beauty and discretion did soon draw the eyes admiration: so that in this the example of her was singular, that whereas the beauty of other fair ladies used to grace and adorn public feasts and assemblies, hers did so far exceed all others as well in action as in excellence, that it drew to her not only the affections, but also the thoughts of all persons, so that all things else that were provided with greatest splendour and curiosity, passed by unregarded and neglected.

From this we understand that Sir Edward (Nearchus) took Venetia with him to London (Corinth) to experience the 'magnificent entertainments' to be expected at such a lavish wedding of a princess, daughter of James, King of England (Morea) and Frederick (one of the princes of Achaya). One presumes that Edward had himself participated in many previous 'magnificent entertainments' at court, perhaps/presumably at least the wedding at Elizabeth's court at Greenwich of his cousin William Stanley in 1595. And he must have known about his cousins-in-law the two Countesses of Derby (Alice, widow of Ferdinando and Elizabeth, wife of William) frequently performing in masques at court during the early years of James's reign, whether he attended any or not.

Venetia obviously attracted a great deal of attention because of her beauty and personality. We should remember, however, that in February 1613 she was only twelve, and at the same time bear in mind that fourteen was considered at the time a suitable age for marriage. As a result of the success of her visit to court Sir Edward installed her in her own establishment at Eynsham, in a house on the estate, where she continued to attract a remarkable amount of attention. According to Aubrey, one of the gallants who courted her was Richard Sackville, 3rd Earl of Dorset. (Or was it his brother? Identifications of both of them have appeared as Venetia's admirer.) In any case this identification of 'Ursatius' in Sir Kenelm's account has often been considered to be historically unsubstantiated. Whether he was Venetia's admirer or not, at that time Richard, 3rd Earl of Dorset was married to Lady Anne Clifford, only daughter and heiress of George Clifford, 3rd Earl of Cumberland, and therefore another Stanley first cousin. (Earl George's half-sister Margaret Clifford was the wife of Henry Stanley, 4th Earl of Derby and therefore Sir Edward Jr's aunt.) But Venetia later found true happiness with Sir Kenelm Digby, son of old family friend Sir Everard Digby, one who, as mentioned above, had unfortunately become involved in the Gunpowder Plot and been executed for his role. Sir Kenelm had disappeared off on various adventures abroad for many years and Venetia assumed he was dead. When he turned up again their childhood friendship was renewed and despite some opposition from their parents (Venetia's father 'Nearchus' and Kenelm's mother 'Arete'), they married secretly in c.1625 and had a blissfully happy marriage in London. We have no idea how aware Sir Edward was of his daughter's indiscretions and subsequent secret marriage, but he certainly discovered about the latter when Venetia arrived at his house pregnant with Kenelm's child.

Their first son Kenelm was born at Eynsham on 6 October, 1625, a somewhat troublesome and premature birth after Venetia had fallen from a horse. Sir Kenelm's account of this leaves no doubt that she had gone to Eynsham to 'her father's house in the country' for the later more visible pregnancy in order to keep this secret, along with their marriage. Although Venetia had planned to return to London to give birth, in fact it perforce took place at Eynsham. As soon as Sir Kenelm heard the news he hurried to Eynsham, and as soon as Venetia was strong enough, took his wife and baby back to London.

The only other record of Sir Edward at Eynsham during this period had been when he appeared as the owner of the Park on a map of 1615 and in 1617 presented 'Thomas Longe to the living', i.e. as minister of the church. 1617 was also the year when Petronella appeared in a court suit concerning Winwick. With her on the contesting side were the Earl of Worcester and her sister Frances Fortescue and husband John. Opposing were 'Ryder, Bishop of Killake and Josiah Herne'. Might this 'Bishop Ryder' have been the 'John Rider' whose initials appeared on the bell at Winwick around 1600? It certainly might. John Ryder (1562-1632) (of Carrington, Cheshire, now in Greater Manchester) had published in 1589 the first Latin-English dictionary in which the English 'langue' took precedence. He was appointed to the living of Winwick by William Stanley, 6th Earl of Derby. He was a favourite of Queen Elizabeth and later Dean of St Patrick's, Dublin and Anglican Bishop of Killaloe, Co. Clare. Hopefully an explanation of this court case and exploration into the implications will emerge in the future from some elusive source. For the moment it happily provides at least the information that sisters Petronella and Frances were still in contact and apparently conducting business on behalf of their father. The previous year William Shakespeare had died and was buried at Stratford on 26 April 1616. One can only presume that Sir Edward mourned the passing of his old friend, who had written the Verse Epitaphs for his tomb.

1626-1632, the last years

On 27 June 1626 Sir Edward appointed Charles Herle, M.A. as Rector of Winwick. (*VCH*, 4, Winwick.) This seems a little odd, if the previous Rector had been appointed by the King and the one before that by cousin Earl William. Yet again, it is difficult to explain this. Did it require Sir Edward's actual presence in Winwick? (In this case he must still have been active and travelling up and down the country.) Or might it have happened by proxy? But in this case, why not allow Cousin William to take over the Advowson? Presumably the lease for 99 years taken out in 1563 by his father Sir Thomas was still valid. However, this is the last mention of Sir Edward in Winwick.

In 1627 Elizabeth née de Vere, Earl William's wife, died at Lathom. One might imagine Sir Edward commiserating with him at the earliest possible opportunity, as one ageing widower to another, but no record of any visits either way has survived. Soon after this William retired to his house in Watergate, Chester to enjoy a pleasant life full of music and theatricals, having handed over all responsibilities to son James.

The MIs in Walthamstow and Tong and the Verse Epitaphs in Tong were already recorded on paper during Sir Edward's lifetime, in c.1626 (or perhaps earlier) by John Weever, who had dedicated his long poem *Faunus and Melliflora* to him in 1600. He did not include any attribution to Shakespeare's authorship, obviously did not visit either monument himself, and got the two MIs and tombs very muddled up. They might also have been recorded on paper again within Sir Edward's lifetime, this time attributing the verses to Shakespeare, by someone whose MS ended up in Warwick Castle and has been dated as c.1630. The Verse Epitaphs were certainly attributed to Shakespeare several more times within the next generation. One who recorded them was (Sir) William Dugdale (another historian with Lancashire origins), who left a record of the Stanley tomb in Tong in 1632, mentioning only Sir Thomas, so before Sir Edward's effigy was placed there. He was later to visit it again in September 1663 as Norroy King of Arms during his Visitation of Shropshire, when he made a detailed record, including complete transcriptions of the MI and the Verse Epitaphs, this time attributing them to Shakespeare, and sending his subordinate herald Francis Sandford to make a drawing of the tomb the following year.

Sir Edward seems to have been cared for in his final years at Eynsham by his unmarried daughter Petronella. Presumably they both survived unscathed from the great fire at Eynsham in 1629. No other direct news of him at Eynsham has survived, but only of events in his immediate and extended family. Cousin William had finally produced two sons, James in 1607 (whom we met above) and Robert in 1610, both of whom were married and still alive at Sir Edward's death in 1632, so the succession of the Earldom of Derby seemed secure, which must have pleased Sir Edward. Sadly Robert, who had married twice, died along with both children, not too long after Sir Edward. The only Stanley great-grandson of Earl Edward at the time of Sir Edward's death was therefore James, Lord Strange. Sir Edward's daughter Frances and John Fortescue completed their family of grandchildren, with the eldest, John Jr, aged sixteen when his grandfather died, and his younger brother Edward there to carry on his grandfather's name. Venetia and Kenelm had two more sons within Sir Edward's lifetime: John on 29 December, 1627 and Everard on 12 January, 1630, who sadly died in his cradle. One wonders – why was there no Edward Digby named after his maternal grandfather?

One old family friend and relative, Sir Rowland Stanley, had survived until 1612, aged 96, the oldest knight in England. He was the last of the original senior Stanley branch at Hooton in the Wirral. Cousin William, 6th Earl was to survive until 1642, aged eighty-one. Perhaps it was just as well that he and Sir Edward did not emulate Sir Rowland's longevity and live until the Civil Wars, when so many of their descendants and in-laws would fight for the Royalist side and suffer accordingly.

Sir Edward wrote his will on 10 June 1632 at Eynsham, leaving everything to Petronella. One assumes he had already settled a third of his property on each of his other two married daughters. He died there on 18 June, in his seventieth year, and was buried in St Leonard's Church by Petronella, with a memorial plaque. For whatever reason, she did not organise the removal of his effigy from its storage place to Eynsham, but had it placed on the tomb of his parents in Tong. As this was where he was already commemorated in an MI and there was a tier waiting for it, this in itself seems logical, but it might well also have been his wish, previously expressed to Petronella. One of his executors was his son-in-law John Fortescue and his other son-in-law Sir Kenelm Digby assisted in the administration of his will in London in December of that year. All the lands received by his father in the settlement shortly after his birth, including Eynsham, went back by reversion to the Earl of Derby.

And so ended this rather short-lived male branch of the Stanleys of Tong and Eynsham. But Sir Edward's name lives on as the recipient of the only Verse Epitaphs by Shakespeare still to be seen today apart from the Bard's own on his gravestone in Stratford Church.

Appendix 1
Was Shakespeare ever in Shropshire?

A word of explanation is required here about Father Thomas Conlan, two quotes from whose letters to Professor Father Peter Milward in Tokyo appear below. Both are/were Jesuit priests. Father Peter has lived for over fifty years in Tokyo, where he became Professor of English Literature at Sophia University (since Emeritus, retired) and founded the Renaissance Institute there. In 1973 he published a seminal book on Catholic Shakespeare, *Shakespeare's Religious Background*, and has continued to publish regularly on this theme ever since (a small selection of his publications is given in the bibliography). He has since become arguably the leading world authority on Shakespeare's Catholicism, but for many years his was a lone voice crying in the wilderness, dismissed by many as partisan: of course, if he was a Jesuit, he would like to believe that Shakespeare was a Catholic. The tide has gradually turned and an ever-increasing number of scholars have started to accept that he might have been right all along.

Father Peter's arguments came mainly from the Works and Father Thomas was determined to provide the genealogical background of all potentially relevant families. He wrote his research in ten airmail letters from 1975 onwards (he died, aged 90, in 2002). These stayed on Father Peter's shelves until he became aware that Carol Curt Enos in the U.S. (author of *Shakespeare and the Catholic Religion*, 2000, among others) and I in Europe were researching in the genealogical area, all details of which provided proof that he was always surrounded by Catholic families, including his own; and that both of us had moved inexorably towards the only logical conclusion that Shakespeare was sympathetic to Catholicism for much if not all of his life, along with his family and many friends and relatives.

Father Peter sent copies of the letters to us both. He valued us particularly because Carol was brought up as a Methodist and I as a Congregationalist – we became his 'non-conformist ladies'. Since then we have transcribed the letters and they are now sitting on our computers, but still unpublished. Like Father Peter for so many years, neither of us was quite sure what to do with them. The first extracts for publication appear below and will be followed by more in my forthcoming book on Shakespeare's Lancashire Links. I will probably put them online, annotated, in the near future. Although the extracts below provide no proof that Shakespeare was ever in Shropshire, they raise some intriguing points about connections with the county of some who have often been associated with him, and the possible performance of some of his plays there.

One well-known boarding school in Tudor England was in Shrewsbury, attended by Sir Philip Sidney (assumed to be one of the main inspirations for Shakespeare to write his Sonnets) and his friend Sir Fulke Greville (later Recorder at Stratford, among many other positions). Father Conlan included the following concerning Shrewsbury and Shropshire.

> The Quarry theatre at Shrewsbury where, says Thomas Churchyard in 1587 'well may sit 10,000 men at ease' & 'At Ashton's plays, who had behelde thys then, might well have seen there 20,000 men' (Thos. Ashton (d. 1578) had been 3rd Headmaster of Shrewsbury - any relation to Alice Ashton, Tho and Alex. Houghton's mother?) Since this was the only theatre in England seating 10,000, it seems clear that Thos. Nash is referring to it in 1592 (the year Sir Gilbert Gerard died) in writing of 'brave Talbot' (buried only a few miles north & ancestor of the Shrewsburys) 'embalmed in the tears of 10,000 spectators, at least, on several occasions'. (Nash in the same passage refers to Talbot's Tomb.) Shrewsbury is less than 25m from Gerard's Bromley. Was *Henry VI* produced there before 1592? (1592 was date Greene published his attack on the 'upstart crow' – Shakescene' etc.)
>
> (Letter 4.)

In a later letter he followed this up:

He (John Shakespeare) must often have junketted & acted with the other officials of Stratford & must have known their wives well. Five of the officials were: 1. Sir Fulke Greville, Recorder (which Inn of Court?) - his wife was Lady Anne Nevelle (Catholic); 2. Sir Greville Verney, High Steward, - his wife was Lady Catharine Southwell (Catholic?); 3. Thomas Russell, Steward - his wife was Mrs. Anne Digges, widow of mathematician Dudley Digges; 4. Abraham Sturley, Deputy Steward (Solicitor - Middle Temple), father of vicar of Broadway - his wife? 4. John Shakespeare, Bailiff - his wife Mary Arden. (One of the Fulke Grevilles was a Catholic - which? The sea-captain one (probably), who was at Shrewsbury with Sir Philip Sydney, both under Thos. Ashton, 3rd Headmaster & dramatist - producer (one play) done by the boys - went on all thro' the holidays (!) at Shrewsbury Quarry & the boys had to act a comedy every Thursday before they were 'off' for the day (this used to be the custom in our S.J. Academy days each term!, i.e. in our boys' colleges).

(Letter 7.)

1a. Shrewsbury Castle and School
(*Shrewsbury*, Rimmer, 1889)

It is worth adding here that this Thomas Russell was appointed one of the overseers of Shakespeare's will in 1616, and that one of his stepsons (Mrs Anne Digges was his second wife) was Leonard Digges, who wrote a prefatory poem in honour of Shakespeare in the *First Folio*, two facts that seem to prove a life-long close relationship between the Shakespeares and the Russells. (These Russells could bear further research, to establish whether they were closely related to the Russells, Earls of Bedford, who enter the 'Shakespeare in Lancashire' story through Lady Anne Clifford's mother Margaret Russell, daughter of the Earl of Bedford.)

Meanwhile we know that the reputation of Thomas Ashton (Headmaster) was great enough to have attracted the attention of the parents of Sir Philip Sydney and Sir Fulke Greville, who sent their sons there. We can also fairly safely assume that his reputation would have been known to the Shakespeares via Sir Fulke Greville when John and Mary were deciding what course young William's education should take. Whether he might have attended or not is another matter, but remains a possibility for future research.

Other Lancashire names and a place mentioned by Conlan are Sir Gilbert Gerard, Gerard's Bromley, Talbots and Shrewsburys. Sir Gilbert Gerard was of Ince near Wigan, Elizabeth's Master of the Rolls and an esteemed personage back in Lancashire, where he appears in many wills receiving bequests for services rendered. His son and heir Sir Thomas Gerard became Elizabeth's and James's Knight Marshal and 1st Baron Gerard of Gerard's Bromley, Staffordshire. (We met them at Preston Guild.) When the Gerards were in London their country house was at Harrow-on-the-Hill.

The Talbots were from the Ribble Valley in Lancashire, and the son of the 'brave Talbot' mentioned above in *Henry VI* was created 1st Earl of Shrewsbury. Always associated with the Midlands from then on, three of the main seats of the 6th Earl in the 1570s were Tutbury, Chatsworth and Sheffield Castle. As we read in a previous chapter, the current Talbot, 6th Earl of Shrewsbury, was the guardian for many years of Mary, Queen of Scots, and it was from his guardianship that another Sir Thomas Gerard (of Bryn) and others planned an aborted scheme in 1570 to free her and spirit her to the Isle of Man, aided and abetted by **Sir Thomas Stanley** and **Sir Edward Sr**. Although the names do not appear in the extracts from Conlan's letters above, in other letters he reveals that he was very aware that one branch of the Stanley family lived in nearby Tong in Shropshire, and was also very aware of the two epitaphs written by Shakespeare.

If Conlan is correct that Nash(e) was referring to audiences of 10,000 at Shrewsbury, rather than in London, this is another bit of the 'conventional' story that requires an overhaul, or at least an insertion. In all major Shakespeare biographies since Sir Sidney Lee's in 1898, it has been assumed that the '10,000 (at several times)' in the audience were at multiple performances in London. Lee includes the text to which Conlan refers:

> On March 3, 1592, a new piece, called 'Henry VI', was acted at the Rose Theatre by Lord Strange's men. It was no doubt the play which was subsequently known as Shakespeare's 'The First Part of Henry VI.' 'How would it have joyed brave Talbot (the terror of the French)' wrote Nash in his 'Pierce Penniless' (1592, licensed August 8), in reference to the striking scenes of Talbot's death (act iv. sc. vi. and vii.), 'to thinke that after he had lyne two hundred yeares in his Tombe, hee should triumphe againe on the Stage, and have his bones newe embalmed with the teares of ten thousand spectators at least (at severall times), who, in the Tragedian that represents his person, imagine they behold him fresh bleeding!'
>
> (Sidney Lee, A Life of Shakespeare, 1898, pp. 56-7.)

Another reason why Shrewsbury and its school is intriguing is that Keen in 1954 (who also knew about the epitaphs) noted that Shakespeare seems to have known the town and surrounding country well.

> Did Shakespeare ever go to Shropshire? There is, as a matter of fact, some reason to suppose that he did. . . As we have seen, if he was well known to the Heskeths and Houghtons, and in touch with their kin, stretching to Herberts and Newports, it would not have been difficult for him to get introductions to that part of the world. . . The idea of a sojourn in Shropshire is supported by the many Shropshire allusions in the plays, from Falstaff's 'long hour by Shrewsbury clock' (put up, incidentally, in 1595) to the 'dancing horse', alluded to in *Love's Labour's Lost*; this apparently was the great sensation of Shrewsbury in 1591. My wife once made a list of one hundred and two Shropshire words that appear in the plays. A curious point is that the name 'Estridge' was borne by a hill to the north of the Vesson in the parish of Habberley, and was there known to be a name for a species of large falcon.
>
> All furnished, all in arms,
All plumed like estridges that wing the wind . . .
>
> Further Shropshire coincidences will be found in Appendix viii.
>
> (Keen, The Annotator, 1954, pp. 90-91.)

The dates given by Keen suggest Shakespeare's knowledge of Shrewsbury later rather than earlier and the main draw would presumably have been the huge theatre. However, to have absorbed so many local dialect words would seem to require a sojourn of longer than a couple of days.

Keen also explored other details about Shropshire families in the hunt for a trail leading from Stratford to Lancashire. If we turn to his Appendix viii, we find the account of the two epitaphs at Tong, already given in a previous chapter, plus one more Shropshire reference:

NEW PLACE DOCUMENTS

In 1886 there came to light the purchaser's and vendor's exemplifications concerning New Place, Stratford-on-Avon, 1597. These papers were found among the papers of the Severne family, of Wallop Hall, Shropshire.

Thomas Severne of Broadway and Powyck, Worcestershire (d. 1592), married in 1587 Elizabeth, daughter of John Nash of Martley, Worcestershire. If hence there sprang a family connexion between the Severnes and the John Nash mentioned in Shakespeare's will, it is easy to see how these papers of his came to be at Wallop.

(Keen, pp. 203-4.)

The main conclusion from these Shropshire details is that there is no proof that Shakespeare was ever there, but enough circumstantial hints that he might well have been. Sheer geographical logic seems to dictate that if he was ever a member of a travelling group of players, then their route must, at some point, have taken them through Shropshire, en route between the main patrons of theatrical performances in neighbouring counties. And even if Shakespeare himself was not there, many of his fellow actors must have been. One might presume that Shakespeare, with all his Stanley contacts, would have been welcome at Tong Castle when (Sir) **Edward Stanley Jr** was in residence.

1b. Shrewsbury
Streets such as this probably looked not very different in the 16th century.

Appendix 2
Was Christopher Marlowe ever in Shropshire?

I was asked some time ago, by a contact at St Bartholomew's, Tong, to write a 'spoof' piece on the local tradition that Christopher Marlowe had visited Tong and that he had written one or more of Shakespeare's plays there. I refused on the grounds that (a) I did not believe for one moment that Marlowe had written any of Shakespeare's plays and (b) before writing anything about Marlowe I would feel obliged to read everything ever written about him, which seemed a rather daunting task.

However, during later reading I came across a few comments and references that MIGHT shed potential light on the origin of any 'local tradition' of Marlowe's presence in Shropshire or neighbouring counties. Although not reported as an actor, he MIGHT have accompanied a troupe of actors that had his works in their repertoire; this troupe MIGHT have been Lord Strange's Men, who certainly performed Marlowe's and Shakespeare's plays in London; his presence in the Midlands – or at least the mention of his name – MIGHT have lingered on in local memory after details of his murder gradually percolated through and became generally known; and this MIGHT over the centuries have been transformed into the 'tradition' that 'Marlowe was here'. This 'tradition' MIGHT have been based on some contemporary reports or MIGHT have been proposed by someone at any time afterwards. 'Traditions' are slippery things unless they are provably old and contemporary. I reject out of hand, along with pretty well everyone else, any suggestion that Marlowe wrote some or all of Shakespeare's plays. His Marlovian supporters claim that he did not die at Deptford in 1593, but was spirited away and lived on for many years. I suppose that if one can believe that he could have survived his own murder, then one can also believe that he could have gone on to perform any number of other miracles. I am not one of these believers.

Reading the following titles was as a background of figures contemporary with Shakespeare in the London theatre, latest explorations on 'Catholic Shakespeare' and/or figures in the Midlands contemporary with **Sir Thomas** and **Sir Edward Stanley** during their years at Tong. In this context, three titles proved very interesting. (I deliberately do not include here any recent books which promote the Marlovian cause.)

Park Honan, *Christopher Marlowe: Poet and Spy* (Oxford University Press, 2005), widely acclaimed as a highly readable and thorough scholarly account of Marlowe's life, work and times. Professor Honan had previously published *Shakespeare, A Life* (Oxford University Press, 1998), in which he had shown a sympathetic interest in, and thorough knowledge of, all previous publications on 'Shakespeare in Lancashire'. Nowhere did he detect any mention of Marlowe in connection with Shropshire.

Clare Asquith, *Shadowplay: The Hidden Beliefs and Coded Politics of William Shakespeare* (PublicAffairs, 2005). This presents the strongest possible case for Shakespeare's Catholicism, as revealed by his Works, and has predictably received wide acclaim from some Shakespearean quarters and provoked cynical rejections from others. Time will tell when the dust settles. She makes several references to Marlowe, but to his works rather than his biography. The first part of the book, however, provides an excellent account of the mood in the country amongst those who deeply regretted the replacement of popular Catholicism and ancient rituals with the Protestant beliefs and practices imposed by Elizabeth's ministers – William Cecil, Lord Burghley, being regarded as the chief culprit. (And Marlowe's death, so the current thinking goes, was engineered by Cecil or others close to him.) So many people played a double-role in this shadowy world that anyone could presumably have popped up anywhere. So why not Marlowe in Shropshire? Although WHY he might have gone to Shropshire in the first place would take a lot of explaining.

Let us take a side-step to Derbyshire, separated from Shropshire only by Staffordshire. Burghley, along with his son, Robert Cecil, later Earl of Salisbury, were amongst the greatest supporters and confidantes of Bess of Hardwick (Derbyshire). This was well known, and probably accounts on its own for her receiving very few visitors who felt themselves under threat of persecution by the Cecils for their religious beliefs or practices.

Mary S. Lovell, *Bess of Hardwick: First Lady of Chatsworth* (2005), has explored this area. Her main aim, admirably fulfilled, was to present Bess in a more sympathetic light than all previous biographers, all men, who had portrayed her as a 'shrew' rather than 'shrewd'. Given that

- Bess's fourth (and last) husband was George Talbot, 6th Earl of Shrewsbury, guardian/jailor of Mary, Queen of Scots in the Midlands from 1569 until her trial and execution in 1587;
- Bess's granddaughter Arbella Stuart, brought up by Bess, was a strong contender as Elizabeth's successor on the throne of England;
- there were so many 'plots' against Elizabeth and pro various other contenders during and after this period, including one in 1570 involving **Sir Thomas Stanley** of Tong and another in 1593 that led to the poisoning the following year of his first cousin Ferdinando, 5th Earl of Derby;
- any potential visit to the Midlands by Christopher Marlowe would most logically have been during the years encompassing his employment as a spy on the continent, the success of his early plays in London and his murder at Deptford (mid-1580s to early-1590s, his murder being in 1593);

then there was hope that any possible appearance of Marlowe in Bess's circles might have been spotted. And indeed, as we will read below, this was the case.

The main and intriguing mention of Marlowe was in a **footnote** from Lovell, in connection with Bess's supervision of Arbella's education. (And at the end of the following extract we have a fascinating glimpse into holiday activities in a large country house in the sixteenth century.) I regard it as highly unlikely to impossible that the **Morley** in the following extract was Christopher Marlowe, but it has been proposed, and is thus worth a mention. It MIGHT be that someone previously had confused Morley and Marlowe, thus helping along the tradition that Marlowe spent time in the Midlands.

> On 5 August 1592, when Bess arrived back at Hardwick, she moved into the Old Hall, where the extensive additions were nearing completion[1]. . . .
>
> Bess had been home only a matter of weeks when she received worrying news from Burghley. A Jesuit had revealed, under torture, a plan to kidnap Arbella. The principals apparently believed that Arbella was 'certain' to be proclaimed Queen should Elizabeth die and schemed 'to convey her with stealth into Flanders; which, if it be done, she shall shortly visit Spain.'[2] Burghley, who always realised Arbella's potential in connection with the throne (even though the Queen chose to ignore it), warned Bess to check the neighbourhood for Jesuits and Catholics.
>
> Bess replied, 'My good Lord, . . . I was at the first much troubled to think that so wicked and mischievous practises should be devised to entrap my poor Arbella and me . . . but will use such diligent care . . . to prevent whatsoever shall be attempted by any wicked persons against the child'.[3] Having had the district searched for 'traitorous and naughty persons', Bess advised that there was a seminary about a mile from Hardwick, but that there was only one man of whom she was really suspicious. He had been Arbella's tutor for the past three and half years.
>
> Bess related to Burghley how, when they visited Chatsworth, this man, **Morley-the-tutor**, had told Arbella he wished to leave her employment. At first he attempted to get Arbella to give him an annuity, or a lease of land 'worth £40 a year', alleging he was much penalised, financially and otherwise, by having left the university (Cambridge) to turn private tutor. Arbella said she could not oblige, so he went to Bess who listened stony-faced before she sent him away empty-

handed. On the following day **Morley** returned, telling Arbella he would work for no recompense if only he could remain in her employment. Ever practical, Bess was immediately suspicious of any man who offered to work for no money,* especially following his remarks of the previous day. She was fair-minded, though, and admitted that she 'could not accuse him of papistry'.

Meanwhile, she advised Burghley, she was maintaining tight security around her grandchild, whom she always called Arbell. '. . . She goeth not to anybody's house at all. I see her almost every hour in the day; [and] she lieth in my bedchamber . . .'⁴ . . .This letter suggests that seventeen-year-old Arbella was almost as much Bess's prisoner as her aunt the Queen of Scots had once been, and within days Bess and Arbella left Hardwick for another visit to Chatsworth.

With the plot discovered, its machinery became useless, and the sense of alarm faded. In early December news was received from London that the great Spanish general, the Duke of Palma, had died. His son was no longer considered of any particular diplomatic value, so the Farnese marriage negotiations [*with Arbella*] were terminated. There is no evidence that this was either welcome or unwelcome news to either Bess or Arbella, and soon afterwards they returned to the Old Hall at Hardwick for the remainder of the winter. No doubt Bess wanted to enjoy the celebrations in the light and beautiful Hill Great Chamber; there was nothing like it at Chatsworth. And perhaps she wanted to keep Christmas and New Year in her usual style, with her favourite son and his family around her. We know from a letter written years later by Sir William that in his mother's home, 'holidays' – feast days birthdays, Christmas and New Year – were always kept with traditional revelry. 'All the old holidays,' he wrote, 'with their mirth and rites . . . May games, Morris dances, the Lord of the May, the Lady of the May, the fool and the Hobby Horse, also the Whitsun Lord and Lady, carols and wassails at Christmas with good plum porridge and pies . . .'⁵

(Lovell, *Bess*, pp. 389-94.)

* [Footnote, *Bess*, p. 393.] Bess's suspicions may have been more justified than she ever knew. In a recent biography of Arbella, the author Sarah Gristwood explores the theory that Morley-the-tutor may have been Christopher Marlowe, the playwright and well-known government spy. Marlowe/Morley; Barlow/Barley – names were often spelled phonetically in the sixteenth century.

[Endnotes, p. 524]
¹ DAJ [*Derbyshire Archaeological Journal*]: vol. XXX, Brodhurst, 'Elizabeth Hardwick, Countess of Shrewsbury', p. 251.
² CSP: [*Calendar of State Papers*] (Domestic), Elizabeth, 591-4, p. 259-60.
³ Hardy, *Arbella Stuart*, pp. 65-6.
⁴ *Ibid*. Also, Bradley, *Life of Arbella Stuart*.
⁵ Gristwood, *Arbella – England's Lost Queen*, p. 85.

[Titles from bibliography, Lovell, *Bess*.]
Bradley, E.T., Life of *Lady Arabella Stuart* (Bentley, 1889).
Gristwood, Sarah, *Arbella, - England's Lost Queen* (Bantam Press, 2003).
Hardy, Blanche Christabel, *Arbella Stuart* (Constable, 1913).

So 'Morley-the-tutor' was based in August 1592 at a seminary a mile away from Hardwick, and had been Arbella's tutor for three and a half years, which takes us back to early 1589. The implication in his statement above is that he had become a private tutor fairly soon after leaving Cambridge, i.e. shortly before this date. Yet Christopher Marlowe had left Cambridge back in 1584, already having done more than a little spying work on the continent, and it is generally assumed that he started writing his plays during the following few years. We know that his *Jew of Malta* was performed in London at the Rose Theatre in early 1592, which was an immediate success. It is therefore highly unlikely that in August of this year, after his London success, he would 'return' to being an impoverished tutor in the country.

Meanwhile, one must search for another mention of a Marlowe-like name in Shropshire or a neighbouring county before any credence might be given to the 'tradition' that he visited Tong.

One intriguing article was found during a search for **Sir Edward Stanley Sr**. Lo and behold, it turned out that there was an Edward Stanley at the Siege of Malta in 1565! Since then I have visited Malta (2007) and read everything available about this Edward Stanley. (See Chapter XXII. Other (Sir) Edward Stanleys.) Presumably he was related in some way to **Sir Edward Sr** and the latter might well have known about the former's exploits. Via an extremely devious route we may follow a hypothetical trail from the Edward Stanley on Malta to Marlowe writing *The Jew of Malta*. In Chapter XXII we already followed a hypothetical trail from Mr Edward Stanley on Malta back to **Sir Edward Sr**, and through him to **Sir Edward Jr** and Tong, for whose tomb Shakespeare wrote two epitaphs. Maybe some rather more fanciful trails lie behind the 'tradition' at Tong that 'Marlowe was here'?

Marlowe and Malta

For the sake of completeness, two whole pages on the internet are quoted, with my gratitude to the anonymous author, whose work appears as referenced below, with all references given there, but here limited to numbers in square brackets. (She/He is presumably on the staff of Millersville University, Pennsylvania, but the author's name of this rather long article completely eluded me.) Some of the Stanley facts are wrong, but this serves as yet another example of how strange 'traditions' arise. The parts of most relevance to the **Marlowe-Stanley connection are in bold**.

> Tydeman and Thomas suggest one principal source for Marlowe's representation of Malta:
>
> For some of the background and 'local colour' which informs his portrait of Malta under siege, Marlowe may well have been indebted to a contemporary account of a visit paid to the island in the course of a journey to Constantinople, undertaken in 1551 by the Lord of Aramont, French Ambassador to the Porte. Among those lords and knights accompanying him was the young French nobleman Nicolas de Nicolay, geographer to King Charles IX; in 1568 Nicolay published at Lyon a narrative of his journey in four books, which appeared in Thomas Washington's translation of 1585 as *The Navigations, Peregrinations and Voyages, Made Into Turkey*...Passages in *Tamburlaine* suggest that Marlowe knew this work, and while composing *The Jew* he might well have recalled from Nicolay...the exotic delights of Malta (which included a plethora of courtesans), the abortive Turkish assault on the island in 1551, and the subsequent siege of Tripoli at which Nicolay was present (an event which involved a stratagem to infiltrate the citadel by effecting an underground entry, a device to which Barabas has recourse in Act V Scene 1).[9]
>
> Marlowe was, however, in a position to have obtained information from other sources beside this. Public interest in Malta ran high in sixteenth-century England, particularly during and immediately after its heroic stand in the Great Siege. Michael Brennan has recently established the existence of at least two English-language newsletter accounts of the siege, though they survive in so fragmentary a state that little can be deduced about their contents or Marlowe's possible awareness of them. [10] The news of the Turks' withdrawal in September 1565 prompted Matthew Parker, Archbishop of Canterbury, to lay down a Form of Thanksgiving for six weeks, and Marlowe, who was later to be a Parker Scholar at Corpus Christi College, Cambridge, could perhaps have known of that. And the history of Malta was in one sense already intimately interconnected with the very location of Marlowe's profession, for the Master of the Revels, whose job it was to censor plays, had his office in the palace of Clerkenwell, historic home of the Order of St John in England. [11]
>
> Roma Gill outlines various possible sources for Marlowe's knowledge of the island, but feels that none of those so far known completely account for the level of his awareness:
>
> Most of this information was available in Marlowe's favourite atlas, the *Theatrum Orbis Terrarum* of Ortelius, which he had used to map the travels and conquests of Tamburlaine. But Malta is a tiny island...and it shows as only a speck in Ortelius's Mediterranean. Marlowe must have had access to some other source for what he knows of the island's topography. The earliest

of all known maps of Malta was drawn by a French knight, Jean Quintin. Its scope includes the 'other petty Iles' - Gozo, Comino, Cominotto, and Filfla - with which Malta is 'contemur'd' (V.iii.9), and it set the example for other sixteenth-century cartographers, who all give the same information (making it impossible to identify any one particular map as the one that Marlowe *must* have used). [12]

In this connection, it might well be worth noting that at the very start of the Great Siege Henry, 2nd baron Paget, commended by Puttenham for his poetic achievements, [13] sent 'a plat of Malta' from Venice to the Earl of Leicester, with an accompanying message still preserved in the Calendar of State Papers, Foreign. [14] It is worth bearing in mind that this kind of source, which has left so slightly-publicised an official record of its existence, might also have been available to Marlowe. Gill also postulates a possible personal connection:

> **"He could have read Malta's history in books - there were several in French, Italian, and Spanish, although little was written in English; and he might have acquired an appreciation of the island's geography through his skill as a map-reader. But books and maps alone cannot explain his interest...I would suggest that Marlowe's experiences as petty spy and go-between somehow equipped him with the insight he needed to create his own world in** *The Jew of Malta*.**"** [15]

This may well be so. There is, however, a more direct link between Marlowe's theatre world and the events dramatised in the play. ***The Jew of Malta* was written when Marlowe '"bore name to serve" Lord Strange as a play-maker', [16] and Lord Strange's uncle Sir Edward Stanley, implicated in a plot to rescue Mary, Queen of Scots in 1571 [*sic*, 1570] and 'listed as a recusant and a "dangerous person" in 1592', [17] is almost certainly identifiable with the Sir Edward Stanley who was one of the only two Englishmen in the relief force (known, because of its small size, as the 'piccolo siccorso') which the Chevalier de Robles brought to the aid of his beleaguered brethren in June 1565. [*WRONG! The one in Malta was Mr Edward, NOT Sir Edward. See Chapter XXII. Other (Sir) Edward Stanleys.* HM]** The 'piccolo siccorso' arrived on the island at a crucial stage in the siege, immediately after the fall of Fort St Elmo, key to the harbour of Marsamxett, a small and poorly-defended fortress which, quite contrary to Turkish expectations that it would fall in five days, had with desperate gallantry resisted for almost a month. . . . and the indigenous Maltese gave them complete support.

Sir Edward Stanley [*to repeat, NOT Sir Edward Stanley Sr, but Mr Stanley.* **HM]**, then, arrived at a vital turning-point of the siege. Spared the lingering horrors suffered by the indomitable defenders of St Elmo, spared too the discussions attendant on the Grand Master's agonised decision to leave them to their fate, spared the sight of the decapitated bodies, their hearts gouged out of their chests, which the current wafted across to St Angelo, **Sir Edward** served not in the living hell of the tiny, ruined fort but in a large, well-supplied garrison fired by furious determination and, thanks to the length of the resistance offered by St Elmo, a reasonable chance of survival, which improved significantly with every extra day they could hold out. When the Turks finally did abandon the siege in September, two and a half months after he arrived, **Sir Edward** also witnessed the withdrawal of their humiliated army, in poor morale and devastated by the loss of some of their ablest commanders, and the ensuing jubilation and thanksgiving of the Knights, the Maltese, and the Sicilians who had brought the final relief force. There is no indication of when he left the island, but he would surely have been aware that Grand Master La Valette had immediately begun making plans for its regeneration and for the foundation of the new capital, to bear his own name of Valletta. Since **Sir Edward did not die until 1609, he would presumably have been well able to give evidence of his experiences.** [*Wrong Sir Edward Stanley; wrong date of death.* HM]

When Marlowe wrote his play, then, he did so in the service of a patron whose own immediate family had significant experience of both the island of Malta in general and the Great Siege in particular, and for an audience who were likely to be well aware of the strategic and historic role that Malta had played. [18] I have dwelt at some length on the probable experiences of Sir Edward Stanley because they seem to me to overlap in some significant respects with Marlowe's dramatisations of the siege, which, intriguingly, is

represented in greater particularity towards its closing stages –precisely those which Sir Edward witnessed. Nevertheless, there is clearly no simple relationship of direct correspondence, if only because the outcome of real siege and fictional one are so radically different. It is these areas of similarity and difference between play-text and historical event which I now propose to trace.

(<marauder.millersville.edu/~resound/*vol1iss2/malta/malta2.html>

And so we end up where we started. With the best will in the world one must dismiss any thought that there is any realistic and provable possibility that Marlowe might have written some of Shakespeare's or his own plays (particularly *The Jew of Malta*) in Tong, Shropshire. Maybe other relevant details will come to light to allow the re-opening of this issue?

Appendix 3
Shakespeare's Dark Lady of the Sonnets –
Sir Edward's cousin-in-law Penelope Rich?

This has been included as a light-hearted spoof. And yet, when I read the novel *Black Jenny* (1992) several years ago, I found this identification of the Dark Lady of the Sonnets fascinating. She was Penelope Rich née Devereux. At the time I found her as good a candidate for the Dark Lady as any of the others proposed - if not better. Several years on, during my research on **Sir Thomas Stanley** and his son **Sir Edward Jr** of Winwick and Tong, I discovered that she was a fairly close relative - sister of a first cousin-in-law, to be precise. Her sister Dorothy Devereux was married to Henry Percy, 9th Earl of Northumberland, the 'Wizard Earl', first cousin of Lucy Percy, **Sir Edward Jr**'s wife. Lucy had grown up with her cousin Henry at Petworth in Sussex under the guardianship of her Uncle Henry, the 8th Earl. He had inherited this title from Lucy's father, his brother, after the latter was executed for treason in 1572 after the Rising of the North in 1569. Lucy's Catholic mother Anne née Somerset had already fled into exile with her youngest daughter and stayed in the Spanish Netherlands for the rest of her life. Her eldest daughters were left in England with Protestant uncle Henry. As far as can be deduced, Lucy always felt close to her cousin Henry, and presumably met his wife Dorothy when they married in 1594 (he was her second husband). One might presume that Lucy's husband (Sir) **Edward Stanley Jr** and Dorothy's sister Penelope were also there, or at least that they all met on many later occasions. Given that Shakespeare wrote the verse epitaphs for **Sir Edward Jr** and given Shakespeare's long connection with the Stanleys, as suggested in this book, it requires no great leap of imagination to envisage many occasions on which Shakespeare might have met Penelope Rich via the Stanley-Percy contacts and become her admirer.

The world of Shakespeare and his Dark Lady must remain in the realms of imagination, and it is appropriate that Dr Wilson presented his candidate in a novel. However, his research might well provide a useful point for further relevant research in the families involved. What is interesting in the current context is that Penelope Rich presents a 'realistic' candidate through her relationship to Lucy Percy Stanley. It should be added that two other aristocratic/upper gentry Dark Lady candidates of long standing present a similar relationship as 'cousins' to **Sir Edward Jr**: Elizabeth Vernon and Mary Fitton. **Sir Edward Jr**'s mother was Margaret Vernon of Derbyshire, and Elizabeth was from a branch of the same family. Mary Fitton's family from Gawsworth, Cheshire, was connected by marriage to many linked to the Stanleys. The same applies to one of the latest Dark Lady candidates, Margaret Radcliffe of Ordsall Hall, Salford (advocated by Georges Bourbaki of Munich, with one article online at *themissingsonnet155.blogspot.com*).

Interestingly, one of Mary Fitton's early supporters was George Bernard Shaw, who wrote a short play on the topic, *Dark Lady of the Sonnets*. His advocacy was rather

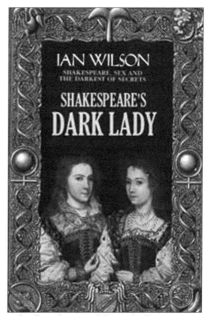

3a. Penelope and Dorothy Devereux
Was Penelope Rich née Devereux Shakespeare's 'Dark Lady'? In any case her sister Dorothy Devereux was married to Henry Percy, 9th Earl of Northumberland, the 'Wizard Earl', who grew up in the same household as his cousin Lucy Percy, wife of Sir Edward Stanley Jr.

light-hearted and readily abandoned when it was established that Mary Fitton had actually been fair-haired! He wrote an amusing account of this, in which one sentence leapt off the page (for me):

> . . . it is by exhausting all the hypotheses that we reach the verifiable one; and after all, the wrong road always leads somewhere.
>
> (George Bernard Shaw, *Dark Lady of the Sonnets*, 1910, Preface, p. 6.)

Maybe Penelope Rich is one of many such 'wrong roads' but this one certainly led somewhere, i.e. in revealing her in-law connection to **Sir Edward Jr**. For what it is worth, my money is on Penny as one of the best possible candidates and I thought she deserved a few pages. Given that Ian Wilson has meanwhile placed his novel online, available free for anyone interested, perhaps a mere reference would have been enough, but nevertheless the introduction appears here. Ian also receives my grateful thanks for permission to use his own Shakespeare portrait – the portrait reproduced on the cover of this book, dubbed the 'Old Player' portrait, for reasons revealed below. An art expert has established the date of painting as the early 1700s, therefore presumably a copy of an earlier portrait. On the website this is intriguingly reversed and placed next to the Chandos portrait for comparison. The cover of his book conveniently provides portraits of Dorothy and Penelope Devereux. The words in **bold** below are as in the online text.

Shakespeare's Dark Lady - a novel by Ian Wilson
Shakespeare's Dark Lady uncovered...

Ian Wilson's novel reveals all the evidence that has led him to solve an enduring mystery by identifying Shakespeare's Dark Lady as the powerful Elizabethan courtesan Lady Penelope Rich.
'A first novel of considerable scientific and historical erudition, entertaining and thought-provoking.'
Anthony Burgess

A woman in search of the identity of Shakespeare's Dark Lady
A man in search of a living descendant of Shakespeare in a bastard line

This novel, first published by HarperCollins under the title *Black Jenny* and now published for the first time on the Internet, explores Shakespeare, sex and the darkest of secrets when past and present meet in an explosive love story.

Author Dr Ian Wilson has come up with a startling theory in *Shakespeare's Dark Lady*, a novel about the love-life of a fictional Shakespeare scholar, Amelia Hungerford. Through Amelia's story, Ian Wilson demonstrates that the Dark Lady was none other than Penelope Rich - the most powerful courtesan of her day and the first cousin of Queen Elizabeth I.

She was born Penelope Devereux around 1563, the daughter of the first Earl of Essex. By her marriage to Lord Robert Rich in 1581 she became Penelope Rich and acquired a surname which would become a favourite pun for many poets. As Stella in Sir Philip Sidney's *Astrophel* and *Stella* sonnets, her name has already survived as more than just a literary footnote.

It is true that Penelope Rich has been put forward before as a possible Dark Lady. There were tentative suggestions from the 1860s up to the 1920s based on the way in which Shakespeare, like some of his contemporaries, repeatedly plays on the name Rich in the plays and 14 times in the *Sonnets*. There was no conclusive evidence, however, and Penelope seemed an unlikely mistress for a humble Stratford player.

On 3 September 1594, a curious narrative poem in 72 cantos was registered at Stationer's Hall in London. It bore the title *Willoughby his Avisa or The True Picture of a **Modest** Maid and of a **Chaste** and **Constant** Wife*.

Canto 44 introduces two of the lecherous suitors of Avisa, the ostensibly virtuous maid and subsequently wife of the title. The first is said to be '***H.W.***' and:
'*...**his familiar friend W.S.**, who not long before had tried the courtesy of the like passion and*

was now newly recovered of the like infection.'

The writer goes on to ask '*whether it would sort to a happier end for this **new actor** than it did for the **old player**.*'

For over a century, Shakespeare scholars have speculated excitedly about the identity of H.W. and W.S. The cuckold's horns decorating the *Avisa's* frontispiece and the lampooning tone of the poem leave little doubt that it is a caricature sending up the adultery of a well-known woman. If Penelope Rich was the object of the attack, this was less than clear to many readers in 1594, which is probably why another short poem entitled *The Victory of English **Chastity** under the Feigned Name of Avisa*, was appended to the 1596 edition. Penelope Rich was the most famous adulteress of her day and her relationship with Sir Charles **Bl(o)unt**, now Lord **Mountjoy**, was all but public knowledge by 1595. This latest poem would have left fewer doubts in contemporary readers' minds as to which woman it was alluding to.

It seemed obvious to commentators on the poem, in which first W.S. and then H.W. attempts unsuccessfully to seduce the temptingly chaste Avisa, that they need only identify the real-life model and they would have solved the riddle of the *Sonnets*, in which first Shakespeare and then his 'Friend' share the carnal charms of the Dark Lady.

In Dr Wilson's own words: 'In the course of my research in the British Library two lines from the *Avisa* suddenly jumped off the page at me. I re-read them to be sure.':
*Yet if you know a bird so **base***
*In this **devise** she hath no place*
'The words come from the *Avisa's* introductory poem, *The Victory of English Chastity*. I knew that *devise* in French could mean a motto, so it might well have meant the same in 16th century English. If I was right, and Penelope Rich was Avisa, her motto would incorporate the word '*base*' or '*basis*'. The Elizabethans loved such word puzzles.

'It took less than five minutes to find what I wanted in the heraldry section. There, in an 18th century leather-bound folio of ancient heraldic emblems and mottos, I found the motto of Penelope's family – the Devereux family:
Basis Virtutum Constantia (The Basis of Virtue is Constancy)

'I thought of the '***Constant Wife***' of the *Avisa's* title. But here before my eyes was ***Basis*** – the very word I had expected if my hunch was correct. From that point on, other clues almost fell out of the *Avisa* to identify her as Penelope Rich. Allusions to Lord **Mountjoy's** name abound in *The Victory of English Chastity*, not least in '***the mounting phoenix***' (a mount was Elizabethan slang for a prostitute, so Charles Bl(o)unt's name lent itself admirably to bawdy innuendo).

'Penelope Rich conceived a child while Blunt was overseas. Ostensibly it was still-born at Leighs Priory, Lord Rich's Essex home, in May 1594. Bl(o)unt had meanwhile returned to England early in 1594 to take up a new post as chief military officer at Portsmouth. Logically the father was neither Lord Rich, from whom Penelope was estranged, nor Charles Bl(o)unt. The question arises: who was the father, and was the child genuinely stillborn? Might it not have been born healthy and the rumour of a stillbirth spread about to avoid a scandal? This is the question I ask in *Shakespeare's Dark Lady*, in which a Harvard Shakespeare scholar, Amelia Hungerford, seeks the answer using genetic fingerprinting to try and trace a living descendant of the Bard.

'Penelope saw herself as a patroness of the arts. A dalliance, but nothing more, with the social-climbing Bard and then Henry Willoughby does not seem beyond the bounds of possibility for this woman with the reputation of a hot-blooded vamp. Nor is it implausible that she dropped Shakespeare like the proverbial hot potato when his *Rape of Lucrece* was published. The virtuous Lucrece of the title could well be Penelope in disguise, and the rapist Tarquin Penelope's lover Lord Mountjoy. The scandalous *Avisa* only made matters worse.'

This is the story of Shakespeare, Willoughby and Penelope Rich as Dr Wilson tells it in *Shakespeare's Dark Lady*, where he also proposes a new key to unlock the mysteries of the *Sonnets*.

~~~~~~~~~~~~~~~~

Appendix 4
SPOOF: Did Sir Edward Stanley write Shakespeare, or collaborate?

If anyone were to be hunting around for yet another daft Shakespeare Alternative Authorship Candidate, at least as a contributor to group authorship, they might consider **Sir Edward Stanley Jr** of Winwick (Lancashire), Tong (Shropshire) and Eynsham (Oxfordshire), of the family of the Earls of Derby (Lancashire), who died and was buried at Eynsham (Oxfordshire) and who had relatives all over the Midlands (even including some Stanleys in Stratford!) and might even have owned an estate in Warwickshire.

I hope that the title of this Appendix has made it very clear that I have no doubt at all that Shakespeare wrote Shakespeare: THIS IS A SPOOF. I hope that this book has made it very clear that my research has led me to believe, however, that young **Edward Stanley** and young William Shakeshafte/Shakespeare almost certainly knew each other from youth onwards, and that they knew each other well enough for Shakespeare to dash off the Stanley Verse Epitaphs for **Sir Edward**, for the Stanley tomb in Tong in the making, or just completed. We are talking here about 1601-4, probably in London. **Sir Edward**, from his grave, might consider it a slight insult that he has not been proposed before now as an Alternative Candidate, even if only in fun.

Previously proposed candidates mentioned in my text below are in **bold**. These come from the list of 24 'Sole or principal authors' or 37 'Contributors to a group authorship' in John Michell, *Who Wrote Shakespeare?* (1996). He also considered the whole matter as a joke but out of them all, his favourite was William Stanley (private communication). And William Stanley, 6th Earl of Derby, was **Sir Edward**'s first cousin, so one could not come much closer. Sadly John Michell died in 2009 (obituaries online). I think he would have enjoyed this SPOOF. His total number of candidates in 1996 came to 61. I believe the number has since risen to over 80!

He would also have enjoyed my including his lists in a review in German of German Roland Emmerich's film *Anonymous* (released September 2011, November 2011 in Germany) in the German magazine *Synesis* Nr. 2/2012. In this I gave a brief overview of the history of the proposals of the main candidates and my opinion of the film, in which Edward de Vere, 17th Earl of Oxford was presented as the author of all of Shakespeare's works. In brief: excellent cinematography, particularly the views of London c.1600, but so many flashbacks to five and forty years previously often left me confused, as did so many 'unhistorical' dates and events. No one but committed Oxfordians could accept the figure of William Shakespeare portrayed in the film as an illiterate buffoon. I particularly regretted the non-appearance of William Stanley, who was married to Elizabeth de Vere, eldest daughter of the main protagonist Edward de Vere. My assessment of the best result to come out of the film was the online Shakespeare Authorship Campaign organised by the Shakespeare Birthplace Trust, including the freebook *Shakespeare Bites Back!* by Stanley Wells and Paul Edmondson. Happily for them, the film was a box-office flop.

Germany plays a rather special role in Shakespeare Studies. Its Romantic writers in the early 19th century were amongst the first to accept Shakespeare as an inspiration and icon; the Deutsche Shakespeare-Gesellschaft/German Shakespeare Society/Association, founded in 1864 in Weimar, is the oldest in the world (the British Shakespeare Association is celebrating its 10th anniversary in 2012 and the Shakespeare Association of America was founded in 1972); and it is the home of one of the largest research libraries in the world dedicated to Shakespeare: the Shakespeare-Forschungsbibliothek at the Ludwig Maximilian University of Munich. Although the German Shakespeare academic community is solidly **Stratfordian**, Germany has, rather interestingly, produced several recent **anti-Stratfordians:**

Oxfordians Roland Emmerich with his film *Anonymous* (2011) and Kurt Kreiler with his book *Der Mann, der Shakespeare erfand* (Insel Verlag, 2009), English translation, *Anonymous Shakespeare: the Man Behind* (Doeling und Galitz Verlag, 2011).

Marlovians Georges Bourbaki *Der Nachruf oder: Es war doch dieser Schlawiner Marlowe* (Eigenverlag, München, 2003), who wrote an article on the subject in *Synesis* Nr. 2/2005. Also Bastian Conrad, *Christopher Marlowe: der wahre Shakespeare* (Buch&media, 2011).

My recommended reading on the subject for any doubters was/is James Shapiro, *Contested Will: Who wrote Shakespeare?* (Simon and Schuster, hardback 2010; Faber and Faber, paperback 2011.) This relates – rather sympathetically - the whole history of the Baconian and Oxfordian theories, followed by all the evidence that leaves virtually the whole of the Shakespeare academic world as Stratfordians.

A Comedy of Errors?

During the course of the twentieth century about sixty others were proposed as principal or group authors. A useful listing of these appeared in John Michell, *Who Wrote Shakespeare?* (Thames and Hudson, 1996, paperback 1998), pp. 37, 38.

* indicates characters who appear named and with speaking roles in *Anonymous*. Some/all of the others might be detected anonymously in the court and theatre scenes.

Sole or principal authors	
William Shakspere*	Henry Wriothesley, Earl of Southampton*
Francis Bacon, Lord Verulam	Cardinal Wolsey
Edward de Vere, Earl of Oxford*	Robert Cecil, Earl of Salisbury*
William Stanley, Earl of Derby	Robert Burton
Roger Manners, Earl of Rutland	Sir John Barnard
Sir Walter Ralegh	Sir Edward Dyer
Christopher Marlowe*	Charles Blunt, Lord Mountjoy, Earl of Devon
Anthony Bacon	Queen Elizabeth*
Michael Angelo Florio	Sir William Alexander, Earl of Stirling
Robert Devereux, 2nd Earl of Essex*	John Richardson of Temple Grafton
William Butts	Anne Whateley
Sir Anthony Shirley	John Williams, Archbishop of York

Contributions to a group authorship		
Barnabe Barnes	John Florio	Mary Sidney, Countess of Pembroke
Richard Barnfield	Robert Greene	William Herbert, Earl of Pembroke
Richard Burbage*	Bartholomew Griffin	Henry Porter
Henry Chettle	Thomas Heywood	Elizabeth Sidney, Countess of Rutland
Samuel Daniel	King James I*	Sir Philip Sidney
Thomas Dekker*	Ben Jonson*	Wentworth Smythe
John Donne, Dean of St Paul's	Thomas Kyd	Edmund Spenser*
Thomas Sackville, Lord Buckhurst, Earl of Dorset	Thomas Lodge	Richard Vaughan, Bishop of London
	John Lyly	William Warner
Sir Francis Drake	Thomas Middleton	Thomas Watson
Michael Drayton	Anthony Munday	John Webster
Walter Devereux, 1st Earl of Essex	Thomas Nashe*	Robert Wilson
Henry Ferrers	Henry, Lord Paget	
John Fletcher	George Peele	

Since 1999 several more candidates have appeared, bringing the current total to 77.

(Helen Moorwood, 'The film *Anonymous*, producer/director Roland Emmerich or Once more unto the breach, dear friends (*Henry V*): Who was Shakespeare?' *Synesis* Nr. 2/2012.)

I now propose, jokingly, Shakespeare Alternative Authorship Candidate Number 78 (or 81?). (A belated google search shows Wikipedia presenting 80 in alphabetical order but, of course, **Sir Edward Stanley** is not amongst them.) Consider the case for **Sir Edward** (and the counter-arguments):

1. His is the only tomb in England, apart from **Shakespeare**'s gravestone at Stratford, to bear an epitaph by Shakespeare. It even has two epitaphs, twice as many as Shakespeare himself! (The other four, covered by Honigmann in *Shakespeare: the 'lost years'*, remained on paper and never made it to a tomb, or at least not to one that has survived.) This seems to prove, somehow, that the two men knew each other. It has generally been accepted that Shakespeare wrote his own epitaph; why could **Sir Edward** not have written his own, but put it about disguised as from Shakespeare the dramatist's hand? Or vice versa? One snag here is that the venerable historian Sir William Dugdale wrote in 1663 that 'the following verses were made by William Shakespeare, the late famous tragedian', with no hint that **Sir Edward** might have been involved in the composition of the verses for himself and his father.

2. He was an exact contemporary of Shakespeare's, so there are no problems, as with other candidates, that he was born or died much too early: **Sir Edward** was born in mid to late-1562 and Shakespeare in early 1564; William died in 1616 after a few years of retirement, whereas **Sir Edward** lived until 1632, which would only mean that he had a much longer period of retirement from play-writing, like his cousin William Stanley, 6th Earl of Derby, (1561-1642) who actually was a recorded playwright c.1600.

3. Most people doubting the authorship of Shakespeare's Works by Shakespeare have rested their case on the playwright's obvious knowledge of court life, many books and many other countries: impossible for the son of a humble glover, in a town without books, who is never known to have travelled abroad, etc. etc., or words and arguments to that effect. **Sir Edward**, as grandson of an earl, was certainly out of the top drawer and was closely related to several other candidates, particularly the earls who have been previously proposed. They, in their desire for anonymity, could have chosen someone who would be even more anonymous and passed their work to him, to pass on to his friend William Shakespeare the actor. Or might **Sir Edward** thus become merely a member in another Group Theory?

4. The most important of these earls is his first cousin, **William Stanley, 6th Earl of Derby**, a candidate, whom he regularly visited in Lancashire and who stayed with him at Eynsham. Like **Sir Edward**, he was an exact contemporary of Shakespeare's: born in 1561 and died in 1642, which would have meant an even longer retirement from the theatre. This William is known to have written plays and might have been the author of some W.S. poems, which – very significantly (!?) – he preferred to keep anonymous. He had also travelled widely in Europe and the Middle East in his youth and we know he spoke fluent French. He could have passed all his best work to his cousin **Sir Edward**, a good friend of William Shakespeare the actor.

5. William Stanley's wife was Elizabeth de Vere, daughter of **Edward de Vere, 17th Earl of Oxford**, another candidate. If there is any truth in his having written plays that were passed off as by William Shakespeare, then to protect his own anonymity de Vere could easily have passed all his work to his daughter's husband's first cousin **Sir Edward**, friend of William Shakespeare, the actor. After Earl Edward de Vere died in 1604, **Sir Edward** continued to write on his own, without the help of material from Oxford.

6. William Stanley's brother, and therefore also **Sir Edward**'s first cousin, was Ferdinando, Lord Strange, later 5th Earl of Derby, whose writings, including plays and poetry, were much admired at the time and who was the patron of Lord Strange's Men, who performed Shakespeare's early plays and in which company Shakespeare himself might well have acted. It is perhaps surprising that Ferdinando himself has not been proposed as a candidate. This is probably because there is no doubt that he was poisoned and buried in 1594, which would make it difficult to account for all the plays known to have been first acted way beyond this date. (Not that this has deterred Marlovian enthusiasts from claiming that Christopher Marlowe survived his own death by murder in 1593.) However, first Ferdinando and then his brother William could have passed their work on to their cousin **Sir Edward**, who was thus the immediate recipient, if not the actual author of all of 'Shakespeare's' plays.

7. Alice née Spencer, Countess of Derby and widow of Ferdinando, was a known patron of poets and a kinswoman of **Edmund Spenser**. After her husband's death in 1594 and Spenser's in 1599, she could easily have continued to find unpublished writings of both of them and passed them on to her former husband's cousin, **Sir Edward**, for him to rework them before passing them on to his friend Shakespeare for performance.

8. **Edmund Spenser** was a protégé of **Sir Philip Sidney**, an accomplished sonneteer whose sonnets in manuscript form were much admired by contemporaries. The latter was mortally wounded at the battle of Zutphen in 1586, but also present at Zutphen was another Edward Stanley, knighted by the Earl of Leicester, who could have delivered Sidney's sonnets in manuscript form and his latest writings in the Netherlands to his kinsman (**Sir**) **Edward Jr** back in England. This might even have been the beginning of Edward Stanley's ingenious plan to rework some of these and then feed them to young Shakespeare, the actor from Stratford who was soon to make a name for himself, even before his arrival in the capital, by plagiarising others' work. **Robert Greene**'s diatribe in 1592 about 'Shakescene' as an 'upstart crow' would fit in here.

9. **Mary Sidney, Countess of Pembroke**, Sir Philip's sister and a noted poetess, could easily be accommodated here, particularly because a later descendant claimed to have seen a letter by her inviting James I to stay at Wilton, with the added incentive that 'the man Shakespeare' was with them. She and her husband, **Henry Herbert, 2nd Earl of Pembroke**, were, of course, the parents of both of the dedicatees of Shakespeare's *First Folio* in 1623. The Pembrokes might well have had **Sir Edward Stanley** staying with them at the same time as Shakespeare and King James, which would have allowed another bit of conspiracy about future publications under Shakespeare's name. And their son Philip Herbert, 1st Earl of Montgomery, was married to Susan de Vere, sister of Elizabeth de Vere, wife of William Stanley, **Sir Edward Jr**'s first cousin, etc. etc. He himself wrote poetry and has in any case been seriously proposed as the 'Fair Youth' of Shakespeare's Sonnets. Shakespeare's *First Folio* was dedicated to him and his brother William Herbert, 3rd Earl of Pembroke. He could easily have collaborated with his brother-in-law William Stanley and his cousin **Sir Edward Jr**.

10. This Wilton incident would allow another meeting between **King James** and Shakespeare, already an actor in the King's Men. They would have had the opportunity, in the country and away from the hectic life in London, to discuss how their collaboration could or should continue. This might have been the time when Shakespeare confessed to the king that he was merely a 'front man' for his friend **Sir Edward Stanley** (who was also in the house party?). James had already created **Sir Edward** a Knight of the Bath at his coronation.

11. **Elizabeth Sidney, Countess of Rutland**, could easily be worked in here with the other Sidneys, because she was the only daughter of Sir Philip Sidney and married to **Roger Manners, 5th Earl of Rutland**. His main credentials were given in the earlier chapter on the Earls of Rutland, with his relationship to Dorothy Vernon, **Edward Stanley**'s aunt. His death in 1612 coincided neatly, but not quite, with the end of the first performance of Shakespeare's last masterpieces. Could Elizabeth have continued to collaborate on the last few works by herself and her husband with **Sir Edward**?

12. The main public claim to fame in the Shakespearean context of **Henry Wriothesley, 3rd Earl of Southampton**, was that he was the dedicatee of Shakespeare's two long poems in 1593 and 1594. It was seen above that he was a close friend of several other earls with easy access to Shakespeare and **Sir Edward Stanley Sr and Jr**. He was at Cambridge with Rutland in 1587. They both joined **Robert Devereux, 2nd Earl of Essex** on some of his campaigns: on the expedition to the Azores in 1597 and Ireland in 1599. Southampton was married to Elizabeth Vernon, lady-in-waiting to Queen Elizabeth, from Hodnet in Shropshire, so she was presumably in close contact with her Vernon kinswoman in Tong Margaret Vernon, **Sir Thomas Stanley**'s wife and **Sir Edward**'s mother. Elizabeth Vernon, incidentally and as a reminder, was one of the early candidates for the Dark Lady of Shakespeare's Sonnets.

13. Another aristocratic candidate for the Dark Lady is Penelope Rich, sister of **Robert Devereux, 2nd Earl of Essex**, whose sister Dorothy was married to Henry Percy, 9th Earl of Northumberland, the 'Wizard Earl', cousin and childhood companion of Lucy Percy, **Sir Edward**'s wife. (See Appendix 3.)

14. The first widely publicised candidate in the 19th century, interestingly, was Mary Fitton of Derbyshire, en route between **Sir Edward**'s journeys from Shropshire to Lancashire, so it would be easy to see her meeting **Sir Edward** on occasion. In fact, it would be easy to claim that **Sir Edward** knew all the upper gentry and aristocratic candidates for the Dark Lady! He was, after all, related to several of them.

15. **Thomas Sackville, Lord Buckhurst, 1ˢᵗ Earl of Dorset**, presents an intriguing link to **Sir Edward**. His grandson Richard, 3ʳᵈ Earl of Dorset, was one of the greatest admirers of Venetia Stanley, **Sir Edward**'s daughter (as we read in the extract from Aubrey, although some suspect he might have been confused with his brother Edward, 4ᵗʰ Earl). If **Sir Edward** met Earl Richard when the latter was visiting Venetia at Eynsham, he might well have met his grandfather earlier. Timing is a little shaky here, because Richard (or brother Edward?) cannot have started visiting Venetia before she was, say, about sixteen, which was in 1616, after Shakespeare had retired from the theatre and died. No doubt ingenuity could explain this away.

16. Finally to a few poets and playwrights. **Christopher Marlowe** is dealt with in Appendix 2. Was Christopher Marlowe ever in Shropshire?

17. **Ben Jonson** wrote a poem about Venetia Stanley, thus proving that he knew her father **Sir Edward**. In this case maybe **Sir Edward** and Ben collaborated on the plays that were performed and published under Shakespeare's name, rather than Ben's own. One snag here is that Jonson was Shakespeare's friend, was with him for a drinking bout shortly before he died and wrote glowingly in praise of him in the *First Folio*. He also published all his works under his own name, so is hardly likely to have allowed them to be published under someone else's.

18. **Michael Drayton**, from Warwickshire, travelled all over England collecting material for his long poem *Polyalbion*. He was a good friend of Christopher Middleton, who dedicated *Chinon* to **Sir Edward** in 1597. He would have had ample opportunity when passing through the Midlands to visit **Sir Edward** at Tong Castle and hand over his latest writings for him to work on before passing them back to his friend Shakespeare for his signature. The main snag is that Drayton also published his works under his own name.

19. **Barnabe Barnes** had to escape from London after a misdemeanour, so would not have dared to use his own name from then on, particularly as his father was the Bishop of Durham. When fleeing to the North (to his father's native Chester?), what better place to stop off than Tong Castle to visit **Sir Edward Stanley**, who would act as middleman before passing on his work for performance and publication by Shakespeare. The main snag, again, is that Barnes published under his own name until his death in 1609.

20. **Samuel Daniel** was tutor to Lady Anne Clifford, daughter of George Clifford, 3ʳᵈ Earl of Cumberland. The latter's sister Margaret Clifford married Henry, 4ᵗʰ Earl of Derby, brother of **Sir Thomas Stanley** of Tong, father of **Sir Edward**. Through this connection **Sir Edward** could easily have received Daniel's best work, reworked it, and handed it on to Shakespeare for performance. The main snag here, yet again, is that Daniel published many works under his own name.

21. John Weever dedicated *Faunus and Melliflora* to **Sir Edward Stanley** in 1600. This would have been in gratitude to him for acting as a middleman for other works he or his aristocratic friends had written, which he/they wished to keep anonymous; **Sir Edward** would have expanded and reshaped these and handed them on to Shakespeare.

Where should we stop? Here is as good a place as any. I do hope that the above is taken in the spirit in which it was intended, as a light-hearted romp though a batty theory, but one, nevertheless, rather less loony than many other candidatures. Apart from Ferdinando and his widow Countess Alice, Lady Anne Clifford and John Weever (potential candidates for yet more Alternative Authors in future), all the **above in bold** have been seriously proposed. One big snag in developing this theory of **Sir Edward**'s role is that there is no surviving record that **Sir Edward** ever wrote anything, not even a letter – although his wife is depicted on her tomb reading. I am sure this problem could be overcome somehow with a little ingenuity. While writing the above, I almost came to believe in his candidature, but would lack the ingenuity required to weave all the contacts and connections to **Sir Edward** into a homogenous whole, centred on him as 'the real Shakespeare'.

There was, however, a serious purpose in grouping all these Alternative Authorship Candidates together. They were all either directly associated with **Sir Edward**, or could easily have been, as mentioned above. He does, therefore, seem to have emerged as a character, rather neglected until now, who might well on occasion have been part of various circles bumping into other circles, all of whom were connected to Shakespeare. He might even have struck up a close friendship with Shakespeare. One requires at least some such explanation for the very existence of the Verse Epitaphs at Tong and the knowledge by Sir William Dugdale one generation later (and several others before him) that the verse epitaphs written for **Sir Edward** were indeed by William Shakespeare.

4a. Sir Edward Stanley
Obviously he did not write Shakespeare's works, but he does have the unique distinction that Shakespeare wrote the only epitaphs for him that can still be seen today.

4b. Shakespeare 'Old Player' portrait
Art experts have dated this to the early 1700s. A juxtaposition (reversed) with the Chandos portrait is given on the Dark Lady website, suggesting that the later may well be a copy of the earlier, one of only two portraits of Shakespeare judged as authentic.

www.shakespearesdarklady.com © Ian Wilson

4c. Edward de Vere,
17th Earl of Oxford, 1575
The current 'loudest' Shakespeare Alternative Authorship Candidate among around 80! Hero of Roland Emmerich's film *Anonymous*, 2011. Of the generation of Sir Thomas Stanley, his eldest daughter Elizabeth de Vere married William Stanley, 6th Earl of Derby, Sir Edward Stanley Jr's first cousin.

Appendix 5
Shakespeare in Lancashire
by Peter Milward SJ
(Renaissance Pamphlets 22, April 1, 2000)

The following article is now more than a decade old, but still serves admirably as an introduction to the 'Shakespeare in Lancashire' or 'Lancastrian Shakespeare' theory, for anyone to whom this is new. Much has been written about this theory since, and it has been incorporated into numerous Shakespeare biographies written in the twenty-first century, but all have basically taken as their source the information contained here, without adding any new facts. The 'new basics' connecting Shakespeare to Lancashire, as presented in this book, which expand on Professor Milward SJ's presentation, are given in footnotes by myself. He is a Jesuit, a retired Professor and the Founder and President of the Renaissance Institute at Sophia University, Tokyo. He can also be called the main advocate for 'Catholic Shakespeare', to which 'Shakespeare in Lancashire' is a vital corollary. We met him briefly in Appendix 1. Was Shakespeare ever in Shropshire?, with his fellow Jesuit Father Thomas Conlan.

An academic conference on Shakespeare, of a wholly unique kind, was held at Lancaster University [from July 21-24, 1999]. Its very theme, 'Lancastrian Shakespeare', was unique, considering how few Shakespeare scholars there are even today who admit that the dramatist was ever in the county of Lancashire. But there is a theory that has been steadily gaining ground, particularly with the publication of Professor E. A. J. Honigmann's study on *Shakespeare: the 'lost years'* in 1985,[i] that the young William Shakespeare is to be identified with the William Shakeshafte mentioned in the will of Alexander Hoghton of Lea Hall[ii] which was drawn up in August 1581 a few months before the testator's death that year.

I need not go into the pages of evidence assembled by Professor Honigmann in support of this theory, which goes back to the 1930s and which had already won the support of not a few scholars, including the late Sir E. K. Chambers, well before the time of Honigmann – while incurring the strong antagonism of Shakespeare's leading biographer in modern times, Samuel Schoenbaum (in his *William Shakespeare: A Compact Documentary Life*, 1977). It is enough for me here to touch on the interesting implication of the theory: that it supports the on-going Catholicism of the young Shakespeare several years before his first appearance in London about the year 1592 as a fully-fledged dramatist, and an object of professional jealousy to other, established dramatists of the time, such as Robert Greene and Christopher Marlowe.[iii]

I say 'on-going Catholicism', since the religious allegiance of both his parents, John Shakespeare and Mary Arden,[iv] namely, their adherence even under persecution to the 'old faith', has already won general recognition in the field of Shakespearian scholarship. Even at Stratford, and the grammar school there, the young William was by no means subjected to a religious training that was - according to Schoenbaum (p. 55) – 'orthodox and Protestant'. After all, Queen Elizabeth had only succeeded to the throne in 1558 and her Protestant policy for England, ratified by a subservient Parliament in 1559, had hardly time enough to impose itself on the devoted allegiance of her subjects by the time William was of an age to profit from the education offered at the local school.

As for this education, consider the probable religious allegiance of the schoolmasters appointed to teach at the grammar school, all with university degrees from 'Oxford, that proverbial home for "lost causes"', such as the Catholic cause was now coming to appear. When William was seven, he would have come under the rod of Simon Hunt, probably the same Simon Hunt (though there is one other man of that name in the area to provide an alternative candidate) who defected - with one of the students, Robert Debdale – in 1575 for the English seminary at Douai (founded in 1568 by William Allen),[v] and who subsequently made his way to Rome to enter the Society of Jesus in 1578. The event must have made quite an impression on the mind of a young lad of twelve, and it has even been suggested - though without any positive evidence - that he accompanied his master and fellow student to Douai. Debdale returned to his native country in 1582 as a seminary priest, and he was put to death as a 'traitor' for complicity in the Babington Plot in 1586.[vi] Hunt remained in Italy as a Jesuit and died in 1585.

The successor of Hunt as schoolmaster was a Thomas Jenkins, who is interesting for my present purpose as having been a fellow with the great Jesuit saint and martyr Edmund Campion[vii] during the 1560s, when they were both at St. John's College, Oxford.[viii] At that time Campion was the darling not just of his own college but also at the university as a whole, and he had attracted the favourable attention of the Queen and her favourite Robert Dudley, Earl of Leicester,[ix] on the occasion of her state visit to the university in 1566. No doubt, Jenkins had many an anecdote to tell his students at Stratford concerning Campion at Oxford and his subsequent defection to Rome and the Society of Jesus - following the same pilgrim route as Simon Hunt, to Douai in 1571, Rome in 1572 and the Society of Jesus in 1573.

Jenkins was in turn succeeded as schoolmaster by his Oxford friend, John Cottam in 1579. Cottam, a Lancashire man from much the same neighbourhood as the above-mentioned Alexander Hoghton,[x] was brother to Thomas Cottam, a seminary priest who came over to England about the same time and in the same group as the two Jesuits, Robert Persons and Edmund Campion, in June 1580. Thomas, who came with a letter from Robert Debdale for his Stratford relatives, was arrested almost immediately on his arrival and so never had an opportunity of visiting those relatives or his brother at Stratford. As for John, his tenure of office at Stratford lasted only till 1582, the very year of his brother's martyrdom at Tyburn, in succession to Campion who had suffered the same fate on December 1, 1581. In any case, it is doubtful if William Shakespeare would have been taught by him, since he was already fifteen in 1579 and of an age to look for further education or employment. In this respect, John Cottam might well have arrived at Stratford at the right time to give him and his concerned parents useful advice, on behalf not only of the Shakespeares but also of his former neighbour in Lancashire, Alexander Hoghton, who is known to have employed young Catholic tutors for his household, whether at Lea Hall on the river Ribble or at the newly built Hoghton Tower a little further inland from Preston. And so Cottam provides us with the necessary link between William Shakespeare of Stratford and William Shakeshafte of Lea Hall.

Now we may return to Edmund Campion, who had by this time moved as a young Jesuit from Rome to Prague, where he spent a few years teaching the classics to the boys at the Jesuit college there - composed at least three Latin plays for them, including one that has come down to us under the title of *Ambrosia* on the famous episode involving St. Ambrose and the emperor Theodosius. When the English mission of the Jesuits was approved by the Father General Everard Mercurian, at the strong insistence of William Allen, Campion was chosen to accompany Robert Persons on this dangerous enterprise. Unlike their companion, Thomas Cottam, the two Jesuits managed to elude the vigilance of spies at the port and to reach London; and from the capital they made their several ways through the provinces - Campion proceeding by way of the Midlands to the many recusant houses in Yorkshire and Lancashire. Something is known of Campion's itinerary as a result of his examination under torture in the Tower of London during the summer of 1581; and so we know that one of his hosts was Sir William Catesby of Lapworth in Warwickshire, some 10 miles to the North of Stratford along what is now the A34.[xi]

There is, moreover, some interesting evidence that on this occasion Campion met Shakespeare's father John, and possibly the young William, too; since one of the major items of evidence that John was a Catholic is his proven possession of a *Spiritual Testament*, such as Campion and Persons had received from the saintly archbishop of Milan, Charles Borromeo, on their way from Rome to England,[xii] for distribution among English Catholics who wished to affirm their loyalty to the Catholic faith in case of sudden death. John's copy of this testament was only discovered in the eighteenth century, in the course of repairs being made to the birthplace on Henley Street; and its authenticity, at first doubted, was only proved to the satisfaction of Shakespeare scholars early in this century. As for the way he came into the possession of this document, what more likely way than a visit to the nearby Lapworth through the introduction of Thomas Cottam's brother John?[xiii] Then William, already sixteen, may well have accompanied him – if he was still at Stratford[xiv] – as a former pupil of Simon Hunt, as a fellow student of Robert Debdale, and as an acquaintance of John Cottam, already perhaps recommended by him to Alexander Hoghton of Lea Hall.

Then from Lapworth we may follow this 'papist and his poet',[xv] the Jesuit and the hopeful dramatist, on their respective ways Northwards: Campion on a twisting road stopping at many recusant houses in Northamptonshire, Derbyshire and Yorkshire, before crossing the Pennines to Lancashire about Eastertime 1581; the young Shakespeare more directly to Lea Hall in Lancashire, perhaps by the early autumn of 1580. As for Campion's residence in Lancashire, it was - as it had been in Yorkshire, according to the evidence extracted from him in the tower - not one but many; and of those many not the least was the house of Alexander's half-brother Richard Hoghton, at Park Hall, near Charnock Richard,[xvi] to the South of Preston, over 10 miles whether from Lea Hall or from Hoghton Tower. It was at Park Hall that Campion had many of the books he used in writing his Latin challenge to the Anglicans, *Rationes Decem*, which he distributed on the seats of St. Mary's church in Oxford that summer. There he remained, while presumably visiting other places in the neighbourhood till Whitsun; and during that time he would have been available for meetings with William, now known as Shakeshafte,[xvii] from Lea Hall - or was it Hoghton Tower?

Only, what evidence is there that the young Shakespeare met the Jesuit Edmund Campion in Lancashire at this time? In the first place, if William had met Campion at Lapworth - whether personally or indirectly through his father John - he might well have informed the other of his plan to stay with the Hoghtons in the near future and learned of Campion's own intention of visiting that family in Lancashire.[xviii] Secondly, it is likely that William would have told the other of his interest in drama, with the probability of furthering this interest in Alexander Hoghton's household, as being one of the tasks committed to a tutor; and so he could have learnt of Campion's past experience in composing Latin plays for his boys at Prague. Thirdly, Campion may well have noted in the young William a suitable recipient of the Spiritual Exercises, one of the principal weapons in the armoury of Jesuits for their spiritual task of winning England back to the fold of the Catholic Church. So it must have seemed providential to both men that they would be staying in the same district of Lancashire, under the auspices of the same Hoghton family, about the same time - from Easter to Whitsun, 1581.

On his arrival at Lea Hall – or Hoghton Tower - possibly in the early autumn of 1580, William Shakeshafte, as he now chose to be known since the name was more familiar to people in that part of England,[xix] would have found his duties not just limited to the task of teaching children in the household, but positively encouraging him in the exercise of his dramatic interests. The former task is attested to by the tradition going back to his colleague Christopher Beeston, of his having been 'a schoolmaster in the country';[xx] while the latter is indicated by his patron Alexander Hoghton, who in his will of 1581 mentions instruments of music and various costumes for the performance of plays in close conjunction with the name of William Shakeshafte. This would have been in perfect accord with Renaissance theories of education, including those practised at Jesuit schools such as that of Prague, which fostered the use of drama in teaching the humanities of Latin and Greek. At the same time the

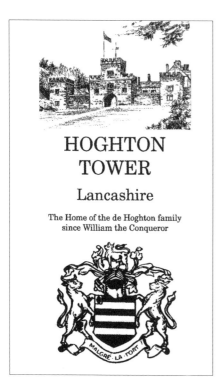

HOGHTON TOWER

Lancashire

The Home of the de Hoghton family
since William the Conqueror

5a. Hoghton Tower

Home of Alexander Hoghton, who named William Shakeshafte three times in his 1581 Will in connection with 'instruments of musics' and 'playclothes', and whose family passed down the oral tradition that young William Shakespeare had been with them 'for a couple of years'.

young man would have been excited at the prospect of a former master of the humanities and drama coming to stay for a few months in the neighbourhood. We, too, at the end of the twentieth century may well feel excited at this possibility of a meeting – not just in passing for a day or two, but for a couple of months - between the budding dramatist and the Jesuit composer of drama, William Shakespeare and Edmund Campion.

But there is much more to their meeting than that. Campion had not come all the way from Prague to Lancashire, at such a dangerous time, to act as tutor in dramaturgy to a promising young dramatist, even if he could have foreseen the future dramatic talent of this promising young man. If he foresaw the young William's greatness, as no doubt he did, it must have been in another context, not so much cultural or literary as spiritual, for the spiritual profit of his fellow Catholics in England. To encourage the others in this great cause, Campion had one principal means at hand - as has been indicated - the Spiritual Exercises of St. Ignatius; and now he had ample time to give them, and the young William to receive them, some time between Easter and Whitsun of 1581.

This is by no means so speculative as it may sound. I myself, as a Jesuit priest, have made these Spiritual Exercises innumerable times, both in their full form of 30 days and in their shorter form of 8 days, and so I have become familiar with their wording in Latin, which is their original language (in two forms, that of St. Ignatius himself and the more polished one of his secretary Juan Polanco). Also, as a Shakespeare scholar, I have perused and studied the plays of Shakespeare innumerable times, though some more frequently than others; and in this task I have been impressed with the number and importance of seeming echoes of the Exercises in the plays. Only, I have come up with the obvious problem: how could Shakespeare have come across the text of the Exercises, which was hardly to be found in England at that time, let alone have been directed in them by a Jesuit priest? The only satisfactory answer to this problem seems to be provided by the above-mentioned simultaneous sojourn of Shakespeare and Campion in Lancashire during the spring of 1581.

Then, where do I find traces of the Exercises in the plays of Shakespeare? To cut a long story short, and to follow the Exercises rather than the plays, I find the cry of wonder in the second exercise on sins, at the way all creatures have permitted us to live and sustained us in life, echoed in Ariel's warning to the three men of sin in *The Tempest* iii.3; I find the retreatant's ideal responses to the invitation of Christ the King echoed in Adam's generous offer to his young master Orlando in *As you Like It* ii.3; I find the wide view of the three divine persons in the contemplation on the Incarnation, 'upon the whole expanse or circuit of all the earth', echoed in the similar view of Isabella in *Measure for Measure* ii.2 and of Michael Williams, the soldier in *Henry V* iv.1; I find the meditation on the Two Standards, of Christ and Lucifer, echoed by Friar Laurence in *Romeo and Juliet* ii.3 and by Belarius in *Cymbeline* iv.2; I find the second class of men, from the meditation on Three Classes, those who wish to rid themselves of an attachment while retaining what they have acquired, in the character of Claudius, especially in his religious soliloquy, in *Hamlet* iii,3; I find the central issue of the Exercises on the election, or at least the reformation of one's state of life already chosen, in the frequent mention of such keywords as 'election', 'reformation' and 'consideration' occurring in plays from *Henry V*, *Hamlet* and *Troilus and Cressida* to *King Lear*; I find the definition of love presented in the concluding contemplation on attaining divine love in the words both of Juliet in *Romeo and Juliet* ii.2: 'My bounty is as boundless as the sea,/My love as deep; the more I give to thee,/The more I have,' and of Cordelia in *King Lear* i.1: 'My love's more richer than my tongue...What I well intend, I'll do't before I speak.'[xxi]

These are just a few indications of places in the plays where Shakespeare may have been inspired by his memory of the time he made the Spiritual Exercises under Campion's personal direction in Lancashire. But of far more importance than these few echoes is the general direction implied in them: that for William Shakespeare his way of working for the kingdom of Christ in England was to be not that of a seminarian, culminating in priesthood and return to his native country, with the high probability of suffering the torture of the rack, followed by execution in the bloody manner of hanging, drawing and quartering, which was the fate of Campion himself and is mentioned more than once in the plays, but that of a crypto-Catholic dramatist working on a variety of plays containing a hidden message to his fellow-countrymen both Catholic and Protestant – an appeal for mercy as well as justice, a warning against the deception of appearances such as 'cunning times put on to deceive the wisest' (*The Merchant of Venice* iii.2), an exhortation to raise the eyes of one's mind from things of earth to things of heaven, according to the ideal of the kingdom of Christ as set forth in the Spiritual Exercises. Such an election made by the young Shakespeare was no easy way out or a concession to his inordinate attachment to the way of drama. In a sense the way of the seminarian and the martyr might have been for him an easy way out; but he chose the more difficult way of dramatic composition in a cause which he could never express in any open manner. As he laments in a seemingly different context in Sonnet 36, 'I may not evermore acknowledge thee'; and as Hamlet complains in his first soliloquy, 'But break, my heart, for I must hold my tongue!' (i.2) In other words, he chose the paradoxical way of dramatic utterance and personal silence: he is always speaking, even shouting, in words, and yet at the heart of all his words there is a secret, if not mystical silence. He can say nothing of what he most wants to say; and yet by this self-sacrifice he hopes to be playing his part in the reconversion of England to the faith of England's past.

All this may well have been foreseen and forechosen by the young William in the making of his election under the wise direction of Edmund Campion. But what he could not have foreseen were the tragic events that were now to follow swiftly one upon another. First, there was the arrest of Edmund Campion at Lyford Grange near Oxford on July 17 1581, followed by his examination under torture in the Tower of London, leading to the revelation of the names and places of many Catholic gentlemen who had given him shelter above all in Yorkshire and Lancashire during the winter and spring of 1580 and 1581. Those gentlemen, including Richard Hoghton of Park Hall, were now in danger of suffering further investigation by government authorities. It was in such a situation that Alexander Hoghton made his above-mentioned will on August 3, 1581, dying not many months later. In his will he specially commends William Shakeshafte, with another young man named Fulke Guillom (apparently connected with the Hathaways of Shottery near Stratford),[xxii] to a Catholic neighbour, Sir Thomas Hesketh of Rufford Hall, whose cousin Bartholomew is also recorded as having given shelter to Edmund Campion.[xxiii] But it is likely that, instead of following this recommendation, William though it more prudent to retire for a time to Stratford; and there some time during the following year he wooed and won a bride some 8 years older than himself, Anne Hathaway, possibly at the introduction of Fulke.[xxiv]

In this connection there is an interesting discrepancy in the diocesan records of Worcester, involving a request by one William Shakespeare for permission to have his wedding in the forbidden season of Advent on two successive days, November 27 and 28. In the first instance the name of the bride is given as 'Anne Whateley of Temple Grafton', but in the second, as 'Anne Hathaway'. The question that naturally occurs is: Are there two women involved on successive days? Or were there two men with the same name, William Shakespeare? Or was there one and the same woman, who is given a different surname in the first case owing to a scribal error? The commonly accepted solution is the third, in which case the church of the bride would have been at a place where we know at this time there was an old Catholic priest from Marian times, one John Frith, officiating; and so, as a firm Catholic, William Shakespeare would naturally have preferred to celebrate his wedding with Anne Hathaway according to Catholic ritual - no doubt several months before applying for the dispensation at Worcester.[xxv] And so it is not so scandalous that his daughter Susanna should have been born in the May of 1583, barely six months after the permisssion from the diocesan authorities. As for the further family life of Shakespeare, it appears in hardly anything more than the bare record of the baptism of his twins, Hamnet and Judith, named after their Catholic godparents Hamnet and Judith Sadler, on February 2, 1585.

So William Shakespeare may now have felt free to follow the recommendation of Alexander Hoghton and to join the Catholic household of Sir Thomas Hesketh. For him this would have been a convenient stepping-stone to higher things, to the country mansion of the Earl of Derby whose son, Lord Strange, had a theatrical group of his own which performed plays not only in Lancashire but also in London. We know that Sir Thomas, like Alexander Hoghton before him, had been a frequent visitor at Derby's mansion, Knowsley House near what is today the great seaport of Liverpool, and that his players also visited that house in the Christmas season of 1587. Sir Thomas died, however, the following year, which was the year of the Armada, 1588; and another victim of death at the same time was the Earl of Leicester, who also had a group of players named Leicester's Men. So Strange's Men came to be fortified by members of both groups, those of Leicester and those of Hesketh, including (it seems) the increasingly proficient William Shakespeare. At least, we know of two plays by Shakespeare performed by Lord Strange's Men at this time, the first part of *Henry VI*, featuring Sir John Talbot, first Earl of Shrewsbury, and *Titus Andronicus*. It is in the latter play that we find an interesting echo of the poem on conscience attributed to the builder of Hoghton Tower, Thomas Hoghton, who chose the path of exile soon after the Tower's completion in 1569. Each stanza of this poem ends with the refrain, 'To keep my conscience'; and in the play Shakespeare puts significant words into the mouth of the villain Aaron the Moor, addressing the good Lucius, where his use of the pejorative 'popish' is for Shakespeare a *hapax legomenon*:

> 'Yet, for I know thou art religious,
> And has a thing within thee called conscience,
> With twenty popish tricks and ceremonies,
> Which I have seen thee careful to observe,
> Therefore I urge thy oath.' (v.1)

And so, it may be said by way of conclusion, the way was open for William Shakespeare - thanks in part to the direction of Edmund Campion – from the simplicity of his country life both at Stratford and in Lancashire to the complexity and sophistication of his city and theatrical life in London. On the other hand, owing to the circumstances of his birth in the Elizabethan age, which was for Catholics from the outset an age of increasing persecution, neither he nor his father could ever enjoy the simplicity of the country life. They both had to learn how to disguise their Catholic identity without ever denying it. In this respect the father may be seen as his son's precursor; and of the son it may be added, that he certainly bettered the instruction in all his plays, which have baffled audiences and critics from his day till today. As is said by Lucio of the duke-friar in *Measure for Measure*, 'His givings out were of an infinite distance/From his true-meant design.' (i.4) In the play the duke is going around in the disguise of a friar, partly for the detection of hypocrisy, partly for the protection of innocence; while behind the play the author himself has assumed the disguise of a dramatist in order to pursue true-meant designs of his own, on behalf of the Catholic cause in England.[xvi]

Notes by HM:

[i] ***'Shakespeare: the 'lost years'***', Manchester University Press, 1985, 2nd ed. 1998, with New Preface. This still stands as THE major scholarly work on the subject. Professor Honigmann mentioned Catholicism in all relevant contexts, although without placing undue emphasis on it. Professor Milward's work, with his Jesuit background, fills in many of these Catholic 'gaps' from his extensive knowledge of the relevant Catholic literature. Papers given at the conference were duly published in:
Theatre and Religion: Lancastrian Shakespeare, 2 Vols, Eds. Richard Dutton, Alison Findlay and
Richard Wilson, Manchester University Press, 2003.

[ii] 'Alexander Hoghton of Lea Hall.' Undoubtedly, his naming 'William Shakeshafte' three times in his will in conjunction with 'instruments of music and play-clothes' is the major key to 'Shakespeare in Lancashire', but he also plays several other roles in the wider story: he was the namesake uncle of Alexander Standish of Duxbury (1567-1622), whose mother Margaret Hoghton was Alexander's half-sister. We met Alexander Standish at Preston Guild in 1602, having previously met his stepfather Thomas Standish there in 1582. Alexander Standish knew John Weever and signed a document with him in London in the early 1600s; he later, as a widower, installed Countess Alice, Ferdinando's widow, during her second widowhood, in one of his properties in Anglezarke, between Duxbury and Hoghton. (His biography has been online on the Duxbury Family History website since

2004; this now needs minor modifications). His 'friend' John Weever had dedicated his *Epigrammes* in 1599 to Sir Richard Hoghton, nephew and heir of Alexander Hoghton. In short, the Hoghtons were even closer than the Stanleys to 'Shakespeare in Lancashire', and the Standishes, as Hoghton in-laws, were only one step away.

They are mentioned here mainly because it was an investigation into the Standishes of Duxbury that brought to my attention the recent work on 'Shakespeare in Lancashire', when the same families turned up over and over again in the Standish, Hoghton, Hesketh and Stanley families as cousins and in-laws. Alexander Standish's other recovered role in history is as the closest relative in Duxbury of Pilgrim Father Captain Myles Standish, who, as is well known, forsook anti-Catholic and anti-Puritan England and joined the Separatists-in-exile in Holland for the voyage on the Mayflower, thus helping to found the future USA. Alexander and Myles were both gt-gt-grandsons of Sir Christopher Standish of Duxbury, who had been knighted along with his kinsman Sir Alexander Standish of Standish by Lord Thomas Stanley (soon to become the 1st Earl of Derby) for Richard III at the Siege of Berwick in 1483. Two years later they were all at Bosworth, where the Standishes were again in the Stanley army, this time opposing Richard III, and won the day for Henry VII. Along with them were the gt-gt-grandfathers of so many who enter the 'Shakespeare in Lancashire' theory, including those of William Shakespeare (a Shakeshafte of Preston and Warwickshire) and Mary Arderne (Thomas Arderne of Harden Hall, Cheshire and Leicestershire). I am afraid that the presentation of the full evidence for this must wait for the publication of *Shakespeare's Lancashire Links*.

[iii] **'Christopher Marlowe.'** He has already speculatively entered the Stanley element of this book through an Edward Stanley fighting at the Siege of Malta and the tradition that he spent time in Tong, Shropshire, where **Sir Thomas** and later **Sir Edward Jr** lived. (See Chapter XXII. Other (Sir) Edward Stanleys and Appendix 2. Was Christopher Marlowe ever in Shropshire?)

[iv] **'. . . both his parents, John Shakespeare and Mary Arden.'** This stands, despite my claim that Mary Arderne was actually John's second (or third) wife. She became William's stepmother in c.1575, in his formative years, and thus must have had a great influence on him and the Shakespeare family through her Catholic Arderne gentry kinsmen of Harden Hall in Cheshire. This family provided the Arderne coat of arms granted to John to impale into his Shakespeare arms in 1599, NOT the Arden family of Park Hall, Warwickshire (which was crossed out to allow inclusion of the correct arms), although they obviously knew of their common origins several centuries previously and still acknowledged each other as kinsmen. (The origin of the Cheshire Ardernes is covered exhaustively in Ormerod's *Cheshire* and Earwaker's *East Cheshire*.)

[v] **'William Allen.'** From Rossall, Lancashire. He was briefly an 'usher' at Stratford Grammar School in the early 1560s, his salary paid by John Shakespeare in his capacity as treasurer for the town council. In exile he was the founder of the school at Douai and later Cardinal in Rome. It was he who sent Edmund Campion and Robert Persons on their Mission to England in 1580. (Notes on William Allen appear in Appendix 7. Carol Enos's *Shakespeare Encyclopedia*.)

[vi] **'The Babington Plot in 1586.'** This led directly to the trial and execution of Mary, Queen of Scots in 1587. This automatically affected the Stanley family, with the record of their planned attempt to free her from imprisonment at Chatsworth in 1570; and Earl Henry was on the 'jury' that condemned Mary to the scaffold.

[vii] **'. . the great Jesuit saint and martyr Edmund Campion.'** Although others before had raised the possibility of Shakespeare's Catholicism and the validity of the traditions of 'Shakespeare in Lancashire', Father Peter was the first to advocate, one might say 'with passion', and certainly deep conviction, the potential involvement of Campion with Shakespeare in Lancashire on his Mission in his book *Shakespeare's Religious Background* (1973). He has followed this up with many publications since then.

[viii] 'St John's, Oxford.' This was the 'Stanley College', attended later by Ferdinando and William, sons of Earl Henry. It is not known whether the previous generation had attended in the persons of the brothers (Earl Henry), **(Sir) Thomas** and **(Sir) Edward Sr**. Nor has any record been detected there of **Sir Edward Jr**. However, another later student at St John's was Sir William Dugdale (father from Lancashire), Norroy King of Arms because of his vast knowledge of Northern gentry families, who recorded the epitaphs in Tong in his notes for his *Visitation of Shropshire* (1663), in which he noted that 'these following verses were made by William Shakespeare, the late famous tragedian'. (See Chapter V. Two early recordings, and VII. 'How reliable was Sir William Dugdale?) Another student at St John's was the historian of Oxford University, Anthony Wood, whose grandfather Wood from Preston, a servant in the Stanley household at Knowsley, had moved to Eynsham to serve in the Stanley household at Eynsham Abbey. (See Chapter XIX. Eynsham.)

[ix] 'Robert Dudley, Earl of Leicester.' He enters the story of this book in several roles, including his presence in Stanley territory as Lord-Lieutenant of Chester and at the head of the English army at Zutphen in 1586, knighting another Edward Stanley there. (See Chapter XXII. Other (Sir) Edward Stanleys.)

[x] 'John Cottam'. Undoubtedly a key figure in young William Shakeshafte/Shakespeare's departure for Lancashire, but I have problems with the dates. He was master at Stratford Grammar School 1579-early 1581, but young William seems to have been with the Hoghtons for 'a couple of years' before the Hoghton will of August 1581, taking him and us back to 1579 and exactly the time when Cottam started at Stratford Grammar School. Some additional explanation is required. See note [xiv].

[xi] 'Sir William Catesby of Lapworth in Warwickshire, some 10 miles to the north of Stratford along what is now the A34.' This was en route to the homes of several other Shakespeares, some of whom, according to the latest research by Stephen Pearsons (webmaster of the Shakespeare Genealogy Forum), were almost certainly close kinsmen of John Shakespeare/Shakeshafte. My claim, in the forthcoming book *Shakespeare's Lancashire Links*, is that John's Shakeshafte great-grandfather was awarded a small estate in North Warwickshire for his role in the Stanley army that won Bosworth for Henry VII. One might assume that John often travelled up and down the 'A34'.

[xii] '. . . the saintly archbishop of Milan, Charles Borromeo, on their way from Rome to England.' It is perhaps not generally known that Saint Carlo Borromeo has a church dedicated to him in Austria, erected by an admirer in the early eighteenth century, on the route from Milan over the Brenner Pass to Munich, and presumably the route taken by Edmund Campion and Robert Persons. It is known as the Karlskirche, Volders, and is directly next to the motorway a few miles east of Innsbruck. It is an impressive baroque building with magnificent frescoes, including one enormous group scene on the ceiling with a depiction of Saint Carlo in the middle. I happen to have passed it rather often because I have lived near Munich for over thirty years and frequently taken this route over the Alps. Only in the spring of 2010 did we finally take time to pay a visit. I felt rather moved that I might be standing in the very footsteps of Campion and Persons, in a church dedicated to one of their greatest inspirations, a copy of whose *Spiritual Testament* was one of the vital pieces of evidence in proving that John Shakespeare was Catholic, with all the implications of this for William. Apologies for including this personal anecdote, but it seemed worth a footnote. (Some notes on Carlo Borromeo appear in Appendix 7. Carol Enos's *Shakespeare Encyclopedia*.)

[xiii] '. . . what more likely way than a visit to the nearby Lapworth through the introduction of Thomas Cottam's brother John?' I suggest that the Catesbys were probably already well known to John Shakespeare through his own minor gentry connections, from the original Stanley link via Bosworth, and his recent marriage to Mary née Arderne, with her Arderne and Stanley links, not to mention his Catholicism, as proved by his receiving a copy of Carlo Borromeo's *Spiritual Testament* around this time. The Karlskirche in Vienna is also dedicated to Carlo Borromeo.

[xiv] 'William, already sixteen, may well have accompanied him [his father] - if he was still at Stratford. . .'. This is a very big IF, particularly when combined with '**the early autumn of 1580**' in each of the following two paragraph. What worries me here is that William turned 16 only in April 1580, Alexander Hoghton wrote his will and died in mid-late 1581, and the family tradition of the de Hoghtons passed down over the generations was that 'young William Shakespeare spent a couple of years' with them (from the mouth of Sir Bernard de Hoghton, Bt, the current incumbent). For 'a couple of years' one might expect him to have arrived at the Hoghtons some time in 1579. This would preclude him living in Stratford in the autumn of 1580. The tradition might be exaggerated, of course, but if he really had arrived as late as the early autumn of 1580 surely the tradition would have been 'stayed a year' with them? Why bother to exaggerate if it wasn't true? The parallel Hesketh oral family tradition did not try to extend the stay beyond 'a short time'. The 'tradition' presumably started within William Shakespeare's own lifetime and that of Sir Richard Hoghton, who would have known him as a boy. It would have been enough just to have the association of a year - unless, of course, it really was 'a couple of years'. An explanation of 'a couple of years', i.e. from 1579, now comes from the 'new discovery' of John Shakespeare's and Mary Arderne's ancestries, and the strong possibility that John spent quite some time in the late 1570s back in Catholic Preston (priest-town), conducting his business from there. More to come in *Shakespeare's Lancashire Links*.

[xv] '. . . this 'papist and his poet'. A phrase used about Robert Persons, a Jesuit leader, and Shakespeare by the historian John Speed in 1611.

[xvi] 'Alexander's half-brother Richard Hoghton, at Park Hall, near Charnock Richard.' He was the only brother to visit Thomas Hoghton 'the Exile' in Flanders, with special licence, and so already well known to the authorities. However he managed it, he convinced his investigators of his innocence in the 'Campion affair', escaped any retribution and lived on to a considerable age. Travellers up the M6 might wish to wave at his memory as they pass the Charnock Richard Services; the grounds of Park Hall today are the home of the theme park Camelot. There are several Arthurian traditions in the neighbourhood, which makes this name appropriate, but they could just as 'traditionally' have created a Shakespeareana world.

[xvii] '. . . now known as Shakeshafte'. My suggestion is that this was merely an absolutely natural 'return' to the original family name of his Lancashire ancestors. 'Shakespeare' was the 'artificial' version, adopted after John Shakeshafte got fed up with always being called Shakespeare in Warwickshire, the local Midlands name - or maybe he even thought it sounded a little more distinguished? Another parallel version in modern times is with my own married surname Moorwood. My family has lost count of the number of times we have been addressed to our faces (with our name on a form in front of the speaker) as Moorehead; and lost count of the variations on letters, ranging from any spelling you wish from Mo(o)r(e)wo(o)d(d)e, along with Moorcroft, Moorfield, Norwood, Horwood and several others, containing EITHER a 'moor' OR a 'wood'. This does not happen in Sheffield, the origin of the name being the hamlet Moorwood, literally 'a wood on the moor' above the city. Today, we stick to the name on all our documents; in Tudor times surnames were still flexible. I find it very easy to understand that John Shakeshafte 'gave in' in Warwickshire and adopted the name Shakespeare when there. Similarly, he would have automatically reverted to Shakeshafte when back in Preston, Lancashire, a county where the name Shakespeare was unrecorded until well into the eighteenth century. (IGI)

[xviii] '. . . his [William's] plan to stay with the Hoghtons in the near future and learned of Campion's own intention of visiting that family in Lancashire.' My suspicion has already been expressed above that young William was already in Lancashire before Campion even landed on the English coast. They could still have met in Lancashire, however, as suggested by Father Peter.

[xix] ' . . .William Shakeshafte, as he now chose to be known since the name was more familiar to people in that part of England.' This point was covered in [xvii].

[xx] '. . . the tradition going back to his colleague Christopher Beeston, of his having been a schoolmaster in the country'. This report came from John Aubrey, *Brief Lives* (written in the 1670s, several published editions, including (Ed.) Richard Barber (Boydell, 1975, 1982), who had the information from William Beeston, actor Christopher's son, so only one generation down the line.

[xxi] The *Spiritual Exercises*. Father Peter has written a monograph devoted entirely to these: Renaissance Monograph 29, 'The Plays and the Exercises - A Hidden Source of Shakespeare's Inspiration?' Obtainable from the Renaissance Institute, Sophia University, Tokyo.

[xxii] '. . . Fulke Guillom (apparently connected with the Hathaways of Shottery near Stratford).' This reference and connection has eluded me, but importantly, Fulke Guillom does appear later in the household of Sir Thomas Hesketh of Rufford, the family with whom Alexander Hoghton hoped that Fulke and William Shakeshafte would find a place, should his brother Thomas Hoghton not be willing to accept them. Professor Honigmann devotes a whole chapter in *'lost years'* to the Heskeths of Rufford. This family, like the Hoghtons, had also passed down a family tradition, completely independent of the Hoghton tradition, that 'Shakespeare had spent a short time with them in his youth'. Historians of Rufford Old Hall (now owned by the National Trust) and the Hesketh family are meanwhile reasonably convinced that this tradition was based on the truth (see Deane, *Guide Book to Rufford Old Hall*; or the website of Rufford Old Hall). This makes it unlikely, as Father Peter suggests, that William Shakespeare went straight from the Hoghtons back to Stratford in late 1581, but spent a short time with the Heskeths, and possibly a short time touring with Strange's Men, patron Ferdinando Stanley, Lord Strange, until mid-1582. Time would also (just) allow him to have been at Preston Guild at the end of August for a few days, which we know was presided over by the Stanleys: Earl Henry, Ferdinando and two brothers, along with **Sir Edward Sr** and **(Sir) Edward Jr**. Also in attendance were Thomas Hoghton of Lea (deceased Alexander's brother), Sir Thomas Hesketh of Rufford and his cousin Bartholomew Hesketh of Aughton (see list in Chapter XV. Preston Guild). 'John Shakeshafte, Glover' was also there, claimed by myself to be most likely one and the same as John Shakespeare, glover of Stratford. William Shakespeare was definitely back in Stratford soon afterwards, however, when he impregnated Anne Hathaway (on the assumption that Susanna was born after a normal nine-month pregnancy). Given that the marriage licence was not obtained until 27/28 November, one likely explanation is that William was away on tour again when Anne realized she was pregnant, and he needed to be contacted elsewhere in the country for a quick return to Stratford to 'do his duty' and 'the honourable thing'. Fulke Guillom, William Shakeshafte's companion with the Hoghtons and the Heskeths, turns up later with his father in Chester.

[xxiii] 'Thomas Hesketh of Rufford, whose cousin Bartholomew is also recorded as having given shelter to Edmund Campion.' Bartholomew was indeed Sir Thomas's 'cousin'. He was of nearby Aughton, and the brother-in-law of Alexander Hoghton, whose wife/widow Elizabeth Hesketh was Bartholomew's sister. It was his brother Richard Hesketh who delivered to Ferdinando, 5th Earl of Derby, the letter from English Catholics in exile, which led to his execution and the poisoning of Ferdinando. These characters appear in the recent book by Leo Daugherty, *The Assassination of Shakespeare's Patron: Investigating the Death of the Fifth Earl of Derby*, Cambria, 2011.

[xxiv] I beg to differ from Father Peter in the explanation of the marriage well into the pregnancy, on which he spends two paragraphs. My tentative explanation was given in Note [xxii] above. However, basically we must accept that we will never know.

[xxv] Current thinking in certain Shakespeare circles sees Shakespeare well established in Derby's Players well before 1587/8. For example John Idris Jones follows Honigmann's suggestion that *The*

Phoenix and the Turtle was written around the time of the wedding of Ursula Stanley/ Halsall (Earl Henry's daughter by his mistress Jane Halsall, installed at Hawarden) and John Salusbury of Lleweni, Denbigh in 1586. He argues this very persuasively, with much local geographical detail and colour, in 'William Shakespeare and John Salusbury: what was their relationship?', *Transactions of the Denbighshire Historical Society*, January 2011. An earlier version of this is online.

[xvi] Thus ends this plea by Peter Milward to accept the historical truth of not only the 'Lancastrian Shakespeare' theory, but also the concomitant 'Catholic Shakespeare' theory. During the dozen years since it was published this plea has received some support, but also much doubt. It remains to be seen what the next few years might bring.

5b. Rufford Old Hall

Home of the Heskeths of Rufford, whose family passed down the oral tradition that young William Shakespeare had spent 'a short time' with them. Owned by the National Trust.

Appendix 6
P.S. Stop Press from Durham in 2010

At the end of July 2010, my daughter, an alumna of Durham University, sent me *Durham First* and later *Durham Newswire*, a service for Durham Alumni, with an item about Shakespeare's *First Folio*. I was interested, of course, not least because one of the dedicatees, Philip Herbert (1584-1650), 1st Earl of Montgomery, 4thEarl of Pembroke, had entered the story of **Sir Edward Jr** by marrying in 1630 (as his second wife and her second husband) Lady Anne Clifford (1590-1676), a cousin of his father **Sir Thomas Stanley** (although of an age closer to **Sir Edward Jr**'s children). Into the story from Durham also came a comment by a recent biographer of Shakespeare, Bill Bryson, who, regrettably but understandably, never even mentioned the Tong Epitaphs in his otherwise 'conventional' but interesting and amusing biography. Despite this, he was appointed Chancellor of Durham University, a worthily amusing successor to Sir Peter Ustinov. And one of the other books mentioned by Durham University was connected with Eynsham Abbey, owned by **Sir Thomas** and **Sir Edward Jr**, to which the latter moved in 1603 and where he died in 1632.

I decided to include excerpts here for the sake of these interests, and in the hope that anyone who reads this book and comes across any 'new' details about anyone named in connection with **Sir Thomas** or **Sir Edward Sr** and **Jr** in Tong, Eynsham, Winwick, Walthamstow or anywhere else, including Durham, will contact me. It could be that there are still a few gems waiting to be discovered which would illuminate further their biographies and more potential contacts of **Sir Edward Jr** with Shakespeare. I also hope, of course, that the remaining invaluable stolen books are recovered and returned to Durham.

Durham University celebrates return of Shakespeare First Folio

Durham University is celebrating after a rare 17th Century First Folio of Shakespeare's plays was returned more than ten years after being stolen. The Folio - the first collected edition of Shakespeare's plays - was returned to the University following the conviction of . . Scott . . . of . . . County Durham, at Newcastle Crown Court. . . Scott was cleared of stealing the Folio but was found guilty of handling stolen goods and removing stolen property from the UK. . . .

The Folio was one of seven books and manuscripts taken from Bishop Cosin's Library, part of the University Library, on Palace Green, Durham City, in December 1998.

The other six have never been recovered and Durham University is appealing for their return.

The Folio resurfaced in the summer of 2008 when it was handed in to the Folger Library, in Washington DC, by a man who asked for it to be valued. Folger Library staff contacted the authorities who subsequently arrested and charged Scott. . . . there is disappointment that it has been damaged. The title-leaf has been torn out and it is generally in a poor condition. As a result the book, which is essentially priceless in terms of its heritage value, has been given an estimated value of £1.5m. . .

The Shakespeare first folio was published in 1623. It was acquired by John Cosin, former Bishop of Durham, and was part of the library he established in Durham in 1669. The Folio is the only one known to have stayed in the same personal library since its purchase. At the time it was stolen experts described it as "the most important printed book in the English language". . .

Bill Bryson, Chancellor of Durham University and author of an acclaimed book on Shakespeare, said: "Shakespeare's First Folio is arguably the most important book in English literature. It is fantastic that Durham's copy is coming home at last . . ."

View the video report here **www.dur.ac.uk/news/shakespearefolio**

Also taken were two printed works by the 10th century scholar Aelfric, **Abbot of Eynsham** (dated 1566 and 1709) . . .

(Reproduced with the kind permission of Durham University.)

~~~~~~~~~~~~~~~~~~~~~~~

The mention of Eynsham Abbey in 1566 excited me, probably/perhaps unduly. In 1566 Eynsham Abbey (near Oxford) already belonged to **Sir Thomas Stanley** of Winwick, having received it along with other Stanley estates from his father Edward, 3ʳᵈ Earl of Derby on the birth of his son **Edward** in 1562, through a settlement in 1562/3. Earl Edward had bought Eynsham Abbey and Manor after the Dissolution of the Monasteries, as the third owner in quick succession in 1535. 1566 was the year when **Sir Thomas** ended a four-year stint as Governor of the Isle of Man and before he became MP for Liverpool in 1568, when Winwick was still his main base on the mainland, but he was Lord of the Manors of Eynsham and Tong. Could he possibly have been living at Eynsham Abbey in 1566, or at least visited it, and been involved in the publication of this medieval gem by a former Abbott of Eynsham? If so, this might tell us a little more about **Sir Thomas**, his level of education and his interests. Possibly the MS had not stayed at Eynsham Abbey between the tenth and sixteenth centuries; the published version in 1566 was almost certainly printed in London; no copy might ever have arrived at Eynsham Abbey; and **Sir Thomas** might have had nothing to do with the MS and the printing. However, the mere thought of the possibility of the MS and a copy of the printed version having been in his hands was exciting enough. (See Chapter XIX. Eynsham.)

There are a few additional connections between the Stanleys and (Bishops of) Durham, apart from a book written in Eynsham and printed in 1566 being bought by a Bishop of Durham, albeit a century later. For starters:

Maybe these will provide clues to further connections?

1. The Protestant Bishop of Durham in 1566 was James Pilkington of Rivington, Lancashire, who founded Rivington Grammar School that very year. Only one list of pupils in the sixteenth century has survived, from 1575, and in that year there were no Stanleys there. (The full list is given in Margaret M. Kay, *History of Rivington and Blackrod School*, 1966.) One would not even expect any sons of Henry, Lord Strange or his brothers **Sir Thomas** and **Sir Edward Stanley** to have been there, because they were educated at home in Lathom House. However, several pupils on the 1575 list appeared as visitors to Henry, 4ᵗʰ Earl of Derby between 1587 and 1590 (the only years for which lists of visitors have survived in the *Derby Household Books*), and they, or other members of their families, also turned up with the Stanleys at Preston Guild in 1582 and 1602.

2. James Pilkington's successor as Bishop of Durham was Richard Barnes (1532-87), whose third son was poet Barnabe Barnes (1571-1609), who was buried at Durham. Richard Barnes was from Bold in Prescot Parish, not far from Lathom, seat of the Stanleys. Barnabe Barnes has enough connections to Shakespeare to have been considered as a Group Authorship Member and also as the 'Rival Poet' in Shakespeare's Sonnets. He was friendly with poet William Spencer, with whom his cousin Lucy Percy had grown up at Petworth.

3. The Rising of the North in 1569 saw a meeting of the Northern rebels in Durham Cathedral. Among them was Thomas Percy, 7th Earl of Northumberland, father of Lucy Percy, who later married **(Sir) Edward Jr**.

6a. Durham, Bishop's Palace
Several Bishops of Durham appear in Stanley stories.

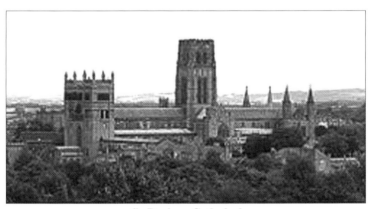

6b. Durham Cathedral
Cathedral Church of Christ, Blessed Mary the Virgin and St Cuthbert of Durham. Lady Lucy's father Thomas Percy, 7th Earl of Northumberland, met with others here in 1569 during the Rising of the North. For his participation he was executed in York in 1572.

Appendix 7
Shakespeare Encyclopedia
Stratford/London/Lancashire Links
by Carol Curt Enos

A compendium of quotes concerning people in the world surrounding Shakespeare.

I was introduced to Carol Curt Enos by Sir Bernard de Hoghton, and through her came in touch with Professor Peter Milward, author of *Shakespeare's Religious Background*, 1973 and prolific author on Shakespeare's Catholicism ever since. Carol and I became his 'Non-conformist ladies', Carol with her solidly Methodist and I with my solidly Congregationalist upbringing. Both of us had come to the conclusion during our totally independent research that Shakespeare's family was Catholic and that he was surrounded by Catholics throughout his life. The results of Carol's research appear in two books: *Shakespeare and the Catholic Religion*, Dorrance, Pittsburgh, Pennsylvania, 2000 and *Shakespeare Setttings: Stratford/Park Hall, Lancashire/Cheshire/the Catholic Mission, and London*, Wheatmark, Tucson, Arizona, 2007.

Between these she had amassed an enormous amount of information, not all of which could be built into her books, and she produced online in 2004 an alphabetical list of characters involved, named *Shakespeare Encyclopedia*, which I have regularly consulted, along with her books. The following are very much 'selected extracts' from her 328 pages online. Her aim was as stated in her Introduction (below); my aim was to extract those items which referred not so much to Shakespeare's surroundings as to those which contributed to the surroundings of the Stanleys around whom this book revolves, and which would therefore provide useful supplementary information concerning probable friends/acquaintances of **Sir Thomas Stanley**, **Sir Edward Sr** and **Sir Edward Jr**, or stories which they almost certainly heard, which in turn might connect them to Shakespeare. This excluded virtually all Stratford and Warwickshire references and many London references, also many of the dozens of references to Catholic priests in exile, and other English exiles, even though so many of these were from Lancashire. 'New' biographies of many have since appeared in the *New/Oxford Dictionary of National Biography* (online 2004, paper 2007), but all make use of the same references given below.

Knowing that Carol had already provided these notes, it seemed sensible to include them as an Appendix, rather than include these details within my own text. Any comments by myself are in [*italics and square brackets*. HM]. All names underlined (by myself) are of those who have already appeared in this book as highly relevant for the **Stanleys of Winwick and Tong** and their wives and cousins. All in bold are from the original online *Shakespeare Encyclopedia* plus, as usual, **Sir Thomas** and **Sir Edward Sr** and **Jr**. The fonts have been adapted to conform to the conventions used in the rest of this book for quotes and quotes within quotes. The original text can be consulted online, of course, along with the additional 300 pages. Carol Enos has given permission for the inclusion of the following text and any format changes at my discretion.

Introduction by Carol Curt Enos

Few direct ties between Shakespeare and any of his contemporaries exist. He left no diary, personal letters, handwritten manuscripts of his plays, or notes in his own handwriting. The list of concrete evidence that he even existed is exceedingly brief: 1. his will; 2. a signature on a deed; one letter addressed, but never delivered to him, and 4. perhaps a part of the play, *Sir Thomas More*. [*Perhaps an exaggeration! One person who amassed an enormous chronological list of documentation was Eric Sams*, The Real Shakespeare 2, *placed posthumously online by his son in 2008*. HM] The personality and convictions of the man himself remain obscure and enigmatic despite the millions of tomes of Shakespeareana that continue to burgeon on library shelves.

The more we can place Shakespeare in his historical setting and the more we can learn about his political, philosophical, and religious beliefs, the closer we can come to understanding his intention. Admittedly, highly respected Shakespeare scholars discount the importance and validity of author's intent, preferring to focus primarily on the timeless, artistic qualities of the plays and sonnets. However, an understanding of the political background that might have provoked a response from Shakespeare as well as some understanding of Shakespeare's perspective and interest in questions he raises on the stage often heighten our appreciation of the art he employed in developing characters, suggesting subtle allusions, and in creating analogous historical situations which paralleled contemporary problems. My greatest frustrations in reading the plays is the realization of how limited we are in knowing anything about the social circles Shakespeare moved in, very little about his youth, next to nothing about how and why he became a playwright, nothing at all about any causes he believed in and might have worked for.

This collection of biographical sketches began as background reading for an extension course at the University at Oxford, England, and grew gradually over approximately sixteen years of extensive reading, often of much-neglected, because tediously detailed, 19th century transcriptions of 16th century primary sources. As the notes amassed, it soon became apparent that some method was essential in my madness, and the best method for organizing, making connections between persons and events, and retrieving information proved to be the simple electronic alphabetical entry by both subject and biographical account.

This is not an unbiased approach, for the more I read, the more clues I saw that substantiated the theory that Shakespeare was raised as a Catholic and that he served for a time in the home of Alexander Hoghton at Hoghton Tower in Lancashire and perhaps in the home of Hoghton's brother-in-law, Sir Thomas Hesketh of Rufford. E. K. Chambers initiated the theory in *Shakespearean Gleanings* (1944), an update of an earlier reference he had made in 1923 to a will that was executed on August 3, 1581, by Alexander Houghton of Lea, Lancashire, in which he named William Shakeshafte and Ffulke Gyllome as 'playeres,' players important enough to be passed on to a good master upon Houghton's demise: either Thomas Houghton of Brynscoules, his brother, or Sir Thomas Heskethe, Knyght, or 'some good master.' Along with the players went 'all my Instruments belonginge to mewsyckes and all maner of playe clothes yf he (brother) be mynded to keepe and doe keppe playeres.' This intriguing reference to a William with a last name so similar to that of the famous playwright, and Shakeshafte's association with a group of players was the basis for *Shakespeare: the 'Lost Years'* (1985) by E. A. J. Honigmann. The very significant possibility that the William Shakeshafte named as a 'player' in the 1581 will of the Catholic Alexander Houghton of Lea and Hoghton Tower, Lancashire, was actually William Shakespeare opens a new area for exploration in the attempt to place William Shakespeare in his contemporary context and to identify subsequent business and personal connections between Shakespeare and Lancashire.

Even now, after all of the exhaustive research on Shakespeare, scholars continue to refer to the years 1577 to 1592 as 'lost years'. If he served as some sort of servant in the Houghton household, perhaps as schoolmaster-turned-playwright and actor, he would have been in contact with the young priests who came to the Houghton home, a focal point of what was called the English Catholic mission. Because of this possibility, it is important to identify those priests and their possible connections with situations and people who logically could have been in touch with Shakespeare. For instance, a logical beginning is to identify and trace the biographies of the legatees named in the Houghton will alongside Shakeshafte.

~~~~~~~~~~~~~~~~~~

A selection of entries of relevance to this book on the tomb at Tong
and those whose effigies appear on it;
text and direct quotes by Carol Curt Enos; extracts selected by Helen Moorwood

Acton, Thomas

His widow married Sir George Vernon, uncle of Elizabeth Vernon (Southampton's wife). She was the mother of Lady Thomas Lucy of Charlecote. Elizabeth Vernon's mother was née Devereux (Fripp, *Shakespeare, Man and Artist* 420).

> "Of this Fire there is no reflection in *King Richard the Second* or *The Merchant of Venice,* which Shakespeare not very long afterwards produced for his gentlemen friends in London and for the Court. The Earl of Southampton was in town. He was two-and-twenty years old on 6 October 1595, and a few days previous it was noted by Roland White, that 'my lord doth with too much familiarity court the fair

Mistress Vernon'. She was <u>Elizabeth, daughter to Sir John Vernon of Hodnet and his wife, Elizabeth Devereux (who was aunt of Robert Earl of Essex and lady Penelope Rich)</u>. Her father's brother, <u>Sir George Vernon,</u> had married for his second wife the widow of Thomas Acton of Sutton Park, the mother of Lady Thomas <u>Lucy</u> of Charlecote. On or after this date Shakespeare could not write to his patron as in Sonnet X, 'that thou none lovest is most evident'" (Fripp, *Shakespeare, Man and Artist* 420).

NOTE: Devereux connections: <u>Robert Devereux (earl of Essex)</u> was a cousin of <u>Elizabeth Vernon</u> (Southampton's wife):

> " . . . Sir Edward Devereux, Baronet, . . . married Catherine, daughter of Edward Arden of Park Hall." Edward Devereux was the half-brother of <u>Robert Devereux Earl of Essex</u> (Enos 107).

[Under **Giles Allen** entry]

"The <u>Earl of Rutland</u> (a close friend of <u>Henry Wriothesley</u>'s) had a town house on part of the old Holywell Priory Estates, of which the other part, granted to Henry Webbe, was eventually sold to Gyles Alleyn and let to <u>James Burbage</u>, who was then in trouble with his landlord" (Stopes, *The Third Earl of Southampton* 93).

Babington (See also: Abington and Habington.)

Habington, Thomas

" . . . antiquary, born at Thorpe, near Chertsey, co. Surrey, Aug. 23, 1560, was the son and heir of John Habington, of Hindlip Castle, co. Worcester, cofferer to Queen Elizabeth. At about the age of sixteen he became a commoner of Lincoln College, Oxford, where he remained three years. Afterwards he spent some years in the universities at Rheims and Paris. On his return to England he became, like his father a zealous partisan of the <u>Queen of Scots</u>, and connected himself with those who laboured to obtain her release. On this account, and for his recusancy, he was sent to the Tower, where he was imprisoned for six years. It is said that had he not been Elizabeth's godson he would have lost his life. He was pardoned, however, and permitted to retire to Hindlip, which his father settled upon him at the time of his marriage with Mary, eldest daughter of <u>Edward Parker, Baron Morley</u>, by <u>Elizabeth, daughter and heiress of William Stanley, Baron Monteagle</u>. <u>Lord Morley</u> was one of the peers who sat in judgment upon the <u>Queen of Scots</u>. [*Along with Henry, 4th Earl of Derby,* **Sir Thomas**'s *brother.* HM]

The laws against Catholics were now rigorously enforced, and it was at great peril that the services of a priest could be obtained. Hindlip is thought to have been erected by John Habington in 1572, as that date appeared in one of the parlours. His son determined that it should afford protection for the persecuted priests. He added much to the mansion, and furnished it with most ingeniously contrived hiding-places. There was scarcely an apartment that had not secret ways of ingress and egress. Trap-doors communicated with staircases concealed in the walls, sliding-panels opened into places of retreat cleverly constructed in the chimneys, and some of the entrances, curiously covered over with bricks and mortar supported by wooden frames black with paint and soot, were actually contrived inside the chimneys. The situation of the house, too, upon the summit of the highest ground in the neighbourhood, with an unintercepted prospect on all sides, afforded peculiar facilities for a timely observance of the approach of dangerous visitors. Nash, on account of its uncommon construction both within and without, gives an engraving of Hindlip as it appeared shortly before it was pulled down. Such was the house which enabled Mr. Habington for many years to offer a comparatively secure refuge to priests and persecuted Catholics.

Shortly after the discovery of the Gunpowder Plot, with which Mr. Habington was not directly (if in any way) concerned, a proclamation was issued for the arrest of suspected traitors, and the facilities of Hindlip for concealment being well known to the government, directions were given for its examination. Sir Hen. Bromley, of Holt Castle, a neighbouring magistrate, was commissioned by the lords of the council to invest the house, and to search rigorously all the apartments. The magistrate surrounded Hindlip with over a hundred soldiers early on Sunday morning, Jan. 19, 1606. Fr. Oldcorne, who usually resided there, had persuaded <u>Fr. Garnett</u> to join him for better security. The two Jesuit lay-brothers, Nicholas Owen and Ralph Ashley, were also in the house. They had barely time to conceal themselves before the doors were broken open. Mr. Habington was from home on a visit to his kinsman, <u>Mr. Talbot</u>, at Pepperhill, but returned on Monday evening. The search lasted for eleven nights and twelve days, until all four had been forced to come forth from their hiding-places through sheer exhaustion, otherwise they would not have been discovered. They were conveyed with Mr. Habington, charged with concealing them, to Worcester, three miles from Hindlip, whence they were forwarded to London and committed to the Tower. Owen died under torture upon the '<u>Topcliff</u>' rack. The rest were brought to the bar at the Lent assizes at Worcester, and all four condemned to death. Mr. Habington, however, who was sentenced for harbouring Frs. Oldcorne and <u>Garnett</u>, was reprieved, owing it is said to the intercession of his father-in-law, <u>Lord Morley</u>. Mrs. Habington is credited with having written the letter warning her brother, <u>Lord Monteagle</u>, of the plot, and this, perhaps, weighed in her husband's favour. Tradition asserts that his pardon was accompanied with the injunction that he should not outstep the precincts of Worcestershire.

During the remainder of his life Mr. Habington devoted himself with great assiduity to the collection of materials for the history of Worcestershire. He surveyed it, says <u>Wood</u>, 'and made a collection of most of its antiquities from records, registers, evidences both public and private, monumental inscriptions and arms'. . . . He died at Hindlip, Oct. 8, 1647, aged 87.

Dodd, Ch. Hist., vol. ii. p. 422; *Bliss, Wood's Athenæ Oxon.,* vol.iii/.p. 222; *Nash, Hist. of Worcestershire,* vol. i. p. 585; *Jardine, Gunpowder Plot; Morris, Condition of Catholics under Jas. I.; Foley, Records S.J.,* vols. iii. iv.; *Butler, Hist. Mem.,* ed. 1822, vol. ii. pp. 176, 441" (Gillow *Thomas Habington*).

[Gillow lists works by Habington and comments on them.]

Blount, Charles, sixth Lord Mountjoy (1563-1606)

". . . was the second son of James and his mother was Catherine Leigh. He went to the Inner Temple to study law. He was created M.A. at Oxford June 16, 1589. He went to court in London in 1583 where he attracted the Queen's attention. She made the <u>Earl of Essex</u> jealous by showing great attention to Charles. On one occasion Elizabeth is said to have rewarded him for his skill at a tilting match with 'a queen at chesse of gold richly enamelled, which his servant had the next day fastened on his arme with a crimson riband.' <u>Essex</u> noticed the token and angrily remarked to Sir Fulke Greville, 'Now I perceive every fool must have a favor.' The speech was reported to Blount, and a duel followed, near Marelybone Park, in which <u>Essex</u> was wounded. Blount was elected M.P. for Beeralston, Devonshire in 1584. He was knighted in 1586 and 'had a company <u>in the Low Countries in 1586</u>.' (Naunton; Cal. Dom. State Papers, Addenda, 1580-1625, p 19). He was present at the skirmish near <u>Zutphen</u> when <u>Sir Philip Sidney</u> received his fatal wound. In 1588 he had his own ship built to join the Armada. He was popular with the poets of his day: John Davies, <u>Barnaby Barnes</u>, <u>Samuel Daniel</u>. He fell in love with <u>Penelope, the wife of Lord Rich</u>. <u>Penelope was the 'Stella' of Sidney's 'Astrophel and Stella.'</u> She had been married against her will to Lord Rich who divorced her" (*DNB*).

Chambers, Sir Edmund

"Perhaps the first (in 1923) to speculate that William Shakeshafte of the <u>Alexander Houghton</u> will was William Shakespeare" (Keen, *The Annotator*, 47). Chambers returned to the idea later in *Shakespearean Gleanings.* Oxford University Press, 1944):

It is clear that if William Shakeshafte passed from the service of <u>Alexander Houghton</u> into that of either <u>Thomas Houghton</u> or <u>Sir Thomas Hesketh</u>, he might very easily have gone into that of <u>Lord Strange</u>, and so later into the London theatrical world, where we find in 1592 William Shakespeare, writing probably for <u>Lord Pembroke</u>'s men, and called by the envious <u>Robert Greene</u> 'the only Shake-scene in a countrey' (Keen 47).

Devereux, Elizabeth, wife of <u>Sir John Vernon</u> was the mother of <u>Elizabeth Vernon</u>; Elizabeth married <u>Henry Wriothesley</u>. [This narrows the relationship between the Earl of Essex, Henry Wriothesley, and Sir Edward Devereux who married Catherine, daughter of Edward Arden and gets closer to Shakespeare. (Enos)]

Dudley, Robert, Earl of Leicester

[Footnote 6:] J. T. Murray, i. 35, 42 (11, 12, 13 July should be 13, 14, 15). Their visit to <u>Lathom</u> House is thus referred to in the House Book: '1587 Week beginning July 8. On Thursday <u>Master Stanley</u> [*this* is **Edward Jr** H.M.] departed, and the same day my Lord of Leicester's Players played. On Friday they played again: which day <u>Master Salesbury</u> came, and also Master Rec'; And on Saturday they departed away, and Master Sorrocolde a preacher came' (*Ib.* ii. 296). Their welcome and entertainment would be not unlike that in *Haml.* II.ii. Thomas Sorrocold was a Lancashire man, M.A. of Oxford, 25 years old (Wood, *Ath.* i. 635)" (Fripp, *Shakespeare, Man and Artist*, 209).

"Early in September 1588 Leicester's players were on the road to London, not a little proud of their master's livery. They performed at Norwich on the 4th, and were there on the 7th when, on their complaint, a cobbler was committed to prison for disrespectful language towards the Bear and Ragged Staff" (J. T. Murray, ii. 336 f.).

At Ipswich, however, on the 14th they made their last recorded appearance as servants of the great Earl. He had died suddenly on the 4th, at Cornbury Park in Oxfordshire, on his journey for his health to Bath.

<u>Dugdale, Sir William</u> (1605-1686)

. . . was born at Shustoke, near Coleshill at Blythe Hall, Warwickshire. <u>His father, John Dugdale, of a Lancashire family</u>, having accompanied some pupils to Oxford, remained at the university for his own purposes, at 30 matriculating at St. John's College, studying civil law, succeeding a kinsman of the same surname as bursar and steward of his college, and after 14 years' residence selling what <u>property he had in Lancashire</u> to settle at Shustoke. He wrote a history of Warwickshire. (*DNB*).

<u>Egerton, Sir Thomas</u> (Baron Ellesmere and Viscount Brackley) (1540?-1617)

. . .<u>Lord Chancellor</u>. Natural son of Sir Richard Egerton of Ridley, Cheshire, by Alice Sparke. He was said to have been a commoner of Brasenose, Oxford, in 1556, but his name does not appear in the register. He was a lawyer and was so good that the Queen enlisted him to work for her after he argued a case against her, saying, 'By my troth, he shall never plead against me again.' He conducted the prosecutions of <u>Campion</u> in 1581, Davison in 1587, and <u>the Earl of Arundel</u> in 1589, and Sir John Perrot in 1592. He became a friend of <u>Essex</u>, and he witnessed the 'boxing of his ears' by the Queen. <u>Egerton</u> tried to dissuade <u>Essex</u> from his plot against Elizabeth when <u>Essex</u> returned from Ireland on Sunday, Feb. 8, 1600-1. <u>Essex</u> had <u>Egerton</u> and the other emissaries locked up. The Great Library at Bridgewater House was founded by the chancellor; some of the books came to him through his third wife, <u>the Dowager Countess of Derby</u>, who as <u>Alice Spencer and Lady Strange</u> was a well-known patron of Elizabethan literature. (*DNB*).

Farington/Ffarington

<u>Farington, William</u> Steward or Comptroller for the <u>Earls of Derby</u>. He recorded the activities of the household between 1586 and 1590 in The Household Books. On 30 December 1587, he noted at Knowsley,

'On Saturday <u>Sr. Tho. Hesketh</u> plaiers went awaie.' (Keen, *The Annotator*, 46, 47).

"<u>Ffarington</u> as [Canon] Raines has shown us [writes Thaler, Profesor Alwin Thaler of the Department of English, Tennessee U in a published thesis, 'The Original Malvolio?' in the *Shakespeare Association Bulletin,* Vol vii, no. 2] was born in 1537 and inherited from his father, Sir Henry Ffarington, a large property, an official connection with the <u>Stanley</u> family, an inordinate 'appetite for law' and nice conduct as a public official (and) an authoritative and unyielding manner which his inferiors and even 'the surrounding gentry . . . felt . . . sometimes to be inconvenient . . . and at other times oppressive.' He increased his property by a prudent marriage to a wealthy young daughter of the house of Stanley and by shrewd legal management. Meanwhile, he had become a Justice of the Peace of his home County and comptroller of the household to <u>Edward, Earl of Derby</u>." (Keen 190, 191).

<u>Fitton, Sir Edward</u> (1550-1605/6)

"This third Sir Edward married <u>Alice Holcroft, daughter of Sir John Holcroft</u> of Lancaster, by whom he had three children, Sir Edward Fitton (the fourth), Anne Fitton and <u>Mary Fitton, the 'Dark Lady.'</u> Alice Holcroft's aunt and namesake married <u>Sir Thomas Hesketh of Rufford</u>, Lancashire, to whom William Shakeshafte was commended by <u>Alexander Houghton</u> of Lea Hall. Her niece Isobel, daughter of her brother Sir Thomas Holcroft, wed the <u>third Earl of Rutland</u>, whose nephew the <u>fifth Earl of Rutland</u> was a friend and fellow member of Gray's Inn with Shakespeare's <u>Earl of Southampton</u>." (Keen 117, 118).

Fletcher, John

"Unfortunately, little is known of the poet and dramatist with whom Shakespeare collaborated in 1612-13. John Fletcher was born in 1579 as the son of an Anglican parish clergyman who later became Bishop of London. He was educated at Cambridge University and apparently brought up as an Anglican. His chief claim to fame is his immortal friendship and collaboration with the poet-dramatist Francis Beaumont (1584-1616), an Oxford student who had tentatively turned to law in London. The close friendship between Beaumont and Fletcher began, as far as is known, about 1607, in which year they published the first direct evidence of their mutual admiration for <u>Ben Jonson</u>. The two dramatists, whose intimacy was closer than that of brothers, were participants in the cultural gatherings led by <u>Jonson</u> and Shakespeare at the Mermaid and other London taverns. Francis Beaumont had connections with the Catholic <u>Fortescues</u> of London: one of <u>John Fortescue</u>'s daughters (the other 'gave eleven daughters to religion,' which means that they became nuns)...

*[This was the family with whom **Sir Edward Stanley Jr** placed his daughters after the death of his wife Lucy Percy; his daughter Frances later married <u>Sir John Fortescue</u>. HM]*

married <u>Francis</u>'s brother Sir John Beaumont of Grace Dieu, whose son Francis (no doubt named after the dramatist) was a Catholic and became a Jesuit. Beaumont died prematurely in his thirty-second year, a month and a half before Shakespeare, in March 1616. John Fletcher—whose name appears in the Southwark 'token' books (listing those receiving the Anglican communion at the church there)—outlived Beaumont by nine years, being carried off at the age of forty-five by the plague in August 1625 and buried in St. Savior's Church, Southwark" (Mutschmann and Wentersdorf 133, 134).

<u>Fortescue:</u> connection with the Blackfriars Gatehouse and Shakespeare's purchase of it:

" . . . . In the Guildhall Library, and the British Museum, London, there can be found respectively the original title-deed and mortgage of Shakespeare's only acquisition of property in London: part of one of the gatehouses to the Blackfriars precinct in which his company operated their Blackfriars theatre. The original documents were first discovered in the late eighteenth century among the papers of the Fetherstonhaugh family, to whom properties in the area had descended, and the two Shakespeare signatures they carry, both universally deemed authentic . . . . Although it can certainly be argued that the gatehouse was convenient for the Blackfriars theatre, with a ferry for crossing to the Globe just down the road, even so it is difficult to regard the purchase as anything other than curious.

. . . . it can be identified as the upper floor of a long-destroyed building that seems to have straddled the Blackfriars precinct's eastern entrance, at or near where a way called Ireland Yard met St Andrew's Hill, leading down to the river.

. . . We are told that the previous owner had been Henry Walker 'citizen and minstrel of London'; and its 'now or late' tenant one William Ireland, who gave his name to Ireland Yard. Henry Walker was presumably another of Shakespeare's musical acquaintances along with the already mentioned Robert Johnson. But, rather more significantly, the document also records that previously the Gatehouse had been 'in the tenure of <u>John Fortescue gent</u>.; this was John Fortescue of Lordington, Sussex, whose uncle was <u>Sir John Fortescue</u>, Elizabeth's Master of the Royal Wardrobe (the repository of royal costumery), just over the way from the Gatehouse, and for whom <u>John the nephew</u> seems to have worked in a minor capacity.

Possibly relevantly, around this particular time, 1613, <u>Sir John</u> married <u>Frances Stanley, daughter of the fiercely Catholic Sir Edward Stanley, cousin of Ferdinando</u> and known shelterer of Catholic priests, *[I have come across no reference for this claim about **Sir Edward Jr**; it might well be a confusion with his father **Sir Thomas** or a previous reference to his uncle **Sir Edward Sr**. HM]* and for whom, as we have seen, Shakespeare seems to have created <u>the epitaphs for his and his father's monuments at Tong</u>. <u>Lucy Percy</u>, <u>Frances</u>' mother, was the second daughter of <u>Thomas, the very Catholic Earl of Northumberland</u>. <u>John Fortescue</u> the nephew was a near overt Catholic, as was his wife Ellen, daughter of the recusant Ralph Henslowe of Boarhunt, Hampshire, a relative of the <u>Earls of Southampton</u>.

Here the further curiosity of the Gatehouse is that it was one of the most notoriously Catholic places Shakespeare could have chosen in all of London. Back in 1586 Blackfriars resident Richard Frith had reported it as having: 'sundry back-doors and byways, and many secret vaults and corners. It hath been in time past suspected, and searched for papists but no good done for want of good knowledge of the backdoors and byways and of the dark corners.'

During the 1590s, the height of the Topcliffe era, the Gatehouse was repeatedly reported for the comings and goings of priests. In 1591, for instance: 'Fennell the priest doth use to come very much to Mr John Fortescue his house.' Richard Topcliffe, to his credit, warned John Fortescue and his uncle that they were courting trouble, culminating in a major raid one day in 1598, when John Fortescue was away, apparently due to a tip-off from an informer, one William Udall. . . . . Once again these 'secret passages' seem to have baffled the searchers, for no priests were found, and although under interrogation Ellen Fortescue and her two very attractive daughter (said to be 'the fairest in London'), admitted they were Catholics they vehemently denied harbouring any priests. This was a clear piece of equivocation if ever there was one since in a later autobiography Jesuit Oswald Greenway recorded how he visited the house the next day, only to be told there had indeed been two priests there, but these had used the hiding places to make their escape.

Seven years later the Gatehouse surfaced again in the annals of the Catholic underground, this time in connection wit the notorious Gunpowder plot. According to a copy of a memorandum of the leading Jesuit Father, John Gerard, preserved to this day at St Cuthbert's College, Ushaw, Durham, shortly before the fateful 5 November 1605 Gerard asked Ellen Fortescue for the use of a private room in the Gatehouse:

where some persons who did not wish to be seen in his company could meet him unobserved. She, being a prudent woman, did not relish this mention of persons likely to come there who did not wish their visits to be known. He [Gerard] replied that they were excellent men of noble birth, and Catholics; and at last, upon her pressing him to say who they were, named Catesby, Percy, Winter, Digby, and several more, all without exception implicated in the Gunpowder Plot.

To her credit Ellen Fortescue, stout Catholic that she was, declined to admit the plotters, remarking of Catesby, whom she acknowledged she knew slightly 'I never approved, nor his habits and loose way of life.' . . . . Arguably weary of all this cloak and dagger business the Fortescues eventually retired to St Omer in France, where Father Persons had founded a school for English Catholics, while one of their two attractive daughters, Elizabeth, married the brother of dramatist Francis Beaumont.

Now in all this the major source of interest is why, with all London to choose from, Shakespeare should have selected, as a purportedly casual investment, this notoriously Catholic Gatehouse, with all its secret hiding places still apparently retaining their secrets. It is not even as though he bought it as a bargain: he paid £140 for it, more than twice the amount he had paid for New Place. So was it really just an 'investment pure and simple?'

[Wilson then provides the details of the complicated sale in which William Johnson, John Jackson, and John Heminges were co-purchasers with Shakespeare. (Enos)]

". . . . the trusteeship arrangement relating to the Blackfriars property had the effect of excluding Anne [Shakespeare's wife] from any rights to it. . . ." (Wilson, Ian, *Shakespeare: the Evidence*, 1993, 372-376).

". . . if Shakespeare did not set down in his will his instructions regarding an interment he clearly cared deeply about, to whom did he entrust them? Here it may be worthwhile to return momentarily to the most over-looked name in Shakespeare's will, and one all the more surprising for its appearing twice, that of John Robinson. This occurs first in reference to the Blackfriars Gatehouse . . . which, in his bequeathing of this to Susanna, Shakespeare specifically describes as 'wherein one John Robinson dwelleth.' The name then recurs among the signatures of the will's witnesses, the third to be so featured. . . . .

It is quite definite that back in the reign of Elizabeth I a John Robinson was working as steward to Sir John Fortescue—Master of the Royal Wardrobe directly opposite Shakespeare's Gatehouse, and the uncle of the Catholic John Fortescue who was associated with the Gatehouse itself. He was described as living 'over against Sir John's door, and thereby in the immediate vicinity of, if not actually in, Shakespeare's Gatehouse. And he was probably the John Robinson listed among those Blackfriars' residents who petitioned against the Blackfriars theatre back in 1596. Like John Fortescue and his family, John Robinson was a very active Catholic. In May 1599, the year in which his wife died, he was reported for sheltering Catholic priest Richard Dudley. Furthermore in 1605, that is at the time of the Gunpowder plot, he sent his thirteen-year-old son, Edward, to the training college for English Catholics at St Omer. This Edward in 1613, at the age of twenty-one, presented himself at the English College in Rome for training to become priest, upon which he told those receiving him that he had 'an only brother, but no sister.' So could this only brother have been named John after his father, and have been not so much Shakespeare's tenant in the Gatehouse, as his appointed guardian of one of London's best places of refuge for Catholic priests? Might he even have been in holy orders like his brother, and have been one and the same as the mysterious Benedictine from whom according to one Catholic tradition, Shakespeare received the last rites of the Catholic Church?" (Wilson, Ian, 396, 397).

Fortescue

"For us, the brightest glories of the house of <u>Fortescue</u> are those which arise from the many and heroic examples which it gave of Catholic faith and loyalty from the day when Blessed Adrian Fortescue sealed his faith with his blood. During several generations, daughters of the house of <u>Fortescue</u> wore the Canoness's white robe in our community, and so I propose to give in this chapter a few brief notices on one branch of this illustrious family, the <u>Fortescues of Salden in Buckinghamshire</u> [*guardians of **Sir Edward Jr**'s three surviving daughters* HM]. One word on the earlier line will suffice. Richard le Fortescu, or 'strong shield,' who is handed down in the family tradition as having saved the Conqueror's life at Hastings, returned to Normandy, but his eldest son, Sir Adam, the ancestor of the English Fortescues, obtained a grant of Wimpstone in the parish of Modbury, a few miles southwest of Totnes, and between the two Devonshire rivers aforesaid, the Dart and the Yealm, there were Fortescues at Preston, Spindlestone, Wood, Norreis, and Fallapit. The family pedigree gives us twelve lords of Wimpstone, whereof six bore the name of Adam, till, at the close of the fourteenth century, Sir John, a younger son of Sir William Fortescue of Wimpstone, gives a wider celebrity to the Fortescues of South Devon. Sir John of Meaux, as he is called, fought at Agincourt, and was made Governor of Meaux after its capture by the English in 1422. He married Eleanor Norreis of Norreis, not far from Wimpstone. Their eldest son, Sir Henry, was Chief-Justice of Ireland, and brought back with him to his Devonshire home a large body of Irish retainers, whose descendants, no doubt, are still there: their second, Sir John, was the renowned Chief-Justice of England, and the direct ancestor of Earl Fortescue of Castle Hill: the third son, Sir Richard, who fell at the first battle of St Alban's, usually called Sir Richard Fortescue of Punsborne, was the grandfather of Blessed Adrian Fortescue, and the ancestor of several of our Louvain nuns. His second son, Sir John, married Alice Boleyn, sister of Thomas, Earl of Wiltshire, the father of the unhappy Queen Anne Boleyn, who was thus the martyr's first cousin.

Sir Adrian Fortescue was beheaded on Tower Hill on the 9th of July (according to some authorities on the 10th) in 1539, three years after his hapless cousin had suffered the same death (but for a far different cause) in the same place. He had been twice married, first to Anne, daughter of Sir William Stonor, and secondly to Anne, daughter of Sir William Reade. . . . . The martyr's eldest son, John**,** was unhappily educated a Protestant, and was Preceptor to Queen Elizabeth, Keeper of the Wardrobe, and Chancellor of the Exchequer. But among his descendants I find many names distinguished for their faith and piety, of whom not a few consecrated themselves to God by the vows of religion. The martyr's grandson, <u>Sir Francis Fortescue of Salden (Sir John's third son)</u>, next claims our attention. Whether he died reconciled to the Church is uncertain, for as <u>Father Gerard </u>wrote, 'he presumed too much on an opportunity of doing penance before death.' The insertion of his name in the Louvain Dirgebook is a strong presumption in his favour.

In his house <u>Father Gerard</u> and other priests lived in safety, preaching and saying Mass, for the mistress was a devout Catholic and the master 'no enemy to religion.' <u>Sir Francis</u> was a Knight of the Bath and in favour at Court. His wife, <u>Grace Manners</u>, who according to one of my authorities was the daughter, according to another the niece, of the <u>Earl of Rutland</u> [*niece of Henry, 2nd Earl of Rutland* HM], her father [*John Manners, second son, brother of Henry, 2nd Earl, married to Dorothy Vernon,* **Sir Edward Jr**'s *sister-in-law* HM], was a convert of <u>Father Gerard</u>'s, and by her influence their children were brought up Catholics. One of these was Sister Frances Fortescue, professed at Louvain in 1622; another, Adrian, entered the Society of Jesus. . . . Let us now return to Blessed Adrian. Through his third son, Sir Anthony, God added still more to His crown by the piety of his descendants. Sir Anthony's wife was Margaret, the granddaughter of Blessed Margaret Pole, Countess of Salisbury and daughter of Geoffrey Pole, the Cardinal's brother. Their second son, <u>John Fortescue</u>, is described in the MS. . . as 'of no great estate but of ancient family,' whose house was a receptacle for all priests and religious 'without partiality or exception.' He married Helen, daughter of Ralph Henslow, of whom our Louvain Records tell us that 'she was near of kin to the <u>Earl of Southampton</u> and a most constant Catholic. . . . This holy couple came over to end their days in Flanders. Their daughter, <u>Mary</u>, made her profession at St Monica's on the same day as Sister Gertrude Winter" (Hamilton, ed., Vol 1, 218-221).

Fortescue, John, Master of the Wardrobe

'Bacon's second tenant there [the Blackfriar's Gatehouse] was a Catholic named <u>John Fortescue of Lordington, Sussex</u> (his father, Sir Anthony Fortescue, was concerned in a conspiracy against Elizabeth in 1562; his mother was one of the Catholic Poles, related to Cardinal Pole). <u>John Fortescue</u>, who held a minor office in the Wardrobe, married Ellen, daughter of Ralph Henslowe, a Catholic recusant of Boarhunt, Hampshire, who was kin to the <u>Earls of Southampton</u>. In 1591, two priests reported that they had presented <u>John and Ellen Fortescue</u> 'with such stuff as we brought from Rome.' In the same year it is said that 'Fennell the priest does use to come very much to <u>Mr. John Fortescue</u> his house.' <u>Fortescue</u> was warned by the Government's priest-hunter, Master <u>Richard Topcliffe</u>, of the danger he was in through his association with priests; but he ignored the warning. In 1598, the authorities received a fresh report about the suspected Catholic activities going on in the house, which was described as having 'many places of secret conveyance in it' communicating with 'secret passages towards the water (i.e., the Thames river). Acting on this report, the authorities had the Gatehouse searched: <u>John Fortescue</u> was absent, but his wife <u>Ellen</u> resisted the searchings, enabling one of two priests who were there to slip away. During the subsequent interrogation, <u>Mistress Fortescue</u> and her daughters Katherine and Elizabeth admitted that they were recusants, but denied the presence of priests in their house. In a letter to the <u>Earl of Essex</u>, <u>John Fortescue</u> repeated this denial: 'I crave no favor either of her Majesty or of any peer within this realm, if any unnatural or disloyal act can be proved against me, either in harboring, maintaining, or abetting either priest or Jesuit, and forbidden by her highness' laws. And . . . if I have retained my conscience at all, her Majesty has been no loser by it, nor myself, God knows, any great gainer.' It is interesting to note that in his autobiography, Father Oswald Greenway, S. J., relates how he paid a surreptitious visit to the Gatehouse on the day following the raid and was there informed that there *had* been priests there but that—by God's grace—their hiding-places had not been discovered. <u>John Fortescue, his wife</u> and their two daughters were imprisoned for a while. After their release, they seem to have maintained their connections with Catholic priests; but when in 1605, <u>Father John Gerard</u> came to <u>Mistress Fortescue</u> and asked for permission to lodge in her house and to use it as a meeting-place with a number of Catholic gentlemen—<u>Catesby</u>, <u>Percy</u>, Winter and others—the good woman declined in her husband's absence to admit them, alleging that she did not approve of <u>Catesby</u>'s loose way of life. A short while after, the Gunpowder Plot was discovered, and among those sought by the Government was <u>Father Gerard</u>, the intimate of the conspirators. To the consternation of the <u>Fortescues</u>, he appeared one day at the Gatehouse, disguised by a false beard and false hair, and asked them to shelter him, as he did not know where to conceal himself. 'Full of sadness', <u>Master Fortescue</u> replied: 'Have you no one to ruin but me and my family?' To escape the continuing persecution, <u>John Fortescue</u> later went abroad and settled in St Omer, France. His son George Fortescue, Catholic essayist and poet, received part of his education at the English college at Douai, and also stayed at the English college in Rome (1609). <u>Fortescue</u>'s daughter Elizabeth married the brother of Francis Beaumont. . . . " (Mutschmann and Wentersdorf 137 – 139). (See also: Sir Adrian Fortescue.) [His father's first wife Anne was a Neville. She was sister and co-heir of John Neville, Marquis of Montacute (Gillow *Sir Adrian Fortescue*).]

<u>Gerard, John</u> (1564-1637)

"He was born 4 Oct 64 at Etwall, Derbys., the younger son of <u>Sir Thomas Gerard</u> [*of Bryn, Lancashire* HM] and Elizabeth, daughter and heiress of Sir John Port. He entered Exeter College, Oxford about 1575 but after less than a year was forced to leave on religious grounds. After two years study at home, with William Sutton (q.v.) as his tutor in Greek, he got a licence to travel. He arrived at Douai 29 Aug 77 (D. 129) and stayed three years. In 1580-1 he was at Cleremont, Paris. About Sep 83 he crossed to Dover (SP, 12/182, no. 19). He was committed to the Marshalsea 5 Mar 84 and released about Easter 85. He arrived in Rome 5 Aug 86 (F. 559) and entered (Vic.) with a dispensation *propter aetatem*, being three months under the canonical age (MB, 25071). A month later, 15 Aug 88, he entered SJ and his long adventurous autobiography is a classic. He died in Rome 27 Jul 1637. cf. P. Caraman, *John Gerard*, 1951" (Anstruther *John Gerard*).

"Jesuit. He was the second son of Sir Thomas Gerard, Knight of Bryn, Lancashire [*the father was the one who planned to rescue Mary, Queen of Scots from Chatsworth in 1570, along with* **Sir Thomas Stanley** *and* **Sir Edward Stanley Sr**; *the first son was Sir Thomas Gerard Jr, knighted by James I at York in 1603, with* **Sir Edward Stanley Jr** *knighted soon afterwards in London,* HM], by Elizabeth, eldest daughter and co-heiress of Sir John Port, Knight, of Etwall, Derbyshire. He received part of his education at the English college at Douay, where he arrived Aug 29, 1577, and apparently accompanied the students to Rheims the following March. He returned to England and was matriculated in the university at Oxford as a member of Exeter College about Oct. 1579. (Boase, Reg of Exeter College. pp 186, 218). Religious reasons forced him to leave the college and return home within a year. In 1581 he went to Clermont College in Paris, which belonged to the Jesuits, but ill health forced him to return home. He tried to leave England without permission and was arrested and put in the Marshalsea Prison, from which he was released in Oct 1585. The next year he went to Rome and was ordained a priest. He joined the Society of Jesus in Rome on 15 Aug 1588. He was sent to the English mission where he was suspected by the government but escaped being arrested. Eventually, while on a visit to London, he was betrayed by a servant and was sent to the Clink and the Tower where he was tortured horribly by being suspended by the wrists. He escaped from the Tower by swinging on a rope suspended over the Tower ditch. He continued to work in the mission and was captured again. He thought he would be able to gain the trust of James, but not so. He had to flee to the continent (dressed in livery of the ambassadors of Spain and Flanders) because he was a suspect in the Gunpowder Plot. He went to Rome and then worked with Father Thomas Talbot in the English Jesuit novitiate at Louvain. He returned to Rome where he died" (*DNB*).

John Gerard was a cousin of Sir William Stanley (Chetham Society, Vol 25, Heywood, ed. iv). (*Not a first cousin, but certainly related*. HM)

"Father Morris, in his *Condition of Catholics under James I.*, gives a letter of Father Gerard, S.J., in which occurs the following passage:—'At the Monastery of St's my cousin Shirley hath requested my coming thither for these three or four months, to bestow one afternoon upon her and some younger nuns whom she hath charge of, that they may all together ask me what spiritual questions they may like best; but I have never yet found a fit time for it.'" (Hamilton, ed., *The Chronicle of St Monica's*, Vol 1, 19).
(See also: Jessop 130).

Gerard, Thomas
"It is true that Ferdinando's [Stanley] followers were mostly Catholic; his bosom-friend Thomas Gerard, for instance, was brother to a famous and much-sought-after Jesuit" (Devlin 82).

Robert Greene (following a synopsis of the *DNB* biography)
" . . . . Green had been courting the favour of the Derbys since 1584, dedicating *The Myrrour of Modestie* to the Countess in that year; but by the time he published *Menaphon* and *Ciceronis Amor* (dedicated to Ferdinando Stanley), his territory was already being invaded, not by other University wits, its previous sole lords, but by an 'upstart crow' of a provincial player. At the end of the few bitter and penurious years left to him, in 1592 the dying Greene dipped his quill in gall and penned a last sneer at the 'absolute *Iohannes fac totum*, in his own conceit the only Shake-scene in a countrey'" (Keen 81).

Hall, John
He, along with Sir Thomas Gerard (father of the Jesuit priest) and two Stanleys [**Sir Thomas** *and* **Sir Edward Sr** HM] had a plot to free Mary, Queen of Scots from Coventry Castle [*actually from Chatsworth House* HM] in 1570 (Fraser 500).

Halsall, Ursula
". . . the phoenix of Shakespeare's *The Phoenix and the Turtle* was almost certainly Ursula Halsall or Stanley, an illegitimate daughter of Henry Stanley, the fourth Earl; Ursula's sister, Dorothy, married (Sir) Cuthbert Halsall (or Halsey), one of the dedicatees of Weever's *Epigrammes*; and Sir

<u>Cuthbert</u>, the phoenix's brother-in-law, was one of several Halsalls engaged in protracted legal battles with the Duddells of Salwick, one of whom was William Duddell, son-in-law of <u>John Cottom,</u> formerly schoolmaster at Stratford" (Honigmann 7).

Lewis, Owen

"Bishop of Cassano, born of an ancient family, Dec. 15, 1533, at Maltrayth, in the hamlet of Bodeon, Isle of Anglesey, became a scholar of Winchester College in 1547, whence he proceeded to New College, Oxford, and was admitted a perpetual fellow in 1554.

At this time <u>St. Charles Borromeo</u>, then Cardinal and Archbishop of Milan, was in Rome, and becoming acquainted with Dr. Lewis, was so impressed with his zeal and abilities that he persuaded him to return with him to Milan to reside in his palace. There he appointed him one of the vicars general of his diocese, June 16, 1580. In this laborious field he laboured for the next four years, enjoying the closest intimacy of his patron, whose last vicar-general he was; indeed, the great saint expired in his arms, in the early part of the night between the 3rd and 4th of November, 1584. Many of the English and Welsh exiled clergy were warmly received by St. Charles. His ordinary confessor was Dr. Gryffyth Roberts, canon and theological of Milan, and Dr. Hugh Gryffyth, nephew of Dr. Lewis, also appears to have resided for a short time with his uncle in the archepiscopal palace at Milan. [*St Carlo Borromeo was the author of the Spiritual Testament, a copy of which, signed by John Shakespeare, was found hidden in the rafters in the house in Henley Street, Stratford.* HM] *Dodd, Ch. Hist.* ii.; *Secret Policy,* 174; *Apol.,* 91, 107, 125, 141 *seq.; Constable, Specimen,* 52, 81, 166; *Plowden, Remarks on Pazani,* 100 *seq.; Tierney, Dodd's Ch. Hist.,* ii. 167 *seq.,* iii. lxxvi.; *Foley, Records S.J.,* vi.; *Watson, Sparing Discov.,* 31, 34 *seq.,* 58, *Decacordon,* 2, 84, 96 *seq.,* 103 *seq.,* 236; *Knox, Records of the Eng. Catholics,* I and ii.; *Estate pf Emg Figitives,* 64 *seq.; Wood, Athenæ Oxon.,* i.; *Butler, Lives of the Saints,* ed. 1812 *seq. ,* xi. 104" (Gillow *Owen Lewis*)

Leyburne, James

". . . martyr, was the eldest son and heir of Nicholas Leyburne, Esq., of Cunswick and Skelsmergh, co. Westmoreland, by Elizabeth Warcopp, of an ancient family of that name, seated at Smardale, co. Westmoreland. His aunt, Elizabeth, daughter of Sir James Leyburne, of Cunswick, knighted at York Place in 1529, (by his second wife, Ellen, daughter of Thomas Preston, of Preston Patrick and Levens, co. Westmoreland, and of the Manor of Furness, co. Lancaster who subsequently became the wife of <u>Thomas Stanley, second Baron Monteagle</u>), married first Thomas fourth Baron Dacre, of Gillesland, and her three daughters, being co-heiresses to their brother George, the last Lord Dacre, became the wives of the three sons of her second husband, <u>Thomas, Duke of Norfolk</u>, and thus conveyed Greystock and Naworth castles to the <u>Howard</u> family. A younger sister of the Duchess of Norfolk, <u>Anne Leyburne, married Sir William Stanley, third Baron Monteagle</u>, of Hornby Castle, by whom she had an only daughter and heiress, <u>Elizabeth, wife of Edward Parker, Baron Morley, whose son, William Parker, became Lord Morley and Monteagle.</u>   ....

In support of his opinions he cited <u>Dr. Allen</u>'s and other works. Of course he would have kept these opinions to himself had he not been purposely put into the logical dilemma of questions as to the Pope's bull of excommunication, etc., questions put with the object of entrapping him to his destruction. Referring to Leyburne and his kinsmen, the <u>Duke of Norfolk</u> and the <u>Earl of Arundel</u>, Ward says:

> 'By plotts, and letters counterfeit,
> By cunning trick, and subtile cheat,
> By suborn'd evidence, and lies,
> Lei'ster and Walsingham devise
> Strange trapst'ensnare the innocent,
> For traitors to the government.'
> *England's Reform,* Canto ii.

The martyr was next sent back to the New Fleet at Manchester, and thence carried to Lancaster, at the charge of the town of Manchester, with other prisoners for conscience. According to instructions from the Council, the judges formally sentenced him to death at the Lenten assizes, and he was hanged, bowelled, and quartered at Lancaster, March 22, 1582-3.

. . . . His quarters were distributed in various towns, Lancaster, Preston, etc., and his head, according to Hollingworth, was set upon the church tower at Manchester.

Sander, De Schism. Angl., ed. 1585, f. 192, 3d. 1586, . 466 and appx.; *Harland, Lanc. Lieut.,* ii.; *Hollingworth, Mancun.,* p. 92; *Heywood, Allen's Defence of Stanley,* p, kxxxv.; *Foser, Cumb. and Westm. Pedigrees; Sharp, Mem. of the Rebel.,* p. 287; *Valladolid Diary, MS.; Pollen, acts of Eng. Mar.; Law, Challoner's Memoirs, Edinb.* ed. i., pp. xxv., xli., 265 *Bridgewater, Cloncertatio,* ed. 1594, ff. 103, 307, 409; *Pollini, L'Hist. Eccles. della Rivol. d'Inghil.,* p. 638; *Norfolk, Lives of P. Howard and A. Dacres,* p. 176; *Dodd, Ch. Hist.,* ii.; *douay Diaries; P.R.O., Dom. Eliz.* civ. n. 35; *Burke, Extinct Peerage; Leyburne, Encycl. Ans.,* p. 8; *Morris, Troubles,* 1st Series; *Foster, Visit. of Yorks; Metcalfe, Book of Knights; Jefferson, Hist. of Carlisle.*

(Gillow *James Leyburne*).

"In vol. I. P. 220, we have given a short biography of this Father; and in page 669 of the same volume some further particulars are added leading to the idea that he was *de jure* the seventh Earl of Westmoreland, and a great grandson to Ralph, the fourth earl, and would have succeeded to the title upon the death of Charles the sixth earl, but for the attainder of the latter.

An antiquarian has subsequently made the following suggestion: 'I should have said that he was Edward, a younger son of Sir John Neville of Leversedge by his second wife Beatrice, daughter to Henry Browne, and that his grandfather, Sir Robert Neville, having married Eleanor Townley, and Sir Robert Hesketh having married Grace Towneley, was the reason of his being brought up with Sir Thomas Hesketh, son of Sir Robert, as stated in Father Neville's autobiography'" (Foley 685).

Neville, Father Edmund

"Edmund Neville, *alias* Eliseus Nelson, is recorded in the year 1648, in chains for the faith. Father Tanner, in his short notice of this venerable Father, calls him a noble confessor of Christ *in vinculis*, and when free an apostle. He states him to have been a native of Lancashire, born in the year 1563, of a family of wealth and station. He was heir to an ample patrimony in Westmoreland, but renounced all in hope of eternal riches, convinced of the vanity of all temporal things, and preferring the reproach of Christ to the delights of princes. Quitting his native land, he went to Rome, and entered the English College at the mature age of forty-three, as an alumnus, in the year 1606, as Edward Neville, under the assumed name of Eliseus Nelson. He took the usual College oath on the 30th of March, 1608, and was ordained priest the 12th of April, 1608.

"During these years [1581 to 1584] the latter [Sir Thomas Hesketh of Rufford] harboured a young son of the famous Neville family: **Edmund Neville**, born 1563, later a Jesuit. After joining the Society Neville praised Sir Thomas Hesketh (to whom he was related) for unusual generosity in rearing him after his own father lost all his property" (Stevenson, Robert 72, 73). (See also: Scarisbrick and Sale.)

Percy, Henry [Close to intrigue surrounding Mary Queen of Scots and plans to marry and free her. Married to Catherine Neville.]

". . . eighth earl of Northumberland, born about 1532, was second son of Sir Thomas Percy, who was executed for his share in the Pilgrimage of Grace. He was M.P. in 1554 for Morpeth, knighted in 1557, and as a soldier distinguished himself before Leith against the Scots (1560). Dodd says that in religion he was an occasionalist. During the life of his elder brother he declared for the new religion, and vigorously supported the Government during the great northern rising of 1569. Nevertheless he was presently in communication with Mary Stuart, who was in confinement at Tutbury, offering to become her 'servant' and to procure her escape. He was arrested in 1571, and after eighteen months' detention in the Tower was brought to trial on a charge of treason. He was fined and forbidden to leave his home at Petworth, but soon after was set at liberty. After his brother's execution in 1571 [*his brother was Thomas, 7th Earl of Northumberland, the father of Lucy Percy, wife of* **Sir Edward Stanley Jr** HM] he succeeded to the title. He took his seat in the House of Lords in 1575-6, but in 1582 he was arrested on the charge of complicity in Throckmorton's plot to release Queen Mary. He was soon released, but was deprived of his post of governor of Tynemouth Castle. In 1583 he received the two Pagets [Thomas and Charles] at Petworth, and offered advice as to the manner of landing French troops; so, at least, it was 'confessed' under torture by William Shelley. Northumberland's aim, it was said, was not only to secure Queen Mary's release, but to extort from Elizabeth religious toleration. In 1584 he was sent to the Tower for the third time. Six months later he was found dead in his bed in his cell, shot through the heart, on June 21, 1585, aged about 52.

The jury returned a verdict of *felo de se*, but there can be little doubt that he was murdered. By his wife Catharine Neville, daughter and coheiress of John, last Lord Latimer, he had eight sons and two daughters, of whom <u>Henry</u>, the eldest succeeded him as ninth earl.

Dodd, ii. 41; 357; *Sharpe, Memorials*, pp. 351-75; *Lee, Dict. Nat. Biog.*, xliv.; *Bridgewater, Concertatio*, ff. 204, 410; *Yepes, Historia*, p. 595; *Persons' edit. of Rishton's sanders*, 1586, p. 474; *Cath. Mag. New Series*, ii. 697.

1. 'Crudelitatis Calvinianæ Exempla Duo recentissima ex Anglia; quorum primum continet barbarum ac sævum Calvinianorum Edictum recenta editum contra Catholicos: Alterum vero, exhibet indignissimam mortem Illustrissimi viri Comitis Northumbriæ in Castro Londinensi occisi mense Julio hujus anni 1585. Præmissa est Præfatio ed Peincipes Populosque Catholicos de Claudibus quas Hæresis infort Rebuspubl. cum Congratulatione de Pace recenter facta in Gallia. Adjectum est in fine Exemplar quarundum Literarum ex Anglia.' (Cologne), 1585, 8vo; Transl. into German, 1586, 4to, English Lond. 1585, 12mo, French, Italian, and Spanish.

In this the Government was charged with Northumberland's murder, and to allay the public excitement a Star Chamber inquiry was ordered, and the following report issued:

2. 'A True and Summarie Reporte of the Declaration of some Part of the Earl of Northumberland's Treasons, with the Examinations and Depositions of sundrie persons concerning the manner of his Murder in the Tower of London,' etc. Lond. C. Barker, 1585, 4to, pp.22 exclus. of preface" (Gillow, *Henry Percy*).

Percy, Sir Josceline Percy A participant in the Essex rebellion.

"<u>Sir Josceline Percy</u> was the seventh son of <u>Henry eighth Earl of Northumberland</u> [*uncle of Lucy Percy, wife of* **Sir Edward Stanley Jr** HM]; he was born in 1578, and knighted in 1599. Having been an adherent of the <u>Earl of Essex</u>, together with his elder brother <u>Sir Charles Percy</u>, they both received the royal pardon in 44 Elizabeth, for any concern they might have had in that Earl's rebellion. The name of <u>Sir Josceline</u> does not occur in the court history of James I.; the whole house of <u>Percy</u> having fallen into disgrace, together with <u>Sir Josceline</u>'s eldest brother the <u>Earl</u>, on account of the Gunpowder Treason. He died unmarried in 1631. <u>Sir Josceline</u> seems to have imagined that the Council acted upon the rule layed down in Magna Charta, that a man should only be fined *salvo contenemento,* that is, saving to a freeholder his freehold, to a merchant his merchandise, to a rustic his plough, to a soldier his arms, and to a scholar his books. But the practice of the Council was as much at variance with Magna Charta as their authority, and many members of <u>the Percy family</u> had sufficient reason to know that it was so. The <u>Earl</u> was fined in the Star Chamber £30,000, besides being sentenced to imprisonment for life, and he actually paid £20,000, . . . " (Camden Society, *Anecdotes and Traditions*, 65).

<u>Percy, Lady Mary</u>

". . . abbess, O.S.B., born June 11, 1570, was <u>the youngest child of Thomas, 7th earl of Northumberland</u> (*q.v.*) and his countess, <u>Anne Somerset</u> (*q.v.*). [*Mary was a sister of Lucy Percy, wife of* **Sir Edward Stanley Jr**. HM] She was carried to the Continent by her mother just after her birth, and educated in various convents. After the death of her mother in 1596, Lady Mary took up her residence in the Low Countries to take possession of what her mother had left. She had vowed virginity and had decided to devote herself to a religious life. With this end in view she lodged at the Augustinian convent called Jericho in Brussels, and subsequently at St. Ursula's convent of the same order in Louvain. Finally she decided to found an English Benedictine convent at Brussels, and purchased premises for that purpose in 1598. It was commenced under the superiorship of Dame Joan Berkeley, from the convent at Rheims, who was consecrated abbess on Nov. 14, 1599, and eight days later <u>Lady Mary</u> received the habit of the order. Upon the death of the lady abbess Berkeley in 1616, <u>Lady Mary Percy</u> succeeded as second abbess, and so continued till her death in 1642, aged 72.

Cath. Mag., New Series, ii. 487, 581; *Cath. Miscel.*, iv. 209; *Tierney's Dodd*, ii. 179 *seq.*, iii. Ap. xc., iv. 103; *Downside Rev.,* iv. 253; *Husenbeth, Notices of Engl. Coll. and Convents*, p. 60; *Chron. Mon. Brussels*" (Gillow *Lady Mary Percy*).

Percy, Thomas, [A leader of the 1569 rebellion.]

". . . 7th <u>earl of Northumberland</u>, [*father of Lucy, wife of* **Sir Edward Stanley Jr** HM] beatified martyr, born in 1528, was the elder son of <u>Sir Thomas Percy</u>, a younger son of <u>Henry Algernon, fifth earl of</u>

Northumberland, and brother and heir-presumptive to <u>Henry Algernon, the sixth earl</u>. <u>Sir Thomas</u> took a prominent part, with his younger brother, Sir Ingelram Percy, in the Pilgrimage of Grace in 1536. Both were taken prisoners. <u>Sir Thomas</u> was attainted and executed at Tyburn, June 2, 1537, being interred in the Crutched Friars Church, London. Thereupon his <u>elder brother, the sixth earl</u>, fearing the effect of the attainder on the fortunes of the family, voluntarily surrendered his estates to the crown, and on his death in 1537 the title fell into abeyance. <u>Sir Thomas</u>' widow was Eleanor, dau. of Sir Guiscard Harbottal, of Beamish, Durham, who fell at Flodden Field in 1513, and had inherited Preston Tower and a large estate, to which she withdrew with her two sons, <u>Thomas</u> and <u>Henry</u>, after her husband's execution.

Subsequently <u>the two boys</u> were entrusted to the care of Sir Thomas Tempest, of Tong Hall, and in 1549 they were restored in blood.

After the accession of Queen Mary, <u>Thomas Percy</u> soon obtained royal favour, and he received the governorship of Prudhoe Castle. In 1557, in consideration of 'his noble descent, constancy, virtue, and valour in arms, and other strong qualifications,' he was promoted to the earldom of Northumberland, and was nominated high marshal of the army in the north. Upon Elizabeth's accession he was harassed by criticism, and in 1560 resigned his office. He was elected K.G. in 1563, but in 1565 was reported 'dangerously obstinate in religion' by Burghley's agents. When <u>Mary Queen of Scots</u> was brought to Carlisle, <u>Northumberland</u> interviewed her and expressed his sympathy. He was suspected of favouring the suggested match between Mary and the <u>Duke of Norfolk</u>. At any rate, he received orders to depart from Carlisle. Indignant that his liberty should be thus hampered, the earl readily lent an ear to the suggestion of one Thomas Markenfield, a gentleman who had lived some time abroad; and together with the <u>earl of Westmorland</u> [*grandfather of Margaret Clifford, wife of Henry, 4th Earl of Derby, brother of* **Sir Thomas** *and* **Sir Edward Sr** HM] he contrived the rising of 1569. Startled into premature action by the preventive measures of the Government, the leaders marched a force through Durham, where mass was for the last time said in the cathedral, to Ripon. After a month of indecisive action their force melted away. The Government treated with rigour all who fell into their hands, some sixty-six being executed. <u>Northumberland</u> fled, and for a time led a hunted life, ultimately taking refuge in Scotland, where he was placed in custody. In Aug. 1572 he was handed by the regent, the earl of Mar, to Elizabeth's officers for a consideration of 2000*l*. He was taken to York, where he was offered his life if he would abandon his religion, but stoutly proclaiming with his last breath his faith in the catholic church, he was beheaded Aug. 22, 1572, aged 44.

The earl married <u>Anne, third dau. of Henry Somerset</u>, [*Lucy Stanley's parents*] second earl of Worcester, by whom he had a son, who died young in 1560, and four daughters. Of the latter, three married [*Lucy to* **Sir Edward Stanley Jr**], and the fourth was <u>Lady Mary Percy</u>, foundress of the English Benedictine Abbey at Brussels (*q.v.*). The title passed to <u>Northumberland's brother Henry, 8th earl</u> (*q.v.*).

After <u>the earl</u>'s flight to Scotland his wife remained on the borders, so that she might the better be able to render him assistance. She made every effort to raise money for his ransom. In Aug. 1570 she arrived at Antwerp with her newly born child, Mary, and obtained funds and devised a plan by which <u>her husband</u> might be sent into Flanders. But her energetic endeavours to purchase his liberty failed. For a time she resided at Liège, and in 1573 she was at Mechlin, and subsequently removed to Brussels. In 1576, at Queen Elizabeth's request, she was temporarily expelled from Spanish territory. She died of smallpox in a convent at Namur, Oct. 17, 1596.

*Dodd, Ch. Hist.m*ii. 18, 38; *Lewis, Sanders' Angl. Schism; Lee, Dict. Nat Biog.,* xliv.; *sharpe, Mem. of the Rebel.,* pp 317-50; *Phillips, Ushaw Mag.* v 331-63, vii. 35-48; *Yepes, Hist. de Inglatera,* pp. 207 – 304; *Bridgewater Concertation,* ed.1594, f. 45 *seq.*, 410; *Records of Eng. Caths.,* i., ii."
[Gillow lists works and a reference to a portrait.] (Gillow, *Thomas Percy*).

Radcliffe, Margaret of Ordsall, Lancashire. ['*Cousin' of* **Sir Edward Jr** *via an earlier Radcliffe-Stanley marriage.* HM]

"The <u>Radcliffes</u> were noted as visitors to Knowsley by <u>Farington</u> in his household book. <u>Margaret</u>'s brother <u>Sir Alexander Radcliffe</u> was a friend of the <u>Earl of Essex</u>, and died in battle in Ireland in 1599. Soon after, Margaret died of a broken heart, and her death was the subject of a touching epitaph by <u>Ben Jonson</u>.

. . . <u>Margaret</u> was one of Elizabeth's Maids of Honour, together with <u>Mary Fitton</u> of Gawsworth, Cheshire, and <u>Elizabeth Vernon</u> of Hodnet, Shropshire, a cousin of <u>Essex</u> and of Shakespeare, and the bride of Shakespeare's patron <u>Southampton</u>; . . . . " [Although the pronoun reference is not clear, Keen apparently means that Elizabeth Vernon was a cousin of Shakespeare.] [*Carol's comment points out a confusing point. They were not first cousins, but were all fairly closely related*. HM] (Keen 61).

Radcliffe, Robert

" . . . second Lord Fitzwater, an earlier collateral of <u>Margaret</u>'s family, took the side of Henry VIII against Catharine of Aragon and was rewarded with the Earldom of Sussex. His second wife was <u>Margaret Stanley, daughter of the second Earl of Derby</u> (Keen 62, 63).

Radcliffe, Thomas Alan Keen quotes from F. E. Halliday's *Shakespeare Companion* (Duckworth, 1952):

"<u>*Sussex's Men*</u>. <u>Thomas Radcliffe, 3rd Earl of Sussex</u>, became Lord Chamberlain in 1572, in which year the company first appeared at Court, and then fairly regularly until his death in 1583. They are sometimes called the Chamberlain's during this period. The year 1583 saw the formation of the favoured Queen's Company, and under the patronage of Henry, 4th Earl, they disappear for the Court records until January 1591. His son Robert became 5th Earl in December 1593, during the plague year when all the companies had to travel. However, they played for Henslowe at the beginning of 1594, in a repertory of twelve plays, one of which was 'titus & ondronicous', Q1 of *Titus Andronicus* being published that year as having been 'Plaide by the Right Honourable the Earle of Darbie, Earle of Pembroke, and Earle of Sussex their Seruants'. In April 'the queenes men and my lord of Sussex together' gave eight performances at Henslowe's theatre. Perhaps they joined the Queen's for they are not heard of again as an independent company until 1602, after which they are traceable in the provinces for many years. It is possible that the 4th Earl was the 'Lord' for whose company Kyd and Marlowe were writing in 1593, and also that Shakespeare wrote *Titus Andronicus* for them' (Keen 63).

<u>**Stanley, Sir Edward**</u> of <u>Winwick and Tong</u>. A cousin of <u>Ferdinando Stanley</u>. Shakespeare is believed by some to have written an epitaph for **Sir Edward**'s tombstone (Honigmann 80). [*All underlinings in the following section on the Stanleys are by Carol Enos; none are by HM. All Stanleys are obviously relevant, so none are underlined.* HM]

Stanley, Ferdinando, Lord Strange [The subject headings in the following are mine (Enos). The text is from the Chetham Society, Vol 25, *Allen's Defence*, from Anstruther, from Fripp, from Keen, from Robert Stevenson, and from Honigmann.]

Claim to English throne.

"Ferdinando, Lord Strange, was third in descent from Henry the Seventh, whilst the Stuarts, though of the older line, were fourth in descent. The Jesuits therefore affirmed that the Stanleys 'were next in propinquity of blood' (Dolman). The claim of the Stanleys to the crown is as early as 1564 (Haynes 412)" (Chetham Society, Vol 25).

William Stanley and plan to put Ferdinando on English throne.

"Lord Strange, and Sir William Stanley, were friends under varied circumstances. There was a difference of twenty-five years in their ages; then Strange was the zealous coadjutor of the puritan Chaderton, (Peck's *Desid. Cur.* i. 147,) though Persons (in Dolman's *Conference* says this Lord was of three religions" (Chetham Society, Vol 25, Allen. *Defence* xlii, footnote 1).

"It is however here shown, that the heirs of the two great Stanley houses of Hooton, and Lathom, were on terms of great and suspicious intimacy; and we cannot doubt that Lord Strange hearkened to proposals to be made king, probably after Elizabeth's death. Yong's confession (Strype's *Annals*, iv. 103,) throws some light on the matter. He was at Seville with Persons 1590. 'At that time he, Persons, was writing to Sir William Stanley, who was shortly to go to Italy, to see Rome, and from thence into Flanders. In this letter he sent him word how now, at length, by the favour of Idiaques, the King had yielded to his request, for the first attempt against England. But not before '93, because of the great hindrances that rose in France daily. Yet they hoped by that time to have Brest in Brittany, where he should have sixteen great ships with 10,000 men. From which place he should have more commodity to come to the Irish Kernes, his old acquaintance, and from thence easily to arrive near his own country, where 19 (Lord Derby) would be ready to assist him, and that young one, 14, (Lord Strange) he hoped would also help, although now he would hold no water, but disclosed every one that seemed to move him in the matter.' Lord Derby died September 25, 1592 [*sic, 1593*]; and Richard Hesketh was sent by Holt, (Collier's *Church History*, vii. 253,) Sir William Stanley, (Appendix, Sadler, iii. 20,) and others, to persuade the new Earl to claim the crown, promising Spanish assistance, and threatening, if the design was divulged. (Camden, lib. 4.) Lord Derby would however 'hold no water,' and delivered Hesketh to justice, who was executed at St. Alban's, Michaelmas 1593, and at the scaffold, 'naming Sir William Stanley, and others, cursed the time he had ever know anie of them.' (Appendix, Sadler, iii. 20.) Lord Derby died, under strange circumstances, April 16, 1594. (Lodge's *Illustrations*, iii. 47; Stowe; Dodd, ii. 160, who denies Hesketh's allegations.) Whether this nobleman's death was the realization of Hesketh's threats, is not clearly ascertained. The Rufford, and Aughton, Heskeths, were both Roman Catholics, and had both a Richard in this generation, so the identification of Lord Derby's unfortunate acquaintance is now difficult" (Chetham Society, Vol 25, *Allen's Defence* xlii, xliii, footnote 1).

Anstruther quotes from a letter addressed to John Cecil and John Fixer from Robert Persons:

"'Again I request you that my cousin's matter be dealt in secrecy, lest it may turn the poor man to hurt, but great desire I have to hear truly and particularly of his estate.' What this refers to we may never know. John Cecil has written in the margin 'by his cousin is meant my lord Strange' and he has added a heading to the letter: 'This letter I brought of purpose that you might see it was no matter framed of mine own head that which they pretend of my lord Strange' (Salisb. IV). In one of his many statements to the government Cecil says, among other wildly improbably accusations against Persons, that he 'was also told to talk about the succession [to the Crown] and persuade catholics to cast their eye upon lord Strange if he would correspond with the cardinal [Allen] and catholics' (SP, 12/238, no. 161). The state papers at this date are teeming with references to lord Strange (i.e. Ferdinando Stanley, 5th earl of Derby) and most of them emanate from John Cecil *alias* Snowden. And the letter from Persons is all the evidence he has to offer! But these letter of Persons could do infinite harm to the priests with whom Cecil had lived in Rome and Spain, and his betrayal of them must rank among the meanest acts of treachery that this book records. There were seven priests besides himself mentioned in the first letter—Blount, Dudley, Fixer, Younger, Francis Lockwood, Rook and Salway. The lives of the first four reflect his action" (Anstruther *John Cecil*).

"Strange's men travelled with *Vetus Comoedia* in the provinces, and returned with it in the autumn [1588? not clear] 'somewhat altered' (*The Return of Pasquil,* McKerrow, i. 100). . . .
. . . . The *Cross Keys* in Gracechurch Street was the 'accustomed' playhouse of Lord Strange's men in winter, as the *Curtain* in the Fields was their usual summer theatre (Chambers, iv. 316: 'My now company of Players have been accustomed to play this winter-time within the City at the Cross Keys in Gracious Street' (Henry Lord Hunsdon, Lord Chamberlain, to the Lord Mayor, Oct. 1594)" (Fripp, *Shakespeare, Man and Artist*, 232).

"Strange's [Ferdinando's] mother, the Countess Margaret, was interested in astrology as well as sorcery (she and her husband the Earl were friends of Dr John Dee of Manchester) and Parker, her Yeoman of the Wardrobe, who was a student of astronomy, designed for her this zodiacal screen or planetarium, which Chaloner described in an obscure laudatory poem of 1576. It served to indicate the diurnal changes of sun, moon and planets" (Keen 70).

" . . . The Stanleys loved plays and their company (Strange's) is known to have been at Coventry, Shrewsbury, Leicester and perhaps at the nearby Chester, that is to say, within easy range of its patron's Lancashire residences, year after year between 1591-1594. . . ..
. . . Stranges's Men may be traced in Ffarington's domain at Knowsley or Lathom or New Parke about 1589-1590 . . . . " (Keen 193).

". . . .   True, he [Henry Stanley, 4th Earl of Derby] had sat in judgment over Mary Stuart. But after her death, some other English Catholic candidates had to be found. Crown agents on the continent reported agitation during 1591 in behalf of 'L. Strange, as one who, if the Spaniards could not prevail [the Spaniards had nominated the Infanta as Elizabeth's successor on the throne] might be made king by the Catholics unanimously.' A year later a plot was brewed 'of the Jesuits by which the Lord Ferdinando . . . should have taken the kingdom.' Though the English refugees knew nothing of his disposition, they did not care 'who be king, so he be of clouts, if he will be a Catholic.'

In 1592 Parsons declared that a military force was ready to strike from Ireland in support of the Earl of Derby and of Lord Strange; the latter 'he hoped would be ready to assist.' Because Ferdinando was in correspondence with Cardinal Allen, Parsons seems to have hoped that Strange might later become an ally. Both Allen and Parsons believed that Thomas Gerard of Bryn, a known intimate of Strange, and brother of a Jesuit, might somehow win him to an uprising. Richard Hesketh, brother of Alexander Houghton's widow, was the personal emissary chosen by the continental party.

This particular Richard Hesketh had fled to the continent in 1590, leaving behind in Lancashire his wife, Isabel, and several children. (He had been party to the assassination of Thomas Houghton of Brynscoules—Alexander Houghton's heir.) In Prague he met Thomas Stephenson, a Jesuit, there allowing himself to be drawn into the conspiracy to place Strange on the throne. Upon returning to Lancashire via Hamburg he immediately looked up the Baron of Newton (with whom he had been involved in the assassination of Thomas Houghton). This baron then introduced him to Lord Strange, whom Richard Hesketh later claimed not to have known personally until his return from the continent. The very day of his meeting Strange, the old Earl died. Scenting the odour of Hesketh's business, Ferdinando, no longer Strange but now 5th Earl of Derby, put him off from day to day on account of his 'sorrows.'

Hesketh, an inexperienced conspirator, allowed the wily Ferdinando to ferret out the true nature of his business. Now bent on securing for himself all the appointive offices in the shift of the crown which his father had held, Ferdinando decided to prove his own loyalty. He therefore induced Hesketh, under a show of affectionate interest, to accompany him to London during early October 1593. Upon their arrival in the capital he delivered Hesketh to justice. During the next few weeks Richard Hesketh's brother, Thomas, lifted not a finger to help save him. On the contrary he went about his accustomed business in Lancashire (collecting subsidy for the crown) with more than usual diligence. Such composure irritated Ferdinando, who was evidently hoping to even some scores with him while at the same time dispatching his brother. On 9 November Ferdinando wrote to Robert Cecil, complaining that Thomas Hesketh had crossed him and adding: 'I would be loth to be thwarted by so mean a man.' Although Thomas's conduct during these trying weeks continued in every respect exemplary (as Heneage's letter, earlier referred to, shows) nevertheless Ferdinando did his best to involve him in his brother's ruin; 'I think he is angry that I used myself so honestly touching his brother,' he told Cecil.

Before death Richard cursed those who had drawn him into the business of negotiating with Ferdinando. Certainly he would never have been set upon so dangerous an enterprise, however, unless Catholics on the continent had really conceived some hope of Ferdinando. In 1594 Parson's book on the succession to the Crown contained this observation; 'The earle of Darbyes religion is held to be more doubtful, so as some do thinke him to be of al three religions, and others of none . . . some do imagin . . . that it will do him hurt, for that no side in deede will esteeme or trust him.' Since Ferdinando died himself only five months after Richard Hesketh's execution, many of the more superstitious, according to Camden, believed that Hesketh's curses had fallen on Ferdinando. During his last illness in April of 1594 Ferdinando did as a matter of fact continuously complain that he was the victim of witchcraft. Since his death occurred when he was only thirty-five (and without any premonitory warnings) there were many who claimed that, if not witchcraft, poison secretly administered was the cause.

Perhaps . . . Ferdinando's death in April 1594 was not inopportune. His players after his death found a more auspicious patron in Hunsdon. Even if Ferdinando's troupe had been the favourite at court during 1592-1593, Hunsdon had gifts to bestow that Derby could not have matched. Shakespeare, who along with Burbage and Kempe, was a payee for performances at Greenwich Palace given during Christmas week of 1594, moved into a larger world when he became a member of the Lord Chamberlain's Company" (Stevenson, Robert 76-79).

Honigmann identified five actors who were members of Lord Strange's Men in a Privy Council Licence, dated 6 May 1593: Will Kempe, Thomas Pope, John Heminges, Augustine Phillips and George Bryan (59).

. . . .

"The Earl of Derby's Men disappear from the records in 1592-3, whereas Strange's Men received payments at court and in the provinces throughout the 1580s" (Honigmann 60).

. . . .

"Shakespeare, I repeat, seems to have served Lord Strange for eight or more years—the crucial years of his apprenticeship in the theatre. . . . [Robert] Greene had himself courted the Stanleys, dedicating his *Mirror of Modesty* (1584) to the Countess of Derby, Lord Strange's mother, and making a bid for Lord Strange's favour in 1589 with *Ciceronis Amor*—while at the same time he published, and probably encouraged, Nashe's sneers at the author of a lost Senecan tragedy called *Hamlet* (Nashe's Preface to Greene's *Menaphon*, 1589). Greene's later attack on Shakespeare, in 1592, adopted some of the very phrases of Nashe's diatribe against the author of *Hamlet*, so it seems that Nashe and Greene believed Shakespeare to be the author of the early (lost) *Hamlet* of 1589, and that Greene had looked upon Shakespeare as a rival for some years before his final outburst in *Groat's Worth of Wit* (1592) (69, 70).

Stanley, Henry, 4th Earl of Derby

"The Lord Lieutenant [of Lancashire] was the Earl of Derby, [in 1571] the magnificent pupil of Wolsey, and yet, not altogether a consistent Roman Catholic. He had assisted in the martyrdom of Marsh, (Fox, iii. 227); and in 1559 was a commissioner for advancing the Reformation; (Dodd, ii. 5.) he was relied upon by Mary, (Queen of Scots;) confided in by Norfolk; invited by the two Earls to join in the rising of the North, whom he denounced, and yet allowed his younger sons to take part in the rebellion (Haynes, pp. 446, 549, 564). In 1562, Elizabeth affected to trust this dangerous peer; but a few years later, and his power was submitted to that of Huntington" (Chetham Society, Vol 25, *Allen's Defence*, lxviii).

"Stranges's [Ferdinando] father, the fourth Earl, was a friend of Leicester; hence the transfer of Leicester's Men to the service of Strange in 1588. This transfer brought into the company the players Augustine Phillips, Thomas Pope, George Bryan, William Kemp, Richard Cowley, Richard Burbage, John Heminges, Henry Condell, William Sly, John Duke, Christopher Beeston, and for a while Edward Alleyn . . . . " (Keen 41, 42).

"Touring companies of actors frequently stopped at Lathom, Knowsley, and New Park, during the late 1580's and early 1590's. Visits by the Earl of Leicester's players (July 1587), Earl of Essex's troupe (September 1589), and Queen's men (October 1588, July and September 1589, June 1590) are recorded in the household books. Lord Strange's troupe—probably acrobats when the group was first formed—seems also to have appeared. Three performances, one on Tuesday, 31 December 1588, another on Sunday, 5 January 1589, and the third on Saturday, 21 February 1590, are noted in the *Derby Household Books*. On Saturday, 30 December 1587, the *Household Books* record that Sir Thomas Hesketh's Players went away. Not until after Sir Thomas's death do the *Household Books* begin to contain notices of players who can be assigned to Lord Strange's patronage" (Stevenson, Robert 74).

". . . . Everywhere in Lancashire, the 'sinke of poperie, manifolde Enormities of the Ecclesiasticall state' flourished in the late 1580's and early 1590's. The abuses included:

I. Continuall recourse of Jesuites and Seminaries Priestes into these parts

II. Masses daily

IV. Popishe ffastes and ffestivalles

VIII. Diuers notoriouse Recusantes not yet reformde; whose presumption
(they being of the better sorte) drawe the inferior sorte into no small bowldnesse . . .

The responsibility for such abuses rested with Henry, Earl of Derby and Lord Lieutenant of Lancashire. Not only his leniency with recusants but also his slackness in attending common prayer caused scandal. The Earl of Huntingdon as early as 24 August 1570 wrote Burghley: 'He with his hole Famylye, never ragyd so muche agaynst Religion as they doo nowe; he never came to comon Prayer for thys Quarter of thys Yeare . . . yf you send sum faythfulle and wyse Spye that woulde dyssemble to cum from *D'Alva*, and dyssemble Poperye, you might understand all.'

Margaret Clifford, his wife, was a lineal descendant of King Henry VII. Their son Ferdinando,

Lord Strange, therefore could claim the right to succeed the childless Elizabeth. In 1571, the year after Huntingdon's disturbing report, Elizabeth sent for a 'hostage' from the Earl—his son and heir, Ferdinando. Shakespeare's Richard III is made to say of Derby's ancestors: 'Cold friends to me: What do they in the North, when they should serve their Sovereign?" The more astute Elizabeth with the Earl's son and heir, Ferdinando, close at hand had less cause for apprehension. Religious training at court so weaned Ferdinando from any incipient recusant sympathies that when he returned to Lancashire he stoutly opposed his father's leniency with all those who did not 'come to Common Prayer,"

On 15 March 1582 Ferdinando wrote to Chaderton, Lord Bishop of Chester, 'I ame *throughe* with my father.' The next year in another letter to Chaderton [16 December 1583] he wrote:

So doubt I not but . . . your lordship will proceide to frame some better reformation in this so unbridled & bade an handfull of England . . . Whereto, my lord, as best becomes me, soe noe man shall shewe himself more forward, to assist with my [ut]most indevor . . . these rebellious minded papists my self will be willinge to geve the first blowe.

He signed himself, 'Youre lordships asured, Yow know *even verie assured*, Fer. Strange.' As if this letter were not strong enough he a few weeks later (21 March 1584) sent a secret one to 'my assured loving frend, the lord bishoppe of Chester' complaining of 'his father Henry E. of Derby's backwardness in prosecuting recusants':

I find him rather an enemye in substance to both actions . . . . To be constant is noe common vertew, althoughe it be most commendable, most fitt, and least founde in noblemen . . . But we must be patient. . . . & mke a vertew of necessitie, & folowe his humor. . . . This secreat letter I sent your lordship. The other his lordship [Earl of Derby] is privie to.

Only under pressure, then, did the Earl of Derby finally begin to prosecute certain of the more notorious recusants. Because he had long been known for his leniency, refugee Catholics began even before the Armada to fasten their eyes upon him and his son, whom they knew little of, as possible candidates for the succession. True, he had sat in judgment over Mary Stuart. But after her death, some other English Catholic candidates had to be found. Crown agents on the continent reported agitation during 1591 in behalf of 'L. Strange, as one who, if the Spaniards could not prevail [the Spaniards had nominated the Infanta as Elizabeth's successor on the throne] might be made king by the Catholics unanimously.' A year later a plot was brewed 'of the Jesuits by which the Lord Ferdinando . . . should have taken the kingdom.' Though the English refugees knew nothing of his disposition, they did not care 'who be king, so he be of clouts, if he will be a Catholic" (Stevenson, Robert 75-77).

"The Earl [Henry, fourth Earl of Derby, father of Ferdinando] officiated as President at the trial of Mary, Queen of Scots, and as Lord High Steward at the trial of the Earl of Arundel, eldest son of the Duke of Norfolk, who was arraigned on a charge of high treason in 1589; his family, however, included an embarrassing number of known or suspected Catholics: `Lady Margaret Clifford [his wife] from whom he was separated was a Catholic—as was also his brother, Thomas Stanley of Winwick. [*Sir Thomas Stanley of the Tong tomb.*] His sisters, daughters of his devout stepmother, Margaret, Countess of Derby, née Barlow, were Catholics also, as were his brothers-in-law, Lords Stafford and Morley, Sir John Arundell and Sir Nicholas Pointz. The Earl, we may suppose, persecuted recusants partly because he felt he had to prove himself" (Honigmann 118, 119).

(See also: Ferdinando Stanley.) (See also: Richard Hesketh.)

Stanley, Margaret, Countess, wife of the fourth Earl of Derby and mother of Ferdinando Stanley, Lord Strange. She was interested in astrology and sorcery. She and the Earl were friends of Dr. John Dee of Manchester. Her Yeoman of the Wardrobe, Parker, a student of astronomy, designed for her a zodiacal screen of planetarium, which Chaloner described in a poem of 1576 (Keen 70).

Stanley, William, 6th Earl of Derby

"Upon the death of Ferdinando Stanley, 5th Earl of Derby, 16 April 1594, the legal heir to the Earldom was William Stanley, second son of Henry, as Ferdinando left only daughters. There were two William Stanleys, the other belonging to the collateral branch of Hooton. The new Earl of Derby was offered

Burleigh's granddaughter in marriage, and Stanley immediately accepted. The marriage was postponed because Ferdinando's wife was pregnant with Ferdinando's posthumous child. If the child turned out to be a boy, William would lose the Earldom to him. Burleigh had chosen Stanley as a good match for the granddaughter who had been waiting five years for <u>Henry Wriothesley</u> to decide if he would marry her. Southampton was fined £5000 to be paid to young <u>Lady Vere</u>, whom he had refused, as a 'breach of promise' fine. When Alice Stanley gave birth to a girl, the marriage could go forward, and on 26 Jan. 37 Elizabeth, William Stanley, Earl of Derby, married the Earl of Oxford's daughter" (Stopes, *The Third Earl of Southampton*, 85, 86).

"William Stanley was born in 1561, younger son of the fourth Earl, whose heir was Ferdinando, Lord Strange. Like him, William went to St. John's College, Oxford, in 1572; and in 1582 at the age of twenty-one he began his travels in France in the charge of a Welsh tutor, Richard Lloyd. In Paris William was received at the Court of Henry III, to whom his father was deputed in 1584, to confer the Order of the Garter. Afterwards he visited the Loire, Orleans, Blois, Tours, Saumur, Angers; then we lose trace of him, but Connes conjectures that Stanley was in Navarre between 1582 and 1587. [*William's appearance at Eynsham in 1584 means that the whole chronology of his travels needs a revision.* HM] Stanley and his tutor Lloyd were back in England and at Lathom House, the other great Stanley mansion, in June 1587, when a great cycle of theatrical representations was given there, lasting more than a month; the Earl of Leicester's company played the chief part in the performances. (This was the company that, on the death of Leicester, was merged into the service of Strange. It included actors who became the fellows of William Shakespeare—Phillips, Pope, Bryan, Kemp, Cowley, Burbage, Heminges, Condell, Sly, Duke, Beeston, Cook, and, for a while, Alleyn.)" (Keen 56, 57).

(See also: Arthur W. Titherley, *Shakespeare's Identity*.)

Stanley, Sir William The following information is drawn from The Chetham Society, Vol 25, Cardinal *Allen's Defence of Sir William Stanley's Surrender of Deventer January 29, 1586-7*. Thomas Heywood, ed. [Footnotes are not included here.]

"Sir William was the son of Rowland Stanley of Hooton. [*Knighted on the same day in 1553 as Sir Thomas Stanley.* HM] William's mother was Margaret Aldersey (d of Hugh) of Chester. Sir William's half sister, Margaret (d. of Ursula Smith and Rowland) married Sir John Egerton of Egerton."

[Was this Egerton related to the Egerton Ferdinando Stanley's widow married?] [*Yes, he was. They were half-brothers because Thomas was illegitimate, although fully recognised by his father.* HM]

"The first service of William was under Alva . . . in 1567. Stanley quitted the Low Countries about 1570 and joined the Queen's forces in Ireland . . .[and] served fifteen years, and he left that island 1585 (Cardinal Allen's Defense iv, v). [Stanley was sent] from Ireland into Holland, where Stanley turned Papist and Traitor (Chetham Society, *Allen's Defence*, vi).

And Ferdinando Stanley (See: Stanley, Ferdinando).

Relationship to Leicester, Essex, Philip Sidney:

"The English auxiliaries arrived in the Dutch provinces December 1585, and with them came Stanley. . . . For some weeks this last [Stanley] remained with Leicester, and on January 24th we find the Knight at the inauguration feast at the Hague, seated next the youthful Lord Essex; and on February 2nd Sir Philip Sidney writes to his uncle, from Bergen op Zoom, ' Therefore, if it please your Excellency, to let old Tutty, and Reade, with Sir William Stanley, and Sir William Russell, with two hundred horse, come hither, I doubt not to send you honourable, and comfortable, news' (Chetham Society, *Allen's Defence*, vii).

[Leicester reposes trust in Stanley to raise and command a force of Irish kerns to be taken from Ireland to fight with English in the Low Countries]: "In March 1585, Shirley suggests the name of a person, who would raise and command this force, and Walsingham recommends Dautrey, to go to Ireland, levy, and bring the men, and to have the rank of Stanley's Lieutenant Colonel; but Leicester replies, 5th April 1586, that Stanley is already set out for Ireland, and that the matter is left to his discretion. . . . Leicester eagerly expected their arrival, with 'our English Master, Sir William Stanley, which, above all other, I desire (viii).

The intrigues of the agents of Mary, and of the Roman Catholic refugees, had free course amongst the followers of Leicester, on their arrival in the Dutch provinces" (viii). Of Christopher Blount, Allen's pupil, and Essex's Mephistopheles, then with Leicester, Morgan, agent of Mary Queen of Scots and imprisoned in Paris wrote: 'He has some charge, and credit, where he is, and his meaning is for the service of God, and advancement of the King of Spain, to further the delivery of some notable townes in Holland, or Zealand, to the King of Spain'(ix).

. . . .

Leicester, his reinforcements having arrived, determined to clear the river Yssel of Spaniards, Zutphen being their principal station. He was led thus to open the campaign because Parma was absent, at the Pope's request, subduing the Electorate of Cologne for Ernest of Bavaria, who had replaced the amatory and protestant duchess. On September 2nd 1586, Stanley was appointed to assist Sir John Norris in storming Doesborg. The place, however, yielded on summons, and the women passing out were plundered and maltreated by the soldiers, whilst Essex and 'other gentlemen interposed, and by smiting and beating the soldiers made them leave off rifling them.' How Stanley, commanding the Irish, carried himself in this affair, may be conjectured; henceforth, he avows, he entertained a dislike to Leicester, 'for his unkynd deling,; and Essex's 'yvill using of him was a grete mislyking to him;' and yet Leicester continued to regard Stanley as a devoted friend (xv).

. . . .

At the glorious battle of Warnsfeld (September 22nd), Stanley distinguished himself. 'There was not,' writes Leicester, in the field of ours, of horse, in the whole two hundred, whereof these Lords, and Gentlemen, with their followers to the number of sixty at the most, did all the feate, with the help only of Sir William Stanley, who had but three hundred for their three thousand foot, and he did most valiantly himself, and his own horse received eight shott of the musquet, and yet himself not hurt. He, and old Reade, are worth their weight in pearl, they be two as rare captains as any living Prince hath.' . . . Stanley next assisted at the taking of Zutphen sconce. This was chiefly owing to the gallantry of his Lieutenant, Edward Stanley, and caused no little surprise to the grateful Leicester, who had ordered the assault against the advice of his captains, and who knighted, and largely recompensed, Edward Stanley [a footnote says Camden identified Edward as of the Elford Stanleys. Seacome identified an Edward who died in Ireland in 1586. [*The Visitation of Cheshire, 1580, gives 1597 for the death in Ireland of Edward Stanley of Elford.* HM] Heywood does not commit himself] (xvi).

[Heywood gives a detailed account of Leicester's plan to take Deventer, a "stubborn" town whose burghers would "admit neither Leicester, nor the States, to govern them" (xvii)].

Leicester entered the town, whose citizens were provoked at the rude manners of the Irish Kerns. With such dissention, it is odd that Leicester placed such responsibility on Stanley. Leicester gave Stanley, on November 18th, authority to act independently of the Governor of the Province, and empowered him to require assistance from the neighbouring garrisons. The apology for thus nominating Stanley, and with such unusual powers, Governor of Deventer, is stated to be 'suspicion of revolt.' . . . Leicester offered to pledge himself, body, and soul, for the loyalty both of Stanley, and York and proceeded to give the States the choice of one of these two men, or *of Pelham, to command in his absence, which offer was immediately declined*' (xix)

Stanley and the Babington Plot:

"In passing through England, on his return to Leicester, Stanley again becomes an object of suspicion. The Babington conspiracy was at this time approaching its denouement, and had so widely extended itself amongst the Roman Catholics, that Stanley could hardly be in England, and not have knowledge of the plot. The statements of Camden and Meteeren, as to Sir William's complicity, are strong; and yet, though Ballard was arrested August 4th, Stanley passed unquestioned into Holland. Burleigh writes to Leicester from Richmond, July 21st 1586: 'At the writing hereof, Sir William Stanley was come hither, and meaneth, with haste, to repaire to your Lordship, judging that his men are before this time at Flushing.'" Leicester indicated the Irish Kerns were 'already objects for Spanish corruption'" (xiii).

Stanley and Ferdinando Stanley (Lord Strange): From the deposition of John Flud (Flood,

Flowde) taken the xv of Marche regarding Sir William's surrender of Deventer:

"Sir Willm Standly willed him [Flud] to tell my L. Strange, that hir Matie is but a shadowe, and one person, if God shoulde will hir Matie, he wolde be one that shoulde stand my L. Strange in stede, one daye, as anny one man, and that hir Matie was Ruled by them, that hath sett hir Matie at warres wth all the worlde.

Also doe yo^u say to my L. Strange, that when the blacke man is owt of hir Maties sight, she is not well plesed, who puttith all men in dispayer in his absens. The Service the blacke man hath done hit is no marvayle of his recompence. This examinat' saith, that the blacke man is ment to be Sir Walter Rawley, and tell my L., if I coulde have written to his L. without int'cepting, he wolde have written more at large, but he lokyth for answere from his Lord by this exammynat" (xli, xlii).

Stanley and the Jesuits:

"Ranke has shown, in his History of the Popes, how Roman Catholicism, mainly by the assistance of the Jesuits, had renewed its strength, and how the Low Countries became the great battle field for the faith, and Elizabeth its most formidable opponent. Parma was surrounded by triumphant ecclesiastics; and the detaching the Walloons, from the Dutch, gave his operations a firmer basis than Alva acquired. The English contributed largely to the Jesuit ranks. 'Now it seems God's will that the company should march to battle against the heresy in England,' said Mercurian, 'since he sends to her such a numerous and valiant host from England'. To the Jesuits Stanley bore a great regard: 'wyth which order he is exceedingly enchanted, and to them wholly subjected. Allen, to the seminaries he had founded, had attracted many Lancashire men; 'but above all the rest, he himself,' (Sir William Stanley,) 'conversed most in kindness of love, and affection, with one Roger Ashton, who had bin his bed-fellow, and the greatest furtherer of him in this enterprize' . . . .Stanley, thus induced by Ashton to surrender Deventer, next communicated his plan to Rowland York, and was by him introduced to Jean Baptiste Tassis, who, eager to recommend himself to the governing powers, reported the matter to Parma, and not to Verdugo, the commandant of the province. Stanley always protested that he was impelled by conscience to deliver up the town. The negociations between Stanley, York, and Tassis, were carried on under the pretext of an interchange of presents . . . . " (Chetham Society, Vol 25, Allen's *Defence*, xxiii-xxv).

"[Roger Ashton (see above)] was probably the third son of Richard Ashton of Croston, (Lancaster) by Anne, daughter of Sir Robert Hesketh of Rufford. . . . Roger Ashton was executed at Tyburn, June 23, 1591, 'for entertaining missioners, as also for applying himself to the see of Rome for a dispensation in a marriage contract,' (Dodd, ii. 154;) Elizabeth keeping back the weightier charges which she had to urge. This Roger had an uncle of the same name, entered as dying in Scotland s.p.; and there is a cotemporary, who followed closely, and profitably, the fortunes of James the Sixth and First, Roger Aston, of the Astons of Aston, (*Cestr.*) generally misspelt Ashton" (xxii, xxiii, footnote 4).

"Stanley however had good friends in the Jesuits, and Persons told Philip 'of the worthiness and virtue' of the Knight, and 'of his experience in the sea coasts of England, and especially of his intelligence as to Ireland;' and in consequence of this, Stanley was sent for to Madrid, and, being introduced into the Council of War, urged Philip to make Ireland the basis of his operations in an attack on England. . . . " (xlviii).

And the Armada:

"Philip, who had rejected the advice of Parma and Idiaques, on the subject of the armada, paid no attention to Stanley, who 'wrote letters to Holt the Jesuite, being in Brussells, (which is his countriman, and one upon whom he chiefly relieth,) of great discontentment, and signifying that his entertainment was far colder than he expected.'

He next went to Corunna to advise Medina Sidonia as to the best method of invading England, and here Burgh, a witness on Perrot's trial, met Stanley, who preferred a debarkation at Milford Haven to landing at Portsmouth; and we find him in 1603 repeating this opinion to Philip the Third. About this time, according to Copley, Lamot offered Stanley a wager, that the English fleet would not abide the attack of the Spaniards; the Knight seems quietly to have replied that he thought otherwise.

Stanley returned to the Low Countries, and although his own regiment hardly existed, yet, in July 1588, he appeared a Nieuport, at the head of seven hundred men, called the English legion, but chiefly consisting of foreigners, ready to join the armada. De Thou makes these men go on shipboard, 'eager to have either the glory or the advantage of landing first in England;' we much doubt however whether they ever embarked. Copley says it was 'supposed,' or 'intended,' and meanwhile, the English refugees 'sorrowed to see how they were disdained by the Spaniards;' and Camden says: 'Interquos septingenti profugi Angli, qui omnium despicatissime habiti.' Parma, mortified at the defeat of the armada, treated them with great neglect; and Stanley returned 'discontented to Antwerp, there hired a house, where four or five months he lived full of melancholy expressions, making evident show that his mind was utterly unable to bear the burthen of so great an indignity'" (xlviii, xlix).

  And later intrigue against England: [From Allen's *Defence*, beginning on p xlix]:
"In 1590 Stanley was again at Madrid, urging some design for the invasion of England; he then went to Rome, (Strype's *Annals,* iv. 281) and must have there known Allen, returning the Easter of 1591. During the visit in Spain, he went to the sea ports, and appears to have taken part in preparing to resist Drake. The invasion, which Persons eagerly promoted, was fixed for 1593. In returning from Rome, Stanley was entertained by the Bishop of ' Montesiaston,' [Montefiascone?] at supper, and there warmly expressed his apprehension, in the event of the Queen's death, of the Lady Arabella being proclaimed as her successor There is a not very clear account of four soldiers being sent into England by Stanley at this time, with passes from Roger Williams, to recruit for the refugee regiment.([1]) We do not find that Stanley took any part in Parma's two French campaigns, or in opposing Maurice, and Vere. Allied to the Jesuit party, the Knight shared in all their desperate projects.([2]) On Garnet's trial, Stanley, Owen, and others, are charged with inviting Cullen to kill the Queen. Grotius states, that Stanley was one of the promoters of the attempt to assassinate Maurice 1594, and from 1591, to about 1604, the Knight shared in the conspiracies of Owen, and Holt, and seems blindly to have followed their guidance. . . . The English exiles were generally in a state of penury from the non-payment of their Spanish allowances. In 1591 Stanley was at Madrid, with six attendants, and two hundred ducats per month. In 1593, he is said to have three hundred ducats from the King of Spain, but 'in May last had received nothing for a year and a half.' The mode in which these English pensioners, who are described as the most 'miserable, and discontented, troupe of gentlemen in the whole world,' were paid, is given in the 'Estate of the English Fugitives,' said to be written by Thomas Scarlett. We find Stanley two years, a year and a half, and six years, in arrear of his pension, and only obtaining the money by repeated journeys to Madrid.
 1) Strype's *Annals*, iv. 106.
 2). . . . Stanley is implicated, and on good evidence, in inciting Cullen, Williams, and York, to kill Elizabeth: 'Qui omnes instigati a Stanleio ejusque vicario Jacobo (Jaques,) et Jesuita Holtio, ac aliis septem vel octo profugis Anglis, pluribus de ea re Bruscellis inter se habitis consultationibus, ingentem ei pollicentes pecuniam.' (Meteeren, lib. 17. p. 575) This accusation is borne out, as respects the three last, by the depositions and confessions given in connection with the processes, in 'Rob. Abbotti *Antilogia*,' &c., Londini, 1613, cap. 8, 9, where Stanley, Holt, Owen, Jaques, and others, are shown to have instigated those attempts at assassination. That Stanley's name is omitted in the requirement Elizabeth proposed to make to the Archduke Ernest, for the giving up of Holt, Owen, Worthington, &c., (Lingard, viii. 388,) occurred probably because he was considered a mere tool of the Jesuits. . . . . We observe Meteeren charges Stanley with being a participator in the Lopez affair.
      In 1596, the English refugees were solicited by Stanley, and Worthington, to sign an attestation to the merits of William Holt, (Strype's *Annals,* iv. 192.) the matter seems to have been regarded by the public with disfavour. Fifty-one officers, and men, of Stanley's legion signed, besides others; and amongst the names are those of Guy Fawkes, and of Elizabeth Allen the widow, late of Rossall. Sir Henry Neville, 27th June 1599, writes to Sir Robert Cecil, that the fugitives abroad are divisible into two classes—those who will not consent to the invasion of England by a foreign Prince, and the Jesuits, who would oppose the existing state of things by every means; and adds, that all the English gentlemen in the Low Countries were of the moderate party, 'excepting Sir William Stanley, Holt, Owen, and three or four more.' (Winwood, i. 51.)

      . . . .
      In the attempt to procure an invasion, on Elizabeth's death, Stanley was an actor, and he sent his subaltern officer, Guy Fawkes, in 1603, to Spain, on this matter, with the emissary of Catesby ([2]). In 1604 Winter arrived in the Netherlands with a two-fold plan; first, of an invasion, which everybody was tired of hearing mentioned, and second, of the gunpowder plot, which, failing the other, was a kind

of dernier ressort. Stanley at this time appears to have been negotiating his own pardon. Winter sought Guy Fawkes as fit 'for councill and execution,' and Owen strongly recommended him; but Fawkes was not at Brussells, and Winter, returning, encountered him at Ostend, with Sir William Stanley, who told him the Archdukes and 'all those parts were weary of war, and desired peace with England . . . . [Fawkes, Winter and Stanley met and] the gunpowder plot was first communicated to Fawkes, (after being sworn and receiving the sacrament, with Catesby, Percy, &c.) behind St. Clement's Church, Strand. . . . In the negotiations preceding the twelve years' truce, 29th March 1609, Stanley was at Madrid; and Cornwallis complains, 7th July 1608, of the information he was affording the King, with whom Stanley 'hath been lately, and yesternight made his return hither,' (Winwood, ii. 416, 417; Birch, p. 293.) and adds, 'Now serves the time for the Jesuite fugitives, who were [Footnote 2]: Examination of Fawkes, November 25, 1605; Jardine, ii. pp. 140, 273; Tierney's Dodd, Appendix, iii. 54. Stanley had previously sent Wright to Madrid, and now despatched Fawkes, to warn Philip against trusting James, and to recommend Milford Haven for debarkation.

'before fallen from their wonted height, to fish newe access, and credit, in this troubled water.' The Jesuit novitiate establishment, founded at Louvain 1607, was partially removed to Liège 1614, and Sir William Stanley took a great interest in the undertaking, to which he largely contributed, recommending his cousin, Father John Gerard, to be set over it. The priests speak of Sir William in the most grateful manner, and he, in return, 'took it exceeding kindly that he should be used in a business so grateful unto him, offered not only his name and countenance, (which only we asked,) but also to concur thereunto.' . . . " (Chetham Society, *Allen's Defence*, xlix – lv).

Stanley and John Flud (Flood):
"About six weeks after the surrender of Deventer, 'John Flud,' sent by Sir William Stanley, with letters and messages, to friends in England, was seized and examined. . . . This Flud must not be confounded with the loyal officer who in these wars laid the foundation of the respectable family of the Irish Floods, and who is designated as 'Captain Flud;' nor with a Father Flud, another actor in these scenes, perhaps the 'Henry Flood, a Jesuit, the chief agent for transporting nuns to Brussells, Graveling, Lisbon, & (*Phoenix Brit.* p 430; for the names of several Floods, 1624, vid. ibid. p. 436.) (xxxiv).
[Flood's depositions in government examinations are given on pp xxxiv – xliv].

After, for three days, thus examining Flud, he appears to have been finally consigned to the Provost Marshal, and the following notice (*Harl. MSS.* 287, fol. 85,) somewhat confusedly describes his fate: 'It is reported that they have charged Sir W. Stanley's lieutenant with receipt of letters, whereuppon he hath been condemned, and executed, on Monday last, by shot, at Dixmude'" (xliii, xliv).

"It is true that Ferdinando's followers were mostly Catholic; his bosom-friend Thomas Gerard, for instance, was brother to a famous and much-sought-after Jesuit" (Devlin 82).

"We now bring the unfortunate Knight to the last scenes of his prolonged life. Wadsworth (*the English Spanish Pilgrim*, James Wadsworth, 4to, 1629.) Wadsworth met Stanley at Madrid in 1624, and states that, at his suggestion, he resolved to follow the wars. The following passage occurs in the book: 'Sir William Stanley, who betrayed Deventer to the Spaniards.' 'This Knight laments now his misfortunes, and says he has outlived his friends; and, in the year 1624, he was constrained to go to Spain in his old age, having now seen ninety-five years, and there to go, cap in hand, to all privy counsellors to crave his pension, which had not been paid him in six years before; and after he had spent three months in petitioning them, they granted him ten thousand crowns, and the title of an earl, to sell, or bestow, on whom he pleased; and thus he returned to Flanders, leaving his money in the hands of a Spanish Jesuit, Father Antonio Vasquez, by name, who promised to return it to him by a bill of exchange, but never did it to this day. Whereupon, seeing himself thus couzened in his old age, turned Carthusian at Austend, and gave the Carthusians there his plate and that little money which he had; where I have heard him often complain of the Jesuits, and say he was sorry to find them such knaves, and that if His Majesty of Great Britain would grant him pardon and leave to live the rest of his days in Lancashire, with beef, and bag pudding, he should deem himself one of the happiest in the world, but this could never be obtained of his aforesaid Majesty, he having been so great and notorious a traitor.' (Randle Holmes's *Book of Funerals*, Harl. MSS. 2129, fol. 96.)" (Chetham Society, Vol 35, lvi, lvii).

Stanley and Francis Jackson: (See: Francis Jackson.)

Account of Funeral (1628-9?) (See: Chetham Society, Vol 25, *Allen's Defence*, lvii – lxi.)

Stanley, Sir William of Hooton.

"Katherine, wife of Ralph Ardern, was daughter of Sir William Stanley of Hooton, according to all authorities, and occurs with him in trust-deeds of the manor of Alvanley, and lands in Bredbury and Stockport, May 2 and 16, 15 Henry VI. He settled lands in Stockport, Romilegh, and Wernith, on his son John, and Alice his wife, Oct., 22 Henry VI, to which Thomas, William, and John Stanley are witnesses, and was deceased before October 3, 27 Henry VI, as by release to his widow from Charles Arderne (Harl. MSS. 2074, 119 b. 120, 134). She had afterwards a licence for an oratory at Alvanley, and married to her second husband John or Jenkin Hyde, before 38 Henry VI, as by award between him and her eldest son John, besides whom she was mother of Thomas, Robert, Hugh, and Ralph, living 13 Henry VII (Ibid. 132 b. 134 b. 133 b.)" (Ormerod, Pedigree of Arderne, of Aldford, Alvanley and Harden, 1066-1701. (Ref DDX 63/2). 91, 92). [*This Arderne family of Cheshire were the ancestors of Mary Arderne, John Shakespeare's second (or third) wife in c.1575.* HM]

"He [Stanley] felt he had been passed over when the Desmond estates in Ireland, which he had helped to win, were divided and he was overlooked. . . . In Dec. 1585 he accompanied Leicester in the expedition sent by Elizabeth to assist the united provinces against Spain. Sir William was dispatched to Ireland to Levy troops among the disbanded troops and native kernes. He raised 1400 men, mostly Irish. As he passed through England, he probably was in contact with the Jesuits. He knew part, at least, of the Babington plot. He communicated with Lord Arundel in the Tower. He secretly wanted Queen Elizabeth to be killed—dallied with his troops in London, and planned to revolt with his troops. Stanley's forces joined Leicester on Aug. 12, 1586, and he joined Sir Norris and took and rifled Doesborg. There was action at Zutphen (Sidney was killed and Stanley displayed great prowess). He was left in charge of the city of Deventer. He surrendered the city to the Spanish governor on Jan. 29, 1587. He was from then on entirely under the influence of the Jesuits. Allen's letter trying to justify Stanley's surrender of the city was probably harmful rather than helpful." [I have misplaced the reference and cannot locate the source. Enos]

"This man, Sir William Stanley, and his agent, Richard Hesketh, were deeply involved in the Catholic unrest that was threatening Elizabeth at the time. The Duke of Guise and the King of Spain had formed a league that was designed to exclude Navarre from the French succession and extirpate heresy in France and the Low Countries. Elizabeth was afraid they were also aiming at heresy in England. She decided against military support in the Netherlands and began negotiations with Scotland and the German Protestant princes for a counter-league. Drake's commission was withdrawn. Then Henry III joined the Leaguers against Navarre, and early in June Philip II seized a large fleet of English merchant ships in Spanish harbours. Elizabeth was angry and considered hiring German troops for Navarre's support. She ordered Raleigh to lead a naval force against Spanish fishermen off the Banks" (Rebholz 68).

"Sidney and Greville made the Queen angry in Aug of 1585 when they planned a secret departure with Drake, ostensibly to join 'a general league among free princes' 'either in Spain or in America, the source of Spanish wealth . . . Greville said the plan to invade and possess all of America was Sidney's idea and that Sidney had chosen Grevill 'of all England' to share in the adventure. Once launched, the expedition was to be commanded jointly by Sidney and Drake. Sidney kept his true role a secret because he knew the Queen or Council would forbid his participation" (Rebholz 68).

Sidney and Greville appear to have been wavering in their loyalty, the intricacies of which would require an entire book to sort out, but Elizabeth seems to have become cautious toward them, keeping Greville at court, out of temptation's way, and sending Sidney off to fight in the Low Countries with Leicester on Dec. 14, 1585. Sidney was wounded Oct 12, 1586, at Zutphen and died three weeks later. All I can offer here is a very strong 'hunch' that these two were involved in the maneuverings that were in progress to put Lord Strange on the throne. This would have encompassed the activities of the Jesuit priests in England, the disagreements that seemed to alienate Elizabeth and Leicester about that time, Leicester's special attention to his old friend Campion who was about to be martyred, the reports by Thoms, recorded by him in 1865 of a troupe of English players who were touring Germany about the time. Elizabeth, Burghley, and Walsingham must have had their hands overflowing. It was not enough that the Catholics had been plotting against her through Spain, Mary, Queen of Scots, Ireland, but it may be that some of her own, Greville, Leicester, Lord Strange, in collusion with the Catholic infiltration that was already in place, were working against her. [I think this is from Rebholtz, but I cannot obtain the book to check it. Enos]

Sir William Stanley of Hooton and Robert Gwillym:

[From the Visitation of Lancashire, 1533, John Atherton of Atherton]:

> "The pedigree of Atherton of Atherton goes back to Robert de Atherton, who was sheriff of Lancashire in the reign of King John. In the reign of Edward III., Nicholas de Atherton, a cadet of the family, married Jane, daughter and heiress of Adam de Bickerstaff, a family of equally ancient date. This line ended in heir female, to wit, Margaret, who married James Scarisbricke, a younger son of the house of Scarisbricke, and had issue an only daughter, Elizabeth, married to Peter Stanley, younger son of Sir William Stanley of Hooton. Margaret, the only daughter of Peter and Elizabeth Stanley, married Henry Stanley of Aughton, son of Sir James Stanley of Cross hall, who was the younger son of the first Earl of Derby. From this marriage descended the line of Stanley of Bickerstaff, baronets, in whom the title of Earl of Derby finally vested.

> . . .

> "John Atherton, the sixth in descent from the John named in this Visitation, married Elizabeth, daughter and heiress of Robert Cholmondley of Vale Royal, by Elizabeth his wife, daughter of Sir Henry Vernon of Hodnet. Their son, Richard Atherton, the last of his line, by Elizabeth his wife, daughter of William Farington of Shaw hall, had an only daughter Elizabeth, who married Robert Gwillym of Langstone in the county of Hereford . . . . " (Chetham Society, Vol 98, 86, 87).

Towneley, John

> "Of him [Edward Alleyn], W. H. Blanch recorded that his mother was Margaret Towneley, daughter of John Towneley, of Towneley in Lancashire. 'Documents at Dulwich College seem to give evidence that Mrs. Alleyn was married a second time to a person of the name of Brown, an actor, and it was owing to this circumstance, doubtless that young Alleyn was (according to Fuller in his *Worthies*) 'bred a stage-player.'

> The Towneleys, incidentally, had some slight connexion with the Houghtons through a marriage in the time of Alexander Houghton's grandfather" (Keen 51, 52).

> ". . . under a portrait of this unconquerable confessor of Christ, formerly at Towneley, was the following inscription: 'This John, about the sixth or seventh year of her Majesty's reign that now is, for professing the Apostolic Roman Catholic Faith, was imprisoned first at Chester Castle; then sent to Marshalsea; then to York Castle; then to the Blockhouses in Hull; then to the Gatehouse in Westminster; then to Manchester; then to Broughton in Oxfordshire; then twice to Ely in Cambridgeshire; and so now, seventy-three years old, and blind, is bound to appear and keep within five miles of Towneley, his house. Who hath, since the stature of the twenty-third, paid into the Exchequer twenty pounds a month, and doth still; so that there is paid already above five thousand pounds, A.D. one thousand six hundred and one. John Towneley of Towneley in Lancashire.' Five thousand pounds in those days would probably be equivalent to £50,000, nowadays. John Towneley died in 1607. The invincible champion of Christ was the father of thirteen children.

> . . .

> John Towneley was succeeded by his son Richard; of the children of the latter the third was Charles, who inherited his father's estates on the death of his brothers, John and Richard. In his 14th year he was sent to St Omer's College, where he spent two years, returning to England till his 19th year" (Hamilton, ed., *Chronicle of St. Monica's,* Vol 2, 171 – 173).

Towneley, Margaret Mother of Edward Alleyn and daughter of John Towneley, of Towneley in Lancashire (Keen 51). (See also: Edward Alleyn.)

Vernon, Elizabeth Daughter of Sir John Vernon of Hodnet and his wife, Elizabeth Devereux (who was aunt of <u>Robert Earl of Essex</u> and <u>Lady Penelope Rich</u>). Her father's brother, <u>Sir George Vernon</u>, had married for his second wife the widow of Thomas Acton of Sutton Park, the mother of Lady Thomas <u>Lucy</u> of Charlecote. Elizabeth eventually became pregnant and <u>Henry Wriothesley, Earl of Southampton</u>, married her secretly. (Fripp, *Shakespeare, Man and Artist*, 420.)

Sir John Vernon of Hodnet, the husband of the Earl of Essex's aunt, had died in 1591, leaving one son and four daughters. The Earl got Elizabeth (one of the daughters) into the royal service, and she sent messages to Essex by way of Southampton because Essex was often out of the country. <u>Southampton</u> and <u>Elizabeth</u> fell in love (Stopes, *The Third Earl of Southampton*, 86).

~~~~~~~~~~~~~~~~~~~~~~

Appendix 8
Father Henry More SJ (1586-1661), Jesuit historian

8-1. Introduction to this search
8-2. The hunt
8-3. The 'facts' behind the quote
8-4. Background to Father Henry More's biography
8-5. Brief biography of Father Henry More
8-6. A close look at More's Historia
8-7. Sorting out some epitaph muddles
8-8. Sorting out some Stanley muddles

8-1. Introduction to this search

This search started after spotting the following notes on a website.

Notes on Two Stanley Monuments

[1] Dugdale's comments as well as these epitaphs and other poetry associated with the Derby family may be found in *The Earls of Derby and the Verse Writers and Poets of the Sixteenth and Seventeenth Century* by Thomas Heywood, available online at Google Books.

[2] Dugdale's ascription of the Stanley monument epitaph to Shake-speare is widely known, but I find another reference to it as written by Shake-speare in the same year, 1660. Father Henry More wrote in his *History of the English Provinces of the Society of Jesus*: 'Lord Stourton called his wife, a daughter of Edward, Earl of Derby, and sister to the Stanley whose epitaph Shakespeare wrote.' This would be Anne Stanley, daughter of Edward the third Earl of Derby, and sister of Sir Thomas Stanley for whom the epitaph was written. I found this reference in *The Poems: Variorum Shakespeare*, 1938, appendix "The Phoenix and the Turtle".

www.rahul.net/raithel/Derby/apocrypha

This was buried in the middle of the site of The URL of Derby, webmaster John Raithel, dedicated to proving, or at least investigating the premise that Shakespeare's works were actually written by William Stanley, 6th Earl of Derby. He knows that I do not believe for one moment that this was the case, but his website has nevertheless produced some interesting points and references to William Stanley. The two Williams undoubtedly knew each other and it may be that some of Stanley's ideas and experiences were adopted by Shakespeare as a basis for his works, most particularly *Love's Labour's Lost*.

My main initial question to myself was: How could it have happened that I had never come across Father Henry More before in any other 'Shakespeare biography literature', or any literature on 'Shakespeare's Lancashire Links', or any literature on 'Catholic Shakespeare', and certainly never in the meagre literature on 'Epitaphs written by Shakespeare'? As a corollary to this question, it is perhaps in order to mention that I had been in regular written contact during the early 2000s with Professor Peter Milward SJ, the major Jesuit advocate of Shakespeare being Catholic. How come Father Peter had never come across this reference to the Stanley epitaph(s)?

It was easy to establish that Father Henry More SJ (1586-1661) had written this in Latin as *Historia Missionis Anglicanæ, ab anno MDLXXX ad MDCXXXV* (1580-1635) (St. Omer, 1660, fol.). His *Historia* therefore started before his own birth, but presumably drew on the intimate knowledge of earlier Jesuits. If this were to be a correct quote, it would be another indication from a learned and highly reputable author of the widespread knowledge of Shakespeare's authorship of the verse epitaphs during his lifetime or shortly after his death. Coming from a Jesuit in exile, this would be even more interesting. The Anne Stanley in question was indeed Lady Stourton, with a well-established brief biography, and she was indeed an elder sister of **Sir Thomas** and **Sir Edward Sr**. The one thing that disturbed me was that it appeared on The URL of Derby in an appendix on *The Phoenix and the Turtle*. Oh dear, I thought, has someone else confused and muddled the epitaphs in Tong with this enigmatic poem, also often (and wrongly) described as an 'epitaph'? Alas, this did indeed turn out to be the case, and the quote above does not appear in *Historia*. However, on the assumption that the quote was not invented out of thin air and that it presumably appears in another piece of Father Henry More's writings, it is a tale worth telling. The puzzle remains about 'two Stanley monuments' in the title, associated with Shakespeare epitaphs. The tomb at Tong is clear – which is the other Stanley monument? I fear this is another muddle.

Indeed, so many muddles emerged that it was difficult to write about them clearly. The muddled reader of this Appendix might wish to jump straight to the concluding sentences!

8-2. The hunt

This se(n)t me off on another paper-chase through Munich Libraries: the Shakespeare Research Library; the Bavarian State Library; the main University Library of the LMU (Ludwig-Maximilian-Universität). Inevitably, this paper-chase also led to a cybernetic hunt on other websites, not least through various books meanwhile 'Digitized by Google'. To my delight there was a copy of the original *Historia*, 1660 in the main Munich University Library, which was ordered for my perusal a few days later. By the time of this appointment I had ordered and received a second-hand copy of the first translation into English of More's *Historia* by another Jesuit priest, Francis Edwards, *The Elizabethan Jesuits* (1981). I already knew his *Plots and Plotters in the Reign of Elizabeth I*. He had, however, only translated the first six 'books', which covered the Elizabethan period, and the quote above certainly did not appear there. There were ten 'books' in total, so I needed to concentrate on the last four, which have never been translated.

The full title of the book in question was *Historia missionis Anglicanae Societatis Jesu, ab anno salutis MDLXXX ad DCXIX et Primum tum Provinciæ eiusdem seculi annum XXV. Collectore Henrico Moro, Eiusdem Societatis Sacerdote, Andomari Typus Thomæ Geubels MDCLX.* The frontispiece appears as an illustration. It was written in Latin in 1647-1660 and published in 1660. I ascertained that this copy arrived in the Jesuit Library in Munich in 1661, where it remained until transferred to the University Library in the nineteenth century. The helpful librarian soon informed me that he had located the *Historia* online (admitting that it was rather well hidden) and so it was waiting for me on my computer when I returned home. At least one other copy has survived, which has been put online by Google Books. This was originally at the Imperial Library in Spain (Libreria del Collegio Imperial), later the Universidad Central de (bottom of stamp disappeared off the bottom of the page, but obviously one of the main research libraries in Spain).

So, I spent several hours in the LMU Library reading Chapters 7-10 of this 500+ page book in Latin and re-read the whole text online back at home to make sure Father Edwards had not omitted 'the quote' from his translation, for whatever reason. I did not find what I was looking for, but did find a few other gems.

8-3. The 'facts' behind the quote

To check the reference given at the beginning in more detail I had first visited the Shakespeare-Forschungsbibliothek München (Shakespeare Research Library, Munich) in the Anglistik Department of the LMU (Ludwig-Maximilian-Universität München). This confirmed the basic text of the quote by Raithel, but revealed at the same time that it was the result of previous paper-chases in the early twentieth century. Reading this quote raised so many questions that it was difficult to know where to start. My considered response was to copy and reproduce the complete quote in Rollins, p. 578, editor of the *Variorum* in 1938 mentioned in the quote above, and add a series of annotations.

> MATTHEW (*Image of Sh.*, 1922 pp. 114 f.)[i] comments on Brown's thesis:[ii] "the title page [of *Love's Martyr*] . . . has been taken as meaning that Sir John Salisbury[iii] and his wife were the Turtle and the Phoenix, and this may have been an old view, for Father Henry More, telling a ghost-story[iv] in his *History of the English Province of the Society of Jesus*,[1] written in 1660,[v] says 'Lord Stourton called his wife, a daughter of Edward, Earl of Derby, and sister to the Stanley whose epitaphs Shakespeare wrote . . .'[vi] Father Henry More may have thought that Poems must be founded on fact and (if he referred to this Poem)[vii] he was probably wrong in thinking that Ursula Stanley and Lady Stourton were sisters.[viii] This Poem was stated to be a poetical essay;[ix] written on a particular theme, and this dedication to Salisbury may have been merely a compliment without any reference to his private affairs. If Shakespeare wrote these beautiful Verses he never wrote anything else like them. . . .[x]
>
> [1] [*Historia missionis Anglicanae Societatis Jesu*, which I have not seen.]
> (Footnote from Rollins, p. 578. 'I' = Rollins had not see More. HM)[xi]
>
> *The Variorum Shakespeare ~ The Poems*, Ed. Hyder Edward Rollins, J. B. Lippincott Co., Philadelphia and London, 1938, p. 578.

Notes by HM:

[i] This refers to Frank Matthew, *An Image of Shakespeare*, London, 1922, the title given in Rollins's bibliography in 1938. This is not amongst the most quoted sources by others later when discussing Shakespeare's biography. It may be worth returning to, but the most important point is that Matthew seems to have been one of the first people interested in Shakespeare's biography to have read Father Henry More's *Historia*, published 1660. This must have been in Latin because it was not translated into English until 1981. Where he found the quote remains a mystery because, as reported, it was not in *Historia*.

[ii] Frank Matthew was referring to Carleton Brown, *Poems by Sir John Salusbury and Robert Chester*, Bryn Mawr Monographs, 1913 (Re-issued by the Early English Text Society, 1914).

This scholarly examination by Brown of the background to *Love's Martyr* has provided the basis for all subsequent commentary, explanation and interpretation of the poem *The Phoenix and (the) Turtle*, including the date of Shakespeare's composition of it, the possible setting referred to, and Shakespeare's potential (social) relationship to Sir John Salusbury of Lleweni and his wife Ursula née Stanley/Halsall (daughter in the 'second family' of Henry Stanley, 4th Earl of Derby and his mistress Jane Halsall, ensconced at Hawarden Castle in Flintshire, N. Wales). The very fact that Brown's monograph was published at Bryn Mawr reveals his Welsh interest and connection.

Two authors who have pursued in detail this work by Carleton Brown are Professor E. A. J. Honigmann, *Shakespeare: the 'lost years'*, Ch. IX 'The Phoenix and the Turtle', pp. 90-113 (1985, 2nd ed. 1998); and John Idris Jones, Welsh poet and historian, whose main (unpublished) work is lodged at the Shakespeare Birthplace Trust, Stratford. An article, 'William Shakespeare and John Salusbury: what was their relationship?' has meanwhile appeared in *Transactions of the Denbighshire Historical Society*, January 2011. Neither of them mentions the Shakespeare/Stanley/Stourton comment by Father Henry More. They both advocate the composition of *The Phoenix and the Turtle* in 1586 for the wedding of (Sir) John Salusbury and Ursula Stanley.

Two who do not believe this, but that the poem was written closer to the date of publication of *Love's Martyr* in 1601 are Professors Katherine Duncan-Jones and Henry Woudhuysen, *Shakespeare's Poems*, 2007. In this they devote pp. 91-124 to an intense analysis of all previous sources of commentary and criticism of *The Phoenix and the Turtle*, including references to Rollins and Honigmann, as above. There is no mention of the Stourton-Stanley-Shakespeare connection, nor of Father Henry More. In their conclusion to this section, when discussing the authenticity of all poems attributed to Shakespeare and covered in their book, the Tong epitaphs receive an interesting mention.

> Assuming cautiously that perhaps 50 per cent of the rest may be Shakespeare's, we are left with an impression of witty concision, like that which characterizes the *Threnos* contributed by Shakespeare to *Love's Martyr*. The single item that seems carefully designed and pondered is AT 3, the verses on the Stanley tomb at Tong. This item also has the strongest claim to authenticity.

> (Duncan-Jones and Woudhuysen, p. 123.)

[iii] It is perhaps superfluous to comment on the spelling of Sir John's family name. It presumably had the same origin as Salisbury, the cathedral city in Wiltshire, and several other places with this name. For whatever reason, the accepted 'modern' spelling of Sir John's surname has become 'Salusbury'.

[iv] 'telling a ghost-story' . . . Intriguing as this is, any commentary on this must await the future hoped-for location of the quote given above. It is not from *Historia*.

[v] We do not know whether More's *Historia* was WRITTEN in 1660. It was certainly published in this year, the year before More's death, but straight common sense indicates that a work of this depth and size, the culmination of his writing career as a historian, must have been based on his notes made during several previous years. His own MS note referring to the composition of an epitaph for a Stanley by Shakespeare might have been written during any previous decade. In any case it pre-dates the MS note by Sir William Dugdale, which can be fairly certainly dated to September 1663, when he visited Tong.

[vi] 'Lord Stourton called his wife, a daughter of Edward, Earl of Derby, and sister to the Stanley whose epitaphs Shakespeare wrote' . . .' Grammatically, this sentence makes no sense on its own and out of context. However, it contains several interesting and separate points:

a) The Stourton/Stanley family link. In itself, the first part of the 'claim' seems to imply that Father Henry had a reasonable knowledge of the Stanley family, Earls of Derby. Genealogical research confirms that he was correct in this claim. The 'Lord Stourton' referred to is covered below.

b) The Stanley/Shakespeare link via epitaphs.

c) It seems that Rollins here, via others, was probably referring to *The Phoenix and the Turtle*. And yet this has rarely been called an 'epitaph', rather a poem; and it is one longish poem, which could hardly be referred to as 'epitaphs' in the plural, although it does have another short poem entitled 'Threnos' following. (Threnos = a lyrical lament over a victim of the catastrophe in a tragedy, Merriam-Webster.)

d) It seems that there are several muddles involved here.

[vii] We are still here in the quote from Matthew (1922) by Rollins (1938), quoting from More (in some otherwise unknown translation into English pre-1981).

[viii] 'he was probably wrong in thinking that Ursula Stanley and Lady Stourton were sisters.' This is Rollins quoting from Matthew. The latter was the one who was probably wrong in thinking More was writing about *The Phoenix and the Turtle*, rather than the Tong verse epitaphs. (See 'Sorting out some Stanley muddles' below.) In any case, Ursula Stanley was indeed NOT Lady Stourton's sister, but her niece.

[ix] 'This Poem was stated to be a poetical essay.' This statement in itself confirms that Rollins was only referring to *The Phoenix and the Turtle* and the 'epitaphs' that More referred to were different. The only sensible alternative was the two short verse epitaphs written for **Sir Edward Stanley Jr**, a nephew of Lady Stourton, for the tomb of his father **Sir Thomas**, a brother of Lady Stourton.

[x] 'If Shakespeare wrote these beautiful Verses he never wrote anything else like them. . . .' Again, it is obvious that Rollins (from Mathew) was here writing only about *The Phoenix and the Turtle*.

[xi] '[Historia missionis Anglicanae Societatis Jesu, which I have not seen.]' Rollins's footnote probably reveals most of the muddles. He was reporting at second or third hand on comments on the original text, without having seen it himself. Let us be grateful, however, that his comments caught the attention of John Raithel researching into William Stanley as an Alternative Authorship candidate, which in turn led to this later exploration.

~~~~~~~~~~

8-4. Background to Father Henry More's biography

Of course, the top priority was to establish as far as possible the biography of Father Henry More, along with the precise details of his various publications in the seventeenth century on church history, most particularly his role in the history of the Jesuits during this turbulent period. The other main priority was to attempt to establish how reliable was his report in a work prior to 1660 in Latin that Shakespeare had written the Verse Epitaphs for **Sir Thomas Stanley** in Tong in c.1603. (We now know that they were actually written for his son **Sir Edward Jr**, with one perhaps in memory of his father. However, enough other people have been confused about this that we can forgive Father Henry for perhaps not knowing the exact dates of father and son.) In any case it would pre-date the handwritten note by Sir William Dugdale, Norroy, written in 1663 when he was conducting his Visitation of Shropshire. Father More must have had a different and earlier source.

The most significant details revealed by this paper-chase were that Father Henry was obviously fully cognizant of some stories about the poet and dramatist William Shakespeare, with the implication that they were well known and circulated within his own lifetime - that is, within the lifetime of Father Henry More, which overlapped with that of William Shakespeare by thirty years. For me this was just one more nut in the bolt of a conclusion and conviction reached several years earlier that several 'anecdotal historical' incidents in several previous 'theories' about William Shakespeare's ancestry and biography might actually have been true. These theories include 'Shakespeare's teenage time in Lancashire in the households of the Hoghtons and Heskeths', otherwise known as 'Shakespeare's Lancashire Connection'; also 'Catholic Shakespeare'; also the 'Shakespeare/Stanley connections', including writing the verse epitaphs in Tong for a Stanley.

Just to remind the reader of the main relevant dates, places and facts under discussion in this Appendix:

1) William Shakespeare was born in 1564 in Stratford to father John Shakespeare, who was very obviously a devout Catholic during certain periods of his life. One of the main pieces of documentary proof of John's Catholicism is the discovery in 1757 in the rafters of the Shakespeare House in Stratford of the 'Catholic Testament', the text of which was written by the Blessed (later St) Carlo Borromeo, Archbishop of Milan. This could only (most sensibly) have come into John Shakespeare's possession in 1580/1 via the English mission of Jesuits Edmund Campion and Robert Persons. (For more details and the full text of this 'Catholic Testament' see a multitude of articles on the internet; also Schoenbaum, *Shakespeare: a Compact Documentary Life*, 2nd ed. 1987, Ch. 5, John Shakespeare's Spiritual Testament, pp. 45-54, which provides the complete text.)

2) Father Henry More was born in 1586, a great-grandson of Sir Thomas More, the English Chancellor and Saint martyred for his faith in 1535, mainly because of his opposition to Henry VIII's divorce/marital plans and his break with the Church in Rome. Father Henry followed the well-established path for sons of eminent Catholic families to flee England to pursue his career in

continued

2) *continuation*

various Catholic strongholds in the Low Countries, Spain, Italy and France. He entered the Society of Jesus, returned to England on Missions, when he was twice arrested and imprisoned (1632 and 1640). He survived to write and publish several historical treatises, including his final work, the one most prominent in the current context, in which someone reported that he actually mentioned the Epitaphs written by Shakespeare for a Stanley (according, that is, to the quote at the beginning of this Appendix).

3) Putting the details from 1) and 2) together, it seems that a reading of all Father Henry More's published writings might be in order, with the main aim being to establish, as far as possible, how reliable was his comment on Shakespeare's epitaph for a Stanley. It would also be interesting to establish which of those involved he had actually known.

A brief check via Google established that Father Henry More was obviously a prominent figure in the stories of so many relevant people in Shakespeare's background. (A brief biography of him appears below.)

I have come to believe, mainly through my own genealogical and other historical research in Lancashire archives and libraries, combined with confirmation from the published results by genealogical researchers on Shakespeares in the Midlands, that the ancestry of William's father John Shakespeare was actually what he (i.e. William's father John Shakespeare) stated in no uncertain terms to heralds at the College of Arms in 1596 and 1599, all of which are recorded in MSS at the College of Arms.

The conclusions emanating from this led to the re-constitution of a rather different picture from the 'conventional ancestry' of Shakespeare emerging from Stratford in the 18th/19th centuries, and still supported by 'Stratford' in the 21st century. In the context of this book, it is with surprise to note the reluctance of 'Stratford' to accept that Shakespeare's immediate ancestry did not lie with grandfather Richard of Snitterfield. (The main proof of this is presented in an article by Stephen Pearson on the Shakespeare Family History website: 'Wherefore art thou, Grandfather?')

Into this new questioning and interpretation of the surviving records of William Shakespeare's ancestry and biography now enters the story of Father Henry More SJ.

8-5. Brief biography of Father Henry More

Henry More (Jesuit)
Wikipedia gives the following source.

Source
This article incorporates text from a publication now in the public domain: Herbermann, Charles, ed. (1913). "Henry More". *Catholic Encyclopedia*. Robert Appleton Company.

Catholic Encyclopedia (1913)/Henry More
From Wikisource
Catholic Encyclopedia (1913)
Henry More

Great-grandson of the martyred English chancellor; b. 1586; d. at Watten in 1661. Having studied at St. Omer and Valladolid, he entered the Society of Jesus, and after his profession, and fulfilling various subordinate posts in the colleges, he was sent on the English Mission where he was twice arrested and imprisoned (1632, 1640), while acting as chaplain to John, the first Lord Petre. He became provincial in 1635, and in that capacity had a good deal to do with the negotiations of Panzani, Conn, and Rossetti, the papal agents at the court of Queen Henrietta

Maria. He was rector of St. Omer in 1649-1652, and again in 1657-1660. During these latter years he wrote his important history of the English Jesuits: "Historia Missionis Anglicanæ, ab anno MDLXXX ad MDCXXXV" (St. Omer, 1660, fol.). Besides translating Jerome Platus's "Happiness of the Religious State" (1632), and the "Manual of Meditations" by Thomas de Villa Castin (1618), he wrote "Vita et Doctrina Christi Domini in meditationes quotidianas per annum digesta" (Antwerp, 1649), followed by an English version, entitled, "Life and Doctrines of our Saviour Jesus Christ" (Ghent, 1656, in two parts; London, 1880).

FOLEY, Records of the English Province S. J., VII, 518; MORRIS, Life of Father John Gerard (London, 1881).
J.H. POLLEN

Also from the *Catholic Encyclopedia* online.

The old trouble about the Oath of Allegiance was revived by the Oath of Abjuration, and the "three questions" proposed by Fairfax, 1 August 1647 (see THOMAS WHITE). The representatives of the secular and regular clergy, amongst them Father Henry More, were called upon at short notice to subscribe to them. They did so, More thinking he might, "considering the reasons of the preamble", which qualified the words of the oath considerably. But the provincial, Fr. Silesdon, recalled him from England, and he was kept out of office for a year; a punishment which, even if drastic for his offence, cannot be regretted, as **it providentially led to his writing the history of the English Jesuits down to the year 1635** ("Hist, missionis anglicanae Soc. Jesu, ab anno salutis MDLXXX", St-Omer, 1660).

It certainly seems that he was in an excellent position to know about **Sir Edward Jr** having received the verse epitaphs from Shakespeare for his father's tomb. We will remember that he was knighted by King James in 1603 at the time of his coronation, shortly after Sir Thomas Gerard Jr of Bryn, Lancashire, had been knighted at York; it was the fathers of both of them who had planned to help Mary, Queen of Scots escape from Chatsworth in 1570, with both spending time in the Tower for this. In 1603 one very active Jesuit in England, operating clandestinely in country houses, was Sir Thomas Gerard Jr's brother Father John Gerard (1564-1637). (Some details in Appendix 7. Carol Enos's *Shakespeare Encyclopedia*.) Amongst other activities during his extended stay in England was a period as chaplain to Sir Everard Digby, a close friend of **Sir Edward Jr**'s until Digby's capture and execution for his role in the Gunpowder Plot. Father John Gerard wrote his autobiography, some details of which must have been known to **Sir Edward Jr** as well as his son-in-law Sir Kenelm Digby and Father Henry More. Perhaps another close look at that will reveal more details, in the light of these newly emerged details about Father Henry More?

8-6. A closer look at More's *Historia*

It seemed that a close look at Gerard's autobiography and More's history, both in Latin, would be in order, in an attempt to track down the phrase in Latin about Lady Stourton, the Stanleys and the Shakespeare epitaphs quoted above (in English). There are several reviews of Gerard's book online, mainly of the English translation published by Philip Caraman SJ in 1951, or recent reprintings. (Some details via Father Garnett are in Appendix 7. *Shakespeare Encyclopedia*.)

As mentioned above, equipped with a copy of the English translation of the first part and two full versions in Latin, I embarked on many hours of hunting. As also mentioned, I could not locate the quote being searched for, but found many other interesting details.

a) Father Francis Edwards's was indeed the first ever translation of More's *Historia* into English, over 300 years after it was written, and there are no obviously discernible translations into any other language.

b) His book was/is *The Elizabethan Jesuits*, 400+ pages, with a reproduction of the original frontispiece (the only illustration) and the following Contents list:

c) The original Folio edition of 1660, in Latin, includes a Praefatio (Preface) and continues after the first six books with Liber 'Seventh', 'Eighth', 'Ninth' and 'Tenth', which take the history down to the dates announced in the title/frontispiece. The title is included within a suitably devotional series of drawings, including portraits in oval miniature form down the sides of four priests who all played an active role on returns to England.

- P. EDMUNDUS CAMPIANVS. (Father Edmund Campion)
- P. ROBERT. PERSONIVS. (Father Robert Persons)
- P. HENRIC. GARNETTVS (Father Henry Garnett)
- P. RICHARD. BLONDVS. (Father Richard Blount)

Edmund Campion has been mentioned elsewhere in this book as being in Lancashire from Easter to Whitsuntide 1581, when young William Shakeshafte/Shakespeare was with the Catholic Hoghtons. His Mission and martyrdom are, of course, covered by More.

Robert Persons (1546-1610), as Head of the English Jesuits in Rome and also on the English Mission in 1580-1, also, of course, appears regularly in More's *Historia*. He wrote under the pseudonym of Nicholas Dolman, and one statement about him by John Speed has been regularly quoted as 'proof' (or not) that Shakespeare was Catholic: 'this papist and his poet', the 'papist' being Persons and the 'poet' being Shakespeare. He was certainly well aware of Shakespeare and his changing the name of Sir John Oldcastle to John Falstaff in three plays.

> The second month of February is more fertile of rubricate martyrs, than January, for that it hath 8 in number, two Wickliffians, Sir John Oldcastle, a ruffian-knight as all England knoweth, and commonly brought in by comedians on their stages: he was put to death for robberies and rebellion under the foresaid King Henry the Fifth.'[14] (Persons in due course drew a contorted riposte from John Speed, who interestingly assumes that the playwright who transformed a Protestant martyr into a comic buffoon must have been a Catholic apologist. In his *History of Great Britain* (1611) Speed writes: 'That N. D. [Nicholas Dolman, Persons's pseudonym] . . . hath made Oldcastle a ruffian, a robber, and a rebel, and his authority, taken from the stage-players, is more befitting the pen of his slanderous report, than the credit of the judicious, being only grounded from **this papist and his poet**, of like conscience for lies, the one ever feigning, and the other ever falsifying the truth . . . I am not ignorant.')

> 14. 'N.D. [Nicholas Doleman, pseudonym of Robert Persons]. The Third Part of a Treatise, Instituted: of three Conversions of England: The Third Part of a Treatise, Intituled: of three Conversions of England: An Examen of the Calendar or Catalogue of Protestant Saints . . . by John Fox (1604). The Last Six Monethes (1604), p. 31; quoted in E. K. Chambers, ii. 213.
> (Schoenbaum, *William Shakespeare: a Compact Documentary Life*, 1987, p. 193, note p. 347.)

Father Garnett (1555-1606) was the one who, amongst many other activities, heard the confessions of the Gunpowder Plotters, but refused to reveal details because of the oath of silence. He, of course, also appears in *Historia*. He presumably knew Sir Everard Digby, whose son Sir Kenelm was later to marry Venetia Stanley. As this was twenty years before the marriage, however, it is not of great relevance for **Sir Edward Jr**.

d) A quote by Edwards referring to husbands of Lady Ann Stourton, although in reference to another Jesuit priest Cornelius. The Earl of Arundell has also entered the Stanley story on occasion, and enters it again here as the second husband of the Lady Stourton née Stanley, referred to somewhere (as yet unascertained) by Father Henry More. She was the sister of **Sir Thomas**.

> Baro de Stourton, p. 219
>
> Ordained priest, Cornelius returned to his old Maecenas, Arundell, who received him into his house and made much of him as long as he lived. On his death, he recommended him to the widow of Baron de Stourton, whom he had taken for his second wife. Arundell was outstanding no less for Catholic faith than for very considerable abilities. . . Cornelius himself, thanks to the goodness of his life, and his winning enthusiasm in preaching, upheld and propagated the Catholic cause in those parts for some 10 years. . . .
>
> (Edwards, p. 171, writing about events in 1594.)

e) It was hardly surprising that there was a copy in Munich, because this was a bastion for the Jesuits, with a large Jesuit complex built in the centre from 1583 onwards and supported by all subsequent Electors (Kurfürste). Wittelsbach Elector Maximilian I (1573-1661) 'the Great', who was Elector from 1591 onwards when his father abdicated, is mentioned several times in the last part of *Historia*. This is also hardly surprising, as he was educated by the Jesuits, and Munich was on one of the standard routes for English priests travelling from Rome to the Low Countries and England. He might even have remembered Edmund Campion and Robert Persons passing through in 1580 when he was a young boy. Maximilian might even also have remembered Campion's brilliant sermons there. As his second wife he married Maria Anna of Austria, daughter of Habsburg Ferdinand II (1568-1637), Holy Roman Emperor. This one was too late to have been the godfather of Ferdinando Stanley, who was probably a Spanish Ferdinando - it was a popular name in both imperial families. Maximilian has gone down in popular history mainly as the Elector during the Thirty Years War, when he allowed the Swedish army under Gustav Adolph to occupy the city rather than risk seeing it destroyed. It took the Allied Bombers in the Second World War to accomplish that, which left the Jesuit church of St Michael as a ruined shell. It has since been restored to much of its original glory.

8-7. Sorting out some 'epitaph' muddles

The quote at the beginning revealed that Rollins in 1938 was quoting from Matthew in 1922, who in turn was quoting from Brown in 1913 about *The Phoenix and the Turtle*. The story above turned out to be mainly a 20th century muddle of dates, people and places in the 16th/17th centuries; also a muddle among those verses by Shakespeare (or others at the same time) which have been variously classified as Sonnets; Poems; Poetical Narratives; Verses; Epitaphs; Eulogies; etc. etc.. This is quite natural because in many instances these categories overlap: a poem might be used as an epitaph, a sonnet might serve as a poetical narrative, or as a eulogy, or obituary, etc.. On occasion a later report of any one of these has often appeared regardless of whether any particular one survived in a form published soon after the time of writing; or existed only in MS form and was therefore only known to readers of the time; or was actually chiselled into or painted onto a tomb; or whether or not that monument has survived to enable checking today; or is only known from reports before the disappearance of the original.

In the context of Father More's writing, as quoted from above, we are concerned with only two of all these compositions by Shakespeare:

1) *The Phoenix and the Turtle*, which by Rollins and Matthew is variously called 'epitaphs', 'a poem', 'a poetical essay', 'a dedication' and 'beautiful verses'. This longish poem was first published in 1601 in *Love's Martyr*, a collection of poems assembled by Robert Chester in praise of Sir John Salusbury. I have come across no better description of this than the following, which also provides the full text of 67 lines, with 13 verses of 4 lines each, and in the *Threnos* 5 verses of 3 lines each.

> An untitled poem now known as *The Phoenix and the Turtle*, first published in Robert Chester's *Love's Martyr* (1601), proves indisputably that Shakespeare was in some way connected with the Stanley family. The poem, signed 'William Shake-speare', was one of several 'poetical essays' by 'the best and chiefest of our modern writers' consecrated (with many flourishes) 'to the love and merit of the true-noble knight, Sir John Salusbury'. Chester's own poems record the lamentations of the turtle and the phoenix, and leave us in no doubt that these two excessively talkative birds represent Sir John Salusbury of Lleweni (in Denbighshire) and his wife, Ursula Halsall or Stanley, an illegitimate daughter of Henry Stanley, fourth Earl of Derby.[1]
>
> [1]Carleton Brown has shown, I think convincingly, that Sir John Salusbury, the dedicatee, must be the turtle, and his wife the phoenix (*Poems of Sir John Salusbury and Robert Chester*, Early English Text Society, Extra Series, no. 113, 1914 (for 1913)). But there are other interpretations: A. B. Grosart, the editor of Robert Chester's 'Loves Martyr' (New Shakespere Society, 1878), argued that the phoenix and turtle represent Queen Elizabeth and the Earl of Essex, and William H. Matchett agreed. (*The Phoenix and the Turtle*, 1965). Matchett, however, could not explain why Shakespeare should refer to Queen Elizabeth in the past tense in 1601; and Matchett seems not to have known J. E. Neale's studies of the Denbighshire elections (cf. p. 93), which contradict his theory that Salusbury could have been an Essex supporter. Roy T. Eriksen has suggested (*Spenser Studies*, 1981, II, 193-215) that Bruno's *De gli eroici furori* (1585) influenced Shakespeare's poem, which is possible; if he is right, 'the theory that Essex was the poem's turtle becomes highly improbable' (p. 210). But Eriksen's idea that the poem also alludes to 'the death of the Italian philosopher-poet at the stake in Rome' is surely far-fetched.
>
> (E. A. J. Honigmann, Shakespeare: the 'lost years',
Manchester UP, 1985, 2nd ed. 1998, p. 91.
Chapter IX. 'The Phoenix and the Turtle', pp. 90-113; footnote, pp. 160-1.)

This footnote provides a flavour of the arguments provoked over the last century about almost every aspect of *The Phoenix and the Turtle*. The arguments are still ongoing. This poem, as far as possible, has been put to one side throughout this book, and it was only someone assuming (falsely) that Father Henry More's reference was to *The Phoenix and the Turtle* that produced this Appendix.

2) The two Verse Epitaphs on the Stanley tomb in Tong. These have nothing at all to do with *The Phoenix and the Turtle*. The Verse Epitaphs could, of course, be described as 'poems', but they were obviously written not to be published in a collection of poems, but to be chiselled or painted on a tomb. The only argument one might have is whether they were written separately, at different times, one in memory of **Sir Thomas** and one specifically for his son **Sir Edward**. As there are two stanzas or verses, it seems that the most accurate, perhaps only, description is 'Verse Epitaphs'.

The only thing that 1) and 2) have in common is that they were both written by Shakespeare for Stanleys (or in the case of Sir John Salusbury, a Stanley in-law), and that both therefore shed more light on Shakespeare's biography, as far as his connections with the Stanleys are concerned. Thankfully, however, for all intents and purposes, we can ignore *The Phoenix and the Turtle* in any further discussion of the Verse Epitaphs in Tong.

8-8. Sorting out some Stanley muddles

'Lord Stourton called his wife, a daughter of Edward, Earl of Derby, and sister to the Stanley whose epitaphs Shakespeare wrote'

Let us start with the Lady Stourton referred to above. The Stanley Family Tree in Appendix 12b makes the relationships clear, and the relevant people were all covered in Chapter XXIII. Immediate ancestors and close relatives of Sir Thomas. We here concentrate on Anne, the eldest daughter (1531-1602) of Edward, 3rd Earl of Derby. She was thus sister of Henry, 4th Earl, **Sir Thomas** and **Sir Edward Sr**, and therefore an aunt of **Sir Edward Jr**. The quote above, about her being '**sister to the Stanley whose epitaphs Shakespeare wrote**' is therefore absolutely accurate, inasmuch as the tomb was built for **Sir Thomas**, and the 'epitaphs' can only refer to those written for the Stanley tomb. Lady Stourton was NOT the sister, but the aunt of Ursula Stanley, for whose husband Shakespeare wrote *The Phoenix and the Turtle*. We will remember that More's dates were 1586-1661, so they overlapped for the last sixteen years of Anne's life.

On 10 February, 1549 Anne married Charles Stourton, 8th Baron Stourton (c.1520-1557), the groom somewhat older than his bride. He was the son of William Stourton, 7th Baron Stourton and Elizabeth Dudley, daughter of Edmund Dudley. Stourton had succeeded his father as baron in 1548. He was a nephew of John Dudley, 1st Duke of Northumberland, and a Catholic. A Wiltshire resident, he was asked for help by Mary Tudor in the succession crisis of 1553, but delayed his support for her until her victory was clear. We will remember that **Sir Thomas Stanley**, his new brother-in-law, was knighted by Queen Mary at her coronation in 1553, so it is likely that both were present at court at the same time. In August 1553 Lord Stourton was described as an 'archpapist' by a London pamphleteer and Lady Stourton was known to have maintained contact with Catholics in London until her death on 22 September 1602. Lord and Lady Stourton had at least two sons: John, who succeeded as 9th Baron in 1557 and Edward, who followed his brother as 10th Baron in 1588. The reason son John Stourton succeeded so early was because his father Charles was executed on 16 March, 1557 at Salisbury for murdering two men.

As a widow Lady Anne married another Catholic - Sir John Arundel of Lamborn, Cornwall, with whom she had a second family, two daughters becoming nuns. She continued to be known as Lady Stourton. Arundel died in 1591, and the events mentioned in a quote by Edwards above were in 1594, so it was indeed his widow who was concerned. (All these biographical details appear on numerous 'Tudor' websites.)

Given Father Henry More's dates (1586-1661), his periods as Rector of St Omer (at a time when **Sir Edward Jr**'s Percy mother-in-law was a Catholic exile in the area) and his two returns on English missions in 1632 and 1640, it seems that he was in an excellent position to know about the Stanley tomb with Verse Epitaphs at Tong, and he obviously had a good knowledge of the Stanley family. To repeat ad. inf., when he referred to the 'epitaphs', he was certainly not confusing them with the poem *The Phoenix and the Turtle*, which can hardly be described as 'epitaphs'.

We now (think we) know that Shakespeare actually wrote the epitaphs for **Sir Thomas**'s son **Sir Edward Jr** in 1601-4 for the tomb in the making or recently completed. This means that in 1602, the last year of Lady Anne's life, we have a very interesting scenario. Her brother **Sir Edward Stanley Sr** (Catholic) was still alive; her nephew William Stanley, 6th Earl of Derby, was writing plays in London alongside Shakespeare; Father John Gerard SJ, son of a dear family friend (Sir Thomas Gerard Sr, mentioned above), was active in country houses and in London; Father Henry More was just beginning his life as a dedicated Catholic and future Jesuit Priest. Her nephew **Sir Edward Stanley Jr** was in mourning for his wife, with his three small daughters placed with the family of his Catholic cousins Sir John Fortescue and Grace née Manners. It seems likely that much of this news would be known in all these circles and that anything reported later by Father John Gerard in his autobiography would have been true, and anything reported later by Father Henry More would therefore also be based on the truth.

'he was probably wrong in thinking that Ursula Stanley and Lady Stourton were sisters.'

This is, I fear, a result of a muddle by Rollins. Ursula Stanley is the one of total relevance to *The Phoenix and the Turtle*, a 'poetical essay', and of very little relevance to the Verse Epitaphs in Tong. Lady Stourton was the sister of **Sir Thomas Stanley** of the Shakespeare Verse Epitaphs in Tong. As we have seen above, Lady Stourton was actually the aunt of Ursula, Ferdinando 5th Earl, William 6th Earl and **Sir Edward Stanley Jr**. If anyone was 'wrong in thinking' about the relationships it is hardly likely that the two Jesuit priests in question were guilty of this - they actually knew all the people involved. The 'wrong in thinking' is much more likely to be the result of a twentieth-century muddle by people writing who had very little knowledge of the Stanley family and never made an adequate distinction between *The Phoenix and the Turtle* and the Tong Verse Epitaphs.

Finally, as an interim conclusion, let us hope that the hunt for the original quote in Latin in one of Father Henry More's other writings will continue and reach a successful conclusion.

8a. Henry More SJ's *Historia*, 1660
Frontispiece of *Historia*, A History of the English Jesuits. More knew about the verse epitaphs by Shakespeare in Tong and knew several in the Stanley family. Left: Edmund Campion, Henry Garnet. Right: Robert Persons, Richard Blount.

Appendix 9
Some Lancashire legends of relevance

9-1. Introduction

Many collections of Lancashire legends were published during the 19th and early 20th centuries. Among them was one in 1873 by John Harland and T. T. Wilkinson, which has seen several facsimile reprints during recent years.

LANCASHIRE LEGENDS,
Traditions, Pageants, Sports, &c.
WITH AN APPENDIX
CONTAINING
A RARE TRACT ON THE LANCASHIRE WITCHES,
&c. &c.
BY
JOHN HARLAND, F.S.A.
AND
T. T. WILKINSON, F.R.A.S. &c.
LONDON :
GEORGE ROUTLEDGE AND SONS.
MANCHESTER : L. C. GENT.
1873

Some of these legends cover places of importance in this book and present an attempted learned approach in assessing the possible/probable veracity of the core elements and what might well have been subsequent accretions. One might assume that all of these legends in one form or another were known to **Sir Thomas** and **Sir Edward Sr** and **Jr**.

The legend behind the crest of the Eagle and Child on the Stanley arms of the line of the Earls of Derby has produced many versions, but all with a central core. The Eagle and Child was, of course, also the crest on the arms of Sir Edward Stanley, 1st Lord Monteagle, hero of Flodden and father of two Thomas Stanleys in this book: Sir Thomas, 2nd Lord Monteagle and Thomas Stanley, Bishop of Sodor and Man. It was the eagle in his crest that apparently prompted Henry VIII to award him the title of Baron Mo(u)nteagle. And so stories and legends by Harland and Wilkinson about this Sir Edward are also included.

Given that John Shakespeare, William's father, chose or was awarded a falcon as his crest in 1596, and not one of the dozens of other possibilities available, and given the numerous Shakespeare-Stanley connections, it is perhaps not too fanciful to imagine that the Stanley eagle might have played a role in this choice.

Anything about Winwick deserves a place because the Rectory in Winwick was the Lancashire base of **Sir Thomas** and his son **Sir Edward** and the latter buried his infant son Thomas here.

9-2. The Eagle and Child I
(Harland & Wilkinson, pp. 19-22)

The fabulous tradition of the Eagle and Child, the crest of the Stanleys, Earls of Derby, associates itself with the family of Lathom, and is thus gravely related: - Sir Thomas Lathom, the father of Isabel, having this only child, and cherishing an ardent desire for a son to inherit his name and fortune, had an intrigue with a young gentlewoman, the fruit of which was a son. This infant he contrived to have conveyed by a confidential servant to the foot of a tree in his park frequented by an eagle; and Sir Thomas and his lady, taking their usual walk, found the infant as if by accident. The old lady, considering it a gift from Heaven brought thither by the bird of prey and miraculously preserved, consented to adopt the boy as their heir.

> "That their content was such to see the hap,
> The ancient lady hugs it in her lap:
> Smothers it in kisses, bathes it in her tears,
> And unto Lathom House the babe she bears."[i]

The name of Oskatel was given to the little foundling, Mary Oskatel being the name of his mother. From this time the crest of the eagle and child was assumed;[ii] but as the old knight approached near the grave, his conscience smote him, and on his death-bed he bequeathed the principal part of his fortune to Isabel, his daughter, now become the lady of Sir John Stanley,[iii] leaving poor Oskatel, on whom the king had conferred the honour of knighthood, only the manors of Islam (*sic*, Irlam) and Urmston, near Manchester, and some possessions in the county of Chester, in which county he settled, and became the founder of the family of Latham[iv] of Astbury. This story is an after-thought, adapted to that which had previously existed. In the Harleian MS (cod. 2151, fol. 4) is an account of some painted windows in Astbury Church, near Congleton, on which a figure is represented, with a sword and spurs, habited in a white tabard, the hands clasped over the head a shield placed angle-wise under a helmet and mantle, emblazoned or, on a chief indented, azure, three bezants, over all a bondlet, gules; crest, an eagle standing on an empty cradle, with wings displayed, regardant or, with the inscription, 'Orate pro anima Philippi Dom. Robert Lathom militis' – (Pray for the soul of Philip, son of Sir Robert Lathom, knight). This Philip Lathom of Astbury was uncle of Sir Thomas, *alias* Oskatel, the father of Isabella; and it would be a strange circumstance if an uncle should have assumed a crest bearing allusion to the adoption of an illegitimate child. Supposing Sir Oskatel to have been the son of Sir Thomas, instead of Sir Thomas himself, the fact of Philip bearing the crest would be still more extraordinary. That there was an Oskel or Oskatel Lathom, who bore as his crest an eagle standing on a child, is proved by the painting formerly in the windows of Northenden Church, 1580, – viz, an eagle sinister, regardant, rising, standing on a child, swaddled, placed on a nest; inscribed, 'Oskell Lathum' (Harl. MS. 2151, fol. 10). But this may have been because it was the old Lathom crest; and the eagle seems to have been from a remote period a favourite cognisance of the family. The Torbocks, the younger branch of the Lathoms, took an eagle's claw for a difference on the family shield; and the grant of Witherington by Sir Thomas Lathom, sen., reputed further [*sic*] of Sir Oskatel, was sealed with the Lathom arms on an eagle's breast. But a legend of the eagle and child is as old as the time of King Alfred - several centuries earlier than the time of the De Lathoms: – 'One day as Alfred was hunting in a wood, he heard the cry of a little infant in a tree, and ordered his huntsmen to examine the place. They ascended the branches, and found at the top, in an eagle's nest, a beautiful child dressed in purple, with golden bracelets (the marks of nobility) on his arms. The King had him brought down and baptized and well educated. From the accident he named the foundling Nestingum. His grandson's daughter is said to have been one of the ladies for whom Edgar indulged an improper passion.' If for Edgar we read Oscital, the Danish prince, this would complete the parallel with the Lancashire tradition, as given by Baines in his history of the county.[v]

Mr Roby,[vi] who expands this tradition into an interesting little romance, states that Sir Oskatel, the Earl of Derby's illegitimate child, palmed upon the Countess, and for a time adopted as heir to the Stanleys, had reserved to him and his descendants the manors of Islam [*sic*, Irlam] and Urmston near Manchester, with other valuable estates. At the same time was given to him the signet of his arms, with the crest assumed for his sake, 'an eagle regardant, proper.' It was only subsequent to the supplanting of Sir Oskatel (continues our author) that his rivals took the present crest of the eagle and child, where the eagle is represented as having secured his prey, in token of their triumph over the foundling, whom he is preparing to devour. This crest the descendants of Sir John Stanley, the present Earls of Derby, continue to hold. – See *Appendix*. (See 9-3.)

Notes by HM:

[i] I have not managed to trace the origin of this verse, but assume it came from a ballad current in the 19th century.

[ii] '**From this time the crest of the eagle and child was assumed.**' Others have claimed that at first only the eagle was assumed, the child in the cradle being added later.

[iii] '**Sir John Stanley**' (c.1340-1414) was a descendant of the first Stanley who moved from Staffordshire to the Wirral in Cheshire. Through his marriage to Isabel Lathom he became the ancestor of all the Stanleys of Lathom, the Lancashire branch that became the Earls of Derby. He fought for many years in Ireland, was 'promoted to' the rank of a Knight of the Garter and in 1405 was appointed Lord (and King) of Man. His biography appears in all the expected places.

[iv] '**Latham**' and Lathom (also Lathum) are used indiscriminately in early documents. The modern spelling of the place-name in Lancashire is Lathom.

[v] '**Baines in his history of the county.**' See bibliography.

[vi] '**Mr Roby.**' See bibliography.

~~~~~~~~~~~~~~~~~~~~~~~~~

9-3. The Eagle and Child II
Harland and Wilkinson's Appendix (pp. 259-261)

Probably the most curious version of this legend is that contained in Hare's MSS., vol. ii; which has been printed by the Lancaster Herald in the seventh volume of the *Journal* of the British Archaeological Association. As the orthography is almost unintelligible to most readers the spelling is here modernised.

> 'THE FAUSE FABLE OF THE LORD LATHOM. A FAYNED TALE.' – When the war was 'twixt the Englishmen and the Irishmen, the power of the English so sore assaulted the Irishmen, that the king of them, being of Ireland, was constrained to take succour, by flight, into other parts for his safeguard; and the queen, being pregnant and great with child, right near her time of deliverance, for dread of the rudeness of the commonalty, took her flight into the wilderness, where her chance was to suffer travail of child; bringing forth two children, the one a son, the other a daughter; when after by natural compulsion, she and such gentlewomen as were with her was constrained to sleep, insomuch that the two children were ravished from the mother; and the daughter, as it is said, is kept in Ireland with the fairies. Insomuch that against the time of death of any of that blood of Stanleys, she maketh a certain noise in one quarter of Ireland, where she useth [to stay].
>
> The son was taken and borne away with an eagle, and brought into Lancashire, into a park called Lathom Park, whereas did dwell a certain Lord named the Lord Lathom; the which Lord Lathom walking in his park heard a child lament and cry, and perceived the skirts of the mantle lying over the next side, and made his servants to bring down the child unto him.
>
> And whereas both he and his wife being in far age, and she past conceiving of child; considering they never could have issue; reckoning that God had sent this child by miracle, they condescended to make this child their heir, and so did. At length this Lord Lathom and his wife deceased, and this young man, which was named Oskell of Lathom, reigned and ruled this land as right heir, and he had to issue a daughter which was his heir and child by the Lady Lathom.
>
> It chanced so that one Stanley, being a younger brother of the House of Wolton [*faulty rendering or mistranscription of Hooton?*] in Cheshire, was servant to the Abbott of West Chester; this young man Stanley was carver to the Abbot, and he would not break his fast on the Sunday till he had heard the High Mass. Insomuch that it chanced one Sunday when the meat was served on the table, he had so great hunger he carved the pig's head, and conveyed one of the ears of the pig and did eat it.

When the Abbot sat down, and perchance missed this pig's ear, he was miscontent and in a great fume, and reviled so extremely and so heinously this young Stanley, that he threw the napkin at his head, and said he would do him no more service and departed. And he came to the king's court and obtained his service, and proved so active a fellow that the renown sprang and inflamed upon him, insomuch that the fame and bruit descended from him around this realm.

And when, as the use then was, that noble adventurers would seek their fortune and chance into divers and strange nations, one renowned gallant came into England, and he called as challenger for death and life, come who list. Insomuch that the king commanded this Stanley to cope with him; and to make short protestation, his chance was to overthrow the challenger and obtain the victory.

Then the king made him knight, and gave him certain lands to live on.

After this foresaid Stanley came for marriage to the daughter of Oskell of Lathom, which was found in the eagle's nest, and obtained her favour, and espoused her. And then after the death of Oskell he was Lord Lathom, and enjoyed it many years. And for such service as he did afterwards the king made him Lord Stanley; and he was the first lord of the name; and so by that reason the Stanleys descended of Lathom give the eagle and child in their arms.

9-4. Hornby Chapel and Sir Edward Stanley (H & W pp. 34-37)

SIR EDWARD STANLEY, fifth son of Thomas, first Earl of Derby, early received the notice and favour of Henry VIII. It is said of him that 'the camp was his school, and his learning the pike and sword.' The King's greeting when they met was, 'Ho! my soldier.' Honour floated in his veins, and valour danced in his spirit. At the battle of Flodden he commanded the rear of the English army, and through his great bravery and skill, he mainly contributed to that memorable victory. A sudden feint inducing the Scots to descend a hill, their stronghold, an opening was caused in their ranks, which Sir Edward Stanley espying, he attacked them on a sudden with his Lancashire bowmen. So unexpected an assault put them into great disorder, which gave the first hopes of success, and kindled fresh courage through the English ranks, ending in the complete overthrow and discomfiture of their enemies. Upon this signal achievement, Sir Edward received from the hand of his royal master a letter of thanks, with an assurance of some future reward. Accordingly, the following year, the King keeping Whitsuntide at Eltham, in Kent, and Sir Edward being in his train, his majesty commanded that, for his valiant acts against the Scots at Flodden - an achievement worthy of his ancestors, who bore an eagle on their crest - he should be created Lord Monteagle; and he had a special summons to Parliament in the same year by the title of Baron Stanley, Lord Monteagle. On various occasions in France, and also in the northern rebellions headed by Aske and Captain Cobbler, he rendered great service both by his bravery and his craft. Marrying into the family of the Harringtons, he resided the latter part of his life at Hornby Castle, engaged in schemes for the most part tending to his own wealth and aggrandisement. Four surmises prevailed, especially during his later years, as to the means by which he possessed himself of the estates which he then held in right of his lady, and those, too, that he enjoyed through the attainder of her uncle, Sir James Harringon. Stanley acknowledged himself a free-thinker and a materialist - a character of rare occurrence in that age, showing him to be as daring in his opinions as in his pursuits. Amongst his recorded expressions are – 'That the soul of man was like the winding-up of a watch; and that when the spring was run down, the man died, and the soul was extinct.' He displayed a thorough contempt for the maxims and opinions of the world, and an utter recklessness of its censure or esteem. Dr Whitaker[i] says of him, 'From several hints obliquely thrown out by friends as well as enemies, this man appears to have been a very wicked person, of a cast and character very uncommon in those unreflecting times . . . There certainly was something very extraordinary about the man, which, amidst the feudal and knightly habits in which young persons of his high rank were then bred, prompted him to speculate, however unhappily, on any metaphysical subject. Now whether this abominable persuasion [of atheism] were the cause or effect of his actual guilt - whether he had reasoned himself into materialism in order to drown the voice of conscience, or fell into the sin of murder because he had previously reasoned himself out of all ideas of responsibility, does not appear; but his practice, as might have been expected, was suited to his principles, and Hornby was too rich a bait to a man who hoped for no enjoyment but in the present life, and feared no retribution in another. Accordingly we find him loudly accused of having poisoned his brother-in-law, John Harrington, by the agency of a servant; and he is suspected also of having, through subornation of perjury, proved or attempted to prove, himself tenant of the Honour of Hornby.' Mr Roby has written a pleasant fiction, based on the character and imputed crimes of Lord Monteagle, in which he represents him as occupying midnight vigils in the castle-turret, in 'wizard spells and rites unholy.' He sends for the parson of Slaidburn, that he may put him to shame in an argument on the authenticity of the Christian religion; but the parson has the better of the argument, and does not fear to taunt the ruthless baron with the murder of John Harrington, whom he styles 'my lady's cousin.' The dispute with the parson ends with an apparition of the murdered man, in the form of a thick white cloud, and the unbelieving baron becomes an altered man. Under the ministrations of the worthy Parson, he becomes gradually more enlightened; his terrors were calmed, and he at length accepted Christianity as truth. Soon afterwards arose that noble structure the chapel of Hornby, bearing on its front the following legend: - 'Edwardus Stanley, Miles, Dñs Monteagle, me fieri fecit' - (Edward Stanley, Knight, Lord Monteagle, caused me to be erected). Its foundation was generally ascribed to some vow made at Flodden; but at that time the bold soldier was not a vower of vows; and Mr Roby thinks that his conversion from infidelity is the more probable cause of his chapel-building. It is recorded that Edward Stanley, Baron Monteagle, died in the faith he had once despised.

[i] '**Dr Whitaker**' was Dr Thomas Dunham Whitaker (1759-1821), from Holme near Cliviger, Burnley, who after his studies was Vicar of Whalley and later Blackburn. He was an esteemed local historian, whose many publications included a *History of Whalley* in 3 parts, 1801 ff. and *History of the Antiquities of the Deanery of Craven*, 1805, 1812, for which J. M. W. Turner, R.A., provided some illustrations.

~~~~~~~~~~~~~~~~~~~~~~~

9-5. Ormskirk Church (H & W pp. 47-49)

(*It is worth reading what Harland and Wilkinson had to say about the burial church of all Earls of Derby after the closure of Burscough Priory during the Dissolution of the Monasteries.* **Sir Thomas** *was buried at Tong and* **Sir Edward Jr** *at Eynsham, but* **Sir Thomas**'s *father Earl Edward and his two brothers, Henry, 4th Earl and* **Sir Edward Sr** *were buried at Ormskirk; as were* **Sir Edward Jr**'s *cousins Ferdinand, 5th Earl and William 6th Earl. A recent description of the church appears in Chapter XIV. 1572: Earl Edward's funeral.*)

This church is a large massive structure, on a slightly rising ground, north-west of the town, and has a tower commanding a fine view of the Irish Sea, Liverpool, Preston, &c., and also a spire at the south-east corner, which is partly modern, but resting on an ancient octagonal base. The church was probably built soon after the Conquest by Orm, the proprietor of Hatton. A local tradition, of no well-ascertained authority, represents it as having been erected at the cost of two maiden ladies [? sisters] named Orm, who, being unable to decide whether it should have a tower or a spire, accommodated their differences by giving it both. A more probable tradition states that the spire was attached to the original edifice, and that, on the suppression of Burscough Priory, the tower was built for the reception of eight of the bells taken hence, the remainder of the priory bells being removed to Croston Church. The tenor bell at Orsmkirk, which is said to have been the third at Burscough, has a Latin inscription in old English letters, 'J. S. de Burscough, Esq., and E. my wife, made [this bell] in honour of the Trinity. R.B. 1497.'

Roby observes that this tradition is an idle and impertinent invention, as the old ladies might each have had her way by building a tower and surmounting it by a spire. But who can say whether, in self-will, one lady would like to see her tower capped, surmounted, and so to speak, extinguished, by the spire of her sister? He suggests as a more probable solution that at the dissolution of the Priory of Burscough, temp. Henry VIII., the bells of its conventual church were removed to Ormskirk; and, as the small tower beneath the spire was not sufficiently capacious to receive them, the present square steeple was added. This suggestion receives some confirmation in the fact that the tenor bell of Ormskirk church, said to have been previously the third bell at Burscough Priory, bears some apparent proof of its translation. Round the circle below the ear is the following inscription, all, except the founder's initials in black letter: - 'J. S. * de Burscough, * Armig. * et * E. * vr. me fecerunt in honoris Trinitatis. * R.B. 1497.' That is, 'J.S. of Burscough, Esq., and E. his wife, made me in honour of the Trinity.' Where each asterisk is marked are the rose, portcullis, and fleur-de-lis. The Lancashire rose and the portcullis (borne by the Countess of Richmond and Derby, as a daughter of the Duke of Somerset) were favourite badges of Henry VII., who, besides the fleur-de-lis of France, being usually quartered at that time in the royal arms of England, had some claim to that bearing as the grandson of Sir Owen Tudor and Catherine of France, relict of Henry V. Henry VII. visited the neighbourhood, at Lathom house, the year before this bell was cast; and hence it was probably presented to the Priory in honour of his visit.

9-6. Winwick Church (H & W pp. 76-77)

The parish church of Winwick stands near that miracle-working spot where St Oswald, King of the Northumbrians, was killed. The founder had destined a different site for it, but his intention was overruled. Winwick had not then even received its name, the church being one of the earliest erections in the parish. The foundation of the church was laid where the founder had directed; and the close of the first day's labour showed that the workmen had not been idle by the progress made in the building. But the approach of night brought to pass an event which utterly destroyed the repose of the few inhabitants around the spot. A pig was seen running hastily to the site of the new church; and as he ran he was heard to cry or scream aloud, 'We-ee-wick, we-ee wick, we-ee-wick.' Then, taking up a stone in his mouth, he carried it up to the spot sanctified by the death of St Oswald, and thus employing himself through the whole night, succeeded in removing all the stones which had been laid by the builders. The founder, feeling himself justly reproved for not having chosen that sacred spot for the site of his church, unhesitatingly yielded to the wise counsel of the pig. Thus the pig not only decided the site of the church, but gave a name to the parish. In support of this tradition, there is the figure of a pig sculptured on the tower of the church,* just above the western entrance; and also the following Latin doggerel: -

> 'Hic locus Oswalde, quondam placint tibi valde;
> Northanhumbrorum fueras Rex, nunc que Polorum
> Regna tenes, loco pupus Marcelde vocato.'

> 'This place, O Oswald, formerly pleased thee greatly;
> Thou wert King of the Northumbrians, and now of the Poles (?);
> Thou holdest the kingdom in the place called Marcelde' [Macer
>   or Mackerfield].

[*This has a different translation in the article following*. HM]

There are other churches in Lancashire besides Winwick whose sites have been changed by the devil, and he has also built some bridges; that at Kirkby Lonsdale owes much of its beauty to the string of his apron giving way when he was carrying stones in it. The stones may be seen yet in the picturesque groups of rock below the bridge. According to some a priest, according to others the devil, stamped his foot into the church wall at Brindle, to prove the truth of Popery; and George Marsh the martyr did the same at Smithell's [*sic*, Smithill's] Hall, to prove the truth of Protestantism. The footmarks still remain on the wall and the flag. There is great sameness in these traditions, one story doing for several places, except that at Winwick it was as a pig, at Leyland as a cat, and somewhere else as a fish, that Satan played his pranks. - *Notes and Queries*, vi. 71.

* The *Oxford Dictionary of English Place-names* (1991, 1996) gives:

> **Winwick**, 'dwelling or (dairy) farm of a man canned Wina' OE pers. name + *wîc*: **Winwick** Cambs. *Wineuuiche* 1086 (DB). **Winwick** Northants. *Winiwican* 1043, *Winewiche* (DB) [= *Domesday Book*].

However, with this 'legend' and the pig sculpture on the wall, one might presume that there was once a pig in Winwick that played some strange and memorable role.

9-7. Some stories of Winwick

From *Stories and Tales of Old Lancashire* by Frank Hird (1911), selected and edited by Cliff Hayes (Aurora, Bolton, 1998).

Although Hird's stories are often romanticised, this account of the history of Winwick is reasonably sober and includes a couple of Stanleys associated with the place long before **Sir Thomas** took the 99-year lease on the Rectory in 1563. These stories were presumably known to him and **Sir Edward Jr**.

> Winwick was the favourite residence of Oswald, King of Northumbria, and it was near this place that he was killed, in A.D. 642, at the Battle of Makerfield. Oswald was a Christian, and he fell not only fighting for his kingdom but for his religion, against the pagan king and army of Mercia. The Venerable Bede, the Anglo-Saxon chronicler to whom we owe so much of our knowledge of the Saxon Heptarchy, tells us that the spot upon which King Oswald's body lay after he was slain became holy ground. Man or beast touching the place where he had lain if they were sick were instantly restored to health. He also says that so many people carried away the earth in order to bestow its miraculous powers upon their friends and relations, that in the course of time a hole, or a fosse as Bede calls it, was formed as large as a man's body.
>
> King Oswald was canonised for his valour against the pagans and for the miracles wrought by the earth. Half a mile from Winwick Church - which is dedicated to the King as St. Oswald - is St. Oswald's Well which, from time immemorial, has been reputed to be holy and health giving. Legend says that this well was formed by the excavation of the earth consecrated by the Saint's blood, mentioned by Bede. Time, instead of lessening the belief in the efficacy of the water of the well and the earth surrounding it, increase it, and all the neighbouring Roman Catholic Chapels took their holy water thence; and into the nineteenth century a man was paid a small annual sum to keep the well clear of weeds in order that the water should not be contaminated.
>
> There are some historians who claim Shropshire as the scene of St Oswald's defeat and death. In that county there was a place called Muserfeld, now Oswestry, and here it is said the great battle took place, and that the head and quarters of the slaughtered king were hung upon a tree on the battlefield - hence the name Oswestry - Oswald's Tree. Further colour is given to this theory by the existence of St. Oswald's Well near Oswestry. But this well comes from a spring, and is not a hole or fosse so distinctly described by Bede. Also the name of Makerfield in Lancashire goes back to the very earliest times. There is further proof of the battle having taken place at Makerfield in the fact that the church, whose foundation is one of the oldest in the kingdom, was dedicated to St. Oswald, the first Christian king amongst the Saxons. In addition there is a Latin inscription on the south wall of the church, which being translated runs: -
>
>> This place, O Oswald formerly delighted you much.
>> You were king of the Northumbrians, now in heaven
>> You possess a Heaven, having fallen in the field of Marcefield.
>> We beseech thee Blessed Saint to remember us.
>
> Then comes a line which has been obliterated, and below three Latin lines which say:-
>
>> In the year fifteen hundred and thirty
>> Sclater restored and built this wall again,
>> Henry Johnson at that time was curate here.
>
> A suggestion accounting for the existence of the St. Oswald legend both at Winwick and Oswestry was put forward by the late Dean Howson in an address he gave at Chester in 1873. He was not going to decide between the claims of the two places, he said, but he was inclined to think both views might be reconciled. 'Oswald had a palace at Winwick, and there was a well there that bore his name and an inscription that recorded his attachment to the locality. Oswestry is said to mean Oswald's Tree. There was no reason why they should not believe that he was killed at Winwick and that his head and arms were taken away and put on a stump of wood at Oswestry. The conflicting statements would then be reconciled.' It is suggested that this opinion

was in no way inconsistent with the character of the King of the Mercians, whose fierce and revengeful nature would not improbably lead him to send the mangled remains of Oswald to his Welsh allies as a proof of his victory over he Northumbrians.

James Stanley, one of the sons of the Thomas Stanley, the first Earl of Derby, by his first wife, was rector of Winwick in 1498, and when Henry VII. made his 'progress into Lancashire there to make merrie with his mother the Countess of Derbie which then laie at Lathom,' the Rector of Winwick entertained him and his Queen and all their Court for one night. Owing to the paramount influence of his stepmother, Margaret, Countess of Richmond and Derby, James Stanley was made Bishop of Ely. He was singularly tall and handsome.

'A goodly tall man he was as any in England.
He did end his life in merry Manchester,
And right honourably he lies buried there.'

But James Stanley was ill-suited for an ecclesiastic. He paid scant attention to his vows of celibacy as a priest of the Roman Catholic Church, and openly acknowledged an illegitimate son who went by the name of John Stanley. Cock-fighting was then a popular pastime, and one to which James Stanley was particularly devoted. It is recorded that he agreed with his neighbour, Thomas Butler of Bewsey, and other friends, to have a cock-fight every Saturday at Winwick. He died in 1515, and was buried at Manchester, where his tomb with his effigy in brass, may still be seen.

The ancient families of Legh and Gerard of Bryn both had their chapels in Winwick Church. In the Gerard chapel is a tombstone over four hundred years old. At the bottom, engraved in the quaint old Church text, is the epitaph: -

'Here lieth Peers Gerard Esquyer, son and heire of Thomas Gerard knyght of the Byrne, which married Margaret daughter to William Stanley of Hoton, knyghte, and one of the heires of John Bromley knyghte, which died the 19th of June 1492, on whose sowle God have mercy. Amen.'[i]

A full-length brass figure in plate armour, with sword and dagger and wearing a surcoat upon which are lions - the crest of the Gerards - stands upon another lion, which is lying on a rock. This is one of the most perfect monumental brasses in England, and shows the appearance of an esquire in the reign of Henry VII. The Legh chapel contains a monumental brass which tells its own story. Upon one side is the figure of Sir Peter Legh clad in armour and wearing the spurs of knighthood, but over this garb of the soldier the chasuble of the priest is engraved. His head is bare and shows the tonsure of the ecclesiastic. On the other side is the effigy of his wife, dressed in a long robe, and wearing the headdress of the time of Henry VII., with long lappets. Between them is a coat-of-arms, which is also engraved on the front of Sir Peter's chasuble. The inscription reads:-

'Pray for the soul of the excellent man, Sir Peter Legh, knight, here buried, and of the Lady Elene his wife, daughter of John Savage, knight, the body of which Elene was deposited at Bellingisett 17th May A.D. 1491. The same Peter after the death of this Elene, having been consecrated to the priesthood, died at Lyme, in Hanley, 11th August 1527.'[ii]

In these bald words, 'after the death of this said Elene, having been consecrated to the priesthood,' lies the tragedy of a life. They loved as devotedly in those far off days as we do now, and when Death took his beloved wife from his side, Sir Peter Legh, the armoured knight, could find no consolation. His position, his possessions were as nothing; his world was empty. He sought refuge in his Church and became a priest, and for thirty-six years out of the desolation of his own heart ministered to others.

Notes by HM:

[i] This was an ancestor of Sir Thomas Gerard of Bryn, who was knighted on the same day in 1553 as **Sir Thomas Stanley**, and was with him in the plan to rescue Mary, Queen of Scots from Chatsworth in 1570. Although Bryn was close to Wigan, they had an estate in Winwick and used their vault under

the Gerard chapel until the Reformation. The wife Margaret Stanley was the daughter of Sir William Stanley of Hooton [Gen. 5] in the Wirral, the original Stanley family in the North West and the senior line.

[ii] The Leghs of Lyme, although with their main seat at Lyme Hall just over the border in Cheshire, had estates in Winwick, still at the time when **Sir Thomas** and **Sir Edward** were leasing the Rectory there. One might imagine that they sometimes attended services together in St Oswald's.

9-8. The Winwick Broad Oak

Although the story told here by Frank Hird took place during the Napoleonic Wars, it is more than possible that the oak tree was already quite a size when **Sir Thomas** and **Sir Edward** lived here. And there was yet another Stanley living in Winwick, or at least the son of another Lady Lucy Stanley - a name passed down from **Sir Edward Jr**'s wife? Perhaps she was still remembered here more than two centuries after she buried her infant son Thomas here?

> There formerly stood at Winwick an old oak of so unusual a size that its branches once served as a canopy for a dinner of one hundred and twenty-four persons, a company 'never exceeded in respectability upon any public occasion in the city of Lancaster.' The dinner was given to Captain Phipps Hornby, who had commanded the *Volage* at the Battle of Lissa, and captured a French flag. The young captain, whose father, the Rector of Winwick, lived at Winwick Cottage, had returned to the village early in August 1811 after five years' absence, and his friends and neighbours, anxious to honour one who had so honoured his native place by his bravery and his services to his country, arranged a princely banquet for him on the 26th. . .
>
> Captain Phipps Hornby, whose mother was Lacy Lucy Stanley, a daughter of the twelfth Earl of Derby, entered the Navy in 1797. . . At the time of the famous dinner under the Winwick Broad Oak, the hero of the festival was only twenty-six. . .
>
> The Winwick Oak stood in a field a little distance to the south of the church. It covered an acre of ground 100 yards in circumference, the lower branches extending 99 feet from north to south, and 87 feet from east to west. The girth of the trunk at the base was 14 feet; and 11½ feet at a height of 5 feet. The first branch was 7½ feet from the ground. This wonderful old tree was blown down in a gale of wind on the 4th February 1850.

9a. The Eagle and Child, Winwick

9b. The Derby Arms, Knowsley Village

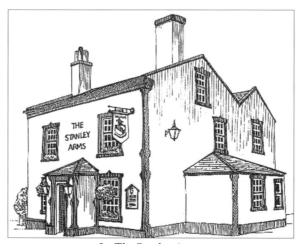

9c. The Stanley Arms
Inns with this and the names in 9a. and 9b. are found all over
Stanley and Derby territory in Lancashire and Cheshire.

Appendix 10
Sir Kenelm Digby's Memoirs

A summary of Nicolas's interpretation of parts of Sir Kenelm Digby's Memoirs was given in Chapter XXVII-4. To do these memoirs full justice it seemed useful to extract and perhaps re-interpret some parts of Sir Kenelm's writings, but only those parts of direct relevance to the biography of his father-in-law **Sir Edward Stanley.**

Private Memoirs of Sir Kenelm Digby, including 'Kenelm Digby',
Nicholas Harris Nicolas, London, Saunders & Otley, 1827

The 'Introductory memoir' by Nicholas Harris Nicolas, first published in 1827, contains 88 pages. At the end it includes a list of his interpretation of the allegorical names given to people and places. It also gives his interpretation of events from Sir Kenelm's somewhat flowery language and often abstruse formulations, resulting in Nicolas's version of Sir Kenelm's biography. Nicolas also helpfully gives (p. x) his location of the source of the first use of 'Anastatia' as a second name for Venetia in Hutchins, *History of Dorset* (1741). There is no contemporary record of her having more than one name. Some of Sir Kenelm's more explicit descriptions of sexual scenes were judged rather too daring for Nicolas's potential readers and are thus presented as 50 pages of 'Castrations from the Private Memoirs of Sir Kenelm Digby, Not published', i.e. they were not published in the first edition in 1827, but included at the end of the second edition of 1828 (by popular request?). Sir Kenelm's memoirs occupy 328 pages, albeit of the small size indicated. Only those passages are reproduced below which are fairly directly relevant to **Sir Edward Stanley Jr**'s biography. The explanation of names and places are Nicolas's; the other comments in the right column are HM's. There are digital versions online from two copies: a Google E-book and California Digital Library. The latest scholarly biographies of Sir Kenelm and Venetia are in the *Oxford Dictionary of National Biography*.

The *italics* in the column on the left indicate the phrases commented on in the right hand column.

p. 13 To deduce then this narration from the very beginning. *Stelliana being born of parents that in the antiquity and lustre of their houses, and in the goods of fortune, were inferior to none in all Peloponesus*; it pleased Heaven, *when she was not many months old, to take her mother from her*, deeming, as I think, the earth and *too negligent a husband*, not worthy of so divine a blessing; who dying left the goodness of her soul and the beauty of her body, in both which she surpassed all others of her time, to her infant daughter.	*Stelliana* = Venetia Kenelm was obviously always very well aware of Venetia's illustrious ancestry on both sides. *Peloponesus* = query Great Britain This is the main source for knowing that her mother Lucy died in early-mid 1601. Venetia was born on 19 December 1600, given in the MI on the tomb in London commissioned by Sir Kenelm, which had disappeared by the late seventeenth century. '*too negligent a husband*'? Was Edward really negligent as a husband? Sir Kenelm never met his mother-in-law Lucy. He was born on 11 July 1603, two years after Lucy's death. So anything he wrote about Edward and Lucy's marriage came from others.
p. 14 *Nearchus* then, for that was the name of Stelliana's father, being like those that through the weakness of their eyes are dazzled with too great a light, and are notable to comprehend it until the absence of it make them lament their loss; began then to be sensible *how happy he might formerly have been* by the *unhappy state* wherein he found himself, being deprived of that jewel whose loss would have made the world poor, if out of her ashes another *Phœnix* had not risen with greater splendour. And then sorrow and discontented thought beginning to take possession of his mind,	*Nearchus* = Sir Edward '*how happy he might formerly have been*'. Was Sir Edward formerly ever in an '*unhappy state*'? Had there been problems in Edward and Lucy's marriage? The '*Phœnix*' was, of course, Venetia, arising from the ashes of her mother.

p. 15 the nature of which is to please themselves in nothing but such objects as may feed and increase them, *he retired himself to a private and recollected life*, where without the troubles that attend upon great fortunes he might give free scope to his *melancholic fantasies*: which to enjoy more fully in the way that he desired, *he judged it expedient by removing his daughter from him to take away such cumbers as might disturb his course, since it was requisite for the education due to her high birth to have many about her, that would ill agree with his affected solitariness.*

Wherefore, *as soon as she had attained to such strength as that her remove might be without danger*, he sent her to *a kinsman of his*, whose wife being a grave and virtuous lady, had given him assurance that no care of diligence should be wanting on her part to cultivate those natural endowments which did al-

This is the only source for knowing about (Sir) Edward's deliberate withdrawal from society, to his *melancholic fantasies*. This was later mirrored by Sir Kenelm's own withdrawal into Gresham College after Venetia's untimely death in 1633, aged 33.

The implication is that Edward kept Venetia – and presumably elder sisters Petronella and Frances – in his own care, presumably at Tong Castle, for some time after Lucy's death. It is anyone's guess as to how long this was. '*as soon as she had attained to such strength as that her remove might be without danger*' could refer to any age during her infancy. One might presume that two major events of 1603 – his knighthood by James I at his coronation on 25 July and his sale of Tong Castle and move to Eynsham – were not unconnected with the decision to place his young daughters in a household which would provide a more suitable setting for them than just the company of their father and his household servants. Eynsham Abbey was also much closer to Salden. The '*kinsman*' was Sir Francis Fortescue of Salden, Bucks, also knighted at James's coronation. As far as is known, he was only related to Kenelm because his wife Grace née Manners was Edward's first cousin. This '*grave and virtuous lady*' (Grace Fortescue) was well known to Sir Kenelm's parents and later to himself, and so his assessment of her can be accepted as being from personal knowledge rather than hearsay.

p. 16 ready shine through her tender age. *Their house in the country* was near to that where *Arete* the mother of *Theagenes* lived, *whose father was then dead*, which gave occasion of frequent interchanging visits between her and Stelliana's guardians, and the affection of the one to her son, which would not suffer her to be long without him, and the respect of the others to this charge, which made them glad to satisfy her, though yet childish desires, in any thing they could, as in the fondness of going abroad and such likes, was the cause that *they seldom came together but that the two children had part in the meeting: who the very first time that ever they had sight of one another*, grew so fond of each other's company, that all that saw them said assuredly that something above their tender capacity breathed this sweet affection into their hearts. They would mingle serious kisses among their

'*Their house in the country*' was Salden House in Mursley, Buckinghamshire
Arete = Mary Digby née Mulsho; *Theagenes* = Sir Kenelm.
His father, who '*was then dead*' was Sir Everard Digby, executed in 1606 for his role in the Gunpowder Plot. This might place Sir Edward's decision to place his daughters with cousin Grace after this date; or it might reflect the fact that Sir Kenelm was born in 1603 and so presumably had few or no memories of his father being at home before his arrest and subsequent execution. He might, therefore, have never known exactly when Venetia had arrived in the Fortescue household.

The Fortescue and Digby families obviously came together quite often, with the children. Kenelm and Venetia immediately formed a close bond. There is no reference to how often Sir Edward visited them. See at the end for more details of this Fortescue family.

p. 17 innocent sports: and whereas other children of like age did delight in fond plays and light toys, these two would spend the day in looking upon each other's face, and in accompanying these looks with *gentle sighs*, which seemed to portend that *much sorrow* was laid up for their more understanding years; and if at any time they happened to use such recreations as were sortable to their age, they demeaned themselves therein so prettily and so affection-

Presumably some of the '*gentle sighs*', portending '*much sorrow*' were Kenelm's retrospective interpretations of their future sorrow caused by their later separation. They might also be a reflection of the memory that Kenelm grew up without his father and Lucy without her mother.

contd

p. 17   ately, that one would have said, love was grown a child again and took delight to play with them. *And when the time of parting came, they would take their leaves with such abundance of tears and sighs as made it evident that so deep a sorrow could not be borne and nursed in children's breasts without a nobler cause than the usual fondness in others.* But I should do wrong unto their riper love, to insist too long upon *these crude*

Sir Kenelm seems to attribute too much from their later passionate love into his memory of the obvious affection they felt for each other in childhood.

p. 18   *beginnings,* therefore, with as much haste as I can I will *run these over,* to come unto the other that calls upon me to keep myself in breath and to summon together my quickest spirits, that I may be able to represent it in as stately and majestic manner as it deserves.

He promises to '*run over*' '*these crude beginnings*', and we therefore omit a page of further eulogy. Later, dozens of pages will be omitted, as of no relevance to Sir Edward's biography.

p. 19   To continue then where I left, Stelliana being of such age that with her tender hand she could scarcely reach to gather the lowest fruit of the loaden boughs; *her father, that yielded daily more and more to his discontents, and fainting under the burden of them which age made to seem heavier, sent for her back to his own house,* hoping that by the presence of such a daughter, who fame delivered to excel in all things belonging to a lady of her quality, and that inherited the perfec-

Did Sir Edward really become more and more 'melancholic'? Or was bringing Venetia back to his home a sign that he wanted to participate more in society for her sake? Surprisingly, Sir Kenelm never mentions sisters Petronella or Frances, neither during the childhood scenes nor later. This is rather surprising not least because John Fortescue and his daughter Frances Stanley married about this time, which might have affected Sir Edward's decision to bring Venetia back to his home.

p. 20   tions of her deceased mother, *whose loss he lamented still as tenderly as at the first day of her death, he might pass the rest of his drooping days with some more content, and to have in her a lively image of his virtuous wife, that being deeply engraved in his heart, did with the continual exercise of his solitary thoughts upon that one subject, almost wear it out and corrode it through.*

     He then perceived that his expectations and desires were not frustrated; for Stelliana's sweet and gentle disposition, that was like a rich soil to sow the best grain in, striving to exceed in capacity the good precepts that were delivered her by *those tutors which her guardian's loving care with singular choice had placed about her,* had made her to *exceed all others of her age* so far, as caused men to doubt that the heavens meaned not to lend her long unto the earth, since she had

Whatever problems Edward and Lucy might have had, she seems to have become ever more saintly in death – at least in his memory of her. We know that he never married again and here we have at least one reason, in this eulogy to Lucy, whether from Sir Kenelm's pen alone, or repeating words that he had heard from Sir Edward. Having Venetia with him again would mean '*to have in her a lively image of his virtuous wife, that being deeply engraved in his heart . . .*'

From this we know that Venetia had had some '*tutors*' while at Salden, as well as enjoying her '*guardian's loving care*'. Did she really '*exceed all others of her age*'? Was Venetia intellectually precocious as well as attractive in looks and personality? She seems to have been, at least in Sir Kenelm's eyes and memory. Sir Edward presumably enjoyed some of this reflected glory on her Stanley and Percy genes.

p. 21   already arrived to that maturity and perfection that most come short of when they have past a long and tedious life so that she was ready to change this wearisome pilgrimage for a happier crown before she knew almost what it was to live.

The King of Morea = James I of England; his daughter was Princess Elizabeth. The wedding was on 24 February 1613.
Achaya = ?; her husband was Frederick V, Elector

contd

p. 21 He had not long enjoyed the fruits of this blessed harvest, when the marriage of *the King of Morea's daughter* with one of the greatest princes of *Achaya*, invited all men of eminence to the court, to contribute their particular joys to the great and public solemnities. Wherefore *Nearchus* being desirous to give his daughter the content of seeing the *magnificent entertainments* that are usual at such times, and also being glad to let the world now see that fame was nothing too lavish in setting out her perfections, took this occasion to bring her to *Corinth* the metropolitan city, where her beauty and discretion did soon draw the eyes

p. 22 admiration : so that in this the example of her was singular, that whereas the beauty of other fair ladies used to grace and adorn public feasts and assemblies, *hers did so far exceed all others as well in action as in excellence, that it drew to her not only the affections, but also the thoughts of all persons, so that all things else that were provided with greatest splendour and curiosity, passed by unregarded and neglected.*

But here one may see how undeservedly that is styled happiness, which subsisteth only in the opinion of others; and how little they are sensible of outward applause, tha have their heart fixed upon other objects ; for in the midst of these joys where Stelliana was the jewel that crowned them all, she could taste nothing that savoured of content ; but *as if happiness had been confined to where Theagenes was, in his absence,* she did languish and think those hours tedious that obliged her by civil re-

p. 23 spect whiles she was in company to suspend and interrupt her thoughts, whose true centre he was and about which they only desired to move. So that one day *Ursatius*, a principal nobleman of the court, whose heart was set on fire with the radiant beams that sparkled from her eyes, took the confidence to speak unto her as he sat next to her at a masque, in this manner : "Fair lady/" quoth he, "I shall begin to endear myself to your knowledge by taxing you with that which I am confident you cannot excuse yourself of; for if by the exterior lineaments of the face, and by the habitude of the body, we may conjecture the frame and temper of the mind, certainly yours must be endowed with such perfections, that it is the greatest injustice and ingratitude that may be, for you to imprison your thoughts in silence, and to deny the happiness of your conversation to those whose very souls depend upon

(Kurfürst) of the Palatinate (Pfalz), with his seat in Heidelberg. Their wedding was on 24 February 1613. Nicolas guessed that Achaya was Bohemia (of which Frederick became King soon afterwards) or Germany.
Nearchus = Sir Edward
One presumes that Edward had himself participated in many previous '*magnificent entertainments*' at court, perhaps/presumably at least the wedding at Elizabeth's court at Greenwich of his cousin William Stanley, 6th Earl of Derby, on 26 January 1595. We know about many court visits by his Uncle Henry when 4th Earl, and his cousins Ferdinando and William. And he must have known about his cousin-in-laws the two Countesses of Derby (Alice, widow of Ferdinando and Elizabeth, wife of William) frequently performing in masques at court during the previous years.
Corinth = London

Venetia's appearance in the courtly scene obviously had an immediate effect in attracting admiration of her beauty and personality. We should remember that in February 1613 she was only 12. Soon afterwards, Sir Edward set her up in her own house on the estate at Eynsham. One should perhaps bear in mind that 14 was considered at the time a suitable age for marriage.

Sir Kenelm rather glosses over the attention that Venetia attracted at this time, even though hidden away in the country. From Aubrey's account we know that she had many admirers. What we do not know is how far Sir Edward was involved in this, nor his reaction to his daughter acting as a magnet. It is difficult to imagine that he was totally unaware of this. Sir Kenelm's explanation for any indiscretions on Venetia's part came from his own absence, '*as if happiness had been confined to where Theagenes was, in his absence*'.

We will soon take a long break from Sir Kenelm's memoirs containing long descriptions of his own teenage years, with studies, travels and adventures. Because of these he did not meet Venetia again until he was in his early twenties. Venetia had meanwhile moved to London, set up her own establishment, had many admirers, and acquired something of a reputation. We have no idea how much Sir Edward was informed of all this, nor whether he and his daughter visited each other during this period, in Eynsham or in London.

However, we know that Sir Kenelm heard about Venetia's admirers. He gives a long description of the enamoured 'Ursatius', whose infatuation he totally understood and whom he later completely forgave. Nicolas did not identify him but John Aubrey, writing in the 1660s (not published until 1898, so unknown to Nicolas except possibly in manuscript), reported the rumour of one of her admirers being Richard Sackville, 3rd Earl of Dorset. This is historically unsubstantiated, but Aubrey was a collaborator with the Oxford historian Anthony Wood, whose great-grandparents had moved to Eynsham from

contd

p. 23
contd

Preston, Lancashire, their children working in the Stanley household. Wood visited his relatives in Eynsham in the 1650s, within living memory of Venetia's residence there. (Chapter XIX. Eynsham, Lilian Wright.)

p. 24   every motion that you make : and so you rob Him of the honour due to Him who is the Author of all good ; and who in retribution expecteth that they unto whom he hath been most liberal of his favours, should by due communication of them most] glorify him."

The following 42 pages cover the period when Kenelm and Venetia lost touch with each other. For details, see any biography of Sir Kenelm. Predictably, there is no mention of Sir Edward until Sir Kenelm returns to his long lost love.

p 66   and principally there, to be concealed: for *Arete, that had long before perceived much affection in her son to Stelliana*, and being *now much averse to it*, as well because of some *unkindesses passed between Nearchus and her*, as that it might be a disturbance to the other that she came about, and infinitely desired; did with watchful eyes, *armed with longing, hatred, and jealousy*, continually observe all passages between her son and Stelliana; so as *the two first days that they were together*, they could have no conveniency of free discourse: whilst their fire increasing by presence and each other's sight, the keeping of it in too narrow a room without any vent, almost smothered their hearts. . .

Arete = Mary Digby, '*had long before perceived much affection in her son to Stelliana*' and did not approve. Various explanations have been offered for this, including that rumours of Venetia's other romances had reached her ears, and she did not want her son to be involved in a scandal. Mary was apparently an extremely gifted and rather commanding, even overbearing person. What the '*unkindesses passed between Nearchus* (Sir Edward Stanley) *and her*' were remain unknown. Whatever the reasons, Mary was '*armed with longing, hatred and jealousy*'. Perhaps it was a classic mother-in-law/potential daughter-in-law situation? No one could ever be good enough for her gifted son.

Their meeting again obviously rekindled their childhood friendship. They spent '*the two first days that they were together*' in the presence of Mary, whether in Salden, Eynsham or London is not known. The intervening and following part of Sir Kenelm and Venetia's story has been told endless times, and has no relevance for Sir Edward's biography, apart from that during this period his daughter committed herself totally to Sir Kenelm. He, however, disappeared again.

Many pages later we pick up the love-story again, in a secret marriage, before or after which she became pregnant. At last we see Venetia back at Eynsham Abbey. She '*was, and had been some time, at her father's house in the country*'.

p. 254   For by a messenger that was sent to him with exceeding haste from Stelliana, *who was, and had been some time, at her father's house in the country*, he understood how, by a *fall from a horse* as she was riding abroad the night before to take the air, she had received some bruises, and being brought speechless home into her chamber, as soon as she came to herself again, she fell suddenly *into labour of childbirth*, she wanting then some few days of her expected time ; which unhappy accident disordered all the long and discreet preparations that were maturely made and contrived by both of them for her fit delivery: *for the next day*

She obviously spent the whole of her late pregnancy at Eynsham before going '*into labour of childbirth*'. She had intended to return to London shortly before the birth, where all had been prepared for her '*lying-in*', but '*a fall from a horse*' had brought on a premature birth.

p. 255   she intended, by coach, which she had with her, to come to Corinth, where a private and fit place, and due attendance, was provided for her lying-in ; and she had remained at her father's all the time that her swelling burden might betray her to strangers' curious eyes, and was now come to the last period that it was safe for her to continue there. But hereby one may take to themselves a lesson, how weak all the wisest propositions of men are, and that

This is 'proof', from Sir Kenelm's pen, that they had both agreed to keep her pregnancy and their marriage secret. One presumes that Sir Edward must have known about her pregnancy and the birth, and the secrecy surrounding this, as '*she had remained at her father's all the time*'.

p. 255 God reserveth to himself the right of dis-
posing all things; and then, when to human
  understandings a business seemeth to be
upon worst terms, he raiseth from the
weakest and least regarded subjects, means
to rectify all again. For what, in all appearance, could be weaker than the tender-
ness of a delicate lady that never knew what
hardness meant, to encounter with dangers,
orments, nay, even death itself, and to
outface suspicion? For thus it hap-

p. 256 pened with Stelliana, who, choosing rather
to suffer death and any other extremity,
than to fail in the least point to what Theagenes desired of her, and what she had
  promised to him, resolved never to acquaint
any one in what state she was while she
had life, more than *one servant she had*,
who was privy to what was between Theagenes and her. And thus, with the help
of that one *fearful and unexperienced maid,
she was delivered of a fair son* after a long
and dangerous labour, in which she had
like to have perished for want of due help ;
and yet she bore it with such a strange and
high resolution, that, being troubled
by times with the visits of her careful
father and others that lived in the house,
she never betrayed any part of her pain by
weak crying, or so much as any languish-
ing sighs. But before Theagenes could
come to her, who, upon the first news of
her danger, made all possible haste thither,

Only her '*one servant*', a '*fearful and unexperienced
maid*', was present during her labour and delivery.

Their first child, '*a fair son*', was thus born at Eynsham.
This was Kenelm, born on 6 October, 1625.

p. 257 she had been so long in the hands of tor-
ment, that her spirits began then to faint,
and to yield themselves to a misty night,
when, of a sudden, his sight brought new
strength and vigour to her dismayed senses ;
so that she, of her side, by undaunted suffering, and he, on his, by providing dis-
creetly for the due carriage of all things,
  wherein he had no easy task, they both
behaved themselves in such sort, that she
soon recovered her perfect health and
strength, and the cause of her sickness was
not so much as suspected. And, if before,
any one might have jealousies what state
she was in, and might doubt the notice of
her first pretending to be indisposed, all
this was now cleared, since what was done
  would seem impossible, and not to be
believed by any that did not know it was
done.
   Theagenes having remained there till
she was perfectly re-established in her

Venetia obviously went through an extremely bad period
after giving birth, and was physically and mentally in such
a serious condition, it seems, for all around to wonder
whether or not she might even survive. Again, we have
no hint as to whether or not Sir Edward was involved in
any way. One can only imagine that he too suffered,
fearing on behalf of his son-in-law a re-enactment of his
own loss of his wife and four daughters, and the
possibility for himself of now losing a fifth child.

This rigmarole is the confirmation that she had kept her
pregnancy and her marriage secret.

As soon as Venetia '*was perfectly re-established in her
health*' Sir Kenelm returned to London.

p. 258 *health*, returned to Corinth; and then *Aris-
tobulus*, taking occasion of this his late
and so long and public having been with
her, to represent to him the wrong that he
did himself in this affection, and how much

There he talked to '*Artistobulus*', his uncle Sir John
Digby, 1st Earl of Bristol. King James had sent him to
Madrid as his ambassador to Spain during the early 1610s,
and Digby had been a leading figure in the recent
unsuccessful Spanish Match, the effort to marry Prince

p. 258
contd
it did prejudice his esteem, did, in a grave and friendly manner, persuade him to cast it from him, and to banish so weak a passion out of his breast ; using words to this effect. 'I have, of late, my worthy cousin, observed in you a great difference from yourself, for I know the natural temper of your mind, and the solidnes of your judgment to be such, *that when you do any thing otherwise than reason would dictate to you, you suffer force from some violent passion*, which, if you give too much scope unto in the way you are, will lessen much, if not altogether lose, the reputation of discretion and prudence which you have gotten among all that know you. I need seek no farther for

p. 259
arguments to prove what I say, than to entreat you to look a little into yourself, . . .'

p. 272
what may be said of the past actions of his wife, and we see it is little regarded by the greatest part and the most solid nations of the world: but in choosing her, he ought to see that she be nobly descended, beautiful to please him, well formed to bear children, of a good wit, sweet disposition, endowed with good parts, and love him; then it will be his fault if he make her not a good wife. These qualities would warrant me in choosing Stelliana; for you know that by both her parents she descendeth from the noblest houses of Greece; and of *her ancestors there have been that have exalted and pulled down Kings in Morea, and some of them might, and their successors still have right to wear a regal crown upon their princely temples. . . . . .*

Charles to the Infanta Maria Anna of Spain. When these plans came to nought, Digby was made the scapegoat. Exactly what advice Sir John was attempting to give to his nephew is up to the reader to decide. Every previous biographer of Sir Kenelm has come to their own conclusion. It certainly involved controlling his temper, because of the '*violent passion*' he apparently displayed on occasion. Here, however, we are only concerned with what effect this might have had on Sir Edward. As usual, there is not even a hint.

We leave *Sir Kenelm's Memoirs* soon, with yet another reflection in retrospect on the virtues of his Venetia, who had died during the night of 30 April/1 May, 1633. His 'narrative', however, stops at the end of 1629. No mention is made of any further contact of either of them with **Sir Edward**, nor his having presented his father-in-law's will for probate in London the December before Venetia's death. No more can be gleaned about **Sir Edward** from this source.

The lines at the bottom of p. 272 recall all the aristrocratic connections on both sides of Venetia's family, with the Percys and Stanleys having played many roles in the royal succession when they '*exalted and pulled down Kings', and 'some of them might, and their successors still have right to wear a regal crown upon their princely temples.*' Unfortunately he makes no mention of these having played so many roles in Shakespeare's 'king' plays.

From the monument erected to Venetia by Sir Kenelm we know that their second son John was born on 29 December, 1627 and their third son Everard on 12 January, 1629/30 (i.e.1630, New Calendar), who died in his cradle.

One can only hope that **Sir Edward** saw his Fortescue and Digby grandchildren often and long enough to enjoy them before he died at Eynsham on 18 June, 1632.

Sir Kenelm's narrative continues to p. 328, covering the years up to 1629, after which come the 60 pages of 'Castrations' performed by Nicolas. Good reading!

Details of the Fortescue family are on several Tudor and family history websites and in Appendix 7. *Shakespeare Ecyclopedia.* Sir Francis's known dates are:

Born c.1563, died 1623/4
1580 Inner Temple
1589 Married Grace Manners
1589, 1593, 1597, MP for Buckingham
1596 Commission of muster for Buckinghamshire
1600 Custos Rotulorum of Buckinghamshire
?? Esquire of the body to Elizabeth
1601 MP for Buckinghamshire
1601-7 Father Sir John Fortescue Chancellor of the Duchy of Lancaster
1603 Knight of the Bath at James's coronation
(Was this when he met Sir Edward and suggested he should send his motherless daughters to join his family?)
1606 Surveyor for Buckinghamshire

1608 Succeeded his father (on his death) in his considerable estates

1608 High Sheriff of Buckinghamshire

1612 On a list of Oxfordshire recusants. He was apparently a committed Catholic all his life.

Grace survived him until 1634, two years after her uncle Sir Edward's death.

The most complete lists of Sir Francis and Grace Fortescue's children include (although not always given in the same order): Mary, John, Robert, Gilbert, William, Adrian, Francis, Roger, Frances, Dorothy, Catherine, one unnamed son, one unnamed daughter, presumably died at birth. This comes to 13. On their tomb in Mursley church are small effigies of 6 sons and 4 daughters, some holding skulls (photos on Flickr). As the tomb was erected by their surviving children, one might presume that the number of children on the tomb is correct. The brief biographies, or at least a few details, appear in local history publications and on websites of at least (Sir) John, the son and heir, Mary (who married John Talbot, 10th Earl of Shrewsbury), Francis and William. None of them appear in Sir Kenelm's *Memoirs*. Sir Edward must have stayed in close touch with the family because John Fortescue, Esquire was named by him as one of the executors of his will in 1632. John was later (1636) created 1st Baronet Fortescue of Nova Scotia, a reflection of King Charles's enthusiasm for the new trading-links with North America.

Nicolas's interpretations of other names of people and places in themselves give a good idea of Sir Kenelm's travels and some of the people he met and found worthy of mention. His account stops in 1629. Names already given above are not included.

PEOPLE

Artesia, widow of Auridonio = Uncertain.

Earl of Arcadia = Henry Rich, Earl of Holland.

Babilinda = Uncertain.

Mufti of Egypt = Query the Archbishop of Toledo.

Faustina = Uncertain, but Lady Venetia's governess or waiting-woman.

Famelicus = Uncertain.

Hephaestion = George Villiers, Duke of Buckingham.

Hydaspes = Uncertain.

Leodivius = Apparently the son of the Countess of Bristol by her first husband, Sir John Dive of Bromham, Co. Bedford ; but the pedigrees of the Dive family are silent as to the issue of that marriage.

Mauricana = Uncertain, but the first lady of the bed-chamber to the Queen of Spain.

Mardontius = Uncertain.

Nugeutius = Uncertain.

Oxicrane = Uncertain, a relation of the Duke of Buckingham.

Rogesilius = Robert Digby, afterward created Lord Digby, and ancestor of the present Earl Digby.

Scanderbret = Uncertain, a relation of the Duke of Buckingham.

Ursatius = Uncertain.

The individual spoken of in page 84, as the paramour of life Queen of France, was the Marquess D'Ancre.

PLACES.

Alexandria = Madrid.

Alexandretta = Scanderoon. [Site of Sir Kenelm's naval victory. HM]

Archiaepelago = Uncertain.

Attica = France.

Athens = Paris, but afterward used also for French, or France. Candle = Uncertain.

Cyprus = Venice.
Egypt = Spain.
Ephesus = Florence.
Greece = Europe.
Ionia = Italy.
Ionian Islands = Uncertain.
Lepanto = Uncertain.
Marathon = Angers.
Milo = Uncertain.
Rhodes = Uncertain, perhaps Sally (today part of Rabat, Morocco), or Algiers.
Syria = Portugal.

~~~~~~~~~~~~~~~~~~~~~

Appendix 11
Epilogue
A never-ending story?

While proofreading the first part of this book, by chance I came across a Google book (pre-view), which provides a partial rendering of a volume of 2007, *Shakespeare's Poems*, which contained a section about the Tong epitaphs. Was this perhaps the one that the Revd Dr Bob Jeffery had advised me about several years ago? The one about which I had said, 'I don't want to read it! I can't bear to read about any more muddles! You and I know we've got it right!' Whether or not it was the same, I was now confronted with a problem: ignore it or tackle it? Given that this was by two such eminent Shakespeare scholars, it could hardly be ignored, and it seemed to call for a commentary. After much thought, and having read the complete text, it seemed most sensible to convert a commentary into the basis of an epilogue. The Shakespeare Research Library in Munich had a copy, which of course included the pages missing from the Google pre-view version. This Epilogue is the result. Whether this puts the whole 'Shakespeare Epitaphs in Tong' story to rest, or leads to the beginning of the next stage of 'a never-ending story' remains to be seen.

It indicates that there is still some way to go before all concerned might agree on all the details, explanations and conclusions given in the book in the reader's hands. Happily, at the same time as ploughing through various muddles, the authors inadvertently provided a few more pieces of the jigsaw puzzle. The writers/editors of the book were Katherine Duncan-Jones, retired Professor of English Literature at Oxford University, and Professor H. R. Woudhuysen, Dean of the Faculty of Arts and Humanities at University College, London. Both have many publications to their credit and are regular contributors of articles and reviews in the *Times Literary Supplement*, which I have read, appreciated and admired over the years. Their chapter on the Tong Epitaphs appeared in a volume in the Arden Shakespeare, a respected series of scholarly editions of Shakespeare's works.

> *Shakespeare's Poems: Venus and Adonis, The Rape of Lucrece and the Shorter Poems*
> Eds Katherine Duncan-Jones and H. R. Woudhuysen, 2007, The Arden Shakespeare, third series, 593 pp.
> ATTRIBUTED POEMS   (Poems with early attributions – title at top of each page in AT.)
> p. 429 ff.
> AT 3 (The Tong Epitaphs) pp. 438-445 (The Google pre-view omits pp. 441, 443 & 444)

The first thing that was obvious was that they based their account and assessment on a rather limited number of sources on the Tong tomb:

a) The only *History of Tong* they refer to is that by George Griffiths (1885, 2nd edition 1894). Although this was exemplary in its thoroughness, with the second edition incorporating many of the changes made during the restoration of St Bartholomew's in 1891/2, it did not, by definition, include any later research. Griffiths was examined and in several places augmented and even supplanted by the Revd J. E. Auden's Notes c.1900, edited by Joyce Frost and published as *Auden's History of Tong*, Volume 1 (2003, 2005), Volume 2 (2005). These were followed by the Revd Dr Robert Jeffery's *Discovering Tong* in 2007, following on from his text in the *Guidebook to St Bartholomew's* (2002). All of these have sections on the Stanley tomb, with Dr Jeffery in 2007 including a summary of recent research.

b) They were obviously unaware of the learned articles on the Stanley tomb in Tong by Mrs Katherine Esdaile (1929) and church historian Simon Watney (2005), the latter including detailed discussions on the Stanley tombs in Tong and Walthamstow.

Two sources for them were, predictably, E. A. J. Honigmann, *Shakespeare: the 'lost years'*, Chapter VII. The Shakespeare Epitaphs and the Stanleys (Manchester UP, 1985, 2nd ed. 1998) and

Honigmann, *Weever* (MUP, 1987). The authors still, however, took very seriously the doubting comments on the Tong Epitaphs by E. K. Chambers, *William Shakespeare: Facts and Problems* (1930), even though he knew very little about the Stanley family. Honigmann had already indicated this. Duncan-Jones and Woudhuysen, also predictably, used the same sources as Honigmann in the manuscript collections of John Weever in The Library of the Society of Antiquaries (LSA, MS 127 & 128, most specifically 128, fo. 382b for the Shakespeare epitaphs) and the relevant pages in 'Dugdale's Diary' at the College of Arms (LCA, C35, 20, 40, 41 – these appear in this book as Illustrations Va, Vb, Vc; also in the colour section).

In addition they also invaluably used other manuscript documents unknown to Honigmann in the 1980s. These are in the Bodleian Library, Oxford: on Dugdale's visit to Tong in 1632 (Bod3, fol. 159r) and another version of the Tong Epitaphs (Bod5, fol. 269v, D-J & W; Rawlinson MSS. Bodleian M32, fol 269v, Campbell). These seem to have come to the attention of the Shakespeare academic world through Professor Gordon Campbell in the 1990s from his work on Milton and his 'Epitaph to Shakespeare' in the *Second Folio*, 1632 (see Chapter VI. Seven seventeenth-century recordings, four attributed to Shakespeare). Other recordings of the Tong epitaphs referred to, also apparently via Campbell, are in the library of the University of Nottingham (Portland MS 9, p. 12) and the Folger Library, Washington (Fo7, fol. 8r).

Based on these sources, Duncan-Jones and Woudhuysen wrote eight dense pages, trying to present what I have needed several hundred pages for. They made the following statements (in reduced font and **bold** below), in the order in which they appear, which demand a comment, whether a query, criticism or word of praise. In no case did they refer to the Stanley tomb at Walthamstow, other than inadvertently. Perhaps more surprisingly, given that the Tong Epitaphs were presented by Honigmann as concomitant to the 'Lancastrian Shakespeare theory', and that 'ye Countie of Lanca:' appears in the Monumental Inscriptions at Tong and Walthamstow, Lancashire does not receive a single mention in their text. Nor is any attempt made to provide even the briefest biographies of **Sir Thomas**, Lady Margaret and their son **Sir Edward Jr**, whose names appear in **bold** below, continuing the convention used throughout this book.

(Extract 1) The text is taken from the incised verse inscriptions, (p. 438)[i]

[i] The inscriptions were not incised, but painted on in gold, with the gold paint renewed several times. Griffiths noted this: see Illustration IIe. Shields on the tomb: 'INSCRIPTION in gilt lettering (not cut in)' (Griffiths, p. 67). This is confirmed by looking at the tomb today.

> **(Extract 2) The 'table part of the tomb' was 'twisted completely round' when the monument was moved from the north side of the chancel to the south transept in the 1760s, at the behest of the new owners of Tong Castle, the Durant family (see Griffiths, 70). The effigies must have been moved separately from their pedestal, and were replaced in the normal position, with feet pointing east, but with the verses that had been at the head now at the feet and vice versa. The pedestal's position was changed to ensure that the inscriptions on the side of the monument were still visible to those who approached it from the aisle.** (p. 438) [ii]

[ii] All very true and I regret not stating this more specifically in some relevant place. The most important point seems to be, however, that during the whole of the seventeenth century, when several people saw it and made notes on the MI and the Verse Epitaphs, the tomb remained in the original position. All subsequent changes affect its appearance today, but do not contribute to our assessment of the relevant events and attributions during the seventeenth century. For the record, the Revd Dr Robert Jeffery's account of the removal was as follows:

> It originally stood on the north side of the High Altar. It was moved from there by George Durant (II) to make way for his father's memorial. This was removed at the 1892 restoration. There are drawings showing the tomb, lying parallel with the east wall of the north aisle, and barred by railings. At the Victorian restoration the tomb was realigned on an east-west axis.
>
> (*Discovering Tong*, 2007, p. 89.)

(Extract 3) Weever had visited Tong in person: 'I heare from the tong of him that show'd me Tong church', he wrote, and referred to 'him that told me' and 'my relatour'. (p. 438)[iii]

[iii] Although John Weever, historian from Lancashire, wrote 'him that show'd me Tong church', his other writings make it absolutely clear that Weever himself never saw the Stanley tomb *in situ*, and was totally muddled about who was depicted by the effigy on the lower tier and what was on the Tong tomb and what on the Walthamstow tomb. The only way Weever 'visited' the Tong tomb was via 'the tong of him', his 'relatour', 'him that told me', who related a rather muddled version, or at least not clear enough to prevent Weever writing his own muddled version. Weever's pun in 'the tong of him that show'd me Tong church' produced, alas, obscurity rather than clarity for later readers.

(Extract 4) He made a copy of the verses, but did not attribute their authorship and neglected to name which members of the family were commemorated by the tomb. (p. 438)[iv]

[iv] Weever did indeed make a copy of a copy of the verses and indeed he did not attribute their authorship. He was, however, rather explicit about who was commemorated on one tomb (**Sir Edward**, his wife and all eight children were named), although he repeated the details from the MI at Walthamstow, thinking that he was writing about Tong, and thought erroneously that **Sir Edward** was also commemorated at Walthamstow (he was not) and that the verses also appeared there (they did not). Weever's notes tell us:

> [Tong here are many goodly monuments.] **Sir Edward Stanley**, Knight of the Bath, hath already made his own monument, whereon is the portraitures of himself, his wife, and his children, which were seven daughters and one son. She and her four daughters, Arbella, Mary, Alice and Priscilla, are interred under a monument in the church of Walthamstow in Essex; Thomas his son died in his infancy, and is buried in the church of Winwick in 'Lancishyre'; Petronella, Frances and Venetia are yet living.
>
> (Honigmann, *Weever*, 69-70.)

(Extract 5) Weever's manuscript account of his visit to Tong is undated.[v] It occurs in a booklet (LSA, fols 368-84), headed 'Lichefeeld and Couentrie', which is evidently copied from the notes he took on his expeditions. […] The latest date in the booklet, which also records his visit to Stratford-upon-Avon, where he copied down the lines on Shakespeare's own grave (see AT lln.), is for an inscription recording the death of Sir Thomas Gerard on 7 October 1617 (see Hasler, 2.184-5). The booklet in MS 128 is the only one of this size and kind in that volume. There are two comparable booklets in MS 127 […]: the latest date recorded on an inscription in these is 1618 from the tomb of Sir Ferdinando Heybourne (alias Richardson). This would suggest that Weever's tours collecting epitaphs were not made much later than 1617-18, in which case the verses on the Stanley tomb could have been made during Shakespeare's lifetime.' (p. 438)[vi]

[v] It has already been mentioned above that Weever obviously did not visit Tong, which makes it unsurprising that his 'account' is undated.

[vi] This is valuable in suggesting a much earlier date than I had assumed. My estimate of c.1626 was based mainly, I confess, on Honigmann's estimate of c.1626 for Weever's transcription of Shakespeare's verses in Stratford, backdated from his presumed date of 1656 for Dugdale's recording of the verses on Shakespeare's own tomb in Stratford.

> Chambers said that 'the verses are transcribed in substantially, but not orthographically, their present form by Dugdale' in 1656. Weever anticipated Dugdale by thirty years.
>
> (Honigmann, *Weever*, p. 70, citing Chambers, *Shakespeare*, II, 181.)

Perhaps erroneously on my part, I transposed this date to that of Weever's transcribing his notes on the Tong tomb. There is, of course, no way of knowing whether Weever's notebooks were based on notes collected on the same or different tours. In any case, if Weever visited Walthamstow, he took very muddled notes, and included under his Walthamstow notes the verse epitaphs, which only appear in Tong. One suspects that he did not visit Walthamstow either, or he would have known that

Sir Edward's effigy (which he certainly knew about) did not appear on this tomb. In brief, Weever could have received notes from others on Tong and Walthamstow any time during the period of his travels, but this suggestion by Duncan-Jones and Woudhuysen of no later than 1617-18 for Weever's own transcriptions directly from tombs seems highly plausible.

Having said all this, it is not obvious whether **'the verses on the Stanley tomb could have been made during Shakespeare's lifetime'** refers to Shakespeare (or someone else) writing and placing on the tomb the Tong verses before Shakespeare's death in 1616, or Weever producing his muddled account of them while Shakespeare was still alive.

It is also interesting that Weever noted, as the last in his series of notes, **'an inscription recording the death of Sir Thomas Gerard on 7 October 1617'**. Weever was presumably interested in this family not least because they had their origins in Lancashire, his own county, and also because he had dedicated the Fifth Book of his *Epigrammes* to this same Sir Thomas Gerard in 1599. He was identified in an endnote by Honigmann, *Weever* (1987), p. 124 as:

> v. *dedication*] Sir Thomas Gerard (c.1564-1617), son of Sir Gilbert Gerard, was at Caius College, Cambridge (1580), became a JP in Lancs., Middlesex, Northants, Staffs., and knight marshal of the [Queen Elizabeth's] Household in 1597. See above, p. 69; Hasler; *Lost Years*, p. 158, n. 3.

(Extract 6) A few years later, in December 1632, the church was visited by the antiquary William Dugdale, who later recorded in a manuscript collection of church notes (Bod3, fol. 159r) that at Tong 'On the North side of the chancel is there a goodly monument lately erected by Sir Edward Stanley KB for his father'.[vii] Dugdale copied the prose and the verse inscriptions in the east-west order (Vpon the east end of the monument this Epitaph ... Vpon the west end this Epitaph').[viii] He visited the church again on 23 September 1663, and from this visit there seem to derive the two versions of the inscriptions in LCA1. (pp. 438, 440) [ix]

[vii] This MS in the Bodleian was unknown to Honigmann (and HM until reading this quote recently) and is invaluable in now establishing beyond all doubt that it was **Sir Edward Jr** who commissioned and erected the tomb at Tong, primarily for his parents - or at least **'for his father'**, according to Dugdale. By implication, **Sir Edward**'s own effigy was not yet in place when Dugdale first saw the tomb in December 1632. Dugdale was presumably unaware that **Sir Edward** was already dead. (He wrote his will on 10 June and died on 18 June, 1632, both at Eynsham Abbey, see Chapter XXVII. Sir Edward Stanley's last will and testament, 1632.) **Sir Edward**'s 'admin' was conducted in London by his son-in-law Sir Kenelm Digby and others on 10 December 1632, but Dugdale, living at that time in Shustoke, Warwickshire and being on tour in the Midlands, was presumably unaware of this. This date is valuable, however, in allowing the conclusion, as long suspected, that **Sir Edward**'s effigy had been in storage since its completion, with instructions for it to be placed on the tomb after his death. It is hardly surprising that this had not yet happened, and presumably would not be organised until after the *Inquisition post mortem*, normally conducted a year after death. **Sir Edward**'s *Ipm* has unfortunately not survived.

[viii] The East-West order was used by Dugdale, but has served for confusion in later discussions before and after the removal in the 1760s and the second removal and restoration in the 1890s. See Note [ii] above.

[ix] The **'two versions of the inscriptions in LCA1'** (London, College of Arms, 'Dugdale's Diary, C35, pp. 20, 40, 41, Illustrations Va, Vb, Vc)) were from two different visits, one by Dugdale on 23 September 1663 (Va) and a follow up visit by Francis Sandford (probably in 1664), who also made a sketch. Sandford wrote first the epitaph 'at the head' (= West, 'Not monumental stone – Standley'), followed by the second 'at the foot' (= East, 'Ask who lies here'). Additional information comes from what I called Transcription 3 (Nottingham University, Portland MS 9) and Transcription 4 (Folger MS7, fol. 8) in my Chapter VI. Seven seventeenth-century recordings. Neither of these gives east-

west or head-foot, but both give first 'Not monumental stone – Standley' as by Shakespeare and written for **Sir Edward** and 'Ask who lies here' written for **Sir Thomas**.

> **(Extract 7)** ... **accompanied by a coloured pen-and-ink drawing of the monument by the then Lancaster Herald, Francis Sandford (Fig. 15).** [Black & white in AT3; in this book as Illustration Vc and also in the colour section. HM] **This shows that the obelisks at this time stood on the floor of the church at the corners of the tomb[x] and that figures of two children[xi] stood at the corners of the upper part of the tomb beside the head and feet of the woman's recumbent body.** (p. 440)

[x] Correct.

[xi] This is the first time that anyone has ever suggested that these figures were of children. No one in the seventeenth century mentioned them specifically, and they were otherwise consistently referred to as 'allegorical figures'. A close scrutiny of Illustration Vc (in the colour section), which is the best quality possible, by a professional photographer of the original manuscript at the College of Arms, reveals two apparently bare-footed female figures in long loose robes, each holding what might be a rather stiff baby. Given that there are only two, with no counterpoint figures on the back corners, it could well be that these are 'allegorical' memorials to the two Stanley sons who both died as infants: Henry, son of **Sir Thomas** (who was perhaps originally in the small coffin found in the Stanley vault when it was opened in the 1890s) and Thomas, son of **Sir Edward**, who was buried at Winwick, Lancashire. **Sir Edward** must have realized when he commissioned the tomb in 1601-3 that unless he re-married and had another son, these two dead sons signalled the end of his Stanley male line. As he could not have known at this early date that he would not have another son, these figures might well have been added to the tomb later, perhaps even as late as when it was very obvious that he was not going to have another son.

Perhaps more light might be shed on these figures (children? allegorical?) if someone takes the two drawings (1664 and pre-restoration) and the following two quotes to the church and investigates:

> Quote 1. There are four marble figures on the top of the monument, but all broke. (*Auden's History*, Vol. 2, p. 132, from his notes shortly after the 1890s restoration.)
> Quote 2. As originally designed, the four pillars had golden balls on the top, and carved figures at each corner (some of these figures are now in the Burgundian Arch to the Golden Chapel).
> (Jeffery, *Discovering Tong*, pp. 90-91.)

In any case, I shall do this myself on my next visit to Tong, about which I will report in some appropriate place.

> **(Extract 8) It is not clear whether the lines represent one or two poems or in what order they should be read.** (p. 442)[xii]

[xii] It has always seemed fairly clear to me that they were written as two separate verses. Dugdale (1605-86) and Sandford (1630-94) chose a different order to present them, so obviously did not consider them as one continuous poem. If they had considered it important to specify any more details about for whom they were intended or in what order they should be read, they could have consulted **Sir Edward**'s son-in-law Sir Kenelm Digby (1603-65) or any of **Sir Edward**'s numerous grandchildren, as the most reliable family fo(u)nts of knowledge about the Stanley-Shakespeare relationship. Alas, not even Sir Kenelm reported on this in his *Memoirs*. The two anonymous transcribers of the verses in the Nottingham and Folger manuscripts, however, were certain that these were two verses, one an epitaph for the father and the other for the son.

> **(Extract 9) Since the only monument to Edward Stanley at Eynsham is a brass plate, this passage probably relates to the tomb at Tong, which then still had the 'portraitures' of his children on the upper part of the tomb as shown in Sandford's drawing.** (p. 442)[xiii]

[xiii] The 'allegorical figures' in the Sandford drawing were covered in Note [xi]. The only genuine portraitures of four of his children are those on the Walthamstow tomb, which displayed then (and

still today) not only a large statue (almost life-size, or she was rather petite) of Lady Lucy, but also four small statuettes of her four daughters who died there with her in mid-1601. This tomb, too, has been moved from free-standing to up against a wall, so the two daughters underneath at the back have been moved to the top at the front. (See Illustrations Xb, Xc.)

> **(Extract 10) However, it is probable that the figures on the tomb represent Sir Thomas, his wife and their son Edward.'** (p. 442)[xiv]

[xiv] Not just 'probable', but definite. Given the text of the MI, no other explanation is possible.

> **(Extract 11) Precisely what Weever had in mind when he wrote the passage about Stanley's having already made his own tomb is not clear;** (p. 442)[xv]

[xv] Yes it is. Weever might have been hopelessly muddled about the Tong and Walthamstow tombs, but it is absolutely clear because of the unified structure of the tomb that **Sir Edward** commissioned the tomb for his parents to lie on the top tier, leaving the bottom tier for his own effigy. The fact that he has the appearance of a man closer to forty (which he was in 1602) rather than sixty-nine (which he was at his death), provides further confirmation of early completion. According to the customs of the time, his own effigy would be kept in storage for placement after his death. Honigmann provides a very good example of a contemporary doing just this. In her case, she prophesied correctly where she would be buried.

> So, too, Bess of Hardwick arranged for her own burial 'in the place appointed', beneath her tomb, which was 'finished and wants nothing but setting up'.
> (Honigmann, *'lost years'* (1998), p. 80, citing D. N. Durant, *Bess of Hardwick* (1977), p. 200.)

> **(Extract 12) [...]; presumably he thought or was told – incorrectly as we believe – by his guide that the couple were Sir Edward and his wife, with the implication that the lower figure was intended for Sir Thomas.** (pp. 442-3)[xvi]

[xvi] No, he didn't think this and wasn't told this. No one in the seventeenth century ever thought that the couple on the top tier of the tomb at Tong was/were **Sir Edward** and his wife. The Memorial Inscription, naming **Sir Thomas** and Lady Margaret first, made it very clear to everyone that they were the couple for whom the tomb was made. This was particularly true for Dugdale, who first saw the tomb in December 1632, when **Sir Edward**'s effigy had not yet been put in place. Also, to repeat *ad nauseam*, Weever's '**his guide**' to the tomb was a guide only by report, NOT in person.

> **(Extract 13) (Chambers, *WS*, 1.554, points out that another Sir Edward Stanley, Sir Thomas's obscure younger brother who died in 1609, had no connection with Tong, and so is unlikely to be the Sir Edward mentioned in the manuscripts or the lower figure on the tomb.)** (p. 443)[xvii]

[xvii] Relying on Chambers (1930) for any details about the Tong tomb and the Stanleys is a non-starter. At the time he was writing very little research on the Stanleys was known in wider circles outside Lancashire. The comment about '**another Sir Edward Stanley**' who '**had no connection with Tong**', therefore '**unlikely to be the Sir Edward mentioned in the manuscripts or the lower figure on the tomb**', presents a strange train of thoughts. No one should ever have even considered him as a candidate for the effigy on the Tong tomb, where the MI states very clearly who it is: **Edward**, son of **Sir Thomas**. '**Sir Edward Stanley, Sir Thomas's obscure younger brother who died in 1609,**' might have been obscure to Chambers, but happily is obscure no longer. He died in 1604 (buried on 4 September at Ormskirk in 'my lord's chapel'), not 1609, and his first-ever biography is meanwhile in Chapter XXI. Sir Edward Stanley Sr's first-ever biography. Other contemporary (Sir) Edward Stanleys are sorted out in Chapter XXII, which is devoted to them. It should be added that Chambers's lack of knowledge of the Stanleys was hardly his fault: the first scholarly study of the family did not appear until 1983 by (later Professor) Barry Coward, *The Stanleys, Lords Stanley and Earls of Derby, 1385-1672*, a re-working of his PhD thesis.

> **(Extract 14) Edward Stanley, their only surviving son, who sold Tong Castle in 1623,**[xviii] was buried, after his death in 1632, at Eynsham in Oxfordshire, having lived for most of his life in Eynsham Abbey. (p. 443) [xix]

[xviii] Sir Edward sold Tong Castle not in 1623 but in 1603 to Sir Thomas Harris/Harries/Harres. See *Auden's History of Tong*, Vol. 2, Note 16, pp. 24-25. Auden's Note 16 gives notes for a biography of Sir Thomas Harris, citing Owen and Blakeway, *History of Shrewsbury* (1825) and others. The notes relevant to his purchase of Tong Castle include:

> 'The king gave licence to **Sir Edward Stanley** to alienate the manor of Tong, Salop to Thomas Harris, serjeant at law, afterwards knight and baronet.'
> 'In 1603 he purchased Tong Castle from **Sir Edward Stanley** and died circa 1628.'
> 'Was made a serjeant at law in 1589, was knighted in 1603 and made a baronet April 12 1623, then of Tong Castle.'
> 'Arms granted to Harries of Tong Castle in July 1604.'

The 'licence to **Sir Edward Stanley** to alienate the manor of Tong' must therefore have been granted between **Sir Edward**'s knighthood on 25 July, 1603 at the coronation of King James and later in the year when Sir Thomas Harris was knighted. Presumably the sale of Tong Castle took place around the same time. As seen above, Harris was definitely 'of Tong Castle' in July 1604, when his arms were granted. It seems that later clarifications of some aspects of the Manor of Tong were made in at least 1607-9, 1613 and 1623, which in turn seem to be the cause of this false assumption about the date of sale of the Castle.

[xix] Sir Edward hardly '**lived for most of his life in Eynsham Abbey.**' He inherited it when his father died in 1576 when **Edward** was only fourteen, and from then on he was usually known as 'of Winwick' or 'of Tong'. To be more precise, it was his mother Lady Margaret who inherited Eynsham on her husband's death, according to the settlement of 1562/3 by his grandfather Edward Stanley, 3rd Earl of Derby. **Sir Edward Jr** might well have visited Eynsham Abbey over the years, given that his parents and later he himself owned it (we know he was living there for some time in 1582 with his uncle **Sir Edward Sr**), but it was only after 1603, when he was in his early forties and sold Tong Castle, that he took up permanent residence at Eynsham.

> **(Extract 15) The lower level of the Tong monument, which might be expected to be occupied by a stone cadaver or cadavers, is presumably an effigy of Sir Edward and a much later addition.[xx] Since his mortal remains lie elsewhere, they cannot therefore be alluded to in AT 3.** (p. 443)[xxi]

[xx] Not just '**presumably**': it IS an effigy of **Sir Edward**. The evidence for his having commissioned his own effigy, aged about forty at the time of commissioning the tomb for his parents, has been given in several places in this book. He did not foresee when he first commissioned the tomb and the effigies, nor when he received the verses from Shakespeare, that he would be buried somewhere else.

[xxi] Epitaphs written in advance for a living person did not oblige them to be commemorated where they died or were buried. It seems reasonable to suppose that Shakespeare wrote both verses at the same time and that **Sir Edward** had them both inscribed at the time of the construction of the tomb. He later died at Eynsham, knowing that the verses had been written for his parents in retrospect and for himself in advance, wherever he might die and be buried.

After taking several other points into consideration and despite all their doubts and dubious statements above, Duncan-Jones and Woudhuysen's concluding sentence is:

> **(Extract 16) Despite the absence of an ascription in Weever's manuscript, the evidence of contemporary attributions, including what appears to be a conscious allusion to the verses in Milton's poem, strongly suggests that they may be by Shakespeare.** (p. 445)

Also, having considered all the problems surrounding *The Phoenix and the Turtle* and other poems discussed in *Shakespeare Poems*, another conclusion is:

> **(Extract 17) The single item that seems carefully designed and pondered is AT 3, the verses on**

the Stanley tomb at Tong. This item also has the strongest claim to authenticity. (p. 123)

So be it. I can only hope that Duncan-Jones and Woudhuysen's '**may be**' has become 'almost certainly' to anyone who has read the biographies of **Sir Thomas** and **Sir Edward Sr** and **Jr** in *Shakespeare's Epitaphs in Tong, Shropshire*. And that their judgment that '**this item has the strongest claim to authenticity**' becomes even more certain in the opinion of the majority of readers. For the sake of comparison, two other 'scholarly' pronouncements of recent years on the authenticity are:

> 'We print below the poems of unknown authorship since the **attribution to Shakespeare has not been disproved.**'
>
>> (*William Shakespeare: The Complete Works*, Second Edition, Eds Stanley Wells and
>> Gary Taylor, Oxford, 2005; 'Various Poems', pp. 805-6.)

> 'Shakespeare had various connections to the Stanley family. It is unclear whether these verses, still visible on the tombstone, memorialize Sir Edward Stanley, Sir Thomas Stanley, or both (with one verse devoted to each).'
>
>> (*The Norton Shakespeare* (Based on the Oxford Edition), Second edition, 2008
>> General Editors: Stephen Greenblatt, Harvard University; Walter Colen, Cornell University
>> Jean E. Howard, Columbia University; Katherine Eisaman Maus, University of Virginia,
>> W.W. Norton & Company, New York, London, p. 2026, Footnote 9.)

Should anyone still have doubts, or come across any other publication or manuscript of relevance to the Tong Epitaphs and not mentioned in this book, I [HM] would be very pleased to hear from them.

This whole book was a preliminary to applying the stories now established to 'Lancastrian Shakespeare' and all the implications for William Shakespeare's 'new' ancestry and early biography.

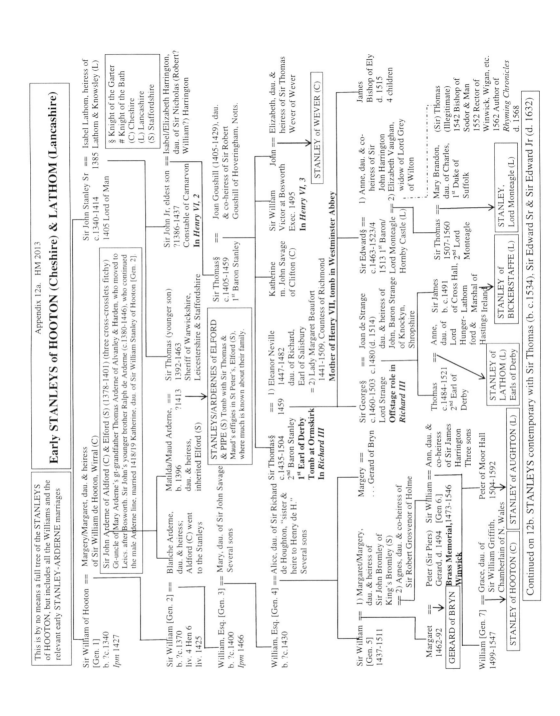

Continued on 12b. STANLEYS contemporary with Sir Thomas (b. c.1534), Sir Edward Sr & Sir Edward Jr (d. 1632)

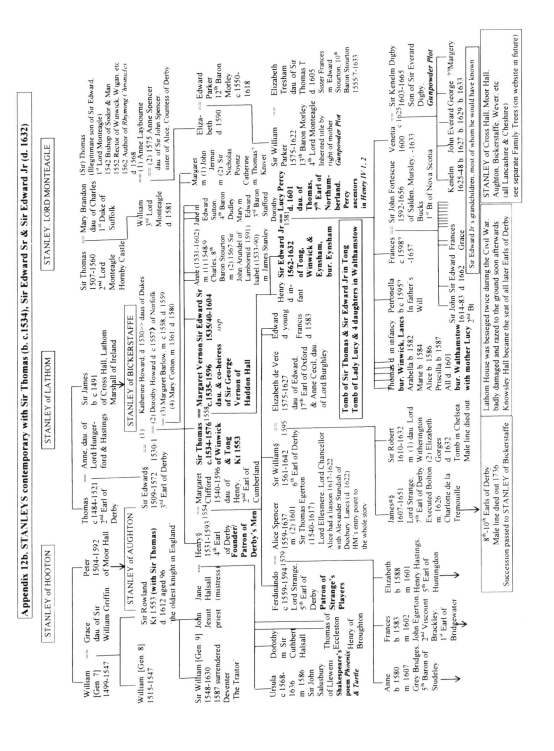

Appendix 12b. STANLEYS contemporary with Sir Thomas (b. c.1534), Sir Edward Sr & Sir Edward Jr (d. 1632)

Appendix 12c.   HM 2013

MANNERS, VERNON, PERCY, FORTESCUE in the fairly immediate family, i.e. close relatives of **Sir Edward STANLEY Jr** of Winwick, Tong, Eynsham, 'friend' of Shakespeare (Tong Epitaphs). The direct bloodlines down to and beyond **Sir Edward STANLEY Jr** and his wife **Lucy PERCY** are shown as dashed lines. N.B. The c. dates of birth inevitably appear slightly differently in various accounts.

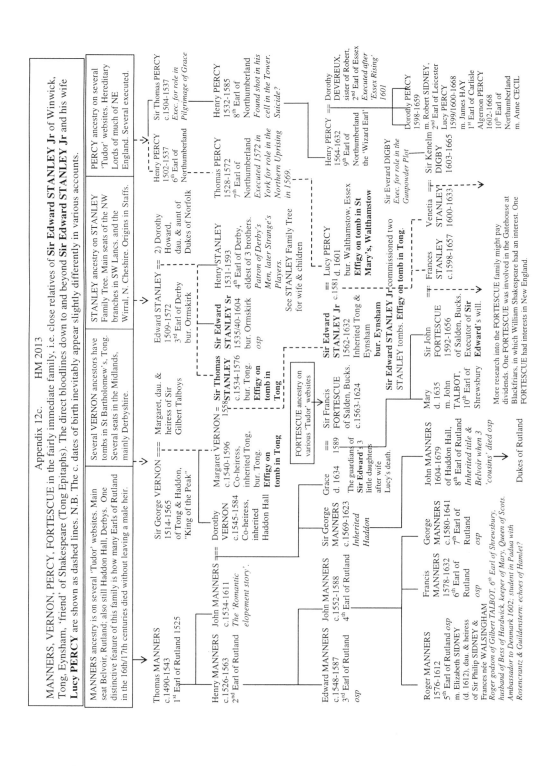

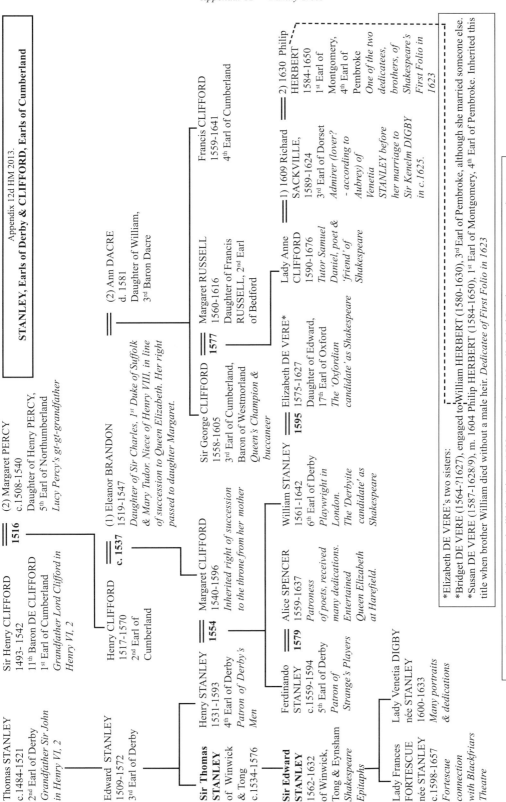

Appendix 12d HM 2013.
STANLEY, Earls of Derby & CLIFFORD, Earls of Cumberland

Elizabeth DE VERE's two sisters:
Bridget DE VERE (1584-?1627), engaged to William HERBERT (1580-1630), 3rd Earl of Pembroke, although she married someone else.
Susan DE VERE (1587-1628/9), m. 1604 Philip HERBERT (1584-1650), 1st Earl of Montgomery, 4th Earl of Pembroke. Inherited this title when brother William died without a male heir. Dedicatee of First Folio in 1623

Those who were adults (and still alive) in the 1590s and early 1600s all visited London, were at court, and must have been aware of Shakespeare's poems, plays and Sonnets (1609). It seems more than likely that they all met him.

Bibliography

Unless indicated otherwise, the place of publication was London.

Abram, W. A. (Ed.), *The rolls of the burgesses at the guilds merchant of the borough of Preston in the county of Lancaster, 1397-1682*, Lancashire and Cheshire Record Society, Vol. 9, 1884. Commonly known as the *Preston Guild Rolls*.

— *A History of Blackburn Town and Parish*, Blackburn, 1877.

Ackroyd, Peter, *Shakespeare: the Biography*, Chatto & Windus, 2005.

Alexander, Peter (Ed.), *William Shakespeare: the Complete Works*, Collins, 1951.

Allen's Defence (see Heywood).

Anstruther, Godfrey, *The Seminary Priests: A dictionary of the secular clergy of England and Wales: I: Elizabethan, 1558-1603*, Ushaw College, Durham, 1964.

Asquith, Clare, *Shadowplay: The Hidden Beliefs and Coded Politics of William Shakespeare*, Public Affairs, 2005.

Aubrey, John: Brief Lives, (Ed.) Richard Barber, Boydell, 1975, 1982.

Auden, J. E./Joyce Frost (Ed.), *Auden's History of Tong, Notes on the History of Tong from the Parish Books. Volume 1. Collected by . . . Volume 2. The third Note Book of John Ernest Auden, Vicar of Tong, 1896-1913*, ed. Joyce Frost, Arima Publishing, Suffolk, 2004/5.

Axon, William E. A., *A Lancashire Treasury: Stories and folk-tales of old Lancashire*, 1890s, re-issued by Aurora Publishing, Bolton, 1995.

Bagley, J. J., *Lancashire Diarists: Three Centuries of Lancashire Lives*, Phillimore, 1975.

— *The History of the Earls of Derby*, Sidgwick and Jackson, 1985.

— & A. G. Hodgkiss, *Lancashire: A History of the County Palatine in Early Maps*, Neil Richardson, Manchester, 1985.

Baines, Edward, *History of the County Palatine and Duchy of Lancaster*, Fisher Son & Co., 1836, Pedigree Charts by Frederick Whatton; 3rd ed. in 5 Vols, (Ed.) James Croston, Manchester, 1888-93.

Baker, Oliver, *In Shakespeare's Warwickshire and the Unknown Years*, Simpkin Marshall Ltd., 1937.

Baldwin, Michael, *Dark Lady*, Little, Brown, 1998; Abacus 1999.

Barber, Richard, see *Aubrey, John*.

Barker, Juliet, *Agincourt: the King, the Campaign, the Battle*, Little, Brown, 2005; Abacus, 2006.

Barns, S. J., 'St Mary the Virgin, Walthamstow: inscriptions in the church and churchyard, 2: memorials in the church', *Proceedings of the Walthamstow Antiquarian Society*, 27 (1932), p. 8.

Bate, Jonathan, *The Genius of Shakespeare*, Picador, 1997.

Bearman, Robert, 'Was William Shakespeare William Shakeshafte? Revisited', *Shakespeare Quarterly*, Vol. 53, No. 1, Spring 2002, pp. 83-94.

Beaumont, William, *A History of Winwick*, Warrington, 1897. (Many extracts in Manx Notebook online.)

Bennett, Michael, *The Battle of Bosworth*, Sutton, Stroud, 1985, 2000.

Bennett, W., *The History of Burnley*, Burnley, 2 vols, 1946-47; facsimile reproduction in one volume, 1980, 1988.

Bevan, Bryan, *King James VI of Scotland & I of England*, The Rubicon Press, 1996.

Bevington, David, *Shakespeare*, Blackwell, 2002.

Bill, Alfred H., *Astrophel, Or the Life and Death of the Renowned Sir Philip Sidney*, Cassell, 1938.

Billing, Joanna, (Ed.), *The Hidden Places of Lancashire, Including the Isle of Man*, Travel Publishing, Aldermaston, Berks, 1998.

Blakeway, J. B. and H. Owen, *A History of Shrewsbury*, 1825.

Boden, G. H., *History of Tong Church*, (referred to by Auden).

Bourbaki, Georges, *Der Nachruf oder: Es war doch dieser Schlawiner Marlowe*, Eigenverlag (published privately), Munich, 2003.

— 'Zu dem Thema des Privatlebens von William Shakespeare', München, den 8. Juli, 2011 (10 pages, as yet unpublished). Proposes Margaret Radcliffe of Ordsall as Shakespeare's 'Dark Lady'.

Bradford, Ernle, *The Siege of Malta, an eye-witness account by Francisco Balbi di Correggio, translated from Spanish in 1965*, Penguin, 2003.

— *The Great Siege: Malta 1565*, Hodder and Stoughton, 1961; Penguin 1964.

Bradley, E. T., *Life of Lady Arabella Stuart*, Bentley, 1889.

Brazendale, David, *Lancashire's Historic Halls*, Carnegie Publishing, Lancaster, 1994.

Bryson, Bill, *Shakespeare: The World as a Stage*, Harper, 2007.

Bryson, Grahame, *Shakespeare in Lancashire*, Sunwards, Liverpool, 1997, 2nd ed. 1998.

Buck, Samuel and Nathaniel, *Views of Ruins and Abbeys in the Midlands*, 1726-1729 (Commonly known as *Buck's/Bucks' Views*), pub. 1760.

Bull, Stephen, *The Civil War in Lancashire,* Lancashire County Books, 1991.

— *The Civil Wars in Lancashire: 1640-1660*, Carnegie, Lancaster, 2009.

Burgess, Anthony, *Shakespeare*, Jonathan Cape, 1970; Vintage, 1996.

Burrow, Colin (ed.), *Shakespeare's Complete Sonnets and Poems*, Oxford, 2002.

Camden, William, *History of the Annals of England*, in Latin 1586, in English 1610.

— *Britannia*, translation Richard Gough, 1789.

Campbell, Douglas, 'Obelisks and Pyramids in Shakespeare, Milton and Alcalà', *Sederi*, 4, 1998, pp. 217-232. (Online)

—'Shakespeare and the Youth of Milton', *Milton Quarterly*, 33.4, 1999, Johns Hopkins University, pp. 95-105. (Online)

Campbell, Lily, *Shakespeare's Histories*, 1947 (quoted by Peter Milward).

Chambers, E. K., *William Shakespeare: A Study of Facts and Problems*, 2 vols, Oxford, 1930.

— *Shakespearean Gleanings*, Oxford University Press, 1944.

Chandler, John, *John Leland's Itinerary: Travels in Tudor England*, Sutton, Stroud, 1993; pb. 1998.

Chester, Robert, *Love's Martyr*, London, 1601. (Includes first publication of *The Phoenix and the Turtle*.)

Christian, Roy, *Notable Derbyshire Families*, The Derbyshire Heritage Series, 1987.

Clark, Sandra (Ed.), *The Penguin Shakespeare Dictionary*, 1999.

Clarke, C. C. (Ed.), *The Poetical Works of Milton*, Allen, 1878.

Coakley, Frances, *Manx Notebook*, website.

Coles, C., *History of Newton*, 1916.

Collins, Arthur, Sir Egerton Brydges, *Collins's Peerage of England*, 1812.

Conlan, Thomas, SJ, Ten unpublished letters to Peter Milward, SJ in Tokyo (1975 ff.).

Conrad, Bastian, *Christopher Marlowe: Der wahre Shakespeare*, BUCH&Media, Munich, 2011.

Cook, A. H., formerly Chief Warden at H. M. Tower of London, *Prisoners in the Tower*, two handwritten vols, 1959.

Coward, Barry, *The Stanleys, Lords Stanley and Earls of Derby, 1385-1672: The origins, wealth and power of a landowning family*, Chetham Society, 3rd Series, Vol. XXX, Manchester, 1983.

Crosby, Alan G., *A History of Lancashire*, Phillimore, Chichester, 1998.

— *Dictionary of Lancashire Dialect, Tradition and Folklore*, Smith, Settle, Otley, W. Yorks, 2000.

— *The History of Preston Guild: England's greatest carnival*, Lancashire County Books, 1991; Carnegie Publishing, Preston, 2012.

Daugherty, Leo, 'Biography of Sir William Stanley, 6th Earl of Derby', *New/Oxford DNB*, 2004.

— *William Shakespeare, Richard Barnfield and the Sixth Earl of Derby*, Cambria Press, US, 2010.

— *The Assassination of Shakespeare's Patron: Investigating the Death of the Fifth Earl of Derby*, Cambria Press, US, 2011.

Dean, E. Barbara, *Bramall Hall: The Story of an Elizabethan Manor House*, Friends of Bramall Hall in conjunction with the Community Services Division, Stockport Metropolitan Borough, 1999.

Dean, R., *Rufford Old Hall*, National Trust, 1991, rev. ed. 1997.

Dee, John, *The Private Diary of Dr John Dee*, (Ed.) J. Halliwell(-Phillips), 1842.

De Groot, John Henry, *The Shakespeares and the Old Faith*, Freeport, Books for Libraries, 1946.

Derby Household Books, see Raines, F. R.

Devlin, Christopher, *Hamlet's Divinity and Other Essays*, Rupert Hart-Davis, 1963.

Dictionary of National Biography, Old, c.1900 & *New/Oxford*, 2004 (digital), 2007 (print).

Digby, Sir Kenelm, *The Private Memoirs of Sir Kenelm Digby, Gentleman of the Bedchamber to King Charles the First, written by himself. Now published from the original manuscript, With an Introductory Memoir*, Sir Nicholas Harris Nicolas, 1827, reprinted 2007. (Online)

Doleman, R. (alias for Robert Parsons), *A Conference about the succession to the Crown of England*, Menston, 1972. A facsimile of a pamphlet dated 1594.

Dover Wilson, John, *Life in Shakespeare's England: A book of Elizabethan Prose*, Cambridge University Press, 1911; Pelican, 1944.

Draper, Peter, *The House of Stanley*, Ormskirk, 1864.

Duffy, Eamon, *The Stripping of the Altars: traditional religion in England c. 1400-c. 1580*, Yale, New Haven, 1992.

Dugdale, Sir William, *Antiquities of Shropshire*, 1664.

— *Antiquities of Warwickshire*, 1659.

— *The life, diary and correspondence of Sir William Dugdale*, (Ed.) William Hamper, 1827.

Duncan-Jones, Katherine, *Ungentle Shakespeare*, Arden Shakespeare, 2001.

— and H. R. Woudhuysen (Eds), *Shakespeare's Poems: Venus and Adonis, The Rape of Lucrece and the Shorter Poems*, Arden Shakespeare, 3rd series, 2007.

Durant, D. N., *Bess of Hardwick: Portrait of an Elizabethan Dynast*, 1978.

Dutton, Richard, Alison Findlay and Richard Wilson (Eds), *Theatre and Religion: Lancastrian Shakespeare*, Manchester University Press, 2003.

— *Region, Religion and Performance: Lancastrian Shakespeare*, Manchester University Press, 2003.

Earwaker, J. P., *East Cheshire Past and Present*, Cheshire Record Office, 1877.

Eccles, Mark, *Shakespeare in Warwickshire*, Madison, Wisconsin, US, 1967.

Edwards, Francis, SJ, *Plots and Plotters in the Reign of Elizabeth I*, Four Courts Press, Dublin, 2002.

Elizabeth, Catalogue to Exhibition, National Maritime Museum, Greenwich, 2003.

Elton, G. R., *Reform & Renewal: Thomas Cromwell and the Common Weal*, Cambridge University Press, 1973.

Encyclopedia Britannica, 1984 (paper), 1911 version online.

Enos, Carol Curt, *Shakespeare and the Catholic Religion*, Dorrance, Pittsburgh, US, 2000.

— *Shakespeare Settings: Stratford/Park Hall, Lancashire/Cheshire/the Catholic Mission, and London*, Wheatmark, Tucson, US, 2007.

— *Shakespeare Encyclopedia*, online, 2004.

Erdeswick, Sampson, *A survey of Staffordshire*, 1596, various reprints (quoted by Auden).

Esdaile, Katherine, 'Shakespeare's Verses in Tong Church', *The Times*, 22 April, 1929.

Espinasse, Francis, *Lancashire Worthies*, Simpkin Marshall & Co., 1874, 2nd Series, 1877.

Every, S. F., *Etchings of the church, monuments and castle of Tong, Salop*, 1841.

Eynsham Manor, from *A History of the County of Oxford*: Volume 12, 1990, British History Online.

Eyre, Kathleen, *Lancashire Legends*, Dalesman Books, Yorks., 1974.

Eyton, Rev. R. W., *Antiquities of Shropshire*, 1841, 7 Vols, 1854-10.

Farmer, David Hugh, *The Oxford Dictionary of Saints*, Oxford University Press, 3rd ed., 1992.

Farrer, W. & J. Brownbill (Eds), *Victoria County History of Lancashire*, 1906-1911.

Fishwick, Henry, *The History of the parish of Preston in Amounderness in the county of Lancaster*, Rochdale, London, 1900.

Flynne, Denis, *The Arch-Conjuror of England: John Dee*, Yale University Press, 2011.

Fraser, Antonia, *Mary, Queen of Scots*, Granada, 1975.

— *The Six Wives of Henry VIII*, Weidenfeld and Nicholson, 1992; Arrow Books, 1998.

— *The Gunpowder Plot: Terror & Faith in 1605*, Weidenfeld and Nicolson, 1996; Arrow Books, 1997, 1999.

French, George Russell, *Shakespeareana Genealogica, Parts I and II*, Macmillan, 1869.

Fripp, Edgar I. *Shakespeare, Man and Artist*, Oxford University Press, 1938.

Frost, Joyce (Ed.), see Auden J. E.

Furnivall, Frederick J., *Child Marriages, Divorce and Ratifications &c. in the Diocese of Chester, AD 1561-6*, pub. for the Early English Text Society, 1897.

George, David, *Records of Early English Drama: Lancashire*, Toronto University Press, 1991.

Gerard, John, *John Gerard: The Autobiography of an Elizabethan*, trans. Philip Caraman, Longmans, 1951.

Gillow, Joseph, *A Bibliographical Dictionary of the English Catholics*, Burns and Oates, London, New York, 1885-1902.

— *Lord Burghley's map of Lancashire in 1590, with notes on the designated manorial lands, biographical and genealogical, and brief histories of their estates traced down to the present day, 1907, Coligite Fragmenta ne Pereant*, printed privately for the Catholic Record Society, the Arden Press, London. Republished Kessinger Publishing Ltd, June 2007.

Glover, Robert, *Ordinary of Arms*, 1570s/1580s; revised and first published by Joseph Edmondson, 1780.

Gough, Richard, *History of Myddle (Shropshire)*, 1700. (Gough's *Middle* quoted by Auden).

Greenblatt, Stephen, *Will in the World: How Shakespeare became Shakespeare*, Jonathan Cape, 2004; Pimlico, 2005.

Greene, Robert, *Greenes, Groats-worth of Witte, bought with a million of Repentance*, 1592.

Greenstreet, James H., 'A Hitherto Unknown Writer of Elizabethan Comedies', *The Genealogist*, July, 1891.

— 'Further Notices of William Stanley Sixth Earl of Derby . . . as a Poet and Dramatist', *The Genealogist*, May 1892. The complete texts are online, placed by John Raithel, The URL of Derby.

Griffiths, George, *A History of Tong and Boscobel*, 1885, 2nd ed.,1894.

Griffiths, Ralph A. and Roger S. Thomas, *The Making of the Tudor Dynasty*, Sutton, Stroud, 1985; Pb. 1993, 1997.

Grindon, Leo H., *A History of Lancashire: From Earliest Times Until 1880, Incorporating Manchester & Liverpool*, 1995, Facsimile of Grindon, *Lancashire; Brief Historical and Descriptive Notes*, 1880s, Aurora, Bolton, 1995.

Gristwood, Sarah, *Arbella, England's Lost Queen*, Bantam, 2003.

— *Elizabeth & Leicester*, Bantam, 2007.

Groot, John Henry de, *The Shakespeares and the 'Old Faith'*, Crown Press, New York, 1946.

Guest, Ken and Denise, *British Battles*, Harper Collins, 1996, pb. 1997 for English Heritage.

Guide to the Lancashire Record Office, 2nd ed., 1962.

Gurr, Andrew, *Playgoing in Shakespeare's London*, Cambridge University Press, 1987; 2nd ed., 1996.

— *The Shakespearian Playing Companies*, Oxford University Press, 1996; reprinted 2003.

— *Shakespeare's Opposites: The Admiral's Company* 1594-1625, Cambridge University Press, 2009.

Haigh, Christopher, *Reformation and Resistance in Tudor Lancashire*, Cambridge University Press, 1975.

Halliday, F. E., *Shakespeare and his World*, Thames and Hudson, 1976.

Halliwell-Phillipps, James Orchard, *Outlines of the Life of Shakespeare*, 1881, 7th ed., 1887.

Halsted, Rachel A. C., *The Pendle Witch-Trial*, 1612, Lancashire County Books, 1993.

Hammerschmidt-Hummel, Hildegard, *Das Geheimnis um Shakespeares >Dark Lady<: Dokumentation einer Enthüllung*, Primus Verlag, Darmstadt, Germany, 1999.

— *Die Verborgene Existenz des William Shakespeare: Dichter und Rebell im katholischen Untergrund*, Herder, Germany, 2001.

Hardy, Blanche Christabel, *Arbella Stuart*, Constable, 1913.

Harland, J. (ed.), T*he Lancashire Lieutenancy under the Tudors and Stuarts*, parts i and ii, Chetham Society Old Series, Vols XLIX, XLVI, 1856-1858.

— *Court Leet Records of the Manor of Manchester A.D. 1586-1602*, Chetham Society Old Series, Vol. LXV, 1865.

Harland, J. and Wilkinson, T. T., *Lancashire Legends* (1873), reprinted 1973.

Haynes, Alan, *The Gunpowder Plot*, Sutton, Stroud, 1994.

Hayes, Cliff, *Stories and Tales of Old Lancashire* (by Frank Hird, c.1911, Selected and Edited), Aurora Publishing, Bolton, 1998.

— *Stories and Tales of Old Manchester*, Aurora, n.d.

Helsby, Thomas, *The History of Cheshire*, 3 vols (1875-82), a revised and enlarged edition of Ormerod.

Heyes, Jim, *A History of Chorley*, Lancashire County Books, 1994.

Heywood, Thomas (Ed.), *Cardinal Allen's defence of Sir William Stanley's surrender of Deventer, January 29, 1586/7*, Chetham Society Old Series, vol. 25, Manchester, 1851.

— *The Earls of Derby and the Verse Writers and Poets of the sixteenth and seventeenth centuries, Stanley Papers Part I*, Chetham Society Old Series vol. 29, Manchester, 1853.

Hilton, J. A., *Catholic Lancashire: From Reformation to Renewal 1559-1991*, Phillimore, Lancaster, 1994.

Hird, Frank, *Lancashire Stories*, see Hayes, Cliff.

Hodkinson, Kenneth, *Old Chorley: In the Footsteps of Wilson*, CKD Publications, 1987.

Holcroft, Fred, *Murder, Terror and Revenge in Medieval Lancashire: The Legend of Mab's Cross*, Wigan Heritage Service publications, 2, 1992.

Holden, Anthony, *William Shakespeare: His Life and Work*, Little, Brown, 1999.

Hollar's Journey on the Rhine, Text by Milos V. Kratochvìl, Artia, Prague, 1965.

Holmes, Martin, *Proud Northern Lady: Lady Anne Clifford 1590-1676*, Phillimore, Lancaster, 1975,1984, pb. 2001.

Honan, Park, *Shakespeare, A Life*, Oxford University Press, 1998.

— *Christopher Marlowe, Poet & Spy*, Oxford University Press, 2005.

Honigmann, E. A. J., *Shakespeare: the 'lost years'*, Manchester University Press, 1985, 2nd ed. 1998.

— *John Weever: A Biography of a Literary Associate of Shakespeare and Jonson, together with a photographic Fascimile of Weever's Epigrammes* (1599), Manchester University Press, 1987.

— 'The Shakespeare/Shakeshafte Question, Continued', *Shakespeare Quarterly*, 2003, Spring Issue, 2002, pp. 83-86.

— 'Catholic Shakespeare? A Response to Hildegard Hammerschmidt-Hummel', *William Shakespeare - Seine Zeit - Sein Leben - Sein Werk*, von Zabern, Mainz, 2003; Connotations 12.1 (2002/2003): 52-60 (online).

Hotson, Leslie, *I, William Shakespeare*, Jonathan Cape, 1937.

Howorth, Nick, 'The Livery Collar of the Duchy of Lancaster', *Lancashire History Quarterly*, Vol. 2, No. 1, March 1998, pp. 37-39.

Hunt, David, *A History of Preston*, Carnegie Publishing, 1992, 2009.

Hunter, Joseph, *A History of Hallamshire*, Sheffield, 1819.

Hyland, Peter, *An Introduction to Shakespeare's Poems*, Palgrave Macmillan, 2003.

Jardine, Lisa & Alan Stewart, *Hostage to Fortune: The troubled life of Francis Bacon 1561-1626*, Gollancz, 1998; Phoenix, 1999.

Jeffery, Robert, *Guidebook to St Bartholomew's Church Tong*, RJL Smith & Associates, Much Wenlock, 2002.

— *Discovering Tong: its History, Myths and Curiosities*, for the Tong Parochial Church Council, Parchment Ltd., Oxford, 2007.

Jirásko, Luděk, *Geistliche Orden und Kongregationen in den boehmischen Kronländern*, Prämonstratenser - Kloster Strahov, 1991.

Jones, J. A. P., *The Medieval World*, Macmillan Education, 1979.

Jones, John Idris, *Where was Shakespeare? The Lancashire theory with new additions*, 2007 (unpublished manuscript lodged at the Shakespeare Birthplace Trust).

— 'William Shakespeare and John Salusbury: what was their relationship?', *Transactions of the Denbighshire Historical Society*, January 2011. (An earlier version is online.)

Kay, Margaret M., *The History of Rivington and Blackrod Grammar School*, Manchester University Press, 1931, 1966.

Keen, Alan and Roger Lubbock, *The Annotator: The pursuit of an Elizabeth Reader of Halle's Chronicle Involving some Surmises about the Early Life of William Shakespeare*, Macmillan, 1954.

Kitto, Tony, *Tracing the Towneleys*, Towneley Hall Art Gallery and Museums, Burnley, 2004.

Knowles, Richard, 'Medieval Livery Collars', Richard III Society Website.

Kreiler, Kurt, *Der Mann, der Shakespeare erfand*, Insel Verlag, 2009.

— *Anonymous Shake-speare: the Man Behind*, Doeling und Galitz Verlag, 2011.

Lancashire Village Book, The, Lancashire Federation of Women's Institutes, 1990.

Lawson Dick, Oliver (Ed.), *Aubrey's Brief Lives*, Secker and Warburg, 1949.

Leatherbarrow, J.S., *The Lancashire Elizabethan Recusants*, Chetham Society, New Series, 110, Manchester, 1947.

Lee, Peter, 'Shakespeare's Hidden Family?', The Shakespeare Family History Site.

Lee, Sidney, *A Life of William Shakespeare*, 1898; Oracle, 1996.

Lefranc, Abel, *Sous le masque de 'William Shakespeare', VIe conte de Derby*, Paris, 1918.

Leland's Itinerary, see Chandler, John.

Lofthouse, Jessica, *West Pennine Highway*, Robert Hale, 1954.

— *Lancashire Countrygoer*, Robert Hale, 1962; reprint 1964.

— *Lancashire's Old Families*, Robert Hale, 1972.

Look Around Lancashire, Lancashire County Books, 4th ed., 1993.

Lovell, Mary S., *Bess of Hardwick: First Lady of Chatsworth*, 1527-1608, Little, Brown, 2005; Abacus, 2006.

Lumby, J. H. (Ed.), *De Hoghton Deeds and Papers*, Lancashire and Cheshire Record Society, 1936.

Manning, Rosemary, *Heraldry*, Black, 1966.

Mantel, Hilary, *Wolf Hall*, Fourth Estate, 2009. (Biography of Cardinal Thomas Wolsey.)

Marshall, T. P., *History of Tong*, 1905 (quoted by Auden).

McDonald, Russ, *The Bedford Companion to Shakespeare*, Boston, US, 1996.

Merriam, Thomas, 'The Misunderstanding of Munday as Author of Sir Thomas More', *Review of English Studies*, New Series, vol. 51, no. 204, 2000. (Quoted by Asquith, 2006.)

Michell, John, *Who Wrote Shakespeare?*, Thames and Hudson, 1996, pb. 1999.

Middleton, Christopher, *Famous Historie of Chinon in England*, 1597.

Miller, George C., *Hoghton Tower: The History of the Manor, the Hereditary lords and the ancient Manor-house of Hoghton in Lancashire*, Preston, 1948.

Milton, Giles, *Big Chief Elizabeth: How England's Adventurers Gambled and Won the New World*, Hodder and Stoughton, 2000.

Milward, Peter, *Shakespeare's Religious Background*, Bloomington, Indiana University Press, 1973, 2nd ed. 1986.

— 'Admissions of an Absent-minded Author', *The Renaissance Bulletin* 15, 1988.

— 'The Catholicism of Shakespeare's Plays', *Pamphlet*, The Renaissance Institute, Sophia University, Tokyo, 1997.

— 'Shakespeare's New World', 'Another Life of Thomas More!', 'Another Life of Shakespeare!', *The Renaissance Bulletin* 25, The Renaissance Institute, 1998.

— 'Was Shakespeare a Catholic?', 'Holden's Shakespeare', 'Catholicism and English Literature, 1558-1660', 'The Catholicism of Shakespeare's Romances', 'A Tale of two Henries', *The Renaissance Bulletin* 26, The Renaissance Institute, 1999.

— 'Another life of Shakespeare!' (review of Park Honan, *Shakespeare, a Life*, 1998), n.d., *Renaissance pamphlet*.

— 'Shakespeare and Religion at Stratford, 2000'; 'Shakespeare and the Reformation'; 'The Challenge of Oberammergau: An Open Letter to the Author', *The Renaissance Bulletin* 27, The Renaissance Institute, 2000.

— 'Shakespeare in Lancashire', *Renaissance Pamphlet*, April 1, 2000.

— 'Shakespeare's Apocalypse', *Renaissance Monographs* 26, The Renaissance Institute, 2001.

— 'The Rise of Puritanism'; 'The Purgatory of Hamlet'; 'A Survey of Shakespeare and Religions'; 'The Political Philosophy of Shakespeare'; Sonnets from Shakespeare (with Apologies), *The Renaissance Bulletin* 28, The Renaissance Institute, 2001.

— 'Shakespeare and Religion at Stratford', 2000, *Renaissance Pamphlets*, April 1, 2001.

— '"The Papist and His Poet" - The Jesuit Background to Shakespeare's Plays', Monograph, *The Renaissance Bulletin*, n.d..

— 'Shakespeare in Lancashire', *Renaissance Pamphlets* 22, April 1, 2000.

— 'A Survey of Shakespeare and Religions', *Renaissance Pamphlets*, April 1, 2002.

— 'The political philosophy of Shakespeare', *Renaissance Pamphlets*, April 1, 2002.

— 'The Purgatory of Hamlet', *Renaissance Pamphlets*, April 1, 2002.

— *The Plays and the Exercises - A Hidden Source of Shakespeare's Inspiration?*, The Renaissance Institute, 2002.

— *Books by Peter Milward, SJ*, Renaissance Centre, 2003.

— 'Shakespeare's Metadrama - *Hamlet* and *Macbeth*', *Renaissance Monographs* 30, The Renaissance Institute, May, 2003.

— 'Shakespeare's Metadrama - *Othello* and *King Lear*', *Renaissance Monographs* 31, The Renaissance Institute, September, 2003.

— 'Shakespeare and Religion - Two New Books' (reviews of collections of papers presented at two Conferences in 1999 (Dutton, Findlay, Wilson, Manchester, 2003) and 200?   (Taylor and

Beauregard, Fordham, 2003), *Renaissance Pamphlets*, April 1, 2004.
— 'The Six Wives of Henry VIII', *Renaissance Pamphlets*, April 1, 2004.
— 'Shakespeare's Metaphysical Heritage'; 'Shakespeare and Ecology'; Shakespeare and Genji";
'The History of William Shakeshafte', *The Renaissance Bulletin* 32, The Renaissance Institute,
2005.
— 'Thirty Years of the Renaissance Institute', *Renaissance Pamphlets*, April 1, 2005.
— 'The History of William Shakeshafte', *Renaissance Pamphlets*, April 1, 2006.
— 'Shakespeare's Passion Play'; 'Evidence Linking Shakespeare and the Jesuits'; 'Notes on
Shakespeare the Thinker, by A.D. Nuttall (Yale UP 2007); *'Notes on Shakespeare'*, by Bill
Bryson (Harper, London, 2007); 'Reflections on the Closing of the Renaissance Centre, and the
opening of the Peter Milward Collection, April 27, 2007', *The Renaissance Bulletin* 34, The
Renaissance Institute, Tokyo, 2007.
— 'Evidence linking Shakespeare and the Jesuits', *Renaissance Pamphlets*, April 1, 2008.
— 'Notes on *The Life and Times of William Shakespeare*, by H. Hammerschmidt-Hummel (Chaucer,
London, 2007), *Renaissance Pamphlets*, April 1, 2008.
— 'Recusant Pilgrimage', Renaissance Pamphlets, April 1, 2009.
— 'Book Reviews': a) *Catholic Resistance in Elizabethan England*, by Victor Houliston;
b) *Catholic Culture in Early Modern England*, ed. by Ronald Corthell, etc.; c) *Catholics Writing
the Nation*, by Christopher Highley;
d) *Burghley, William Cecil at the Court of Elizabeth I*, by Stephen Alford; e) *The Enigma of the
Gunpowder Plot*, by Francis Edwards, *The Renaissance Bulletin* No. 35, Pamphlets, April 1,
2009.
— 'Shakespeare and Western Culture', *The Renaissance Bulletin* No. 36 Pamphlets, April 1, 2010.
— 'The Heart of His Mystery', *Renaissance Pamphlets*, April 1, 2010.
Moorhouse, Geoffrey, *The Pilgrimage of Grace: the rebellion that shook Henry VIII's throne*,
Weidenfeld and Nicholson, 2002; Phoenix, 2003.
Moorwood, Helen, 'Duxbury of Duxbury', *Lancashire*, journal of the Lancashire Family History &
Heraldry Society, 1998.
— 'Pilgrim Father Captain Myles Standish of Duxbury, Lancashire and Massachusetts', Parts 1-6,
Lancashire History Quarterly, 1999-2000.
— 'In search of Sir Edward Stanley Sr' Parts 1, 2, *Lancashire History Quarterly*, 2008.
— 'Die Shakespeare-Stanley Epitaphe in Tong, Shropshire', *Synesis-Magazin* 2/2011, Munich.
— 'Der Film "Anonymus" von Roland Emmerich. Die entscheidende Frage: Wer eigentlich war
William Shakespeare?', *Synesis-Magazin* 2/2012, Munich.
Morton, Nathaniel, *New Englands Memoriall*, Massachusetts, 1669.
Morton, Thomas, *New English Canaan*, Amsterdam, 1637.
Mutschmann, H. and K. Wentersdorff, *Shakespeare and Catholicism*, New York, 1969.

Nelson, Alan H., Monstrous Adversary: *The Life of Edward de Vere, 17th Earl of Oxford*, University
of Liverpool Press, 2003.
Newdigate, Bernard H., *Michael Drayton and his Circle*, Oxford, 1941.
Nicholl, Charles, *The Reckoning: The Murder of Christopher Marlowe*, Picador, 1992.
Nicholls, Mark, *Investigating Gunpowder Plot*, Manchester UP, 1991.
Norman, Marc and Tom Stoppard, *Shakespeare in Love*, (the script), Faber and Faber, 1999.
Norton, Peter A., *Railways and Waterways to Warrington*, Cheshire Libraries and Museums, 1984.
Norwich, John Julius, *Shakespeare's Kings*, Viking, 1999; Penguin, 2000.

Ormerod, George, *The History of the County Palatine of Chester*, 3 vols, 1816-19, 2nd Ed. revised
and enlarged by Thomas Helsby, 1877-82.

Ormskirk Parish Church: A Guide and Short History, Revised 1990.

Ormskirk Parish Registers, Lancashire Record Society, 1902.

Owen, H. and J. B. Blakeway, *A History of Shrewsbury*, 1825.

Parry, Glyn, *The Arch-Conjuror of England: John Dee*, Yale University Press, US, 2011.

Pearce, J. P., *Lancashire Legends*, Howell, 1928.

Pearson, Stephen, 'Wherefore Art Thou, Grandfather?', 2004, The Shakespeare Family History Site.

Perry, Maria, *Sisters to the King: The Tumultuous Lives of Henry VIII's Sisters: Margaret of Scotland & Mary of France*, André Deutsch, 1998.

Porteus, T. C., *A History of the Parish of Standish*, Wigan, 1927.

— *A Calendar of the Standish Deeds 1230-1575, preserved in the Wigan Public Library, together with Abstracts made by the Revd Thomas West in 1770 of 228 Deeds not now in the Collection*, Wigan Public Libraries, 1933.

Potter, Lois, 'Having our Will: Imagination in recent Shakespeare Biographies', *Shakespeare Survey, Writing about Shakespeare* (ed. Peter Holland), Cambridge University Press, 2005.

Preston Guild Rolls, see Abram, W. A.

Pritchard, R. E. (Ed.), *Shakespeare's England: Life in Elizabethan & Jacobean Times*, Sutton, Stroud, 1999, 2003.

Raines, F. R., (Ed.) *The Stanley Papers, pt. ii. The Derby household books; comprising an account of the household regulations and expenses of Edward and Henry, third and fourth Earls of Derby, together with a diary containing the names of the guests who visited the latter Earl at his houses in Lancashire, by William Ffarington, esquire, the comptroller [1561-90]* (Chetham Society, Old Series, 31, 1853). Commonly known as *The Derby Household Books*.

Raithel, John, website The URL of Derby.

Reaney, P. H. & R. M. Wilson, *A Dictionary of English Surnames*, Oxford University Press, 1995.

Rebholz, Ronald A., *The Life of Fulke Grevill, first Lord Brooke*, Oxford, 1971.

Records of Early English Drama (REED) 2 vols., (Eds) Alan H. Nelson, John R. Elliott, Jr., Alexandra F. Johnston, Diana Wyatt. Toronto: University of Toronto Press, 2004.

Rimmer, Alfred, *A History of Shrewsbury School*, from the Blakeway MSS, etc., Shrewsbury, 1889.

Roberts, Brian S., Stanley Family Genealogy website http://www.fintco.demon.co.uk/stanley

Roby, John, *Lancashire Myths & Legends*, Vols 1 & 2, repub. of *Roby's Traditions of Lancashire*, 1829, Book Clearance Centre, Bury, 2002.

Rylands, John Paul (Ed), *The Visitation of Cheshire in the year 1580 made by Robert Glover, Somerset Herald, for William Flower, Norroy King of Arms, with numbers, additions and continuations, including those from The Visitation of Cheshire made in the year 1566 by the same Herald, with an appendix, containing the Visitation of a Part of Cheshire in the year 1533, made by William Fellows, Lancaster Herald for Thomas Benolte, Clarenceux King of Arms, and a fragment of The Visitation of the City of Chester in the year 1591, made by Thomas Chaloner, Deputy to the Office of Arms*, The Harleian Society, Vol. CVIII, London, 1882

Sams, Eric, *The Real Shakespeare: Retrieving the Early Years, 1564-1594*, Yale University Press, 1995. The sequel has been published posthumously as an Ebook by his son.

Savage, Richard and E.I. Fripp (Eds), *Minutes and Accounts of Stratford-upon-Avon and Other Records*, Vol. 1, 1553-6, Stratford, 1921-30.

Scarisbrick, J. J., *Henry VIII*, Pelican, 1967.

Schabert, Ina, *Shakespeare Handbuch*, Kroener, Stuttgart, Germany, 2000.

Schiffhorst, Gerald. J., *John Milton*, New York, 1990.

Schoenbaum, Samuel, *Shakespeare's Lives*, Oxford and New York, 1970.

— *William Shakespeare: a compact documentary Life, Revised Edition with a New Postscript,*

Oxford University Press, New York, Oxford, 1987.

Seacome, John, *Memoirs: containing a genealogical and historical account of the ancient and honourable house of Stanley; from the Conquest to the death of James late Earl of Derby, in the year 1725; as also a full description of the Isle of Man, etc.*, Liverpool, 1741. Updates and reprints (later ones sometimes under another title), Manchester 1767, Manchester 1783, Preston 1793, Liverpool 1801, the last one including *A brief account of the Travels of the celebrated Sir William Stanley, son of the fourth Earl of Derby, of Latham-Hall, Lancashire*, anonymous, added by this editor of Seacome, Printed by J. Nuttall, 38, Denison-street, Liverpool, 1801.

Sergeantson, R. M., *A History of the Church of St Peter Northampton*, Northampton, 1904 (online).

Seward, Desmond, *The Hundred Years War: The English in France, 1337-1453*, Robinson, 1978, 2003.

Shapiro, James, *1599: A Year in the Life of William Shakespeare*, Faber and Faber, 2005.

— *Contested Will: Who Wrote Shakespeare?*, Faber and Faber, 2010.

Shaw, William A., *The Knights of England*, 2 Vols, printed and published for the Central Chancery of the Orders of Knighthood, Lord Chamberlain's Office, St James's Palace, Sherratt and Hughes, 1906.

Somerset, Anne, *Elizabeth I*, Weidenfeld and Nicholson, 1991; Fontana, 1992.

Speed, John, *The Counties of Britain: A Tudor Atlas by John Speed*, published in Association with the British Library, Intro. by Nigel Nicolson, County Commentaries by Alasdair Hawkyard, 1988, Pavilion in Association with the British Library, 1999.

Spenser, Edmund, *Tears of the Muses*, 1591.

Stanley, Peter Edmund, *The House of Stanley from the 12th century*, Pentland Press, 1998.

Stevenson, Robert, *Shakespeare's Religious Frontier*, Routledge, 1958.

Stonyhurst Museum Guide, by Janet Graffius, Curator of Stonyhurst College, n.d.

Stopes, Charlotte C., *Shakespeare's Family*, 1901, reprinted 2007.

— *Shakespeare's Environment*, 1918, reprinted 2010.

Strong, Roy, *Henry Prince of Wales and England's Lost Renaissance*, Thames and Hudson, 1986; Pimlico, 2000.

Strype, John, *Annals of the Reformation and Ecclesiastical Memorials*, Vol. III. Pt I, Oxford UP, 1820.

Sumner, Ann, 'Venetia Digby on her deathbed', chapter from *Catalogue* accompanying an Exhibition at Dulwich Picture Gallery, London, 1995-6.

Taylor, Gary, *Reinventing Shakespeare: a Cultural History from the Restoration to the Present*, Hogarth, 1989; Vintage, 1991.

Tey, Josephine, *A Daughter of Time*, 1951, 1995.

Thaler, Alwin, 'The Original Malvolio?', *Shakespeare Association Bulletin*, Vol. vii, no. 2, 1932.

Thoms, William J, *Shakespeare in Germany 1, Three Notelets on Shakespeare*, London, 1865.

Thornber, Craig, Cheshire Antiquities Website.

Thornton, Canon Kenneth, *Guidebook of Ormskirk Church*, 1990.

Tillyard, E. M. W., *Shakespeare's History Plays*, Chatto and Windus, 1944; Peregrine, 1962.

Titherley, Arthur W., *Shakespeare's Identity*, Winchester, 1952.

Trevelyan, G. M., *Trinity College: an Historical Sketch*, Trinity College, Cambridge, 2001.

Trutt, David, *Haddon Hall's Dorothy Vernon: the story of the legend, 2006*, an ebook online.

Tupling, G. H., *The Royal and Seignorial Bailiffs of Lancashire in the Thirteenth and Fourteenth Centuries*, Chetham Society, 1945.

Turner and Dr. Whitaker, Catalogue of an exhibition at Towneley Hall, 1982, compiled by Stanley Warburton.

Tylden-Wright, D., *John Aubrey: a life*, Harper Collins, 1991.

Victoria County History, see Farrer, W.

Walker, W., *Duxbury in Decline 1756-1932: A story of the decline of a Lancashire Estate and the families associated with it*, Palatine Books, Preston, 1995.

Webb, Nicholas, *Standish: Eight Hundred Years of History*, Wigan Heritage Service Publications: 6, 1993.

Weever, John, *Ancient Funeral Monuments within the United Monarchy of Great Britain*, 1631.
— *Epigrammes*, 1599.
— *Faunus and Melliflora*, 1600.

Weir, Alison, *Lancaster and York: The Wars of the Roses*, Jonathan Cape, 1995; Vintage, 2009.
— *Elizabeth the Queen*, Jonathan Cape, 1998; Pimlico, 1999.

Wells, Stanley, *Shakespeare Around The Globe*, International Shakespeare Association, Occasional Paper No. 6, 1998.
— & Gary Taylor (eds), *Shakespeare: The Complete Works*, Oxford, 1973, 2nd ed., 2005.
— & Paul Edmondson, *Shakespeare Bites Back!*, ebook, 2011.

Whitaker, T. D., *A History of Whalley* in 3 parts, 1801 ff.
— *History of the Antiquities of the Deanery of Craven*, 1805, 1812.

Williams, Neville, *The Life and Times of Henry VII*, Weidenfeld and Nicholson, 1973, reissued 1994.

Wilson, Ian, *Shakespeare: The Evidence*, St Martin's Press, 1999.
— 'Shakespeare the Catholic', *The Renaissance Bulletin* 28, The Renaissance Institute, Tokyo, 2001.

Wilson, (Dr) Ian, *Black Jenny: Shakespeare, Sex and the Darkest of Secrets*, Paladin, 1992, online as *Shakespeare's Dark Lady*.

Wilson, John, *Verses and Notes*, Chorley, 1903.

Wilson, Richard, *Secret Shakespeare: Studies in theatre, religion and resistance*, Manchester University Press, 2004.

Wood, Anthony, *Athenae Oxonienses: an Exact History of all the Writers and Bishops who have had their Education in the University of Oxford from 1500 to 1690*, 2 vols folio, 1691-2.

Wood, Michael, *In Search of Shakespeare*, BBC, 2003; to accompany the 4-part TV Series by Maya Vision, broadcast by BBC2, 2003.

Woodcock, Thomas and John Martin Robinson, *The Oxford Guide to Heraldry*, Oxford University Press, 1988, pb., 1990.

Woudhuysen, H.R. and Katherine Duncan-Jones (eds), *Shakespeare's Poems: Venus and Adonis, The Rape of Lucrece and the Shorter Poems*, Arden Shakespeare, 3rd series, 2007.

Wright, James, *The History and Antiquities of the County of Rutland*, mid-18th century.

Wright, Lilian, 'The 1584 quarrel between William Stanley and Thomas Peniston', *Eynsham Record*, Volume 1, 1984, pp. 22-26.
— 'The Stanleys in Eynsham: an outline of the Stanley connection, 1545-1643', *Eynsham Record*, Volume 2, 1985, pp. 32-38.
— 'Venetia Anastasia Stanley', *Eynsham Record*, Volume 27, 2012, pp. 4-9.

Zevin, Edward, 'The early marriages of Edward Stanley, third Earl of Derby', Historic Society of Lancashire and Cheshire, Vol. 134, 1985.

N.B. Only main entries in the Shakespeare Encyclopedia (Appendix 7) are given, indicated by (Sh. Enc.). Those in the Index who appear on a Family Tree in Appendix 12 are given the appropriate number in square brackets and **bold [12a, 12b, 12c, 12d]** at the beginning of their page references.